Point/Counterpoint sections focus on areas of controversy or disagreements within HRM, offering the arguments for and against a position, along with some conclusions that leave room for interpretation by the student.

Outsourcing (Ch. 1)
Privacy or Security (Ch. 2)
Wages and Conditions in Foreign Plants (Ch. 3)
Best Practices or Contingency Approach? (Ch. 4)
Employee Retention (Ch. 6)
Selecting for Fit Versus Skill (Ch. 7)
Should Our Society Move from the "Melting Pot" to Pluralism? (Ch. 8)
What Should Be the Basis for Compensation? (Ch. 9)
360-Degree Feedback (Ch. 10)
Are Labor Unions Still Necessary? (Ch. 11)
Not Enough Stress? (Ch. 12)
Reinforcement Versus Free Will (Ch. 13)
Team Versus Individual Incentives (Ch. 14)

 HR Legal Brief describes specific legal issues that are especially important and related to the chapter topic. Relevant laws and regulations are discussed throughout the text, but this section calls attention to issues that either are the focus of significant public interest, or are so important that they are likely to dominate HR practice in the future.

Paying the Price (Ch. 1)
Child Labor and International Business (Ch. 3)
The Merits of Diversity Training? (Ch. 8)
Identifying a Firm's "Worst" Employees (Ch. 10)

 HR Around the Globe discusses HR practices from outside the United States, offering a useful background for students who will be working in a global economy.

Toyota Wants Only the Best (Ch. 3)
Blending the Multinational Mix (Ch. 4)
International Relations 101 (Ch. 5)
Exporting Jobs? (Ch. 6)
Too Little Diversity? (Ch. 8)

 HR in the 21st Century identifies a trend or practice that the authors see as growing, and then discusses why it is expected to become more common in the future.

A Shortage in the Work Force (Ch. 1)
Trends in the Affirmative Action Debate (Ch. 2)
Easy Come, Easy Go (Ch. 5)
Absenteeism as an Entitlement? (Ch. 6)
Internships Go Virtual as Firms Seek Ways to Save (Ch. 7)
Negotiating Salaries on the Web (Ch. 9)
Minimum Wage . . . or Minimum Wages? (Ch. 9)
Emerging Trends in Unionization (Ch. 11)
Building the Perfect Work Environment (Ch. 12)
Too Much Technology? (Ch. 12)
The Noble Choice (Ch. 13)
Creating Humane Work Schedules (Ch. 14)

 Taking HR to the Next Level are discussions at the end of every section that supplement the previous chapter material. These discussions take the subject of HRM to a different level of depth or provide a more strategic or managerial perspective of the HR process in organizations.

Part I: The Strategic Context of Human Resource Management
Part II: Contingent Workers, Reliability, and Validity
Part III: Knowledge, Social Issues, and Human Resource Management
Part IV: Psychological Contracts and Work: Human Resource Management and Executives

edition
3

HUMAN RESOURCE
MANAGEMENT

Angelo S. DeNisi
Tulane University

Ricky W. Griffin
Texas A&M University

edition

3

HUMAN RESOURCE MANAGEMENT

Houghton Mifflin Company

Boston   New York

For Adrienne, Jessica, and Rebecca
the women who mean the most to me (AD)

For Matt, who makes my daughter smile (RWG)

Executive Publisher: George Hoffman
Executive Sponsoring Editor: Lisé Johnson
Senior Marketing Manager: Nicole Hamm
Senior Development Editor: Joanne Dauksewicz
Project Editor: Shelley Dickerson
Art and Design Manager: Jill Haber
Cover Design Manager: Anne S. Katzeff
Senior Photo Editor: Jennifer Meyer Dare
Senior Composition Buyer: Chuck Dutton
New Title Project Manager: James Lonergan
Marketing Associate: Karen E. Mulvey
Editorial Assistant: Anthony D'Aries

Cover image: © Digital Vision/Veer

Photo credits appear on page 533, except for pages 11, 37, 113, 297, 324, and 464.

Printed in the U.S.A.

Library of Congress Control Number: 2007927195

Student Edition (use for ordering)—
ISBN 13: 978-0-618-79419-5
ISBN 10: 0-618-79419-0

Exam Copy—
ISBN 13: 978-0-618-83358-0
ISBN 10: 0-618-83358-7

1 2 3 4 5 6 7 8 9 – CRK – 11 10 09 08 07

Brief Contents

Contents

Angelo S. DeNisi

Angelo S. DeNisi is Dean of the A.B. Freeman School of Business at Tulane University. After receiving his Ph.D. in Industrial/Organizational Psychology from Purdue University, Angelo taught at Kent State University, the University of South Carolina, Rutgers University, and Texas A&M University (where he was Head of the Department of Management) before moving to Tulane as Dean. He has taught HR courses for undergraduates, MBAs, Executive MBAs, MS in HR students, and Ph.D. students. He has also taught classes and conducted seminars on various HR topics in Singapore, Madrid, Jerusalem, Beijing, Kuala Lumpur, Hong Kong, Seville, Jerez, Santo Domingo, and Jakarta. He is President-Elect of the Academy of Management, a Fellow of the Academy of Management, and has served as Editor of the *Academy of Management Journal,* as well as the Chair of both the Human Resources Division and the Organizational Behavior Division. He is a Fellow of The Society for Industrial and Organizational Psychology (SIOP) and the American Psychological Association, and a past SIOP President. In addition, he is a Fellow of the Southern Management Association, and he served on the Board of Governors of the Southern Management Association. Most of his research has focused on issues of performance appraisal and feedback, but he has also written on job analysis, managing persons with disabilities at work, and problems associated with expatriate management. His research has been funded by such organizations as the National Science Foundation and the Army Research Institute, and has appeared in such journals as the *Academy of Management Journal, Academy of Management Review, Journal of Applied Psychology, Psychological Bulletin, Journal of Personality and Social Psychology,* and *Industrial and Labor Relations Review.* He has also published a book about his research entitled *Cognitive Approach to Performance Appraisal: A Program of Research,* and is co-editor of *Managing Knowledge for Sustained Competitive Advantage,* as well as *Performance Management Systems: A Global Perspective.*

Angelo has received a number of honors over the years, including being named Honorary Professor, Department of Management, City University of Hong Kong; and External Examiner, Human Resource Consulting/Management, Nanyang Business School, Nanyang Polytechnic University, Singapore. His research has also been honored, including winning awards such as the William Owens Award for the Outstanding Publication in Industrial and Organizational Psychology, 1998; Outstanding Publication in Organizational Behavior, Organizational Behavior Division of the Academy of Management, 1997; and Best Paper in Organizational Communications, Organizational Communications Division of the Academy of Management, 1992.

Ricky W. Griffin

Ricky W. Griffin is Distinguished Professor of Management, holds the Blocker Chair in Business, and currently serves as the Executive Associate Dean at the Mays Business School at Texas A&M University. He formerly served as Director of the Center for Human Resource Management and as the Head of the Department of Management at Texas A&M. His research interests include workplace aggression and violence, executive skills and decision making, and workplace culture. Ricky's research has been funded by the Office of Naval Research and the Global Research Consortium and has been published in such journals as *Academy of Management Review, Academy of Management Journal, Administrative Science Quarterly,* and *Journal of Management.* He has also served as Editor of *Journal of Management.* Ricky has served the Academy of Management as Chair of the Organizational Behavior Division. He has also served as President of the Southwest Division of the Academy of Management and on the Board of Directors of the Southern Management Association. Ricky is a Fellow of both the Academy of Management and the Southern Management Association. He has also co-edited several scholarly books, including *Dysfunctional Behavior in Organizations* and *The Dark Side of Organizational Behavior.*

 Ricky has been a visiting scholar at the Warsaw School of Management in Poland and at the University of South Africa in Pretoria, South Africa. He has won numerous awards for his research, including the Outstanding Publication in Organizational Behavior award and the Best Paper award, each presented by the Organizational Behavior Division of the Academy of Management. He is also the author of several market-leading textbooks, including *Management* (9th Edition), *Organizational Behavior* (8th Edition), *Business* (8th Edition) and *International Business* (5th Edition). In addition, his texts are widely used in dozens of countries, adapted for use in countries such as Australia and Canada, and have been translated into numerous foreign languages, including Russian, Chinese, Spanish, and Polish.

The Evolution of a Textbook

It has been interesting to note how a textbook can evolve over time. In our first edition, we tried to present the most up-to-date information in a manner that made it easy to digest and somewhat interesting. We tried to include a number of features that would add to the interest and the relevance of the book, but we stayed pretty close to the format of a traditional HR text. By the second edition, a lot had happened in the world. September 11th had forever changed the way Americans would view their world, and we tried to incorporate some of this in our revision. We also brought in more information about the role of electronic systems in HR, and we included even more features that we hoped would add to the reader's interests.

Now, as we launch our third edition, the world has changed even further. Not only do Americans view their world differently, but now much of the world also views Americans differently. As we write this, the United States is engaged in a war in Iraq, which has colored the world's perceptions of us, and notions of security and safety have become much more important than they were a few years ago. But it is also more apparent than ever that we live in a larger global environment and that any discussion of management and human resource management must take that larger view into account. We have tried, therefore, to do a better job of representing the global business environment, and we have also tried to deal with some of the security concerns that face organizations everywhere. These concerns include having to deal with natural disasters, such as the hurricane and flooding that has had such an impact upon New Orleans (which one of us calls home) as well as the entire gulf coast.

What's Changed in the Third Edition?

In addition to trying to incorporate these changing aspects of the world into our new edition, we have also made some fundamental changes in the content itself. We have combined some topics, eliminated some, and cover a number of areas in more depth than we did previously. We have also reorganized the text around a conceptual model of the HRM process in most organizations.

Our emphasis in this third edition is managing human resources for competitive advantage. We have shifted the focus of several chapters to reflect that emphasis and we have added new material to help readers see more clearly how effective human resource management can be a critical source of competitive advantage.

We begin the new structure with a section we call "An Overview of Human Resource Management," and here we deal with the context in which HR takes place. We have updated Chapter 2, "The Legal Environment," and expanded Chapter 3, "The Global Environment," but we have also shifted the focus a bit in Chapter 4, "The Competitive Environment," which deals with strategic issues. We now focus on strategy as part of the process of managing a competitive environment. Therefore, we emphasize how one uses strategy and HR strategy to gain competitive advantage, rather than simply discussing strategy per se.

We have called Part Two "Decision Making in Human Resource Management," and here we deal with the major decisions that must be made regarding human resources.

We begin with a new chapter, Chapter 5, "Information for Making Human Resource Decisions," which covers some general sources of information for making those decisions. We discuss the role of HR planning, and consider organizational strategy and the general economy as important sources of information. We also discuss how job analysis (and planning) work together to provide critical input for HR decisions. Chapter 6, "Organizational Form and Structure," deals with how organizational structures and forms also serve as inputs for HR decisions. We also cover issues of "rightsizing" the organization in this chapter. Chapter 7 combines coverage of recruitment and selection, topics we previously dealt with separately, as we see these as major decisions that face an organization.

Part Three, "Managing the Existing Workforce," deals with HR activities needed to maintain the workforce that has been chosen. It begins with a revised Chapter 8, "Managing the Diverse Workforce," which emphasizes that organizations must decide how to deal with diversity rather than decide whether to deal with it at all. Chapter 9 combines coverage of compensation and benefits and emphasizes the roles these activities play in workforce management. Chapter 10 deals with performance appraisal and career development activities. Again, we've combined material from several chapters in our last edition here, as we discuss these activities in the context of developing better employees over time. Chapter 11, "Managing Labor Relations," has been updated and kept in the text because we still believe that it is important for managers to understand the role of unions in today's workforce, especially when we think more globally. Finally, Chapter 12, "Safety, Health, Well-Being, and Security," ends the section. This chapter combines material from several other chapters in our previous edition, but it also adds coverage dealing with the increased security issues facing employees and employers everywhere.

The final section of this third edition is almost completely new. Part Four, "Enhancing Performance," re-emphasizes our theme of HR a source of competitive advantage. Here, we take notions of HR and discuss how they can be used to enhance performance, first at the level of the employee, and later at the level of the organization. There are two chapters in this section, the first being a completely new chapter on motivation. This chapter, Chapter 13, draws on some material we had scattered throughout the book before and adds new material to provide a practical discussion of how to motivate employees to improve their performance. The final chapter, Chapter 14, "Performance Enhancement Techniques," takes many of the concepts discussed earlier in the text and demonstrates how they can be used to enhance performance. This chapter includes discussion of techniques for job enrichment, incentive schemes, work flexibility, and performance management; and these topics serve to bring together our ideas of using HRM to gain competitive advantage.

In addition to the new structure and the new chapter material, we have also added a feature we call *Taking HR to the Next Level*. Each of the four sections of the text ends with this feature, which is intended to supplement the rest of the material in that section. An instructor who is interested in spending more time on a specific issue related to the coverage in that section can use these features to do so; but this will really involve taking the discussion of HRM to a different level than is usually found in a book such as this. This feature, then, will deal with issues that are either very specific or issues that are very broad.

Specifically, the feature at the end of Part One delves more deeply into some strategic issues that form the context for *Human Resource Management*—strategy and expatriate managers and HRM and the merger and acquisition process. The feature at the end of Part Two focuses on more specialized staffing issues, specifically, contingent workers and validity and reliability. The third feature addresses some broader issues, dealing with managing the knowledge function, as well as human resource management and social issues. Finally, the feature at the end of Part Four covers psychological contracts and work, and HRM and executives. In each case, the material is meant to enhance the general discussion. It can be assigned, or students can read it on their own. However, if it is not covered, the student will still be exposed to the major issues in HRM today.

Finally, we have updated references and sources and changed and updated other features throughout the text. We hope that these changes will keep the text relevant and interesting. It is the more basic changes, however, that we believe really set apart this third edition. We believe that we have placed HRM into a context where it can do the most good. We have tried to move away from a purely administrative discussion of the field (although legal issues remain important) to a more truly strategic discussion where managers can learn how to leverage their human resources to gain competitive advantage. We are excited about this new approach and hope that you will be as well.

Text Features

There are a number of things that have *not* changed in this third edition. These are features we believe we got right the first time around. Therefore, although we've updated the entire book, there are things we hope you liked in the previous editions that have been retained and enhanced. Therefore, you will find that every chapter includes

- an opening real-world case highlighting a recent event, issue, or trend that illustrates a major point or theme in the chapter.
- a more detailed closing case with questions to guide discussion.
- a *Point/Counterpoint* feature that focuses on an area of controversy or disagreement within HRM, offering arguments for and against a position, along with some conclusions that leave room for interpretation by the student.
- a Chapter Summary and Review & Discussion questions that help students review, test, and apply what they have learned.
- two sets of Key Points, one for HR managers and one for other readers.
- a Building HR Management Skills exercise that requires students to apply the information from the chapter to a specific problem.
- an Ethical Dilemmas in HR Management scenario that presents a situation related to the chapter material and asks students to discuss what they believe would be the response of most managers.
- an HR Internet Exercise encouraging website investigation to see how organizations are really approaching issues discussed in the chapter.

We have included other features throughout the book where relevant:

- *HR in the 21st Century* features identify a trend we see as growing, then discuss why the trend or practice is expected to become more common in the future when students are ready to move into management.
- *HR Legal Brief* features describe specific legal issues that are especially important and relevant to the chapter topic. Relevant laws and regulations are discussed throughout, but this section calls attention to legal issues that either are the focus of significant public interest or are so important that they are likely to dominate HR practice in the future.
- *HR Around the Globe* features discuss noteworthy HRM practices from outside the U.S., offering a useful background for students who will be working in an increasingly global economy.
- *The Lighter Side of HR* features reinforce important points made in the chapter with amusing cartoons accompanied by expository captions.

An Effective Teaching and Learning Package

We are pleased to provide a comprehensive set of supplements to help both instructors and students:

- *Online Study Center.* The student site includes the Internet exercises from the text (with updates as necessary), hyperlinks to the companies highlighted in each chapter, complete and chapter-by-chapter glossaries, flashcards for reviewing key terms, and ACE self-tests.

- *Online Teaching Center.* The instructor site provides downloadable versions of the complete *Instructor's Resource Manual* (in PDF format) as well as by chapter (in MS Word) that can be edited or used as is. It also provides a set of Basic PowerPoint slides and Premium PowerPoint slides for each chapter. In addition, the site includes sample syllabi, a Content Correlation Chart (relating text material to content in the PHR and SPHR certification exams), and the complete Video Guide.

- *Instructor's Resource Manual.* This resource includes the list of learning objectives for each chapter, a detailed lecture outline, and suggested answers to all text questions and end-of-chapter activities.

- *Test Bank.* The *Test Bank* includes both recall and application oriented multiple-choice, essay, short answer, and scenario-based questions.

- *HM Testing CD.* The electronic version of the printed *Test Bank,* HM Testing, (powered by Diploma™) allows instructors to easily generate and edit tests. The program includes an online testing feature instructors can use to administer tests via their local area network or over the Web. It also has a gradebook feature that lets users set up classes, record and track grades from tests or assignments, analyze grades, and produce class and individual statistics.

- *PowerPoint Slides.* PowerPoint slides on the instructor website provide an effective presentation tool for lectures. The Basic PowerPoint program provides an outline of each chapter with key figures and tables from the main text. The Premium PowerPoint program includes all of the basic slides as well as additional slides that contain unique content that supplements text material.

- *Video Package.* To illustrate important concepts from the text, real-world video examples from leading organizations are provided. The video segments run from ten to twenty minutes to allow time for classroom discussion. The Video Guide provides suggested uses, teaching objectives, an overview, and issues for discussion for each video segment.

A Final Word

As we noted in the preface to our first edition, what sets our book apart from many others you may have seen is not the content, but the approach. It is always our goal to present the most current information, based on the best research we can find, and to present that information in a way that is engaging and easy to understand. We make extensive use of cases and special features to try to bring the topics we cover to life for students. These were our goals in the first edition, and they remain so for this edition. What we have done is to take these ideas and update and expand how we apply them to the topic of human resource management. As a result, the new edition has a new look, and covers some new topics and includes some new features, but we hope that it remains a well-informed, user-friendly text. We also hope that both students and instructors will benefit from what we have done.

Acknowledgments

A project such as this is never the result of just one or two people's efforts. There are many people who have contributed to this book in different ways over the years. First, we must thank the many (indeed, more than we would like to admit) students who have taken our classes over the years. They endured the process of climbing a learning curve as we learned how and what to teach, and they were the "guinea pigs" whenever we decided to try new ideas or approaches. But, more than that, authors form ideas about how a text should be written only by spending a lot of time observing students using other texts. So, to all the students who complained about the texts we assigned them, we apologize, and hope that this book will better meet students' needs, challenge their minds, and engage their interest.

Our colleagues have also helped us form ideas through discussions, as well as through the feedback they provided over the years. These discussions and conversations were critical for crystallizing the concepts that appear in this book. Other feedback from colleagues helped develop better writing skills and allowed each of us to be able to communicate our ideas more clearly. Therefore we thank all those colleagues from the University of Houston, Purdue University, the University of Missouri, Kent State University, the University of South Carolina, Rutgers University, and of course from Texas A&M University. Somewhere along the line, though, some people played an even greater role in guiding and developing our ideas. We must therefore specifically thank and acknowledge the efforts and help of our mentors John Ivancevich and Ernest McCormick.

As we actually started writing this book, a number of other people played a role that should be acknowledged. We want to thank the reviewers of this text for spending time reading drafts of chapters and providing useful feedback for us on how to make them better. In particular, we want to thank:

Ron Abernathy
University of North Carolina—Greensboro

Paula Becker Alexander
Seton Hall University

Debra A. Arvanites
Villanova University

Sheila R. Baiers
Kalamazoo Valley Community College

Janet C. Barnard
Rochester Institute of Technology

Lynda Brown
University of Montana

Kevin Carlson
Virginia Tech

Jennifer Carney
(MBA candidate)
Georgia State University

Suzanne Clinton
Cameron University

Gwendolyn M. Combs
University of Nebraska—Lincoln

Mary L. Connerley
Virginia Tech

Robert R. Cordell
West Virginia University at Parkersburg

Barbara J. Durkin
SUNY, College at Oneonta

Dyanne J. Ferk
University of Illinois—Springfield

John Fielding
Mount Wachusett Community College

Maureen J. Fleming
The University of Montana

Donald G. Gardner
University of Colorado

Carol B. Gilmore
University of Maine

Audrey Guskey
Duquesne University

Barbara L. Hassell
University of North Texas

Micki Kacmar
Florida State University

David L. Kaiser
Hamline University

Gundars Kaupins
Boise State University

Noel McKeon
Florida Community College

Alice E. Nuttall
Kent State University, Tuscarawas Campus

Stephen Owens
Western Carolina University

Robert Paul
Kansas State University

Alex Pomnichowski
Ferris State University

Paul R. Reed
Sam Houston State University

Shelton Rhodes
Bowie State University

Joan B. Rivera
West Texas A&M University

Anna C. Smith
McKendree College

Emeric Solymossy
Western Illinois University

Paul Stimmler
The Pennsylvania State University

Rebecca A. Thacker
Ohio University

Charles N. Toftoy
George Washington University

J. Bruce Tracey
Cornell University

Carolyn Wiley
The University of Tennessee at Chattanooga

We also want to thank the professionals at Houghton Mifflin, especially Lisé Johnson, George Hoffman, Joanne Dauksewicz, and Shelley Dickerson, who at various times encouraged, threatened, supported, and browbeat us to get the book finished, and to make it the best we could. We hope you are pleased with the final product.

Finally, we must thank family and friends for their support through the entire process. These are the folks who had to listen to brilliant ideas (even when they weren't so brilliant), and our complaints about unreasonable reviewers (who truly weren't) and those editors who kept pressuring us to get the book finished (who really did). Without their help, this book would never have been completed. We are especially indebted to Glenda Griffin and Adrienne Colella, who play the multiple roles of wives, partners, collaborators, colleagues, and best friends. It is with all our love, respect, and appreciation that we dedicate this book to them.

Angelo S. DeNisi
Ricky W. Griffin

An Overview of Human Resource Management

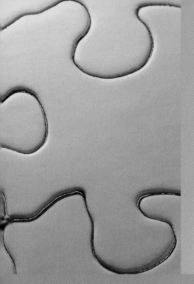

1

The Nature of Human Resource Management

CHAPTER OBJECTIVES

After studying this chapter you should be able to:

■ Characterize contemporary human resource management perspectives.

■ Summarize the evolution of the human resource function in organizations.

■ Identify and discuss the fundamental goals of human resource management in organizations.

■ Discuss the responsibilities for human resource management, describe the human resource management department, and discuss the human resource management system.

■ Discuss human resource managers in terms of their professionalism and careers.

Southwest Airlines is one of the most successful firms in the world today. Unlike other major airlines, however, Southwest does not fly international routes, serve meals on its flights, subscribe to any computerized reservation system, or have preassigned seating or business or first-class compartments, and it refuses to transfer bags to other airlines. It boasts the lowest costs and highest profits and regularly has the highest levels of efficiency, productivity, and customer satisfaction in the airline industry today. It is also consistently recognized as one of the most-admired companies in the United States (ranking third in 2006).

One key to Southwest's success is the culture created by the firm's legendary cofounder and long-time chief executive officer (CEO) Herb Kelleher, affectionately known as "Uncle Herbie" to Southwest employees. From the company's earliest days, Kelleher decided to make all his employees feel like part of one big team. For instance, Kelleher established a policy that no employee would be laid off, and he sometimes pitched in when a ticket counter or luggage conveyor became too crowded. And for years Southwest has offered innovative compensation and advancement opportunities and stressed employee involvement in every phase of the firm's operations. As a result of this unique culture, Southwest routinely makes *Fortune* magazine's annual list of the best places to work.

What does it take to work for Southwest Airlines?

> *"We are committed to provide our Employees a stable work environment with equal opportunity for learning and personal growth. Creativity and innovation are encouraged for improving the effectiveness of Southwest Airlines. Above all, Employees will be provided the same concern, respect, and caring attitude within the organization that they are expected to share externally with every Southwest Customer."*
>
> From the Southwest Airlines Mission Statement, southwest.com.

Obviously, candidates need to have the requisite skills necessary to perform the job for which they are being considered. But beyond technical skills, successful applicants must also demonstrate the capacity to get along with others, to be a team player, and to be willing to pitch in wherever needed. In return for these qualities, Southwest provides a flexible, stimulating, and enjoyable work environment; reasonable pay; good benefits; opportunities to advance; and job security.

Southwest's approach to dealing with its employees has paid big dividends. For instance, they do indeed view themselves as part of one big team and strive to work together in the best interests of the company. The firm has the lowest turnover in the industry and a workforce committed to flexibility and innovation. During the Persian Gulf Crisis in 1990–1991, more than one-third of the airline's employees took a voluntary pay cut to help offset higher jet-fuel prices so the firm could remain profitable. And Southwest reciprocated in 2001 when it became the only major U.S. airline not to eliminate jobs in the wake of the September 11, 2001, terrorist attacks.

When Kelleher recently retired, some observers worried that the firm's culture might falter. But so far, at least, that has not been the case. Under the leadership of Colleen Barrett, president, and Gary Kelly, CEO, Southwest hasn't missed a beat. Indeed, Southwest's current leadership shows every indication that the best is yet to be.[1]

outhwest Airlines clearly recognizes the value of people in the success of its business. If Southwest needs a new airplane or a new information system for managing its flight operations, it can just buy them. Neither of these assets can give the firm a sustained competitive advantage, however, because JetBlue, United, or American can easily buy the exact assets. But the people who work for Southwest have an unusual relationship with their employer and provide the firm with a rare and valuable set of resources that its competitors cannot easily duplicate or sustain. Indeed, it is the quality and character of these human resources that sets Southwest apart from other airlines and has helped Southwest to be the only airline to consistently show a profit in the aftermath of September 11 and the surge in fuel costs in 2005 and 2006.

Regardless of their size, mission, market, or environment, all organizations strive to achieve their goals by combining various resources into goods and services that will be of value to their customers. But many different resources are available. Economists traditionally thought in terms of concrete physical resources. In this view organizations draw on financial resources such as ownership investment, sales revenues, and bank loans to provide capital and to cover expenses necessary to conduct business. Material resources such as factories, equipment, raw materials, computers, and offices also play an important role in the actual creation of goods and services and are easy to think

Southwest Airlines has been at the forefront of its industry for years. Gary Kelly, the firm's CEO, has continued to build impressively upon the solid competitive foundation laid by the legendary Herb Kelleher. The cornerstone of that foundation, in turn, is the firm's human resources. Southwest recruits employees who fit its climate of high morale and high customer satisfaction, and then rewards these people for working harder and smarter by providing job security and profit sharing.

about when we discuss a firm's resources. But increasingly managers are beginning to view less tangible resources as the most critical for gaining a competitive advantage.

For example, successful organizations need information about consumers and the firm's competitive environment to help managers make decisions, solve problems, and develop competitive strategies. Many people refer to such resources as knowledge-based resources.[2] That is, organizations need to know how to get information and how to use that information. We will discuss knowledge-based resources and knowledge workers later in this chapter, and throughout the book, but for now it is sufficient to note that most (but not all) of this critical knowledge tends to reside in the people in the organization. Therefore, many experts in the field have come to recognize that no set of resources is more vital to an organization's success than its human resources.[3]

An organization's **human resources** are the people it employs to carry out various jobs, tasks, and functions in exchange for wages, salaries, and other rewards. The chief executive officer responsible for the overall effectiveness of the organization, the advertising manager responsible for creating newspaper ads, the operations manager sent to open a new manufacturing facility in Taiwan, the financial analyst who manages the organization's cash reserves, and the custodian who cleans the offices after everyone else goes home are all human resources. And in his or her own way, each is a vital ingredient that helps determine the overall effectiveness—or lack of effectiveness—of the organization as it strives to accomplish its goals and objectives. At Southwest Airlines, Colleen Barrett and Gary Kelly, working in concert with the firm's pilots, flight attendants, ground staff, maintenance workers, and myriad other employees comprise the firm's human resources.

Human resource management refers to the comprehensive set of managerial activities and tasks concerned with developing and maintaining a qualified workforce—human resources—in ways that contribute to organizational effectiveness. As we will see, organizations that once paid only lip service to human resource issues are increasingly recognizing the dramatic impact that effective human resource management can have in all areas of an organization. Indeed, effective human resource management is becoming a vital strategic concern for most organizations today.[4]

In this chapter we will explore the nature of human resource management in a way that provides a useful framework for the more detailed discussions in subsequent chapters. We begin by looking at a contemporary view of human resource management and the important role this process plays in organizational effectiveness. But the human resource function was not always held in such high esteem, and so we briefly trace how human resource management has evolved to its present role in modern organizations. The goals of the human resource management function are then identified and discussed. Next, we examine how the responsibilities for human resource management are shared as staff and management functions. The human resource department in different kinds of organizations is then discussed. Finally, we focus on the professionalism and career development of human resource managers themselves.

Human resources *are the people an organization employs to carry out various jobs, tasks, and functions in exchange for wages, salaries, and other rewards.*

Human resource management *is the comprehensive set of managerial activities and tasks concerned with developing and maintaining a qualified workforce—human resources—in ways that contribute to organizational effectiveness.*

Contemporary Human Resource Management Perspectives

In most of today's organizations the role of human resource management has become quite important.[5] The real emergence of human resource management as a critical management function probably came with the passage in 1964 of the Civil Rights Act. This law and the court cases that followed from it made it clear that organizations had to find ways to hire, reward, and manage people effectively while ensuring that they worked within the limits of the law. In this context, the human resource management function came to require dedicated professionals who could balance legal and ethical concerns with the need that organizations have to survive and be profitable.

But the human resource management function has become much more than the legal enforcement arm of the organization. Top management has come to understand that, if properly managed, human resources can be an important source of competitive advantage in an increasingly competitive world. In fact, as noted earlier, human resources are the organization's most important resources. Hiring the right people, equipping them with the right skills, and then providing an environment where they can truly contribute can substantially affect the quality and quantity of whatever goods or services the organization produces. And properly motivated and committed employees can add immeasurable value to an organization's bottom line. Given the shift in competitiveness, top executives in most firms now see that human resource management practices and policies significantly affect their ability to formulate and implement strategy in any area, and that other strategic decisions significantly affect the firm's human resources as well.

It was only natural, therefore, that human resource management would eventually be elevated to the same level of importance and status as other major functional areas of the firm.[6] The top human resource executive at most companies today has vice presidential or executive vice presidential status and is a fully contributing member of the firm's executive committee, the executive body composed of key top managers that makes major policy decisions and sets corporate strategy. Today, most firms use a term such as *human resource management* to reflect more accurately the sophistication and maturity of the function. But some argue that even this term is outdated and does not do justice to the role the human resource manager plays. Instead, some organizations have moved toward using more specialized terminology that fits their corporate culture more closely. The top human resource executive at Southwest Airlines, for example, has the title of Vice President for People, while other firms, recognizing the importance of human resources as knowledge resources, have started using titles such as Chief Knowledge Officer. To keep things simple, though, we will use the human resource management terminology throughout this book.

Many aspects of the modern human resource management function actually date back to the 1980s and 1990s. During this period, it became apparent to many firms that they were not able to compete effectively in the global marketplace. Some of these firms went out of business and the employees lost their jobs. Some were acquired by other, more successful firms, and in the aftermath many employees of the acquired firm were seen as redundant and so were let go. Still other firms sought mergers with former or potential competitors in the hope of forming a new joint enterprise that could compete successfully. But again, in most cases, following such mergers companies often did not find the same need for as many employees, and many workers lost their jobs. Finally, those firms struggling to be competitive often concluded that they could be more efficient with fewer employees, and we saw the beginning of an era of downsizing, right-sizing, or reengineering. Whatever it was called, though, fewer and fewer jobs were available. Note, however, that a "no layoff" policy is one of the major features of management at Southwest Airlines.

Each of these responses resulted in a profound impact on the human resource management function. It was often the job of the human resource management department to determine how and when layoffs would take place. This is not a pleasant part of anyone's job, and a lot of hard feelings were associated with these decisions (we will discuss these issues in more detail in Chapter 6). When firms went out of business, the human resource management department was usually charged with making sure that applications for unemployment were filed and that employees received due notice of closings. When a merger or acquisition took place, it was often the role of the human resource manager to help integrate the two workforces and workplace cultures. And as our feature *HR in the 21st Century* illustrates, it will be human resource managers who, ironically, will take the lead in addressing a projected future shortage of workers.

But in the last few years human resource managers began taking on a much more strategic role in organizations. Instead of simply managing the layoff process following a merger or acquisition, human resource managers became part of the team deciding which firms to merge with or to acquire outright. Human resource managers could help identify the critical human resources that the firm would need in the future, and they could also help identify other firms that might already have those resources and so would be prime targets for takeovers or mergers. As knowledge became a more critical factor for gaining competitive advantage, human resource managers helped define strategies to acquire knowledge resources or develop them. They also developed strategies for ensuring that any knowledge acquired was fully dispersed throughout the organization.

Yet, at the same time human resource managers were taking on a more strategic role, many organizations began shrinking the more traditional roles played by human resource managers. As these organizations looked for new ways to be competitive by

---

HR IN THE 21ST CENTURY

A Shortage in the Work Force

 Layoffs have become common in the U.S. economy as businesses face cyclical demand and increased pressure to reduce costs. However, James E. Oesterreicher, labor expert, says, "The U.S. faces a worker gap and a skills gap—and both are right around the corner." Even as layoffs continue to the automobile industry, for instance, labor shortages are beginning in health care and construction. Harvard economist Dale W. Jorgenson claims, "If employers thought the [last ten years] was the decade of the worker, the next decade will be even more that way."

Retirement of aging baby boomers is just one reason for the shortage. Another factor is the lower numbers of twenty-somethings entering the workforce. There are no untapped pockets of labor supply, such as women or immigrants, that contributed workers during the 1990s. In addition, work attitudes have shifted, and workers are more willing to leave jobs to gain time for leisure or family. The productivity gains that occurred over the last decade may be at a limit. "It would be almost impossible to match the increases of the past 20 years," says David T. Ellwood, Harvard economist. Finally, the pool of new labor entrants, such as welfare-to-work recipients, is almost depleted.

> *"The U.S. faces a worker gap and a skills gap. . . ."*
>
> (James E. Oesterreicher, labor expert)*

Employers may choose to offer incentives to attract applicants, or they may concentrate on better retention of current employees. Workers can best prepare themselves for the change by seeking higher education, especially in technical or professional fields. Ellwood states, "If you believe that technological change isn't going to slow down, we're not going to have enough college-educated workers to meet the demand." While layoffs grew in 2004, they grew much more rapidly for low-skilled workers than for professionals. John Challenger, CEO of an outplacement firm, claims, "Even when the economy is fully recovered and companies are back in expansion mode, we may not see a revival in hiring of the rank-and-file worker." The proverb "A rising tide raises all boats" may be true, but it may not raise all boats equally.

Sources: "Hot Careers for the Next 10 Years," *Fortune,* March 21, 2005, p. 131; Aaron Bernstein, "Too Many Workers? Not for Long," *Business Week,* May 20, 2002 (*quote on p. 78); "Lower Paid Workers Face Job Cuts," *CNN Money,* September 10, 2002; "Statement of U.S. Secretary of Labor Elaine L. Chao on Unemployment Numbers for October 2002," U.S. Department of Labor, November 23, 2002, www.dol.gov; Peter Cappelli, "Will There *Really* Be a Labor Shortage?" *Organizational Dynamics,* Vol. 32, No. 3, 2003, pp. 221–233.

reducing costs, they often looked for activities within the company that could be done more efficiently by outsiders. For example, it became common for companies to eliminate cleaning and maintenance units and contract with an outside cleaning firm that could perform the task more efficiently.

This trend has spread to other areas as well. Today, many large organizations hire outside firms to handle payroll, insurance and benefits, and even recruitment and selection in some cases.[7] This practice, commonly known as **outsourcing,** has resulted in smaller human resource staffs within companies and more reliance on outside consultants to provide the services that were once provided by those staffs. Thus, while the importance of human resource management activities is growing, the importance of human resource departments may be shrinking, and the kind of work performed by human resource managers is certainly changing as the size of the human resource function is shrinking.

Outsourcing can indeed be an important competitive weapon for organizations. If done properly, outsourcing results in more efficient operations as outside firms are hired who benefit from the fact that they perform the same tasks for many companies. Also, outsourcing tends to eliminate jobs that tend to be more repetitive and can be dull. As a result, the employees who work on these jobs are more likely to be dissatisfied at work, which can have tremendous cost for the firms (see Chapter 6). But any function that is outsourced cannot possibly be a source of competitive advantage for a firm. Thus it is very important that a firm retains any function that is either of strategic importance in its own right (i.e., strategic planning) or that can lead to some advantage because the firm is especially expert at this function (e.g., selection or training). Therefore, the issue for most firms today is not whether to outsource but rather what to outsource and what to keep in-house.

In recent times, the trend for human resource management to become more strategic and more complex has continued. Today, when mergers, acquisitions, or divestitures occur, they often involve firms from different countries. For instance, a few years ago IBM sold its PC business to a Chinese firm called Lenovo. Even without a formal merger between parties, the number of joint ventures, especially with firms from China and other emerging economies, is growing at a rapid pace. Thus, the challenges of how to manage a proper-size workforce as well as the challenges involved in integrating workforces from different cultures (national as well as corporate) will continue to be important for human resource management in the future.

In addition, the legal imperatives that in large part helped elevate the importance of the human resource management function are changing and becoming more complex. In what has been termed a post–affirmative action world, issues regarding differential test performance of members of different ethnic and racial groups, especially in high-stakes situations (where jobs or entrance into academic institutions are involved), are becoming more rather than less complex. How do we address differences in test scores in a society where credentialing and accountability are becoming more important, and when we still haven't figured out how to deal with the diversity our society presents us?[8]

Furthermore, following the events of September 11, 2001, and their aftermath, employers and employees need to deal with entirely new challenges.[9] Questions of security (in every sense of the word) have become more important. For example, issues related to how to select, train, and motivate airport security personnel, who are the first line of defense against terrorism, fall squarely under the purview of human resource management. Following Hurricanes Katrina and Rita, and the devastating impact they had on the Gulf Coast of the United States, firms are becoming much more concerned about the security of their data (such as employee records), as well as their buildings and equipment, and how to protect them from natural disasters. Those hurricanes also demonstrated how important it is to have evacuation plans for employees and contingency plans for how to conduct business if a firm's buildings are destroyed or inaccessible.

Outsourcing *is the process of hiring outside firms to handle basic human resource management functions, presumably more efficiently than the organization.*

POINT | COUNTERPOINT

Outsourcing

 Outsourcing refers to an organization contracting with an outside provider for services formerly provided inside the organization. Typically, the organization determines its core functions and then outsources all other activities. In some cases all human resource activities are outsourced, but more typically, only activities that are fairly routine, such as enrolling employees in benefits programs, or even administering those programs, are outsourced.

POINT... Outsourcing makes sense for organizations because...	**COUNTERPOINT...** On the other hand, outsourcing could be a problem because...
The need for full-time, permanent employees is reduced.	Higher-paid jobs within large corporations will be replaced by low-paying jobs with vendors.
Jobs that deal with routine and dull tasks are eliminated from the organization.	Organizations will have fewer entry-level jobs, making it more difficult for some people to start careers.
Fewer employees are working in marginal jobs, where satisfaction might be low.	Employees providing outsourced services will have fewer benefits and less security.
When budgets get tighter, costs can be reduced by dropping programs, but no permanent employees will lose their jobs.	No new human resource managers will be gaining important experience to replace those managers dealing with strategic issues when necessary.
Managers in human resources can spend their time dealing with larger strategic issues that are better suited to their abilities.	An activity that is outsourced can no longer be a source of competitive advantage because many other organizations that use the same vendor will have the same programs.
Vendors who provide services for several organizations can provide those services at a lower cost than if the organization provides the services itself.	Fewer employees will feel committed to their organizations.

So... It probably makes sense for an organization to outsource certain activities, especially those that are totally routine, can be performed more efficiently by outside vendors, and are not seen as a potential source of competitive advantage. However, an organization must also recognize the downsides to outsourcing so that it is not the solution to all human resource problems. It is especially critical to ensure that some new managers are always gaining experience and are ready to move up to the level of strategic decision making when they are needed.

Yet, at the same time, organizations must find a balance between these different types of security needs and the need (both ethical and legal) to recognize the rights and privileges of all employees and not to engage in stereotyping or illegal profiling. The U.S. Congress ended its 2005 session by refusing to extend the Patriot Act permanently, voting for a one-month extension instead. The Act, which was passed to help the U.S. government coordinate information about potential terrorist activities, has, in some critics' opinions, gone too far in the direction of infringing on citizens' rights of privacy and individual freedom. The importance of the human resource management function will clearly grow over the years in all these areas, as the issues and challenges facing any organization involving people become more complex.

Before moving on to a more detailed discussion of the tasks and functions of modern human resource management, it is useful to consider how we arrived where we are today. The struggle of human resource management for legitimacy within the organization, and how that legitimacy came about, is due in large part to the history of how human resource management developed.

Evolution of The Human Resource Function

Even though businesses have existed for literally thousands of years, the practice of management itself has only been of special interest and concern for about 100 years or so.[10] Many early businesses were small enterprises and farms run by families interested only in supporting themselves and in providing security for family members. The industrial revolution of the eighteenth century, however, sparked a greater interest in business growth and expansion, and large-scale business operations began to emerge throughout Europe and the United States. As these businesses grew and became increasingly complex, owners began to step aside and turn the operation of their firms over to full-time professional managers. Owners who remained in control of their businesses still found it necessary to rely on managers to oversee a portion of their operations. This transition, in turn, resulted in greater awareness of the various functions of management that were necessary for long-term organizational success.[11]

While a few early management pioneers and writers like Robert Owen, Mary Parker Follette, and Hugo Munsterberg recognized the importance of people in organizations, the first serious study of management practice—set during the early years of the twentieth century—was based on scientific management.[12] **Scientific management,** in turn, was concerned with how to structure individual jobs to maximize efficiency and productivity. The major proponents of scientific management, such as Frederick Taylor and Frank and Lillian Gilbreth, had backgrounds in engineering and often used time-and-motion studies in which managers used stopwatches to teach workers precisely how to perform each task that comprised their jobs. In fact, scientific management was concerned with every motion a worker made, and there were many examples of how changes in movements or in the placement of some piece of equipment led to increased productivity.

The Lighter Side of HR, however, illustrates an argument made by critics of scientific management—that labor would use the production standards established by management as a way to work even more slowly. Other critics argued that individual workers were generally valued only in terms of their capacity to perform assigned tasks as efficiently and as productively as possible. Still, scientific management helped augment the concepts of assembly-line production, division of labor, and economies of scale that gave birth to the large businesses that transformed domestic and international economies throughout the twentieth century.[13]

Scientific management, *one of the earliest approaches to management, was concerned with how to structure individual jobs so as to maximize efficiency and productivity.*

Origins of the Human Resource Function

As businesses such as General Motors (started in 1908), Bethlehem Steel (1899), Ford Motor Company (1903), Boeing (1916), and the other industrial giants launched during this era expanded rapidly and grew into big companies, they obviously needed to hire more and more workers. Ford, for example, increased its manufacturing capacity from 800 cars per day in 1910 to 9,109 cars per day by 1925.[14] At the same time, its workforce increased from less than 200 workers to several thousand workers. This same pattern of growth and hiring was being repeated in literally hundreds of other businesses across dozens of industries. These workers were needed to perform operating jobs created to produce ever-greater quantities of the products sold by the businesses. In the early days of this business explosion, the foreman, or first-line supervisor, usually hired new workers. Office workers were also needed, so people with titles such as office manager hired clerks and secretaries.

As these businesses became more complex and as their hiring needs became more complicated, however, the task of hiring new employees became too time-consuming for a first-line supervisor or an office manager to perform. In addition, extra administrative duties were being added. For example, in 1913 Ford was paying its unskilled employees $2.34 per nine-hour day. Because the pay was so low

THE LIGHTER SIDE OF HR

Some people might think that the popularity of workplace comic strips such as Dilbert and Cathy is a recent phenomenon. But in reality, the workplace has been a source of comic humor for over a century, dating back to political and editorial cartoon features often centered on labor and labor-management conflicts. The cartoon below, for example, is from around the turn of the last century. It depicts how some critics of scientific management thought that labor might use Taylor's time-and-motion study ideas against management. The bricklayers in the cartoon, for example, have apparently been successful in getting work rules approved that allow them five minutes between motions. They are now waiting for the timer to hit the five-minute mark again, so that they can perform their next task.

MODERN BRICK-LAYING IN CHICAGO.

Source: Image © Bettmann/Corbis

and the work was both monotonous and tiring, the firm was also experiencing a turnover rate of almost 400 percent per year. Thus, the firm had to replace its average worker four times each year. It was hiring workers to fill new jobs while also hiring workers to replace those who quit. In 1914 Henry Ford made a dramatic effort to attract and retain higher-quality workers by boosting the firm's pay to a minimum of $5 for an eight-hour day.[15] This action attracted a groundswell of new job applicants and almost overwhelmed first-line supervisors, who were then hiring new employees while overseeing the work of existing workers.

As a result of growth and complexity, most large businesses, including Ford, started to hire their new employees through newly created specialized units. Ford, for example, called this unit the employment department. While these units were initially created to hire those new employees, they also began to help manage the existing workforce. For example, the emergence and growth of large labor unions like the United Auto Workers and the passage of the Fair Labor Standards Act in 1938 (which established a minimum wage) and the National Labor Relations Act in 1935 (which dealt with unionization procedures) made it necessary for businesses to have one or more managers represent the interests of the business to organized labor and to administer the emerging set of laws and regulations that governed labor practices.

Meanwhile, other developments, many taking place in other parts of the world, provided organizations with some of the tools they would need to manage these employment processes more effectively. For example, in England, the work of Charles Darwin popularized the idea that individuals differed from each other in important ways. In France, the work of Alfred Binet and Theophile Simon led to the development of the first intelligence tests, and, during the course of World War I, several major armies tried

As noted in the text, in 1913 Ford was paying workers like these $2.34 per nine-hour day. Because this wage was so low and the work so boring, the average worker only stayed on the job for a few months before seeking better opportunities. But very shortly after this photograph was taken, Ford revolutionized by boosting pay to a minimum of $5 a day and shortening the workday itself to eight hours. As a result, turnover dropped sharply, and Ford could have its pick of the droves of workers who showed up looking for jobs. This trend, in turn, led directly to the creation of what would eventually evolve into one of the first "personnel" departments anywhere.

using these tests to assign soldiers to jobs. These attempts at staffing continued in the private sector after the end of World War I, and by 1923 *Personnel Management* by Scott and Clothier was already spelling out how to match a person's skills and aptitudes with the requirements of the job.

Another important ingredient in the origins of the human resource function during this period was the so-called **human relations era,** which emerged following the **Hawthorne studies.** Between 1927 and 1932, the Western Electric Company sponsored a major research program at its Hawthorne plant near Chicago. This research, conducted by Roethlisbeger and Mayo, revealed for perhaps the first time that individual and group behavior played an important role in organizations and that human behavior at work was something managers really needed to understand more fully. One of the Hawthorne studies suggested, for example, that individual attitudes may have been related to performance, while another suggested that a work group may have established norms to restrict the output of its individual group members.[16] Prior to this work, many managers paid almost no attention to their employees as people but instead viewed them in the same way they viewed a machine or a piece of equipment—as an economic entity to be managed dispassionately and with concern only for resource output.

Stimulated by the findings of the Hawthorne studies, managers began to focus more and more attention on better understanding the human character of their employees. During this era, for example, Abraham Maslow popularized his **hierarchy of human needs** (see Chapter 13 for a further discussion of this model).[17] And Douglas McGregor's well-known **Theory X** and **Theory Y** framework also grew from the human relations movement.[18] The basic premise of the human relations era was that if managers could make their employees more satisfied and happier, they would work harder and be more productive. Today, researchers and managers alike recognize that this viewpoint was overly simplistic and that both satisfaction and productivity are complex phenomena that affect and are affected by many different factors. Nonetheless, the increased awareness of the importance of human behavior stimulated during this period helped

The **human relations era** *supplanted scientific management as the dominant approach to management during the 1930s.*

The human relations era was stimulated by the **Hawthorne studies.**

Abraham Maslow's **hierarchy of human needs** *was developed during the human relations era.*

Douglas McGregor's **Theory X** *and* **Theory Y** *framework also grew from the human relations movement.*

organizations to become even more focused on better managing their human resources. These organizations saw effective management of human resources as a means of potentially increasing productivity and, incidentally, as a way of slowing the growth of unionism, which was beginning to gain popularity.

Personnel Management

We noted earlier that as organizations grew, they began to create specialized units to cope with their increasing hiring needs, to deal with government regulations, and to provide a mechanism for better dealing with behavioral issues. During the 1930s and 1940s these units gradually began to be called **personnel departments** (the word *personnel* was derived from an Old French word that meant "persons"). They were usually set up as special, self-contained departments charged with the responsibility of hiring new workers and administering basic human resource activities like pay and benefits. The recognition that human resources needed to be managed and the creation of personnel departments also gave rise to a new type of management function—**personnel management.**[19]

During this period, personnel management was concerned almost exclusively with hiring first-line employees such as production workers, salesclerks, custodians, secretaries, blue-collar workers, unskilled labor, and other operating employees. Issues associated with hiring, developing, and promoting managers and executives did not surface until later. The manager who ran the personnel department was soon called the **personnel manager.**

Personnel management took another step forward in its evolution during World War II. Both the military and its major suppliers developed an interest in better matching people with jobs. That is, they wanted to optimize the fit between the demands and requirements of the jobs that needed to be performed and the skills and interests of people available to perform them. Psychologists were consulted to help develop selection tests, for example, to assess individual skills, interests, and abilities more accurately. During the 1950s the lessons learned during the war were adapted for use in private industry. New and more sophisticated techniques were developed, especially in the area of testing, and companies also began to experiment with more sophisticated reward and incentive systems. Labor unions became more powerful and demanded a broader array of benefits for their members. In addition, government legislation expanded and continued to add complexity to the job of the personnel manager.

Still, from the first days of its inception until the 1970s, personnel management was not seen as a particularly important or critical function in most business organizations. While other managers accepted personnel as a necessary vehicle for hiring new operating employees, personnel management was also seen primarily as a routine clerical and bookkeeping function. For example, personnel was responsible for placing newspaper ads to recruit new employees, filling out paperwork for those employees after they were hired, and seeing that everyone was paid on time.

While other organizational units like marketing, finance, and operations grew in status and importance, the personnel department of most organizations was generally relegated to the status of necessary evil that had to be tolerated but that presumably contributed little to the success of the organization. Its offices were often drab and poorly equipped and were often located away from the central activity areas of the organization. And personnel managers themselves were often stereotyped as individuals who could not succeed in other functional areas and who were assigned to personnel either because the organization had nothing else for them to do or as a signal that the individual was not deemed to be a candidate for promotion to a higher-ranking position.

Personnel departments, *specialized organizational units for hiring and administering human resources, became popular during the 1930s and 1940s.*

Personnel management, *a new type of management function, grew from the recognition that human resources needed to be managed.*

The manager who ran the personnel department was called the **personnel manager.**

Human Resource Management Today

As noted earlier, the first real impetus for the increased importance for the role of human resource management came with the passage in 1964 of the Civil Rights Act. This law made it illegal for employers to consider factors such as gender, religion, race, skin color, or national origin when making employment-related decisions. The 1964 Civil Rights Act, combined with several subsequent amendments, executive orders, and legal decisions, made the processes of hiring and promoting employees within the organization far more complex. Thus, it quickly became critically important to organizations that those responsible for hiring and promoting employees fully understand the legal context within which they functioned. For example, ethical and moral issues aside, improper or inappropriate hiring practices left the organization open to lawsuits and other legal sanctions, accompanied by large fines, judgments, and new expenses. (We discuss the 1964 Civil Rights Act and related regulation more fully in the next chapter.)

But, as we discussed earlier in the chapter, the human resource manager's role as a compliance officer has grown into the role of strategic partner. As firms continue to recognize the importance of human resources it becomes critical that they do more than just obey the laws. Firms are increasingly competing to attract and retain the best talent they can, and then to develop strategies or tactics that leverage those talented people into a competitive advantage. At the same time, however, human resource management is changing in response to new technological innovations, and so it is important to consider how the electronic age has affected the human resource management function.

Human Resource Management in the Electronic Age

Through the years, as social and market dynamics changed, dramatic changes in technology also affected how we manage human resources. Some of these changes were related to the technologies available for measurement, although new technologies such as television, videotaping, and facsimile machines were also important for the development of the human resource management function. In recent years, however, the popularity of the Internet has had a profound impact on the human resource management function, and that impact is still developing and growing.

The widespread use of electronic technology and the Internet has not drastically affected the basic approach to how we manage human resources, but it has certainly had a major effect on how many human resource management systems are delivered. For example, in Chapter 5 we discuss methods for conducting job analysis, but we also note that the new O*NET system may allow many organizations to obtain the job analysis information they need online from a database. Chapter 7 discusses issues of recruiting, but one of the more popular ways for job seekers to search for jobs is by accessing one of the many job-search websites (like Monster.com). As a result, most organizations have come to realize that they must post job openings online with these services, in addition to using more traditional methods. Our examination of selection techniques in Chapter 7 also includes discussion of online testing and other ways in which the Internet has changed how organizations select employees. Training programs can now be purchased from vendors and provided to employees online, allowing them to take classes and training programs on their own schedule. Information systems, including information on benefits, make it easier for employees to check their benefit coverage and change it if desired.

Have these new applications of technology made human resource management easier? Clearly, it is easier now for management to deliver information and communicate with employees. But the openness of communications also means that employees can communicate with management, and this presents new challenges to managers. Electronic systems for communication and monitoring also bring up new challenges for the legal system (discussed in Chapter 2) and have led to new discussions about ethics and privacy. Thus, the new technology has made human resource management easier in some ways but more complicated in others. Have these new applications of technology made the management of human resources more effective? This question is important, but there is little data addressing it. Nonetheless, we will discuss the opportunities and challenges presented by new technology and the Internet throughout the book.

One other way in which technology has affected the human resource management function needs to be mentioned. As organizations introduced new technologies for manufacturing, communication, and human resource management, they also increased their need for more specialized employees. **Knowledge workers** include any employees whose jobs are to acquire and apply knowledge, and they contribute to the organization by the nature of what they know and how well they can apply what they know. Although knowledge workers include more than workers who deal with computer technology (scientists and lawyers, for example, are usually considered knowledge workers), the explosion of technology at work has led to a huge increase in the need for workers who can learn and apply the management of this technology. These employees present special problems for recruitment, retention, and compensation, as well as for motivation; we will discuss these challenges throughout the book.

Knowledge workers *are employees whose jobs are primarily concerned with the acquisition and application of knowledge, and they contribute to an organization through what they know and how they can apply what they know.*

Goals of Human Resource Management

This modern view of human resource management has also meant that these departments have taken on increasingly important goals. Understanding the goals of human resource management not only helps us to put human resource management in the proper perspective, but it also provides a framework for evaluating any activities carried out by this area.[20] Figure 1.1 illustrates the four basic goals of the human resource management function in most organizations today.

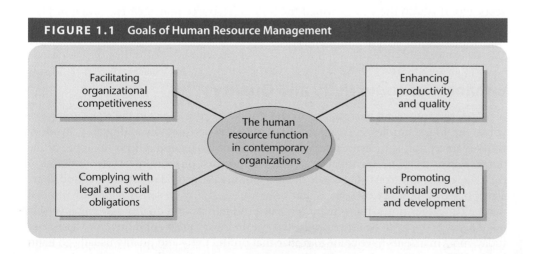

FIGURE 1.1 Goals of Human Resource Management

- Facilitating organizational competitiveness
- Enhancing productivity and quality
- The human resource function in contemporary organizations
- Complying with legal and social obligations
- Promoting individual growth and development

Facilitating Organizational Competitiveness

All organizations have a general set of goals and objectives that they try to accomplish. Regardless of the time horizon or the level of specificity involved in these goals, they are generally intended to promote the organization's ability to be competitive in its efforts to fulfill its purpose or mission. For example, business organizations like Microsoft, Wal-Mart, Nestlé, and Toyota exist primarily to make a profit for their owners. Thus, their goals and objectives usually deal with sales or revenue growth, market share, profitability, return on investment, and so forth. Other organizations exist for different purposes and so they have goals other than increased profitability. Educational organizations like Ohio State University, Houston Community College, and the St. Louis Independent School District have their unique purposes, for example. The same can be said for health-care organizations like the Mayo Clinic, governmental organizations such as the U.S. Federal Bureau of Investigation (FBI), State of Missouri's Revenue Department, and charitable organizations like the United Way.

Even though people often associate competitiveness only with businesses, each of these other types of organizations must also be managed effectively and compete for the right to continue to work toward fulfillment of its purpose. For example, a state university that misuses its resources and does not provide an adequate education for its students will not be held in high regard. As a result, the university will have difficulty competing for high-quality faculty and students, which are needed to enhance the university's reputation and thus make it more competitive. Similarly, a hospital that does not provide technical support for its doctors or adequate health care for its patients will find it more difficult to compete for the doctors and patients who might use its services and so pay for those services.

Given the central role that human resources play in organizational effectiveness, it is clear that the organization needs to employ those individuals most able to help it accomplish its goals and to remain competitive. The human resource management function in any organization must therefore have as one of its basic goals a clear understanding of how the organization competes, the kinds of human resources necessary to promote its ability to compete, and the most appropriate methods for attracting and developing those human resources.[21] This goal relates clearly to the strategic perspective developed more fully in Chapter 4.

We believe that facilitating organizational competitiveness must be the most important goal for modern human resource management. This is the goal that sets the modern function apart even from the human resource management function of twenty years ago. It is also the way in which the human resource management function provides the most value to the organization. Of course, the second goal we will discuss also contributes to this goal of competitiveness.

Enhancing Productivity and Quality

Productivity *is an economic measure of efficiency that summarizes and reflects the value of the outputs created by an individual, organization, industry, or economic system relative to the value of the inputs used to create them.*

Quality *is the total set of features and characteristics of a product or service that bears on its ability to satisfy stated or implied needs.*

A related but somewhat narrower concern for most organizations in the world today involves the issues, hurdles, and opportunities posed by productivity and quality. **Productivity** is an economic measure of efficiency that summarizes and reflects the value of the outputs created by an individual, organization, industry, or economic system relative to the value of the inputs used to create them.[22] **Quality** is the total set of features and characteristics of a product or service that bears on its ability to satisfy stated or implied needs.[23] In earlier times, many managers saw productivity and quality as being inversely related; the best way to be more productive was to lower quality and therefore costs. But today, most managers have come to realize that productivity and quality usually go hand in hand. That is, improving quality almost always increases productivity.

Organizations around the world have come to recognize the importance of productivity and quality for their ability not only to compete but also to survive. But actually improving productivity and quality takes a major and comprehensive approach that relies heavily on human resource management. Among other things, an organization that is serious about productivity and quality may need to alter its selection system to hire different kinds of workers. It will definitely need to invest more in training and development to give workers the necessary skills and abilities to create high-quality products and services, and it will need to use new and different types of rewards to help maintain motivation and effort among its employees. Thus, human resource management also has the goal in most organizations of helping to enhance productivity and quality through different activities and tasks.

Complying with Legal and Social Obligations

A third fundamental goal of the human resource management function today is to ensure that the organization is complying with and meeting its legal and social obligations. We noted earlier the impact of the 1964 Civil Rights Act and other regulations on hiring and other related human resource management practices and activities. More recently, the Americans with Disabilities Act has also had a major impact on human resource management. It is clearly important that organizations stay within the relevant legal boundaries whenever they deal with their employees. An organization that does not comply with government regulations and various legal constraints risks huge financial penalties, as well as considerable negative publicity and damage to its own internal corporate culture. This point is amply illustrated on the next page in the *HR Legal Brief*.

Beyond the strict legal parameters of compliance, however, more and more organizations today are also assuming at least some degree of social obligation to the society within which they operate. This obligation extends beyond the minimum activities necessary to comply with legal regulations and calls for the organization to serve as a contributing "citizen." Such efforts might include outreach programs to help attract individuals—often from minority populations—who may lack the basic skills necessary to perform meaningful jobs, or even the divestiture of holdings in countries with poor records on human rights. These activities are becoming increasingly important as financial management firms offer investment funds that specialize in socially responsible organizations, and corporate social performance (CSP) is often considered another dimension of organizational performance.

Promoting Individual Growth and Development

Finally, a fourth goal for human resource management in most contemporary organizations is to help promote the personal growth and development of its employees.[24] As a starting point, this goal usually includes basic job-related training and development activities. But in more and more organizations, it is increasingly going far beyond basic skills training. Some firms, for example, now offer basic educational courses in English, math, and science for their employees. Many organizations also include some provision for career development—helping people understand what career opportunities are available to them and how to pursue those opportunities. Formal mentoring programs are also commonly being used to help prepare women and minorities for advancement in the organization.[25]

Individual growth and development may also focus on areas that do not relate directly to job responsibilities. For example, some organizations provide stress-management programs to help their employees better cope with the anxieties and tensions of modern

Paying the Price

Just how important is the human resource department? Experiences at Rent-A-Center clearly show what can happen when a firm minimizes the importance of the human resource function. Thorn Americas, a unit of London-based Thorn EMI, had prospered as a large player in the rent-to-own industry. The firm had a large, professionally staffed human resource department and was known for its progressive hiring and employment development practices.

In 1998 Thorn merged with another large rent-to-own business, Renters Choice. The new firm was renamed Rent-A-Center, and an outsider named J. Ernest Talley was brought in to run the combined business. But Talley had some unusual views of the human resource function. Specifically, he saw human resources as an expense, bristled at the notion of government regulation, and allegedly had a strong bias against women. For example, he was quoted by one employee as saying, "Get rid of women any way you can." Another indicated that he said, "Women should be home taking care of their husbands and children, chained to a stove, not working in my stores."

Even though Rent-A-Center had 2,300 stores and 13,000 employees, Talley essentially eliminated the firm's human resource function. For example, he fired the firm's top human resource executive and dropped all training and employee relations activities. He kept only enough clerical support to handle payroll and benefits activities.

"Women should be home taking care of their husbands and children, chained to a stove, not working in my stores."

(Quote attributed to J. Ernest Talley by a Rent-A-Center employee*)

But his stance on women and the culture he created proved to be costly. Thousands of talented women left the company, and thousands of potentially valuable new employees were systematically blackballed. Talented males also left in droves, at least in part because they wanted no part of what Talley was trying to do.

Not surprisingly, Talley's stance soon prompted legal action. Several women charged that they had been demoted or forced to resign because of their gender. Others charged that Talley had created a hostile work environment, a key form of sexual harassment. For instance, at one national sales meeting in Las Vegas, Talley hired scantily clad go-go dancers for entertainment. Many of the men in attendance got drunk, while the women felt humiliated.

The lawsuit against Rent-A-Center represented 5,300 current and former employees, as well as approximately 10,000 rejected job applicants. One attorney involved in the case said, "I've never seen a case in which so many women and men tell the same kind of story all across the country. It's remarkable." Faced with overwhelming evidence, Rent-A-Center forced Talley to retire and settled the suit for $47 million in payments. The firm also agreed to re-establish a human resource department, hire a human resource vice president, and take numerous other steps to change its employment practices and culture.

Source: Robert Grossman, "Paying the Price," *HRMagazine,* August 2002, pp. 28–37 (*quote on p. 30).

---

life. Wellness and fitness programs are also becoming more common as organizations seek new and different ways to help their employees remain physically, mentally, and emotionally fit and better prepared to manage their lives and careers. Still another common area for continuing education is personal financial planning, which may even include assistance in writing a will or retirement planning.

But, increasingly, organizations are viewing this goal much more broadly. For many, it means that the firm should do everything it can to ensure that employees are personally fulfilled on the job. This may involve designing jobs that are more challenging and provide more personal satisfaction (see more in Chapter 14), or it may involve providing employees opportunities to be more creative at work (see Chapter 13). In general, more firms are seeing human resource management as part of the psychological contract that they provide a personally rewarding work experience for their employees in return for the employees' working toward the firm's strategic goals. A **psychological contract** is the overall set of expectancies held by the employee with regard to what he or she will contribute to the organization and held by the organization with regard to what it will

A **psychological contract** is the overall set of expectations held by the employee with regard to what he or she will contribute to the organization and that are held by the organization with regard to what it will provide to the individual in return.

provide to the individual in return. These firms know that they will get the most out of employees as sources of competitive advantage when the employees feel that their work experience is meaningful and helps them meet their potential. It is interesting to note how this has largely come full circle to the early days of human resource management and the human relations movement.

The Setting for Human Resource Management

Another important factor to consider in the modern view of human resource management is the setting in which the human resource manager operates. Traditionally, all human resource activities resided in a separate human resource department, but this model is becoming rare. Instead, human resource activities are carried out by both line and staff managers. Furthermore, we are seeing differences in the way human resource management operates in larger versus smaller companies. We will explore some of these different settings.

Human Resource Management as a Staff Versus Line Function

Organizations historically divided their managers into two groups: line management and staff management. Human resource management was traditionally considered to be a staff function. **Line managers** were those directly responsible for creating goods and services. That is, their contributions to the organization can generally be assessed

Line managers *are those directly responsible for creating goods and services.*

The most visible competitive arena for multinational businesses includes customers and revenue. But just as important is the competition for talent. Take Sophia Zhu, for instance. After she graduated from the People's University of Beijing, she had her pick of several job offers. Even though the firm offered a bit less money than some others, General Electric attracted Ms. Zhu because of its clear commitment to employee development and career opportunity. Among its other initiatives, GE recently opened a new training facility in Shanghai.

in terms of their actual contributions and costs to the organization's bottom line. The performance of a sales manager whose unit costs $500,000 per year to support (for salaries, administration, and so forth) and that generates $3.5 million per year in revenue can be evaluated this way. Operations managers, financial managers, and marketing managers were generally considered to have line functions.

Staff managers, on the other hand, were those responsible for an indirect or support function that would have costs but whose bottom-line contributions were less direct. Legal, accounting, and human resource departments were usually thought of as staff functions. Their role was to support line management's efforts to achieve organizational goals and objectives.

Today, however, many organizations have blurred this distinction. New forms of organizational design (such as teams and an emphasis on flatter and more decentralized organization) have made it more likely that many human resource management activities are actually carried out by line managers. For example, it is fairly common today for line managers to be involved in recruiting new employees for a work group, and sometimes for actually making the selection decision (although a staff member might help collect information needed to make that decision). Line managers are intimately involved in most of the interventions designed to enhance performance, and they often make decisions about pay raises and promotions.

In some organizations, the human resource management function is structured in a completely different way. In these firms, there is a human resource management department, but that department is structured around "centers of excellence." In these cases, the human resource department is responsible for providing services only in those cases where they can provide higher-quality services than can be purchased on the outside (i.e., through outsourcing, discussed earlier). When they cannot provide higher-quality services, they are often asked to identify and then manage the outside consultants who are brought in to perform the services. In still other cases, the human resource department itself functions as a consulting operation within the organization. These departments are expected to be responsive to the needs of the other functional areas, but they have to be able to demonstrate their added value, and they must actually "sell" their services to the line managers. In these arrangements, the human resource management department budget is very small, and the only way to hire and retain employees in that area is to provide services that other managers are willing to pay for (literally). Thus, the human resource management department becomes a self-funding operation, or it could even become somewhat of a profit center.

The Human Resource Department in Smaller Versus Larger Organizations

There are also noteworthy differences in the way human resource management operations are carried out in larger versus smaller organizations. As noted, responsibilities for carrying out human resource functions may reside in a separate human resource department, but many smaller organizations do not have such departments and must deliver the required services in different ways.[26]

Human resource management in smaller organizations   Most small organizations require line managers to handle their basic human resource functions. In the case of a franchised operation, like a single McDonald's or Pizza Hut restaurant, or an individual retail outlet such as a Gap or Limited clothing store, the store manager generally hires new employees, schedules and tracks working hours for all employees, and

Staff managers *are those responsible for an indirect or support function that would have costs but whose bottom-line contributions were less direct.*

disciplines problem employees. The franchiser or home office, in turn, generally suggests or mandates hourly wages, provides performance appraisal forms for local use, and may handle payroll services as well.

A small independent business is generally operated in the same way, with the owner or general manager handling human resource duties. Payroll and other basic administrative activities may be subcontracted to businesses in the local community that specialize in providing such services for other local organizations. Relatively little training is provided in these small organizations, and other human resource issues are relatively straightforward. Very small organizations are exempt from many legal regulations (again, we cover this topic more fully in Chapter 2). Thus, a single manager can usually handle the human resource function in smaller firms without too much difficulty.

Human resource management in larger organizations   As the firm grows beyond a certain size, however, a separate human resource unit becomes a necessity. At first, the manager who had been handling the human resource duties may delegate them to a special assistant, or even to an individual human resource manager. But when an organization reaches a size of around 200 to 250 employees, it generally establishes a self-contained human resource department. While there is no standard approach, a firm of this size might have one full-time manager and a single secretary or assistant to function as its human resource department. These individuals handle all of the firm's human resource administration.

All businesses—from the very largest to the smallest—need effective human resource management. To help meet this need, Lisa Bing recently left a lucrative job at Prudential Insurance to launch her own human resource consulting firm. During her fifteen-year career at Prudential, she had an opportunity to develop expertise in all facets of management in general and human resource management in particular. Now she is putting that experience to work by helping other companies.

As the firm continues to grow, however, more assistance is needed to staff the human resource department, and so that department also grows. Indeed, in very large organizations, human resource functions are themselves likely to specialize into subunits. For example, large firms might have one department to handle recruiting and selection, one to handle wage and salary administration, one to handle training and development, and still another to handle labor relations. Figure 1.2 shows how Texas Instruments has organized its human resource function.

The Human Resource Management System

The modern view of human resource management is also a systems-oriented view. That is, by its very nature, a strategic perspective requires the coordination of the various human resource management activities to ensure that they are consistent with corporate strategy. If those services are provided primarily internally by the human resource management department, this coordination can be fairly simple. As those activities move outside the organization, perhaps by contracting with outside vendors, the coordination problem becomes much more complex. But, in any case, a strategic perspective means understanding that a decision made in any one area of human resource management will affect what happens in every other area. If an organization needs highly skilled, knowledgeable workers to carry out its strategy, then all staffing activities must be coordinated toward identifying and attracting such employees. But, once these employees join the firm, performance appraisals, compensation, and performance management systems must all be changed to reflect the nature of the new employee.

Thus, while we will often discuss various tasks and functions of human resource management from the perspective of discrete, self-contained activities, this is not the case in practice. In fact, these tasks and functions are highly interrelated and do not unfold in a neat and systematic manner. Each of the various tasks and functions can affect and/or be affected by any of the other tasks and functions. And most basic human resource functions are practiced on an ongoing and continuous basis.

Indeed, it is truly appropriate to think of human resource management as a system. A system is an interrelated set of elements functioning as a whole. A **human resource management system,** then, is an integrated and interrelated approach to managing human resources that fully recognizes the interdependence among the various tasks and functions that must be performed. This viewpoint is illustrated in Figure 1.3. The basic premise of this perspective is that every element of the human resource

A **human resource management system** *is an integrated and interrelated approach to managing human resources that fully recognizes the interdependence among the various tasks and functions that must be performed.*

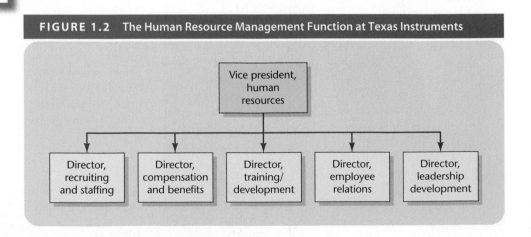

FIGURE 1.2   The Human Resource Management Function at Texas Instruments

Vice president, human resources

Director, recruiting and staffing

Director, compensation and benefits

Director, training/ development

Director, employee relations

Director, leadership development

FIGURE 1.3   A Systems View of Human Resource Management

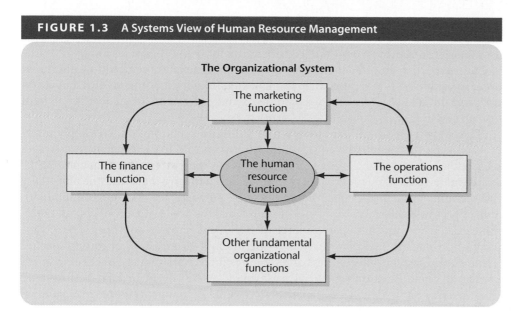

management system must be designed and implemented with full knowledge and understanding of, and integration with, the various other elements. For example, poor recruiting practices will result in a weak pool of applicants. Even if the organization has sophisticated selection techniques available, it will not make much difference without a pool of truly qualified applicants from which to choose. As a result, there will be a greater need for training before a new employee starts work to provide him or her with the necessary skills. Subsequent performance appraisals will also be more difficult because it may take longer before these employees are truly proficient in their jobs, and this situation will affect how much they are paid.

Figure 1.3 also illustrates another useful systems-based perspective on human resource management. Many systems are themselves composed of subsystems—systems within a broader and more general system. By viewing the overall organization as a system, human resource management then can be conceptualized as a subsystem within that more general organizational system. As the figure shows, the human resource management subsystem both affects and is affected by the other functional subsystems throughout the organization. This perspective can help reinforce the idea that human resource management must be approached from the same strategic vantage point afforded the other areas within the organization. Failure to do so can result in unanticipated consequences, poor coordination, and less effective performance.

To illustrate, if the organization makes a strategic decision to compete on the basis of high-quality service, it will almost certainly need to use several mechanisms to do so. For example, the organization will need to recruit and subsequently hire more qualified new workers and to provide more training to both new and current workers. Similarly, if the financial function of an organization dictates that major cost cutting be undertaken, some portion of those costs may come from the human resource area. Thus, human resource managers may need to reduce the size of the workforce, attempt to renegotiate labor contracts for a lower pay rate, defer payment of some benefits, and so forth.

The increasing globalization of business also reinforces the need to view the human resource management function from a systems perspective. That is, human resource managers must take a global perspective in managing people. Within the borders of their own country, human resource managers must consider the social norms, individual expectations, and so forth that shape worker behaviors. Cross-national assignments for managers are also an important consideration for many businesses today. Thus, the global perspective on human resource management includes the need to understand domestic similarities and differences in managing human resources in different countries and the role of international assignments and experiences in the development of human resource skills and abilities.

This systems approach has also led to organizations becoming increasingly interested in ways to evaluate the effectiveness of human resource management activities relative to the firm's strategic goals. Traditionally, many experts believed that human resource management practices could not be assessed with anywhere near the objectivity that we could evaluate the effectiveness of a sales campaign, for instance. But the 1980s and 1990s saw further developments in utility analysis that made it possible to determine exactly how much human resource management activities contributed to a company's bottom line.[27] **Utility analysis** is the attempt to measure, in more objective terms, the impact and effectiveness of human resource management practices in terms of metrics such as a firm's financial performance. The advent of high-performance work systems resulted in broader metrics for evaluating human resource management activities,[28] and as a result, it is now possible to develop fairly objective measures of the impact and/or effectiveness of human resource management practices. It remains the role of the human resource management department, however, to develop these metrics and to apply them to all human resource management activities undertaken on behalf of the organization. We will return to this topic again in Chapter 4.

Utility analysis   *is the attempt to measure, in more objective terms, the impact and effectiveness of human resource management practices in terms of such metrics as a firm's financial performance.*

Human Resource Managers

Who are today's human resource managers? Given the rapid and dynamic changes that have characterized this field, it should come as no surprise that human resource managers represent a diverse set of professionals with a variety of backgrounds, experiences, and career objectives. A human resource executive today needs to understand different specialized areas, such as the legal environment, the process of change management, labor relations, and so forth. In addition, contemporary human resource executives must also possess general management skills and abilities reflecting conceptual, diagnostic, and analytical skills. It is important that they fully understand the role and importance of the human resource function for their organization.[29] Thus, both a solid educational background and a foundation of experience are necessary prerequisites for success.[30]

Consistent with these changes, it is often more useful to conceptualize human resources as a center of expertise within the organization. That is, everyone in the organization should recognize human resource managers as the firm's most critical source of information about employment practices, employee behavior, labor relations, and the effective management of all aspects of people at work. This view of human resource management is illustrated in Figure 1.4, which builds upon the systems view of human resource management presented earlier in Figure 1.3.

Professionalism and Human Resource Management

Accompanying the shifts and changes in human resource functions and importance is a greater emphasis on professionalism, reflected by a clear and recognized knowledge base and a generally understood way of doing business.[31] Human resource managers are no longer regarded as second-class corporate citizens. And more and more organi-

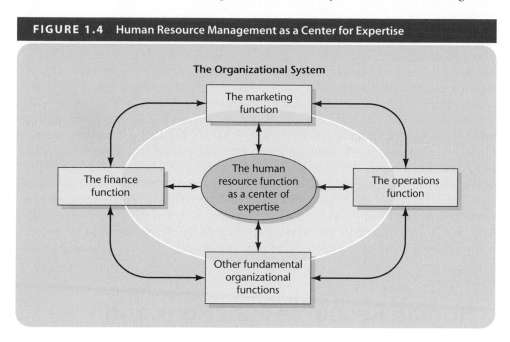

FIGURE 1.4   Human Resource Management as a Center for Expertise

zations are including a stint in human resources as a normal step on a person's way to the top. Senior human resource executives in large firms earn six-figure salaries and receive the same sorts of perquisites once reserved only for executives of operating units. Indeed, the salaries for human resource executives continue to rise at an impressive rate. Human resource departments are also being viewed more and more as cost centers, with the goal of providing clear and measurable financial benefits to the organization.[32]

Many human resource managers today belong to the Society for Human Resource Management (SHRM), the field's largest professional association. SHRM publishes professional journals that enable members to stay abreast of the newest developments in the field, sponsor workshops and conferences, and so forth. To help establish human resource management as a recognized profession, SHRM has created the Human Resource Certification Institute (HRCI). The HRCI is expected to become the recognized symbol of accreditation in much the same way that the accounting profession uses the certified public accountant (CPA) exam and credential to designate those individuals who have formally achieved basic minimal competencies in prescribed areas.

The HRCI currently has two levels of accreditation. To become a Professional in Human Resources, a manager must have four years of professional experience and pass an examination covering the basic body of human resource knowledge (having a college degree in an appropriate field such as human resource management or industrial/organizational psychology reduces the experience requirement base to two years). To become a Senior Professional in Human Resource Management, an individual must pass the same exam and have eight years of professional experience. The three most recent years of experience must be at a policymaking (senior executive) level in an organization.

Careers in Human Resource Management

How does one become a human resource manager? Career opportunities in human resource management continue to grow and expand and are expected to continue to do so. One obvious way to enter this profession is to get a degree in human resource management (or a related field) and then seek entry-level employment as a human resource manager. Alternative job options may be as the human resource manager for a small firm or as a human resource specialist in a larger organization. Some universities also offer specialized graduate degree programs in human resource management. For example, a master of science or master of business administration degree with a concentration in human resource management would likely lead to a higher-level position in an organization than would a bachelor's degree alone.

Another route to human resource management would be through line management. As described earlier, more and more firms are beginning to rotate managers through the human resource function as part of their own personal career development program. Thus, people who go to work in marketing or finance may very well have an opportunity at some point to sample central human resource management responsibilities. Regardless of the path taken, however, those interested in human resource management are likely to have a fascinating, demanding, and rewarding experience as they help their organization compete more effectively through the power of the people who comprise every organization in every industry in every marketplace in the world today.

Human Resource Functions and the Organization of This Book

It should be clear by now that the human resource management function has changed over the years, and it continues to change at a rapid pace. As human resource management was becoming more important because of the increasingly complex legal environment, other changes in the world of work led to other pressures to manage human resources more effectively. Changes in the competitive landscape, combined with rapid advances in technology and communication, made it more important than ever for organizations to use their resources wisely and to capitalize on the full value of those resources. At the same time, however, there was increasing concern over what was called quality-of-work-life issues. While managers were becoming increasingly concerned with ways to improve productivity and competitiveness, they also began to realize that it was important for workers to feel that their jobs were a source of personal satisfaction and growth. Successful organizations were those that could maximize effectiveness while making work more meaningful and fulfilling.

As noted earlier, human resources are an organization's most important resources. Hiring the right people and then equipping them with the right skills and abilities can substantially affect the quality and quantity of whatever goods or services the organization produces. Properly motivated and committed employees can add immeasurable value to an organization's bottom line. Given the shift in competitiveness, top executives in most firms began to see that human resource management practices and policies significantly affected their ability to formulate and implement strategy in any area and that other strategic decisions significantly affected the firm's human resources as well.

Thus, a combination of historical forces, legal pressures, and the increased need to gain competitive advantage has led to our contemporary view of human resource management. Figure 1.5 shows the major tasks and functions that comprise human resource management today. This figure also represents the framework around which this book is organized. After this overview chapter, we start with the environment in which the human resource manager must function.

The legal environment of human resource management, as already noted, is a very important aspect of the context for the area. Organizations that do not understand their legal environment are almost certain to encounter difficulties in almost every aspect of human resource management and may face financial and legal penalties as a result. Understanding the legal environment begins with equal employment opportunity and requires a complete understanding of protected classes in the workforce and what organizations must do to ensure that members of those classes have the same chances for success in the organization as do any other employees. Numerous special legal issues regarding compensation, benefits, labor relations, working conditions, training practices, and other related areas of human resource management must also be understood and considered by all managers. Chapter 2 provides in-depth coverage of these and other legal issues confronting human resource managers today.

Another vital dimension of the environment of human resources is the global context in which the organization functions. Large multinationals like Ford, Sony, and Unilever clearly have numerous international human resource issues to manage. But many smaller firms are also venturing into foreign markets. Even purely domestic firms may find themselves buying from, selling to, and/or competing with businesses in other countries. Thus, all managers today must have an appreciation of the international business environment. Chapter 3 explores the various issues associated with managing human resources in an international company and with taking a global approach to human resource management itself.

To function effectively within the environment, most experts today agree that it is necessary to adopt a strategic perspective on human resource management.[33] That is, all aspects of the human resource management system should be coordinated, and together they should support the strategic goals of the organization. We will discuss strategic human resource management in more detail in Chapter 4.

Part Two of the book focuses on the decisions that are made in the human resource management area. We begin by discussing various sources of information used by the human resource manager to make those decisions. Thus, in Chapter 5 we discuss how human resource planning interacts with strategy to provide important input for the human resource management decision maker. We also discuss the economy and job analysis as important sources of information for decisions in this area.

The first general decision we discuss regards the form and structure of the organization, as discussed in Chapter 6. Here we explore rightsizing and issues of voluntary and involuntary turnover, as well as other decisions that can affect how the organization will operate. Next we turn to staffing in Chapter 7, where we examine issues related to both recruitment and selection. Staffing decisions also require input about the form and structure of the organization, and staffing decisions provide significant input for the next set of decisions—those involving diversity. Chapter 8 discusses diversity, not in terms of deciding whether or not to have a diverse organization, but relative to decisions about how to best develop diversity in a way that it serves the organization's strategic goals.

Part Three deals with managing the workforce. We begin with an examination of basic compensation and benefits in Chapter 9, since pay and benefits are an important part of managing and retaining valued employees. Chapter 10 is where we discuss performance appraisal and development. In this chapter we begin with a review of issues in the measurement of performance, but then broaden our discussion to deal with developing employees and managing their careers. Chapter 11 deals with labor relations and various issues associated with managing a unionized workforce, while Chapter 12 covers issues of safety, well-being, and health on the job. We also deal with some of the more recent challenges in terms of security in this chapter.

Part Four is devoted exclusively to enhancing performance, critical for achieving the goal of improved competitiveness. Chapter 13 presents an overview of human motivation and discusses several major models of how to motivate employees to exert greater effort on the job. Chapter 14 discusses specific performance enhancement techniques

FIGURE 1.5   The Human Resource Management Process

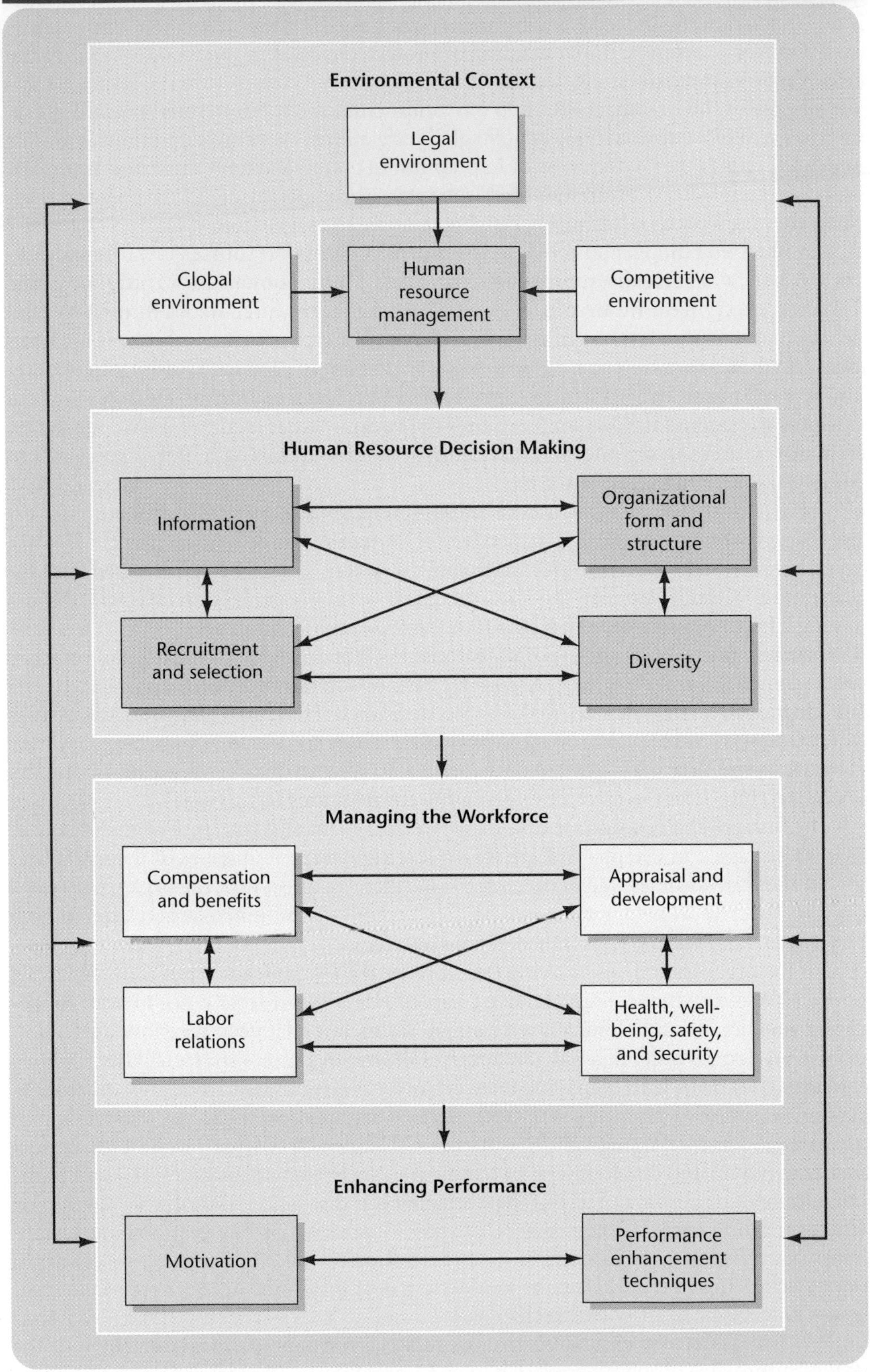

Environmental Context

Legal environment

Global environment → Human resource management ← Competitive environment

Human Resource Decision Making

Information ↔ Organizational form and structure

Recruitment and selection ↔ Diversity

Managing the Workforce

Compensation and benefits ↔ Appraisal and development

Labor relations ↔ Health, well-being, safety, and security

Enhancing Performance

Motivation ↔ Performance enhancement techniques

that are critical for achieving competitive advantage. Chapter 14 discusses job design and job enrichment as tools for enhancing performance, as well as the importance of incentive pay plans, and it also discusses the role of training and development, as well as flexible work systems and general performance management techniques, as ways of enhancing performance and productivity.

In addition to following this framework throughout the book, another perspective also shapes the material covered here. Many human resource functions are the responsibility of managers who may not have had formal training in the fundamentals of human resource management. In fact, many students who elect or who are required to take a survey course in human resource management do not plan to become human resource management professionals. On the other hand, many other students may plan to work in the human resource field. Regardless of your specific intentions, both future and current managers need to know the basic concepts about the management of human resources.

The level of detail and the importance of specific elements of an area will vary, however, depending on whether you plan to be a professional human resource manager or not. Therefore, we will end each chapter with two different Key Point lists after the chapter summary. One Key Points list will present the major learning points for the human resource management professional. You will need to understand these points if you plan to do this kind of work for a living. The second Key Points list will present learning points for the reader who is not planning to become a human resource manager. We assume that these readers plan to move into some type of management position, however, and so we will outline the points that any manager should take away to be effective in his or her job.

Finally, in each section we also include additional topical material for the student (or instructor) who wants to gain more depth in a specialized topic in human resource management. This material goes above and beyond what most students (whether they are planning to go into human resource management or not) will need, but it does provide the opportunity to dig a bit deeper in a few selected areas.

Chapter Summary

Human resource management is a relatively new functional area in many organizations. As today's large organizations began to emerge around 100 years ago, they found it necessary to establish specialized units to handle hiring and the administration of current employees. These units were usually called personnel departments and were headed by personnel managers. Contemporary human resource management deals with different complex and strategic issues.

Human resource management generally has four basic goals to pursue: facilitating organizational competitiveness, enhancing productivity and quality, complying with legal and social obligations, and promoting individual growth and development. Each goal is an important ingredient in organizational effectiveness.

Line (or operating) managers and staff managers (or specialized human resource managers) typically share the responsibility for effective human resource management. Both sets of managers must work to deal with the conflict that often occurs. The owner or general manager still often handles human resource management in smaller firms, but as organizations grow, they usually establish separate human resource departments. Managers should also adopt a systems perspective on the human resource function.

Today's human resource managers are becoming more and more professional in both their training and their orientation toward their work. A variety of career paths are also available for people wanting to work in the human resource function.

Key Points for Future HR Managers

- Modern human resource managers must function as strategic partners. That is, they must understand the nature of the business and how human resource activities can help support and foster business goals.

- Traditionally, human resource management was not viewed in such high esteem, and those responsible for these activities were instead seen primarily as recordkeepers.

- The passage of the Civil Rights Act of 1964 and the increasing global competition of the 1980s resulted in a fundamental change in the importance of the human resource management function.

- Many traditional human resource management activities are now being outsourced, but human resource management departments are still generally responsible for tying human resource practices to a firm's strategic goals and for measuring the effectiveness of human resource management practices.

- Human resource management has become a true profession, and a career in this field typically requires formal education.

- Human resource management practices differ fairly dramatically between smaller and larger organizations.

Key Points for Future General Managers

- The effective management of a firm's human resources is probably the most important source of sustained competitive advantage for a modern organization.

- The changing legal environment has made it critical that an organization be aware of the legal requirements involved in all human resource management practices. Failure to do so can be quite costly.

- Effective human management practices support corporate strategic goals.

- Everyone who deals with people has a need to understand some basic notions of human resource management.

Review and Discussion Questions

1. Identify five examples of human resources in your college or university.

2. Summarize the evolution of the human resource function in organizations.

3. Summarize the basic ideas underlying the human resource management system concept.

4. What are the goals of human resource management?

5. Who is responsible for human resource management?

6. Why do you think human resource management (or personnel) was previously held in such low esteem in many organizations?

7. Do you think human resource management would have become more important even if laws such as the 1964 Civil Rights Act had never been passed? Why or why not?

8. Identify several consequences of an organization's failure to recognize that its human resource management practices comprise an interrelated system.

9. Do you think some human resource management goals are more important than others? Why or why not? What implications might be drawn if a particular manager felt that certain goals were indeed more important than others?

10. Do you think it might be possible for a large company today to function without a human resources department?

Enterprise Builds on People

When most people think of car-rental firms, the names Hertz and Avis usually come to mind. But in the last few years, Enterprise Rent-A-Car has overtaken both of these industry giants, and today it stands as both the largest and the most profitable business in the car-rental industry. In 2006, for instance, the firm had sales in excess of $8.2 billion and employed 61,000 people.

Jack Taylor started Enterprise in St. Louis in 1957. Taylor had a unique strategy in mind for Enterprise, and that strategy played a key role in the firm's initial success. Most car-rental firms like Hertz and Avis base most of their locations in or near airports, train stations, and other transportation hubs. These firms see their customers as business travelers and people who fly for vacation and then need transportation at the end of their flight. But Enterprise went after a different customer. It sought to rent cars to individuals whose own cars are being repaired or who are taking a driving vacation.

The firm got its start by working with insurance companies. A standard feature in many automobile insurance policies is the provision of a rental car when one's personal car has been in an accident or has been stolen. Firms like Hertz and Avis charge relatively high daily rates because their customers need the convenience of being near an airport and/or they are having their expenses paid by their employer. These rates are often higher than insurance companies are willing to pay, so customers who use these firms end up paying part of the rental bill themselves. In addition, their locations are also often inconvenient for people seeking a replacement car while theirs is in the shop.

But Enterprise located stores in downtown and suburban areas, where local residents actually live. The firm also provides local pickup and delivery service in most areas. It also negotiates exclusive contract arrangements with local insurance agents. They get the agent's referral business while guaranteeing lower rates that are more in line with what insurance covers.

In recent years Enterprise has started to expand its market base by pursuing a two-pronged growth strategy. First, the firm has started opening airport locations to compete with Hertz and Avis more directly. But their target is still the occasional renter rather than the frequent business traveler. Second, the firm also began to expand into international markets and today has rental offices in the United Kingdom, Ireland, and Germany.

Another key to Enterprise's success has been its human resource strategy. The firm carefully targets a certain kind of individual to hire: its preferred new employee is a college graduate from the middle-to-bottom half of the graduating class, and preferably one who was an athlete or who was otherwise actively involved in campus social activities. The rationale for this unusual academic standard is actually quite simple. Enterprise managers do not believe that especially high levels of achievement are necessary to perform well in the car-rental industry, but having a college degree nevertheless demonstrates intelligence and motivation. In addition, since interpersonal relations are important to its business, Enterprise wants people who were social directors or high-ranking officers of social organizations such as fraternities or sororities. Athletes are also desirable because of their competitiveness.

Once hired, new employees at Enterprise are often shocked at the performance expectations placed on them by the firm. They generally work long, grueling hours for relatively low pay. And all Enterprise managers are expected to jump in and help wash or vacuum cars when a rental agency gets backed up. All Enterprise managers must adhere to a stringent set of dress and grooming requirements. For instance, men must wear coordinated dress shirts and ties and can have facial hair only when "medically necessary." And women must wear skirts no shorter than two inches above their knees or creased pants.

So what are the incentives for working at Enterprise? For one thing, it's an unfortunate fact of life that college graduates with low grades often struggle to find work. Thus, a job at Enterprise is still better than no job at all. The firm does not hire outsiders—every position is filled by promoting someone already inside the company. Thus, Enterprise employees know that if they work hard and do their best, they may very well succeed in moving higher up the corporate ladder at a growing and successful firm.[34]

Case Questions

1. Would Enterprise's approach to human resource management work in other industries?

2. Does Enterprise face any risks from its human resource strategy?

3. Would you want to work for Enterprise? Why or why not?

Building HR Management Skills

Purpose: The purpose of this exercise is to serve as an icebreaker at the beginning of the course while simultaneously getting you to think about how human resource management will affect you personally.

Step 1: Your instructor will ask you to form small groups of four to five members each. Each member of the group should first introduce him- or herself to other group members.

Step 2: Group members should write their majors and career objectives on a sheet of paper and place the sheets in the center of the group so that everyone can read them.

Step 3: Working in concert with your group members, respond to the following questions and ideas:

1. How does human resource management affect each academic major and set of career objectives represented in the group?

2. How would group members feel about starting their careers in a human resource department?

3. How would group members feel about taking a position in human resources later in their careers?

4. What specific skills and abilities do group members believe are most important for someone who wants to work in human resources?

5. What will group members expect from the human resources department at the organization where they begin their career?

Step 4: Each group should select one member to serve as its representative. Your instructor may ask each representative to summarize the responses of her or his group to these questions either verbally or in writing.

Step 5: Reconvene with your group and discuss areas of agreement and disagreement among the various groups and group members.

Ethical Dilemmas in HR Management

Assume that you are a top human resource executive for a large, privately held company. Your specific area of responsibility is managing all aspects of compensation and benefits for the company; you report to the executive vice president of administration. This individual, in turn, is from the finance department and oversees HR, finance, and environmental regulation and shows little interest in HR per se as long as things are going smoothly.

The firm employs over 20,000 workers, has operations in fifteen countries, and has a long and stable history of growth and profitability. The owners of the firm, the descendants of the original founder, are not actively involved in management and express satisfaction with the firm's current and projected financial performance. Indeed, all components of financial performance are excellent, and the firm is widely respected for the quality of its management. The owners also have often expressed an interest in protecting their workers and maintaining as much job security as possible. The firm has not been forced to lay off any of its employees in more than twenty years.

About a year ago you read some research extolling the benefits of outsourcing. You have been quietly looking into how outsourcing might benefit your company. Your findings are troubling, and you are now trying to decide how to proceed. Specifically, you have determined that outsourcing parts of the firm's human resource function could yield some modest cost savings for the firm. Unfortunately for you, compensation and benefits also seem to be the area most conducive to outsourcing.

On the one hand, as a manager you feel obligated to consider anything that might lower costs and/or improve the financial performance of the firm. Outsourcing does seem almost certain to improve financial performance, albeit only in relatively small ways. Thus, if you present your findings to your boss, the firm and its owners will benefit. On the other hand, if outsourcing were to be implemented, you estimate that approximately fifteen employees would lose their jobs, and your own position would be substantially diminished in importance.

Questions

1. What are the ethical issues in this situation?

2. What are the basic arguments for and against out-sourcing in this situation?

3. What do you think most managers would do? What would you do?

HR Internet Exercise

 Each year *Fortune* magazine publishes a list of what it calls "The Best Companies to Work for in America." The editors of the magazine base their list on extensive reviews of the human resource practices of many different firms and surveys of current and former employees.

As the first step in this exercise, use the Internet to identify the ten very best places to work as reflected in the most recent *Fortune* list. Next, visit the websites for these ten organizations and review the material at these sites through the eyes of someone looking for a job. Be sure to visit all the links to each company's different webpages at its website. Use the information you find to answer the following questions.

Questions

1. What specific information on each website most interested you as a prospective employee?

2. Based solely on the information you located, which company scores best, in your mind, as a potential employer?

3. What are the advantages and disadvantages to both employers and individuals seeking employment of using the Internet as a potential recruiting tool?

2

The Legal Environment

CHAPTER OBJECTIVES

After studying this chapter you should be able to:

- Describe the legal context of human resource management.

- Identify key laws that prohibit discrimination in the workplace and discuss equal employment opportunity.

- Discuss legal issues in compensation, labor relations, and other areas in human resource management.

- Discuss the importance to an organization of evaluating its legal compliance.

For years Omar Belazi, a former RadioShack store manager, enthusiastically logged sixty-five-hour workweeks, stayed late to clean the store's restrooms and vacuum the floor, and worked all weekend just to help meet the store's sales goals. Regardless of the hours he worked, however, he received the same monthly salary. Belazi gradually grew tired of the long hours, extra work, and stress and left Radio-Shack.

He eventually became part of a class-action lawsuit against RadioShack that included 1,300 current and former California store managers. Their contention was that they were managers in title only. More specifically, the lawsuit argued that all true management decisions were made at higher levels in the organization, leaving those with the title of store manager as little more than sales workers. But because they had a managerial title and were paid salaries, the company did not have to pay them overtime. The lawsuit was settled when RadioShack agreed to pay $29.9 million to the plaintiffs.

At the heart of the argument was a decades-old law that mandates overtime payments for hourly operating workers who work more than forty hours a week but allows firms to pay salaries to professionals regardless of how many hours they work. The Fair Labor Standards Act specifically exempts those in executive, administrative, or professional jobs from overtime payments. But because so many jobs have shifted from manufacturing settings to service settings, and because the nature of so many jobs has changed, the lines between different kinds of work have blurred.

And whether intentional or not, many firms now routinely use general titles such as "manager," "administrator," or "analyst" but assign employees with those titles tasks that do not always fit the title. For instance, Mr. Belazi was not specifically directed to work extra on weekends or to clean the restrooms. But if an hourly worker had been hired, that person's time would have been charged against the store's weekly labor budget. If he didn't maximize the labor hours he and his employees devoted to selling, his store's sales would drop and he would be reprimanded.

RadioShack, of course, is not the only employer who has had to confront this problem. Starbucks and SBC Pacific Bell both settled similar charges in California with payments to plaintiffs. In Louisiana, Eckerd Drugs also settled a case involving 1,100 pharmacists. In this case the pharmacists charged that their pay was docked if they worked less than forty hours per week but that they received no overtime if they worked in excess of forty hours. Eckerd denied guilt and maintained that it settled only to avoid a lengthy court battle. And in one of the most closely watched battlegrounds of all, retailing giant Wal-Mart is currently fighting literally dozens of similar lawsuits in thirty states.[1]

"It gets to be very stressful, very tiring. You just get up and go to RadioShack and go home and go to sleep."

(Omar Belazi, ex-RadioShack employee)

L ike every other organization today, RadioShack must adhere to the laws and regulations that govern its employment practices. In general, organizations try to follow such laws and regulations for several reasons. One is an inherent commitment in most organizations to ethical and socially responsible behavior. Another is to avoid the direct costs and bad publicity that might result from lawsuits brought against the organization if those laws and regulations are broken. But as the opening case illustrates, these laws and regulations are sometimes ambiguous and open to different interpretations. As we will see, failure to follow the law, even because of a well-intentioned misunderstanding, can be enormously costly to an organization.

As we noted in Chapter 1, the proliferation of laws and regulations affecting employment practices in the 1960s and 1970s was a key reason for the emergence of human resource management as a vital organizational function. Managing within the complex legal environment that affects human resource practices requires a full understanding of that legal environment and the ability to ensure that others within the organization also understand it.[2] This chapter is devoted to helping you understand the legal environment of human resource management. First we establish the legal context of human resource management. We then focus on perhaps the most important area of this legal context—equal employment opportunity—and review several key court cases that have established the law in this area. Subsequent sections introduce legal issues in compensation and in labor relations. Various emerging legal issues are also introduced and discussed. Finally, we conclude by summarizing how many organizations today evaluate their legal compliance.

The Legal Context of Human Resource Management

The legal context of human resource management is shaped by different forces. The catalyst for modifying or enhancing the legal context may be legislative initiative, social change, or judicial rulings. Governmental bodies pass laws that affect human resource practices, for example, and the courts interpret those laws as they apply to specific circumstances and situations. Thus, the regulatory environment itself is quite complex and affects different areas within the human resource management process.[3]

The Regulatory Environment of Human Resource Management

The legal and regulatory environment of human resource management in the United States emerges as a result of a three-step process, starting with the actual creation of new regulation. This regulation can come in the form of new laws or statutes passed by national, state, or local government bodies; however, most start at the national level. State and local regulations are more likely to extend or modify national regulations than create new ones. In addition, as we will see later, the president of the United States can also create regulations that apply to specific situations.

The second step in the regulation process is the enforcement of these regulations. Occasionally the laws themselves provide for enforcement through the creation of special agencies or other forms of regulatory groups. (We will discuss one important agency, the Equal Employment Opportunity Commission, later in the chapter.) In other situations enforcement might be assigned to an existing agency, such as the Department of Labor. The court system also interprets laws that the government passes and provides another vehicle for enforcement. To be effective, an enforcing agency must have an appropriate degree of power. The ability to levy fines or bring lawsuits against firms that violate the law are among the most powerful tools provided to the various agencies charged with enforcing human resource regulations.

The third step in the regulation process is the actual practice and implementation of those regulations in organizations. That is, organizations and managers must implement and follow the guidelines that the government has passed and that the courts and regulatory agencies attempt to enforce. In many cases, following regulations is a logical and straightforward process. In some cases, however, a regulation may be unintentionally ambiguous or be interpreted by the courts in different ways over time. Regardless of the clarity of the regulation, the actual process of implementing and demonstrating adherence to it may take an extended period of time. Thus, organizations are sometimes put in the difficult position of figuring out how to follow a particular regulation and/or needing an extended period of time to enact full compliance. The Lighter Side of HR highlights this point.

THE LIGHTER SIDE OF HR

The regulatory environment of human resource management imposes numerous constraints on organizations. Laws regarding employment practices have become so complicated in recent years that many employers are unsure of their own rights when it comes to hiring or terminating employees. For example, a firm that uses discriminatory practices can be sued for not hiring someone or for firing a current employee, and the burden of proof is often on the employer to prove that it is not using discriminatory practices. Not surprisingly, many employment decisions today are routinely reviewed by human resource experts and/or attorneys. And the opinions of these experts and attorneys often determine whether or not someone will be hired or fired.

"I've been speaking to my attorneys, Larson, and this time we think we've got you fired."

Source: Danny Shanahan, c/o Riley Illustrations

Basic Areas of Legal Regulation

Regulations exist in almost every aspect of the employment relationship. As illustrated in Figure 2.1, equal employment opportunity intended to protect individuals from illegal discrimination is the most fundamental and far-reaching area of the legal regulation of human resource management. Indeed, in one way or another, almost every law and statute governing employment relationships is essentially attempting to ensure equal employment opportunity. But equal employment opportunity has been interpreted to include protection that goes beyond ensuring that a person has a fair chance at being hired for a job for which the person is qualified. As also illustrated in Figure 2.1, this protection extends to preventing illegal discrimination against current employees with regard to performance appraisal, pay, promotion opportunities, and various other dimensions of the employment relationship. In addition, several related legal issues warrant separate discussion as well.

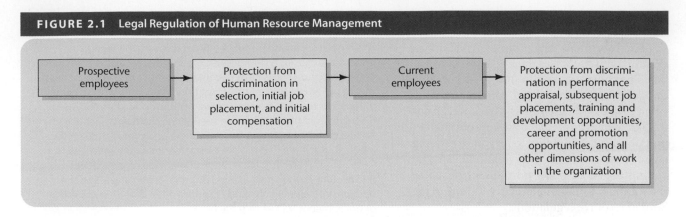

FIGURE 2.1   Legal Regulation of Human Resource Management

Equal Employment Opportunity

Some managers assume that the legal regulation of human resource management is a relatively recent phenomenon. In reality, however, concerns about equal opportunity can be traced back to the Thirteenth and Fourteenth Amendments to the Constitution of the United States. The Thirteenth Amendment, passed in 1865, abolished slavery; the Fourteenth Amendment, passed in 1868, made it illegal for government to take the life, liberty, or property of individuals without due process of law. The Fourteenth Amendment goes on to prohibit states from denying equal protection to their residents, and it has actually been cited in a limited number of cases where reverse discrimination (discussed later in the chapter) has been alleged. The Reconstruction Civil Rights Acts of 1866 and 1871 further extended protection offered to people under the Thirteenth and Fourteenth Amendments, and together with those amendments, these laws still form the basis for present-day federal court actions that involve the payment of compensatory and punitive damages.[4]

Discrimination and Equal Employment Opportunity

The basic goal of all equal employment opportunity regulation is to protect people from unfair or inappropriate discrimination in the workplace.[5] However, most laws passed to eliminate discrimination do not explicitly define the term itself. It is also instructive to note that discrimination per se is not illegal. Whenever one person is given a pay raise and another is not, for example, the organization has made a decision to differentiate the first person from the second. It can be said that the organization has discriminated between these two employees. As long as the basis for this discrimination is purely job-related, however, such as basing it on performance or seniority, and is applied objectively and consistently, such an action is legal and appropriate. Problems arise, though, when differentiation between people is not job-related and the resulting discrimination is illegal. Various court decisions and basic inferences about the language of various laws suggest that **illegal discrimination** is what results from behaviors or actions by an organization or managers within an organization that cause members of a protected class to be unfairly differentiated from others. (We discuss protected classes later in this chapter.)

Although numerous laws deal with different aspects of equal employment opportunity, the Civil Rights Act of 1964 clearly signaled the beginning of a new legislative era in American business. The act grew out of the growing atmosphere of protest for equal

Illegal discrimination *results from behaviors or actions by an organization or managers within an organization that cause members of a protected class to be unfairly differentiated from others.*

Title VII of the Civil Rights Act of 1964 is probably the single most important piece of legislation affecting human resource management. President Lyndon Johnson is shown here signing the bill into law on July 2, 1964. The Civil Rights Act legislates non-discrimination at work; subsequent court decisions relating to Title VII have defined the meanings of disparate impact, job relatedness, bona fide occupational qualification, sexual harassment, and other factors. The Act continues to play a major role in corporate HR practices, and the importance of the statutes contained in the Act were reaffirmed with the passage of the Civil Rights Act of 1991.

rights in the early 1960s and contains several "titles"(or sections) that deal with different areas of application of the Civil Rights Act. Our discussion will focus on Title VII, which deals with work settings under the heading of Equal Employment Opportunity.

Title VII of the Civil Rights Act of 1964   The most significant single piece of legislation specifically affecting the legal context for human resource management to date has been **Title VII of the Civil Rights Act of 1964.** Congress passed the Civil Rights Act and President Lyndon Johnson signed it into law in 1964 as a way to ensure that equal opportunities are available to everyone. Title VII of the Civil Rights Act states that it is illegal for an employer to fail or refuse to hire, to discharge any individual, or to discriminate in any other way against any individual with respect to any aspect of the employment relationship on the basis of that individual's race, color, religious beliefs, sex, or national origin.

The law applies to all components of the employment relationship, including compensation, employment terms, working conditions, and various other privileges of employment. Title VII applies to all organizations with fifteen or more employees working twenty or more weeks a year and that are involved in interstate commerce. In addition, it also applies to state and local governments, employment agencies, and labor organizations. Title VII also created the Equal Employment Opportunity Commission (EEOC) to enforce the various provisions of the law (we discuss the EEOC later in this chapter). Under Title VII, as interpreted by the courts, several types of illegal discrimination are outlawed. These types are discussed next and are illustrated in Figure 2.2.

Title VII of the Civil Rights Act   *states that it is illegal for an employer to fail or refuse to hire or to discharge any individual or to in any other way discriminate against any individual with respect to any aspect of the employment relationship on the basis of that individual's race, color, religious beliefs, sex, or national origin.*

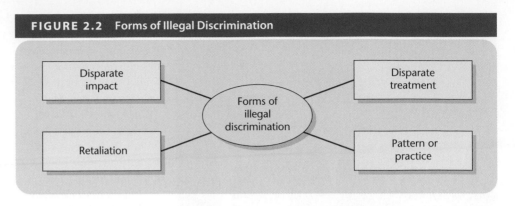

FIGURE 2.2   Forms of Illegal Discrimination

Disparate treatment   **Disparate treatment** discrimination exists when individuals in similar situations are treated differently *and* when the differential treatment is based on the individual's race, color, religion, sex, national origin, age, or disability status. For example, if two people with the same qualifications for the job apply for a promotion and the organization decides which employee to promote based on one individual's religious beliefs or gender, the individual not promoted is a victim of disparate treatment discrimination. To prove discrimination in this situation, an individual filing a charge must demonstrate that there was a discriminatory motive; that is, the individual must prove that the organization took the individual's protected class status into consideration when making the decision.

One circumstance in which organizations can legitimately treat members of different groups differently is when there exists a **bona fide occupational qualification (BFOQ)** for performing a particular job. This condition means that some personal characteristic, such as age, legitimately affects a person's ability to perform the job. For example, a producer casting a new play or movie can legally refuse to hire an older person to play a role that is expressly written for a very young person. There are few BFOQs, however. For example, a restaurant cannot hire only young, attractive people as servers based on the argument that their customers prefer young, attractive servers. In fact, customer and/or client preference can never be the basis of a BFOQ. As we shall see, however, this situation can become quite complex.

To claim a BFOQ exception, the organization must be able to demonstrate that hiring on the basis of the characteristic in question (e.g., age) is not simply a preference but a **business necessity.** That is, the organization must be able to prove that the practice is important for the safe and efficient operation of the business. But what if customers at a casino would prefer female card dealers or if customers at an automobile dealership would prefer male salespersons? These customers might go elsewhere if these preferences were not satisfied, and those decisions could surely hurt the business involved. In general, neither of these cases would qualify as a BFOQ; however, reality is rarely this simple.

The case of *Diaz* v. *Pan American World Airways,* for example, was filed after Celio Diaz (a male) applied for the job of flight attendant with Pan American Airlines (Pan Am).[6] He was rejected because Pan Am had a policy of hiring only women for this position (as did many airlines in 1971). Diaz filed suit for discrimination, but Pan Am argued that gender was a BFOQ for the job of flight attendant. This argument was based on Pan Am's own experience with male and female flight attendants and on the fact that Pan Am's customers overwhelmingly preferred to be served by female attendants. A lower court accepted the airlines' argument that ". . . an airline cabin represents a unique [and stressful] environment in which an air carrier is required to take account of the special psychological needs of its passengers. Those needs are better attended to by females."[7] The appeals court reversed that decision, however, citing that Pan Am's data on the relative effectiveness of male and female flight attendants was not very compelling and noting that customer preference was not relevant because no evidence existed that hiring male flight attendants would substantially affect the business performance of the airlines. But while this ruling may seem clear, Asian restaurants are routinely allowed to hire only Asian-American waiters because they add to the authenticity of the dining experience and are therefore deemed a business necessity.

Disparate impact   A second form of discrimination is disparate impact. **Disparate impact** discrimination occurs when an apparently neutral employment practice disproportionately excludes a protected group from employment opportunities. This argument is the most common for charges of discrimination brought under the Civil Rights Act. For example, suppose a restaurant determined that, for health reasons, no one who had hair long enough to cover his or her ears would be hired to handle food. Although this practice would be applied to all applicants and would certainly result in some long-haired males not being hired, it would have a much greater impact on female applicants because they are more likely to have longer hair. As a result, even though all applicants would be treated the same, this practice would result in the rejection of many more female applicants. This situation would be an example of disparate impact discrimination because the organization, even with no direct intention of discriminating against women, is using a particular employment practice that results in discrimination against women. In this situation, intent to discriminate is irrelevant (and the proper solution is to have all employees wear hairnets).

One of the first instances in which disparate impact was defined involved a landmark legal case, *Griggs* v. *Duke Power*. Following passage of Title VII, Duke Power initiated a new selection system that required new employees to have either a high school education or a minimum cutoff score on two specific personality tests. Griggs, a black male, filed a lawsuit against Duke Power after he was denied employment based on these criteria. His argument was that neither criterion was a necessary qualification for performing the work he was seeking. After his attorneys demonstrated that those criteria disproportionately affected blacks and that the company had no documentation to support the validity of the criteria, the courts ruled that the firm had to change its selection criteria on the basis of disparate impact.[8]

The important criterion in this situation is that the consequences of the employment practice are discriminatory, and thus the practice in question has disparate (sometimes referred to as *adverse*) impact. In fact, if a plaintiff can establish what is called a prima facie case of discrimination, the company is considered to be at fault unless it can demonstrate another legal basis for the decision.[9] This finding doesn't mean that the company automatically loses the case, but it does mean that the burden of proof rests with the company to defend itself, rather than with the plaintiff trying to prove discrimination. Therefore, it is extremely important to understand how one establishes a prima facie case.

There are several avenues for establishing a prima facie case, but the most common approach relies on the so-called **four-fifths rule**. Specifically, the courts have ruled that disparate impact exists if a selection criterion (such as a test score) results in a selection rate for a protected class that is less than four-fifths (80 percent) than that for the majority group. For example, assume that an organization is considering 100 white applicants and 100 Hispanic applicants for the same job. If an employment test used to select among these applicants results in sixty white applicants (60 percent) being hired, but

Disparate impact
discrimination occurs when an apparently neutral employment practice disproportionately excludes a protected group from employment opportunities.

The **four-fifths rule**   *suggests that disparate impact exists if a selection criterion (such as a test score) results in a selection rate for a protected class that is less than four-fifths (80 percent) of that for the majority group.*

only thirty Hispanic applicants (30 percent) being hired, disparate impact is likely to be ruled because Hispanics are being hired at a rate that is less than four-fifths than that of whites. At this point, the organization using the test would be required to prove that its differential selection rate of whites versus Hispanics could be justified (the basis for this justification will be explained below).

But demonstrating that an organization's policies have violated the four-fifths rule can sometimes be complicated. In the case of *Wards Cove Packing* v. *Antonio,* the defendant, a salmon cannery in Alaska, had two distinct types of jobs for which people were hired.[10] Cannery jobs were seen as skilled (administrative and engineering) while noncannery jobs were viewed as unskilled. The plaintiff's attorneys argued that since the noncannery jobs were predominantly filled by Filipino and Native Alaskans, while the cannery jobs were held predominantly by whites, the company had violated the four-fifths rule and they had therefore established a prima facie case for disparate impact. The defendant did not dispute the statistics but argued that the policies in place did not lead to apparent disparate impact and therefore there was no prima facie case. The Supreme Court agreed with the defendant, ruling that the statistical proof alone was not sufficient for establishing a prima facie case. Therefore, the burden of proof did not shift to the defendant but rested with the employee involved. Wards Cove won the case. In addition to illustrating the problems with establishing a violation of the four-fifths rule, the *Wards Cove* case was also widely seen as dealing a major blow to the enforcement of the Civil Rights Act of 1964—a topic to which we will return shortly.

A plaintiff might be able to demonstrate disparate impact by relying upon so-called **geographical comparisons.** These involve comparing the characteristics of the potential pool of qualified applicants for a job (focusing on characteristics such as race, ethnicity, and gender) with those same characteristics of the present employees in the job. Thus, if the potential pool of qualified applicants in the labor market for the job of bank teller is 50 percent African-American, a bank hiring from that market should have approximately 50 percent African-American tellers. Failure to achieve this degree of representation is considered a basis for a prima facie case of disparate impact discrimination. This comparison requires a clear understanding of the labor market from which the organization typically recruits employees for this job since, even within the same organization, different jobs might draw on different "relevant" labor markets with different characteristics. For instance, a university might rely on a national labor market for new faculty members, a regional labor market for professional staff employees, and a local labor market for custodial and food-service employees. It is also important to note that the definition of the "potential pool of qualified applicants" draws heavily on census data for the area.

Finally, the **McDonnell-Douglas test,** named for a Supreme Court ruling in *McDonnell-Douglas* v. *Green,* is another basis for establishing a prima facie case.[11] Four steps are part of the McDonnell-Douglas test:

1. The applicant is a member of a protected class (see below).
2. The applicant was qualified for the job for which he or she applied.
3. The individual was turned down for the job.
4. The company continued to seek other applicants with the same qualifications.

Pattern or practice discrimination   The third kind of discrimination that can be identified is pattern or practice discrimination. **Pattern or practice discrimination** is a form of disparate treatment that occurs on a classwide or systemic basis. Although an individual can bring charges of practice discrimination, the question is whether the organization engages in a pattern or practice of discrimination against all members of a protected class instead of against one particular member. Title VII of the 1964 Civil

Geographical comparisons *involve comparing the characteristics of the potential pool of qualified applicants for a job (focusing on characteristics such as race, ethnicity, and gender) with those same characteristics of the present employees in the job.*

The **McDonnell-Douglas test** *is a test that is the basis for establishing a prima facie case of disparate impact discrimination.*

Pattern or practice discrimination *is similar to disparate treatment but occurs on a classwide basis.*

Rights Act gives the attorney general of the United States express powers to bring lawsuits against organizations thought to be guilty of pattern or practice discrimination. Specifically, Section 707 of Title VII states that such a lawsuit can be brought if there is reasonable cause to believe that an employer is engaging in pattern or practice discrimination. A good example of pattern or practice discrimination allegedly occurred several years ago at Shoney's, a popular family-oriented restaurant chain with operations and locations throughout the South. A former assistant manager at the firm alleged that she was told by her supervisor to use a pencil to color in the "o" in the Shoney's logo printed on its employment application blanks for all black applicants. The presumed intent of this coding scheme was to eliminate all those applicants from further consideration.[12]

To demonstrate pattern or practice discrimination, the plaintiff must prove that the organization intended to discriminate against a particular class of individuals. A critical issue in practice or pattern discrimination lawsuits is the definition of a statistical comparison group or a definition of the relevant labor market. A labor market consists of workers who have the skills needed to perform the work and who are within a reasonable commuting distance from the organization. The definition of the labor market is a major issue then in resolving lawsuits brought under pattern or practice discrimination suits.

Retaliation   A final form of illegal discrimination that has been occasionally identified in some reorganizations is retaliation for "participation and opposition." Title VII states that it is illegal for employers to retaliate against employees for either opposing a perceived illegal employment practice or participating in a proceeding that is related to an alleged illegal employment practice. If an employee's behavior fits the legal definition of participation and/or opposition and the organization takes some measure against that particular employee, such as a reprimand, demotion, or termination, the employee can file a lawsuit against the organization under Title VII.

Employer defense   Our discussion so far has focused on the types of illegal discrimination and the ways in which a plaintiff can establish a case of discrimination. As noted earlier, however, once a prima facie case has been established, the burden of proof shifts to the defendant. That is, the defendant has to provide evidence for nondiscriminatory bases for the decisions made. Therefore, it is critical to understand that just because a prima facie case has been established, it does not necessarily mean that the defendant (typically the company) will be found liable. The company can defend itself by providing evidence that the selection decision (or employment decision of any type) was based on criteria that are job related. That is, the defendant (usually an organization) must be able to prove that decisions were made so that the persons most likely to be selected (or be promoted, or receive a pay raise) are those who are most likely to perform best on the job (or who have already performed best on the job). This situation is also referred to as validation of the practice in question. In the *Taking HR to the Next Level* at the end of Part Two, we will discuss how one validates a selection technique and therefore establishes that it is job-related. Many of these issues are also based on the court ruling in the *Albermarle Paper Company* case, which is discussed in Chapter 7.

Protected Classes in the Workforce

We have made several references so far to protected classes. It is now time to turn our attention to what that term means in practice. Many of the discriminatory practices described above stemmed from stereotypes, beliefs, or prejudice about classes of individuals.

For example, common stereotypes at one time were that black employees were less dependable than white employees, that women were less suited to certain types of work than were men, and that disabled individuals could not be productive employees. Based on these stereotypes, many organizations routinely discriminated against blacks, women, and disabled people. Although such blatant discrimination is rare today, that does not mean that discrimination at work has disappeared. Instead, as we shall see, it has found new targets and, in many cases, a much more subtle approach.

To combat this past discrimination, various laws have been passed to protect different classes or categories of individuals. While varying from law to law, a **protected class** consists of all individuals who share one or more common characteristics as indicated by that law. The most common characteristics used to define protected classes include race, color, religion, gender, age, national origin, disability status, and status as a military veteran. As we will see, some laws pertain to several protected classes, while others pertain to a single protected class. Class definition generally involves first specifying the basis of distinction and then specifying which degree or category of that distinction is protected. For example, a law may prohibit discrimination on the basis of gender—a basis of distinction—and then define the protected class as females. This distinction does not mean that an organization can discriminate against men, of course, and in some cases men could even be considered members of a protected class. But the law was almost certainly passed on the assumption that most gender-based discrimination has been directed against women and thus it is women who need to be protected in the future.

At the same time, an important issue is the extent to which an organization can give preferential treatment to members of a protected class. While exceptions can be made in certain circumstances, by and large the intent of most equal employment opportunity legislation is to provide fair and equitable treatment for everyone, as opposed to stipulating preferential treatment for members of a protected class.[13] This interpretation becomes a bit complicated, though, and can result in charges of reverse discrimination, our next topic.

> A **protected class** *consists of all individuals who share one or more common characteristic as indicated by that law.*

Affirmative Action and Reverse Discrimination

When charges of illegal discrimination have been supported, courts sometimes impose remedies that try to reverse the effects of past discrimination. Most frequently, these remedies have taken the form of some type of affirmative action. (As we shall see below, some organizations are also required to file affirmative action plans even without charges of illegal discrimination.) **Affirmative action** refers to positive steps taken by an organization to seek qualified employees from underrepresented groups in the workforce. When affirmative action is part of a remedy in a discrimination case, the plan takes on additional urgency and the steps are somewhat clearer. Three elements make up any affirmative action program.

The first element is called the utilization analysis. A **utilization analysis** is a comparison of the racial, sex, and ethnic composition of the employer's workforce compared to that of the available labor supply. For each group of jobs, the organization needs to identify the percentage of its workforce with that characteristic (i.e., black, female, etc.) and identify the percentage of workers in the relevant labor market with that characteristic. If the percentage in the employer's workforce is considerably less than the percentage in the external labor supply, then that minority group is characterized as being underutilized. Much of this analysis takes place as part of the discrimination case, if one is involved, and the affected groups are defined by the specifics of the case.

The second part of an affirmative action plan is the development of goals and timetables for achieving balance in the workforce concerning those characteristics, especially where underutilization exists. Goals and timetables generally specify the percentage of

> **Affirmative action** *represents a set of steps, taken by an organization, to actively seek qualified applicants from groups underrepresented in the workforce.*

> A **utilization analysis** *is a comparison of the racial, sex, and ethnic composition of the employer's workforce compared to that of the available labor supply.*

In many ways, equal employment opportunity is the central element in the legal context of human resource management. Equal employment opportunity, in turn, emerged from the struggles of such pioneers of the Civil Rights movement as Ms. Rosa Parks and Dr. Martin Luther King, Jr. Ms. Parks, for instance, took a stand against prejudice by refusing to give up her seat on a bus for a white passenger. When she died in 2005, mourners from across the country came to her funeral to pay homage.

protected classes of employees that the organization seeks to have in each group and the targeted date by which that percentage should be attained, but these are much more flexible than quotas, which are illegal (except is rare cases where these have been imposed by courts). The idea underlying goals and timetables is that if no discriminatory hiring practices exist, then underutilization should be eliminated over time.

The third part of the affirmative action program is the development of a list of action steps. These steps specify what the organization will do to work toward attaining its goals to reduce underutilization. Common action steps include increased communication of job openings to underrepresented groups, recruiting at schools that predominantly cater to a particular protected class, participating in programs designed to improve employment opportunities for underemployed groups, and taking all steps to remove inappropriate barriers to employment. In some cases this third part might also include preferential hiring. That is, given two equally qualified applicants for a job, the organization would be required to hire the member of the underrepresented group in every case until its goals and targets are met.

In the late 1990s, the courts began to impose many more restrictions on what was acceptable (or required) in the way of preferential hiring and quotas. We will discuss representative relevant court decisions shortly, but the impetus for some of these decisions was the concern that affirmative action *could* in some cases appear to be a form of reverse discrimination. Reverse discrimination refers to any practice that has a disparate impact on members of *nonprotected* classes. Thus, charges of reverse discrimination typically stem from the belief by white males that they have suffered because of preferential treatment given to other groups.

The two most famous court cases in this area help to illustrate how complicated this issue can be. In the *Bakke* case a student, white male Allen Bakke had applied to medical school at the University of California Davis but was denied admission.[14] At issue was the fact that the university had set aside 16 of its 100 seats for an incoming class for minority students to promote diversity and affirmative action at the school. Bakke's attorneys argued that he was not necessarily more qualified than those admitted for the eighty-four "white" openings, but that he was more qualified than those admitted to the sixteen openings set aside for minorities. Since the school had imposed this system on its own (to correct past injustice), the Court ruled that this "set-aside" program constituted reverse discrimination because it clearly favored one race over another, and it ruled in favor of Bakke.

In the *Weber* case a white male, Brian Weber, applied for a temporary training program that would lead to a higher-paying skilled job at a Kaiser Aluminum facility.[15] He was not accepted into the program; he then sued because he claimed that African-American applicants with less seniority were admitted into the program strictly because of their race. In fact, Kaiser and United Steelworkers had agreed to a contract whereby 50 percent of the openings for these programs would be reserved for African-Americans in an attempt to address the fact that African-Americans had been systematically excluded from these programs in the past. The Supreme Court found in favor of Kaiser and the union, acknowledging that a collective-bargaining agreement such as this one was binding and was a reasonable means of addressing past discrimination.

Given these two legal decisions, one might question the current status of reverse discrimination cases. In fact, it is by no means clear. Within the space of a few years, the Supreme Court:

- Ruled against an organization giving preferential treatment to minority workers during a layoff.[16]
- Ruled in support of temporary preferential hiring and promotion practices as part of a settlement of a lawsuit.[17]
- Ruled in support of the establishment of quotas as a remedy for past discrimination.[18]
- Ruled that any form of affirmative action is inherently discriminatory and could be used only as a temporary measure.[19]

It would appear that the future of affirmative action is unclear, suggesting that the courts will be leaning more toward interpretations in line with reverse discrimination in the future.

Indeed, there is growing evidence that the concept of affirmative action is increasingly being called into question. In 1996, for instance, a circuit court judge ruled that a goal of increasing student diversity at the University of Texas was not sufficient grounds for giving preference to racial minorities in terms of admission or financial aid.[20] And in 1998 California voters ratified a proposition called the California Civil Rights Initiative, which outlawed any preferential treatment on the basis of race, gender, color, ethnicity, or national origin for all public employment, education, and contracting activities. However, in 2003 the Supreme Court ruled that the University of Michigan could use diversity as one of several factors in making its admissions decisions, while saying that explicit rules which awarded extra points to underrepresented groups in the student population were not allowed. Other recent developments are discussed in *HR in the 21st Century*.

Sexual Harassment at Work

One final area of coverage for the Civil Rights Act that is critical for the human resource manager is sexual harassment. This area is particularly important in this context because much of the litigation and the organization's liability in these cases depend on the initial responses to charges of sexual harassment, and these responses are typically the responsibility of someone in human resources. Sexual harassment is defined by the EEOC as unwelcome sexual advances in the work environment. If the conduct is indeed unwelcome and occurs with sufficient frequency to create an abusive work environment, the employer is responsible for changing the environment by warning, reprimanding, or perhaps firing the harasser.[21]

Trends in the Affirmative Action Debate

As noted in the text, affirmative action is coming under growing scrutiny today. Some experts suggest that political shifts in the U.S. Supreme Court will have a major impact. Specifically, it is likely that the Supreme Court will be moving more to the right politically. In July 2005 Justice Sandra Day O'Connor (most of whose decisions would be considered "middle of the road") announced her retirement. President Bush announced that his choice to replace O'Connor was John Roberts, a conservative judge with a great deal of judicial experience. But then, in September 2005 Chief Justice William Rehnquist died after a long battle with cancer. President Bush subsequently switched his nomination of John Roberts to replace Rehnquist as chief justice, and Roberts was confirmed as chief justice at the end of September 2005. President Bush next announced his choice of Samuel Alito to fill the remaining opening; Alito was subsequently confirmed in early 2006. Alito is seen as a rather conservative judge who will likely move the Court further to the right.

By 2006 the affirmative action debate had also be-

". . . affirmative action is coming under growing scrutiny today."

come linked to a discussion of a "new racism" by both sides of the debate. Many conservatives, for instance, were arguing that affirmative action was itself a form of racism whereby people were classified according to their race and stereotyped because of that classification. Individuals opposed to affirmative action argued that it made more sense for organizations to deal with everyone on the basis of individual ability and potential. They also claimed that affirmative action condemned black Americans to second-class status because it assumed that they could not get ahead on their own.

Interestingly, advocates of affirmative action also started to invoke charges of racism in arguing their case. These individuals suggested that the conservatives arguing against affirmative action were guilty of a new form of racism. Specifically, they argued that while opponents of affirmative action were calling for decisions based on merit, those decisions would open the door to the same types of discrimination that had occurred in the past. These arguments are certain to continue with no clear answer likely to emerge.

The courts have ruled that there are two types of sexual harassment and have defined both types. One type of sexual harassment is **quid pro quo harassment.** In this case, the harasser offers to exchange something of value for sexual favors. For example, a male supervisor might tell or imply to a female subordinate that he will recommend her for promotion or provide her with a salary increase, but only if she sleeps with him. Although this type of situation definitely occurs, organizations generally have no problem in understanding that it is illegal and knowing how to respond.

But a more subtle (and probably more common) type of sexual harassment is the creation of a **hostile work environment,** and this situation is not always so easy to define. For example, a group of male employees who continually make off-color jokes and lewd comments and perhaps decorate the work environment with inappropriate photographs may create a hostile work environment for a female colleague, to the point where she is uncomfortable working in that job setting. Most experts would agree that this situation constitutes sexual harassment. But what if an employee has an inappropriate magazine in a desk drawer and a coworker sees it only when she (or he) happens to walk by when the drawer is open?

In *Meritor Savings Bank* v. *Vinson* the Supreme Court noted that a hostile work environment constitutes sexual harassment, even if the employee did not suffer any economic penalties or was not threatened with any such penalties.[22] In *Harris* v. *Forklift Systems* the Court ruled that the plaintiff did not have to suffer substantial mental distress to receive a jury settlement.[23] Hence, it is critical that organizations monitor the situation and be alert for these instances because, as noted, it is the organization's responsibility for dealing with this sort of problem.[24]

Quid pro quo harassment *is sexual harassment in which the harasser offers to exchange something of value for sexual favors.*

A **hostile work environment** *is sexual harassment resulting from a climate or culture that is punitive toward people of a different gender.*

Therefore, the human resource manager must play a major role in investigating any hint of sexual harassment in the organization. The manager cannot simply wait for an employee to complain. Although the Court had ruled in the case of *Scott* v. *Sears Roebuck*[25] that the employer was not liable for the sexual harassment because the plaintiff did not complain to supervisors, the ruling in the *Meritor* case makes it much more difficult for the organization to avoid liability by claiming ignorance (although this liability is not automatic). This responsibility is further complicated by the fact that, although most sexual harassment cases involve men harassing women, there are, of course, many other situations of sexual harassment that can be identified. Females can harass men, and in the case of *Oncale* v. *Sundowner* the Supreme Court ruled unanimously that a male oil rigger who claimed to be harassed by his coworkers and supervisor on an offshore oil rig was indeed the victim of sexual harassment.[26] Several recent cases involving same-sex harassment have focused new attention on this form of sexual harassment.[27] Regardless of the pattern, however, the same rules apply: sexual harassment is illegal and it is the organization's responsibility to control it.

Other Equal Employment Opportunity Legislation

In addition to the Civil Rights Act of 1964, a large body of supporting legal regulation has also been created in an effort to provide equal employment opportunity for various protected classes of individuals. Although the 1964 act is probably the best known and most influential piece of legislation in this area, a new civil rights act was passed in 1991 and numerous other laws deal with different aspects of equal employment or are concerned with specific areas of work, and these are discussed in this section. Some of them apply only to federal contractors, and these are discussed separately, while others apply more widely.

The **Equal Pay Act of 1963** *requires that organizations provide men and women who are doing equal work the same pay.*

The Equal Pay Act of 1963   The **Equal Pay Act of 1963** requires that organizations provide the same pay to men and women who are doing equal work. The law defines equality in terms of skill, responsibility, effort, and working conditions. Thus, an organization cannot pay a man more than it pays a woman for the same job on the grounds that, say, the male employee needs the money more because he has a bigger family to support. Similarly, organizations cannot circumvent the law by using different job titles for essentially the same work, such as a school district giving a man the title of assistant superintendent and a woman the title of curriculum coordinator. If the work is essentially the same, then pay differentials on the basis of difference in titles alone is illegal.

This does not mean, of course, that men and women must be paid the same if there are legitimate, job-related reasons for pay differences. That is, a man may be paid more than a woman doing the same job if there are legitimate organizational practices to support such a differential. For example, suppose a firm gives a 5 percent seniority raise every year. A man who has worked for the firm for ten years may therefore legitimately be paid more than a woman who has worked at the same firm for only five years. Of course, for these practices to be legal the organization must also be paying the woman more than it is paying another man who has worked in the organization for only two years. Other potential differences in pay might be made on the basis of merit, quantity or quality of performance, or any other work- or performance-related factor.[28]

The **Age Discrimination and Employment Act** *(or* **ADEA***) prohibits discrimination against employees over the age of forty.*

The Age Discrimination and Employment Act   The **Age Discrimination and Employment Act (ADEA)** was first passed in 1967 and later amended in 1986. The ADEA prohibits discrimination against employees forty years old or older. The ADEA is very similar to Title VII of the 1964 Civil Rights Act in terms of both its major provisions and the procedures that are followed in pursuing a case of discrimination. Like Title VII, enforcement of the ADEA is the responsibility of the Equal Employment Opportunity Commission.

The ADEA was felt to be necessary because of a disquieting trend in some organizations in the early 1960s. Specifically, these firms were beginning to discriminate against older employees when they found it necessary to lay people off or otherwise to scale back their workforce. By targeting older workers who tended to have higher pay because of their seniority with the firm, companies were substantially cutting their labor costs. In addition, there was some feeling that organizations were also discriminating against older workers in their hiring decisions. The specific concern here was that organizations would not hire people in their forties or fifties because (1) they would have to pay those individuals more based on their experience and salary history and (2) they would have a shorter potential career with the organization. Consequently, some organizations were found guilty of giving preferential treatment to younger workers over older workers. These concerns have been raised again with recent new efforts to downsize workforces. The issue is that organizations may focus especially on older workers for the reasons noted above. It is vital that firms who are downsizing, be aware of this and ensure that their efforts are not differentially impacting older workers.

The other area where the ADEA has generated a fair amount of controversy relates to mandatory retirement ages. The Supreme Court has indicated that an agency or an organization may require mandatory retirement at a given age *if and only if* it could be shown that age was a BFOQ. Thus, the organization in question would have to demonstrate the inability of persons beyond a certain age to perform a given job safely. But, in several decisions, the Court has indicated that it will interpret this BFOQ exception very narrowly. In fact, in *Johnson* v. *Mayor and City of Baltimore,* the Court ruled that not even a federal statute requiring firefighters to retire at age fifty-five constituted a BFOQ exception to the law.[29]

The Pregnancy Discrimination Act of 1979   As its name suggests, the **Pregnancy Discrimination Act of 1979** was passed to protect pregnant women from discrimination in the workplace. The law requires that the pregnant woman be treated as any other employee in the workplace. Therefore, the act specifies that a woman cannot be refused a job or promotion, fired, or otherwise discriminated against simply because she is pregnant (or has had an abortion). She also cannot be forced to leave employment with the organization as long as she is physically able to work. Finally, the Pregnancy Discrimination Act also specifies that if other employees have the right to return to their jobs after a leave, then this benefit must also be accorded to pregnant women. In one high-profile case a few years ago, actress Hunter Tylo won a $5 million judgment against the producers of her television show *Melrose Place* after they used her pregnancy as a basis for writing her out of the show.[30]

> The **Pregnancy Discrimination Act of 1979** *protects pregnant women from discrimination in the workplace.*

The Civil Rights Act of 1991   The **Civil Rights Act of 1991** was passed as a direct amendment of Title VII of the Civil Rights Act of 1964. During the twenty-five years following the passage of the original act, the U.S. Supreme Court handed down several rulings that helped define how the Civil Rights Act would be administered. But in the course of its 1989 Supreme Court session, several decisions were handed down that many felt seriously limited the viability of the Civil Rights Act of 1964.[31] In response to this development, the Civil Rights Act of 1991 was passed essentially to restore the force of the original act. Although some new aspects of the law were introduced as part of the

> The **Civil Rights Act of 1991** *makes it easier for individuals who feel they have been discriminated against to take legal action against organizations and provides for the payment of compensatory and punitive damages in cases of discrimination under Title VII.*

Civil Rights Act of 1991, the primary purpose of this new law was to make it easier for individuals who feel they have been discriminated against to take legal action against organizations. As a result, this law also reinforced the idea that a firm must remain within the limits of the law when engaging in various human resource management practices.

Specifically, the Civil Rights Act of 1991 prohibits discrimination on the job and makes it easier for the burden of proof to shift to employers (to demonstrate that they did not discriminate). It also reinforces the illegality of making hiring, firing, or promotion decisions on the basis of race, gender, color, religion, or national origin; it also includes the *Glass Ceiling Act,* which established a commission to investigate practices that limited the access of protected class members (especially women) from attaining the top levels of management in organizations. For the first time, the act provides the potential payment of compensatory and punitive damages in cases of discrimination under Title VII. While the law limited the amount of punitive damages that could be paid to no more than nine times the amount of compensatory damages, it also allowed juries rather than federal judges to hear these cases.

This law also makes it possible for employees of U.S. companies working in foreign countries to bring suit against those companies for violation of the Civil Rights Act. The only exception to this provision is the situation in which a country has laws that specifically contradict some aspect of the Civil Rights Act. For example, Moslem countries often have laws limiting the rights of women. Foreign companies with operations in such countries would almost certainly be required to abide by local laws. As a result, a female employee of a U.S. company working in such a setting would not be directly protected under the Civil Rights Act. However, her employer would still need to inform her fully of the kinds of discriminatory practices she might face as a result of transferring to the foreign site and then ensure that when this particular foreign assignment were completed, her career opportunities would not have been compromised in any way.[32]

The **Americans with Disabilities Act of 1990 (**or **ADA)** *prohibits discrimination based on disability and all aspects of the employment relationship such as job application procedures, hiring, firing, promotion, compensation, and training, as well as other employment activities such as advertising, recruiting, tenure, layoffs, and leave and fringe benefits.*

The Americans with Disabilities Act of 1990   The **Americans with Disabilities Act of 1990 (ADA)** is potentially one of the most important pieces of equal employment opportunity legislation to affect human resource management. The ADA was passed in response to growing criticisms and concerns about employment opportunities denied to people with various disabilities. For example, one survey found that of 12.2 million Americans not working because of disabilities, 8.2 million would have preferred to work. Similarly, another survey found that almost 80 percent of all managers surveyed found the overall performance of their disabled workers to be good to excellent. In response to these trends and pressures, the ADA was passed to protect individuals with disabilities from being discriminated against in the workplace.[33]

Specifically, the ADA prohibits discrimination based on disability and all aspects of the employment relationship such as job application procedures, hiring, firing, promotion, compensation, and training, as well as other employment activities such as advertising, recruiting, tenure, layoffs, leave, and benefits. In addition, the ADA also requires that organizations make reasonable accommodations for disabled employees as long as the accommodations themselves do not pose an undue burden on the organization. The act initially went into effect in 1992 and covered employers with twenty-five or more employees. It was expanded in July 1994 to cover employers with fifteen or more employees.

The ADA defines a *disability* as (1) a mental or physical impairment that limits one or more major life activities, (2) a record of having such an impairment, or (3) being regarded as having such an impairment. Clearly included within the domain of the ADA are individuals with disabilities such as blindness, deafness, paralysis, and similar disabilities. In addition, the ADA covers employees with cancer, a history of mental illness, or a history of heart disease. Finally, the act also covers employees regarded as having a disability, such as individuals who are disfigured or who for some other reason an employer feels will prompt a negative reaction from others. In addition, the ADA covers mental and psychological disorders such as mental retardation, emotional or mental illness (including depression), and learning disabilities.

On the other hand, individuals with substance-abuse problems, obesity, and similar non-work-related characteristics may not be covered by the ADA.[34] But because the ADA defines disabilities in terms of limitations on life activities, myriad cases continue to be raised. For example, in recent years workers have attempted to claim protection under the ADA on the basis of ailments ranging from alcoholism to dental problems! These activities have led some to question whether the ADA is being abused by workers rather than serving to protect their rights.[35]

In fact, the definition of a disability and what constitutes a "reasonable accommodation" pose the greatest potential problems for the human resource manager. Individuals who are confined to wheelchairs, are visually impaired, and/or have similar physical disabilities are usually quite easy to identify, but many employees may suffer from "invisible" disabilities that might include physical problems (e.g., someone needing dialysis) as well as psychological problems (acute anxiety) and learning disabilities (such as dyslexia). Thus it is not always obvious who among a group of employees is actually eligible for protection under the ADA.[36]

One area of coverage where the courts and EEOC (the agency charged with the administration of the ADA) have taken a fairly clear position deals with AIDS and HIV in the workplace. Both AIDS and HIV are considered disabilities under the Americans with Disabilities Act, and employers cannot legally require an HIV test or any other medical examination as a condition for making an offer of employment. After an offer of employment has been extended, however, organizations can make that offer contingent on the individual taking a physical examination. If an individual is found to be HIV positive, an employer cannot discriminate against that job applicant in a hiring decision, although it might be permissible to reassign the person in certain industries such as food services.

Essentially, organizations must follow a certain set of guidelines and employ common sense when dealing with AIDS-related issues. For example, they must treat AIDS like any other disease that is covered by law, they must maintain confidentiality of all medical records, they cannot discriminate against a person with AIDS, they should strive to educate coworkers about AIDS, they cannot discriminate against AIDS victims regarding training or consideration for promotion in the organization, and they must accommodate or make a good-faith effort to accommodate AIDS victims.

While taking a fairly clear position on AIDS and HIV, the EEOC is still working to develop guidelines and interpretations to allow organizations to comply more effectively in other areas of coverage. The U.S. Supreme Court took a major step toward clarifying the ADA in mid-1999, however. In a landmark decision, the Court ruled that individuals who can correct or overcome their disabilities through medication or other means are not protected by the ADA. For example, if a worker can correct his or her vision by wearing corrective lenses but prefers not to do so, an employer no longer must make accommodation for that individual.[37]

In addition, the reasonable accommodation stipulation adds considerable complexity to the job of human resource manager and other executives in organizations. Clearly, for example, organizations must provide ramps and wide hallways to accommodate individuals confined to a wheelchair. At the same time, however, providing accommodations for other disabilities may be more complex. If an applicant for a job takes an employment test, fails the test (and so is not offered employment), and *then* indicates that he or she has a learning disability (for example) that makes it difficult to take paper-and-pencil tests, the applicant probably can demand an accommodation. Specifically, the organization would likely be required either to find a different way to administer the test or to provide the applicant with additional time to take the test a second time before making a final decision. Likewise, an existing employee diagnosed with a psychological disorder may be able to request on-site psychological support.

Recently, yet another issue involved with granting accommodations has been identified.[38] The nature of many accommodations granted to employees is such that other employees who are not disabled and who are not requesting an accommodation are unlikely to be envious or resentful about the accommodation. But this is not the case for all requested accommodations. For example, a woman claimed that having every Friday off was the only accommodation that would help to reduce her stress at work.[39] What if the organization granted her that accommodation? Surely other employees would wonder why they could not have Fridays off, especially since stress is not typically a visible disability. This situation would lead to resentment and potentially to other problems. Therefore, although the ADA does not consider coworker reactions as relevant to determining whether or not an accommodation is reasonable, the knowledgeable human resource manager will at least think about how others might react to an accommodation when trying to deal with the legal requests of employees with disabilities.

The Family and Medical Leave Act of 1993   The **Family and Medical Leave Act of 1993** was passed in part to remedy weaknesses in the Pregnancy Discrimination Act of 1979. The law requires employers with more than fifty employees to provide up to twelve weeks of unpaid leave for employees after the birth or adoption of a child; to care for a seriously ill child, spouse, or parent; or in the case of an employee's own serious illness. The organization must also provide the employee with the same or comparable job upon the employee's return.[40]

The law also requires the organization to pay the health-care coverage of the employee during the leave. However, the employer can require the employee to reimburse these health-care premiums if the employee fails to return to work after the absence. Organizations are allowed to identify key employees, specifically defined as the highest paid 10 percent of their workforce, on the grounds that granting leave to these individuals would grant serious economic harm to the organization. The law also does not apply to employees who have not worked an average of twenty-five hours a week in the previous twelve months.[41]

Clearly, a substantial body of laws and regulations govern equal employment opportunity. As we shall discuss a bit later, there are other areas where legislation has been enacted that affects what happens in the workplace, but, for the foreseeable future, equal employment issues will continue to be a major part of the job of the human resource manager.

Regulations for federal contractors   In addition to the various laws described above, there are also numerous regulations that apply only to federal contractors. It should be noted, however, that the definition of a federal contractor is quite broad. For instance, all banks (that participate in the U.S. Federal Reserve system) and most universities (that have federal research grants or that accept federal loans for their students) would qualify as federal contractors.

Executive Order 11246 was issued by President Lyndon Johnson, who believed that Title VII of the 1964 Civil Rights Act was not comprehensive enough. This order prohibits discrimination based on race, color, religion, sex, or national origin for organizations

The **Family and Medical Leave Act of 1993** *requires employers having more than fifty employees to provide up to twelve weeks unpaid leave for employees after the birth or adoption of a child, to care for a seriously ill child, spouse, or parent, or in the case of an employee's own serious illness.*

Executive Order 11246 *prohibits discrimination based on race, color, religion, sex, or national origin for organizations that are federal contractors and subcontractors.*

that are federal contractors and subcontractors, and it requires written affirmative action plans from those organizations with contracts greater than $50,000. **Executive Order 11478** was issued by President Richard Nixon and required the federal government to base all of its own employment policies on merit and fitness and specifies that race, color, sex, religion, and national origin should not be considered. The executive order also extends to all contractors and subcontractors doing $10,000 or more worth of business with the federal government. These executive orders are enforced by the Office of Federal Contract Compliance Procedures (OFCCP), which is discussed later.

The **Vocational Rehabilitation Act of 1973** requires that executive agencies and subcontractors and contractors of the federal government receiving more than $2,500 a year from the government engage in affirmative action for disabled individuals. This act is administered by the Department of Labor. Finally, the **Vietnam Era Veterans' Readjustment Act of 1974** requires that federal contractors and subcontractors take affirmative action toward employing Vietnam-era veterans. Vietnam-era veterans are specifically defined as those serving as members of the U.S. armed forces between August 5, 1964, and May 7, 1975. This act is enforced through the Office of Federal Contract Compliance Procedures (OFCCP).

Enforcing Equal Employment Opportunity

The enforcement of equal opportunity legislation generally is handled by two agencies. As noted earlier, one agency is the Equal Employment Opportunity Commission (EEOC) and the other is the Office of Federal Contract Compliance Procedures (OFCCP). The EEOC is a division of the Department of Justice. It was created by Title VII of the 1964 Civil Rights Act and today is given specific responsibility for enforcing Title VII, the Equal Pay Act, and the Americans with Disabilities Act. The EEOC has three major functions: (1) investigating and resolving complaints about alleged discrimination, (2) gathering information regarding employment patterns and trends in U.S. businesses, and (3) issuing information about new employment guidelines as they become relevant.

The first function is illustrated in Figure 2.3, which depicts the basic steps that an individual who thinks she has been discriminated against in a promotion decision might follow to get her complaint addressed. In general, if an individual believes that she or he has been discriminated against, the first step in reaching a resolution is to file a complaint with the EEOC or a corresponding state agency. The individual has 180 days from the date of the incident to file the complaint. The EEOC will dismiss out of hand almost all complaints that exceed the 180-day time frame for filing. After the complaint has been filed, the EEOC assumes responsibility for investigating the claim itself. The EEOC can take up to sixty days to investigate a complaint. If the EEOC either finds that the complaint is not valid or does not complete the investigation within a sixty-day period, the individual has the right to sue in a federal court.

If the EEOC believes that discrimination has occurred, its representative will first try to negotiate a reconciliation between the two parties without taking the case to court. Occasionally, the EEOC may enter into a consent decree with the discriminating organization. This consent decree is essentially an agreement between the EEOC and the organization that stipulates that the organization will cease certain discriminatory practices and perhaps implement new affirmative action procedures to rectify its history of discrimination.

On the other hand, if the EEOC cannot reach an agreement with the organization, two courses of action may be pursued. First, the EEOC can issue a right-to-sue letter to the victim; the letter simply certifies that the agency has investigated the complaint and found potential validity in the victim's allegations. Essentially, that course of action involves the EEOC giving its blessings to the individual to file suit on his or her own

Executive Order 11478 *requires the federal government to base all of its own employment policies on merit and fitness and specifies that race, color, sex, religion, and national origin should not be considered.*

The **Vocational Rehabilitation Act of 1973** *requires that executive agencies and subcontractors and contractors of the federal government receiving more than $2,500 a year from the government engage in affirmative action for disabled individuals.*

The **Vietnam Era Veterans' Readjustment Act of 1974** *requires that federal contractors and subcontractors take affirmative action toward employing Vietnam era veterans.*

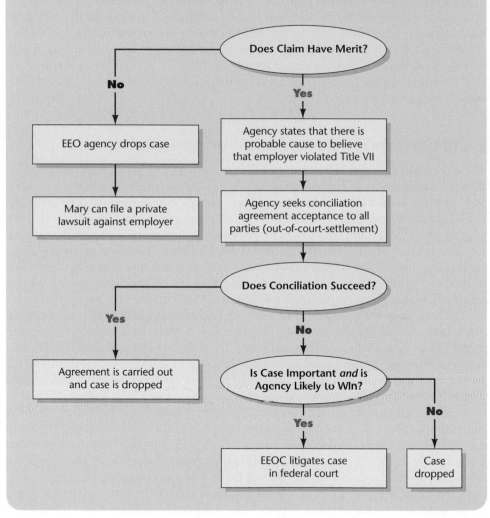

FIGURE 2.3   Investigating and Resolving a Discrimination Complaint

MARY SMITH believes she has been discriminated against at work. She was passed over for a promotion to supervisor, and believes it was because she was a woman, rather than because she was unqualified. Specifically, all candidates for promotion must be approved by their immediate supervisor, and most of these supervisors are older white men who have been heard to say that women should not be promoted. In fact, almost no women have been promoted to supervisor in this organization. What can Mary do?

STEP 1:   Mary files a complaint with her local or state EEO agency.
STEP 2:   Local/state EEO agency agrees to investigate Mary's claim on behalf of EEOC, and the agency contacts Mary's employer to determine whether the claim has any merit.

Does Claim Have Merit?

No

Yes

EEO agency drops case

Agency states that there is probable cause to believe that employer violated Title VII

Mary can file a private lawsuit against employer

Agency seeks conciliation agreement acceptance to all parties (out-of-court-settlement)

Does Conciliation Succeed?

Yes

No

Agreement is carried out and case is dropped

Is Case Important *and* is Agency Likely to Win?

Yes

No

EEOC litigates case in federal court

Case dropped

behalf. Alternatively, in certain limited cases, the EEOC itself may assist the victim in bringing suit in federal court. In either event, however, the lawsuit must be filed in federal court within 300 days of the alleged discriminatory act. The courts follow this guideline very strictly, and many valid complaints have lost standing in court because lawsuits were not filed on time. As already noted, the EEOC has recently become backlogged with complaints stemming primarily from the passage of the newer civil rights

FIGURE 2.3 (Continued)

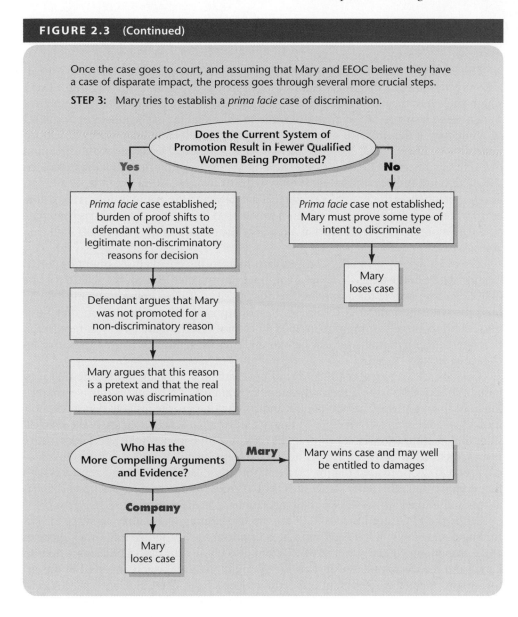

Once the case goes to court, and assuming that Mary and EEOC believe they have a case of disparate impact, the process goes through several more crucial steps.

STEP 3: Mary tries to establish a *prima facie* case of discrimination.

Does the Current System of Promotion Result in Fewer Qualified Women Being Promoted?

Yes

Prima facie case established; burden of proof shifts to defendant who must state legitimate non-discriminatory reasons for decision

Defendant argues that Mary was not promoted for a non-discriminatory reason

Mary argues that this reason is a pretext and that the real reason was discrimination

Who Has the More Compelling Arguments and Evidence?

Mary

Mary wins case and may well be entitled to damages

Company

Mary loses case

No

Prima facie case not established; Mary must prove some type of intent to discriminate

Mary loses case

act. One recent court case that involved the implementation of a discriminatory seniority system was settled in such a way that it helped provide the grounds for amending Title VII to provide exceptions to the 300-day deadline for filing a lawsuit.

The EEOC recently announced a new policy for prioritizing pending complaints to help clear its backlog and to provide better enforcement of the law. When a new complaint is filed, a case officer quickly reviews it and makes a judgment about its merits. Cases that appear to reflect a strong likelihood of discrimination are then given higher priority than are cases that appear to have less merit. Even higher priority is given to those cases that appear to have the potential for widespread or classwide effects.[42]

The second important function of the EEOC is to monitor the hiring practices of organizations. Every year all organizations that employ 100 or more individuals must file a report with the EEOC that summarizes the number of women and minorities that the organization employs in nine different job categories. The EEOC tracks these reports to identify potential patterns of discrimination that it can then potentially address through class-action lawsuits.

The third function of the EEOC is to develop and issue guidelines that help organizations determine whether their decisions are violations of the law enforced by the EEOC. These guidelines themselves are not laws, but the courts have generally given them great weight when hearing employment discrimination cases. One of the most important set of guidelines is the uniform guidelines on employee selection procedures developed jointly by the EEOC, the U.S. Department of Labor, the U.S. Department of Justice, and the U.S. Civil Service Commission. These guidelines summarize how organizations should develop and administer selection systems to avoid violating Title VII. The EEOC also frequently uses the *Federal Register* to issue new guidelines and opinions regarding employment practices that result from newly passed laws.[43] This activity has been particularly important in recent years as a result of the passage of the Americans with Disabilities Act.[44]

The other agency primarily charged with monitoring equal employment opportunity legislation is the Office of Federal Contract Compliance Procedures (OFCCP). The OFCCP is responsible for enforcing the executive orders that cover companies doing business with the federal government. Recall from our earlier discussion that businesses with contracts of more than $50,000 cannot discriminate based on race, color, religious beliefs, national origin, or gender, and they must have a written affirmative action plan on file.[45]

The OFCCP conducts yearly audits of government contractors to ensure that they have been actively pursuing their affirmative action goals. These audits involve examining a company's affirmative action plan and conducting on-site visits to determine how individual employees perceive the company's affirmative action policies. If the OFCCP finds that its contractors or subcontractors are not complying with the relevant executive orders, then it may notify the EEOC, advise the Department of Justice to institute criminal proceedings, or request that the Secretary of Labor cancel or suspend contracts with that organization. This latter step is the OFCCP's most important weapon because it has a clear and immediate impact on an organization's revenue stream.

While the EEOC and the OFCCP are the two primary regulatory agencies for enforcing equal employment legislation, it is important to recognize that other agencies and components of our government system also come into play. The Department of Labor and the Department of Justice, for example, are both heavily involved in the enforcement of equal employment opportunity legislation. The U.S. Civil Service Commission is also actively involved for government organizations where civil-service jobs exist. The U.S. judicial systems reflected by our courts also play an important role in enforcing all human resource management legislation.

Other Areas of Human Resource Regulation

As noted earlier, most employment regulations are designed to provide equal employment opportunity. However, some legislation goes beyond equal employment opportunity and really deals more substantively with other issues. We will touch on these different areas of legislation here, but we will discuss them in more detail when we discuss the content area involved. So, for example, while we will begin with a discussion of legislation dealing with compensation and benefits, we will discuss these laws in more detail in Chapter 9.

Legal Perspectives on Compensation and Benefits

The most basic, and yet far-reaching law dealing with compensation at work is the Fair Labor Standards Act. The **Fair Labor Standards Act (FLSA),** passed in 1938, established a minimum hourly wage for jobs. The rationale for this legislation was to ensure that everyone who works would receive an income sufficient to meet basic needs. The first minimum wage was $0.25 an hour. Of course, this minimum wage has been revised many times, most recently in 2007.

The FSLA also established, for the first time, the workweek in the United States as forty hours per week. It further specifies that all full-time employees must be paid at a rate of one and a half times their normal hourly rate for each hour of overtime work beyond forty hours in a week. Note, however, that the law makes no provision for daily work time. Thus, while a normal workday might be considered eight hours, an employer is actually free to schedule, say, ten or twelve hours in a single day without paying overtime as long as the weekly total does not exceed forty hours. The FLSA also includes child labor provisions, which provide protection for persons eighteen years of age and under. These protections include keeping minors from working on extremely dangerous jobs, as well as limiting the number of hours that persons under sixteen can work.

Another important piece of legislation that affects compensation is the **Employee Retirement Income Security Act of 1974 (ERISA).** This law was passed to protect employee investments in their pensions and to ensure that employees would be able to receive at least some pension benefits at the time of retirement or even termination. ERISA does not mean that an employee must receive a pension, rather it is meant to protect any pension benefits to which the employee is entitled. (This topic will be discussed in somewhat more detail in Chapter 9.) ERISA was passed in part because some organizations had abused their pension plans in their efforts to control costs or to channel money inappropriately to other uses within the organization and in part because of corruption.

Two other emerging legal perspectives on compensation and benefits involve minimum benefits coverage and executive compensation. Recent publicity about the poor benefits Wal-Mart provides some of its employees, for example, led the Maryland General Assembly to pass a bill requiring employers with more than 10,000 workers to spend at least 8 percent of their payroll on benefits or else pay into a fund for the uninsured. At the time the bill was passed (in early 2006) Wal-Mart was the only company to be affected. Moreover, several other states are exploring similar legislation. On another front, the Securities and Exchange Commission (SEC) is also developing new guidelines that will require companies to divulge more complete and detailed information about their executive compensation packages.[46]

Legal Perspectives on Labor Relations

There are also a number of laws and acts that deal with labor relations—a term generally used to refer to the formal and legal relationship between an organization and some or all of its workers who have formed and joined a labor union. (We will discuss this topic in more detail in Chapter 11.)

The **National Labor Relations Act,** or Wagner Act, was passed in 1935 in an effort to control and legislate collective bargaining between organizations and labor unions. Prior to this time the legal system in the United States was generally considered hostile

*The **Fair Labor Standards Act (FLSA),** passed in 1938, established a minimum hourly wage for jobs.*

*The **Employee Retirement Income Security Act of 1974** (or **ERISA**) was passed to guarantee a basic minimum benefit that employees could expect to be paid upon retirement.*

*The **National Labor Relations Act** (or **Wagner Act**) was passed in 1935 in an effort to control and legislate collective bargaining between organizations and labor unions, to grant power to labor unions, and to put unions on a more equal footing with managers in terms of the rights of employees.*

to labor unions. The Wagner Act was passed in an effort to provide some sense of balance in the power relationship between organizations and unions. The Wagner Act describes the process through which labor unions can be formed and the requirements faced by organizations in dealing with those labor unions. The Wagner Act served to triple union membership in the United States and granted labor unions significant power in their relationships with organizations.

Following a series of crippling strikes, however, the U.S. government concluded that the Wagner Act had actually shifted too much power to labor unions. As a result, businesses had been placed at a significant disadvantage. To correct this imbalance, Congress subsequently passed the **Labor Management Relations Act (Taft-Hartley Act)** in 1947 and the **Landrum-Griffin Act** in 1959. Both of these acts regulate union actions and their internal affairs in a way that puts them on an equal footing with management and organizations. The Taft-Hartley Act also created the National Labor Relations Board (NLRB), which was charged with enforcement of the act.

Although the basic issues of unionization and collective bargaining have become pretty well established, some legal issues have emerged in this area. The Taft-Hartley Act guarantees these rights but also guarantees that these unions should be independent. This issue has come up in two fairly recent cases. More important for the future, in both these cases, the company was involved in setting up autonomous work teams that were empowered to make certain decisions about employees. In *Electromation* v. *NLRB*,[47] the NLRB ruled that the company's "action committees," formed to deal with employee working conditions and staffed by employees, actually constituted a threat to the union already in place in the company. These action committees, which the NLRB ruled were dominated by management, were seen as an alternative way to deal with problems concerning working conditions and could allow the company to circumvent the union and the collective-bargaining process. As such, the company was found in violation of the Taft Hartley Act. In a similar case, *E.I. Du Pont de Nemours* v. *NLRB*,[48] the board ruled that Du Pont's safety committees were essentially employer-dominated labor organizations and thus were in violation of the Taft Hartley Act.

Employee Safety and Health

Employees also have the right to work in safe and healthy environments, and these rights continue to be important in organizations. The **Occupational Safety and Health Act of 1970 (OSHA)** is the single most comprehensive piece of legislation regarding worker safety and health in organizations. OSHA granted the federal government the power to establish and enforce occupational safety and health standards for all places of employment directly affecting interstate commerce. The Department of Labor was given power to apply the standards and enforce the provisions of OSHA. The Department of Health was given responsibility for conducting research to determine the criteria for specific operations or occupations and for training employers to comply with the act itself. OSHA also makes provisions through which individual states can substitute their own safety and health standards for those suggested by the federal government.

The basic premise of OSHA (also known as the *general duty clause*) is that each employer has an obligation to furnish each employee with a place of employment that is free from hazards that can cause death or physical harm. OSHA is generally enforced through inspections of the workplace by OSHA inspectors, and fines can be imposed on violators. We will deal with these issues in more detail in Chapter 12.

The **Labor Management Relations Act (*or* Taft-Hartley Act)** *was passed in 1947 in response to public outcries against a wide variety of strikes in the years following World War II; it curtailed and limited union powers and regulates union actions and their internal affairs.*

The **Landrum-Griffin Act** *was passed in 1959, and was focused on the elimination of various unethical, illegal, and/or undemoctratic practices within unions themselves.*

The **Occupational Safety and Health Act of 1970 (*or* OSHA)** *grants the federal government the power to establish and enforce occupational safety and health standards for all places of employment directly affecting interstate commerce.*

Employee safety and health are important considerations in organizations today. The Occupational Safety and Health Act is the major law that governs safety and health today. Take this steel worker, for example. He is evaluating the quality of molten steel before it is poured into molds for fabrication. OSHA provides detailed specifications for the safety equipment he is wearing (the gloves, goggles, and helmet), the distance he should maintain from the vat, and the procedures he should use to carry out the key elements of this particular task.

Drugs in the Workplace

The **Drug-Free Workplace Act of 1988** was passed to reduce the use of illegal drugs in the workplace. This law applies primarily to government employees and federal contractors, but it also extends to organizations regulated by the Department of Transportation and the Nuclear Regulatory Commission. Thus, long-haul truck drivers and workers at most nuclear reactors are subject to these regulations. The actual regulations themselves are aimed at establishing a drug-free workplace and include the requirement, in some cases, for regular drug testing.

But concerns over the problems of drugs at work have also led many other companies not covered by this law to establish drug-testing programs of their own. In fact, drug testing is becoming quite widespread, even though there is little hard evidence addressing the effectiveness of these programs.[49] The issue for the present discussion is whether these testing programs constitute an invasion of employee privacy. Many opponents of drug-testing programs argue that drug testing is clearly appropriate for cases where there is some "reasonable" basis for suspected drug use, but not otherwise. Others argue that organizations that test for drug use often do not test for alcohol use. Of course, alcohol consumption is not illegal, but this related issue then raises the question of the purpose of drug testing. Presumably organizations are concerned about drug use on the job because they believe that it affects performance. If this belief is true, then surely alcohol consumption on the job should be of equal concern, but it is not. On the other hand, do organizations have a right to investigate the behavior of employees when they are *not* on company time if the behavior does not affect performance on the job?

There are no easy answers to these questions, and so drug testing will likely continue to be an issue of employee versus employer rights. Of course, what makes the privacy issues here even more salient is the method generally used to test for drugs on the job.

*The **Drug-Free Workplace Act of 1988** was passed to reduce the use of illegal drugs in the workplace. It applies primarily to government employees and federal contractors, but it also extends to organizations regulated by the Department of Transportation and the Nuclear Regulatory Commission. The actual regulations themselves are aimed at establishing a drug-free workplace and include the requirement, in some cases, for regular drug testing.*

Urinalysis (by far the most common method) is extremely invasive and has been known to result in a fair number of false positive tests (i.e., employees are incorrectly identified as drug users). As a result, several alternatives have begun to appear in organizations, including testing of one's individual hairs.[50] Perhaps these new technologies will reduce some of the concerns over drug testing while providing employers the protection they deserve from drug use on the job.

Plant Closings and Employee Rights

The **Worker Adjustment and Retraining Notification (WARN) Act of 1988** stipulates that an organization employing at least 100 employees must provide notice at least sixty days in advance of plans to close a facility or lay off fifty or more employees. The act also provides for warnings about pending reductions in work hours but generally applies only to private employers.

The **Worker Adjustment and Retraining Notification (WARN) Act of 1988** stipulates that an organization employing at least 100 employees must provide notice at least sixty days in advance of plans to close a facility or lay off fifty or more employees. The penalty for failing to comply is equal to one day's pay (plus benefits) for each employee for each day that notice should have been given. An organization that closes a plant without any warning and lays off 1,000 employees would be liable for sixty days of pay and benefits for those 1,000 employees, which could translate into a substantial amount of money. The act also provides for warnings about pending reductions in work hours but generally applies only to private employers. There are exceptions to the WARN requirements; those exceptions are related to unforeseeable business circumstances such as a strike at a major employer or a government-enforced shutdown.[51]

We will discuss other issues related to reductions in the workforce in Chapter 6, but the events of September 11, 2001, constitute a clear example of an exception to the requirements about notification. It has been obvious in all cases that no business could have reasonably foreseen and planned for such an attack, and therefore there is no issue about a failure to warn employees about closings and layoffs.

Privacy Issues at Work

In recent years issues of privacy are more important to Americans than ever before. Therefore, it is not surprising that privacy at work has become more important as well. The history of legislation dealing with privacy at work, however, actually goes back several years. The **Privacy Act of 1974** applies directly to federal employees only, but it has served as the impetus for several state laws. Basically, this legislation allows employees to review their personnel file periodically to ensure that the information contained therein is accurate. Prior to this privacy legislation, managers could place almost any information they pleased in a personnel file and only certain other managers could see those files.

The **Privacy Act of 1974** applies directly to federal employees only, but it has served as the impetus for several state laws. Basically, this legislation allows employees to review their personnel file periodically to ensure that the information contained therein is accurate.

But the larger concerns with privacy these days relate to potential invasions of employee privacy by organizations. For example, organizations generally reserve the right to monitor the e-mail correspondence of employees. Presumably employees should be using company e-mail only for company business, so this practice may not be a problem, but it does mean that employees who receive unsolicited e-mails from suspect vendors (such as pornographic websites) may also have that information shared with their employer. These issues have become more important, however, in light of the Patriot Act.

The **Patriot Act** was passed shortly after the terrorist attacks on September 11, 2001, to help the United States more effectively battle terrorism worldwide.

The **Patriot Act** was passed shortly after the terrorist attacks on September 11, 2001, to help the United States more effectively battle terrorism worldwide. Many of the act's provisions expand the rights of the government or law enforcement agencies to collect information about and/or pursue potential terrorists. Some major provisions include those that:

- Allow law enforcement agencies to use surveillance to gather information related to a full range of terrorist crimes
- Allow law enforcement agencies to carry out investigations of potential terrorists without having to inform the targets of those investigations

- Allow federal agents to seek business records related to terrorist activities (such as lists of who purchased certain products)
- Allow law enforcement agencies to obtain search warrants any place a terrorist activity might occur
- Facilitate the sharing of information about suspected terrorists among law enforcement and government agencies

Although most of these stipulations are necessary in the fight against terrorism, there is concern that some of them represent important limits on individual rights to privacy at work and at home. In fact, these concerns led to the Congress failing to reinstate the Patriot Act at the end of 2005, even with new assurances from the government concerning civil rights. The act was finally reauthorized in early 2006, but the debate about privacy versus security continues and is the focus of our Point-Counterpoint feature for this chapter.

Ethics and Human Resource Management

Another important and related issue for all managers, not just human resource managers, is ethics.[52] Ethics is a separate concept from the law but is closely intertwined. **Ethics** refers to an individual's beliefs about what is right and wrong and what is good and bad. A person's set of ethics is formed by the societal context in which people and organizations function. In recent years, ethical behavior and ethical conduct on the part of managers and organizations have received increased attention, a trend fueled by scandals at firms such as Enron, Worldcom, Imclone, and Tyco International. The basic premise is that laws are passed by the government to control and dictate appropriate behavior and conduct in a society. The concept of ethics serves much the same purpose because of its premise about what is right and what is wrong.

But ethics and law don't always coincide precisely. For example, it may be perfectly legal for a manager to take a certain action, but some observers might find his or her action to be unethical. For example, an organization undergoing a major cutback might be able legally to terminate a specific employee who is nearing retirement age. But if that employee has a long history of dedicated service to the organization, many people could consider termination ethically questionable. Managers from every part of the organization must take steps to ensure that their behavior is both ethical and legal. Some organizations develop codes of conduct or ethical statements in an attempt to communicate their stance on ethics and ethical conduct publicly.

Ethics *refers to an individual's beliefs about what is right and wrong and what is good and bad.*

Evaluating Legal Compliance

Given the clear and obvious importance as well as the complexities associated with the legal environment of human resource management, it is critically important that organizations comply with the laws and regulations that govern human resource management practices to the best of their ability. The assurance of compliance can best be done through a three-step process. The first step is to ensure that managers have a clear understanding of the laws that govern every aspect of human resource management. That is, all managers must understand and be intimately familiar with the various laws that restrict and govern their behavior vis-à-vis their employees.

Privacy or Security?

What Price Security? Ever since the September 11 attacks on the World Trade Center, Americans have become much more aware of the threats to their security. The Patriot Act, described above, is really just one tangible outcome of these new concerns. In addition, people have been pulled from airline flights if they were on some list of suspected terrorists (including the singer formerly known as Cat Stevens who sang about the "peace train"), our bags are x-rayed and inspected at the airports, and we can't even go through security wearing shoes in many airports. In addition, government agencies have searched library records to determine who has checked out certain kinds of books. For many people around the world, these measures sound like normal life, but they are not "normal" for Americans. We have been forced to give up certain rights and freedoms, especially some privacy rights, in the name of security. No one suggests that we should not be concerned about security, but is it worth giving up all our rights to be more secure? Some? None?

POINT... National and personal security are so important that we should maximize security at almost any price because...	COUNTERPOINT... Security issues are important, but not as important as our rights and freedoms because...
Our country is at war with terrorists and we are all potential targets. Therefore, we must all be protected.	If we give up our freedom, the terrorists win.
The people we are fighting want to destroy our democratic system and we must defeat them at all costs.	We may help terrorists destroy our system by dismantling it. Our citizens need protection from other threats as well, and that is what our laws do.
Innocent people will die if we do not maintain the necessary levels of security.	Innocent people will suffer if we begin dismantling our rights to privacy. Such actions will make some people in our country easy targets for hate groups inside the United States.
Terrorists can hide behind some of the kinds of protection that our laws have guaranteed our citizens and this was not the intent of those laws.	These laws were passed to protect our citizens and this need is paramount.
We have always made tradeoffs between freedom and protection, and this is just one more (rather serious) example of this.	We can never protect our citizens from all threats, so we need to guard their rights as best we can.

So... This is a debate that will intensify in years to come. As noted, Americans are fairly unique in the sense that most of us grew up expecting certain rights and privileges, and now we see that we may have to give some of them up. It is foolish to suggest that we can return to the innocence that we once knew—some rights and freedoms must be limited, including some of our privacy rights. Yet we must also be sure that no one in the government or anywhere else forgets that those laws also protect our citizens in other ways and that we cannot just ignore them just because the threat of terrorism has increased.

Ethical conduct in the workplace has come under increased scrutiny in light of problems at firms like Enron and Tyco. One of the more recent scandals involved Hewlett-Packard's former Chair, Patricia Dunn. The problems started when it became apparent that someone associated with HP's board of directors was leaking confidential material to the press. Ms. Dunn hired a private investigator to identify the source of the leaks. But the investigator resorted to unethical practices, apparently with her tacit approval. The resulting media firestorm eventually forced Ms. Dunn to resign from her position.

Second, managers should rely on their own legal and human resource staff to answer questions and to review procedures periodically. Almost all larger organizations have a legal staff consisting of professionals trained in various areas of the legal environment of business. A human resource manager or other manager with a legal question regarding a particular employment issue or practice is well advised to consult the firm's attorney about the legality of that particular action.

And third, organizations may also find it useful to engage occasionally in external legal audits of their human resource management procedures. This audit might involve contracting with an outside law firm to review the organization's human resource management systems and practices to ensure that they comply with all appropriate laws and regulations. Such an external audit will, of course, be expensive and somewhat intrusive into the organization's daily routine. When properly conducted, however, external audits can keep an organization out of trouble.

Chapter Summary

The legal context of human resource management is shaped by various forces. The first step in this process is the actual creation of new regulation. The second step is the enforcement of those regulations. The third step is the actual practice and implementation of those regulations in organizations. Regulations exist in almost every aspect of the employment relationship.

The basic goal of all equal employment opportunity regulation is to protect people from unfair or inappropriate discrimination in the workplace. Illegal discrimination results from behaviors or actions by an organization or managers within an organization that cause members of a protected class to be unfairly differentiated from others. Four basic kinds of discrimination are disparate treatment, disparate impact, pattern or practice discrimination, and retaliation. Depending on the specific law, a protected class consists of all individuals who share one or more common characteristic, as indicated by that law.

The major laws and related regulations that affect equal employment opportunity include Title VII of the Civil Rights Act of 1964, Executive Order 11246, Executive Order 11478, the Equal Pay Act of 1963, the Age Discrimination and Employment Act (ADEA), the Vocational Rehabilitation Act of 1973, the Vietnam Era Veterans' Readjustment Act of 1974, the Pregnancy Discrimination Act of 1979, the Civil Rights Act of 1991, the Americans with Disabilities Act of 1990 (ADA), and the Family and Medical Leave Act of 1993. The enforcement of equal opportunity legislation generally is handled by the Equal Employment Opportunity Commission (EEOC) and the Office of Federal Contract Compliance Procedures (OFCCP.)

The most far-reaching law dealing with total compensation is the Fair Labor Standards Act, which was passed in 1938. This law established a minimum hourly wage for jobs. Another important piece of legislation that affects compensation is the Employee Retirement Income Security Act of 1974 (ERISA).

The National Labor Relations Act, or Wagner Act, was passed in 1935 in an effort to control and legislate collective bargaining between organizations and labor unions. Congress subsequently passed the Taft-Hartley Act in 1947 and the Landrum-Griffin Act in 1959 to regulate union actions and their internal affairs.

Several related areas of human resource management are affected by laws and associated legal issues. These related areas include employee safety and health (especially as related to the Occupational Safety and Health Act [OSHA]), various emerging areas of discrimination law (especially sexual harassment), ethics, and human resource management.

Key Points for Future HR Managers

- Dealing with legal issues has become the most critical part of the human resource manager's job, and it is an area where a great deal of expertise is needed.

- Human resource managers must balance the needs of the organization with the need to obey the law.

- Human resource managers are generally responsible, under the law, for communicating the duties and responsibilities of line managers to those managers and for making sure that those line managers act appropriately.

- The Civil Rights Act remains the single most important piece of legislation for human resource management. Title VII outlaws discrimination on the basis of race, gender, color, religion, or national origin.

- The Civil Rights Act outlaws disparate treatment as well as disparate impact discrimination against members of protected classes under the law.

- Disparate treatment cases involve policies that systematically treat members of some groups differently than members of other groups. The only clear exception is called a bona fide occupational qualification (BFOQ), which is a narrow basis for what would otherwise be disparate treatment.

- Disparate impact cases involve using policies that, although they are applied equally to all employees, will have a more adverse impact on employees who are members of protected classes.

- Three methods are available for establishing a prima facie case of discrimination: violation of the four-fifths rule, population comparisons, and the McDonnell test. Once such a case has been established, the burden of proof shifts to the defendant.

- Reverse discrimination occurs when a practice or policy has a disparate impact on the majority group (such as white males). The potential for reverse discrimination exists when certain voluntary quotas are implemented.

- Sexual harassment is an important issue in organizations. Different types of sexual harassment exist, but all involve either unwanted attention or an uncomfortable workplace. Once the management of an organization has been notified that sexual harassment has occurred, the organization is legally responsible for correcting the offending practices.

- The Americans with Disabilities Act outlaws discrimination against individuals with disabilities. It also requires that an organization provide a reasonable accommodation to anyone who has a disability and requests such an accommodation. The definition of disability under this law is quite broad, and so the potential liability is quite large.

- The Fair Labor Standards Act provides for a minimum wage and overtime provisions and establishes child-labor laws.

- The Employee Income Security Act (ERISA) requires that an organization guarantee employee pension rights in certain ways if the organization plans to deduct the cost of pensions from its taxes.

- The Taft-Hartley Act recognizes employee rights to organize and bargain collectively, and organizations must be careful not to violate those rights.

- The Occupational Safety and Health Act (OSHA) requires that employees work in a safe work environment. It stipulates substantial penalties if these rights are violated.

- Employees' rights to privacy usually involve statements in personnel files but also involve other issues relating to invasions of privacy by employers.

- Employers' rights to administer drug tests are somewhat limited because they can clash with employees' rights to privacy.

Key Points for Future General Managers

- The law represents a major constraint on corporate human resource practices.

- The Civil Rights Act is probably the single most important piece of legislation that addresses which human resource practices are allowed under the law.

- Under the Civil Rights Act, policies that are applied equally to all employees but have a different (and adverse) effect on employees based on race, gender, religion, color, or national origin are potentially illegal.

- Sexual harassment is outlawed under the Civil Rights Act, and the scope of activities covered here is quite broad.

- Laws also outlaw discrimination on the basis of disability and age.

- Still other laws regulate how people are paid, how organizations deal with unions (or attempts to unionize), and worker safety and privacy.

- No human resource decision should be made without consulting someone knowledgeable about the legal implications of the action. These consultations should include a professional human resource manager as well as a lawyer.

Review and Discussion Questions

1. Describe the process through which the legal context of human resource management is created.

2. Summarize the role of the Thirteenth and Fourteenth Amendments to the U.S. Constitution in equal employment opportunity.

3. What is illegal discrimination? What is legal discrimination?

4. Identify and summarize the various forms of illegal discrimination.

5. Identify and summarize five major laws that deal with equal employment opportunity.

6. Why is most employment regulation passed at the national level, as opposed to the state or local level?

7. Which equal employment opportunity laws will likely affect you most directly when you finish school and begin to look for employment?

Questions

1. What are the ethical issues in this situation?

2. What are the pros and cons for keeping this information to yourself versus telling your plant manager what you heard?

3. What do you think most managers would do? What would you do?

HR Internet Exercise

 One of the most critical issues facing all human resource managers today is compliance with various legal regulations. The following website summarizes most current lawsuits in federal courts involving claims of various forms of discrimination: http:www.nyper.com.

Visit this website and select any two categories of pending lawsuits. Then visit those locations and review some of the lawsuits. Choose two lawsuits from each area that seem interesting to you (for a total of four). Write a brief description of each lawsuit. Then describe the potential implications for you as a future human resource manager for each potential outcome of the lawsuits.

Questions

1. How useful is the Internet in keeping human resource managers informed about legal actions that may affect them?

2. Does relying on the Internet for legal information pose any risks?

3. What other legal information would you like to see on the Internet?

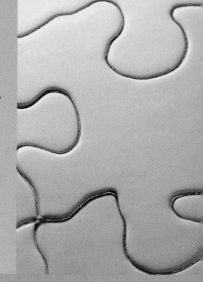

3

The Global Environment

CHAPTER OBJECTIVES

After studying this chapter you should be able to:

- Describe the growth of international business.

- Identify and discuss global issues in international human resource management.

- Discuss the human resource management function in international business.

- Identify and discuss domestic issues in international human resource management.

- Describe the issues involved in managing international transfers and assignments.

- Summarize the issues in international labor relations.

One of the most significant trends in U.S. business today is the growing practice of moving production to foreign factories in an effort to capitalize on lower labor costs. General Motors (GM) has been very successful with this practice, especially in Mexico. Almost 20 percent of the firm's North American manufacturing workforce is now based in Mexico. Indeed, GM and Delphi Automotive Systems, GM's huge parts-making subsidiary, are among the most attractive—and important—employers in Mexico.

> **"It's the turn of the [twentieth] century all over again, now, south of the border."**
>
> (Charles Robinson, U.S. auto industry consultant)*

The benefits of producing in Mexico are clear. Local wage standards mean that Mexican workers are paid about one-tenth the pay rate of their counterparts in Flint, Michigan, GM's other big North American production center. They also expect fewer benefits, and the government imposes fewer regulations on employers. The products that come out of the Mexican plants can be exported tariff-free back to the United States.

Mexican workers also seem to agree that they are getting a good deal. For example, while their wages may seem low by U.S. standards, most of them are actually earning far more than they would be if they were working for Mexican firms in other parts of the country. They also generally feel that they have better benefits, more job security, improved job training, and greater opportunities for advancement than if they were employed elsewhere. Indeed, some observers feel that the northern Mexico region today is very much like Detroit was seventy years ago because it has become a magnet for motivated but undereducated workers looking for a better way of life.

One factor that continues to support GM's growing pressure in Mexico, however, is that it does indeed generally benefit both the company and its workers. Provisions of NAFTA (the North American Free Trade Agreement) provide protection for domestic workers, and GM seems to be a good employer. Unlike corporate practices in other parts of the world (some of which are discussed later), GM's human resource strategy in Mexico seems to be well-conceived and effectively implemented.

But not everything is perfect. GM's biggest union, the United Auto Workers (UAW), is seriously concerned about what GM is doing and sees it as a major threat to the long-term job security of its own members in the United States. GM's plants in Mexico experience very high turnover—as much as 50 percent a year—in large part because many of their workers leave their families behind when they come north to work and then get lonely and return home. And many of the workers are poorly educated and must first be taught to read and write before true job-related training can even begin. In the event of a long-term slowdown in the auto industry, any major job cuts by GM could seriously undermine its current reputation as a major employer of choice in Mexico. And finally, while wages are low in Mexico, they are actually somewhat lower in certain other countries such as India and China. As a result, GM is also exploring other areas for low-cost production in order to remain competitive.[1]

t's no secret that international business is booming these days. Almost every large firm located anywhere in the world is always on the alert for new business opportunities anywhere else in the world. Such opportunities include new markets where products and services can be sold; new locations where products and services can be created for lower costs; and areas where new information, financing, and other resources may be obtained. To manage international expansion effectively, firms need skilled and experienced managers and employees who understand both specific individual foreign markets (such as Japan or Germany) and general international issues (including areas such as exchange rate fluctuations, political risk, and the cost of labor). One of the fastest-growing and most important concerns for human resource managers in many companies today is preparing other managers for international assignments. In reality, however, this is only one part of international human resource management.

This chapter will explore international human resource management in detail. We begin with a general overview of the growth of international business. Global issues in international human resource management are then introduced and discussed. Next we examine the human resource function in international business. Domestic issues in international human resource management are identified and described, and then we describe the management of international transfers and assignments. Finally, we summarize the basic issues in international labor relations.

The Growth of International Business

International business is not a new phenomenon. Indeed, its origins can be traced back literally thousands of years as merchants plied their wares along ancient trade routes linking southern Europe, the Middle East, and the Orient. Silks, spices, grains, jade, ivory, and textiles were among the most popular goods forming the basis for early trade. Even in more recent times Columbus's voyages to the so-called New World were motivated by the economic goal of discovering new trade routes to the Far East. Wars have been fought over issues arising from international commerce, and the British Empire was built around the financial and business interests of the British nobility. In more recent years, however, several specific trends have emerged in international business that provide a meaningful context for the study of human resource management.

The forces that shaped today's competitive international business environment began to emerge in the years following World War II. As a result of that global conflict, Japan and most of Europe were devastated. Roads and highways were destroyed and factories were bombed. The United States was the only major industrial power that emerged from World War II with its infrastructure relatively intact. Places not devastated by the war, such as South and Central America and Africa, were not major players in the global economy even before the war, and Canada had yet to become a major global economic power.

Businesses in war-torn countries had little choice but to rebuild from scratch. They were in the unfortunate position of having to rethink every facet of their business, including technology, productions, operations, finance, and marketing. Ultimately, however, this position worked to their advantage. During the 1950s the United States was by far the dominant economic power in the world. Its businesses controlled most major marketplaces and most major industries. At the same time, however, Japan, Germany, and other countries were rebuilding their own infrastructures and developing new industrial clout.

During the 1960s this newly formed industrial clout first began to exert itself in the world marketplace. Firms from Germany (like Siemens, Daimler-Benz [now Daimler-Chrysler], and Bayer) and Japan (like Toyota, NEC, and Mitsubishi) began to take on new industrial strength and slowly but surely began to challenge the dominance of U.S. firms in markets ranging from automobiles to electronics. Firms from other parts of Europe had also fully recovered and were asserting themselves in areas ranging from petroleum and energy (e.g., Shell and British Petroleum) to food (e.g., Nestlé and Cadbury), to luxury goods (e.g., LVMH and Gucci). By the late 1970s businesses from other countries emerged as major players in the world economy, and by the 1980s many of them had established dominant positions in their industries. At the same time, many U.S. firms had grown complacent, their products and services were not of high quality, and their manufacturing and production methods were outdated and outmoded.

Eventually, U.S. firms decided that they had little choice but to start over as well. Thus, during the latter part of the 1980s and into the early 1990s, many U.S. firms practically rebuilt themselves. They shut down or renovated old factories, developed new manufacturing techniques, and began to focus renewed emphasis on quality. By the mid-1990s, global competitiveness seemed to have become the norm rather than the exception. The United States, Japan, and Germany remained the three leading industrial powers in the world. However, other western European countries such as France, England, the Netherlands, Spain, and Belgium were also becoming increasingly important. In Asia, Taiwan, Singapore, and Malaysia were also emerging as global economic powers. Of course, China and India are clearly emerging as global powers. Few events illustrate this last statement better than the acquisition by Lenovo (a Beijing-based personal computer company) of IBM's Personal Computing division in May of 2005 and the growth of call-center operations in India.

Substantial developments in Europe (which we will discuss below) have strengthened the position of countries there. In North America, Canada and Mexico also began to show promise of achieving economic pre-eminence in the global marketplaces, and many countries in South America have also begun to globalize their operations. Figure 3.1 illustrates the regions of the world that are especially significant in today's global economy, and Table 3.1 shows the world's largest industrial corporations.

But several other developments in the world also have an impact on the new global economy. First, many developed countries, such as the United States, Japan, and the countries of western Europe have experienced slowing rates of growth in their populations. This trend has implications for the demand for certain types of consumer goods as well as for the availability of individuals to work producing those goods. On the other hand, countries such as Mexico, India, Indonesia, and China (despite its one-child-per-couple policy) continue to experience rapid population growth. This growth is fueling a demand for international goods and also makes these locations attractive sites for new businesses or joint ventures. Furthermore, the collapse of the Japanese markets in the late 1990s and the downturn in the U.S. stock market in 2002 (especially the high-tech sector), and the effects these events had on world markets, made it clear exactly how interdependent global economies really are. No global organization can ignore elections in Iraq, the developments in the Gaza Strip, or the valuation of the Chinese RMB. All of these events, once seen as far removed from the concerns of American businesses, now have a strong and immediate impact on how firms in this country and other countries around the world do business. Finally, as we discuss below, the growth of regional economic alliances has also had a substantial impact on the global business community.

FIGURE 3.1   Global Business Centers

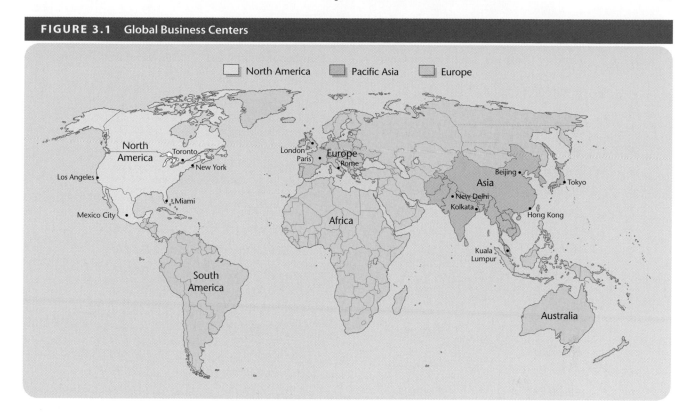

Global Issues in International Human Resource Management

Various global issues in international human resource management must be addressed by any international firm. As shown in Figure 3.2 on page 76, one issue is the development of an international human resource management strategy.[2] Another is developing an understanding of the cultural environment of human resource management. A third is developing an understanding of the political and legal environment of international business.

International Human Resource Management Strategy

The overall strategy of a business has to be logical and well-conceived, and so too must the effective management of a firm's international human resources be approached with a cohesive and coherent strategy. As a starting point, most international businesses today begin by developing a systematic strategy for choosing among home-country nationals, parent-country nationals, and third-country nationals for various positions in their organization.[3]

Some firms adopt what is called an **ethnocentric staffing model.** Firms that use this staffing model primarily use parent-country nationals to staff higher-level foreign positions. This strategy is based on the assumption that home-office perspectives and

The **ethnocentric staffing model** *primarily uses parent-country nationals to staff higher-level foreign positions.*

TABLE 3.1   The World's Largest Multinational Firms

Ranking	Name of Company	Home Country	Number of Employees	2006 Revenues (millions)
1	Exxon Mobil	USA	83,700	339,938
2	Wal-Mart Stores	USA	1,800,000	315,654
3	Royal Dutch Shell	Netherlands	109,000	306,731
4	BP	UK	96,000	267,600
5	General Motors	USA	335,000	192,604
6	Chevron	USA	59,000	189,481
7	DaimlerChrysler	Germany	382,724	186,106
8	Toyota Motor	Japan	285,977	185,805
9	Ford Motor	USA	300,000	177,210
10	Conoco Phillips	USA	35,600	166,683
11	General Electric	USA	316,000	157,153
12	Total	France	112,877	152,360
13	ING	Netherlands	115,300	138,235.30
14	Citigroup	USA	303,000	131,045
15	AXA	France	78,800	129,839
16	Allianz	Germany	177,625	121,406
17	Volkswagen	Germany	344,902	118,376.60
18	Fortis	Belgium	54,245	112,351.40
19	Crédit Agricole	France	136,848	110,764.60
20	American Intl. Group	USA	97,000	108,905.00
21	Assicurazioni Generali	Italy	61,561	101,403.80
22	Siemens	Germany	461,000	100,098.70
23	Sinopec	China	730,800	98,784.90
24	Nippon Telegraph & Telephone	Japan	199,113	94,869.30
25	Carrefour	France	440,479	94,454.50
26	HSBC Holdings	UK	284,000	93,494.00
27	ENI	Italy	72,258	92,603.30
28	Aviva	UK	54,791	92,579.40
29	Intl. Business Machines	USA	329,373	91,134.00
30	McKesson	USA	26,400	88,050.00
31	Honda Motor	Japan	144,786	87,510.70
32	State Grid	China	844,031	86,984.30
33	Hewlett-Packard	USA	150,000	86,696.00
34	BNP Paribas	France	101,917	85,687.20
35	PDVSA	Venezuela	48,919	85,618.00
36	UBS	Switzerland	69,569	84,707.60
37	Bank of America Corp.	USA	176,638	83,980.00

TABLE 3.1 (Continued)				
Ranking	**Name of Company**	**Home Country**	**Number of Employees**	**2006 Revenues (millions)**
38	Hitachi	Japan	355,879	83,596.30
39	China National Petroleum	China	1,090,232	83,556.50
40	Pemex	Mexico	139,171	83,381.70
41	Nissan Motor	Japan	182,273	83,273.80
42	Berkshire Hathaway	USA	192,012	81,663.00
43	Home Depot	USA	289,800	81,511.00
44	Valero Energy	USA	22,068	81,362.00
45	J.P. Morgan Chase & Co.	USA	168,847	79,902.00
46	Samsung Electronics	South Korea	80,594	78,716.60
47	Matsushita Electric Industrial	Japan	334,402	78,557.70
48	Deutsche Bank	Germany	63,427	76,227.60
49	HBOS	UK	63,685	75,798.80
50	Verizon Communications	USA	217,000	75,111.90

Source: "The World's Largest Multinational Firms" from *Fortune*, July 24, 2006. Copyright © 2006 Time Inc. Reprinted by permission. All rights reserved.

issues should take precedence over local perspectives and issues positions and that parent-country nationals will be more effective in representing the views of the home office in the foreign operation.[4] The corporate human resource function in organizations that adopt this mentality is primarily concerned with selecting and training managers for foreign assignments, developing appropriate compensation packages for those managers, and handling adjustment issues when the manager is reassigned back home. Local human resource officials handle staffing and related human resource issues for local employees hired to fill lower-level positions in the firm. Sony Corporation's operations in the United States follow this model. Sony Corporation of America, a wholly owned subsidiary of Sony Corporation, handles local human resource issues, but top executives at the firm's operations around the United States are Japanese managers from the firm's Japanese home office.

Other international businesses adopt what is called a **polycentric staffing model,** which calls for a much heavier use of host-country nationals throughout the organization, from top to bottom. Thus, the use of the polycentric staffing model is based on the assumption that such individuals (that is, host-country nationals) are better equipped to deal with local market conditions. Organizations using this approach usually have a fully functioning human resource department in each foreign subsidiary that is responsible for managing all local human resource issues for lower-level and upper-level employees alike. The corporate human resource function in such companies focuses primarily on coordinating relevant activities with their counterparts in each foreign operation. U.S. energy companies operating in Asia often adopt this model, especially because these operations are often joint ventures between the U.S. company and one or more local companies.

The **polycentric staffing model** *calls for heavy use of host-country nationals throughout the organization.*

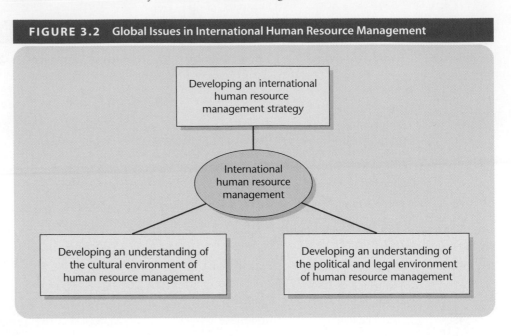

FIGURE 3.2   Global Issues in International Human Resource Management

Developing an international
human resource
management strategy

International
human resource
management

Developing an understanding of
the cultural environment of
human resource management

Developing an understanding of
the political and legal environment
of human resource management

The **geocentric staffing model** *puts parent-country nationals, host-country nationals, and third-country nationals all in the same category, with the firm attempting to always hire the best person available for a position.*

Still other firms adopt what is called a **geocentric staffing model.** The geocentric staffing model puts parent-country nationals, host-country nationals, and third-country nationals in the same category. The firm then attempts to hire the best person available for a position, regardless of where that individual comes from. The geocentric staffing model is most likely to be adopted and used by fully internationalized firms such as Nestlé and Unilever.[5] In many ways, the corporate human resource function in geocentric companies is the most complicated of all. Every aspect of the human resource management process—planning, recruiting, selection, compensation, and training—must be undertaken from an international perspective. Each foreign subsidiary or operation still needs its own self-contained human resource unit to handle ongoing employment issues.

Understanding the Cultural Environment

A country's **culture** *is the set of values, symbols, beliefs, and languages that guide human behavior within that culture.*

The cultural environment of international business also poses a variety of more applied challenges and opportunities for human resource managers. A country's **culture** can be defined as the set of values, symbols, beliefs, and languages that guide behavior of people within that culture. A culture does not necessarily coincide precisely with national boundaries, but these two different constructs are sometimes similar in terms of geographic area and domain. While all managers in an international business need to be aware of cultural nuances (by definition human resource managers are concerned with people), they must be especially cognizant of the role and importance of cultural differences and similarities in workers from different cultures.

Cultural beliefs and values are often unspoken and may even be taken for granted by those who live in a particular country. When cultures are similar, relatively few problems or difficulties may be encountered. Human resource managers can extrapolate from their own experiences to understand their function in the other culture. Thus, U.S. managers often have relatively little difficulty doing business in England. Managers in both countries speak the same language and a common framework exists for understanding both commercial and personal relationships.

Change is increasingly becoming a way of life in every part of the globe. Take Santosh Kumar, for example. Mr. Kumar is from a remote village in India. He worked hard and studied diligently to gain admission into one of India's most prestigious universities, and today he is pursuing a doctorate in chemistry. Mr. Kumar is the first person from his village to attend a university, making him a hero in the eyes of others. His example, meanwhile, is likely to motivate others to pursue similar opportunities.

More significant issues can arise, however, when considerable differences exist between the home culture of a manager and the culture of the country in which business is to be conducted. Thus, there is a higher likelihood of culturally related problems and difficulties between managers from, say, Canada and India. Differences in language, customs, and business and personal norms increase the potential for misunderstandings, miscommunication, and similar problems. In these instances, human resource managers must be careful to avoid overgeneralizing from their own experiences or perspectives.

Cultural differences can also have a direct impact on business practices in international situations. For example, the religion of Islam teaches that people should not make a living by exploiting the problems of others and that making interest payments is immoral. As a result, no outplacement consulting firms exist in Saudi Arabia and the Sudan (because outplacement involves charging a fee to help terminated workers cope with their misfortunes). As a result of these and myriad other cultural differences, then, managers may encounter unexpected complexities when doing business in countries where these sorts of cultural differences exist.

Language is another important cultural dimension that affects international human resource management practices. Most obviously, differences in specific languages such as English, Japanese, Chinese, and Spanish dramatically complicate the issues involved in dealing with international business. Unfortunately, U.S. managers who are fluent in different languages still tend to be relatively rare. When a U.S. organization does find such an employee, that individual usually becomes a valuable asset. On the other hand, it is fairly common for Asian managers to learn English in school, and most European managers are multilingual. It is interesting to note that several years ago many U.S. colleges and universities (and especially business schools) began dropping foreign-language requirements. As it turns out, those decisions may result in some competitive disadvantage for managers educated in the United States.

Another cultural factor that is most directly related to human resource management practices has to do with roles that exist in different cultures. The United States has seen considerable change over the last few decades regarding the role of women in our society. For example, women have made considerable strides in pursuing and achieving career opportunities previously closed to them. In some parts of the world, however, the situation is quite different. In Japan, for example, women may still find it fairly difficult to launch a successful career. Similar situations exist in some European countries, as well as in almost all the countries in the Middle East. Some role differences are related to status and hierarchy. In the United States, for example, relatively little psychological distance exists between managers and subordinates, resulting in a certain degree of familiarity and informality. But in many Asian countries, this psychological distance is much greater, resulting in more formalized roles and less informal communication across levels in the organization.

Perhaps the most systematic study of national values was undertaken by a Dutch scholar named Geert Hofstede, who studied cultural differences among managers in fifty-three countries.[6] He defined five dimensions of culture:

- *Power distance* (status and authority differences between a superior and a subordinate)
- *Individualism versus collectivism* (the extent to which persons define themselves as individuals rather than as members of groups)
- *Masculinity versus femininity* (assertive, competitive, success-driven values versus quality of life, relationship-oriented values in society)
- *Uncertainty avoidance* (preference for structured rather than unstructured situations)
- *Time orientation* (emphasizing long-term values such as thrift and persistence versus short-term values such as fulfilling social obligations)

Hofstede's work has been influential in the field of international management and provides some useful general guidelines for what to expect when dealing with managers or employees from different countries.

But Hofstede's work has some limitations as well. The initial sample, although quite large (100,000), was drawn from a single organization (IBM). Thus, it is difficult to tell if some of the effects found in the study were due to country cultures or one or more elements of the corporate culture that all respondents shared. Even though the sample was large, it is still difficult to make generalizations across the entire populations of countries. For example, the United States was described as being the highest on individualism, in the middle on masculinity versus femininity and on time orientation, and quite low on power distance and uncertainty avoidance. But is this description true of all Americans? Surely not. It is not even clear that they describe the "typical" American (whoever that might be). Even within countries, for instance, regional and ethnic differences account for large differences in values. Thus, one must be careful not to overgeneralize from these results. Nonetheless, Hofstede's work provides some interesting and useful ideas about differences across cultures that are relevant to human resource managers.

Yet another significant cultural factor has to do with children. In the United States child labor is closely regulated and children traditionally attend school until they become young adults. In other countries, however, this practice may be quite different. For example, in Bangladesh it is quite common for children to be a major source of income for their families. Many children do not attend school at all and begin seeking jobs at a very young age. A business operating in an environment like Bangladesh, therefore, faces a significant dilemma. On the one hand, local cultural factors suggest that it is acceptable to hire young children to work for low wages because other businesses do the same. On the other hand, this practice would be illegal and/or unethical by the standards that exist in most industrialized countries.

The human resource manager dealing with international issues thus faces two fundamental cultural challenges. One challenge is simply understanding and appreciating differences that exist in different cultures. The value of work, attitudes, orientation

POINT | COUNTERPOINT

Wages and Conditions in Foreign Plants

 Wages and working conditions in some foreign plants are different from those in U.S. plants, even when the two plants are run by the same organization and are performing the same functions. The press has reported about the working conditions in Latin American plants that manufacture clothing for a company owned by Kathy Lee Gifford and about the working conditions in Asian plants that make the Nike sneakers touted by Michael Jordan. Why do these differences exist, and should U.S. companies be forced to do something about them? The differences exist because of different expectations about wages and working conditions. U.S. firms simply pay workers in a Third World country what the workers there would otherwise earn, which is usually less than what U.S. workers doing the same job would earn.

POINT... **It makes sense for organizations to allow and even to encourage these difference because...**	COUNTERPOINT... **But on the other hand, this behavior is wrong, and U.S. firms should be forced to make changes because...**
Lower labor costs are exactly the reason the U.S. firm opens operations in these countries, and these savings allow the firm to be more competitive.	These jobs would otherwise be given to U.S. workers. The failure to do so leads to problems of unemployment and underemployment in the United States.
Wages are lower in these countries, so paying workers there what U.S. workers make would create inequalities.	U.S. companies could become a source of change, forcing other firms to raise wages and improve conditions for all workers.
Although wages are lower and conditions poorer, the cost of living is much lower in many of these countries, so that workers actually live fairly well.	Employees in foreign countries are often required to work under appalling conditions, and their wages are often not enough to alleviate their poverty.
Wages paid by U.S. firms and conditions in U.S.-owned operations are already much better than the alternatives for these foreign workers. Why should a company pay more or improve conditions more than it has to?	This is the basic issue—should U.S. firms have some social responsibility in the countries where they do business, or are these countries simply resources to be exploited?
U.S. firms are already helping these workers by providing jobs that otherwise would not be available.	This system deprives U.S. workers of jobs.

So... This issue is complex. When most Americans see how workers in Third World plants live and work, they are upset and call for change. We like to think of our country as being a source of positive change in the world, but should U.S. companies be held to a higher standard than foreign firms are in their own countries, especially if such a standard hurts competition? The answer is really a function of one's personal value system. How important is it to protect the rights and try to improve the lives of others? If one believes our country stands for something important, perhaps paying foreign workers more is a way to demonstrate it. On the other hand, if U.S. companies become less successful, they may not be in a position to help anyone. This issue is one we will continue to debate. What do you think?

toward work, and common work-related attitudes and practices vary significantly from culture to culture, and the human resource manager needs to develop an understanding of these differences if she or he is to function effectively.[7]

The second challenge is more ethical in nature. On the one hand, many businesses relocate manufacturing facilities to other countries to capitalize on lower labor costs. Indeed, it is quite possible for a business from a country like Japan or the United States to set up a factory in Bangladesh, Pakistan, or other regions of the world and have minimal labor costs there. The ethical issue, however, is the extent to which this situation becomes exploitation. Many people, for instance, would agree that it is reasonable for a company to take advantage of low prevailing wage and benefit costs to achieve low-cost production. But if a company goes too far and truly begins to exploit foreign workers, problems may subsequently arise. This issue is illustrated in this chapter's Point/Counterpoint feature.

Understanding the Political and Legal Environment

It is also important for human resource managers in international businesses to understand the political and legal environment of the countries in which they do business. Figure 3.3 illustrates four fundamental aspects of the political and legal environment of international business that are of primary concern for human resource managers: government stability, potential incentives for international trade, controls on international trade, and the influence of economic communities on international trade. In addition, laws that affect the management of human resources are basic issues, but we will say more about those issues later.[8]

Government stability can be thought of as either the ability of a given government to stay in power against opposing factions or as the permanence of government policies toward business. In general, companies prefer to do business in countries that are stable in both respects because managers have a higher probability of understanding how those governments affect their business. In recent years, several governments in the Middle East

One of the most contentious business issues today involves the use of cheap labor in foreign factories. Some argue that steady jobs that offer modest but secure wages are a boon to local economies and to people accustomed to earning virtually nothing. But others argue that it exploits people who have no other options. These protestors are symbolizing the "faceless" exploited workers critics believe some manufacturers used to make the clothing and athletic gear used in the recent Olympic Games in Athens, Greece.

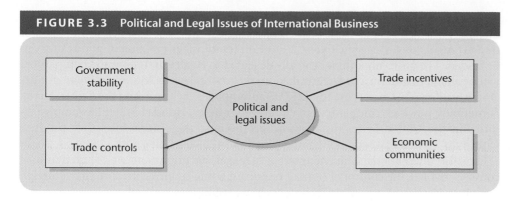

FIGURE 3.3   Political and Legal Issues of International Business

have been facing mounting pressure from Muslim fundamentalists to establish governments more in line with the teachings of the Koran; it is not clear, at this time, how stable (or effective) the newly elected Iraqi government will be; and the Israelis and Palestinians continue to struggle. These events have made the Middle East a less attractive region for doing business. On the other hand, the easing of tensions between the Chinese and the government on Taiwan has made that entire region more attractive.

A major human resource issue relating to the topic of government stability is the extent to which expatriate managers, or any other representatives of a U.S. firm, may be put at risk as a result of political instability. For years extremist groups have targeted U.S. executives for terrorist activities. But since September 11, 2001, these fears have grown considerably. The kidnapping and assassination of journalist Daniel Pearl, for example, provided graphic evidence that U.S. employees assigned overseas can face considerable danger. In the post–September 11 world, many U.S.-based managers are more uncomfortable about traveling to parts of the world where they fear they may be threatened. Heightened security measures on planes and in airports have made these dangers salient to anyone undertaking foreign travel.

In addition, some firms continue to face situations where their managers are closely watched and/or even harassed by local government officials on the grounds that they are alleged illegal informants and/or spies for the U.S. government. Still another risk is the extent to which a business itself might become nationalized. The process of nationalization occurs when a government seizes the facilities of a company and declares them to be its own. Nationalization has occasionally occurred in the Middle East and in certain countries in South America.

Another aspect of the political and legal environment involves the incentives for international trade that are sometimes offered to attract foreign business. Occasionally, municipal governments offer foreign companies tax breaks and other incentives to build facilities in their area. Over the last few years, for example, both BMW and Mercedes have announced plans to build new assembly factories in the United States. In each instance, various state and local governments started what essentially became bidding wars to see who could attract the manufacturing facilities. Examples of incentives include reduced interest rates on loans, construction subsidies and tax incentives, and the relaxation of various controls on international trade. Some countries have also offered guaranteed labor contracts with local unions as a form of incentive designed to reduce the uncertainties an entering foreign business might face in negotiating its own initial labor contract.

A third dimension of the political and legal environment of international business consists of those very controls that some countries place on international trade. Several different controls exist. One is a *tariff*, essentially a tax collected on goods shipped across national boundaries. Tariffs may be levied by the exporting country, countries through which goods pass, and/or the importing country. The most common form of trade control, however, is the *quota,* a limit on the number or value of goods that can be traded. The quota amount is typically designed to ensure that domestic competitors will be able to maintain a predetermined market share. Honda Motors in Japan, for example, is allowed to export exactly 425,000 automobiles each year into the United States. Sometimes, however, companies can circumvent quotas. Honda has built assembly factories in the United States for this purpose because the automobiles they produce within the United States do not count against the 425,000-unit quota.

For the international human resource manager, an important set of international controls involves the control of human resources. Some countries require that a foreign business setting up shop within its borders hire a minimum percentage of local employees to work there. For example, a country might require that 80 percent of the production employees and 50 percent of the managers of a foreign-owned business come from among the local citizenry. A less common but still salient factor is the control of international travel. For instance, some countries limit the number of trips that foreign managers can make in and out of their country in a given period of time. The *HR Legal Brief* in this chapter discusses a variation on this issue related to child labor in other countries.

HR LEGAL BRIEF

Child Labor and International Business

For years, large juice distributors like Minute Maid, Tropicana, and Nestlé have bought fruit juices from suppliers in South America. But a few years ago, it was learned that many of these suppliers relied heavily on child labor to harvest oranges, lemons, and other fruit. Children as young as nine were commonly taken out of school by their impoverished parents and put to work in the citrus groves. The parents often saw no problem with this action because they themselves had also picked fruit when they were children.

In recent years, though, the situation has begun to change. For example, in 1997 the U.S. Congress amended a 1930 trade law to ban the importation of products made with child labor. Similarly, the International Brotherhood of Teamsters has also taken on a watchdog role to ensure that Brazilian exporters are held accountable for adhering to the law. Of course, critics claim that the Teamsters' motivation is self-interest, but regardless of its reasons, the union is having a positive effect.

And many South American countries are also trying to stamp out child labor. For example, child advocacy groups in Brazil have helped pass a new labor code. One of its

"You can't take juice companies seriously about trying to eradicate child labor when they are promoting a system that clouds accountability in the workplace."

(Raimundo Limao de Mello, Brazilian attorney)*

provisions is a ban on child labor; another is the payment of $45 per month per child who stays in school and maintains good attendance records—the sum is about the same that the child might earn picking fruit. The juice companies themselves also claim to be imposing more stringent controls on their suppliers, although watchdog groups question their real commitment to eradicating child labor.

While it is difficult to trace accurately the activities of child fruit-pickers, most experts do agree that, slowly but surely, conditions are improving. For example, Brazilian government statistics suggest that child labor in general is down about 15 percent over the past three years. And more adults in Brazil also seem to be more aware of the importance of education and are actively discouraging fruit picking by children. But there is still a long way to go.

Sources: "U.S. Child-Labor Law Sparks a Trade Debate Over Brazilian Oranges," *Wall Street Journal,* September 9, 1998, pp. A1, A9 (*quote on p. A9); "Chile's Labor Law Hobbles Its Workers and Troubles the U.S.," *Wall Street Journal,* October 15, 1997, pp. A1, A14; "Sweatshop Police," *Business Week,* October 20, 1997, p. 39.

A final aspect of the political and legal environment is the growing importance of the influence of economic communities. Economic communities consist of sets of countries that agree to reduce or eliminate trade barriers among their member nations. One of the most commonly cited economic communities is the European Union (EU). The original EU members included Belgium, France, Luxembourg, Germany, Italy, and the Netherlands. Denmark, Ireland, the United Kingdom, Greece, Portugal, and Spain joined later. Austria, Finland, and Sweden have also been admitted, and quite recently, Poland, Hungary, and other former Soviet-bloc countries joined as well. For the past several years, these countries have been systematically working toward a unified market in which trade barriers and controls are gradually eliminated.

This European Union became much more formidable with the introduction of the euro, a common currency designed to eliminate exchange rate fluctuations and to make cross-national transactions easier. Twelve of the original members of the EU (all except Denmark, Sweden, and the United Kingdom) officially converted their domestic currencies to the euro on January 1, 2002. These twelve countries now comprise what is called the Eurozone. From a human resource management perspective, the advent of the euro brings up two issues: (1) individuals and employers in the Eurozone can more readily compare their compensation packages to those of their peers in other countries because they are all paid in the same currency, and (2) it is easier for firms in the Eurozone to transfer managers to other countries.

Nonetheless, the rejection by French and Dutch voters of the new EU Constitution in 2004 raises some question about the long-term viability of the union. Furthermore, with the admission of countries such as Romania and Hungary, subsidies long enjoyed by Spain and Ireland are rapidly disappearing and are being transferred to these newer, and economically poorer, members. These shifts are also putting new strains on the EU.

Another less comprehensive economic community was created by the North American Free Trade Agreement (NAFTA). NAFTA attempts to reduce the trade barriers that exist among Canada, the United States, and Mexico, making it easier for companies to do business in each of the three countries. Extending NAFTA to other countries in Latin America, especially Chile, has been discussed, but for now at least it remains a three-country union. No plans for a single currency have been implemented, and human resource management practices and laws remain independent. But NAFTA also includes separate labor agreements, which have the potential to affect human resource management practices dramatically. The Commission on Labor Cooperation, for example, was established to hear cases dealing with these labor agreements in areas such as child labor, occupational safety and health, and union-management relations. Some of these standards are more stringent than those imposed by U.S.-based legislation (see Chapter 2). Although it is not clear how much enforcement power the Commission on Labor Cooperation will have, it is possible that human resource managers will have to deal with an even more complex set of regulations in the future. It is interesting to note that these standards would apply not only to U.S. companies doing business in Mexico and/or Canada but also to U.S. companies doing business solely in this country.

The Human Resource Function in International Business

All basic international functions—marketing, operations, finance, and human resources—play a vital role in international business. The human resource function, for example, must deal with several general, fundamental management challenges in international business.[9] These challenges are illustrated in Figure 3.4. In addition, specific human resource management implications exist for the different forms of international business activity that firms can pursue.

General Human Resource Issues in International Business

One general set of challenges relates to differences that may exist in culture, levels of economic development, and legal systems that typify the countries where the firm operates. These differences may force an international organization to customize its hiring, firing, training, and compensation programs on a country-by-country basis. A particularly difficult set of issues arises when conflict exists between the laws and/or cultures of the home country and those of the host country.

For example, as described in Chapter 2, it is illegal in the United States to discriminate in an employment relationship on the basis of gender. In Saudi Arabia, on the other hand, such discrimination is not only allowed but is expected. Women are highly restricted in their career opportunities, and a firm doing business in that country has to balance its own affirmative action efforts with the legal and cultural restrictions imposed by that country. And overt discrimination is still actively practiced in many other countries as well.[10] As we noted, the Civil Rights Act of 1991 allows employees of U.S. firms working abroad to sue their employers if they violate the Civil Rights Act. But exception to this privilege exists when a country has a law that specifically contradicts the Civil Rights Act. For example, a woman could not sue a U.S. company operating in Saudi Arabia for sex discrimination because some discrimination against women is actually prescribed by law in that country. On the other hand, Japan has no laws institutionalizing such discrimination, so a woman could bring suit against a U.S. firm operating there if it were guilty of discriminatory practices.

A second fundamental human resource challenge in international business (a topic introduced earlier) is the determination of the most appropriate source of employees: the host country, the home country, or a third country. The ideal combination of employees differs according to the location of a firm's operations, the nature of its operations, and

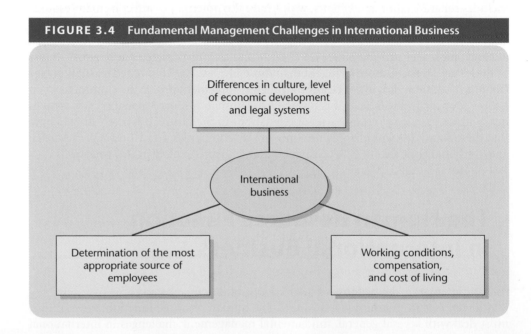

FIGURE 3.4   Fundamental Management Challenges in International Business

Differences in culture, level of economic development and legal systems

International business

Determination of the most appropriate source of employees

Working conditions, compensation, and cost of living

myriad other factors. A company is more likely to hire local employees, for example, for lower-level jobs with minimal skill requirements and for which there is a reasonable local supply of labor. Again, it is also necessary to consider local laws and/or customs that may limit or constrain hiring practices. For instance, immigration laws may limit the number of work visas that a firm can grant to foreigners, or employment regulations may mandate the hiring of local citizens as a requirement for doing business in a particular country.

But this situation is changing to some extent. Twenty-five years ago, companies doing business in places such as Singapore would have relied on the local labor market for hourly employees only. Over the years, however, Singapore and other countries have made significant investments in their human capital. As a result, a large pool of well-educated (often at western universities), highly motivated locals who are qualified for and interested in management positions now exists in these same countries. Some U.S.-based organizations are taking advantage of these relatively new labor pools by hiring local employees and then transferring them to the United States for training before returning them to their home country, where they can play a key role in managing the global enterprise. U.S.-based universities are increasingly opening branches for graduate study in places such as Singapore and China, as are European universities, especially INSEAD.

Third, international businesses must also deal with complex training and development challenges. At one level, for example, human resource managers need to provide cross-cultural training for corporate executives who are chosen for overseas assignments. In addition, training programs for production workers in host countries must be tailored to represent the education offered by local school systems. Dramatic differences in the skill and educational levels within a labor force make it necessary for international business to pay close attention to the training and development needs of all its employees in foreign markets.[11] But again, the establishment of institutions of higher education from the United States, the United Kingdom, France, and Australia has changed the face of local training and education in many countries, especially in Asia.

Yet another important international human resource management question relates to working conditions, compensation, and the cost of living. It costs more for people to live and work in some countries than in others. A general stance adopted by most international businesses is that an employee should not suffer a loss of compensation or a decrease in his or her standard of living by virtue of accepting an international assignment. Thus, human resource managers must determine how to compensate executives who accept overseas assignments and who face higher costs of living, a reduction in their quality of life, and/or unhappiness or stress because of separation from family or friends. This stance, however, can create some additional complications that we will address later when dealing with issues for expatriate managers.

Specific Human Resource Issues in International Business

Organizations can adopt a wide variety of strategies for competing in the international environment. Each strategy poses its own unique set of challenges for human resource managers. One common strategy is **exporting,** which is the process of making a product in the firm's domestic marketplace and then selling it in another country. Exporting can involve both goods and services. U.S. agricultural cooperatives export grain to Russia while major consulting firms sell their services to companies in Europe and Asia. Other businesses ship gas turbines to Saudi Arabia, locomotives to Indonesia, blue jeans to Great Britain, computers to Japan, disposable diapers to Italy, and steel to Brazil; others sell airline service, information technology support, and various other service products.

Exporting *is the process of making a product in the firm's domestic marketplace and then selling it in another country. Exporting can involve both goods and services.*

Such an approach to international business has many advantages. First, it is usually the easiest way to enter a new market. In addition, it typically requires only a small outlay of capital. Because the products are usually sold "as is," there is no need to adapt them to local conditions. Finally, relatively little risk is involved. On the other hand, products exported to other countries are often subject to taxes, tariffs, and high transportation expenses. In addition, because the products are seldom adapted to local conditions, they may not actually address the needs of consumers in local markets, and consequently the products may not achieve their full revenue potential. The shipment of some products across national boundaries is also restricted by various government regulations. For example, textile products made in Turkey cannot be exported easily to the United States due to complex regulations developed to protect U.S. cotton producers.

If the firm functions solely as an exporter, the human resource function faces no meaningful differences in responsibilities from those in a domestic business. An exporting company usually has an export manager, and that manager likely has a staff to assist in the various parts of the exporting process. Human resource managers usually play a role in hiring people for these jobs and oversee other aspects of their employment, such as compensation and performance appraisal. But other than perhaps some exporting-specific skills required for workers in this department, these employees are treated the same as employees in the operations, sales, or finance departments. Thus, when a domestic firm begins to export to a foreign market, the human resource function may be extended to include another set of employees, but it does not change in any other meaningful way.

Licensing *involves one company granting its permission to another company in a foreign country to manufacture and/or market its products in its local market.*

Another popular form of international business strategy is called **licensing.** Under this agreement, a company grants its permission to another company in a foreign country to manufacture and/or market its products in the foreign country's local market. For example, a clothing manufacturer might allow a manufacturer in another country to use its design, logo, and materials to manufacture clothing under the original firm's name. Under such an agreement, the licensing firm typically pays a royalty or licensing fee to the original firm based on the number of units it actually sells. Microsoft licenses software firms in other countries to produce and distribute software products such as Office and Windows in their local markets.

The major advantage of this strategy is that, again, it allows the firm to enter a foreign market with relatively little risk. It also makes it possible for the firm to gain some market exposure and develop name recognition that will make it easier for it to enter the market more aggressively in the future. On the other hand, its profits are limited to those it receives from the royalty payment. Likewise, the firm must also be vigilant to ensure that its quality standards are upheld.

If a firm is involved in international business activities exclusively via licensing, the human resource function is approached in the same way as in a pure exporting enterprise. That is, no meaningful differences in the human resource function likely exist, but human resource managers need to extend their existing services and responsibilities to employees associated with the licensing activities. The human resource function itself does not really change in any meaningful way.

Direct investment *occurs when a firm headquartered in one country builds or purchases operating facilities or subsidiaries in a foreign country.*

A third international strategy for doing business is **direct foreign investment.** A direct investment occurs when a firm headquartered in one country builds or purchases operating facilities or subsidiaries in a foreign country. That is, the firm actually owns physical assets in the other country. Kodak, for example, constructed a research and development laboratory in Japan. This business activity represents a direct investment on the part of Kodak. Other examples of direct investment include Disney's recent construction of a new theme park near Hong Kong, BMW's construction of a new assembly plant in South Carolina, and Ford's acquisition of Jaguar and Volvo.

As implied above, there are actually two different forms of direct investment. First, the firm can simply acquire an existing business in the foreign country. This has been the primary strategy enacted by Wal-Mart as it entered Germany and the United Kingdom— it bought existing retail chains and then converted them to Wal-Marts. This approach provides very quick access to new markets, but it may require protracted negotiations over the acquisition; afterward, the firm also faces the challenge of how to integrate the new acquisition into its other operations. Alternatively, the firm can create or build a new wholly owned subsidiary, factory, or other unit. This takes much more time, carries much greater risk, and is much more expensive, yet it also represents the path to the greatest potential profits.

In either case, direct investment has the advantage that it provides the firm its own company-owned facilities in the foreign country and allows it to become truly integrated in a particular foreign market. Considerably more profit potential can be realized in direct investment because the company itself keeps all the profits its investment earns in that country. On the other hand, considerably more risk is attached to this strategy. Just as the investing firm can keep all its profits, so too must it absorb any and all losses and related financial setbacks. In addition, of course, the costs of direct investment are also quite high and are borne solely by the investing firm.

At this level of international business activity, the human resource function changes substantially from that of a domestic firm or business using a pure exporting or licensing strategy. This difference stems from the fact that in a direct investment situation, employees of the firm are working in foreign locations. Depending on the nationalities reflected in the foreign workforce (i.e., whether the firm uses a polycentric, geocentric, or ethnocentric approach to hiring), the corporate human resource function will need to extend and expand its scope and operations to provide the appropriate contributions to firm performance as determined by the philosophy used for staffing the foreign operations.

A fourth form of international strategy is a **joint venture** or **strategic alliance.** In this case, two or more firms cooperate in the ownership and/or management of an operation, often on an equity basis. A joint venture is the traditional term used for such an arrangement and describes a situation in which actual equity ownership exists. A strategic alliance might not involve ownership but still involves cooperation between firms. Joint ventures and strategic alliances are rapidly growing in importance in the international business environment. They represent a way for two or more firms to achieve synergy from working together, they reduce risk, and they provide mutual benefit to both partners. The airline industry has seen several strategic alliances. One of the largest is known as the Star Alliance. This group includes United Airlines, Lufthansa, All Nippon Airlines, Singapore Airlines, and several other airlines from all over the world. This alliance makes it easier for travelers to place reservations, purchase tickets, and make connections between any two of all the partners in the alliance. This flexibility also makes the group itself more competitive relative to other airlines.

Human resource managers in a firm that uses this strategy face an even more complex set of issues and challenges. If the new operation is a separate legal entity that functions as a semi-autonomous enterprise, the corporate human resource staff of each strategic partner needs to determine how to link and coordinate with their counterparts in both the new venture (seen as a separate entity) and their partner. If the new venture is operated within the context of one of the existing partner's organization structures, the human resource function becomes more complicated still because of the disparate relationships among the human resource staff for the new venture and its counterparts in both the partner within which it operates and the other partner (this latter relationship is somewhat more distant).

A **joint venture (strategic alliance)** *refers to when two or more firms cooperate in the ownership and/or management of an operation on an equity basis.*

Joint ventures are booming today. These often involve partnerships between businesses in different countries. Among the significant management challenges that joint ventures have to address is how to create, develop, and retain a strong workforce. FieldFresh is a joint venture between E.L. Rothschild, a European firm, and Bjarti, an Indian company. The two businesses are working together to grow fruits and vegetables for export from India to foreign markets. These women are harvesting carrots for export. By relying heavily on local employees and then paying them competitive wages, FieldFresh has enjoyed strong productivity and low turnover.

Domestic Issues in International Human Resource Management

Regardless of their level of internationalization, all firms dealing in foreign markets must confront three sets of domestic issues in the management of their human resources. These domestic issues, shown in Figure 3.5, are local recruiting and selection issues, local training issues, and local compensation issues.

Local Recruiting and Selection Issues

Nonmanagerial employees, such as blue-collar production workers and white-collar clerical and office workers, are usually host-country nationals in international business. Basic and fundamental economic reasons explain this pattern. Simply put, host-country nationals are usually cheaper to employ than are parent-country nationals or third-country nationals. Host-country nationals are also frequently used because local laws usually promote the hiring of locals.[12] Immigration laws, for example, may restrict jobs to citizens and legal residents of a country. Thus, an international business must develop and implement a plan for recruiting and selecting its employees in a host-country market. This plan must include assessments of the firm's human resource needs, primary sources of labor in that country, labor-force skills and talents, and training requirements. In addition, the plan should also account for special circumstances that exist in the local markets. When firms hire parent-country nationals for foreign assignments, they must obviously adhere to their home-country hiring regulations. But when hiring host-country nationals, they must also be aware of the regulations, laws, and norms that govern employment relationships within the host country. Thus, while the reliance

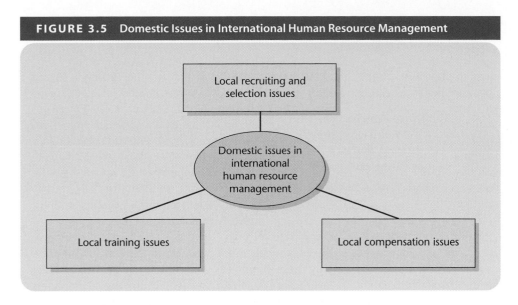

FIGURE 3.5   Domestic Issues in International Human Resource Management

on parent-country nationals may be less expensive, it also adds complexity to the employment relationship.[13]

Local Training Issues

Human resource managers must also understand the training and development needs of the host country's workforce to help host-country nationals perform their jobs most effectively. The training and development needs of a local workforce depend on several factors. One, of course, is the location of the foreign market. In highly industrialized markets, such as England or Japan, organizations can usually find a cadre of capable employees who may need only a small amount of firm-specific training. But in a relatively underdeveloped area, training and development needs will be much more extensive.

For example, when Hilton first began opening hotels in eastern Europe, it found that restaurant waiters, desk clerks, and other customer-service employees lacked the basic skills necessary to provide high-quality service to guests. Because eastern European employees were accustomed to working in a planned economy in which they did not have to worry about customer satisfaction, they had difficulty recognizing why it was important to shift their focus. As a result, Hilton had to invest considerably more than originally planned in training employees to provide customer service. Training is also important if international business wants to take full advantage of locating production abroad. Many firms move production facilities to areas with low labor costs, such as Malaysia and Mexico, but then find that the productivity of the labor force is relatively low. Thus, they have to invest additional training and development dollars to bring the workforce up to the performance standards they expect. Some of the methods that Toyota uses both to select and to train workers in the United States are described in this chapter's *HR Around the Globe* feature.

Local Compensation Issues

Compensation must also be addressed at a local level for international businesses. Some countries, such as the United States, focus compensation on assessing individual

Toyota Wants Only the Best

When Toyota decided to open its first automobile assembly plant in the United States several years ago, the firm knew it faced real challenges in staffing the facility. In its native Japan, many high school students go through special training programs funded by businesses to teach them various work skills. And high school graduates not heading off to college usually enroll in apprenticeship programs to develop their skills further. Because no such programs exist in the United States, Toyota realized that it would not have as large and talented a labor pool from which to hire as it did back home.

The firm initially had over 100,000 applicants for 2,700 production jobs. Many were initially screened out due to lack of education and/or experience. Most of those who remained under consideration underwent over fourteen hours of testing. Finalists from this pool then participated in various work simulations under the watchful eyes of Toyota managers. And after all this screening, only the very best were hired. All told, Toyota estimated that it spent over $13,000 hiring each worker for the factory.

> *"Those exercises are pretty close to what they'll experience on the assembly line."*
>
> (Mark Daugherty, Toyota assistant personnel manager)*

After the plant was up and running, however, Toyota didn't slack off in its hiring rigor. Indeed, it still maintains the same high standards today. For example, applicants today who meet minimum education and experience qualifications are invited to the factory for a difficult twelve-hour assessment that the company calls the "day of work." Throughout this day, the applicants simulate work in various settings, meet with existing employees, and undergo detailed tests. The plant's managers try to make the work simulations as realistic as possible, and they hire only those employees who perform at the very highest levels. Does the hiring process pay off? Toyota managers believe that it does, and they point to the fact that product quality in the United States is comparable to what it achieves at home.

Sources: "Toyota Devises Grueling Workout for Job Seekers," *USA Today,* August 11, 1997, p. 3B (*quote on p. 3B); "Toyota Takes Pains, and Time, Filling Jobs at Its Kentucky Plant," *Wall Street Journal,* December 1, 1987, pp. 1, 29; "San Antonio Aims to Build Toyota-Caliber Workforce, *Bryan-College Station Eagle,* March 9, 2003, p. A7; *Hoover's Handbook of World Business 2006* (Austin: Hoover's Business Press, 2006), pp. 628–629.

performance and then compensating that individual accordingly. In other countries, however, such as Japan, the emphasis is based more on group work and less on individual performance. Dramatic differences in life styles, standards of living, and regulation also cause a wide variation in the way in which firms compensate their employees in different foreign locations.

Of course, dramatic differences in benefit packages are offered to workers in different countries as well. In countries with socialized medicine, such as the United Kingdom, firms do not have to worry as much about paying all or part of employee health-insurance premiums (although they pay higher taxes to help support the government program). In Italy, most workers expect to have several hours off in the afternoon. In Germany, most workers get six weeks of paid vacation time a year, and many work only thirty hours a week. German autoworkers earn $39 an hour in wages and benefits, compared to $25 in the United States and $27 in Japan.[14] Italy and Britain legally mandate four weeks of vacation time per year, while France mandates 5 weeks. In contrast, U.S. firms are not legally required to provide any vacation leave.[15]

It is also important for international human resource managers to look at the total picture of compensation rather than some simple index such as the hourly wage. For example, as already noted, some firms choose to move production to Mexico to take advantage of lower labor costs. While it is true that labor costs in Mexico are cheaper than they are in the United States (when compared on an hourly basis), it is also true that

Mexican law requires employers to pay maternity leave to their employees, provide a Christmas bonus equal to fifteen days' pay, and provide at least three months of severance pay for workers who are terminated. Thus, lower labor costs may be at least partially lost due to these and other higher costs for other benefits.

Managing International Transfers and Assignments

Another extremely important part of international human resource management is the effective management of expatriate employees.[16] **Expatriates** are employees who are sent by a firm to work in another country and may be either parent-country nationals or third-country nationals. Particularly key areas of importance here include selecting, training, and compensating expatriates.[17]

Expatriates   *are employees who are sent by a firm to work in another country; they may be either parent-country nationals or third-country nationals.*

Selecting Expatriates

Recruiting and selecting employees for an international business requires that the human resource manager address two sets of questions.[18] The first set of questions involves the definition of skills and abilities necessary to perform the work that the organization needs to have done. The second set of issues relates to defining the skills and abilities that are needed to work in a foreign location.

The first step, then, is to define the actual skills necessary to do the job. Different types of assignments typically require different types of skills for success. Traditionally, expatriate managers were sent abroad to provide some technical expertise that was not available in the local economy. In such cases, it is extremely important that the manager selected has the requisite technical skills and communication skills needed to work with less technically adept workers. Because these assignments are often for a limited time, however, it may be less critical that the manager possess extensive cultural skills. But multinational enterprises (MNEs) more and more often send managers overseas, not to help the overseas operation, but to help the manager. That is, they see expatriate assignments as a critical developmental opportunity that is essential for career progress.[19] Clearly, success in these assignments is based less on technical skills, and cultural skills would be far more critical because the expatriate manager is supposed to learn from his or her experience and carry this information back to the home country. Some of the more common skills and abilities assumed to be necessary in this regard include adaptability, language ability, overall physical and emotional health, relatively high levels of independence and self-reliance, and appropriate levels of experience and education. We will say more about required skills and abilities a bit later in the chapter.

The recruitment of employees for international business is an important step in the human resource management process. International businesses attempt to recruit experienced managers through various channels. One common source of recruits is the firm itself. That is, a good starting place may be to seek employees already working for the firm and in the host country who might be prepared for international assignment. In some cases, the firm may be selecting individuals for their first international assignment, but in other cases they may be selecting people for their second or third international assignment. Nestlé, for example, maintains a cadre of approximately 200 managers who are capable of and willing to accept an international assignment anywhere the firm does business.[20]

International businesses also frequently look to other organizations as a source of prospective managers. These may be home-country managers who are qualified for an international assignment, or managers already working in an international assignment for another firm. For higher-level positions in an organization, international businesses often rely on professional recruiting firms to help them identify prospective managerial candidates. These recruiters, often called *headhunters,* are recruiting firms that actively seek qualified managers and other professionals for possible placement in positions in other organizations. Headhunting has long been an accepted practice in the United States. In both Japan and Europe, headhunting was considered unethical until recently. Within the last decade or so, however, headhunting has become a more accepted practice in most industrialized countries.[21]

Increasingly, many firms are finding it necessary to hire new college graduates for immediate foreign assignment. Traditionally, this practice has been relatively unpopular because organizations believed that managers needed to develop experience in a firm's domestic operations before taking on an international assignment. Because of both the shortage of global managers and the recent emphasis that many colleges of business are placing on training international managers, however, firms are finding that they can hire younger managers and place them in foreign assignments more quickly than was the case in the past. Potential managerial candidates with foreign-language skills, international travel experience, and course work in international business or related fields are especially attractive candidates for firms in this position.[22]

After a pool of qualified applicants has been identified, the organization must then select the managers that it needs for international assignments. In general, organizations look at three sets of criteria for selecting people for international assignments: managerial competence, language training, and adaptability to new situations. It is extremely important that organizations select managers for international assignments with deliberate care. The cost of a failed international assignment is extremely high. Expatriate failure is defined as the early return of an expatriate manager to his or her home country because of an inability to perform in the overseas assignment.[23]

Experts suggest that a failed expatriate assignment for a top manager might cost the organization as much as $250,000, in addition to any salary losses. This figure includes the expatriate's original training, moving expenses, and lost managerial productivity. Failure of expatriate assignments is quite high. Estimates place the expatriate failure rate in U.S. companies at between 20 and 50 percent. Japanese and European firms appear to do a somewhat better job of selecting international managers and, as a result, experience a lower expatriate failure rate.[24]

Several factors may contribute to this pattern. One is the inability of the manager and/or the manager's spouse and family to adjust to a new location. Evidence suggests that this inability interferes with the manager's ability to adjust to the new setting and subsequently contributes to failure.[25] As a result of this pattern, some firms are beginning to pay more attention to helping spouses and children adjust to the new environment, and many other firms are placing a greater emphasis on the nontechnical aspects of a prospective manager's suitability for a foreign assignment. For example, they look closely at a person's cultural adaptability, as well as the adaptability of their families. It is also important to consider the perspective of international managers' motivation for and real interest in the foreign assignments. Some managers are attracted to foreign assignments because they relish the thought of living abroad or perhaps they see the experience as being useful in their career plans.[26] In addition, personality and international experience (of any type) also seem to be important determinants of expatriate success.[27]

Regardless of their motives in seeking international assignments, and regardless of their skills and abilities to carry out those assignments, many managers who don't have a realistic preview of what an international assignment really is become disillusioned

The management of foreign assignments is often a major element of international human resource management. Kazuo Hyodo (left) is a thirty-year veteran of Toyota's manufacturing operations in Japan. When the firm built a new assembly plant in South Africa, it sent several veterans like Mr. Hyodo to help train new Toyota employees like Ray Hawley (right). Deciding who to send on this assignment, how long he would stay in South Africa, how his compensation would be affected, and whether to send his family with him were all decisions made by Toyota human resource managers in Japan.

within a few months of accepting such an assignment. Thus, it is critical that organizations prepare managers completely for what they might expect when they move overseas. It is also becoming clear that, once expatriate managers arrive at their new assignments, it is critical that they receive support and help from the host-country nationals with whom they will be working.[28] This realization is quite important because it may have far-reaching implications for other expatriate human resource policies. Specifically, as we shall see below, a great deal of attention is given to the problem of how to compensate expatriate managers. Most of the policies and practices result in expatriate managers earning considerably more than any host-country counterparts. In the past, this problem was not that serious because few local managers had the background and training of the expatriates. In fact, it was this very lack of local competence that led many organizations to assign expatriate managers. But, as noted above, organizations increasingly see expatriate assignments as helpful to the home-country manager. As a result, he or she may be assigned to a foreign post even though other host-country nationals (HCNs), or local employees are capable of doing the same job. As many countries more routinely send potential managers abroad for training and education, the local employee may well be as qualified in every way as the expatriate. To date, however, most expatriate policies dictate that the expatriate manager would earn more than the local doing the same or a similar job. This situation can lead to resentment on the part of the HCN and can potentially lead the HCN to withhold the help and support the expatriate needs to be successful. Does this situation mean that expatriates should not be compensated for their overseas assignments? Surely not, but it does mean that organizations may have to take a closer look at their expatriate policies and practices and evaluate them in light of the importance of obtaining HCN support for the expatriate once he or she arrives in the new assignment.[29]

Training Expatriates

Given the potential costs involved in failure, it is not surprising that organizations also spend a great deal of time and money on training expatriate managers. General Motors spends almost $500,000 a year on cross-cultural training for 150 or so U.S. managers and their families heading to international assignments. The firm reports that less than 1 percent of its expatriate assignments fail, and it attributes much of its success to its training program.[30] Training (as we will cover more fully in Chapter 14) is instruction directed at enhancing specific job-related skills and abilities and most often focuses on operating employees and technical specialists. For example, a training program might be designed to help employees learn to use a new software package as part of an international communication network. Development (we will also cover this topic more fully in Chapter 14) is general education devoted to preparing future managers for higher-level positions and/or new assignments within the organization. For example, a development program might span several months or even years and be targeted to helping managers improve their ability to make decisions, to motivate subordinates to work harder, and to develop more effective strategies for the organization.[31]

Training for expatriate managers may be as "simple" as language training (which is not very simple if it involves a completely unfamiliar language, such as Japanese for the English speaker) or it can be rather involved. For example, language-training programs and other forms of language training from cassette tapes, videotapes, and similar media are very common and fairly inexpensive.[32] In addition, it is common to have some type of classroom training dealing with the history of the country or the area and with daily living conditions (e.g., how to make a phone call or hail a taxicab). It is also typical to have some training component that deals with social manners and issues involved in social exchanges (when should you shake hands and when should you avoid shaking hands, for example, or how deeply to bow).[33]

The *Cultural Assimilator* is a more complex training program built around short case studies and critical incidents. It asks the manager how he or she would react to different situations, and it provides detailed feedback on the correct responses.[34] In addition, firms are more and more often sending prospective expatriates to their ultimate foreign destination for short periods of time before their permanent move. This experience allows them to become acculturated on a gradual basis and to obtain a truly realistic picture of what life will be like. But whatever the exact nature of the training, the goals of expatriate training are becoming clearer and more consistent. Increasingly, multinational organizations are recognizing that managers given overseas assignments must be able to communicate with others in the host country and must be able to adapt to different life styles and values. When we consider all the factors that seem to go into expatriate success, it becomes clearer why some have suggested that a manager given an assignment in a foreign country must possess "the patience of a diplomat, the zeal of a missionary, and the language skills of a U.N. interpreter."[35]

Compensating Expatriates

As noted above, another important issue in international human resource management is compensation. To remain competitive, an organization must provide compensation packages for their managers that are comparable to those in a given market. Compensation packages include salary and nonsalary items and are jointly determined by labor-market forces such as the supply and demand of managerial talent, professional licensing requirements, the standard of living, occupational status, government regulations, and so forth.[36]

Most international businesses find it necessary to provide expatriate managers with differential compensation to make up for differences in currency valuation, standards of living, life-style norms, and so on. When managers are on short-term assignments at a foreign location, their salary is often tied to their domestic currency and home-country living standards. Of course, these managers are reimbursed for short-term living expenses, such as the cost of hotel rooms, meals, and local transportation. If the foreign assignment is for a longer time period, however, compensation is usually adjusted to allow the manager to maintain her or his home-country standard of living. This adjustment is particularly important if the manager is transferred from a low-cost location to a high-cost location or from a country with a relatively high standard of living to one with a relatively low standard of living.[37]

Differential compensation usually starts with a cost-of-living allowance. This basic difference in salary is intended to offset the differences in the cost of living between the home country and the host country. The logic is that if managers accept a foreign assignment, they should enjoy the same standard of living as they would have enjoyed had they remained in their home country. If the cost of living in the foreign country is higher than that at home, then the manager's existing base pay alone will result in a lower standard of living. The firm may therefore need to supplement the base pay to offset the difference. On the other hand, if the cost of living at a foreign location is lower than that at home, no such allowance is needed (few companies would actually lower the manager's salary).

Occasionally, organizations might have to provide an additional salary inducement simply to convince people to accept a foreign assignment. Many employees may be relatively interested in accepting assignments to countries such as England, France, Italy, or Japan, but it may be more difficult to entice people to accept a position in Haiti, Pakistan, or Vietnam. Thus, organizations sometimes find it necessary to provide what is called a **hardship premium,** or a **foreign-service premium.** Total Fina Elf S.A. is a large French oil company. The firm has substantial holdings in the African country of Angola. During a recent bloody civil war in the country, however, Total pulled its employees out. When the war ended Total began to again assign managers to run its Angolan operations. But because of lingering violence and other concerns, the firm had to provide them with a 25 percent salary premium as well as numerous other incentives in order to get the desired mix of managers to agree to accept their new assignments. Likewise, during the reconstruction efforts in Iraq in 2004–2007, U.S. contractors such as KBR (a Halliburton subsidiary) also paid substantial premiums to attract and retain employees willing to work there. This premium (called an *uplift* by the firm) was sometimes more than the individual employee's base salary.

Many international businesses also find that they must set up a tax-equalization system for their managers on foreign assignments. A tax-equalization system is designed to ensure that the expatriates' after-tax income in the host country is comparable to what the person's after-tax income would have been in the home country. Every country has its own unique income tax laws that apply to the earnings of its citizens and/or to earnings within its borders by foreign citizens, and companies must develop plans to make sure that the tax burden for individuals is equalized relative to the amount of salary they earn.

The other part of compensation besides salary is benefits. Most international businesses find that, in addition to salary adjustments, they must also provide benefit adjustments. Special benefits for managers on foreign assignments usually include housing, education, medical treatment, travel to the home country, and club membership. Housing

*A **hardship premium** (also called a **foreign service premium**) is an additional financial incentive offered to individuals to entice them to accept a "less than attractive" international assignment.*

and they may be less likely to do so if they feel resentment toward the expatriate manager.

■ A strategic approach to expatriation must include a strategy for repatriation.

Review and Discussion Questions

1. Summarize recent growth and trends in international business.

2. What are the basic international business strategies that firms can pursue?

3. What are the basic human resource management functions in international business?

4. What are the basic human resource management issues to be addressed by an international business?

5. What are the basic domestic issues in international human resource management for the firm in its home country?

6. What are the human resource management implications of each strategy for international business?

7. What do you see as the basic similarities and differences in the human resource function between domestic and international businesses?

8. Which do you think is more critical for international human resource management: understanding the cultural environment or understanding the political and legal environment?

9. When a basic incongruence exists in the ethical context of human resource management between the foreign-country environment and a firm's home-country environment, which do you think should take precedence, the foreign-country environment or the firm's home-country environment?

10. Would you be interested in an international assignment as part of your employer's management development strategy? Why or why not? What factors would be most important to you in making such a decision?

CLOSING CASE

Human Resources and International Mergers

Mergers and acquisitions are nothing new, of course, but a new slate of megamergers between international giants may well portend a new era in global consolidation. Two of these mergers, in particular, have the potential to reshape international competition. And each also has significant implications for international human resource practices. One megamerger involved Chrysler Corporation and Daimler-Benz. The other involved Amoco and British Petroleum.

The news about Chrysler and Daimler-Benz made headlines around the world when the deal was announced in midsummer 1998. Most experts agreed at the time that it was a good match. Chrysler made moderately priced cars and light trucks, was strong in North America but weak in Europe, and had distinctive competencies in design and product development. Daimler-Benz, on the other hand, made luxury cars and heavy trucks, was very strong in Europe, and had distinctive competencies in engineering and technology. While billed as a merger, Daimler-Benz actually bought Chrysler for $38 billion. The new company, called DaimlerChrysler AG, remained headquartered in Germany and became the fifth-largest automobile company in the world.

Myriad strategic, technical, and operational systems had to be integrated before the two firms truly become one, and these problems proved to be dramatically more complex than originally thought. Indeed, Integration problems persist today and the new firm has yet to capture the efficiencies and economies of scale and scope that the firm's managers intended. Blending the two firms' human resources also presented a formidable challenge. Prior to merging, Chrysler and Daimler-Benz had a combined worldwide workforce of 421,000 employees. After the merger was complete, however, not all these workers were needed. Hence, job cuts occurred at the production, technical, operations, and executive levels. But the two firms also had to deal with powerful unions, the United Auto Workers (UAW) for Chrysler in the United States and IG Metall in Germany.

Some issues were associated with employment conditions. Consider, for example, representative conditions at three plants. In Germany, prior to the merger, Daimler-Benz auto workers had an hourly wage range of from $15 to $20 per hour, got six weeks of annual vacation and twelve sick days, and worked an average of thirty-five hours a week. The Mercedes-Benz plant in Alabama, however, had substantially different conditions. Its workers earned from $14.05 to $19.20 an hour, got twelve days of vacation time and ten sick days, and worked an average of forty hours per week. At Chrysler's biggest plant, in Detroit, meanwhile, workers earned between $19.37 and $23.22 an hour, got four weeks of vacation time and five sick days, and worked an average of 50.5 hours per week (of which 10.5 hours were compensated at a rate of time and a half). Clearly, then, integrating these disparate conditions under a single employment umbrella was a challenge.

A second big international merger was announced later the same year, this one between Amoco and British Petroleum (BP). At the time of the announcement, Amoco was the fourth-largest oil producer in the United States, while BP was the third largest in the world, behind Royal Dutch/Shell and Exxon. Like the Chrysler and Daimler deal, this one was also not a true merger—BP was actually the buyer, with a 60 percent ownership stake in the new company. The firm remained headquartered in London, but all of its U.S. operations shifted to the Amoco organization and brand name.

Again, the firms had to address significant human resource issues as the integration of the two operations unfolded. BP's operations in the United States were based in Cleveland, while Amoco operated out of Chicago. BP an-

nounced that it would shut down most of its Cleveland operation, with some employees there transferred to Chicago. To make room, Amoco also indicated that several jobs in its own headquarters would be eliminated. All told, the firms cut about 6,000 of their combined 99,000 jobs. Most of these cuts were in marketing and exploration. But no one can really say for sure exactly how many cuts will eventually be made, or when full integration will be achieved. And, of course, integrating compensation, benefits, and other human resource practices will also be a complex task.[44]

Case Questions

1. What are the likely advantages and disadvantages that firms in these kinds of mergers can expect?

2. What are the advantages and disadvantages for individual workers at firms that merge with international partners?

3. What basic human resource issues, besides those mentioned in the case, must be addressed as a result of these mergers?

Building HR Management Skills

Purpose: The purpose of this exercise is to provide you with some critical insights into the complexities associated with international human resource management.

Step 1: Your instructor will divide your class into small groups of four to five members each. Begin by reading and discussing the context description that follows.

Assume that your group is the human resource management executive team of a large electronics firm. Your firm has several factories located throughout North and South America. The company has just decided to open its first Asian factory in Thailand. Plans call for the plant to open in two years. The plant will require a general manager, four associate managers, and ten other relatively high-level managerial positions (a purchasing manager, a warehouse manager, etc.). The plant will also require approximately thirty first-line supervisors, 600 operating employees, and thirty maintenance and custodial work-

ers. Finally, approximately twenty-five office and clerical workers will also be needed.

Step 2: Your boss has asked your team to develop a staffing plan for the new plant. She wants to know where each type of employee should come from, when they should be hired, and how they should be trained. Spend about twenty minutes discussing this step as a group and outlining the basic issues that you will need to meet this request adequately. That is, your task is not to develop the actual plan; instead, your task is to decide what information you need to develop the plan and where you might go to get that information.

Step 3: Report the results of your group's deliberations to the entire class. Identify areas of agreement and disagreement across groups and explore why there were differences.

Ethical Dilemmas in HR Management

Assume that you are a senior human resource management executive for a large multinational firm. Your firm routinely buys products manufactured in factories in Asia, and it also operates three foreign plants itself, one each in Malaysia, Thailand, and Pakistan. The company hired a new chief executive officer (CEO) a few months ago. The CEO, in turn, has a reputation for being an outspoken advocate for the rights of foreign workers. He routinely proclaims that your company's foreign workers are treated exceptionally well, that he is proud of your firm's record in this area, and that he is willing to stake his personal reputation on the ethical and humane treatment of workers employed by both your firm and your firm's suppliers.

You recently returned from a fourteen-day inspection of your three international plants, plus four plants operated by two of your major suppliers. While you did not see any major problems, you have become quite concerned that your firm's treatment of its foreign workers is not as good as it once was. For example, the weak economy in Thailand has resulted in your plant manager there increasing work hours and withholding pay increases that had been planned. More troubling is what you saw in a supplier factory. What once was a comprehensive educational center for younger workers has been greatly reduced in scope, and you detected hints that it might be shut down altogether.

After your return, you spoke with the CEO and relayed to him your concerns. He seemed to be genuinely bothered by the news, but indicated that he wanted to delay taking any actions. He noted, for example, that your firms' annual shareholder meeting was coming up next month. If news of your concerns were to leak out, the firm's stock price might drop and the proposed slate of bonuses for senior managers, including you, might be jeopardized. He indicated that he would prefer to keep things quiet for now, but he promised to take some action to improve the situation in the foreign plants shortly after the meeting. Meanwhile, you have observed him to continue making boastful proclamations about the company's treatment of its foreign workers.

Questions

1. What are the ethical issues in this situation?

2. What are the arguments for and against following your CEO's suggested approach?

3. What do you think most managers would do? What would you do?

HR Internet Exercise

Identify five companies that are foreign owned but that have large U.S. operations. For example, Toyota, a Japanese firm, has a large U.S. subsidiary that is legally incorporated as Toyota Motor Sales, U.S.A., Inc. Nestlé, a Swiss firm, owns Carnation Foods in the United States. Search the Internet to see if you can locate separate websites for both the parent company and its U.S. subsidiary. Next, determine the extent to which the two websites contain any information regarding human resource issues. If you can locate this information, see if you can identify any parallels, extensions, or even inconsistencies between them.

Questions

1. What role might the Internet play in helping an international business coordinate its international human resources?

2. What risks does an international business run by relying on the Internet to address human resource issues?

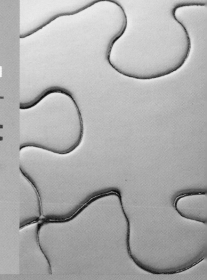

4

The Competitive Environment

CHAPTER OBJECTIVES

After studying this chapter you should be able to:

■ Describe the strategic context of human resource management.

■ Identify three types of strategies and relate each to human resource management.

■ Discuss human resource strategy formulation and relevant organizational factors.

■ Discuss the processes through which human resource strategy is implemented.

■ Discuss how the human resource function in organizations can be evaluated.

For the past several years Starbucks Corporation has been the highest-profile and fastest-growing food and beverage company in the United States. Howard Schultz bought Starbucks in 1987 when it was still a small mail-order operation. Schultz promptly reoriented the business away from mail-order sales and emphasized retail coffee sales through the firm's coffee bars. Today, Starbucks is not only the largest coffee importer and roaster of specialty beans, but it is also the largest specialty coffee-bean retailer in the United States.

> *"One reason a lot of youths don't find corporate America so attractive is because of the IBM image: I'll become a blue suit. Starbucks makes you feel like a partner."*
>
> (Karen Hunsaker, Starbucks employee)*

What are the keys to Starbucks' phenomenal growth and success? One important ingredient is its well-conceived and implemented strategy. Starbucks is on a phenomenal growth pace, opening a new coffee shop somewhere almost every day. But this growth is planned and coordinated each step of the way through careful site selection. And through its astute promotional campaigns and commitment to quality, the firm has elevated the coffee-drinking taste of millions of Americans and fueled a significant increase in demand. Another key to Starbucks' success is its near-fanatical emphasis on quality control and operations efficiencies. For example, milk must be heated to precise temperatures before it is used, and every espresso shot must be pulled within twenty-three seconds or else it is discarded. And no coffee is allowed to sit on a hot plate for more than twenty minutes. Schultz also refuses to franchise his Starbucks stores, fearing a loss of control and a potential deterioration of quality.

The people who work for Starbucks have also played a major role in the firm's success. Managers at each store have considerable autonomy over how they run operations, as long as the firm's basic principles are followed. Starbucks also uses a state-of-the-art communication network to keep in contact with its employees. The firm hires relatively young people to work in its restaurants and starts them at hourly wages that are somewhat higher than most entry-level food-service jobs. The company also offers health insurance to all of its employees, including part-timers, and it has a lucrative stock-option plan for everyone in the firm. In addition, a state-of-the-art information system allows every employee to keep abreast of what's happening in the company.

Its phenomenal growth rate notwithstanding, Starbucks is continually on the alert for new business opportunities. One area of growth is international markets. It was only about a decade ago (1996, to be exact) that Starbucks opened its very first coffee shops outside the United States: two in Japan and another in Singapore. By the end of 2006, there were over 3,000 company-owned or licensed Starbucks stores in thirty-six foreign countries.

Another growth area for the company is brand extension with other companies. For instance, the firm collaborates with Dreyer's to distribute five flavors of Starbucks' coffee ice cream to grocery store freezers across the country. Starbucks also collaborates with Capital Records on Starbucks jazz CDs, which are available in Starbucks' stores. Redhook Brewery even uses Starbucks' coffee extract in its double black stout beer. And Jim Beam recently introduced Starbucks Coffee Liqueur.[1]

Starbucks has achieved undeniable success through an astute combination of strategy, control, and human resources. Under the leadership of Howard Schultz, the firm has been on a phenomenal growth and expansion pace, with everything dictated by an overarching strategy. Precise operations systems and control standards ensure consistent product quality, and highly motivated people throughout the organization keep everything running according to plan. Take away any of the three elements—strategy, operations, and motivated people—and both the company and its remarkable performance would not be the same. Indeed, more and more managers today are recognizing the important links that exist among strategy, operations, and human resource management. Further, a strategic orientation to human resource management provides a useful and effective perspective on how to create these linkages.

Thus, this chapter is devoted to the strategic human resource environment. The first section discusses the strategic context of human resource management in terms of the organization's purpose, mission, and top management team. The next section focuses on corporate, business, and functional strategies and their relationship to human resource management. We then address the increasingly important area of strategic human resource management in terms of, first, its formulation and, second, its implementation. Important organizational characteristics that affect and are affected by these processes are also described. Finally, we provide a framework for how organizations evaluate the human resource function.

The Competitive Environment for Human Resource Management

Human resource management does not occur in a vacuum but instead occurs in a complex and dynamic milieu of forces within the organizational context.[2] A significant trend in recent years has been for human resource managers to adopt a strategic perspective on

Starbucks owes its success to a variety of strategic goals and standards. For instance, the firm has very specific guidelines to help maintain the uniform quality of its coffees. This inspector is first smelling and then tasting several blends of Starbucks coffee. As a result of practices such as this, Starbucks has been able to achieve continuous growth around the world.

FIGURE 4.1   Strategic Human Resource Management

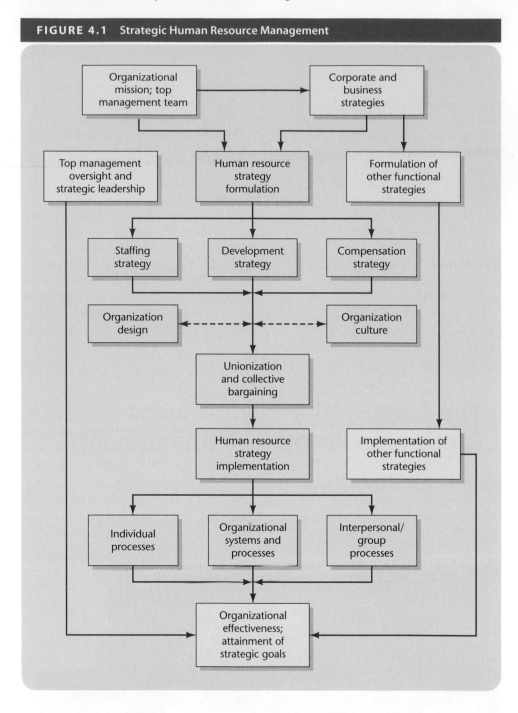

their job and to recognize the critical links between organizational strategy and human resource strategy. In this way, it may be possible for an organization to gain a competitive advantage through its management of human resources. Figure 4.1 illustrates the framework we will use in discussing strategic human resource management. As the figure shows, this process starts with an understanding of the organization's purpose and mission and the influence of its top management team and culminates with the human resource manager serving as a strategic partner to the operating divisions of the organization. That is, under this new view of human resource management, the human resource manager's job is to help line managers (at all levels) achieve their strategic goals. In this way, the human resource manager adds value to the organization by providing expertise concerning how to use the firm's human resources to accomplish its objectives and gain competitive advantage.

But this view also has important implications for how human resource managers are trained and how human resource management courses are designed. Traditionally, managers, scholars, and textbook authors have discussed the newest—and presumably the best—ways to interview candidates or to select employees, as well as the best models for compensation and performance appraisal. But when we begin to consider the role of the human resource department as being that of a strategic partner, does it still make sense to talk about the single best way to do anything? Are there truly "best practices" that all firms should adopt, or should the practices adopted by a firm depend exclusively on the firm's specific strategic goals? The "truth" probably lies somewhere between these two extremes, but there have been loud debates within the human resource community over whether a best-practices approach or a contingency approach (based on the strategy pursued) is most logical.[3] Our *Point/Counterpoint* feature for this chapter addresses this controversy.

POINT | COUNTERPOINT

Best Practices or Contingency Approach?

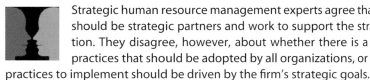 Strategic human resource management experts agree that human resource managers should be strategic partners and work to support the strategic goals of the organization. They disagree, however, about whether there is a set of best human resource practices that should be adopted by all organizations, or whether the choice of which practices to implement should be driven by the firm's strategic goals.

POINT... There is one set of best practices that should be adopted by all firms because...	COUNTERPOINT... All practices should depend upon the firm's strategic goals because...
Research has indicated that some practices tend to work better than others.	Research has indicated that there is no practice that always works.
Best practices lead to outcomes such as higher commitment and higher individual goals.	Desired outcomes depend on the firm's strategic goals.
It is easier to defend the use of practices that others have found successful.	What works for one firm may not work for another.
A body of sound scientific data supports the effectiveness of these practices.	It is impossible to assess effectiveness without considering organizational goals.
If there are no best practices, there are no principles to teach and there are no right answers.	There are no right answers (not any simple ones).

So... Some human resource practices probably work better than others, but how they are applied will depend on a firm's strategic goals. Also, it does make sense for any firm to consider its own goals rather than copy someone else's practices when designing a human resource management system.

The adaptation model also identifies a fourth strategic alternative called the *reactor*. The reactor is really seen as a strategic failure, however, and is not held up as a model that any firm should emulate. A reactor is a firm that either improperly ignores its environment or else attempts to react to its environment in inappropriate ways. During the early 1980s Kmart was guilty of using the reactor strategy. It failed to keep pace with Wal-Mart, for example, and spread itself too thin by investing heavily in specialty retailing. Human resource managers in organizations functioning as reactors may lack a clear understanding of exactly what qualities they are seeking in their employees. And, indeed, this lack of understanding may contribute to the firm's poor performance.

Other competitive strategies   The other dominant approach to business-level strategies identifies three specific competitive strategies, namely differentiation, cost leadership, and focus. These three are presumed to be appropriate for a wide variety of organizations in diverse industries.[20]

*A company that uses a **differentiation strategy** attempts to develop an image or reputation for its product or service that sets the company apart from its competitors.*

A company that uses a **differentiation strategy** attempts to develop an image or reputation for its product or service that sets it apart from those of their competitors. The differentiating factor may be real and/or objective, such as product reliability or design, or it may be more perceptual and/or subjective, such as fashion and appearance. Regardless of its basis, however, a firm that can differentiate its products or services from those of its competitors can charge higher prices for those products or services, thereby earning a larger profit. Rolex and BMW are both examples of firms that have used a differentiation strategy successfully. Human resource managers contribute to the successful use of a differentiation strategy by recruiting and retaining employees who can perform high-quality work and/or provide exemplary customer service. Likewise, employee training will likely focus on quality improvement, and reward systems may be based on factors such as quality of work and customer satisfaction.[21]

*A **cost leadership strategy** is one that focuses on minimizing the costs as much as possible.*

A **cost leadership strategy** is one that focuses on minimizing the costs as much as possible. This strategy allows the firm to charge the lowest possible prices for its products, thereby presumably generating a higher overall level of revenue. Low cost may be achieved through production efficiencies, distribution efficiencies, or product design efficiencies. Timex and Hyundai are examples of businesses that have used a cost leadership strategy successfully. Human resource contributions here focus on recruiting and retaining employees who can work as efficiently and productively as possible. On the other hand, more experienced employees may demand higher wages, and so it might also be possible to reengineer jobs so that they require minimal skills, and then select employees who can perform the jobs but who may not remain with the organization long. Fast-food restaurants often control labor costs using an approach such as this one. In any case, training may emphasize efficient production methods, and reward systems may be based more on quantity than on quality of output. One popular approach to reducing costs today is moving production to other countries where labor costs are lower.

*The **focus strategy** is undertaken when an organization tries to target a specific segment of the marketplace for its products or services.*

Finally, when an organization uses the **focus strategy,** it tries to target a specific segment of the marketplace for its products or services. This focus may be toward a specific geographic area, a specific segment of the consuming population based on ethnicity or gender, or some other factor that serves to segment the market. Within that focus, a firm may attempt either to differentiate or to cost lead its products or services. Fiesta Mart is a Houston-based grocery store chain that has prospered by focusing its marketing on the large number of immigrants, especially Hispanics, who live in the Southwest. These stores sell Mexican soft drinks, cornhusks for wrapping tamales, and many other products that are not carried in general-purpose grocery stores. The key human resource goal in this instance is recruiting and retaining employees who understand the focal market. For example, Fiesta Mart must recruit, hire, and retain employees who really understand the products they are selling and who speak Spanish, the language of most of its customers.

Functional Strategies and Human Resource Management

The third level of strategy formulation and implementation is at the functional level. Functional strategies address how the organization will manage its basic functional activities, such as marketing, finance, operations, research and development, and human resources. Thus, at this level human resource strategy formulation formally begins to take shape. It is clearly important that a human resource functional strategy be closely integrated and coordinated with corporate, business, and other functional strategies. Indeed, without such integration and coordination, organizational competitiveness will clearly suffer.[22]

Much of our discussion throughout the remainder of this text explicitly or implicitly addresses the human resource function from a contextual perspective that includes other fundamental business functions. As you saw in Figure 4.1, human resource strategy is, of course, our primary concern. Keep in mind, however, that other functional strategies are also developed and (as you saw in the figure) combine with the human resource strategy and top management strategic leadership to determine the firm's overall performance.

Human Resource Strategy Formulation

Using the organization's overarching corporate and business strategies as context, managers can then formally develop the organization's human resource strategy, as noted above. As illustrated earlier in Figure 4.1, this strategy commonly includes three distinct components—a staffing strategy, a development strategy, and a compensation strategy. These dimensions are shown in more detail in Figure 4.3.

Staffing refers to the set of activities used by the organization to determine its future human resource needs, to recruit qualified applicants interested in working for the

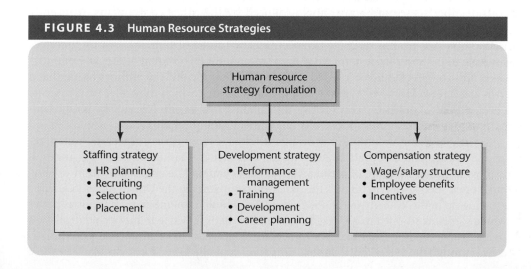

FIGURE 4.3   Human Resource Strategies

organization, and then to select the best of those applicants as new employees. Obviously, however, this process can be undertaken only after a careful and systematic strategy has been developed to ensure that staffing activities mesh appropriately with other strategic elements of the organization. For example, as already noted, if the business employs a growth strategy, the staffing strategy must be based on the aggressive recruiting and selection of large numbers of qualified employees.[23] But if retrenchment is the expectation, the staffing strategy will focus instead on determining which employees to retain and how to handle best the process of terminating other employees.

Similarly, human resource managers must also formulate an employee development strategy for helping the organization enhance the quality of its human resources. This strategy usually involves performance management, the actual training and development of employees and managers, and career planning and development for appropriate employees. As with staffing, the development strategy must be consistent with corporate and business strategies. For example, if an organization uses a differentiation strategy, the firm needs to invest heavily in training its employees to produce the highest-quality products and/or provide the highest-quality service. Performance management must also be focused on recognizing and rewarding performance leading to improved quality. But if cost leadership is the strategy of choice, the firm may choose to invest less in training (helping to keep overall costs low) and orient what training is offered toward efficiency and productivity improvement methods and techniques.

Third, the compensation strategy must likewise complement other strategies adopted by the firm. Basic compensation, performance-based incentives, and employee benefits and services—the major components of the compensation strategy—must all be congruent with their relevant strategic contexts to be effective. For example, if a firm uses a strategy of related diversification, its compensation system must be geared to, first, rewarding those employees with different skills that allow them to transition across businesses and, second, be flexible enough to facilitate those same cross-business transfers. If a manager moves from one division to another, for instance, that manager's pension plan should be readily portable to the new assignment. If the firm uses unrelated diversification, on the other hand, compensation may instead be focused on depth of knowledge and skills. Hence, the firm may choose to pay a premium salary to a highly talented expert with unusual skills relevant to one of the firm's businesses. The ability of this expert to transition across businesses is less important and thus is not likely to be a factor in compensation.[24]

Of course, these three components cannot be treated independently of each other. Each component must be tied to the overall human resource strategy, and each must consider the factors and constraints produced by the other components. A recently proposed theoretical model attempts to look at the entire array of interrelationships with employees from a strategic perspective. The model of human resource architecture suggests that not all employees possess capabilities of equal strategic value to a firm, and so they should be treated differently.[25] Specifically, the authors argue that a firm can have at least four types of employment modes, which they refer to as internal development, acquisition, contracting, and alliance, for its employees. The model suggests strategic imperatives for establishing these different relationships.

To help explain the complexities of the interchange among these aspects of human resource strategy and corporate strategy, we can consider a situation where an organization is moving into a new line of business, or at least changing its emphasis within existing businesses. A good case in point is the major oil companies in the United States. Someone growing up in this country in the 1960s and 1970s would remember gas stations as places where someone stopped to get gas for a car and perhaps was able to buy a cold drink or a snack from a vending machine. Over time, the image of the gas station changed dramatically. Through the 1980s and 1990s oil companies expanded the services available at these stations, and many of them became minimarts offering a wider variety of food and beverages. By the beginning of the twenty-first century, many oil companies entered into alliances with fast-food chains (such as McDonald's and Kentucky Fried Chicken) so that patrons could buy a meal as well as gas.

These services were viewed as a means to get potential customers to stop at a given gas station. Although the oil companies made money from products sold at the mini-marts, they did not see these products as a primary line of business. But at the end of the 1990s and in the earlier years of the twenty-first century, several large mergers occurred between major oil companies (e.g., British Petroleum and AMOCO, Exxon and Mobil), and as a result the new merged companies discovered that they owned a large number of food marts around the country. The feature *HR Around the Globe* describes how BP-AMOCO has sharpened its thinking regarding its human resources as a result of their merger.

When attempting to formulate the human resource strategy as well as its three basic components, human resource managers must also account for other key parts of the

---

HR AROUND THE GLOBE

Blending the Multinational Mix

As the merger between British Petroleum and AMOCO was being completed in 1998, the firm's executives realized that the combined company actually owned more retail outlets than McDonald's! The business then began developing strategies to exploit these resources, and several of them related to human resource issues.

*"There's no ocean wide enough to keep two oil companies apart."**

First, BP-AMOCO, as the new company was called, needed to recruit a new type of employee—a retail sales employee. Although each firm had employed many of these people in the past, their function was not central to the company's strategic goals (which focused on oil and gasoline). But if retailing was going to be a major business in the future, the company wanted to make sure they recruited top salespeople. This change also necessitated new human resource policies designed to retain the retail employees they already had and to train those employees to provide better services. This situation is also complicated by the fact that many of these retail outlets are actually franchised to other owners. Since the company traditionally focused more on employees directly involved in the drilling and refining of oil, this change required new systems and new policies.

This was only the beginning, however. If the company wanted to be a major retailing power, it needed a presence everywhere in the United States. An examination of where the company owned stations, however, indicated that it was extremely weak in California and the Pacific coast. How could it penetrate that market quickly? BP-AMOCO could obviously build new stations in California, but starting from scratch would take a long time. Instead, managers identified a target for another acquisition. ARCO was another large oil company with energy holdings in Alaska that were attractive, but with something else BP-AMOCO needed even more—most of ARCO's service stations were located on the West Coast. If BP could acquire ARCO, it would have the market penetration it needed.

In order to get the acquisition approved by the Justice Department, the company ended up having to sell ARCO's Alaskan operations but was able to retain its West Coast retailing business. Hence, BP, as the firm renamed itself, may now move even faster into retailing as a major part of its strategy and will continue to need new types of employees. The human resource function at the new company will have to work to meld the cultures of a traditional British company (BP), a Midwest-based U.S. oil company (AMOCO) and a West Coast–based oil company (ARCO). Clearly, the decision to exploit BP's retail outlets in a more meaningful way will have far-reaching implications for the firm's human resource function.

Source: Hoover's Handbook of World Business 2006 (Austin, Tex.: Hoover's Business Press, 2006), pp. 118–119 (*quote on p. 118).

Key Points for Future HR Managers

- All human resource management activities must be aligned with an organization's strategic goals.

- Corporate level strategy is often stated in a company's mission statements and is influenced by the firm's top management team, who sets the strategic directions.

- Human resource strategy must be consistent with corporate strategy and with the design of the organization and its technology, unionization, and culture.

- Formulating strategy is important, but the implementation of human resource strategy is even more critical for the human resource management function.

- Modeling high-performance work systems may be a good start for the design of a human resource management system, but the specific policies should reflect the unique strategy and environment of the organization.

Key Points for Future General Managers

- Corporate and business strategies define how an organization will operate and compete in the market.

- Common strategies at the corporate level include a growth strategy, a retrenchment (or turnaround) strategy, and a stability strategy.

- A diversification strategy is one where an organization decides to operate different related or unrelated businesses.

- The adaptation model of strategy suggests that organizations should match their strategy to the environment. The model includes defender, prospector, analyzer, and reactor strategies.

- Major competitive strategies include differentiation, cost leadership, and focus strategies (i.e., targeting a specific segment of the market).

- Human resource management strategy is determined by organizational level strategy as well as by organizational design, culture, technology, and the workforce.

- Certain specific human resource practices may be capable of providing a competitive advantage to organizations.

Review and Discussion Questions

1. Discuss the influence of organizational purpose, mission, and the top management team on human resource strategy.

2. Distinguish among corporate, business, and functional strategies. How does each general level of strategy relate to human resource management?

3. Specify the circumstances under which from a strategic perspective a firm's human resources might be seen as an organizational strength. Specify the circumstances under which human resources might be seen as a weakness.

4. Discuss how the specific business strategies relate to human resource management.

5. What are the advantages and disadvantages to an individual who accepts a job as a human resource manager in a firm that is in the midst of a retrenchment corporate strategy? A reactor business strategy?

6. If you were hired as a human resource manager in a large firm where the human resource function was poorly integrated with other functional areas, what steps would you take to improve this integration?

7. Explain how organization design, culture, and unionization issues are related to human resource management.

8. How does the firm's human resource strategy interact with other functional strategies and the strategic leadership of top management to affect organizational effectiveness?

9. Why is it important for all managers to understand behavioral forces in organizations? Why might it be especially important for human resource managers to understand these forces?

10. What are the two primary reasons many businesses today are interested in evaluating the effectiveness of their human resource management function?

Home Depot's Changing Competitive Landscape

Home Depot was facing growing competition from Lowe's and Wal-Mart. In 2001, the firm hired Robert Nardelli, an executive at General Electric, to turn things around. At a time when many companies are exploring collaboration and decision making by consensus, Nardelli started pushing Home Depot to become more centralized. At a time when many companies are eliminating layers of management and reducing dependence on the formal organization hierarchy, Nardelli emphasized a military-like discipline and obedience. At a time when many focus on progressive policies and experimentation, Nardelli rewarded those who implemented stringent plans to a high standard.

Nardelli's type of organization was one that used to be called command-and-control. Although widely popular throughout the economic expansion days of the 1950s and 1960s, its strict reliance on hierarchy and centralized decision making fell out of favor by the 1970s. Globalization, workplace diversity, rapid technological innovation, and even management consultants gradually shifted managerial attention toward more "soft" topics, such as corporate culture and employee empowerment.

Nardelli adopted command-and-control to help the firm recover from problems with its former decentralized structure that gave store managers tremendous autonomy. Home Depot founders Bernie Marcus and Arthur Blank wanted to encourage innovation and initiative, but instead, the company grew so fast that the firm lacked any unifying direction or approach. Nardelli moved the company back to where many firms started.

The principles that Nardelli used are simple. First, centralize control over functions such as purchasing and information technology for better coordination and control, as well as lowered expenses due to high purchase volume. Second, slow growth to allow more time to recover from changes and to slow expansion expenses. Third, control by measuring every input and output carefully, instead of relying on instinct, as the founders often did. Fourth, ruthlessly eliminate underperforming managers. Nardelli replaced 98 percent of top managers at Home Depot between 2001 and 2005.

But Nardelli's ideas aren't solely focused on cost cutting. He made a gutsy move into wholesale supply to contractors. The sales margins are lower, and professional customers demand service and quality. Yet this industry is very fragmented, so Nardelli believed Home Depot could gain an advantage by being the first large-scale competitor to enter. The CEO also increased Home Depot's service offerings, again, to move the company into an industry with weaker competitors. The firm started to do its own product testing and new-product development. "Soft" issues weren't neglected entirely. For example, potential new hires who had passed an interview then underwent a role-playing exercise. Only the best problem solvers and implementers made the cut.

Home Depot's sales increased by 30 percent between 2002 and 2006, yet the share price has dropped 20 percent, and customer satisfaction ratings are lower than Lowe's. One former manager claims that Nardelli measured good customer service instead of inspiring it: "The mechanics are there. The soul isn't." The CEO was forced to find a way to answer critics who said that he turned a flexible, entrepreneurial employer into "a factory."

Nardelli knew that he was zigging when the rest of the industry was zagging, but he bet on the strategic power of difference. Rarely does any advantage over competitors come from following the same strategy that everyone is using. Winning is almost always associated with unusual or contrary strategies. For years, observers have criticized many participants in the discount retail industry, asking, "Why try to out-Wal-Mart Wal-Mart? Why try to cut costs lower than the master at cost cutting?" Unfortunately, in early 2007 Home Depot's board of directors decided that Nardelli's plans were not working. Talented managers were leaving the firm in droves, and the company was having trouble attracting well-qualified people. So, in January of this year Nardelli was fired. But don't feel too sorry for him—Nardelli received a severance package valued at over $200 million![41]

Case Questions

1. Discuss the impact of top management on Home Depot before, during, and after Nardelli's tenure as CEO.

2. Describe how and why Home Depot has chosen previous and its current approaches to confronting its competitive environment.

3. What are the implications of Home Depot's current strategy for human resource management at the firm?

Building HR Management Skills

Purpose: The purpose of this exercise is to enhance your appreciation of the links among human resource strategy and corporate, business, and other functional strategies.

Step 1: Your instructor will ask you to form small groups of four to five members each. Read the introductory scenario below and then proceed through the remaining steps in order. Develop brief, overview answers to the various questions as they are posed.

Your group has just been hired as the top management team for a midsize firm. The firm has been floundering in recent years—market share and profits have dropped, morale is low, and the firm's stock price is at an all-time low. The board of directors has come to realize that retrenchment is needed to turn the firm around. Thus, the board fired the old team, hired your team, and gave you total responsibility for the anticipated turnaround. The facts are as follows: your firm has been making home appliances such as refrigerators, stoves, and microwaves. Ten years ago, the company had 20 percent of the market, annual revenues of $500 million, and a workforce of 15,000 employees. Today, the company has 7 percent of the market, annual revenues of less than $300 million, and a workforce of 14,500. (No new employees have been hired in three years, but few have left.) As a first step, the board wants the workforce trimmed, product quality improved, and a more effective marketing strategy developed. In the long term, the board wants the firm to diversify into other, less competitive markets.

Step 2: Identify three fundamental human resource strategy issues, challenges, and opportunities facing your firm immediately.

Step 3: Fast-forward five years: your turnaround has been successful. The firm has increased its market share to over 15 percent, sales are over $450 million, and the

workforce has been trimmed. The situation is looking bright, but your team and the board believe that it is still a bit too soon to launch a diversification effort. Identify three fundamental human resource strategy issues, challenges, and opportunities facing your firm now.

Step 4: Fast-forward another five years: your firm has continued to prosper and has just launched a diversification program. The core business now has almost 25 percent of the home appliance business, sales are approaching $750 million, and the workforce has grown to almost 20,000 employees. As first steps in diversification, the firm has bought another firm that makes home-electronics products (televisions, stereos, etc.) and is starting its own new small appliances business (can openers, coffeemakers, etc.). Identify three fundamental human resource strategy issues, challenges, and opportunities facing your firm now.

Step 5: Fast-forward another five years: your firm has continued to prosper and now sees itself as a mature, diversified home-products company. In addition to the businesses noted above, your company also now owns businesses that make telephones and related communication equipment (facsimile machines, copiers, etc.), cable-related television operations (regional cable television companies, pay-per-view businesses, etc.), and related automotive accessories (CD players, portable facsimile machines, etc.). But your management team believes that the firm has now entered a period of stability. Little new growth is foreseen, for instance, and the company wants to maintain its status quo for the next few years. Identify three fundamental human resource strategy issues, challenges, and opportunities facing your firm now.

Step 6: Report your ideas and suggestions through whatever form your instructor assigns (in-class presentations, written notes to be turned in, general discussion).

Ethical Dilemmas in HR Management

Assume that you are a project manager in the human resource department for a large manufacturing business. All told, your firm's human resource department employs about 120 people. As part of a strategy calling for related diversification, the firm has recently announced a merger

with one of its largest competitors. That firm has about 100 people in its human resource department. Your firm will be the dominant partner in the merger, controlling 56 percent of the new enterprise.

Your boss just informed you that you will be responsible for developing plans to integrate the two human resource departments during the merger. He estimates that the new, combined department will need about 160 people, necessitating a layoff of about 60 people. Your most critical task, therefore, will be to decide who stays and who has to leave. Your boss has given you clear and unambiguous written instructions that you are to select the best people possible from the two current departments, regardless of current affiliation. After he gave you these instructions, however, he also lowered his voice and said, "Of course, we should try to take care of as many of our own people as we can."

Questions

1. What are the ethical issues in this situation?

2. What criteria might you find it necessary to use in making your decisions?

3. What are your personal feelings about how to prioritize individual employees in a situation like this?

HR Internet Exercise

 AT&T maintains what it calls a "factbook" on the Internet. Its Web address is http://www.att.com/att/factbook.html. The factbook includes a wide array of information about the firm, its mission, its strategy, and other elements of its operations. It also has information about careers and jobs at AT&T. Visit the website and read and study the information that you find. Focus especially on information regarding the firm's strategy and its human resources. Use the information you find to answer the following questions.

Questions

1. What relationships, if any, do you see between AT&T's corporate or business strategies and its human resource strategy?

2. This chapter suggests that overall strategy affects human resource strategy, and that human resource strategy also affects overall strategy. Can you make any inferences about which of these two viewpoints AT&T seems to have adopted?

2. If AT&T changed its corporate or business strategies, would it necessarily have to change its human resource strategy? Why or why not?

from the table, knowledge transfer requirements under an exporting arrangement are rather straightforward. Expatriates would only be needed if they were to oversee marketing or distribution. They would need to learn local markets to some degree, and the transfer of knowledge may be expected to be primarily from the foreign operation back to the firm via the expatriate.

Knowledge transfer requirements would only be slightly more complicated under a licensing arrangement. Here expatriate managers would have the added dimension of monitoring local production to ensure quality control and to guard the firm's reputation. Thus, one would expect a significant degree of two-way information exchange, and the expatriate manager would need to have reliable sources of information about local practices and norms. Strategic alliances are likely to have the most complex knowledge transfer requirements because such ventures only survive when both parties are able to exhibit some level of trust. Therefore, an open flow of information that will facilitate trust-building and cooperation is most effective in this mode. Local employees will be called upon to communicate information regarding how to compete in the local environment, and both firms will be expected to share core competencies upon which the alliance is built. Expatriate managers play a critical role in this mode of entry. They will be required to both transmit and acquire information, and to do so as honest brokers.

The last two modes of entry both result in a subsidiary that is entirely owned by the parent company. Therefore, they have similar knowledge transfer requirements. The first, acquisitions, typically require expatriate managers. Their function in this case typically revolves around the communication of information about strategic coordination and management practices to local managers who, in turn, are responsible for daily operations and for communicating operational activity back to the parent company. The expatriate would also need to acquire information about local markets and customs that might precipitate some level of customization.

The establishment of a new wholly owned subsidiary would also have strong expatriate demands. This mode of entry would encompass similar knowledge transfer requirements with respect to strategic coordination and management practices, but with the addition of transferring specialized knowledge regarding the firms' products or services that would allow the subsidiary to compete effectively. In this case, we may expect an even greater flow of information from the parent firm to the new subsidiary although, again, expatriate managers would also need to acquire information about local markets that might necessitate local responsiveness.

Repatriation   The final piece in the strategic management of expatriate managers is their **repatriation.** Repatriation is often seen as more difficult than the original expatriation. Problems with repatriation often lead to the premature departure of the returning expatriate from the parent firm. Unfortunately, however, repatriation has received relatively little attention from scholars in human resource management.[7]

There are several challenges that make repatriation so difficult. As we discuss, though, it is absolutely critical that multinationals manage this part of the process well. Otherwise, many of the goals in the original expatriate assignment will not be reached. Repatriation problems can often be traced back to the time of the original assignment. Although the company plans to employ the manager back at the parent firm upon completion of the foreign assignment, often insufficient thought is actually given to exactly what role the returning manager will play. Moreover, during the period of the assignment, changes may also occur that alter the intended purpose. For instance, a manager may be sent abroad to better prepare him or her to take over a certain division within the company. But for a variety of reasons, during the time of the assignment that division might be

Repatriation   *refers to the process where expatriates are returned to their home country and assigned to jobs there.*

sold, closed, downsized, or strategically redirected. In any of these cases the role for which the expatriate manager is being prepared will have substantially changed.

So, while the manager is experiencing new challenges and developing new global skills, she or he is also "out of the sight" of decision makers in the home office. Thus, they may not always consider the expatriate manager when they think about new opportunities or assignments. As a result, the manager returns home only to find that the most interesting jobs (and those that are best for career advancement) have been given to managers who remained home—simply because they were there and so were more obvious choices to the decision makers. Instead, the returning manager is given a job similar to the one he or she left. But the returning manager is more energized and looking for new challenges—not a return to the way things were.

As a result, many returning managers leave the firm not long after they are repatriated. This is potentially disastrous for the multinational firm for several reasons. First, of course, it is always costly when a valued manager leaves the firm and needs to be replaced. In this case, however, the problem is exacerbated by the fact that the firm has invested a large amount of money in the manager as part of the international assignment. But the real cost comes in terms of the knowledge transfer discussed above. In those cases where the transfer of knowledge was intended to be primarily from the parent firm to the foreign operation the loss of knowledge may not be so high. But when information must be transferred from the foreign operation to the parent company, this failure to transfer information is quite costly. Information about special aspects of the local markets are lost, as well as a person who has actually established relationships with local employees.

A strategic approach to expatriate assignments is therefore extremely important for any multinational firm. The international strategy being pursued and the mode of entry a firm chooses will have serious implications for the importance of knowledge transfer and the nature and direction of that transfer. Success, then, should usually be measured relative to the amount and importance of the knowledge transferred rather than in terms of the length of assignment (or even in terms of performance ratings). In such cases, the only way for the assignment to be successful is for the returning manager to remain with the firm long enough to share the information she or he has gathered. Although there are a number of factors to be considered when trying to manage employee turnover in any setting (see Chapter 6), when dealing with expatriate managers one of the most important considerations is the repatriation process. Thus, strategically, a firm can help ensure the success of its overseas assignments by deciding beforehand how the manager will be assigned upon return, discussing this with the manager, and reviewing and updating that decision as circumstances dictate.

Human Resource Management and the Merger and Acquisition Process

Every few years it seems as though we experience another wave of mergers and acquisitions. Several years ago, for instance, a number of mergers and acquisitions occurred in the oil industry. These resulted in the creation of four "megafirms" now—BP-AMOCO, Exxon/Mobil, Shell, and Chevron/Texaco—that control a large portion of that industry. We have also seen a number of acquisitions in the casino industry so that now, between them, MGM and Harrah's control almost 60 percent of all the casino business in the United States.

But, whereas a lot of attention is paid to the big mergers and acquisitions, there is less public awareness of the fact that many of these mergers and acquisitions actually fail.

Failure (or success) can be assessed by looking at stock prices, accounting measures, or indicators such as R&D expenditures. For each of these measures the data (with few exceptions) have shown that mergers and acquisitions, overall, typically fail. That is, they result in lower stock prices, lower returns, and lower levels of R&D expenditures.[8]

There is considerable speculation and even some research on why mergers and acquisitions fail, but much of the attention has been paid to financial aspects of the deal (e.g., the acquiring firm paid too much), or to strategic aspects (e.g., the new business was too far from the firm's areas of expertise). Whereas these issues are certainly important, it is becoming increasingly clear that the successful management of human resources during the merger and acquisition process is also quite important for the overall success of the project.[9] In fact, several aspects of human resource management may be critical for the successful implementation of mergers and acquisitions.

When a merger or acquisition is announced, a number of interesting processes begin. The most obvious is that employees in the firms involved become concerned about their jobs. This is especially the case among employees of a firm that is being acquired by another company. In many cases, for example, a merger or acquisition is known to result in a certain amount of redundant human resources. Therefore, it is not unusual for layoffs to occur following the merger or acquisition. This awareness causes employees to become more stressed and to worry about their security, and it leads some employees to seek other employment before they become victims of a layoff. Unfortunately, in these cases, it is often the more valued employees who have the market value that makes such a job change easy.

But mergers and acquisitions also threaten the very way employees think about themselves. This core belief is known as a person's self-identity, and a great deal of our self-identity is tied up with what we do and for whom we work. For example, in Chapter 4 we related the story about how the employees at General Foods reacted when their new parent company, Philip Morris, handed out cartons of cigarettes. This example may be extreme, but it illustrates the more general problem. Employees involved in mergers and acquisitions must abandon one self-identity and then develop a new one—that of an employee of the acquiring firm or an employee of the new, merged firm. This is not a trivial manner. When people perceive threats to their self-identity, they actually work to reinforce that self-identity. In this case, an employee in a firm about to be acquired would feel his or her identity threatened and, as a reaction, would develop even stronger feelings of identity with the firm about to be acquired. Then, when employees of the acquiring firm were there, they would be seen as the "enemy"—as the people responsible for threatening the employee's self-identity. In intergroup research, these feelings have been found to be associated with a "we versus them" mentality, which results in competition between groups and even dislike for the other group members.[10]

Of course, this is exactly what the organizations involved want to avoid. They must move to integrate the two firms into one and create a new self-identity for all employees—as employees of the newly merged firm. That is, in order for a merger or acquisition to be successful, one thing that should happen is for all the employees to identify with the new firm, and therefore to work with one another and cooperate to help make the new firm the best it can be—especially since it is even more rewarding to be associated with a really successful firm.

What Can Be Done? The description of the situation thus far does not sound very promising. It would seem as though all mergers and acquisitions are doomed to fail because of these issues about identity. Yet we know that many mergers and acquisitions are successful. Moreover, we believe that in those cases the human resource manager functioned in such a way as to increase the likelihood that the merger or acquisition was successful. One critical role the human resource manager can play during this process is to serve as the center of communications. As noted above, there is a great deal of uncertainty, on everyone's part, during a merger or acquisition, and the human resource manager can work to communicate openly, honestly, and frequently with the employees. Research has shown that realistic information during the merger or acquisition process can reduce stress, increase job satisfaction and commitment, and can even reduce turnover, so this communication process can be very useful.[11]

In addition, it is important to build identification with the new corporate identity. This can be accomplished with simple measures such as distributing shorts or caps with the new corporate logo, or it might involve orientation sessions where all the reasons and details of the merger or acquisition are explained. It is easier to do this when the policies and procedures in the new firm are not based solely on the policies and procedures of one party in the merger or acquisition. That is, if some policies are based on one firm's policies, and some on the other firm's policies, and still other policies might be a blending of the two, it is easier for the employees from each firm to retain some good feelings about their former employer and also feel good about the newly created firm.[12]

Through programs such as these, the human resource manager can be an important player in the merger and acquisition process, and thus can add value to the organization in yet another way. Perhaps the human resource manager should never become the final arbiter of which mergers or acquisitions should be pursued, but input from that manager might be useful. For example, input from human resources might help decide how much should be paid for an acquisition, or what terms should be agreed to for a merger, with an eye toward how easy it would be to implement the merger or acquisition from the perspective of dealing with the problems identified above. In any event, once a merger or acquisition is begun, it should be clear that the close involvement of the human resource manager is critical for the ultimate success of the endeavor.

Decision Making in Human Resource Management

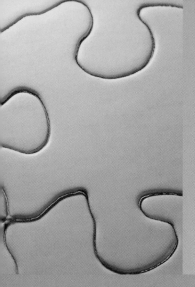

5

Information for Making Human Resource Decisions

CHAPTER OBJECTIVES

After studying this chapter you should be able to:

■ Describe human resource planning as a source of information for decision making.

■ Discuss strategy as a source of information for making human resource decisions.

■ Discuss economic conditions as a source of information for making human resource decisions.

■ Describe job analysis as a source of information for making human resource decisions.

■ Discuss the job analysis process

■ Identlfy and summarize common Job analysis methods.

Coleman Peterson is facing a mission that's almost impossible. As executive vice president of Wal-Mart Stores' "people" division, he was recently charged with hiring more than one million employees over a period of five years. That's like hiring the entire population of Rhode Island or the city of San Antonio.

About 800,000 global new hires will be added, and other hires will take the place of current employees expected to leave because of natural turnover. That will bring Wal-Mart's total global workforce—already the largest private labor force in the United States—to more than 2 million, up from 1.3 million. That would eclipse the population of the U.S. armed forces, which is about 1.4 million.

> *"The biggest challenge is the numbers. The numbers are just so large. But the issue is no different than the one [founder] Sam Walton faced. We have to focus on one associate at a time."*
>
> (Coleman Peterson, Wal-Mart executive)

While the stumbling economy put a chill on hiring at most companies, that's not the case at Wal-Mart. Instead, Wal-Mart executives see any downturn as a catalyst for growth because cash-strapped consumers are likely to turn to discounters. The Bentonville, Arkansas–based company's ability to meet its ambitious hiring goal is critical to its continued dominance in the retail market, analysts say. It needs people to maintain its aggressive push into other profitable areas, such as the $680 billion retail grocery business.

But there are challenges. The mass merchandiser will have to expand quickly while still being selective about whom it hires. It will have to overcome attacks in lawsuits and from unions on its reputation as an employer. And it will face mounting wage pressures that run counter to the retailer's focus on keeping operational costs low. "The biggest challenge is the numbers," Peterson says. "The numbers are just so large. But the issue is no different than the one [founder] Sam Walton faced. We have to focus on one associate at a time."

Wal-Mart's aggressive hiring plan will seek to continue bringing in minorities and female applicants and turn part-time, college-age workers into long-term employees. Some keys to success are offering competitive salary programs that are still cost-effective and retaining workers by promoting them through the ranks. While officials won't disclose pay information, unions that have pressed the company for wage increases put front-line workers' salaries at $7 to $8 an hour. Analysts say wages may be higher in some cases because they vary by location and job position.

Wal-Mart executives remain confident that their hiring needs will remain relatively constant. The company's net income has grown by over 10 percent per year for the last decade and even began to increase in recent years as the economy faltered. "If you study this company, we always perform best in tough economies," says Tom Coughlin, CEO of Wal-Mart stores division. As the economy gets tougher, he says, more people live paycheck to paycheck. "More and more people are looking for value."

Wal-Mart will have to grapple with ways to increase pay and benefits. It's a critical issue for the company's workers. About 60 percent of employees have told Wal-Mart in surveys that one of the main reasons they joined was because of the company's health benefits, according to information posted on Wal-Mart's website. But the company is not known as a generous spender, analysts say. Lawsuits have been filed by workers who say they were forced to work overtime for no pay, and the company keeps such a tight rein on spending that executives occasionally share hotel rooms on business trips.

The company will also have to remain selective—adding tens of thousands of workers who can deliver customer service, not just fill a hiring quota. Customer care is critical to the success of a deep discounter such as Wal-Mart. Already, that is an area where the company's image has been faltering, analysts say. "It used to be you could walk up to any Wal-Mart employee and they'd either help you or find a person who could," says David Schehr, research director at GartnerG2, a research service for business strategists, adding that the customer service has since faltered.

But Wal-Mart executives remain convinced that their multifaceted hiring approach will reap gains in the marketplace along with a growing labor pool. "How are we going to fuel this growth? The major source is internal," Peterson says. "Every time we open a Wal-Mart store or a Sam's Club, it's a recruiting outpost."[1]

Source: "While Hiring at Most Firms Chills, Wal-Mart Heats Up," by Stephanie Armour from *USA Today,* August 26, 2002, p. 3B. Copyright © 2002. Reprinted with permission.

Wal-Mart continues to grow rapidly, both in the United States and key foreign markets such as China. This new store recently opened in Jinan, the capital city of Shandong Province. Since it first started doing business in China in 1996, the firm has opened 34 stores and hired 18,000 sales associates. The retailing giant's future expansion plans will necessitate the hiring of thousands of more employees over the next several years.

Wal-Mart executives face the daunting task of hiring over a million new employees. This number was not selected at random, though. Instead, it came from a logical and systematic analysis of the firm's current and projected human resource needs. And as the hiring process continues, it will be critical that company officials monitor the environment and the firm itself and make any midcourse adjustments that may be required. Both the original hiring goal and its implementation have one major thing in common: information. Indeed, it is critical that firms have the information they need to make informed human resource management decisions.

With an understanding of the nature of human resource management and the human resource environment as a foundation, it is now possible to begin a more focused and detailed analysis of the kinds of decisions that human resource managers must make and the information they need to make those decisions. Chapter 5 opens this section with a discussion of the critical information needs of the human resource manager. Chapter 6 begins dealing with the decisions themselves and addresses decisions concerning size and structure of the organizational form. This involves decisions about who to let go and who to retain, and how we make sure that the right people are retained and separated.

Finally, Chapter 7 deals with staffing by discussing issues involved in recruiting and selecting employees. These are critical decisions for the human resource manager since they will determine the nature of the workforce available to try to meet strategic objectives.

We begin, then, with the information human resource managers need to make the decisions required. The most basic type of information deals with the supply and demand for labor in the marketplace, and so we begin with human resource planning and forecasting as input for decision making.

Human Resource Planning as a Source of Information

Probably the most important factor that affects the human resource management function is the labor force or workforce. An organization may pursue a growth strategy, and the human resource manager may attempt to recruit and hire new employees, but if there are not enough people in the labor force with the required skills or background, the efforts to recruit and hire will fail and so will the overall growth strategy. Thus, the composition of the labor force is a major limiting factor in pursuing strategic goals. The successful management of this component requires what is called **human resource planning,** and this planning can often make the difference between organizational success and failure.[2] Human resource planning, illustrated in Figure 5.1, can be defined as the process of forecasting the supply and demand for human resources within an organization and developing action plans for aligning the two. This section examines that process in more detail.

Human resource planning *is the process of forecasting the supply and demand for human resources within an organization and developing action plans for aligning the two.*

Forecasting the Supply of Human Resources

An important first step in human resource planning is forecasting the future supply of human resources—predicting the availability of current and/or potential employees with the skills, abilities, and motivation to perform jobs that the organization expects to have available. Several mechanisms can be used to help managers forecast the supply

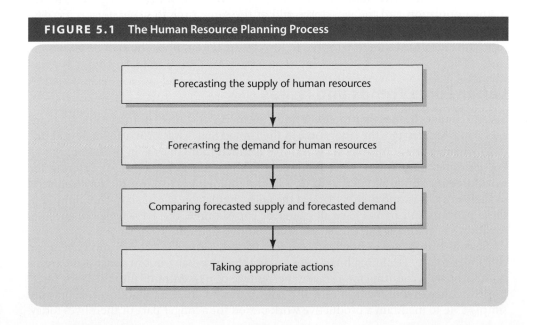

FIGURE 5.1   The Human Resource Planning Process

Forecasting the supply of human resources

↓

Forecasting the demand for human resources

↓

Comparing forecasted supply and forecasted demand

↓

Taking appropriate actions

of human resources vis-à-vis its current employees. By looking internally at its own records, the organization is likely to be able to draw on considerable historical data about its own abilities to hire and retain employees. In addition, the organization can glean information about the extent to which people leave their jobs voluntarily or involuntarily. All of this information, in turn, is useful in predicting the internal supply of human resources in the future.

Suppose, for example, that Atlas Industries, a regional manufacturing and supply business serving the plumbing industry, has averaged 15 percent turnover for each of the last ten years, with little variation from year to year. When Atlas's human resource manager attempts to predict the future supply of existing workers, at least initially it seems reasonable to predict a relatively similar level of turnover for the forthcoming year. Thus, the internal supply of the human resources at Atlas will likely decline by about 15 percent during the next year. Assuming the firm plans to maintain its current operations and will need a workforce comparable to what it has today, it becomes necessary for the organization to plan to replace those individuals who will depart by recruiting and hiring new employees.

*A **human resource information system** is an integrated and increasingly automated system for maintaining a database regarding the employees in an organization.*

An increasingly important element in this part of the human resource planning process for most organizations is the effective use of the organization's **human resource information system.** While we discuss the concepts associated with human resource information systems more completely in Appendix 1, it is relevant to introduce and briefly discuss them here, particularly as they pertain to human resource planning. A human resource information system is an integrated and increasingly an automated system for maintaining a database regarding the employees in an organization. For example, a properly developed human resource information system should have details on every employee regarding date of hire, job history within the organization, education, performance ratings, compensation history, training and development profile, and various special skills and abilities that each employee possesses.[3] Of course, the human resource manager also needs to look carefully at impending retirements and the firm's experiences with involuntary turnover. We will discuss these issues more fully in Chapter 6.

Because a firm often expects to need new employees in the future, it is also important to forecast the supply of human resources outside the firm that will be potentially available for it to recruit and hire. Here it is important to consider both general trends in the population and the workforce and at the same time to generate specific data about availability as it relates to the specific firm. Specifically, these trends and issues serve as valuable information related to forecasting the supply of human resources.

Labor Force Trends and Issues

Several changes in the labor force continue to emerge and affect human resource management. Decades ago, the labor force in the United States was primarily male and primarily white. Now, however, the workforce is much more diverse in numerous ways.[4] For example, most people once followed a fairly predictable pattern of entering the workforce at a young age, maintaining a stable employment relationship for the period of their work lives, and then retiring at the fairly predictable age of sixty-five. But today, these patterns and trends have all changed. For example, the average age of the U.S. workforce is gradually increasing and will continue to do so.

Several reasons have contributed to this pattern. First, the baby-boom generation continues to age. Declining birth rates among the post-baby-boom generation are simultaneously accounting for a smaller percentage of new entrants into the labor force. Improved health and medical care also contributes to an aging workforce. People are simply able to maintain a productive work period for a longer part of their lives today.

And finally, mandatory retirement ages have been increased or dropped altogether, allowing people to remain in the labor force for a longer period of time.

Gender differences in the workforce also play an important role. More and more women have entered the workforce, and their presence is felt in more and more occupational groupings that were traditionally dominated by men. In 2005 the composition of the workforce in the United States was almost 50 percent female, although some critics claim that a glass ceiling still exists in some organizations. A glass ceiling refers to an invisible barrier that keeps women from progressing to higher levels in the organization.

Changing ethnicity is also reflected in the workforce today. The percentage of whites in the workforce is gradually dropping, while the percentage of Hispanics in the workforce is climbing at an almost comparable rate. The percentage of African Americans and Asians in the workforce is also growing but at a much smaller rate. In addition to age, gender, and ethnicity, other diversity forces are also affecting the labor force. For example, country of national origin is an important diversity dimension. Physically challenged employees and employees with other disabilities are also an important part of workforce trends. And many other dimensions of diversity, such as single-parent status, dual-career couples, gays and lesbians, people with special dietary preferences, and people with different political ideologies and viewpoints are each playing an important role in organizations today. We cover diversity more fully in Chapter 8.

In addition, external data can also be used to predict the supply of labor in specific regions. Over the last several years, for example, there has been a gradual movement of population away from the northern and northeastern parts of the United States and toward the southern, southeastern, and southwestern parts of the country. Thus the supply of labor in the North and Northeast is gradually declining, while the supply of labor in the southern parts of the United States is gradually increasing. In other parts of the world, wherever immigration rules permit, workers are gradually shifting away from developing parts of the world and toward industrialized and economically prosperous regions. For instance, many workers in eastern regions of Europe continue to move into western areas in anticipation of better employment prospects.[5]

In any case, immigration patterns are important inputs for forecasting the supply of labor. But borders are not as open as they once were, even in the United States. Concerns over homeland security have made it much more difficult for individuals from certain parts of the world to even visit the United States. Young males from predominantly Arab countries have had an especially hard time coming to the United States to work, or even to study, and some business leaders have become concerned about this and argue that security concerns are taking precedence over the need for qualified people to fill jobs. Furthermore, several critics, such as Dr. Robert Gates (former director of the CIA and president of Texas A&M University and currently Secretary of Defense) have warned that these policies can hurt the long-term productivity of the United States and cut the country off from an important pool of talent. His opinions are summarized in *HR Around the Globe.*

Future labor supplies are typically forecasted by developing mathematical trend models using data from the past, with appropriate adjustments for migratory trends and predictions. These models, which essentially assume that trends will continue in a linear (i.e., straight-line) fashion, are usually reasonably accurate. But they can be far less accurate when some unforeseen event or trend disrupts expectations. An example was the unexpected increase in the labor-force participation rates for women during the 1980s. Although women's participation rates had been climbing for years, statistical predictions based on simple trend lines substantially underestimated the growth rates in the 1980s. In retrospect, observers realized that new (i.e., first-time) entries by women into the labor force were being substantially supplemented by other women already in the labor force but who were previously underemployed.

HR AROUND THE GLOBE

International Relations 101

Osama bin Laden and other terrorists are on the brink of achieving an unanticipated victory, one that could have long-term consequences for the United States. Over the decades, millions of young people from other countries have come to America to study at our colleges and universities. Many have remained here to start companies, to keep us at the forefront of scientific and technological discovery, to teach in our schools and to enrich our culture. Many others have returned home to help build market economies and to lead political reform.

Thousands of legitimate international students are being denied entry into the United States or are giving up in frustration and anger.

Robert M. Gates,
U.S. Secretary of Defense

After 9/11, for perfectly understandable reasons, the federal government made it much tougher to get a visa to come to the United States. Sadly, the unpredictability and delays that characterize the new system—and, too often, the indifference or hostility of those doing the processing—have resulted over the last year or so in a growing number of the world's brightest young people deciding to remain at home or go to other countries for their college or graduate education. Thousands of legitimate international students are being denied entry into the United States or are giving up in frustration and anger.

At 90 percent of American colleges and universities, applications from international students for fall 2004 are down, according to a survey by the Council of Graduate Schools that was released earlier this month. According to a recent article in *The Chronicle of Higher Education*, applications from China have fallen by 76 percent, while those from India have dropped by 58 percent. Applications to research universities from prospective international graduate students are down by at least 25 percent overall; here at Texas A&M, international student applications have fallen by 38 percent from last year.

Not surprisingly, universities in Australia, Britain, France and elsewhere are taking advantage of our barriers and are aggressively recruiting these students. According to the *Chronicle*, foreign student enrollment in Australia is up 16.5 percent over last year; Chinese enrollment there has risen by 20 percent.

Why should we be concerned? For starters, it is a sad reality that relatively small numbers of American students pursue graduate degrees in engineering and science. As a result, the research efforts at many American universities depend on international graduate students. They do much of the laboratory work that leads to new discoveries.

More troubling is the impact that declining foreign enrollments could have in the war on terrorism. To defeat terrorism, our global military, law enforcement, and intelligence capacities must be complemented with positive initiatives and programs aimed at the young people in developing nations who will guide their countries in the future. No policy has proved more successful in making friends for the United States, during the cold war and since, than educating students from abroad at our colleges and universities.

I take a back seat to no one in concern about our security at home in an age of terrorism. I am now the president of Texas A&M, but I spent nearly 30 years at the Central Intelligence Agency, ultimately serving as director under President George H. W. Bush. I learned during that time that protecting our security requires more than defensive measures; we have to win the war of ideas, too. For this reason, we simply cannot tolerate a visa process that fails to differentiate quickly and accurately between legitimate scholars and students—and individuals who may pose genuine security risks.

Senior officials in the White House and in the Departments of State and Homeland Security understand the importance of solving the visa processing problem. But carrying out post-9/11 visa policies and procedures has been badly hamstrung by a lack of resources, unrealistic deadlines and shortcomings in scanning technologies and background checks. American universities have had a difficult time tracking foreign student applicants as they move through the screening process—and there are just too many people in visa offices who are indifferent to the importance of these students to America.

Universities are willing partners in strengthening homeland security. This is not the 1960's. We are working with the government to keep track of international students. But averting a serious defeat for the United States—and serious problems for all its research universities—will require urgent action by Congress and the administration. Beyond the risk to economic, scientific and political interests, we risk something more: alienating our allies of the future.

Source: Robert M. Gates is the former director of Central Intelligence and served as president of Texas A&M University. Mr. Gates became Secretary of Defense in early 2007. "International Relations 101," by Robert M. Gates from The *New York Times*, March 31, 2004. Copyright © 2004 The New York Times Co. Reprinted by permission.

Finally, we should also note the special forecasting situation generally known as **executive succession.** Executive succession involves systematically planning for future promotions into top management positions. This process is much more complicated because it is often critical that exactly the right type of person is selected for a top position, the development costs to groom this person are very high, and the actual decision may have a major impact on the firm's future. Thus, many organizations try to bring as much order and logic to the process as possible. For example, senior executives usually indicate well in advance when they expect to retire—sometimes several years in advance. The firm can then draw on its cadre of up-and-coming managers for replacement candidates. Sometimes a specific set of individuals may be moved into special high-profile jobs, with the expectation that whoever does the best job will receive the promotion when the senior person steps down. In other cases, the most likely successor is moved into the number two spot to eliminate all uncertainties and to allow this person to concentrate on learning as much as possible about the senior position.[6]

This latter approach may be advantageous because the new person is already in line should the organization need to move more quickly than anticipated. For example, Procter & Gamble's board of directors realized that the firm was facing substantially greater competition than in the past and that its performance was beginning to slide. To accelerate the change in strategy, it promoted its new heir apparent to the top spot earlier than originally planned. But the reason Procter & Gamble had this option was that it had already done an effective job of succession planning.[7]

Executive succession
involves systematically planning for future promotions into top management positions.

Forecasting the Demand for Human Resources

In addition to supply, strategic planning requires that human resource managers must also develop forecasts about future demand. That is, they need to ascertain the numbers and types of people the organization will actually need to employ in the future. One important ingredient in this assessment is the organization's own strategic plans regarding anticipated growth, stability, or decline, described below.

But it is also necessary to consider larger, broader trends in the economy when forecasting the demand for human resources. For example, the chart illustrated in *HR in the 21st Century* shows how some jobs, like retail salespersons, have remained in high demand since 1900. But other jobs, like tailors, masons, tobacco factory workers, and butchers, have dropped sharply. Still others, such as nurses, hotel and restaurant managers, and moving equipment operators, have seen demand increase significantly. These general demand trends influence the availability of human resources for two reasons. First, employees for jobs in high demand will be more difficult to hire and will be more expensive to hire. In addition, students and future employees who track these demand trends often make decisions about what majors to pursue in college based on their anticipated employability. Thus, general trends like the ones described here must be part of the planning process.

It should now be clear that the planning process, and the associated forecasting of supply and demand relative to labor, is an important source of information for the human resource manager. Information about what kinds of people will be in demand in general, as well as information about what kinds of people will be available, is critical as the human resource manager begins thinking about staffing decisions, downsizing or rightsizing decisions, and how to develop a diverse organization. This information will serve as a set of constraints on what the manager can accomplish, but can also help the manager to identify ways to meet the organization's strategic goals. A related source of information for the human resource manager comes out of the strategic planning process itself.

Human resource managers must often understand projected growth rates in certain occupational fields as well as the number of people entering those fields. Nursing is a field where the number of new jobs is expected to grow rapidly over the next several years. As a result, nurses such as this one may be able to select from a number of different jobs. Moreover, they might also expect their pay to steadily increase. Employers of nurses, meanwhile, need to be prepared to aggressively recruit the nurses they need and to offer incentives to first attract and then retain them.

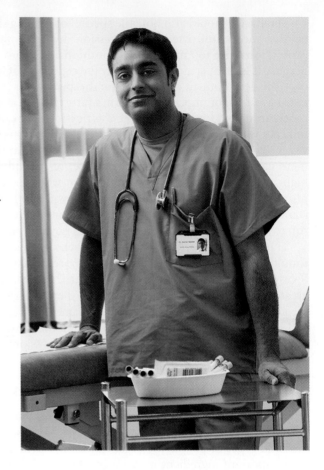

Strategy as a Source of Information

We touched on the relationship between strategic planning and effective human resource management in Chapter 4 but there are some specific aspects of the strategy formulation process that are also important as sources of information for human resource decision making. Specifically, the need for human resources in an organization will depend, to a large extent, upon the organization's overall strategy.

For example, as we described in Chapter 4, organizations often adopt corporate strategies aimed at growth, stability, or retrenchment. Clearly if an organization intends to grow, it will most likely need to hire additional human resources in the future.[8] Likewise, if the organization expects to enter a period of stability, its human resource demand is also likely to be relatively stable.[9] And finally, of course, if a period of decline or retrenchment is anticipated, then the organization may be confronting a decreased demand for human resources. Clearly, the choice of a strategy will be an important input for any decision making, since it is up to the human resource manager to implement the strategy that is chosen. Therefore, we will discuss the implications of each strategy for human resource management decisions.

Easy Come, Easy Go

Managers attempting to forecast the future supply of and demand for jobs and employees face numerous uncertainties. One major uncertainty for long-term planning is the extent to which any given job may become more or less popular in the future. The following graph clearly illustrates this point. The graph rank orders the top thirty jobs (by millions of workers) for the years 1900, 1960, and 1995. Only eight job categories among the most popular in 1900 are still on the list by 1995.

". . . The structure of U.S. employment has changed enormously."

Some jobs, like carpenters, have consistently dropped further down the list, whereas others, such as police officers and guards, have steadily risen. But most striking is simply the array of jobs on the 1995 list that did not appear previously—jobs such as computer programmers, health technicians, and lawyers and judges.

Over the century, the structure of U.S. employment has changed enormously. Only eight top job categories have survived throughout. And many more top job categories now require substantial education.

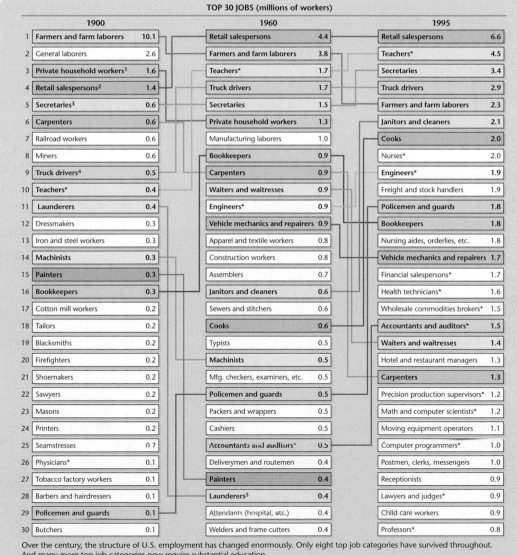

TOP 30 JOBS (millions of workers)

	1900		1960		1995	
1	Farmers and farm laborers	10.1	Retail salespersons	4.4	Retail salespersons	6.6
2	General laborers	2.6	Farmers and farm laborers	3.8	Teachers*	4.5
3	Private household workers[1]	1.6	Teachers*	1.7	Secretaries	3.4
4	Retail salespersons[2]	1.4	Truck drivers	1.7	Truck drivers	2.9
5	Secretaries[3]	0.6	Secretaries	1.5	Farmers and farm laborers	2.3
6	Carpenters	0.6	Private household workers	1.3	Janitors and cleaners	2.1
7	Railroad workers	0.6	Manufacturing laborers	1.0	Cooks	2.0
8	Miners	0.6	Bookkeepers	0.9	Nurses*	2.0
9	Truck drivers[4]	0.5	Carpenters	0.9	Engineers*	1.9
10	Teachers*	0.4	Waiters and waitresses	0.9	Freight and stock handlers	1.9
11	Launderers	0.4	Engineers*	0.9	Policemen and guards	1.8
12	Dressmakers	0.3	Vehicle mechanics and repairers	0.9	Bookkeepers	1.8
13	Iron and steel workers	0.3	Apparel and textile workers	0.8	Nursing aides, orderlies, etc.	1.8
14	Machinists	0.3	Construction workers	0.8	Vehicle mechanics and repairers	1.7
15	Painters	0.3	Assemblers	0.7	Financial salespersons*	1.7
16	Bookkeepers	0.3	Janitors and cleaners	0.6	Health technicians*	1.6
17	Cotton mill workers	0.2	Sewers and stitchers	0.6	Wholesale commodities brokers*	1.5
18	Tailors	0.2	Cooks	0.6	Accountants and auditors*	1.5
19	Blacksmiths	0.2	Typists	0.5	Waiters and waitresses	1.4
20	Firefighters	0.2	Machinists	0.5	Hotel and restaurant managers	1.3
21	Shoemakers	0.2	Mfg. checkers, examiners, etc.	0.5	Carpenters	1.3
22	Sawyers	0.2	Policemen and guards	0.5	Precision production supervisors*	1.2
23	Masons	0.2	Packers and wrappers	0.5	Math and computer scientists*	1.2
24	Printers	0.2	Cashiers	0.5	Moving equipment operators	1.1
25	Seamstresses	0.2	Accountants and auditors*	0.5	Computer programmers*	1.0
26	Physicians*	0.1	Deliverymen and routemen	0.4	Postmen, clerks, messengers	1.0
27	Tobacco factory workers	0.1	Painters	0.4	Receptionists	0.9
28	Barbers and hairdressers	0.1	Launderers[5]	0.4	Lawyers and judges*	0.9
29	Policemen and guards	0.1	Attendants (hospital, etc.)	0.4	Child care workers	0.9
30	Butchers	0.1	Welders and frame cutters	0.4	Professors*	0.8

Over the century, the structure of U.S. employment has changed enormously. Only eight top job categories have survived throughout. And many more top job categories now require substantial education.

* Requires education. [1]Servants and housekeepers in 1900. [2]Merchants and salespeople in 1900. [3]Clerks in 1900. [4]Teamsters and coachmen in 1900. [5]Launderers and dry cleaners in 1960.

Source: "Top 30 Jobs" from *Forbes,* May 6, 1996, p. 17. Reprinted by permission of Forbes Magazine. © 2003 Forbes, Inc.

Implications of a Growth Strategy

A strategy of growth is indicative of growing sales, increasing demand, and expanding operations for the organization. When the organization is growing and expanding, it most likely will need to hire new employees in the future.[10] In some cases, the organization may be able to hire employees readily without additional work. For example, if the organization is currently receiving 1,000 qualified applications per year and has been hiring only 50 of those individuals, it may be able to meet its growth rate by simply increasing the number of people that it hires. Instead of 50, the firm may begin hiring 75 or 100 people a year.

In other situations, implementing a growth strategy may be more difficult. Market conditions may be such that qualified employees are hard to find. For example, if the firm is receiving 100 qualified applications per year and is currently hiring as many as 90 of those individuals, then it is unlikely that it will be able to hire dramatically larger numbers of them without taking some additional actions. The organization may have to increase its recruiting efforts to attract more job applicants and even perhaps to begin to provide additional support to apprentice or training programs. Support of various college and university programs might also be a way of increasing the supply of available labor talent in the future.

A related incident recently involved United Parcel Service (UPS), the giant delivery business. UPS is based in Louisville, Kentucky, and maintains a huge operation there. The firm recently wanted to launch a major expansion but was concerned about its ability to attract enough new workers, especially those who might be interested in working the night shift. The firm threatened to build its expansion in another state unless Kentucky would help. Facing the threat of losing such a big employer, the state passed and funded major job training legislation and programs to help it attract and develop capable workers of the type that UPS needed.[11]

Some firms occasionally need to reduce the size of their workforce, while others may be hiring new workers. Ford Motor Company has recently undergone a major downsizing. Ford has been forced to offer various incentives to workers to give up jobs guaranteed to them under long-standing union contracts. These Ford workers, all considering contract buy-outs, listen to a recruiter from Union Pacific Railroad at a Ford-sponsored job fair as he discusses job opportunities with the railroad.

Implications of a Stability Strategy

In many ways, a stability strategy may be the easiest for the human resource manager to implement because the organization presumably must do what it has been doing all along. But even here specific and subtle planning nuances must be considered. For example, the organization will naturally experience a certain amount of attrition in its employee ranks each year. As noted earlier, some people will leave for better jobs, some people will retire, some will leave because of poor performance, and others will leave for reasons such as career relocation on the part of a spouse or significant other. Thus, even an organization that is projecting a period of stability is likely to need to augment its human resource labor force to replace those individuals who leave the organization for various reasons. In such cases, the organization can implement programs such as training to upgrade the skills of current employees and therefore make them more valuable to the organization. Alternatively, the organization might implement programs designed to reduce turnover among current employees, making stability easier to maintain.

Implications of a Reduction Strategy

In some cases, an organization may find itself facing reductions. Perhaps an organization is experiencing cutbacks, such as many organizations in the United States have faced over the last several years. Organizations such as IBM, General Motors, Chrysler, and others reduced their workforce by the thousands. Levi Strauss cut over 6,395 jobs, and many Wall Street investment firms have laid off stockbrokers and analysts.[12] SBC Communications recently announced plans to cut 11,000 jobs.

Sometimes these reductions can be handled through normal attrition processes as described above. For example, if the organization currently has 1,000 employees and it knows from experience that approximately 100 of those individuals will retire, resign, or be fired next year, and if it forecast that it will need only 900 employees following next year, then it may need to do very little. But if the actual forecast calls for only 700 employees, the organization must figure out how to eliminate the other 200 jobs in addition to the 100 that will disappear automatically. This sort of situation may call for laying people off, or terminating them, and we will discuss some important issues associated with this downsizing process in Chapter 6.

A popular alternative to terminations and layoffs, especially for managers, is early retirement. The idea is to make offers to employees to enhance their retirement benefits so that people might consider retiring at an earlier age than they would have done otherwise. Of course, this process involves costs to the organization. The organization may be forced to pay additional benefits to those employees above and beyond what they would have ordinarily expected to pay. It is also possible that the organization might lose people that it would have preferred to keep. That is, its highest-performing employees may be those who opt for early retirement. In fact, they may see early retirement as an opportunity for increasing their income by taking retirement benefits from their current employer but using their high-performance credentials to gain new employment with another organization. On the other hand, lower-performing employees are less likely to have this option and thus may be more likely to remain with the current organization.

Clearly, the actual strategy chosen is an important source of information for decision making, since it determines what kinds of decisions will need to be made. It will determine whether the human resource manager needs to be concerned with recruiting new talent or finding ways to reduce the workforce. Strategy will also determine whether the human resource manager needs to worry about reducing turnover or encouraging it.

believe that this technology will become commonly used in the foreseeable future, they may need to incorporate into the job analysis the ways in which this technology can alter the job being studied.

Specific Job Analysis Techniques

Several job analysis techniques are used in organizations, although the trend is away from these more traditional methods and toward competency modeling, which we will discuss later. The most commonly used methods are the straight narrative, Fleishman job analysis system, task analysis inventory, functional job analysis, the Position Analysis Questionnaire (PAQ), the Managerial Position Description Questionnaire (MPDQ), and the critical incidents approach.[23]

Narrative job analysis   The most common approach to job analysis is simply to have one or more SMEs prepare a written narrative or text description of the job. These narratives can vary in terms of length and detail. To some extent the quality of the information depends on the writing skills of the job analyst. Although it is possible to specify the format and structure of these narratives, they are typically individualistic, making it difficult to compare the tasks on one job with the tasks on another. They are relatively inexpensive, however, and it generally does not require a great deal of training for someone to complete a narrative job analysis.

*The **Fleishman job analysis system**   is a job analysis procedure that defines abilities as the enduring attributes of individuals that account for differences in performance; it relies on the taxonomy of abilities that presumably represents all the dimensions relevant to work.*

Fleishman job analysis system   Another popular method for job analysis is the **Fleishman job analysis system**.[24] This approach defines abilities as enduring attributes of individuals that account for differences in performance. The system itself relies on the taxonomy of abilities that presumably represents all the dimensions relevant to work. The taxonomy includes a total of fifty-two abilities. In general, these fifty-two specific abilities are presumed to reflect cognitive, psychomotor, and sensory abilities.

Examples of the specific abilities included in the Fleishman system include oral comprehension, written comprehension, oral expression, written expression, fluency of ideas, night vision, depth perception, auditory attention, and speech clarity. The actual Fleishman scales consist of descriptions of each ability, followed by a behavioral benchmark example of the different levels of the ability along a seven-point scale. An organization using this job analysis technique relies on a panel of SMEs (again, incumbent workers and/or supervisors are most commonly used) to indicate how important the ability is for the job, and the actual level of ability required for a particular job. Because of its complexity, job analysts who use this method require training, but it is also much closer in operation to the notion of competency modeling, which we will discuss below.

*The **task analysis inventory** is a family of job analysis methods, each with unique characteristics; each focuses on analyzing all the tasks performed in the focal job.*

Task analysis inventory   Another method of job analysis is the task analysis inventory. The **task analysis inventory** method actually refers to a family of job analysis methods, each with unique characteristics. However, each one focuses on analyzing all the tasks performed in the focal job. Any given job may have dozens of tasks, for example. Again relying on SMEs, this method requires the generation of a list of tasks performed in a job. Once the list has been developed, a job analyst—frequently the job incumbent— evaluates each task on dimensions such as the relative amount of time spent on the task, the frequency with which the task is performed, the relative importance of the task, the relative difficulty of the task, and the time necessary to learn the task.

Task inventories require a fair amount of effort to develop. Once they are developed, however, they are relatively easy to use. This approach to job analysis is often used in municipal and county governments and is also the most common form of job analysis used in the U.S. military. The information generated by this approach to job analysis is often detailed, and it is useful for establishing KSAs and training needs. The military has used these inventories to establish career paths and job families, where the jobs clustered together have a large amount of overlap in terms of the important tasks.[25] Managers then use a single task inventory to analyze all the jobs in the family. It is more difficult, though, to make comparisons across job families, and this drawback reduces the usefulness of task inventories to some degree.

Functional job analysis   One attempt to have a single job analysis instrument that can be used with a wide variety of jobs resulted in the development of functional job analysis.[26] According to this approach, all jobs can be described in terms of the level of involvement with *people*, *data*, and *things*. For example, employees on a job at a Halliburton manufacturing site might be said to "set up" machines (things), "mentor" people, and "synthesize" data. All are high levels of involvement and would indicate a complex job. The exact definition of each of these terms is provided to the job analyst. The Department of Labor relies on functional job analysis for some of its classifications of jobs, but it is not used widely in private industry. Nonetheless, this approach is important because it represents the first attempt to develop a single instrument that can describe all jobs in common terms.

Position Analysis Questionnaire   One of the most popular and widely used job analysis methods is the **Position Analysis Questionnaire (PAQ).** The PAQ was developed by Ernest McCormick and his associates, and it is a standardized job analysis instrument consisting of 194 items. These items reflect work behavior, working conditions, or job characteristics that are assumed to be generalizable across a wide variety of jobs.[27] The items that comprise the PAQ are organized into six sections. *Information inputs* include where and how a worker gets information needed to perform his or her job.

The **Position Analysis Questionnaire (PAQ)** *is a standardized job analysis instrument consisting of 194 items reflecting work behavior, working conditions, or job characteristics that are assumed to be generalizable across a wide variety of jobs.*

Job analysis helps managers better understand the essential elements of jobs as well as the skills needed to perform them. The Americans With Disabilities Act, meanwhile, has caused organizations to pay even more attention to exactly what skills are required to perform a job. Take Staff Sgt. Josh Olson (foreground), for example. Sgt. Olson lost his leg while serving in the Army in Iraq in 2003. In earlier times, Sgt. Olson would have been dismissed from further military service. Job analysis, however, determined that Sgt. Olson could still perform certain jobs very effectively. As a result, he is currently assigned to duty as a marksmanship instructor at Fort Benning, Georgia.

Mental processes represent the reasoning, decision-making, planning, and information-processing activities involved in performing the job. *Work output* refers to the physical activities, tools, and devices used by the worker to perform the job. *Relationships with other people* include the relationships with other people that are required in performing the job. *Job context* represents the physical and social contacts where the work is performed. Finally, *other characteristics* include the activities, conditions, and characteristics other than those previously described that pertain to the job.

Job analysts are asked to determine whether each scale applies to the specific job being analyzed. The analyst rates the item on six scales: extent of use, amount of time, importance of the job, possibility of occurrence, applicability, and special code. Special code refers to unique and special rating scales that are used with a particular item. These ratings are then submitted to a centralized location indicated on the questionnaire where computer software compiles a report regarding the job scores on the job dimensions.

A major advantage of the PAQ is that, like functional job analysis, its dimensions are believed to underlie all jobs. This feature allows a wide variety (although probably not all) jobs to be described in common terms. In the case of the PAQ, this feature results from the items and dimensions of the PAQ that describe what a worker does on the job rather than what gets done. For example, a baker bakes bread and a pilot flies an airplane, but when we examine how these workers get the information they need to do their jobs, we find that they both rely heavily on dials and instruments for critical information. We do not mean to suggest that the two jobs are related, just that workers perform similar functions even on diverse jobs. Unlike functional job analysis, the PAQ can provide information on 187 separate items, allowing a much richer picture of what happens on a job (the PAQ actually includes 194 items, but the remaining items deal with methods of pay). Finally, another strength of the PAQ is the fact that, because it has been widely used for many years, a considerable database of information exists, attesting to its validity and reliability.

In general, research supports the validity and reliability of the instrument. Research also suggests that the PAQ measures thirty-two dimensions and thirteen overall job dimensions. A given job score on these dimensions can be useful in job analysis.[28] Because the instrument has been so widely used, it has also been statistically related to other measures, including the scores of job applicants on standardized selection tests, compensation rates on various jobs, and even the importance of various abilities.[29]

Even though it is widely used, however, the PAQ also has some noteworthy shortcomings. The PAQ instrument itself is relatively complex, and an employee must have the reading level of a college graduate to be able to complete it. Although the PAQ is supposed to be applicable to most jobs, there is reason to believe that it is less useful for higher-level managerial jobs, and it is less useful for describing white-collar jobs.[30] Despite these limitations, the PAQ remains the most popular standardized job analysis instrument available and is commonly used by firms such as Kodak, Nestlé USA, and Delta Airlines.

Management Position Description Questionnaire (MPDQ)   The **Management Position Description Questionnaire (MPDQ)** is a standardized job analysis instrument , similar in approach to the PAQ, which also contains 197 items. The focus here, however, is on managerial jobs, and the analysis is done in terms of thirteen essential components of all managerial jobs.[31] These essential components are supervision, staff service, internal business control, complexity and stress, coordination of other units, public and customer relations, HR responsibility, autonomy of action, advanced consulting, advanced financial responsibility, approval of financial commitments, product and service responsibility, and product market and financial planning. The information generated by the MPDQ can be used to classify managerial positions as well as to estimate reasonable compensation for them.

The **Management Position Description Questionnaire (MPDQ)** *is a standardized job analysis instrument , similar in approach to the PAQ, which also contains 197 items. The focus here, however, is on managerial jobs, and the analysis is done in terms of thirteen essential components of all managerial jobs.*

Critical incidents approach   Critical incidents are examples of particularly effective or ineffective performance.[32] When used for job analysis, the **critical incidents approach** focuses on the critical behaviors that distinguish between effective and ineffective performers. Although this approach to job analysis is most widely used in connection with the development of appraisal instruments, it is generally useful because it focuses the organization's attention on aspects of the job that lead to more or less effective performance.

*The **critical incidents approach** to job analysis focuses on critical behaviors that distinguish between effective and ineffective performers.*

The O*NET   The **Occupational Information Network, or O*NET,** is technically not a job analysis procedure; it is a database that provides both basic and advanced job analysis information. As such, it can be viewed as an alternative to conducting job analysis.[33] The O*NET presently has information for over 1,000 occupations and is organized according to a system known as the standard occupational classification. The O*NET content model is presented in Figure 5.5.

For each occupation, then, information is provided about the relative importance of worker characteristics, including fifty-two separate abilities for effective job performance

Occupational Information Network (O*NET) *is technically not a job analysis procedure, but a database that provides both basic and advanced job analysis information and, as such, can be viewed as an alternative to conducting job analysis.*

FIGURE 5.5   O*NET Content Model

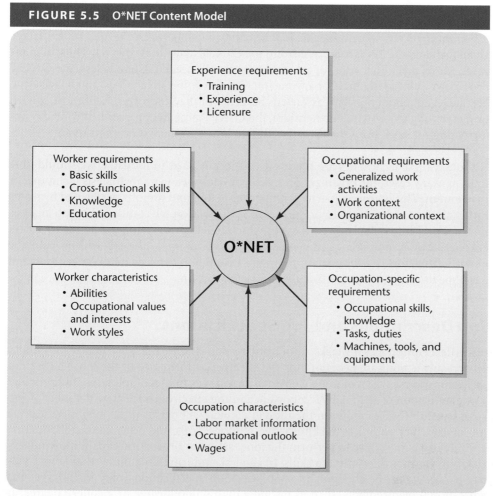

Source: "Understanding Work Using the Occupational Information Network (O*NET)" by Peterson et al., from *Personnel Psychology*, 2001, Vol. 54 (2), p. 458.

(classified as representing cognitive abilities, such as oral comprehension, deductive reasoning, and spatial orientation; psychometric abilities, such as manual dexterity and reaction time; physical abilities, such as explosive and static strength, and stamina; and sensory abilities, such as peripheral vision, heat sensitivity, and speech clarity), occupational interests (such as interests in artistic occupations, realistic occupations, and social occupations) and values (such as achievement, status, and comfort), and work styles (such as achievement orientation, conscientiousness, and practical intelligence). Information is also included regarding general occupational characteristics and occupation-specific requirements.

In addition, information is provided about appropriate worker requirements such as knowledge (fifty-two cross-occupation knowledge areas), skills (including ten basic skills, such as writing and speaking, and thirty-six cross-functional skills, such as negotiating, persuading, and time management), and education. There is also information about the experience requirements (including requirements regarding training and licensure), as well as occupational requirements, including general work activities (such as getting information needed to do the job, and thinking creatively), work context (such as environmental conditions), and organizational context (such as type of industry, organizational structure, and organizational culture). Links to other resources are provided, and they yield information about legal requirements, job hazards, and environmental conditions.

Although this is quite an array of information, and, in fact, new information is being added all the time, it is still possible that the O*NET does not have information that an organization needs about a specific job. Also, the match between the job as it exists in a given firm and the job as it is classified in the O*NET may not be perfect. Thus, in many cases, more traditional types of job analyses are still needed. Nonetheless, the O*NET provides a valuable resource for anyone interested in doing job analysis, and it is likely to become even more important as various branches of the U.S. government move toward implementing the system. Furthermore, the O*NET provides an excellent source of information for small firms that cannot afford to hire a job analyst or a consultant.

Although these techniques are the most commonly used in industry, we should note that, in many cases, the organization simply develops its own job analysis technique or instrument. This is especially true for managerial jobs and for jobs performed by teams rather than by individuals. In both cases, no widely accepted standardized job analysis instruments are available. Regardless of which job analysis technique an organization employs, however, at some point a narrative description of the job will probably be needed. Therefore, it is important to draw a distinction between a job description and a job specification, which we discuss in the next section.

Job Descriptions and Job Specifications

A **job description** lists the tasks, duties, and responsibilities that a particular job entails. Observable actions are necessary for the effective performance of the job. The job description specifies the major job elements, provides examples of job tasks, and provides some indication of the relative importance in the effective conduct of the job.[34] A **job specification** focuses more on the individual who will perform the job. Specifically, a job specification indicates the knowledge, abilities, skills, and other characteristics that an individual must have to perform the job. Factual or procedural capabilities and levels of proficiency refer more to skills. In general, enduring capabilities that an individual possesses can be thought of as abilities. Job specifications may include general educational requirements, such as having a high school degree or a college degree, as

A **job description** lists the tasks, duties, and responsibilities for a particular job and specifies the major job elements, provides examples of job tasks, and provides some indication of the relative importance in the effective conduct of the job.

A **job specification** focuses on the individual who will perform the job and indicates the knowledge, abilities, skills, and other characteristics that an individual must have to be able to perform the job.

well as the specifications of job-related skills, such as the ability to keyboard seventy words a minute, or the requirement that an individual be fluent in Japanese or Spanish.

Taken together then, the job description and the job specification should provide a parallel and mutually consistent set of information and details that focuses on the job itself and the individual most likely to be successful performing that job. This information should then inform all subsequent recruiting and selection decisions. Figure 5.6 illustrates an actual job description and job specification for a particular kind of accountant at Johnson & Johnson. This description and specification were created as part of a job analysis and are used to communicate to job applicants and managers what skills and abilities are necessary to perform the job.

Modeling Competencies and the End of the "Job"

Given the rate of change in work, some scholars and other human resource experts have argued that the nature of work is changing so much that the concept of a "job" is becoming obsolete. Although many people will continue to have "jobs" for some time to come, in some work settings it may well be true that the traditional view of jobs and work is no longer applicable. In these settings people usually work on teams where the focus is on getting tasks accomplished rather than on specific task requirements. Thus, there is reason to suggest that we should think about roles that have to be filled within the organization, and that employees will need to emphasize flexibility, teamwork, and accomplishing tasks, rather than job descriptions and sets of duties. In light of these developments, then, some have argued that traditional methods of job analysis (including the O*NET) have little place in the modern organization, and that the information needed by human resource managers can be better provided by modeling competencies instead of by describing jobs.

In fact, data from a survey conducted in 1998 indicated that 75 percent of the companies surveyed were using some type of competency modeling.[35] Nonetheless, there is little agreement about what exactly is meant by the term *competency*. Some view competencies as being broader than abilities, while others suggest that competencies exist at a deeper level and really underlie abilities. Generally, however, experts view competencies

---

FIGURE 5.6   Example Job Description and Job Specification

Job Title: Accounts Payable and Payroll Accountant, Johnson & Johnson Corp.

Job Description: Business partner with Accounts Payable and Payroll Departments to develop expense forecasts and commentary; prepare Accounts Payable and Payroll shared services charge-outs to affiliates; ensure Accounts Payable and Payroll inputs are posted weekly; perform account analysis/reconciliations of Cash, Liability, and Employee Loan accounts related to Accounts Payable and Payroll; submit routine reports to Corporate; identify and implement process improvements relative to all responsibilities listed above.

Job Specification: BS degree in accounting or finance; 2+ years of accounting/finance experience; sound knowledge of Integral Accounts Payable and General Ledger Systems; working knowledge of Hyperion Software, PACT; good communication skills; able to work independently at off-site location.

as characteristics of employees (or teams of employees) that lead to success on the job. Thus, abilities such as decisiveness and adaptability are seen as competencies that might underlie more specific abilities such as decision making or coping with change.[36]

Clearly, this approach has the potential for providing critical information to the human resource manager in a more useful form, since it emphasizes what a person needs in order to be successful. Thus, it may not be important to know whether an employee will type letters or run a lathe, but it may be very important to know that an employee needs to be adaptable. Competencies are determined in a number of ways, but typically, teams of top managers, working with consultants, identify the competencies necessary to compete in the future. These competencies are then described in clear behavioral terms, measures are designed, and each is rated according to its relative importance for future success. Employees who have these competencies are then sought through the recruiting and selection process, or current employees are provided training opportunities to acquire these competencies and are then rewarded when they do acquire them. (See the discussion of skill-based pay and knowledge-based pay in Chapter 9.) The critical difference is that the human resource manager no longer focuses on what is needed to be successful at one job, but instead focuses on what is needed to be successful at any and all jobs within the organization. There are also some applications of competency modeling to selection, which we will discuss in Chapter 7.

Legal Issues in Job Analysis

Because job analysis is a critical building block for much of the human resource management process, it should not be surprising that numerous legal issues have been raised with regard to job analysis. In fact, federal government guidelines on selection include discussion of the appropriate ways to conduct job analysis and state that any attempt to establish the job relatedness of a selection instrument must begin with a careful analysis of the jobs in question. Most of the specific cases, in fact, have been concerned more with the *failure* of an organization to perform a job analysis. For example, in *Albermarle* v. *Moody* the Albermarle Paper Company argued that tests found to be job related for one set of jobs could be used to select employees for another set of jobs that they argued were similar.[37] The Court found that, in the absence of clear job analysis information to support such a claim (and there was no job analysis information), it was unacceptable to assume that the jobs in question were the same.

The Americans with Disabilities Act of 1990 (ADA) raises additional legal issues associated with job analysis. As noted in Chapter 2, the ADA states that an employer must offer a reasonable accommodation to any employee who has a disability and who can perform the "essential functions" of the job. Basically, essential functions are those that take up a significant part of the employee's time, are performed regularly, and have consequences for other parts of the job. Organizations need to rely on careful job analysis to determine exactly what those essential functions are and thus determine if the employee is entitled to an accommodation under the law.

Finally, several issues regarding the accuracy of job analysis information have potential legal implications.[38] Perhaps the most troubling of these issues relates to potential gender discrimination in job analysis. Specifically, evidence suggests that jobs occupied primarily by male incumbents are more likely to be rated as more complex and higher level than are similar jobs occupied primarily by female incumbents.[39] One striking result that has been published relates to different job analysis information generated for the jobs of "prison guard" and "prison matron," which are simply the traditional titles for persons of different gender doing the same job (these different titles are no longer used, incidentally). Because the information from job analysis can be used for determining appraisal systems as well as compensation rates, this problem is potentially serious.

Finally, as discussed in Chapter 2, the creation of autonomous work teams has presented a new legal challenge. In the *Electromation* decision, the National Labor Relations Board (NLRB) ruled that the autonomous work teams and action committees created at the company were illegal labor organizations.[40] That is, they were labor organizations because they scheduled work, determined wages, and made selection and promotion decisions; and they were illegal because they were created and controlled by management.

In summary, job analysis can provide extremely important information for the human resource manager since it reveals what a person does on the job. This information can be used for a variety of applications, and it can be collected using a variety of techniques and job analysts. Recently, a number of organizations have moved toward competency modeling to replace traditional job analysis, and this approach has the potential to provide even more useful information about what is required for someone to be successful on the job. Finally, because job analysis information is a basic building block for human resource management decisions, a number of legal issues have been raised relative to the applications of job analysis information.

Chapter Summary

Human resource executives rely on a number of sources of information to make decisions and to manage human capital. Human resource planning, for example, draws from forecasts of the supply of human resources, labor force trends and issues, and forecasts of the demand for human resources.

The organization's strategy is also a critical information source. Growth, stability, and reduction strategies, for example, each carry substantially different implications for human resource managers. Another important source of information comes from various economic conditions. Unemployment rates, market wage rates, and human capital investments each provide useful information to human resource executives.

Job analysis is one of the building blocks of the human resource planning process and is also a fundamental source of information for that same planning process. Job analysis involves the gathering and organizing of detailed information about various jobs within the organization so that managers can better understand the processes through which jobs are most effectively performed. Job analysis provides input to the human resource planning process by helping planners better understand exactly what kinds of work must be performed.

Job analysis itself generally follows a three-step process: determining information needs, determining methods for obtaining information, and determining who will collect information. The responsibility of analysis is jointly shared by line managers, the human resource group or department, and the job analyst(s).

Commonly used methods of job analysis include the narrative approach, Fleishman job analysis system, task analysis inventory, functional job analysis, Position Analysis Questionnaire, Management Position Description Questionnaire, and critical incidents approach. The O*NET, while not technically a job analysis procedure, provides advanced job analysis information.

Job analysis results in a job description and a job specification. The changing nature of work and of jobs must also be understood and appreciated by managers. Finally, there are also important legal implications related to job analysis.

Key Points for Future HR Managers

■ Human resource planning is a critical source of information for making decisions.

■ The organization's strategy is an important source of information for human resource managers.

■ Various economic conditions provide useful information for human resource decisions.

■ Job analysis provides critical information about what people do on their jobs.

■ Job analysis information provides the basis for recruitment, selection, compensation, appraisal, and training.

■ Various sources of job analysis information are available and each has advantages and drawbacks. You must match the job analyst to your needs.

■ Several job analysis methods are available. The Position Analysis Questionnaire is the most widely used

structured instrument, but you should be aware of the strengths and weaknesses of each technique and choose a technique based on your needs.

■ The O*NET is a potentially revolutionary approach to job analysis that may replace other job analysis techniques, especially in smaller companies.

■ Competency modeling is a new approach to job analysis. It focuses on broader requirements and on those requirements that might be applicable for a wide variety of jobs within an organization.

■ The Americans with Disabilities Act has made job analysis an even more critical part of the system because the act emphasizes the establishment of the "critical functions" on a job.

Key Points for Future General Managers

■ Planning is as important for human resource management as for any other function in an organization.

■ Human resource management should be an integral part of the organization's strategy.

■ Job analysis is and should be the basic cornerstone for all other human resource management functions.

■ It is essential to understand the strengths and weaknesses of different job analysis approaches because one is not better than the others.

■ Competency modeling is concerned with identifying broader sets of requirements that may cut across individual jobs within an organization.

Review and Discussion Questions

1. Describe the essential elements of forecasting the supply of and demand for human resources.

2. Summarize the basic implications for human resource decisions of three different strategies.

3. What are the basic economic conditions that are especially relevant to human resource managers?

4. List the steps in job analysis.

5. Compare and contrast job descriptions and job specifications.

6. Compare and contrast the major techniques that organizations use for job analysis.

7. Can all jobs be analyzed? Why or why not?

8. Are there circumstances when managers might choose not to have job descriptions and/or job specifications?

9. Distinguish between job behaviors and job competencies.

10. Summarize the basic legal issues related to job analysis.

Doing the Dirty Work

Business magazines and newspapers regularly publish articles about the changing nature of work in the United States and about how many jobs are being changed. Indeed, because so much has been made of the shift toward service-sector and professional jobs, many people assume that the number of unpleasant and undesirable jobs has declined.

In fact, nothing could be further from the truth. Millions of Americans work in gleaming air-conditioned facilities, but many others work in dirty, grimy, and unsafe settings. For example, many jobs in the recycling industry require workers to sort through moving conveyors of trash, pulling out those items that can be recycled. Other relatively unattractive jobs include cleaning hospital restrooms, washing dishes in a restaurant, and handling toxic waste.

Consider the jobs in a chicken-processing facility. Much like a manufacturing assembly line, a chicken-processing facility is organized around a moving conveyor system. Workers call it the chain. In reality, it's a steel cable with large clips that carries dead chickens down what might be called a "disassembly line." Standing along this line are dozens of workers who do, in fact, take the birds apart as they pass.

Even the titles of the jobs are unsavory. Among the first set of jobs along the chain is the skinner. Skinners use sharp instruments to cut and pull the skin off the dead chicken. Toward the middle of the line are the gut pullers. These workers reach inside the chicken carcasses and remove the intestines and other organs. At the end of the line are the gizzard cutters, who tackle the more difficult organs attached to the inside of the chicken's carcass. These organs have to be individually cut and removed for disposal.

The work is obviously distasteful, and the pace of the work is unrelenting. On a good day the chain moves an average of ninety chickens a minute for nine hours. And the workers are essentially held captive by the moving chain. For example, no one can vacate a post to use the bathroom or for other reasons without the permission of the supervisor. In some plants, taking an unauthorized bathroom break can result in suspension without pay. But the noise in a typical chicken-processing plant is so loud that the supervisor can't hear someone calling for relief unless the person happens to be standing close by.

Jobs such as these on the chicken-processing line are actually becoming increasingly common. Fueled by Americans' growing appetites for lean, easy-to-cook meat, the number of poultry workers has almost doubled since 1980, and today they constitute a workforce of around a quarter of a million people. Indeed, the chicken-processing industry has become a major component of the state economies of Georgia, North Carolina, Mississippi, Arkansas, and Alabama.

Besides being unpleasant and dirty, many jobs in a chicken-processing plant are dangerous and unhealthy. Some workers, for example, have to fight the live birds when they are first hung on the chains. These workers are routinely scratched and pecked by the chickens. And the air inside a typical chicken-processing plant is difficult to breathe. Workers are usually supplied with paper masks, but most don't use them because they are hot and confining.

And the work space itself is so tight that the workers often cut themselves—and sometimes their coworkers—with the knives, scissors, and other instruments they use to perform their jobs. Indeed, poultry processing ranks third among industries in the United States for cumulative trauma injuries such as carpal tunnel syndrome. The inevitable chicken feathers, feces, and blood also contribute to the hazardous and unpleasant work environment.[41]

Case Questions

1. How relevant are the concepts of competencies to the jobs in a chicken-processing plant?

2. What information sources would be of most significance regarding jobs in a chicken-processing plant?

3. Are dirty, dangerous, and unpleasant jobs an inevitable part of any economy?

Building HR Management Skills

Purpose: The purpose of this exercise is to provide you with insights into the processes associated with job analysis.

Step 1: Your instructor will divide the class into small groups of four to five members each.

Step 2: Your group should select a job with which group members have some familiarity. Examples might be cook at McDonald's, retail clerk at The Gap, or a similar job.

Step 3: Based on group members' understanding of the job, outline how you would conduct a job analysis for that job.

Step 4: Draft a job description and a job specification that you think represent the job.

Step 5: Assume you are managers in the company you chose for analysis. Develop planning scenarios for growth, stability, and reductions.

Ethical Dilemmas in HR Management

Assume you are a plant manager for a manufacturing company. For years your low-wage workers (about 250 people in a total workforce of 1,500) have complained about their pay and general working conditions. They have recently presented you with a list of demands, calling for an immediate wage increase of 25 percent, an upgrade of the factory's heating and air-conditioning system, and remodeling the plant's restrooms and cafeteria. All of your low-wage employees have signed a petition supporting the demands and have threatened to quit if their demands are not met. In addition, several people holding higher-income jobs have expressed sympathy for the concerns of the low-wage workers.

You know the following things: (1) another large manufacturer in the area is about to close down, putting about 500 low-wage employees out of work; (2) the corporation that owns your manufacturing company is about to implement a reduction strategy and call for an overall reduction in the workforce of 15 percent; (3) general un-employment rates are also growing, increasing the number of people who will be looking for jobs.

You feel that you have two choices. One is to meet with all of your workers, inform them of the things you know, and advise them to back off their demands. The other choice is to do nothing and see what happens. This may result in some (but not all) of your workers quitting. But given that you may have to lay some people off anyway and that there will be plenty of other people looking for jobs this is not likely to be a major problem.

Questions

1. What are the ethical issues in this situation?

2. What are the basic arguments for each course of action?

3. What do you think most managers would do? What would you do?

HR Internet Exercise

Use the Internet to see what information you can obtain about the jobs listed below:

1. Sanitation workers

2. Coffee brewers

3. Petroleum refinery workers

4. Retail clerks

5. Restaurant cooks

Questions

1. Identify the essential skills and competencies needed to perform each of these jobs.

2. How valuable do you think the Internet is for job analysis and job design?

3. Do you need any additional information that you could not find on the Internet?

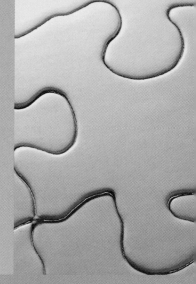

6

Organizational Form and Structure

CHAPTER OBJECTIVES

After studying this chapter you should be able to:

■ Understand the concept of rightsizing and describe organizational strategies for rightsizing.

■ Identify and discuss temporary solutions for increased demand for employees.

■ Describe approaches to dealing with declining needs for employees.

■ Discuss termination options and issues.

■ Describe the issues associated with employment-at-will.

■ Identify the major reasons for voluntary turnover in organizations.

■ Understand the determinants of job satisfaction and how satisfaction relates to turnover.

■ Discuss how organizations can evaluate rightsizing strategies.

With increased competitive pressures, an uncertain political climate, and the rapid pace of change in all sectors of the economy, U.S. companies need all the help they can get. Among other things, market pressures compel businesses to continuously look for ways to lower their costs and increase their revenues. One way that managers lower costs is to reduce the size of their workforce. This often results in events known as terminating, downsizing, rightsizing, or getting the pink slip.

> *"A lot of us are unhappy, but what are we going to do—go somewhere else?"*
>
> (A long-time Dell employee)*

A quick review of business headlines from the last decade conveys a stark picture: "American Airlines Cuts 7,000 Jobs," "United Slashes 9,000 Jobs in Bid for Solvency," "IBM Laid Off 15,600 in Second Quarter." Indeed, almost 1.5 million workers were laid off in 2002. And these layoffs came on top of 1.96 million terminations in 2001. While layoffs slowed from 2003 through 2006, few companies seem eager to begin replacing jobs they had eliminated. And those that are hiring are doing so with caution and deliberation. Industries such as telecommunications and auto production have been especially hard-hit, with lower-paid workers suffering the most. Surveys also indicated that many firms in these sectors are likely to make additional layoffs, and few plan to increase hiring dramatically.

This period of job cuts, coupled with higher productivity and better use of automation, has made U.S. firms more efficient. But at what price? The remaining workers, who must learn new tasks and work harder to replace their laid-off colleagues, are prone to stress. Hamilton Beazley, a management consultant, calls such additional duties *ghost work*. He describes ghost work as challenging for employees, saying, "It can be totally demoralizing and can cripple the individual as well as the organization."

Not surprisingly, most workers are not pleased with having to pick up the slack for laid-off coworkers. Some workers refer to ghost work as *speed up,* because each remaining worker has to work harder, or *stretch out,* because they have to put in longer hours. Land Windham, a labor spokesperson, says, "*They* call it productivity," referring to management.

Given the uncertain job market today, however, many workers are willing to endure the stress and discouragement of ghost work. Computer maker Dell recently laid off 6,000 of its 40,000 workers, allowing the firm to cut personal computer (PC) prices and increase sales and profits. A long-time employee says, "A lot of us are unhappy, but what are we going to do—go somewhere else?" The danger for employers is that, if the job market improves, many disgruntled workers may do just that.[1]

Layoffs are an increasingly common part of the competitive landscape of business today. Businesses need to hire judiciously so as to not hire more workers than they need, but even so, conditions may require that workers be laid-off or terminated altogether. These workers were previously employed at a Boeing plant in Long Beach, California. Unfortunately, they have just been informed that their jobs are being eliminated.

n Chapter 5 we discussed the human resource planning process and noted that an organization may forecast growth, stability, or reductions in its workforce needs. As will be described in Chapter 7, growth and stability scenarios ultimately require the organization to recruit and hire more employees for the future, but this can take time, and the organization may need to rely upon a more temporary strategy for dealing with increased demand in the short run. Also, the reduction scenario essentially means that the organization will need fewer workers in the future than it does at present. In all cases, therefore, it is essential that the organization, through the human resource management function, manage the size of its workforce effectively. This process is called rightsizing. More specifically, **rightsizing** is the process of monitoring and adjusting the organization's workforce to its optimal size and composition.

Rightsizing *is the process of monitoring and adjusting the composition of the organization's workforce to its optimal size.*

Managing the size of the workforce, in turn, may involve layoffs or early-retirement programs to reduce the size of the workforce; it may involve retention programs to maintain the size of the workforce; and it may involve using temporary workers as a bridge between the present state of affairs and either growth or reduction. In any case, it is essential that the organization take care to ensure that it has the "right" people. That is, reduction, retention, or any other strategy affecting the size and composition of the workforce must target the specific types of employees the organization would like to eliminate or keep. For the most part, organizations choose to retain highly committed, highly motivated, and productive employees and would prefer to lose less committed and less productive employees. How an organization achieves this goal while staying within the limits of the law will be one major focus of this chapter.

Rightsizing the Organization

Over the past three decades people in the United States have witnessed firsthand the cyclical nature of economic forces. In the 1980s numerous layoffs and workforce reductions occurred at U.S. firms, primarily as the firms adjusted to increased global competition. Both academic researchers and the popular press discussed at length the best ways to manage layoffs and the challenges of dealing with the survivors of layoffs. Then, in the 1990s, the economy began to grow at an unprecedented rate, and expert opinion began to focus more on recommendations for recruiting and retaining valuable employees. Then came September 11, 2001, and its aftermath—the economy slowed and workforce reductions began again. By the middle of 2002, the Dow Jones Industrial Average had its sharpest decline since the Great Depression, and layoffs and reductions were again the order of the day. This time, however, most organizations took a more strategic approach than they had in the 1980s, and as a result, many were in a good position to capitalize when markets turned around again (this time in the positive direction in 2006).

Thus, organizations face a real challenge in managing the size of their workforces as a way to deal with their current needs and potential future economic realities. Initially, a firm might react to the need for more workers by asking workers to work overtime, or by hiring temporary or contingent workers as a way of dealing with this uncertainty. These contingent workers help provide a buffer for the organization. When facing declining needs for employees, the organization can simply decide not to renew the contracts of temporary workers or end their relationship with contingent workers in other ways. When facing increasing demand for employees, the organization can increase overtime or hire contingent workers until it determines if it will need more permanent workers. Once the need for permanent employees is established, we must deal with the recruitment and selection issues discussed in the next chapter. This chapter, on the other hand, is more concerned with temporary fixes for increased demand and the special issues that face an organization with declining demands for employees—these are the true focus of any discussion of rightsizing. We begin with an examination of the easiest ways to deal with an increased demand for employees.

Temporary Solutions for Increased Demand for Employees

When an organization anticipates an increased need for employees, it typically begins the process of recruitment, which will lead to new permanent employees. But that process takes time and, in some case, it is not clear if the increased demand for employees will last. For example, if the increased need is part of a growth strategy, it might make sense to invest the time and effort into finding permanent employees. But if the increase in need is the result of unanticipated new demand for products or services, the firm may not wish to hire new employees but may try instead to deal with the need on a temporary basis. This is almost always the solution when the increased need for employees is part of a known cycle (e.g., the demand for employees in the retail industry during November and December). These temporary solutions can range from offering overtime to hiring employees in some context other than permanent employee status, and we will begin with a discussion of the simplest way of dealing with the problem—overtime.

Overtime

The easiest way to deal with a temporary increase in the demand for employees is to offer **overtime,** which simply means asking current workers to put in longer hours. As noted, this alternative is especially beneficial when the increased need for human resources is short term. For example, a manufacturing plant facing a production crunch might ask some of its production workers to work an extra half-day, perhaps on Saturday, for two or three weeks to get the work done.

    This method has two basic advantages. One is that it gives employees the opportunity to earn extra income. Some employees welcome this opportunity and are thankful to the organization for making it available. In addition, it keeps the organization from having to hire and train new employees. Since the existing employees already know how to do their work, the organization does not have to provide them with additional training.

    On the other hand, overtime has some disadvantages. Labor costs per hour are likely to increase. The Fair Labor Standards Act (described earlier in Chapter 2 and discussed further in Chapter 9) stipulates that employees who work over forty hours a week must be compensated at a rate of one and a half times their normal hourly rate. Thus, if an employee is making $10 an hour for a normal workweek, the organization may have to pay that same individual $15 an hour for the extra hours beyond forty each week. Another disadvantage of relying on overtime relates to the potential problems for conflict and/or equity considerations. For example, the organization may not really need all the members of a work group for overtime, and it may face a complicated situation in deciding who gets to work the overtime. Unionized organizations often have contracts that specify the decision rules that must be followed when offering overtime. Yet another problem is the potential for increased fatigue and anxiety on the part of employees, particularly if the overtime is not particularly welcome and if they have to work the overtime for an extended period of time.

    Nonetheless, overtime is often a reasonable solution. For example, Corning has a small ceramics plant in Blacksburg, Virginia. Because the plant is quite small, Corning is reluctant to add new workers whenever production requirements increase temporarily. As a result, the firm routinely offers overtime to its employees. While not everyone is eager to accept this offer, enough employees do accept so that the firm can function effectively. For example, one of its employees, Joe Sizemore, routinely works between sixty and seventy hours a week. He points out that the extra income has allowed him a better life style. Corning, meanwhile, keeps a highly productive worker happy and avoids having to hire a new employee.[2]

Overtime   *refers to hours worked above the normal 40 hour workweek, for which there is usually a pay premium.*

Temporary Workers

Another increasingly popular alternative to hiring permanent employees is a growing reliance on temporary employees. The idea behind temporary employment is that an organization can hire someone for only a specific period of time. A major advantage of temporary employment to the organization is that such workers can usually be paid a lower rate, although they are now more likely to be entitled to the same benefits as full-time workers.[3] Considerable flexibility comes from the fact that employees themselves realize their jobs are not permanent and therefore the organization can terminate their relationship as work demands mandate.[4] On the other hand, temporary employees tend not to understand the organization's culture as well as do permanent employees.

In addition, they are not as likely to be as productive as are permanent full-time employees of the organization.

Employee Leasing

Employee leasing *involves an organization paying a fee to a leasing company that provides a pool of employees who are available on a temporary basis. This pool of employees usually constitutes a group or crew intended to handle all or most of the organization's work needs in a particular area.*

Another increasingly popular alternative to hiring permanent workers is **employee leasing.** In this circumstance the organization pays a fee to a leasing company that provides a pool of employees to the leasing firm. This pool of employees usually constitutes a group or crew intended to handle all or most of the organization's work needs in a particular area. For example, an organization might lease a crew of custodial and other maintenance workers from an outside firm specializing in such services. These workers appear in the organization every day at a predetermined time and perform all maintenance and custodial work. To the general public, they may even appear to be employees of the firm occupying the building. In reality, however, they work for a leasing company.

The basic advantage of this approach to the organization is that it essentially outsources to the leasing firm the human resource elements of recruiting, hiring, training, compensating, and evaluating those employees. On the other hand, because the individuals are not employees of the firm, they are likely to have less commitment and attachment to the organization. In addition, the cost of the leasing arrangement might be a bit higher than if the employees had been hired directly by the firm itself.

Part-time Workers

Part-time workers *refers to those who are regularly expected to work less than forty hours a week. They typically do not receive benefits and they afford the organization a great deal of flexibility in staffing.*

A final alternative to hiring permanent workers is to rely on part-time workers. **Part-time workers** are those individuals who routinely expect to work less than forty hours a week. Among the major advantages of part-time employment is the fact that these employees are usually not covered by benefits, thus lowering labor costs, and the organization can achieve considerable flexibility. That is, the part-time workers are routinely

Firms often find it useful to use part-time workers. This practice provides increased flexibility while also tapping a segment of the labor force that isn't necessarily interested in full-time permanent employment. Dan Young, shown here dipping an ice cream cone, is the co-owner of Young's Dairy, a Midwestern restaurant/ice cream company. At any given time Young's Dairy employs about 300 high school and college students as part-time workers.

called on to work different schedules from week to week, thereby allowing the organization to cluster its labor force around peak demand times and have a smaller staff on hand during down times. Part-time workers are common in organizations like restaurants. Wait staff, bus persons, kitchen help, and other employees of such an organization might be college students who want to work only fifteen or twenty hours a week to earn spending money. Their part-time interest provides considerable scheduling flexibility to the organization that hires them.

Each of the groups of employees described above can be considered part of the *contingent workforce.* The contingent workforce includes all temporary, part-time, and leased employees who are employed by organizations to fill in for permanent employees during times of peak demand. Thus, these contingent workers are considered alternatives to recruiting, but usually as alternatives that are less desirable. Some recent views of staffing take a more strategic perspective, however, and suggest that there may be situations where it would be preferable to hire temporary or contingent workers instead of permanent employees.[5]

   In this view, whenever a firm requires additional human resources who are not related to its core competencies or who are required to have skills or knowledge that is generally available in the marketplace, it may be to the firm's competitive advantage to add resources through some other arrangement besides permanent hires. Yet, eventually, it may become clear that the firm needs to hire more permanent employees and that is the focus of the next chapter. For now, we turn instead to the situation where rightsizing requires the firm to reduce the number of employees.

Dealing with Declining Need for Employees

The discussion thus far has focused on ways of dealing with a temporary increased need for employees. But there are also cases where the organization faces a relatively permanent decrease in the need for employees. In these cases, the exercise of rightsizing really becomes one of downsizing and is much more problematic. However, as we shall see, a number of strategies are available for reducing the size of a workforce as well as increasing it.

Planning for Declines and Early Retirement

When it is possible to plan systematically for a gradual decrease in the workforce, one way to deal with the reduction is through early retirements and natural attrition. That is, in some cases organizations can conduct planning exercises that suggest the need to reduce the size of the workforce over the next few years. This reduction may be due to anticipated changes in technology or customer bases or even to anticipated changes in corporate or business strategies. The organization can attempt to manage the reduction first by simply not replacing workers who leave voluntarily and/or by providing incentives for other employees to retire early.

   Clearly, in any mature organization a certain number of employees will retire every year, and the organization can reduce the size of the workforce by simply not replacing those retired employees. But what if normal retirement rates are not expected to be enough to produce the necessary reductions? In those cases, the organization can offer certain types of incentives to convince some employees to retire earlier than they had planned.

For example, in organizations that have a defined benefit retirement plan (see Chapter 9), the pension that an employee earns at retirement is a function of (among other things) the number of years that person has worked and her or his salary. An organization could simply announce that anyone who is thinking about retiring will automatically have, say, three years added to their years of service if they make a decision to retire by a certain date. As a result, an employee could feel comfortable about retiring three years earlier than he or she had planned. An organization could also increase the rate at which it matches employee contributions to 401(k) plans (also discussed in Chapter 9) or in some other way make it financially more attractive for employees to retire early.

Some organizations plan for early retirement in other ways. For example, for many years IBM provided programs for all new managers in the area of wealth accumulation. That is, the company provides experts who counsel managers on ways to build their personal wealth (i.e., increase their net worth). If there is some pressure on managers to retire early, the company can feel comfortable knowing that those managers will not be hurt by an early retirement. Traditionally IBM also offered retiring managers consulting arrangements in which the managers could be hired on a contingent basis as needed after their retirement.

It is critical to remember, however, that these plans must truly be voluntary or the organization may encounter legal problems. By definition early-retirement plans target older workers, so any attempt—real or perceived—to coerce them into leaving can be construed as age discrimination. As noted in Chapter 2, age discrimination toward older workers is illegal.

Strategies for Layoffs

Early retirement may not always be a sufficient way to reduce the size of an organization's workforce, however. In some situations the need for a reduction may arise too fast to be managed systematically through retirement of employees, or the need may be greater than originally forecasted. In these cases it is usually necessary to reduce the workforce through layoffs.

People often react badly when they are told they will no longer have jobs. Some may decide to sue, for instance. Wrongful termination suits involve employees who believe that the organization acted illegally in terminating the employment relationship. Sometimes these suits revolve around contracts but more often they revolve around potential discrimination. For example, in many cases layoffs tend to have a greater impact on older employees, which can be in violation of the Age Discrimination in Employment Act.

Aside from legal complexities, many employees who have lost their jobs develop negative feelings toward their former employer. These feelings usually manifest themselves through negative comments made to other people or refusing to conduct personal business with their former employer. For example, employees laid off by a struggling retailer such as Kmart may avoid shopping there themselves and they might encourage their families and friends to take all their business to a competitor such as Target or Wal-Mart. Sometimes, tragically, an employee who has been laid off reacts by attacking the manager and/or coworkers perceived to be responsible. Hundreds of such attacks occur each year, and several dozen result in the loss of life. Therefore it is critical that any layoffs be carried out humanely and carefully.

Much of people's reactions to layoffs are determined by perceptions of the justice involved in the layoff process. Three types of justice seem to be related to reactions to layoffs.[6] **Distributive justice** refers to perceptions that the outcomes a person faces are

Distributive justice *refers to perceptions that the outcomes a person faces are fair when compared to the outcomes faced by others.*

fair when compared to the outcomes faced by others. This type of justice is often important in determining an employee's reactions to pay decisions, for example. Most experts believe that these perceptions are based on both the actual outcomes faced (e.g., how much I am paid, whether or not I lose my job) and the perceptions of what others have contributed.[7] For example, a person may be paid less than his coworker, but if he can see that she contributes more to the company than he does and that the difference in the pay is proportional to the difference in contributions each makes, he can still view the outcome as fair. Others argue, however, that unequal outcomes alone lead to perceptions of low distributive justice and when someone loses his or her job and someone else does not, it is difficult to see how this difference in outcome can be linked to differences in contribution.[8]

Nonetheless, someone who loses his or her job may still react reasonably as long as he or she feels that the organization has not also violated another type of justice. **Procedural justice** refers to perceptions that the process used to determine the outcomes was fair. Thus, an employee who loses his or her job may be less angry if everyone in a department also lost their jobs or if layoffs were based on objective and accepted criteria. Several models of procedural justice have been proposed, and these models have yielded the dimensions of procedural justice presented in Table 6.1.

Procedural justice *refers to perceptions that the process used to determine the outcomes was fair.*

It is also clear, however, that an employee (or anyone) will judge a process to be fair when it leads to an outcome that is favorable.[9] This perspective explains why most students generally consider fair tests to be the ones they perform best on. It is also why employees who do not lose their jobs are more likely to view the basis for layoff decisions as being more just (see, however, the discussion on survivor guilt).

Finally, a third dimension of justice, **interactional justice,** refers to the quality of the interpersonal treatment people receive when a decision is implemented.[10] Thus, a person losing his or her job will feel that the decision was more just if the decision is communicated to them in a considerate, respectful, and polite manner. In fact, scholars have proposed more recently that there are two separate dimensions to interactional

Interactional justice *refers to the quality of the interpersonal treatment people receive when a decision is implemented.*

TABLE 6.1   Critical Dimensions of Procedural Justice

Voice: The perception that the person had some control over the outcome, or some voice in the decision.

Consistency: The perception that the rules were applied the same way to everyone involved.

Free from Bias: The perception that the person applying the rules had no vested interest in the outcome of the decision.

Information Accuracy: The perception that the information used to make the decision was accurate and complete.

Possibility of Correction: The perception that some mechanism exists to correct flawed or inaccurate decisions.

Ethicality: The perception that the decision rules conform to personal or prevailing standards of ethics and morality.

Representativeness: The perception that the opinions of the various groups affected by the decision have been considered in the decision.

Source: Adapted from Jason Colquitt, Donald Conlon, Michael Wesson, Christopher Porter, and K. Yee Ng, "Justice at the Millennium: A Meta-Analytic Review of 25 Years of Organizational Justice Research," *Journal of Applied Psychology,* 2001, Vol. 86, pp. 425–445.

justice. The first deals with the extent to which the person was treated with respect and dignity when he or she was told about the decision, while the second refers to the extent to which the decision maker provides information about the decision rules used and how they were applied. These two dimensions have been called interpersonal justice and informational justice, respectively.[11]

The human resource manager who has to deal with layoffs should consider these justice issues. Basically, they suggest that when layoffs are necessary, they should be implemented using a well-formulated strategy that can be communicated to and understood by the employees and that follows the rules implied by the dimensions of procedural justice in Table 6.1. Finally, the decisions should be communicated in a way that conveys respect and caring for the people involved.

Of course, the actual strategy used for determining who will be laid off must also be reasonable. As noted above, a layoff strategy that targets older workers is probably illegal and would rarely be considered as fair. Thus, if layoff decisions are to be made on the basis of seniority, it should be the least senior employees who are let go, even though the most senior employees are probably the highest paid and the organization could thus save the most money if they were no longer employed. Also, layoff decisions are often made on the basis of performance. That is, the organization decides to lay off its poorest performers. But how does an organization decide who are the poorest performers? Typically, this decision is based on past performance appraisals, and we will discuss the important issues associated with performance appraisals in Chapter 10. But performance appraisals are far from perfect (as we shall see in Chapter 9), and they are prone to various biases. When layoff decisions are based on performance ratings, those ratings take on the role of employment tests. In other words, because the organization is making a decision based on the performance ratings, the courts consider the performance ratings to be employment tests. Thus if there is evidence of disparate impact in the layoffs, the organization will need to demonstrate that the performance ratings are job related or valid. This process is not always simple, as we shall discuss below.

Finally, the layoff strategy must also include some plan for callbacks if the demand for labor increases again. For example, will the first to be laid off also be the first to be called back? This option doesn't have to be followed by the organization, but it is most likely to be perceived as a fair strategy. It is also likely that the demand grows in some areas before it does in others, and so callbacks could be based on organizational needs. Decisions must also be made about whether an employee continues to receive benefits when he or she is laid off and how long those benefits last. Thus, a strategy for layoffs must include rules for who is let go as well as rules for who is called back.

Legal Issues in Layoffs

When employees who lose their jobs in a layoff perceive that the decision was unjust (using the rules discussed above), they are more likely to take some type of action. As noted, if the layoff strategy produces some form of disparate impact (i.e., members of protected classes are more likely to lose their jobs), legal actions can become problematic. Decisions to lay off more senior employees cannot be based on stereotypes about older workers and their ability to perform the job. In fact, many advocates of older workers argue that decrements in performance associated with aging actually take place at a much slower rate than most people believe. Therefore, strategies that have a greater impact on older workers are generally difficult to defend. In fact, Storage Technology was sued in late 1990 for age discrimination when employees charged that layoffs were targeted toward employees over the age of forty. The company paid $5 million in a settlement.

Strategies based on performance can also be difficult to defend. We discussed ways to establish the job relatedness of selection techniques, but it is more difficult to establish the job relatedness of a performance appraisal system. As we shall see in Chapter 10, many organizations use a single appraisal instrument to rate all employees. As a result, the content of the appraisal system does not always reflect the nature of the job in question. This method makes a content validity approach difficult. A criterion-related validity approach also requires the organization to demonstrate a relationship between performance ratings and job performance. But job performance is typically measured using performance ratings, so this approach requires the organization to develop a separate measure of job performance to carry out the validation process. If the organization could develop a separate measure of job performance, however, it would probably be using that measure instead of performance ratings. Thus, it is critical for the layoff strategy to appear fair, and to minimize disparate impact to avoid legal problems.

Finally, as noted in Chapter 2, when an organization is about to undertake a large-scale layoff or site closure, it is necessary to announce this step far enough in advance to allow employees (and others) to take some action to adjust to the coming changes. The Worker Adjustment and Retraining Notification (WARN) Act requires at least sixty days' notice for a facility closure or a mass layoff (see Chapter 2 for a more precise definition of *mass layoff*). Failure to provide this notification can result in serious financial penalties, especially for a firm facing pressure to reduce costs. From the organization's perspective, however, some potential costs come with announcing planned layoffs. Once this plan is made known, many employees will seek alternative employment to avoid being out of work (which is the intention of the law). The employees most likely to find alternative employment are the best employees, however, and the firm is most likely to want to retain these employees. It is difficult to balance the requirements of the law (and of the individual employees) with the needs of the organization that desires to retain its top talent. Additional legal issues may arise in the future if the current trend toward exporting jobs to foreign countries continues to expand. This issue is discussed in *HR Around the Globe*.

Is Downsizing Effective?

Given the prevalence of downsizing as a response to pressures to reduce labor costs and make a firm more efficient, it would seem that a lot of support would be forthcoming for the effectiveness of downsizing as a strategy. Why else would so many firms turn to this strategy as a means of becoming more competitive? The data on the effectiveness of downsizing is rather mixed, however, and most of the data suggest that downsizing is *not* an effective strategy.

A major study of the effects of downsizing was conducted in the 1990s.[12] The authors compared several groups of companies that were tracked from 1980 through 1994, but our discussion will focus on only three. "Stable employers" were defined as those firms where changes in employment throughout these years fell between plus and minus 5 percent. (This was the largest group in the study.) "Employment downsizers" were firms where the decline in employment was more than 5 percent during this time *and* the decline in plant and equipment was less than 5 percent during the same period. "Asset downsizers" were defined as firms where the decline in employment was less than 5 percent during this time, but the decline in plant and assets was at least 5 percent greater than the decline in employment. They examined the impact of these strategies over time on two indices of performance: return on assets (a financial index of profitability) and common stock prices. The results are shown in Figure 6.1 on page 188.

As you can see in the figure, employment downsizers had the lowest levels of return on assets over time and also did quite poorly on stock price. In both cases, the asset downsizers produced the greatest performance over the period. Most of the pressure on management to downsize the workforce comes from stockholders, who believe that

HR AROUND THE GLOBE

Exporting Jobs?

 American workers have become used to the fact that large organizations will occasionally downsize their workforce and some people will lose their jobs. But in recent years, workers in the United States have also had to deal with the fact that some of the jobs that are lost are actually being exported to other countries where workers expect and are paid much less than their American counterparts. Quite recently, however, this problem has spread to groups of workers that have not been affected by the exportation of jobs in the past.

Specifically, many Americans are aware of the fact that a person who receives an MBA from a reasonable program can earn a great deal of money. In fact, a typical MBA with three years of experience will earn about $100,000 per year. But, of course, that is for someone who earns an MBA from a school in the United States and who works in the United States. In India, an MBA with three years of work experience earns an average of $12,000 a year. Although this may sound like a good reason to pursue an MBA in the United States, many American workers are finding that this salary differential is turning into a serious disadvantage.

For quite a few years, U.S.- and European-based companies have been exporting low-level manufacturing jobs to Latin America and Asia. Everything from designer polo shirts to cars are often manufactured for U.S. (or European) companies at some offshore location, and then shipped back here for sale. But now, while U.S. companies are continuing to export low-paying, semiskilled jobs overseas, they are also beginning to export white-collar jobs overseas. In 2000, it was estimated that the United States exported white-collar jobs that generated $4 billion in payroll. By the year 2015, it is expected that the United States will export 3.3 million white-collar jobs and $136 billion in wages abroad.

Large U.S. companies are in fact leading this trend, with companies such as IBM, Microsoft, and Procter & Gamble exporting thousands of white-collar jobs to lower-wage markets. The types of jobs that are being exported cover a wide range. As already noted, for instance, manufacturing jobs have been exported for a number of years; in recent years many call center jobs have also been exported overseas. But now, jobs such as financial analysts, architectural drafters, and accountants are being ex-

"By the year 2015, it is expected that the U.S. will export 3.3 million white-collar jobs and $136 billion in wages abroad."

ported as well. For example, data from the Department of Labor indicate that in the year 2000, there were essentially no management jobs being sent overseas but that by 2005 there were almost 40,000 such jobs that have been lost to American workers. This is in addition to the over 100,000 computer jobs and almost 300,000 office jobs exported by 2005. This is outsourcing on a huge global scale, and not surprising, many people are upset about it.

Of course, workers themselves are worried. Halfway through the fiscal year of 2006 the unemployment rate in the United States was about 6 percent, which fueled worker concerns about the loss of their jobs and actually led to higher unemployment rates. Even when companies are growing and can assure workers that exporting some jobs will not affect them in any way, workers worry about the future. Organized labor is also concerned about this trend, which they argue is a threat to the American middle-class workforce. As a result, unions such as the Communications Workers of America have actually called for a congressional investigation into the large-scale exporting of these jobs. It will be interesting to see how this trend and the labor movement's reactions to it might translate to gains in unionization among white-collar workers in the future.

The reason for exporting these jobs is actually quite simple. The wage differentials between workers in the United States and workers in countries such as India are huge. Yet Indian workers are well-educated and highly motivated and, with a little training, can speak colloquial American English quite well. The combination is one that is difficult for many firms to resist. Clearly, if they can provide quality goods and services at a lower cost, they can increase sales and profits as they increase their competitive stance relative to other firms in this country and abroad.

Although some experts claim that the real threat to American jobs is not great and that it will become more apparent as the economy improves, others see it as a real problem and have actually refused to send jobs overseas even though they can save money. It is difficult to see any reason why this trend should slow down in the future, unless there is much more pressure from legislative bodies and groups of workers (organized labor and others). Without such pressure we must assume that the problem will become more serious and we will have to see exactly

(continued)

what the impact is on the American workforce and American economy.

Sources: "USA's New Money-Saving Export: White-Collar Jobs," *USA Today,* August 5, 2003, pp. 1B–2B; *Hoover's Handbook of World Business 2006* (Austin, Tex.: Hoover's Business Press, 2006); Thomas Friedman, *The World is Flat* (New York: Farrar, Strauss & Giroux, 2005).

this method is a good way to cut costs and increase profitability. But the results of this study suggest that firms facing increased competition or some other need to downsize should consider reducing plants and assets rather than their workforce.

Other studies have also reported negative effects on stock prices and other financial indexes as a result of downsizing.[13] Given these findings, why do firms continue to downsize as a reaction to the need to cut costs? Some evidence suggests that, in the short run, the stock market reacts positively to these cuts, and so managers are reinforced for their decisions. But other potential costs, not only potential direct financial costs, are also associated with downsizing.

Earlier in this chapter we emphasized issues that can occur in conjunction with those employees who lose their jobs in a layoff, but issues related to those who avoid losing their jobs in the layoff also crop up. A phenomenon known as *survivor syndrome* can counteract many of the presumed cost savings that led to the layoffs in the first place.[14] This syndrome describes employees who feel guilty over keeping their jobs (that is, they survived) when others lost their jobs. Their morale and commitment to the organization drops dramatically. In fact, according to a study of firms implementing layoffs through the 1990s, almost 70 percent of the human resource managers surveyed reported declines in employee morale, more than 40 percent reported increased voluntary turnover, and over 10 percent reported an increase in disability claims—all within the first year of the layoff.[15] These data may underestimate the total costs of increased layoffs. As discussed in *HR in the 21st Century* on page 200, evidence suggests that the increasing rates of layoffs and the resulting joblessness are causing serious emotional problems for employees—both those actually affected by layoffs and those who think they *might* be affected by layoffs.

Given these data, we must close with a discussion of some alternatives to layoffs as ways of reducing costs. Downsizing the number of employees is a tangible way of demonstrating that a firm is serious about cutting costs, but as noted, it may not be the most effective. Reducing assets is an alternative. This could include reducing investments in new machinery, stretching out maintenance schedules for equipment, or actually getting out of some lines of business. Although closing plants will also result in job loss, a firm might be able to sell some of its less productive assets. Thus, some alternatives to layoffs may also result in job loss, but that outcome isn't a foregone conclusion. Some firms find even more productive ways to reduce costs. Some years ago, one of the authors of this textbook learned about a DuPont plant that was facing layoffs or closure because of high labor costs. The plant manager (subsequently promoted several times) asked the employees to get involved in the decision about reducing costs. The employees suggested a combination of job sharing, salary reductions (the plant was nonunion), early-retirement plans, and part-time work, which resulted in almost no employees losing their jobs. At the same time, the plant became extremely profitable and the employees developed a loyalty to the company that was the envy of the manufacturing sector.

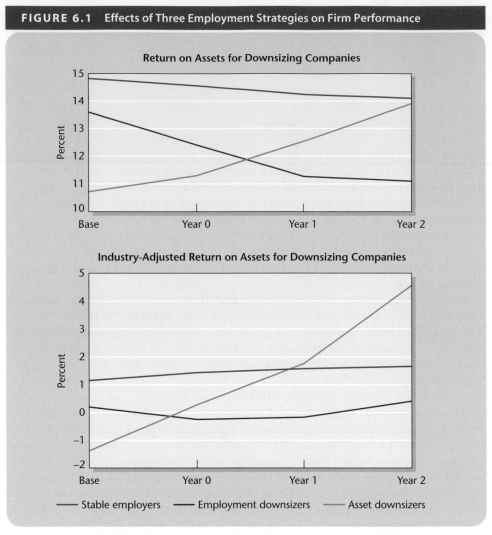

FIGURE 6.1   Effects of Three Employment Strategies on Firm Performance

Source: Wayne Cascio, Clifford Young, and James Morris, "Financial Consequences of Employment Change Decisions in Major U.S. Corporations," from *Academy of Management Journal,* 1997, Vol. 40, pp. 1175–1189. Copyright © 1997 by Academy of Management. Reprinted by permission of Academy of Management via Copyright Clearance Center.

Termination

Rightsizing or downsizing refers to strategies designed to reduce the overall size of the workforce. The size of the workforce can also be reduced in other ways. Later, we shall talk about the voluntary turnover problem, where (presumably) valuable employees decide to leave the organization and seek employment elsewhere. But sometimes the organization wants to sever the employment relationship, not with a large number of employees but with specific employees. We turn our attention now to the various issues involved in terminating employees whose services are no longer desired—also known as involuntary turnover.

Managing Involuntary Turnover

Effective human resource practices are supposed to ensure that most employees perform their job satisfactorily. Recruitment and selection practices are aimed at attracting people who can perform the jobs to which they are assigned, and training and development activities are designed to achieve the same goals. Nonetheless, sometimes an employee is simply not performing up to acceptable standards or presents enough of a disciplinary problem that he or she must be terminated.

Anytime an employee is terminated, however, it represents a failure of some part of the human resource system. It can also be costly because the firm must then seek to recruit, hire, and train a replacement. Therefore, in all the situations we will describe in this section, we should view termination as the last resort. Before terminating an employee, we must try everything reasonable to salvage the situation. These attempts begin with trying to ascertain the reasons for poor performance.

The most common reason for an employee failing to perform up to standard is that the employee simply does not know how or cannot perform at that level. It may be a problem due to a lack of ability, for example. That is, the employee should never have been hired for the job because he or she is simply not capable of performing it effectively. A simple example would be the case where someone was hired to be a reporter but he or she cannot write effectively. The original decision to hire the person was an error, and in such cases it is in everyone's best interests for the employee to leave the company or to be reassigned to another job.

In other cases, the person might have the potential to perform effectively but he or she was never properly trained. Perhaps the training program was ineffective or the employee has never been properly supervised. In these cases, a lot can be done to bring the employee's performance up to standard, such as retraining or reassignment to a supervisor who is better at developing employees.

In still other cases, the employee may be suffering from various physical or psychological problems. Perhaps the employee is suffering from too much stress on the job or outside the job. It is also possible that the employee is suffering from severe psychological problems or is abusing drugs or alcohol. Finally, it is possible that the employee is suffering from a physical ailment that is interfering with work. Obviously, in each of these cases the organization should seek to help the employee deal with the problems.

Most organizations have some type of employee assistance program (EAP) designed either to help the employee directly or to refer the employee to competent professionals who can provide that help. Originally, many EAPs focused on alcoholism, but more recently they have expanded to deal with drugs and more general problems of mental health.[16] Considerable evidence suggests that effective EAPs can help employees and reduce the costs associated with lost workdays and poor productivity.[17] These plans can also save costs by serving as gatekeepers for employee health plans because they determine what types of services are best suited for each employee.[18] But, more important, these programs make it possible for potentially valuable employees to be brought back to productive levels, thus ensuring their continued employment and yielding savings for the organization.

In still other cases, poor performance is due to motivational problems, not to personal or ability problems. For whatever reasons, the employee chooses not to perform at expected levels, even though he or she is capable of doing so. In such cases, organizations typically resort to some type of disciplinary action in an attempt to convince the employee to improve his or her performance.

Progressive Discipline

Most organizations try to correct problems of poor performance (broadly defined to include tardiness, absenteeism, dishonesty, or any other problems on the job) through the use of punishment. **Punishment** simply refers to following unacceptable behavior with some type of negative consequences. **Discipline** refers to the system of rules and

Punishment *simply refers to following unacceptable behavior with some type of negative consequences.*

Discipline *refers to the system of rules and procedures for how and when that punishment is administered and how severe the punishment should be.*

procedures for how and when that punishment is administered and how severe the punishment should be. Note that in all cases the goal of the disciplinary program is to convince the employee to stop the ineffective or undesired behavior and to engage in more accepted or desired behavior. As we shall discuss a bit later, some have argued that disciplinary programs may be effective at getting the employee to drop the undesired behavior, but they are generally less effective at getting the employee to adopt more desired behavior.

Progressive disciplinary plans *are organizational disciplinary programs where the severity of the punishment increases over time or across the problem.*

We refer to these programs as **progressive disciplinary plans** because, almost invariably, the severity of the punishment increases over time or across the seriousness of the problem. (We will define each of the steps in more detail below.) For example, if an employee is late for work one day, a supervisor may simply issue a verbal warning. After several more infractions, the supervisor might issue a written warning, which will be added to the employee's personnel file. Continued tardiness could result in suspension and eventually in dismissal or termination. Other types of problems, however, might incur more severe penalties from the outset. For example, it is common in manufacturing facilities to have rules about sleeping on the job. The penalty for an infraction is always quite severe, but in many organizations an additional distinction is made. If an employee simply falls asleep at his or her workstation, the penalty might be two weeks' suspension without pay for the first infraction. But if the employee "makes a bed"— that is, the employee leaves the workstation and lies down to sleep somewhere else—the penalty is immediate dismissal for the first infraction.

What types of problems can be specified in a disciplinary program? Typical examples are provided in Table 6.2. Each infraction, as well as the schedule of penalties, should be spelled out clearly to employees, both in the form of an employee handbook and orally at employee orientation. Whatever the infractions, the steps in the disciplinary process are almost always the same.

TABLE 6.2 Typical Disciplinary Problems	
Problems with performance	▪ Failure to complete work on time
	▪ Errors in work products
	▪ Work products that do not meet established tolerances
Problems with attendance	▪ Repeated unexcused absences
	▪ Tardiness
	▪ Leaving work early
Problems with ethics or honesty	▪ Taking credit for the work of others
	▪ Falsifying records
	▪ Soliciting and/or accepting bribes or kickbacks
Other behavior problems	▪ Gambling
	▪ Vandalism
	▪ Use of drugs or alcohol on the job
	▪ Sexual harassment
Problems that could lead to immediate termination	▪ Major theft
	▪ Sleeping on the job
	▪ Selling narcotics on the job

The first step in most progressive disciplinary programs is verbal warning. **Verbal warnings** are cautions conveyed to the employee orally rather than in writing. The supervisor or manager should keep a written record of the fact that a verbal warning was given to document the fact that all required steps were taken in dealing with an employee. **Written warnings** are more formal and are the second step in the process. Here, the supervisor gives the warning to the employee in writing and provides a copy to the human resource department. As a result, a written warning becomes part of the employee's permanent record.

At each of these steps, the manager should discuss with the employee ways for the employee to correct the problem. In some cases this discussion might be quite simple, but in others it might include a recommendation that the employee seek additional help such as referral to the EAP. **Suspension,** or a temporary layoff, is the next step in the process. The suspension could last a day or a few weeks; it is rare for a suspension to last as long as a month. In some cases, the employee is suspended with pay, but this step is usually taken when an ongoing investigation involves the employee, such as the case where the employee is charged with theft. More typically, suspension is without pay. This step is meant to impress on the employee the organization's willingness to punish the infraction involved. The final step in the process is **termination**. At this point, the organization faces potential legal problems as well as potentially violent reactions by the employee. This final step should be taken only after serious consideration and the decision that the employee is not salvageable.

> **Verbal warnings,** *the first step in most progressive disciplinary programs, are cautions conveyed orally to the employee.*
>
> **Written warnings** *are the second step in most progressive disciplinary programs. Warnings are given to the employee in writing and become part of the employee's permanent record.*
>
> **Suspension,** *as part of a progressive disciplinary program, is a temporary layoff, usually with pay, while there is an ongoing investigation.*
>
> **Termination,** *as part of progressive disciplinary program, is an act by the organization to end the employment relationship.*

Employment-at-Will

It is not always easy to terminate an employee, no matter how problematic he or she may be. Considerable publicity has surrounded the issue of employees suing organizations for wrongful termination, and so you might suspect that the formal law dealing with this issue is quite complicated. It might be surprising, therefore, to learn that the only real legal perspective on employee termination is a nineteenth-century common-law rule known as **employment-at-will.** Basically, this view asserts that, because an employee can terminate an employment relationship at any time (i.e., quit a job), the employer should have similar rights. Therefore, employment-at-will states that an employer can terminate any employee, at any time, for any reason (good or bad), or for no reason at all. This view differs dramatically from the situation in many European countries, where employees can be terminated for criminal behavior only.[19]

> **Employment-at-will** *states that an employer can terminate any employee, at any time, for any reason (good or bad), or for no reason at all.*

In the United States companies are relatively free to terminate employees anytime they wish; thus, in most cases the employee has no legal recourse if he or she is terminated. Several important exceptions to the employment-at-will doctrine exist. These exceptions define situations where an employee who was discharged can sue for wrongful termination and thus get his or her job back. These exceptions are important to keep in mind and are presented in Table 6.3.

The first exception is the existence of a law forbidding termination for a specific reason. For example, it would be a violation of the Civil Rights Act to terminate an employee because he or she is an African-American, and it is a violation of the Taft-Hartley Act to terminate an employee because he or she advocated joining a labor union. Most regulations dealing with the workplace also forbid termination of employees who are whistle blowers. That is, a firm cannot dismiss an employee because he or she informs the government or law enforcement agencies about a violation that has occurred in the company.

Another exception exists when someone has a contractual right to his or her job. Therefore, an organization cannot terminate someone with a valid contract (unless the organization is willing to pay off the contract). Following this logic, in some cases, courts have actually stated that some employees are protected because they have an implied

TABLE 6.3   Exceptions to the Doctrine of Employment-at-Will

1. **The Termination Would Violate a Specific Law:** Various laws forbid termination for a specific reason. Some of the most common reasons are termination based on gender or race (violates the Civil Rights Act) or termination because of union activity (violates the Taft-Hartley Act).

2. **The Employee Has a Contractual Right to His or Her Job:** The contract might be a formal contract or an implied contract guaranteeing or implying a guarantee of employment.

3. **The Employee's Rights of Due Process Have Been Violated:** For example, if an employee is accused of theft, the employee has the right to know of the charges and to refute those charges—in a court of law if necessary.

4. **Public-Policy Exception:** This exception has been less common but involves cases where an employee is discharged for refusing to commit a crime or for reporting a crime or unethical or unsafe behavior on the part of the organization. Thus, whistle blowers are protected under this exception.

5. **Breach-of-Good-Faith Exception:** The most difficult exception to establish because it involves a breach of promise, such as terminating an employee to avoid promised commissions or bonuses.

Note: These exceptions have been cited in various court cases, but there is no guarantee that any specific state will recognize any one of these exceptions in its jurisdiction.

contract. An implied contract might exist, for example, if a contract employee had his or her contract renewed every year for the past twelve years and was told that his or her performance was good, but he or she was still terminated. It is also possible for a discussion about an annual salary to be construed as an implied contract for one year. In one of the more interesting cases, an employee sued after being terminated, asserting that he had been promised he could remain with the company until retirement as long as his performance was satisfactory.[20] Since his subsequent dismissal was not for cause (e.g., poor performance), the court ruled that it was improper, and the employee was given his job back.

Another exception exists when a person's rights to due process have been violated. Most often, this situation means that the organization has failed to follow all the steps in its progressive disciplinary program before terminating the employee. This situation explains why it is so critical that managers and supervisors follow all the steps in the disciplinary process and document the fact that each step has been followed.

Yet another exception that has been used in some cases is the public-policy exception. Under this exception, an organization cannot terminate an employee because of failure to obey an order that could be considered illegal or because of failure to take a bribe, even though the company may lose important business. In one case, a nurse at a plant in South Carolina was terminated because she complained that the company was pressuring her to send injured workers back to work before they were ready. The court found that the company's behavior was a public-policy violation because it would be better for society if organizations did *not* try to force injured workers back to their jobs prematurely.

Finally, a breach-of-good-faith exception is the most difficult to prove because it involves a breach of promise. In one of the best-known cases, an employee claimed that he was terminated after twenty-five years of employment so that the company could avoid paying him his sales commission.[21]

These exceptions vary so much from state to state that it is easier for employers to terminate an employee in some states than it is others. In any case, the exceptions to the employment-at-will doctrine signify a substantial limit on the organization's ability to terminate employees. It is important to note that, even with these exceptions, employers can terminate employees for cause. That is, if the employee violates a rule or is a poor performer, he or she can always be terminated.

The key to successful termination of an employee is documentation. An organization can terminate any employee at any time, but if the employee claims that the termination was wrong, the employer may have to prove otherwise. If an employee is dismissed for poor performance, it may be necessary to document that most (if not all) of the employee's recent performance appraisals were poor or below standard. If in fact the employee has received generally acceptable evaluations, it will be extremely difficult to terminate the employee for poor performance. Thus, supervisors must understand that if they give overly lenient ratings to a poor employee, the employee cannot be terminated later.

If an employee is terminated because of a rule violation, a written record should be made of all the steps taken along the way. If the company has a progressive disciplinary program, it will be necessary to prove that each step was followed before the employee was terminated. If an employee is terminated because of theft, the organization must prove that an honest investigation was held and that clear evidence demonstrated the employee's guilt before he or she was terminated.

If an employer does not follow the proper steps and document each one, the employee may well get his or her job back. This situation may be annoying to the employer, but it is actually far more serious than annoyance. Progressive discipline can work only if the employee truly believes that he or she will be fired without improvement in performance. If the threat of termination is not a credible one, either because procedures were not followed correctly or because of some other reason (perhaps the employee is a civil-service employee), it is extremely difficult to correct a problem employee. The credible threat of termination is actually an important part of the process through which an organization can turn a poorly performing employee into a productive one.

Some organizations have begun to adopt an approach referred to as positive discipline, which has a somewhat different orientation.[22] This approach integrates discipline with performance management. (We will discuss this more fully in Chapter 14.) Positive discipline emphasizes positive changes rather than punishment. Typically, the process is still somewhat progressive in nature, with warnings leading to eventual termination if the problem is not corrected. The major difference, however, is that a great deal of counseling and problem solving are integral to the process. Therefore, the employee is given as much help as is reasonable to help him or her identify the behaviors desired by the organization and to eliminate undesirable behaviors.

As we noted at the beginning of this section, most discipline systems have the following shortcoming: they can help eliminate undesired behavior but they do not help the employee to understand what he or she should be doing instead. Thus, positive discipline seems to represent a real advantage over more traditional systems. It is not clear, however, whether the performance management aspect of the system needs to be an integral part of the disciplinary system or it can work just as well on its own. In any case, aligning disciplinary practices with performance management may be an important approach to remember.

Employee Retention

Thus far, we have discussed ways to temporarily increase the size of the workforce, as well as ways to decrease the size of the workforce, but there is another aspect of right-sizing that we must discuss as well. We just discussed the case where the employee does not necessarily want to leave the organization, but the organization no longer wants to retain the employee either because of excess labor supply or because of poor performance. Managing the flow of human resources would be relatively easy if the only employees who left were the people we wanted to see leave and who left when it was most convenient for the organization. But, sometimes, employees who we would like to retain take matters into their own hands and make their own decisions to leave the organization. Employees might decide to leave perhaps because of a better offer, a spouse's job, or a sick parent. In some of these cases, the human resource manager can do little. But, in many cases, employees leave voluntarily because they are unhappy with some aspect of their working environment.

Interestingly, one of the authors of this book works at a university in New Orleans where this problem was played out in a rather dramatic fashion. Following Hurricane Katrina and the breaching of the New Orleans levee system (in August 2005), the university had to close for a semester and it lost a great deal of money. When the university was ready to reopen, it became clear that it would be necessary to reduce the size of the staff (and the faculty) in order to survive. Deans and heads of programs were therefore asked to determine what staff positions were critical for the future of the university and to prioritize layoffs among the remainder of the staff. Lists of potential layoffs were thus generated across the university, and hundreds of staff members were scheduled to lose their jobs. But no one really understood the situation from the perspective of the staff employees. Many of them had been forced to evacuate New Orleans and they had to enroll their children in schools in other cities. Many of them had lived in areas that had been flooded and could not be rebuilt in time to return to work in January 2006. Still others had found jobs elsewhere or had spouses who had found jobs elsewhere and were not planning to return to New Orleans. As a result, hundreds of staff employees voluntarily left their jobs. Unfortunately, these were often not the same people whom the university had planned to lay off. Instead, these were valued employees whose jobs were critical to the future of the organization. As a result, all the planned layoffs had to be canceled (with a few exceptions), and the university had to scramble to make sure that all critical positions were filled.

This experience illustrated, quite graphically, that there are two sides to every rightsizing exercise—the termination of employees who are no longer needed, and the retention of those employees who are still needed, and who may become even more critical in the light of planned layoffs. Therefore we turn our attention now to the problems of retaining valued employees. These strategies are always important if the firm hopes to gain competitive advantage through its human resources, but they are especially critical as part of any rightsizing.

Managing Voluntary Turnover

As noted, managers cannot always control who leaves the organization or why they leave, but they should not assume that all turnover is negative, even in the case of voluntary turnover. In fact, although the organization does not want to force someone out, management may not be totally disappointed that the person left, and a certain amount of voluntary turnover is probably healthy for the organization.[23] Yet it is important to manage this turnover as much as possible. High rates of turnover cost the organization a great deal in terms of the expense associated with employee replacement, and such turnover can hurt the organization's reputation as a good place to work. Some of the positive and negative aspects of turnover are discussed in this chapter's *Point/Counterpoint* feature.

To manage turnover, it is important to understand why people leave. A major cause for turnover is **job dissatisfaction,** or being unhappy with one's job.[24] We will discuss some causes for job dissatisfaction later in the chapter (we will also discuss some additional consequences of dissatisfaction later in the chapter), but for now it is enough to say that the human resource manager plays a major role in ensuring that employees remain reasonably satisfied with their jobs. It is also the role of human resources to help reduce turnover and retain valued employees. As we shall see, job dissatisfaction is often the key to turnover. Different views explain why dissatisfied workers decide to leave.

> **Job dissatisfaction** *is the feeling of being unhappy with one's job. It is a major cause of voluntary turnover.*

Models of the Turnover Process

The basic reason why people leave their jobs is because they are unhappy with them. Thus, the simplest view of the employee turnover process would suggest that, if we increase job satisfaction, we will decrease turnover. Although this basic view is correct, the processes involved are somewhat more complex.

POINT | COUNTERPOINT

Employee Retention

 We usually assume that an effective human resource manager works to retain employees who are performing well. We also assume that poor performers are given enticements to leave and that it is desirable to retain all other employees. But this situation is not always clear, and there are some arguments for not retaining employees who might be interested in leaving.

POINT... **Organizations should seek to retain employees because...**	COUNTERPOINT... **Organizations should not seek to retain employees because...**
It is expensive to replace employees.	Keeping dissatisfied employees can cost more if they "infect" other employees.
High turnover reduces general morale in the organization.	Morale could go up if troublesome employees leave.
Experienced employees are better able to contribute to the organization.	New employees can bring fresh ideas to the organization.
A shortage of qualified employees can result in decreased efficiency.	Turnover creates new opportunities for advancement for those who stay.

So... The key is to manage the turnover process because some turnover is definitely healthy for the organization. Of course, some employees are more difficult to replace than others, but a certain amount of turnover ensures that new ideas can be introduced into the organization.

First, the economy and the labor market play a role. It has been noted that the prevailing unemployment rate is as big a factor in whether or not a person leaves a job as is the level of dissatisfaction.[25] Clearly, this explanation makes a great deal of sense. Even if an employee is extremely dissatisfied, he or she is not likely to quit without real prospects of finding another job.

Recognizing this fact, several turnover models emphasize the role of dissatisfaction in the decision to look for alternatives, and it is seen as a necessary (but not sufficient) first step in the decision to quit. At least two major streams of research have proposed models incorporating these ideas, and the basic concepts of these models are present in Figure 6.2.[26] As you can see in the figure, the process begins with factors leading to job dissatisfaction (which will be discussed below). Job dissatisfaction causes the employee to begin thinking about quitting, which leads to a search for alternatives. Only if those alternatives look better does the employee decide that he or she will quit, a decision first manifested by an intention to quit.

Of course, the implication of this type of model is that managers should reduce the sources of job dissatisfaction. It is best to stop the turnover before the employee begins searching for alternatives because he or she might find an alternative that is more attractive. Once an employee begins searching for alternatives, it may still be possible to retain the employee by convincing him or her that the present job really is better than the alternatives. In fact, the search for alternatives sometimes leads to increased satisfaction on the present job after the employee discovers that the alternatives were not as positive as once believed.

Other models have proposed similar mechanisms but have also suggested that job dissatisfaction must reach a critical level before anything happens and, at that point, it may be too late to do anything. In other words, this approach suggests that, as levels of job dissatisfaction increase, there is little change in the employee's intentions to leave.

FIGURE 6.2   A Model of the Turnover Process

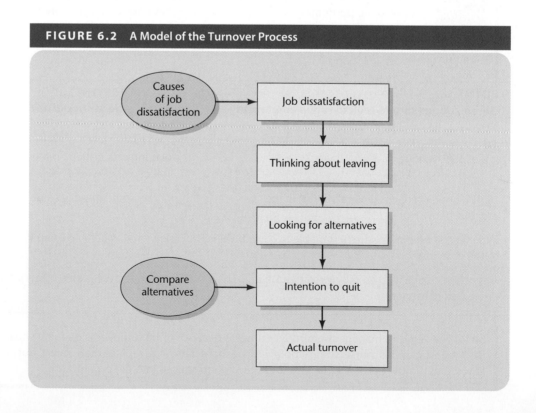

Those levels of job dissatisfaction finally reach a critical level, however, and the intention to leave becomes so strong that the employee is almost guaranteed to leave.[27]

Another interesting model that deviates a bit from the basic model in Figure 6.2 revolves around the notion of "shocks" to the individual.[28] First, this model proposes that several paths can lead to turnover, and they do not all require shocks. Nonetheless, the major focus is on a shock—an event that can be either positive or negative but is so profound that it causes the employee to think about the organization, the job, and how he or she fits with both. This model begins with shock and not with job dissatisfaction. In fact, the dissatisfaction occurs only because the employee started thinking about the job in response to the shock. The decision to leave is largely based on the perception that the employee does not really fit with the company—that is, the present job in the present company is not consistent with the image the employee has of him- or herself. In some cases, the employee will leave without even considering alternatives, but in all cases the decision to leave takes place over time.

The model includes other aspects of cognitive processing, but the shocks include events such as winning the lottery or losing a loved one, as well as job-related events such as missing a promotion or receiving an offer from another company. This model has interesting implications for understanding how difficult it is to manage the turnover process, but recently the authors of the model have added one more wrinkle. Although the model was originally proposed as a way of understanding why people leave their jobs, it can also help understand why others stay. The notion of **job embeddedness** has been proposed as an explanation for why some people stay on their jobs, even when they decide they are unhappy and should leave.[29] Some employees are simply tied too strongly to their jobs to leave. Perhaps they are deeply involved in the neighborhood, or perhaps they cannot sell their houses. Whatever the reason, they feel that they cannot quit. These employees may be quite unhappy, which can cause resulting problems. This state is not always a desirable state. Nonetheless, the notion of job embeddedness adds a great deal to our potential understanding of the turnover process.

Job embeddedness *refers to the fact that some people stay on their jobs, even when they decide they are unhappy and should leave. Other ties in the community or obligations keep the employee on the job.*

The Causes of Job Dissatisfaction

A common thread in these models of the turnover process is job dissatisfaction. Wherever and however in the process the dissatisfaction occurs, reducing job dissatisfaction is likely to reduce turnover. Therefore it is important to understand the causes of job dissatisfaction. Although most of the sources of job dissatisfaction that have been studied are related to the job, some of the more creative approaches have focused on factors that have little or nothing to do with the job.

One interesting line of research has focused on the study of pairs of identical twins. Identical twins are a useful source of data because they are identical genetically, although they may well work at very different types of jobs. In one particular study, the authors found that identical twins reported quite similar levels of job satisfaction, regardless of the jobs they had. Although the authors have interpreted their results with due caution, these results raise the distinct possibility that a certain component of job satisfaction may be genetic.[30]

Others have proposed a similar but less radical approach, suggesting that some individuals are simply disposed toward being satisfied, while others are disposed toward being dissatisfied. Thus, they argue that individuals differ in their tendencies to be happy and unhappy and, although conditions on the job play a role, these tendencies are potentially as important in determining the levels of job dissatisfaction an employee will experience and report.[31] As a result, for some individuals, the organization can do little to make them happy; for other individuals, the organization can do little

When she was attending Princeton, Gretchen Tonnesen was captain of the school's rugby team. She loved the competitiveness and the rush she got when she succeeded. A knee injury ended her athletic career, but she has found the same excitement as a Wall Street broker with JP Morgan. She loves going to work each day and is on the fast track toward career advancement. And she credits, in part, her athletic activities for helping her understand what she wanted from her work as she was selecting the right job offer.

that will make them unhappy. More typical approaches to job dissatisfaction, however, tend to focus on job-related factors.

Nature of the work   One of the most important sources of dissatisfaction on the job is the nature of the work that a person does.[32] For example, a consistent relationship exists between job complexity (and job challenge) and job satisfaction such that employees with more complex and challenging jobs are more satisfied. We will discuss how jobs can be redesigned to make them more motivating and satisfying in Chapter 14.

In addition, job satisfaction tends to be higher when the job is less physically demanding. We don't want to suggest that a boring job is preferred—quite the contrary—but a job that requires constant physical exertion and strain tends to lower levels of job satisfaction. Also, jobs that help employees achieve something of value tend to result in higher levels of job satisfaction. That is, if an employee feels that he or she is accomplishing some good on the job, satisfaction tends to be higher. In addition, if an employee values status, and a job provides him or her with more status, levels of satisfaction are also likely to be higher.[33]

Pay and benefits   Perhaps not surprisingly an employee's level of satisfaction on the job is affected by the extent to which the employee is satisfied with pay and benefits. In general, higher levels of pay and more attractive benefits tend to result in greater satisfaction, and we will discuss issues of both compensation and benefits in Chapter 9. But other considerations also determine satisfaction with pay. Earlier in the chapter, we discussed issues of fairness and justice relative to decisions about laying off employees. We noted that distributive justice was concerned with the level of outcomes received, and although we discussed processes underlying distributive justice perceptions earlier, we need to elaborate a bit on those perceptions now.

An important factor in determining satisfaction with an outcome such as pay is what other people are making, and not just anyone, but other employees who are at similar levels in the organization. In fact, the models of distributive justice suggest that we compare our pay with another "comparison person." We note not only what each of us makes but also what we make relative to what we contribute. Contributions might include years on the job, education, performance, or some combination of these and other factors. We assess our own contributions relative to what we are paid. And we compare the ratio of contribution to pay to the contributions that our comparison person makes relative to his or her pay. Note that we are making all the judgments, and the judgments may be incorrect. Nonetheless, if our input/outcome ratio (the ratio of contribution to pay) is the same (or better) than the comparison person's ratio, we will be satisfied with our pay. If our ratio is not high, then we will be dissatisfied. These ideas will also be explored in more depth in Chapter 13.

Supervisors and coworkers   Supervisors and coworkers represent two additional potential sources of job dissatisfaction. An employee may be satisfied (or dissatisfied) with coworkers for several reasons. An important one is that the employee believes that he or she shares certain values and attitudes with coworkers. This perception that everyone has some shared vision of the world and can work together as a team is an important determinant of job satisfaction.[34] Clearly, the impression that coworkers do not share values and attitudes can lead to dissatisfaction. In addition, coworkers can be seen as sources of social support, which can also lead to increased job satisfaction.

Employees can be satisfied with supervisors for many of the same reasons. That is, shared values and social support can be important determinants of satisfaction with a supervisor as well as with a coworker. In addition, an employee can be satisfied (or dissatisfied) with a supervisor's leadership ability. How a supervisor leads (i.e., his or her leadership style) and the effectiveness of the work group are important determinants of satisfaction with the supervisor.[35]

Each of these sources of job dissatisfaction can be measured and thought of independently or as part of a whole. That is, studying and considering satisfaction with pay in its own right has some value, while others consider it simply as one source of overall satisfaction with the job. We will return to this issue below when we discuss methods of measuring satisfaction. Before turning to that topic, however, we turn our attention to some of the outcomes of dissatisfaction on the job.

The Effects of Job Dissatisfaction

We began our discussion of job satisfaction by noting that it is a major determinant of voluntary turnover and thus our major reason for discussing job satisfaction, but it is worth noting that job dissatisfaction can have other negative effects. Furthermore, some of these effects are related to topics we will discuss later in the text.

For now our primary concern with job dissatisfaction is that it leads to increased voluntary turnover. As noted earlier, job dissatisfaction is a major determinant of turnover, but it is also predictive of other types of withdrawal behavior. For example, a strong relationship exists between job dissatisfaction and absenteeism.[36] Part of this relationship is due to the fact that employees who are dissatisfied may not always be able to leave their jobs (because of a lack of alternatives), and so they choose to withdraw partially, by being absent. In addition, it is possible to withdraw even more gradually (or partially) by simply being late. *HR in the 21st Century* presents an interesting view

HR IN THE 21ST CENTURY

Absenteeism as an Entitlement

Earlier in the chapter, we discussed the notion of distributive justice; that is, people must believe they are getting their fair share in any relationship. As organizations become leaner through downsizing, however, they are forced to do more with fewer employees. As a result, some companies are cutting back on vacations and paid sick days. In fact, a survey conducted by the Society for Human Resource Management indicates that the number of firms that offer paid vacations and personal days is steadily declining. Moreover, some evidence also suggests that more companies are telling employees that if they don't use their vacation days by the end of the fiscal year, they will forfeit those days.

One result of the various trends and policies is a sharp increase in unscheduled absenteeism. In fact, evidence suggests that just as "legitimate" time off is decreasing, unscheduled absenteeism and its associated costs are increasing. There is reason to believe that employees feel they are entitled to these extra days off because the company has not kept its end of the bargain or because of the

> *"Employers have gotten stingier about [granting] time off, so people are thinking, 'I'll take it anyway.'"*
>
> (Jennifer Gwaltney, laid-off conference planner in Virginia Beach, Virginia)

extra stress at work. Unscheduled absences because of personal reasons rose 21 percent in one recent year alone, and 20 percent of employees in another recent poll indicated that they have tried to take more vacation days than they were entitled to.

Although these trends may simply be a different manifestation of job dissatisfaction, they seem to go beyond that simple explanation. Employees feel that they are being shortchanged by their employers and that those employers are too demanding. One of the few ways they can seek to restore equity without losing their jobs is to be absent. Should organizations clamp down even tighter or should they allow this form of equity restoration? What would be the consequences if employees did not feel they could take this time off? This issue will remain an interesting challenge for human resource managers over the next few years.

Sources: Stephanie Armour, "Faced with Less Time Off, Workers Take More," *USA Today,* October 29, 2002, p. 1A; Ricky Griffin and Gregory Moorhead, *Organizational Behavior,* 8th Ed. (Boston: Houghton Mifflin, 2007).

---

of the causes of absenteeism—a view that considers several issues discussed elsewhere in this chapter.

A more subtle form of withdrawal that doesn't involve being away from the job is a reduction of commitment to the organization. **Organizational commitment** is the degree to which an employee identifies with an organization and is willing to exert effort on behalf of the organization.[37] Employees lacking organizational commitment are excellent candidates for turnover when a workable alternative presents itself. They are also unlikely to exert extra effort or even to encourage others to join the organization.

Dissatisfied employees are also more likely to join unions. Several studies support this relationship and, although the process of joining a union is fairly complex, job dissatisfaction has consistently been found to be a good predictor of who joins unions.[38] We will discuss the implications of this relationship in more detail in Chapter 11.

Finally, dissatisfied employees are less likely to engage in behaviors on the job known broadly as organizational citizenship behaviors,[39] sometimes called contextual performance.[40] **Organizational citizenship behaviors (OCBs)** include those behaviors that are beneficial to the organization but are not formally required as part of an employee's job. These behaviors include activities such as volunteering to carry out extra tasks, helping and cooperating with others, following rules even when such behavior is inconvenient, and endorsing and supporting organizational goals. We will discuss contextual performance further in the next chapter, but clearly the organization benefits when employees engage in these types of behavior, and dissatisfied employees are simply less likely to do so.

Organizational commitment *is the degree to which an employee identifies with an organization and is willing to exert effort on behalf of the organization.*

Organizational citizenship behaviors (OCBs) *include employee behaviors that are beneficial to the organization but are not formally required as part of an employee's job.*

In addition, considerable evidence suggests that job dissatisfaction imposes a different type of cost on an organization. Job dissatisfaction has been found to be strongly linked to stress (discussed more fully in Chapter 12), job burnout (the condition of physical, emotional, and mental exhaustion on the job[41]), and (through the first two processes) employee health.[42] Thus, happier workers are healthier workers. Dissatisfied employees are more likely to be absent for health reasons.

The most intriguing possibility, however, is the link between job satisfaction and productivity. The notion that happy workers may be productive workers has attracted scholars for almost 100 years. Although there are cases where performance and satisfaction have common determinants, and even cases where the most productive employees are also the most satisfied, no consistent causal relationship between job satisfaction and performance has been found. Thus, higher levels of job satisfaction do not necessarily lead to higher levels of performance, and an organization should not target increases in job satisfaction in the hope of raising productivity.

Measuring and Monitoring Job Satisfaction

As should be clear by now, job satisfaction is extremely important for managing the size and the effectiveness of the workforce. As a result, organizations spend a fair amount of time and effort monitoring the levels of job satisfaction among their employees. This monitoring is done primarily through the use of attitude surveys that are distributed to employees once or more a year. The responses from these surveys are used to track changes in employees' attitudes—such as job satisfaction—so that the organization can respond to them before they become problematic.

Although many organizations design their own attitude surveys (or hire consulting firms to design them), some widely used measures of job satisfaction often show up as part of these surveys. By using standard measures of job satisfaction, an organization not only tracks changes in its employees' levels of satisfaction, it can also compare satisfaction levels with other organizations that use the same measures.

The job descriptive index (JDI) is the most commonly used measure of job satisfaction.[43] It measures satisfaction with specific aspects of the job such as pay, the work itself, and supervision; however, it does not have a single overall measure of job satisfaction (although it is easy to assess overall satisfaction using the JDI). For each aspect of the job, a series of descriptors might apply. For example, for the work itself, adjectives such as *routine* and *satisfying* are listed, among others. Employees are asked to indicate if each adjective "describes your work," "does not describe your work," or if the employee "can't decide." The employee indicates the level of agreement by placing a Y, N, or ? next to each item. The instrument is scored so that agreement with a positive adjective (e.g., satisfying) is given a 3, disagreement with a positive item is given a 0, and the question mark is given a 1 (indicating a moderate level of dissatisfaction).

Other instruments do include direct measures of job satisfaction, and some include questions about the levels desired versus what is experienced. One instrument, known as the faces scale, presents a series of faces that are either happy or sad, and the employee is instructed to check the face that best reflects his or her feelings about the job.[44]

Whatever the measure, most organizations are interested in changes in the levels of job satisfaction over time. Before leaving this discussion, it is important to make a final note. The primary reason for measuring job satisfaction is because dissatisfied employees tend to quit their jobs. Thus, over time, employees who are the most dissatisfied will quit the soonest. The next time the organization surveys its employees, the survey will not include those employees who have already quit. As a result, it is quite likely that the overall levels of job satisfaction will go up, even if the organization does nothing to improve job satisfaction, because only the more satisfied employees are still on the job.

The others have already left, indicating a serious problem that the organization could overlook if managers are not paying attention.

Retention Strategies

The purpose of discussing job satisfaction is to provide some insights into how to manage voluntary turnover. At the simplest level, one could say that the way to manage turnover is to increase the levels of satisfaction among employees. But the key is in understanding exactly how to do that. First, when an organization learns of a potential problem, most likely through a survey, it is important that *something* be done. Employees are less likely to respond honestly to survey questions if they feel that no one will respond to their concerns. More specifically, two other types of interventions (both discussed previously in different contexts) have been found to increase levels of job satisfaction.

Job enrichment, discussed in Chapter 14 as a strategy for enhancing performance, has been consistently linked with higher levels of job satisfaction. By making the work more challenging and meaningful, and by granting employees more autonomy and more opportunity to use their skills, the work itself becomes both motivating and satisfying (and more satisfied employees are also more productive). These employees are also more likely to find the work itself more satisfying, which in turn reduces turnover rates.

Realistic job previews (RJPs), are pre-employment previews providing accurate and realistic information to the job applicant. They are often used with new employees as a means of socializing them in their new job roles (and they will be discussed further in this context in the next chapter), but they are also effective in reducing turnover. The link to turnover reduction is the result of several aspects of RJPs. First, because potential employees who receive RJPs have more complete information about the job (including the nature of the work, supervision, pay, etc.), those who are more likely to be dissatisfied with the job characteristics are less likely to accept the jobs. Therefore, RJPs help ensure that the people on the job are those most likely to be satisfied and thus remain. In addition, when new employees are made aware of potential sources of dissatisfaction prior to encountering them, the employees can prepare themselves (psychologically or even physically) so that, when they encounter the problem, they are ready to deal with it. In fact, when employees learn that they can cope with various problems on the job by preparing, this knowledge can be a source of job satisfaction and thus promote retention.

Another retention strategy involves issuing stock options to new employees at all levels of the organization (these options have typically been given to executives only). **Stock options** are rights, given to employees, to purchase a certain number of shares of stock at a given price. That stock option price is often just slightly lower than the selling price of the stock when the option is issued. If the stock appreciates in value, these options can become very valuable. The employee can exercise the option, buy the stock at an option price that is lower than the present selling price, and then can sell the stock for an immediate profit (some firms don't even require the employee to purchase the stock at that point but simply pay out the profit). But by the end of the 1990s, some firms began adding a new wrinkle aimed specifically at retention. Although the employee was issued stock options early in the employment relationship, the options were restricted so that the employee could not exercise the options for five (or so) years. If the stock was climbing, the employee who left before he or she had completed five years of employment would forgo potentially large profits because he or she would not be able to exercise the stock options. Thus, there was a real incentive for the employee to remain with the firm (at least long enough to exercise her or his stock options). Of course, if the stock price falls below the option price (and the option is said to be "under water"), there is no reason to exercise the option, and the incentive to remain with the company is lost.

Realistic job previews (RJPs) *are pre-employment previews that provide accurate and realistic information to the job applicant. They can also be used with new employees as a means of socializing them in their new job roles, and they are effective in reducing turnover.*

Stock options *are rights, given to employees, to purchase a certain number of shares of stock at a given price.*

Evaluating the Rightsizing Process

Organizations increase or decrease the size of the workforce in response to changes in markets. As discussed in Chapters 4 and 5, this process should be the result of continuous strategic planning. Therefore, if the process is effective, the organization should never be seen as doing anything out of the ordinary. That is, the organization should be projecting increases or decreases in the need for labor and addressing these projections in the most painless ways. The use of overtime, part-time workers, or temporary workers can help solve problems in the short run, as the company prepares to deal with the longer-term problem. Early-retirement plans and estate-planning programs make it easier for older employees to ease out of the company and either make room for new employees or obviate the need for cutbacks. Managing the voluntary turnover process (as well as the involuntary turnover process) is another way to reduce the size of the workforce without taking drastic measures.

When a downturn (such as the general downturn in the U.S. economy following September 11, 2001) simply cannot be anticipated, an organization must conduct layoffs in ways that are compassionate, recognizing that the affected employees are now unemployed, and perceived as fair. A critical part of the entire process, though, is the retention of valued employees. It is difficult to tell, however, how well a company is doing in retaining employees until the employees decide to leave, and then it is a bit too late. It is possible, and advisable, however, to conduct exit interviews of all employees who leave voluntarily. An exit interview is simply a formal discussion with an employee who has announced his or her decision to quit. Because the employee will no longer be working with the company, he or she will presumably be honest about the reasons for leaving. Individuals leave their jobs for a wide variety of reasons, so it is always useful to learn why any individual decided to quit. More important, if several employees quit and most of the people leaving cite the same or similar reasons for leaving, the organization can get a good idea of the problem that needs to be fixed.

Chapter Summary

Organizations strive to maintain the right number of employees. Options for such rightsizing include hiring new employees when there is a long-term need for more employees (discussed in the next chapter), responding to temporary demands for additional employees using various methods, and reducing the size of the organization's workforce. When organizations have temporary or short-term needs for additional employees, instead of hiring permanent workers managers can generally use overtime, temporary workers, leased employees, and/or part-time employees.

Organizations that need to reduce the number of employees can achieve these reductions through early retirement and plans to encourage early retirement or through layoffs. Layoffs can bring legal problems (especially concerning potential age discrimination), and the survivors of layoffs often experience guilt. Furthermore, evidence suggests that downsizing is not an effective strategy. A final way to reduce the size of the labor force is through termination—that is, some people can be fired. Although employment-at-will is the law, there are enough exceptions to this doctrine that organizations are often sued for wrongful termination.

While organizations seek to eliminate some employees, they must also strive to retain valued employees. This process involves reducing voluntary turnover and requires an understanding of the causes of voluntary turnover. The major determinant of voluntary turnover is usually job dissatisfaction, or being unhappy in one's job.

Several models of the voluntary turnover process

Building HR Management Skills

Purpose: The purpose of this exercise is to help you develop a better understanding about how experts retain valuable employees.

Step 1: Working with a small group of your classmates, select a local employer to serve as a hypothetical client. An example might be a neighborhood Italian restaurant, a family-owned discount store, or an independent coffee shop.

Step 2: Assume that your group represents a consulting firm specializing in employee retention. You have been approached by the client identified in step 1. The problem is that a large national firm is planning to move in across the street. (Examples might be Olive Garden, Target, or Starbucks for the three businesses noted earlier.)

Step 3: Your client is only somewhat concerned about business competition with the new firm because of its large and loyal customer base. However, the client is more concerned about the new business luring away its best employees. You are asked to develop a retention plan.

Step 4: Develop answers to the following questions:

1. What information will you need to help your client?

2. Where can you obtain this information?

3. What kinds of retention ideas come to mind first?

Ethical Dilemmas in HR Management

Assume that you are working as the human resource manager for a large manufacturing firm. An area supervisor terminated an employee recently for poor performance, and this employee has threatened to take legal action. The employee maintains that she was terminated because she had attended a meeting of employees who were thinking about a union organization campaign. The supervisor claims that the union organization meeting had nothing to do with the termination and that he had documented poor performance over a period of almost six months. When you spoke to the supervisor, he showed you the documentation, and he also made it clear that he did know the employee had attended the union meeting. He stated that she had been a "troublemaker" all along. You have been told to resolve this situation as quickly as possible.

Questions

1. What are the ethical issues in this situation?

2. Do you believe that the termination was due to poor performance alone?

3. How important is the fact that the company lawyers have suggested this case is a sure win for the company?

HR Internet Exercise

Assume that you are the human resource manager for a large telecommunications company. Your firm plans to reduce its workforce by approximately 10,000 workers (out of a total workforce of 140,000). Use the Internet to locate details about at least three recent major downsizing programs in your industry and/or in related industries.

Questions

1. What, if anything, can you learn from the experiences of the firms that you researched?

2. Do you think it is better to model a layoff plan after other firms or to develop your own? Why?

3. In what ways is it easier and in what ways is it harder to lay off people when other firms in your industry are doing the same thing?

7

Recruitment and Selection

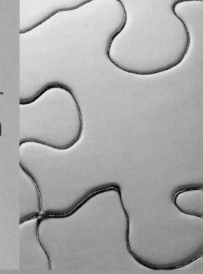

CHAPTER OBJECTIVES

After studying this chapter you should be able to:

- Describe the relationships among planning, recruiting, and selection.

- Identify and discuss the basic sources for recruiting.

- Discuss realistic job previews and their role in effective recruiting.

- Describe the steps in the selection process and identify and summarize basic selection criteria that organizations use in hiring new employees.

- Discuss popular selection techniques that organizations use to hire new employees.

- Discuss the selection decision itself.

- Identify and summarize the basic legal issues in selection.

- Discuss the importance of evaluating recruiting and selection activities.

One of the many consequences of the terrorist attacks of September 11, 2001, was that the U.S. government decided to take over passenger security screening at most of the nation's commercial airports. Screening had previously been handled by various private firms hired by individual airports (at larger airports) or by airline employees themselves (primarily at smaller airports). The purpose behind the change was to bring greater control and a higher level of competence and consistency to the screening process and thus boost security and airline safety.

> *"Initial difficulties in hiring and training the passenger screener work force made it a challenge for TSA to meet the deadline for federalizing this work force."*
>
> (Gerald Dillingham, the GAO's director of civil aviation issues)*

The Transportation Security Administration (TSA), created in response to the September 11 attacks, was assigned responsibility for hiring and maintaining a workforce of screeners at the nation's 429 commercial airports. Five airports continued to have privately employed screeners under a pilot program approved by Congress, but the other 424 were mandated to have an all-federal workforce by November 19, 2002.

When the government first tried to recruit screeners, officials found that a surprisingly high percentage of the applicants were unqualified. And there were far fewer female candidates than expected. The TSA had initially set a goal of filling half of all the screening positions with women. But because so few qualified women could be recruited, the agency eventually had to reduce this goal to one-third.

Officials also had to step up advertising and recruitment campaigns—job fairs were launched in various cities, for example. The TSA also began trying to attract more qualified applicants—and women in particular—by offering part-time positions or seasonal work. In addition, there has been more online advertising and increased listings with both private and public employment agencies.

There was even doubt for a while that the agency would be able to meet its federally mandated deadline. "Initial difficulties in hiring and training the passenger screener work force made it a challenge for TSA to meet the deadline for federalizing this work force," said Gerald Dillingham, the General Accounting Office (GAO) director of civil aviation issues. But that problem may be the tip of the iceberg. That is, given the difficulties in attracting qualified applicants to begin with, it may be even harder to attract new applicants in the future when the job market begins to improve in other sectors of the economy.[1]

Managers at the TSA face a real dilemma because they are charged with attracting qualified applicants to fill important jobs but have had difficulties in doing so. In one way or another, all organizations must address the problems and opportunities faced by the TSA—the need to recruit new people who are both interested and capable of working for them.

In this chapter we examine the recruiting process in more detail. We start by assessing the goals of recruiting. We then look at the sources and methods of recruiting. After describing the importance of realistic job previews in effective recruiting, we discuss the recruitment of part-time and temporary workers, as well as alternatives to recruiting. Finally, we briefly note how organizations evaluate the effectiveness of their recruiting efforts.

Planning, Recruitment, and Selection

In Chapters 4 and 5 we discussed planning for growth strategies and planning for stability strategies. In both cases, an organization needs to attract and hire new employees. In the case of a stability strategy, the organization needs to hire new employees to replace those who might quit or retire. In the case of a growth strategy, the organization simply needs more employees in the future than it does now, and this situation clearly requires acquiring new human resources from the outside. The processes of recruitment and selection are the means by which organizations acquire those new human resources. The two processes work together, and if they are carried out effectively, the organization will have not only the number but also the type of human resource it needs to carry out its overall strategy. These two processes are the focus of this chapter, and we begin with the recruitment process.

The Transportation Safety Administration (TSA) has found it difficult to recruit, hire, and retain qualified safety inspectors. This safety inspector at Washington Dulles Airport is among those who have come to see safety inspection as a career. Unfortunately for the TSA, though, there continues to be a real shortage of qualified and motivated candidates for jobs such as this.

Recruiting *is the process of developing a pool of qualified applicants who are interested in working for the organization and from which the organization might reasonably select the best individual or individuals to hire for employment.*

Recruiting is the process of developing a pool of qualified applicants who are interested in working for the organization and from which the organization might reasonably select the best individual or individuals to hire for employment.[2] As we will see, however, and as illustrated in Figure 7.1, it is important to remember that recruiting is a two-way street. That is, just as the organization is looking for qualified job applicants, those applicants are also likely to be looking at various potential employment opportunities. Thus, both organizations and individuals have recruiting goals.[3] The best hiring opportunities for organizations and employment opportunities for job seekers emerge when these different goals match.

Both parties in the recruiting process—the organization and the prospective employee—have goals they are trying to accomplish in the recruiting process. The most basic and fundamental goal of an organization's recruiting effort is essentially to fulfill the definition of recruiting—to develop a pool of qualified applicants. This overriding goal, however, also suggests several related goals that are important to the recruiting process.

One of these goals is to optimize the size of the pool of qualified applicants. That is, the organization should have more applicants than it has openings so that it can select the applicants it feels are best suited for the jobs. But if there were literally thousands of applicants for each job, the organization will need to process the large number of applicants for the positions, which is, in itself costly. Thus the organization wants enough candidates to be able to choose, but not so many that processing would become overwhelming.

Second, the recruiting process should generate a pool of applicants that is both qualified and interested in working for the organization. A final goal of the recruiting process from the organization's viewpoint is to offer an honest and candid assessment to prospective applicants of what kinds of jobs and what kinds of opportunities the organization can potentially make available to them. It does no one any good to trick or mislead job applicants into thinking that they will have more challenging or higher-level jobs than are actually available or that they will be earning higher salaries than the organization is prepared to pay. Thus, the recruiting process needs to paint a realistic picture of what the potential job entails. We examine this issue in more detail later when we discuss realistic job previews.

Of course, it is also important for the organization to remember that the prospective employee in the recruiting pool also has goals that affect the process. Indeed, human resource managers must never forget that recruiting is a two-way process. Just as the organization is seeking qualified applicants who are interested in employment with the firm, so too are individuals likely to be approaching several organizations and trying to entice as many of them as possible to offer employment.[4]

Thus, the organization is attempting to develop a pool of qualified applicants, and individuals are simultaneously attempting to create a pool of potentially interesting and attractive job opportunities from which they can select. As a result, it is important

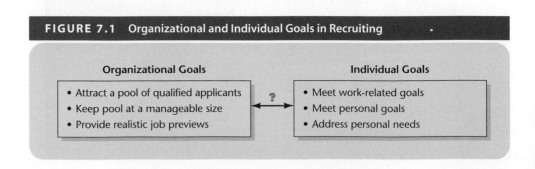

FIGURE 7.1   Organizational and Individual Goals in Recruiting

Organizational Goals		Individual Goals
• Attract a pool of qualified applicants • Keep pool at a manageable size • Provide realistic job previews	?	• Meet work-related goals • Meet personal goals • Address personal needs

for the human resource manager to understand prospective employees' goals as part of their own recruiting process. During the economic downturn in 2002, many job seekers turned to creative and unusual ways to attract the attention of potential employers.

In many cases a prospective employee's goals are relatively straightforward. Individuals work for several reasons, but the most common are financial income, job security, promotion opportunities, benefits, challenging work assignments, and so forth. In addition to these goals, however, individuals can also have idiosyncratic goals. For example, some people put extra emphasis on the location of a particular job opportunity. They may want to work close to their hometown, close to where they went to school, in a big city, in a small city, near family, near the ocean, or near recreational opportunities.[5]

Sources for Recruits

One fundamental decision that an organization must make as part of its recruiting strategy is whether to focus recruiting efforts internally or externally. As summarized in Table 7.1 and discussed below, both internal and external recruiting have unique advantages and disadvantages.

Internal Recruiting

Internal recruiting is the process of looking inside the organization for existing qualified employees who might be promoted to higher-level positions. This situation may not seem particularly useful for increasing the size of the workforce, but internal recruiting can play a role even in growth strategies. If an organization can fill higher-level openings with present employees who are ready to move up, it will have to fill lower-level positions from the outside later. These lower-level positions would presumably be easier and less costly to fill. Using this approach in an ideal situation, in which the organization could fill all of its needs, except those for entry-level jobs, from the inside and then recruit externally for entry-level job openings.

In any event, it is generally important that an organization always uses internal recruiting as part of its overall planning process because internal recruiting has several advantages over external recruiting. A major advantage of internal recruiting is motivation. Many employees want—and some expect—to advance and move up the organizational ladder to higher-level positions. An opportunity to do just that is likely to be seen as a viable reward and an important source of motivation for many people. Hence,

Internal recruiting is the process of looking inside the organization for existing qualified employees who might be promoted to higher-level positions.

TABLE 7.1 Advantages and Disadvantages of Internal and External Recruiting		
	Advantages	**Disadvantages**
Internal recruiting	■ Increases motivation	■ May foster stagnation
	■ Sustains knowledge and culture	■ May cause a ripple effect
External recruiting	■ Brings in new ideas	■ May hurt motivation
	■ Avoids the ripple effect	■ Costs more

an organization that routinely promotes from within through internal recruiting will usually find that it is more likely to have a committed and motivated workforce.

Another advantage of internal recruiting is that employees promoted to higher-level positions bring with them an existing familiarity and understanding of the organization: its heritage, culture, policies and procedures, strategies, and ways of doing business. As a result, their transition to higher-level positions is somewhat easier and the organization can often rely on the fact that these individuals will continue to promote and enhance the corporate culture in a positive and beneficial manner.

On the other hand, a disadvantage of internal recruiting is that it may foster stagnation and stifle creativity and new ideas. People tend to develop a certain mindset and way of doing business, and they tend to maintain that outlook as they progress in the organization. If the corporate culture is not what managers would really like, they should recognize that promoting from within is not necessarily likely to be a positive force for change.

Another disadvantage of internal recruiting is the so-called ripple effect. For example, if a person is promoted from one level of the organization to a higher-level position, then the job that that individual vacates must be filled. If that job is filled from someone still lower in the organization, an open position that the organization has to fill still exists. A relatively few promotions can sometimes result in a large-scale set of transfers and movements from position to position within the organization. As noted above, however, if an organization approaches this process strategically, only the lowest-level positions will remain vacant and, at that point, the organization can turn to external recruiting.

Methods for Internal Recruiting

The two most common methods used for internal recruiting are job posting and supervisory recommendations.

Job posting is a mechanism for internal recruiting in which vacancies in the organization are publicized through various media such as company newsletters, bulletin boards, internal memos, and the firm's intranet.

Job posting   Perhaps the most common method that organizations use for internal recruiting is a process called **job posting.** Job posting is a relatively simple procedure. Vacancies in the organization are publicized through various media such as company newsletters, bulletin boards, internal memos, and/or the firm's intranet. Any individual who is interested in being considered for the position simply files an application with the human resource department. Some organizations that rely heavily on internal recruiting go so far as to require that jobs be posted internally before any external recruiting is undertaken. Note that a candidate hired through a job posting could be applying for a promotion or merely for a transfer.

Supervisory recommendations is a mechanism for internal recruiting where, when a new position needs to be filled, a manager simply solicits nominations or recommendations for the position from supervisors in the organization.

Supervisory recommendations   Another method of internal recruiting is through **supervisory recommendations.** In this case, when a new position needs to be filled, a manager simply solicits nominations or recommendations for the position from supervisors in the organization. These supervisors look at the employees for whom they are responsible, and if any are particularly well suited for the new job opening, then the supervisors recommend those individuals to the higher-level manager.

It is important, however, that supervisors give equal consideration to all potential candidates in these cases. In a landmark decision, *Rowe* v. *General Motors,* the Supreme Court found General Motors (GM) guilty of discrimination because, under a system where supervisory recommendations were needed for promotions, supervisors failed to recommend qualified black candidates as frequently as they recommended white candidates. As a result, at the time of the suit, almost no black supervisors were working at most GM facilities.

We should also point out that, given the large numbers of layoffs and workforce reductions (from downsizing) in recent years, some potential applicants are somewhere between the classifications of internal and external candidates. Individuals who have been laid off (as opposed to terminated) are usually considered first when openings occur in the organization (and indeed this procedure may be mandated by certain union contracts). These individuals may not be active employees at the time, but they would still be considered internal candidates. On the other hand, individuals who actually lost their jobs during downsizing—that is, they were officially terminated—are technically no longer employees of the organization and so would be considered external candidates. Because they had worked for the organization previously, however, they would share more characteristics in common with internal candidates and might constitute a good source of potential applicants.

External Recruiting

External recruiting involves looking to sources outside the organization for prospective employees. Not surprisingly, external recruiting has advantages and disadvantages that are directly counter to those of internal recruiting. For example, external recruiting has the advantage of bringing in new ideas, new perspectives, and new ways of doing things. Hence, the organization can enhance its vitality, creativity, and potential ability to innovate by routinely bringing in people from the outside. External recruiting also avoids the ripple effect. In some cases, no internal employees may be able to fill new positions, thereby making external recruiting the only option.

A few years ago the managers and owners of a small software computer company in Iowa were frustrated because they could not make the major breakthroughs necessary to fuel growth for the firm. After considerable discussion, they decided that it was simply a case of no one inside the firm having the managerial skills needed to take the company to the next stage in its growth. All current managers were professional engineers, and none really had much managerial experience. Consequently, the firm decided to hire an outsider to come in and run the business. Within a couple of years, he had increased the firm's sales from $750,000 a year to over $11 million.[6]

On the other hand, external recruiting may result in motivational problems in the organization. Current employees may feel that they have been denied opportunities and that outsiders who are brought into the organization at higher levels may be less qualified than the current employees themselves. External recruiting also tends to be a bit more expensive than internal recruiting because of the advertising and other search processes that must be undertaken.

Many organizations prefer to rely on both internal and external recruiting strategies. This combined approach allows an organization to match the advantages and disadvantages of each particular recruiting effort to its own unique context. For example, during its dramatic growth period in the 1990s, Compaq Computer recruited both internally and externally. The firm wanted to ensure that current employees had ample promotion opportunity, but it also felt that it needed to hire people at a faster rate than could be accommodated by internal recruitment alone. Thus, each major hiring phase was carefully assessed and decisions were made in advance about the sources to be used. In some instances almost all recruiting was done internally, while in others only external recruiting was used. In still other cases, the firm looked both inside and outside at the same time for new recruits.

External recruiting   *is the process of looking to sources outside the organization for prospective employees.*

While organizations seek applicants, unemployed persons are seeking jobs. Finding creative ways to get the two groups together and get a potential employer to notice a potential employee can sometimes be more rewarding than more traditional methods of recruiting and job hunting. The man in this photo is attending a Pink Slip Party in the Silicon Valley in California. As the dot-com bust led to increased layoffs in the area, the frequency of parties where employers and the unemployed were invited to meet in a relaxed setting also increased. When times get tough for job seekers, creative approaches such as this man's sign on his back are more likely to get attention than more common approaches such as simply handing out his resumé.

Methods for External Recruiting

Somewhat different methods are likely to be used by an organization engaged in external recruiting because the organization needs to reach potential applicants from outside the company.

Word-of-mouth recruiting *is when the organization simply informs present employees that positions are available and encourages them to refer friends, family members, or neighbors for those jobs.*

Word-of-mouth recruiting   Referrals come to an organization via **word-of-mouth recruiting.** In most cases, the organization simply informs present employees that positions are available and encourages them to refer friends, family members, or neighbors for those jobs.[7] From the organization's perspective, this method is an inexpensive way to generate a large number of applicants. In addition, if we assume that the present employees are satisfactory and that people generally associate with people who are similar to them, the organization should also have a reasonable chance of generating high-quality applicants with this method, and some portion of the applicants for any job come through word-of-mouth recruiting. If an organization relies on this recruiting technique exclusively, however, problems may arise. If the present workforce is almost completely white and male, for example, the individuals referred will most likely be primarily white males as well, and this situation might represent discrimination in recruitment.

Advertisements   Advertisements in newspapers and related publications are also popular methods for external recruiting. Any local newspaper is likely to have help wanted sections ranging from perhaps a few listings to as many as several pages, sometimes organized by different kinds of job openings such as sales, health care, professional, nonprofessional, technical, and so forth. Depending on the job, these advertisements might be placed in local newspapers or national newspapers such as the *Wall Street Journal.*

Some professional periodicals and publications also have similar kinds of spaces set aside for help wanted recruiting ads. This form of advertising tends to be relatively expensive and, perhaps surprisingly, attracts somewhat fewer qualified applicants than some of the other methods of recruiting. It does enable the organization to cast a wide net, however, in its efforts to publicize its affirmative action programs and to reach every sector of the labor market. By targeting specialized publications that might appeal primarily to members of groups that are underrepresented in the workforce, the organization might also advance its affirmative action goals. On the other hand, restricting advertisements to publications that are not widely available could be considered discriminatory.

Employment agencies   Reliance upon employment agencies is another common method for external recruiting, but there are different types of employment agencies that serve different purposes. *Public employment agencies* became a formal part of the recruiting process with the passage of the Social Security Act of 1935. This law requires that anyone who is paid unemployment compensation must register that fact with a local state employment office. These state agencies work closely with the U.S. Employment Service to get unemployed individuals off state aid as quickly as possible and back in permanent jobs.

Employers register their job openings with the local state employment agency. At the same time, the employment agency collects data (mostly regarding skills, experience, and abilities) from unemployed persons and uses these data to match qualified individuals with available jobs. Two significant advantages of public employment agencies are that (1) they are free, and (2) they are a particularly useful source of job applicants for minorities, handicapped individuals, and other protected classes. Because they are state agencies, they are fully cognizant of the requirements that organizations must face, and they work hard to maintain an adequate labor pool of all classes of employees.

Private employment agencies are more likely to serve the white-collar labor market (although some serve specialized niches such as office workers), and they charge a fee for their services. Sometimes this fee is paid by the individual; sometimes it is paid by the organization if it hires an individual referred to it. In a public employment agency, all potential employee job applicants are currently unemployed, but many employed individuals use the services of private employment agencies in an effort to find government work while maintaining their current job. Since private employment agencies are supported by the firms and individuals that use their services, however, they may be able to devote more resources to performing their function.

Finally, *executive search firms* specialize in finding applicants for high-level positions. An individual working for an executive search firm is also known as a **headhunter.** An organization that wants to hire a top-level manager can go to an executive search firm and explain exactly what kind of individuals it is looking for. This explanation, for example, might specify the kind of work experience the organization wants the individual to have, the degree that is necessary, the number of years of experience, and perhaps a salary profile as well. The executive search firm then attempts to locate individuals who fit this profile for the organization. Typically, the search firm screens potential candidates and then presents the organization with a small number of candidates, all of whom are highly qualified and interested.

Executive search firms can perform rather exhaustive searches for qualified candidates, and they allow both parties in the process to maintain confidentiality. Yet they tend

A **headhunter** *is an individual working for an executive search firm that seeks out qualified individuals for higher-level positions.*

to be among the most expensive methods for external recruiting. In addition, one caveat that applies to any type of agency relates to potential discrimination. Many stories have been published in the popular press about employment agencies (both public and private) that referred individuals of one race, ethnicity, or gender for some jobs but not for others. If an organization engages the services of an employment agency that discriminates, the organization itself (not the employment agency) almost certainly will be held liable for the discrimination.

College placement offices   Another method of external recruiting is to utilize the placement offices that most colleges and universities sponsor. Most large organizations visit college campuses every year to interview graduates for jobs within the organization. Large firms may visit many different colleges and universities scattered across the country, or they may choose to visit only regional or local colleges and universities.

An advantage of this method for the organization is that it can specify qualifications such as major, grade point average, work experience, and so forth. It is also a relatively inexpensive method of recruiting because the colleges and universities typically provide the facilities, schedule the appointments, and so forth. The organization sends the interviewer to the campus, and that individual sits in the interview room during the course of the day and meets prospective applicants. For students, this job search method is also quite efficient. The student can visit his or her local placement office on a regular basis, keep apprised of which companies are coming to interview, and sign up for interviews using whatever methods and protocols the college or university has established.

Microsoft relies heavily on college recruiting in its efforts to bring in new talent every year. The firm has a staff of twenty-two full-time campus recruiters who visit schools each year. These recruiters conduct half-hour interviews with thousands of prospective employees, selecting about 450 for follow-up visits to company headquarters.[8]

Electronic Recruiting

The Internet has had an impact on a number of human resource management activities, but there are few areas where the Internet has had a greater impact than on the recruiting function. In fact, many of the techniques discussed above for external and internal recruiting can be and are being replaced by the Internet. The importance of electronic recruiting would be hard to overestimate. A recent article noted that in 1998, 29 percent of the Fortune 500 companies generated applicants through their websites, but that rate rose to 88 percent in less than three years. This same article also reported that 34 percent of these companies accepted applications only through their websites.[9] Several key reasons explain why we have experienced such an explosion in electronic recruiting.

Perhaps the most important reason for the growing reliance on electronic recruiting is that it is cost-effective. It does not cost much to post a job opening on a job board like those available at the websites monster.com and hotjob.com, and these websites are visited by literally millions of people a year. Not everyone who visits these websites is looking for a new job, and many might not be qualified for a given job, but the level of exposure offered by these services is unprecedented. In addition, many organizations who are starting their own websites for recruiting find that they can reach potential applicants more easily and that they can use these websites as marketing tools.[10]

Electronic ads can also reach a large number of applicants. Only a few years ago, the effectiveness of electronic recruiting was somewhat limited by the numbers of potential job applicants who had easy access to the Internet. Although accessibility varies around the world and within every country, the number of people who search the Internet is growing dramatically, and many people use the Internet when searching for jobs. Recent estimates show 160 million Internet users in the United States and 1.2 billion Internet users worldwide. In the United States approximately 74 percent of those with access to the Internet use it to search for jobs.[11] Thus, the Internet allows an organization instant access to a global pool of potential applicants. In this country, many organizations have reported that advertising on the Internet has also produced a more diverse group of applicants and job seekers than they had reached using more traditional methods.[12] Furthermore, there is no question that the numbers of persons reached by ads on the Internet will continue to grow dramatically.

Finally, electronic recruiting saves time. A potential applicant who sees an interesting opening can e-mail questions and answers as well as electronically submit resumés—all in a matter of minutes. This can be contrasted with the more traditional types of recruiting where there are several steps and iterations and each one can take days. In fact, this time savings has helped electronic recruiting to become much more popular for internal recruiting as well. For example, at Gillette Co. all current employees can read the company philosophy, learn about openings within the company, and apply for the jobs for which they are qualified in a few minutes on the company intranet. Office workers can do so on their work computers, while manufacturing employees can do so at computer kiosks located around the shop floor.

Of course, although electronic recruiting offers many advantages, some costs are involved. The obvious problem with reaching a broad set of potential applicants is that many people may apply for a job when they are not really qualified. In fact, nearly one-third of the human resource managers in a recent survey indicated that Internet recruiting caused additional work because staff members had to sift through resumés from unqualified people and had to respond to the barrage of e-mail messages that some job postings can generate.

As noted above, many companies are pleased with the increased diversity that electronic recruiting seems to provide, but differences in access to computers and the Internet still exist in the United States. A study by the Department of Labor notes that fewer Hispanic-American and African-American applicants have regular access to computers, and as a result, members of these groups are more likely to rely on more traditional sources of job information.[13] It is not clear what the impact of this differential access is if companies continue to post ads in both traditional and electronic sources, but it is an issue to consider when deciding whether to move to electronic recruiting.

Finally, although electronic recruiting can offer a company many advantages, it seems that potential job seekers who visit company websites do not always come away happy. Many users report that company websites are difficult to navigate or are sloppy, while others complain that it is difficult to apply for a job at the website.[14] It is important for organizations to recognize that, in this electronic age, a company website may actually be the first point of contact for an applicant. The potential applicant should find the experience pleasant because this first positive impression will make the company seem more attractive as an employer. On the other hand, if the experience is a frustrating one, many potentially valuable applicants could be lost.

Internships: A Mixed Model

Although it is easier to think about recruiting having either an internal or external focus, it is possible to take an approach that really combines elements of the two. Many students try to obtain internships that will provide real-world experience, but internships are also quite useful from the organization's perspective. Of course, an internship is a form of temporary employee (see later in this chapter) who can help respond to work demands in the short term. But, more important, internships can be an important recruiting tool.

The intern is hired, in essence, on approval. That is, if the organization does not think that the person is someone who will be able to contribute to the organization or that the person is a good fit, the organization simply allows the internship to end. The intern is not really rejected because he or she has never really applied. On the other hand, if the intern is someone whom the organization is interested in, the organization can offer the person permanent employment. Even if the intern is a student who must complete his or her studies, the organization might want to offer a contract to the person that would become effective on graduation. At that point, this contract would really become a form of internal recruiting but because the intern is not a permanent employee, it is also a form of external recruiting.

In fact, using internships to bring people into the organization and then hiring them allows the organization to obtain the best of both internal and external recruiting. The interns bring in a fresh perspective, the organization knows a lot about the intern, and the intern is somewhat familiar with the organization. This practice is becoming more common, and in some cases, interns who do not receive permanent job offers may even feel as if they have been rejected. Even if that feeling becomes more common among interns generally, recruiting interns on a tryout basis is an effective way of combining internal and external recruiting. *HR in the 21st Century* discusses how some organizations have started using virtual interns.

Realistic Job Previews

*A **realistic job preview** is an effective technique for ensuring that job seekers understand the actual nature of the jobs available to them.*

Many organizations today find it increasingly important to provide prospective employees with what is called a **realistic job preview.** In the past, many recruiters were guilty of painting a glowing picture of what a particular job might entail. They made the job sound glamorous, exciting, fun, challenging, and rewarding in different ways. Once employees accepted the job, however, they found just the opposite: the job they were hired to fill proved to be boring, tedious, monotonous, and routine. Because their expectations were set so high, and because the reality they faced proved to be so different, they were extremely dissatisfied with their work and consequently were prone to high turnover. These problems can be partly minimized, however, if recruiters paint a more realistic picture of the job. If the job is relatively routine, then prospective job applicants should be told that fact. The idea is simply to present as realistic a preview of the actual job and its working conditions as possible without glossing over some of the more unpleasant characteristics of the job or the working conditions for that job.[15]

One relatively straightforward method for providing a realistic job preview is to provide job applicants with an opportunity to observe others performing the work. Job applicants can go to the job site and watch people work or they can watch a videotape of people performing the job. If neither of these alternatives is feasible, then at a minimum the recruiter should describe in as realistic terms as possible the job itself and the circumstances under which it will be performed.

Disney has found that using realistic job previews has greatly improved its recruiting and selection processes. At its vast Disney World complex, the firm has an employment office it calls its casting center. Before being interviewed or asked to complete a job application, people who visit the center seeking employment are instructed to watch a videotape. The video informs job seekers about the firm's strict appearance guidelines and the difficult and rigorous working conditions. The goal is to provide a candid and realistic introduction to the working conditions at Disney.[16]

Considerable research has been done to document the benefits of realistic job previews. If applicants are given realistic previews before they make a decision, some potential applicants will be discouraged and withdraw from consideration.[17] At the same

Internships Go Virtual as Firms Seek Ways to Save

Some cost-cutting employers are trying a novel alternative to the traditional student apprenticeship: virtual internships. Companies are hiring college students to work on projects from afar rather than relocating them for short-term assignments. The programs, dubbed e-internships, represent a new way for companies and pending graduates to get connected.

Employers are experimenting with the idea because more college students have access to computers, virtual work has become more commonplace, and companies want to tap more affordable labor sources. Firms can save money because the internships may be short in duration or unpaid. For example:

"It tests your communication skills and shows you can work virtually."

(Dennis Joseph, virtual intern)

- At Cardinal Health in Dublin, Ohio, college students in states such as Arkansas and Ohio have been hired for virtual internships. Using school computers, they have worked on data warehousing and other projects and searched for errors on websites. The students are paired with a mentor and are paid. The company is a provider of health-care products and services. Dennis Joseph, twenty-three, is a senior at Southern Arkansas University in Magnolia who is testing applications as a virtual intern. "It tests your communication skills and shows you can work virtually," he says.

- International Truck and Engine, a maker of commercial trucks and diesel engines based in Warrenville, Illinois, has launched a virtual internship program. Last year, four students at Hiram College in Hiram, Ohio,

worked for the company and were supervised by phone and e-mail. The students, who each received $500, worked on a Web-marketing project. "We get a lot of great work at a low cost," says Jim Clarke, manager of channel development in used truck operations. "The only thing is [that] they don't learn anything about the company culture. But it's a good recruiting tool."

- At Edwards & Hill Communications in Baltimore, Maryland, about ten college students have participated in virtual internships. Using their own computers, the students post casting notices online for the multimedia company, which runs a website that caters to the entertainment industry.

No one knows how many companies are offering virtual internships, but hiring experts say that they're a creative approach that could catch on. And even though students may never set foot in the companies that hire them, the e-internships often retain the hallmarks of traditional programs. Students often have mentors, projects to work on, and online brainstorming sessions with colleagues. "It was a pretty cool experience," says Guru Pinglay, twenty-six, a technical support analyst at Cardinal Health who previously worked as a virtual intern and was hired in June. "The communication problems were more, but that was the only disadvantage."

Source: "Internships Go Virtual as Firms Seek Ways to Save," by Stephanie Armour from *USA Today,* October 22, 2002, p. 1B. Copyright © 2002 *USA Today.* Reprinted with permission.

---

time, however, those who know what to expect and still choose to join the organization generally are more successful. The results of this research include, among other things, the fact that newly hired employees who have received realistic job previews have a higher rate of job survival than those who are hired without realistic previews. Those newcomers who received a realistic job preview reported higher levels of job satisfaction, higher levels of trust in the organization, and a more realistic set of expectations about the job. A recent meta-analysis of several studies of realistic job previews reported that they are generally associated with higher performance and lower turnover.[18] Not only do realistic job previews seem to work, their effectiveness has been demonstrated with jobs as diverse as bank teller,[19] army recruit,[20] and prison guard![21] Nonetheless, realistic job previews represent a much different approach to traditional recruiting. For that reason, some people have argued that they are not the best way to recruit new people.

The Selection Process

Selection *is concerned with identifying the best candidate or candidates for jobs from among the pool of qualified applicants developed during the recruiting process.*

Once the recruitment process has identified a pool of qualified applicants, it is time to begin the selection process. **Selection** is concerned with identifying the best candidate or candidates for jobs from among the pool of qualified applicants developed during the recruiting process.

Steps in Selection

At a general level, the selection process involves three distinct steps (see Figure 7.2).[22] The first step is to gather information about the members of the pool of qualified recruits (as created by the recruiting process described earlier) regarding the levels of requisite knowledge, skills, and abilities (KSAs) possessed by each applicant. However, in addition, information about factors such as education and experience, as well as attitudes of the individuals toward work and the impressions of current managers about the individual's likelihood of success are also collected.

The second step in the selection process is to evaluate the qualifications of each applicant from among the recruiting pool. This evaluation process occurs through the application of explicit or implicit standards to the information gathered in step 1. For example, if the standard for hiring is that the person must be able to keyboard seventy words per minute, a manager can give each applicant a keyboarding test and compare applicants' scores to that standard. Similarly, if the standard calls for a certain personality type, a manager can give personality tests, interpret test scores based on test norms, and then assess how closely the individual fits the desired profile.

Interviews are a fairly common method for selecting among job applicants. They allow organizational representatives to see the applicant and interact with him or her, and they allow the applicant to ask questions and learn about the company. In the U.S. interviews are usually scheduled for one applicant at a time, and there may be a sequence of multiple interviews for each applicant. Employers at this job fair in Shanghai use a different approach. Job applicants stand in line for a chance to be interviewed. The interview is conducted on the spot, and applicants are contacted about results soon after.

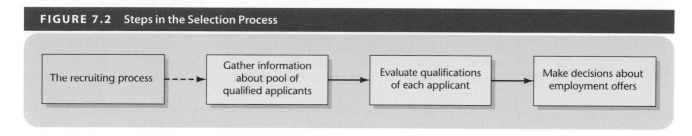

FIGURE 7.2   Steps in the Selection Process

But sometimes applying standards is not so straightforward. For example, if the standard is ten years of relevant work experience, someone must make the decision about whether or not people who exceed that standard are more qualified than individuals who simply meet it. For example, is an applicant with fifteen years of experience a more desirable candidate than another applicant with ten years and one month experience, or are these two candidates to be treated as equal on this dimension because they each meet the standard? We will discuss some important implications of decisions such as this one later in the chapter.

The third step in the selection process is making the actual decision about which candidate or candidates will be offered employment with the organization. This decision involves careful assessment of the individuals' qualifications relative to the standards of the job and the extent to which those qualifications best prepare and give an individual the requisite skills and abilities for the position. In some cases, an organization may need to select large numbers of people to hire simultaneously. For example, a firm opening a new factory may be hiring hundreds of operating employees from a pool of thousands of applicants, or a rapidly growing restaurant chain may need to hire dozens of management trainees to assume management positions in new restaurants in a year or two. In both cases the manager doesn't necessarily have to make fine gradations between, say, candidate number 11 and candidate number 12. The only decision is determining the extent to which a candidate is in the set of desirable people to hire or is outside that set because of job-relevant characteristics.

But if the selection decision involves hiring a specific single individual for a specific position in the organization, such as a new director of marketing or a vice president of human resources, then one individual must be selected. It is sometimes helpful at this point to rank-order the candidates who are being considered for the job. If the organization does not succeed in hiring its top choice for the job, then decisions will have already been made regarding the relative acceptability of candidate number 2, candidate number 3, and so on. In some cases, for example, if the recruiting process has been handled effectively, the organization may want to hire more than one qualified applicant in the pool. Thus, it may be helpful to develop a backup plan in case the top choice cannot be employed.

Basic Selection Criteria

What exactly are the bases for evaluating the applicants during the selection process? A number of possible criteria can be used in the selection decision, and these often differ in terms of how objectively they can be assessed.

Education and experience   For example, education and experience are criteria that are relatively straightforward to assess. In a selection context, **education** refers to the formal classroom training an individual has received in public or private schools and in a college, university, and/or technical school. Some jobs require high school diplomas, while others might require advanced degrees. For some jobs, the educational fields (a person's major) are open; in other cases they must be within a specified area, such as mechanical engineering, French, or human resource management.

Experience refers to the amount of time the individual may have spent working, either in a general capacity or in a particular field. Experience is presumably an indicator of an individual's familiarity with work and his or her ability to work, and a surrogate measure of a person's competencies as an employee. In some cases it may be necessary that the individual have a predetermined level of experience in a certain field of study. For example, if a large organization is looking to hire someone to be director of advertising, it will quite likely expect applicants to have substantial experience in the advertising field. In other cases, however, the experience requirement may be more general. Simply having a certain number of years' experience in full-time work activities might be sufficient evidence of an individual's employability. And some entry-level jobs may require no experience at all.

Skills and abilities   The assessment of skills and abilities, on the other hand, are rather mixed in terms of objectivity. It is relatively straightforward to assess someone's typing ability, and it is even possible to measure an ability such as spatial relations (the ability to manipulate three-dimensional objects in one's mind) objectively. But as organizations move toward teamwork and team-based operating systems, many of them are also putting more emphasis on hiring individuals with the skills necessary to function effectively in a group situation.[23] These skills are much more subjective and therefore more difficult to assess accurately.

Personal characteristics   Some personal characteristics, which are believed to reflect the applicant's personality, are also difficult to assess objectively. Assessments of characteristics such as friendliness, the ability to deal with others, and perseverance are usually quite subjective and are obtained as part of the interview process (discussed below). More recently, however, a great deal of attention has been paid to assessing applicants in terms of the **big five personality traits.** These five personality traits tend to be more behavioral than cognitive or emotional, and so can be assessed in a fairly objective manner. Furthermore, recent research has suggested that they are likely to be more important for job performance than are more traditional personality traits.[24] The big five traits are *neuroticism* (disposition to experience states like anxiety and guilt rather than being better adjusted emotionally), *extraversion* (tendency to be outgoing, sociable, and upbeat), *openness to experience* (tendency to be imaginative and intellectually curious), *agreeableness* (tendency to be altruistic and cooperative), and *conscientiousness* (tendency to be purposeful and dependable and to pay attention to detail).

Hiring for "fit"   A rather unique and interesting criterion for selection is referred to as "fit." When a firm decides to hire someone on the basis of fit, it is choosing not to hire someone because he or she is the most qualified for a specific job, but because she or he is a good fit for the larger organization. Thus, rather than hire someone for a programming position because of his or her computer skills alone, the firm might consider hiring persons whose personal values or personality fit with the rest of the organization.

Note that the firm likely would not hire an unqualified person simply because of fit, but from among a group of reasonably qualified persons, the company would select the person who it thought would fit in best. But fit for a specific job is likely to be based on KSAs, and can probably be assessed rather objectively, while organizational fit is likely to be based on values and personality, which are more difficult to assess objectively.[25] In some cases, the organization might assume that the requisite KSAs can actually be learned after the person has been hired, resulting in even more reliance upon selection based on fit. This trend has developed into a growing controversy in selection today. Human resource managers traditionally believed that they should hire the person with the best set of job-specific skills relative to the work that needed to be performed, but today many argue that the best hires are those who fit into the overall organization based on personal characteristics, values, and so forth.[26] The *Point/Counterpoint* feature for this chapter outlines some of the arguments on both sides of this controversy.

POINT | COUNTERPOINT

Selecting for Fit Versus Skill

 The basis for a selection decision has traditionally been whether or not a person can do the job. That is, organizations would identify the knowledge, skills, and abilities (KSAs) needed to do a job and then select the best-qualified candidate(s). More recently, organizations have begun basing selection decisions on whether or not a person fits with the organization. That is, the decision is based on whether the applicant seems to share values and personality traits with the organization as a whole. We don't want to suggest that KSAs have become irrelevant; they are simply of secondary importance.

POINT... **Organizations should select people primarily on the basis of fit because...**	COUNTERPOINT... **Organizations should select people primarily on the basis of KSAs because...**
Even if they are qualified, people who don't fit in the organization will probably never succeed.	No matter how well someone fits in, he or she will never perform as well as someone who is more qualified.
A strong organizational or corporate culture depends on hiring people with consistent values.	Organizations that rely on fit simply hire more of the same kind of people.
Teams are easier to form and are more likely to be successful when all team members share some basic values.	Lack of diversity in backgrounds and interests can result in fewer ideas and less originality, and perhaps can even lead to discrimination.
People will be more attracted and committed to organizations with which they believe they share values.	Diverse populations will be committed to organizations that value diversity.
It is easier to determine whether or not an applicant is "one of us."	Determinations of fit are always subjective, whereas determinations of KSAs can be more objective and thus less biased.

So... Organizations will always use both factors to some extent, but the issue is which one is given precedence. As long as all persons selected are reasonably qualified, there would seem to be no problems with selecting people on the basis of fit, and such an approach would surely reap some benefits. The biggest potential downside to a reliance on fit is that it can lead to the exclusion of people who are different (on the basis of race and/or gender), which is illegal. Of course, a tolerant, diverse culture might be exactly the culture the organization is trying to foster.

Popular Selection Techniques

Organizations use different techniques for gathering information that reflects an individual's education and experience, skills and abilities, and personal characteristics. Indeed, most organizations rely on a comprehensive system involving multiple selection techniques to ensure that they gather all the relevant data and that they assess this data rigorously, objectively, and in a nondiscriminatory fashion. In the sections that follow we will identify and discuss some of the more popular and commonly used selection techniques. Logic may underlie the sequence in which organizations use these techniques, but at the same time many organizations vary the order to fit their own particular needs, circumstances, and beliefs. Figure 7.3 illustrates one example selection sequence that an organization might employ.

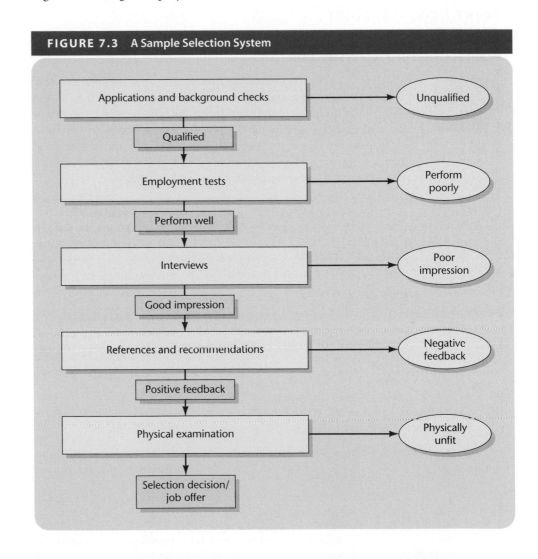

FIGURE 7.3   A Sample Selection System

Applications and Background Checks

One of the first steps in most selection systems is to ask applicants to complete an employment application or an application blank. An **employment application** asks individuals for various facts and information pertaining to their personal background. Commonly asked questions on an employment application include details such as name, educational background, personal career goals, experience, and so forth.

Of course, all questions on an employment application must relate to an individual's ability to perform the job. For example, an employment application cannot ask for a person's gender, age, or marital status because these questions have no bearing on that person's ability to perform specific jobs. Such questions could even serve as a basis for applicants' claims of discrimination on the basis of age or gender. An organization may need this information after someone is hired, but it is illegal to make selection decisions based on these variables and they should be avoided on application blanks. Figure 7.4 presents an example of an application blank.

Application blanks provide a quick and inexpensive mechanism for gathering several kinds of objective information about an individual and information of a type that can be easily verified. As discussed in HR in the 21st Century, some organizations today are even using electronic screening devices to review applications. Even on a traditional paper application, however, if an individual states that she has a bachelor's degree in electrical engineering from a given university, the organization can verify this information with a simple call to that university's registrar's office. Organizations can also use application blanks to quickly determine if an applicant meets minimum selection criteria (e.g., years of experience).

There have also been a number of innovations that have extended the usefulness of application blanks. One of these is the so-called **weighted application blank**.[27] A weighted application blank relies on statistical techniques to determine the relative importance of various personal factors for predicting a person's ability to perform a job effectively. Using information gathered from current high and low performers in the organization, it is often possible to determine whether specific levels of education, experience, and so on that are gathered on the application blank are related to a person's ability to perform a job effectively. The **biodata application blank** focuses on the same type of information found in a regular application, but it also goes into more complex and detailed assessments about that background.[28] For example, in addition to asking about an applicant's college major, a biodata application might ask questions about which courses the applicant enjoyed most and why a particular field of study was chosen. As with weighted application blanks, responses to these questions are then studied to see if they differentiate between employees who have done well and who have done poorly on the job. This information is then used to predict the performance of new applicants from their application blanks. Thus, in both cases, the organization is interested in determining if any of the information collected on application blanks can be used to provide direct predictions of performance on the job.

Employment Tests

Another popular selection technique used by many organizations is an employment test.[29] An **employment test** is a device for measuring the characteristics of an individual. These characteristics may include personality, intelligence, or aptitude. Although employment tests are generally traditional question-and-answer exercises that applicants complete on paper or online, the courts consider any device used to make an employment decision, including interviews, to be a test. Typically, though, employment tests per se are either paper or computer-administered. For a paper test the organization

*An **employment application** asks individuals for various bits of information pertaining to their personal background.*

*A **weighted application blank** relies on the determination of numerical indices to indicate the relative importance of various personal factors for predicting a person's ability to perform a job effectively.*

***Biodata application blanks** focus on the same type of information that is found in a regular application but go into more complex and detailed assessments about that background.*

*An **employment test** is a device for measuring the characteristics of an individual, such as personality, intelligence, or aptitude.*

Regardless of the merits of these arguments, however, both personality and cognitive ability remain popular criteria in selection techniques, as do all employment tests in general.[35]

A somewhat different but related approach to testing prospective employees is the use of an integrity test. **Integrity tests** attempt to assess an applicant's moral character and honesty. Most of these tests are fairly straightforward and include questions such as "Do you think most people would cheat if they thought they could get away with it?" and "Have you ever taken anything that didn't belong to you at work?" Other tests are less obvious and are based more on personality measures. The use of integrity tests is growing dramatically, with several million administered annually in the United States.[36] The likelihood is that the number will continue to increase as the cost of employee theft rises.[37] Despite their popularity, however, there are some important issues involved with their use in selection settings. First, most of the evidence about their accuracy has been supplied by the publishers of the tests, which raises the possibility of conflict of interests. Second, these tests may do a good job of identifying potential "thieves," but many other individuals not identified by the tests steal and simply do not get caught. Finally, some applicants find these tests invasive and respond negatively to them.[38]

Integrity tests *attempt to assess an applicant's moral character and honesty.*

Work Simulations

Work simulations (sometimes referred to as **work samples**) require the applicant to perform tasks or job-related activities that simulate or represent the actual work for which the person is being considered. For example, suppose an organization needs to hire a new data-entry specialist. The organization has determined that the data-entry specialist must be proficient with Microsoft Office software and must be capable of keyboarding seventy-five words a minute. A relatively easy method for assessing a candidate's qualifications, then, is to seat the individual at a computer, ask him or her to perform various data-entry tasks and activities using Microsoft Office software, and then keyboard a letter or document to measure how quickly the person can keyboard. Other jobs for which work simulations are appropriate might be machinist jobs, where the individual can work on the machine under close supervision, a driving test for taxi drivers or school-bus drivers, and an audition for a performing-arts organization such as a musical group. **In-basket exercises,** which consist of collections of hypothetical memos, letters, and notes that require prioritization and responses, are sometimes used as part of management simulations.

Work simulations (*or* **work samples**) *involve asking the prospective employee to perform tasks or job-related activities that simulate or represent the actual work for which the person is being considered.*

In-basket exercises *are special forms of work simulations for prospective managers. They consist of collections of hypothetical memos, letters, and notes that require responses.*

Personal Interviews

While tests are popular, the most widely used selection technique in most organizations is the employment interview. *Interviews* are face-to-face conversations between prospective job applicants and representatives of the organization.[39]

Types of interviews   Not all interviews are the same, and we can think about three types of interviews that are commonly encountered: structured, semistructured, and unstructured interviews. In a **structured employment interview,** the interviewer either prepares or is given by others a list of standard questions to be asked during the interview. All interviewers ask the same questions of each candidate to achieve consistency across interviews. Also, since the questions are presumably prepared based on a

A **Structured employment interview** *is a type of interview where the interviewer either prepares or is given by others a list of standard questions to be asked during the interview. All interviewers ask the same questions of each candidate to achieve consistency across interviews.*

careful study of the job, these questions are more pertinent than are those that many interviewers would generate on their own. In some cases, after the questions are determined, potential answers are also devised and given scores, so that the interviewer can assign overall grades based on a scoring key.

The **semistructured employment interview** involves advance preparation of major or key questions to be asked. This method provides a common frame of reference for all people who are interviewed for a job and requires that they all answer a predetermined set of specific questions. However, the interviewer is also given the prerogative to ask additional follow-up questions to probe specific answers that the interviewee provides, and so forth. For example, a popular strategy used in some firms today, especially high-tech firms, is to ask challenging and unusual questions designed to assess creativity and insight. For example, Microsoft interviewers sometimes ask applicants "Why are manhole covers round?" This question has four different, relatively correct answers, each of which allows the interviewer to probe more in different areas.[40]

The **unstructured employment interview** involves relatively little advance preparation. The interviewer may have a general idea about what she or he wants to learn about the job applicant but has few or no advance questions that are formally constructed and ready to be asked. Thus, the interview is likely to be more spontaneous, to be more wide ranging in its focus, and to cover a wide variety of topics.

In addition to these basic types of interviews, another has been gaining popularity. A **situational interview** asks the applicant questions about a specific situation to see how the applicant would react. For example, an interviewer might ask the applicant something like:

- Think back to a situation where a personal conflict between a supervisor and a subordinate was interfering with the work of both parties. How did you deal with this conflict? Was the problem resolved?

In other cases, rather than ask about something that has already happened, the interviewer might ask the applicant to imagine a situation that has not yet occurred. In such cases, the interviewer might ask something like:

- Suppose you had a subordinate who you knew had the abilities to perform his or her job but who simply chose not to exert any effort on the job. How would you approach this problem? What kinds of approaches might you try?

Research results indicate that situational interviews are better predictors of future job performance than are more traditional interviews.[41] They also change the focus of the interview more explicitly from a KSA approach to a job-fit approach.

Interviewers generally prefer unstructured interviews because they believe these interviews allow them to gather richer information, and give them the freedom to make employment decisions on their own. But evidence suggests that structured interviews are much better predictors of subsequent job performance (i.e., they are more valid or job related) than are unstructured interviews, and situational interviews are even better at predicting future job performance.[42] None of them do as well predicting future performance as some paper-and-pencil tests, but only interviews are effective at assessing KSAs such as interpersonal skills, and interviews are generally effective at allowing organizations to decide who fits best in the organization.

For these and other reasons, interviews will continue to be a popular means for making selection decisions. It is important to note, however, that the Supreme Court, in *Watson* v. *Forth Worth Bank,* ruled that interviews used for making selection decisions had the same requirements concerning demonstrating job relatedness as did any

Semistructured employment interview *is a type of interview that involves advance preparation of major or key questions to be asked, so that all applicants will be asked essentially the same questions. However, the interviewer is also given the prerogative to ask additional follow-up questions to probe specific answers that the interviewee provides.*

Unstructured employment interview *involves relatively little advance preparation. The interviewer may have a general idea about what she or he wants to learn about the job applicant but has few or no advance questions that are formally constructed and ready to be asked.*

Situational interview *is a type of interview, growing in popularity, where the interviewer asks the applicant questions about a specific situation to see how the applicant would react.*

other selection technique.[43] But, as we noted above, it is more difficult to establish the job relatedness of interviews, in part, because of the prevalence of interview errors.

First impression error   *occurs when an interviewer makes a decision too early in the interview process. This error may significantly affect a decision even when subsequent information indicates the first impression may have been wrong.*

Contrast error   *occurs when the interviewer is unduly influenced by other people who have been interviewed. For example, suppose an interviewer meets with one candidate who is extremely good or extremely bad. The next person interviewed may suffer or benefit by the contrast with this person.*

Similarity error   *occurs when the interviewer is unduly influenced by the fact that the interviewee is similar to the interviewer in one or more important ways. As a result of the perception of similarity, the interviewer may be more favorably disposed toward the candidate than the candidate's credentials warrant.*

Nonrelevancy   *is a type of error that occurs when an interviewer really doesn't know enough about the job for which he or she is interviewing candidates. As a result, the interviewer bases an assessment of the individual's abilities to perform the job on incomplete or inaccurate assessments of the nature of that job.*

Interview errors   One such error that occurs in interviews is known as the **first impression error.**[44] Interviewers who make this mistake are those who tend to make a decision early in the interview process. For example, the candidate being interviewed might arrive a minute or two late or might have a few awkward moments at the beginning of the interview. This situation, in turn, may cause the interviewer to make a negative decision about that individual, even though later evidence in the interview may have been more positive. The **contrast error** occurs when the interviewer is unduly influenced by other people who have been interviewed. For example, suppose an interviewer meets with one candidate who is extremely good or extremely bad. The next person interviewed may suffer or benefit by the contrast with this person. That is, if the first candidate was extremely good and the second candidate is only slightly above average, the interviewer may be prone to provide a lower evaluation for the second person than would have otherwise been the case. Similarly, if the first candidate was poor, the second candidate, who again may be about average, may appear to be even better in the eyes of the interviewer and receive a more positive evaluation than is warranted.

Similarity errors, on the other hand occur when the interviewer is unduly influenced by the fact that the interviewee is similar to the interviewer in one or more important ways. For example, consider the case of a person who was graduated from a particular college or is from a certain town and who interviews someone who was graduated from the same college or who is from the same hometown. As a result of the perception of similarity, the interviewer may be more favorably disposed toward the candidate than the candidate's credentials warrant.

Another type of error that interviewers can make is that of **nonrelevancy.** For example, the interviewer may be inappropriately influenced by an individual's posture, dress, or appearance. An interviewer may rely too heavily on the extent to which an interviewee can maintain eye contact for an extended period of time. The interviewee may be shy or bashful or simply doesn't want to seem too aggressive. By not maintaining eye contact with the interviewer, however, the individual may create a false impression that she or he isn't assertive enough to do the job.

A final type of error that is common in interview situations has to do with the interviewer's knowledge of the job. Some organizations do not pay adequate attention to selecting appropriate interviewers. They may select employees to interview candidates for a particular job even though the interviewers know little or nothing about that job. Thus, the interviewer may base her or his assessment of the individual's abilities to perform the job on incomplete or inaccurate assessments of the nature of that job.

These problems exist, to a greater or lesser extent, in all interviews. Their effects can be minimized, however, with proper training of interviewers. Experience itself is not a good substitute for training, and this training should focus on the occurrence of the problems outlined above, making the interviewer aware of what he or she says and does. In addition, the training should provide interviewers with the means to replace behaviors that lead to errors with behaviors more likely to lead to their deciding on the best person for the job.

Other Selection Techniques

Application blanks, tests, and interviews are part of most selection systems, but these techniques are often enhanced by several other techniques that are part of the selection process.

References and recommendations   One of these other techniques is the use of references and recommendations. The job applicant is usually asked to provide either letters of recommendation or the names and addresses of individuals who may be contacted to write such letters. Presumably, the organization can use this information as a basis for knowing about a person's past experiences and work history. References and recommendations, however, are often of little real value. If a job applicant selects the people to write recommendations, the individual is likely to pick people who she or he knows will write positive letters of recommendation. For example, a student is more likely to ask a professor who gave him an A for a recommendation than a professor who gave him a D. Likewise, a former boss who gave the individual high performance evaluations is a more likely reference than is a former boss who gave the individual average or below-average recommendations. Thus, the organization must be somewhat skeptical about a set of glowing recommendation letters that a job applicant submits for consideration.

There is also a growing concern about legal liability in the preparation of recommendation letters. Job applicants have sued someone who wrote a negative letter of recommendation that was, in turn, the basis for the individual subsequently not being offered employment. Organizations themselves have sued people who wrote favorable recommendations for job candidates who were then found to be highly unsuitable. As a result of these legal concerns, many individuals have begun to take the position that they will provide only objective information about a job candidate as part of a reference letter. Thus, they might be willing to verify dates of employment, salary, history, job title, and so forth, but they may be unwilling to provide any assessment regarding the person's performance, capabilities, or the likelihood for success in a new setting.[45]

Assessment centers   Another selection technique that is used widely, but only for the selection of managers, is the assessment center.[46] An assessment center is not a physical location but is instead an approach to selecting managers based on measuring and evaluating their ability to perform critical work behaviors. Individuals participating in an assessment center are likely to be either current managers who are being considered for promotion to higher levels or a pool of external recruits such as upcoming college graduates whom the firm is considering hiring for management positions.

The individuals to be assessed are brought together in a single place such as the company's training headquarters or perhaps a conference facility at a hotel. While there, they undergo a series of tests, exercises, and feedback sessions. A normal assessment-center schedule lasts two to three days and involves about ten to fifteen individuals at any one time. During the assessment-center schedule, these individuals may undergo experiential exercises; group decision-making tasks; case analyses; individual employment tests, such as personality inventories and so forth; role-playing exercises; and other methods for assessing their potential skills and abilities. A panel of current managers oversees the assessment and serves as the evaluators. At the conclusion of the assessment center, each of these evaluators provides an in-depth evaluation of each person attending the assessment center and makes an overall evaluation about the person's suitability for promotion.

AT&T was one of the first companies in the United States to use the assessment-center concept, and since 1956 over 200,000 of its employees have attended various assessment centers. AT&T's evaluation of its assessment centers indicates that this method for selecting managers is a fairly effective technique for differentiating between those who are more and those who are less likely to be successful in the organization. This suggests that assessment centers may be quite useful, but there are some disadvantages as well. The most critical is that assessment centers are rather expensive to run, especially when we consider the lost productivity of both the candidates and the assessors.[47]

The Selection Decision

The final step in the process is to make the actual decision about whom to hire. If there is only one position to fill, the organization can simply hire the highest-ranked candidate and the decision is relatively easy. Likewise, if there is a need to hire dozens of employees for similar kinds of positions, the selection decision may simply consist of choosing where to draw the line between those who qualify for employment and those who do not.

Multiple Indicators

Since every selection technique has its limitations, most organizations actually rely on several selection techniques and, in fact, may use all or most of the selection techniques discussed above. Hence, a person who applies for a job may be subjected to a preliminary screening interview to make sure that she meets the minimum qualifications necessary for the job. Then she may have to complete an application and be subjected to background checks, followed by employment tests and/or work simulations. For example, almost all of the 100 best companies to work for in America (as determined by *Fortune* magazine), ranging from Southwest Airlines to The Container Store, rely heavily on multiple predictors when making hiring decisions.[48]

By using multiple approaches, the organization is able to counterbalance the measurement error in one selection technique against another, and it is also able to base decisions on the basis of more complete information. This fact can complicate matters, however. The organization must decide if a candidate must pass some minimum requirement on every selection technique (i.e., "multiple hurdles") or if a high score in one area can compensate for a lower score somewhere else (i.e., a compensatory model). Thus, when an organization uses multiple approaches, it is not always clear who really is the "best" candidate.

The hiring decision may also be complicated by the fact that the person hired may not be the one who is ranked first on the selection criteria. As noted earlier, an organization might select a person who has "acceptable" levels of the requisite KSAs but who is a better "fit" with the culture and style of the organization. Furthermore, it is fairly common for organizations to cluster applicants who may differ somewhat in terms of KSAs but who don't differ enough from one another to be critical. Thus, the organization could use any decision rules it wished to select among the people in such a cluster without sacrificing performance on the job. This procedure, known as *banding,* allows an organization to select an applicant, for example, from some underrepresented group in the organization while still ensuring high performance standards. A variation on this approach can also be used to ensure that candidates selected because they fit can also perform the jobs in question.

Selection Errors

But, in fact, no selection system is perfect, and an organization will always make at least an occasional selection error and decide to hire the wrong person. Actually, there are two basic types of selection errors that can be made: **false positives** and **false negatives.** In each case, the decision maker examines the information available, predicts whether the applicant will ultimately succeed or fail on the job, and then decides to hire or re-

False positives   *are applicants who are predicted to be successful and are hired but who ultimately fail.*

False negatives   *are applicants who are predicted to fail and are not hired, but if they had been hired, they would have been successful.*

ject (not hire) the person on that basis. In each case, some of the predictions are correct and others are incorrect; these situations are illustrated in Figure 7.6.

The figure shows that some of the people predicted to be successful and who are hired will in fact succeed. These are "hits" (shown in quadrant II) because the right decision was made. The bottom left quadrant (quadrant III) also shows hits. These people are rejected; if they were hired, they would fail. But the other two quadrants illustrate the two types of selection errors. Quadrant I represents the false positives: the applicants who are predicted to be successful and who are therefore hired, but who ultimately fail. Quadrant IV represents the false negatives: the applicants who are predicted to fail and so are not hired. If they had been hired, however, they would have been successful.

It would seem obvious that selection systems that minimize selection errors will be more effective for the organization, but it is not possible to minimize both types of errors at the same time, and so decisions must be made concerning which type of decision is more costly for the organization. Specifically, it is possible to minimize the number of poor performers that are hired by using more rigorous tests or more challenging interviews to make selection decisions. Indeed, the organization may set its standards for selection so high it may rarely hire anyone who fails. But, if decisions are based on more and more stringent criteria, there will also be fewer people hired overall, and the organization will miss opportunities by rejecting people who could have done the job and been successful. Again, it depends on which error the organization sees as more costly.

The information in Figure 7.6 also provides some insight into the issue of **test validity.** The specific techniques for establishing validity in a formal manner are provided in the *Taking HR to the Next Level* feature at the end of Part Two, but we can provide a simpler view of the process for now. Validating a test essentially means determining if the test measures what was intended. In the case of a selection test, this means that scores on the test should be able to predict who will be successful on the job. As noted in Chapter 2, sometimes this is referred to as establishing that the selection device is "job related." But looking at Figure 7.6, we have information about exactly what we need. If a test is valid, then there should be many more "hits" than errors. As noted, there are tradeoffs between the types of errors we can make, but a test cannot be valid unless it predicts subsequent success more often than it misses. The actual information needed to successfully defend a selection technique in court is provided in the *Taking HR to the Next Level* feature, found at the end of Part Two.

> **Test validity**   *means that scores on a test are related to performance on a job. This must be determined empirically, and it is critical to defending against charges of discrimination in hiring.*

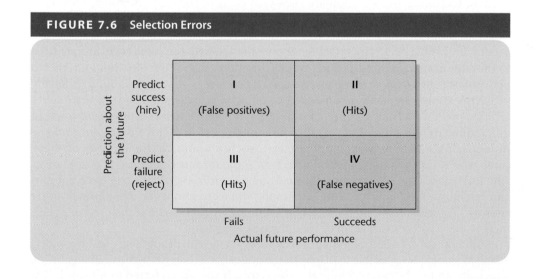

FIGURE 7.6   Selection Errors

Legal Issues in Selection

In Chapter 2 we discussed the Civil Rights Act and the various pieces of legislation dealing with discrimination in the workplace. Although this legislation covers the full range of employment decisions, you may have noticed in that discussion that most of the cases involved discrimination in selection. There is little doubt that an organization faces the greatest legal liability in this area, and, therefore, it has received a great deal of attention. We also noted in Chapter 2 that an organization faced with a prima facie case of discrimination must prove that the basis for the selection decision was job related. The organization must demonstrate that persons scoring higher on the selection instrument are those who are most likely to perform best on the job.

Establishing this relationship is essentially what the validation process is about. In fact, the courts have made it clear in a series of key decisions that validating a selection instrument is the way to establish job relatedness.[49] Since the *Griggs* decision, the courts have become less lenient about how validation studies should be conducted and thus found acceptable.[50] Therefore, it is critical that the human resource manager understand the process of validating a selection instrument and the importance of carrying out this process in all cases, rather than just those cases with evidence of disparate impact.

Helping the organization defend itself in discrimination cases is one of the most important areas where a human resource manager can make a contribution to the firm. It is just as critical, however, for the human resource manager to help the organization avoid legal problems in the first place. Table 7.2 illustrates some critical questions that the human resource manager should ask concerning any selection system when trying to select the best employees and still work within the law.

Evaluating Recruiting and Selection Activities

Because recruiting and selection are such vital parts of the human resource management process for most organizations, it stands to reason that the organization will periodically evaluate their effectiveness. As far as recruiting is concerned, an effective process is one that results in a reasonable pool of qualified employees who are available to the organization and from which the organization can hire people whom it wants to perform various jobs, at a reasonable cost. Therefore, if the organization is having problems attracting qualified candidates or filling jobs, this would suggest that the recruiting process was not working. In addition, it is possible to assess the effectiveness of different recruiting sources the organization might be using. This assessment could be in terms of the number of applicants generated, or in terms of the number of applicants who accept jobs when offered. In fact, some evidence suggests that applicants who learn about the organization through some sources are more likely to accept jobs and remain in those jobs than are applicants who learn about the jobs through other sources.[51] Therefore, it might be reasonable for an organization to target recruiting efforts at those sources that seem to yield the best applicants.

Evaluation of the selection system is a bit more complicated, but there are some widely accepted techniques available to help with the evaluation. To begin with, recall Figure 7.6, which illustrated the two types of selection errors. If you also referred to Appendix 2 at that point in the chapter discussion, it might have occurred to you that the number of

TABLE 7.2 Critical Questions to Ask About a Selection System

1. Was a job analysis conducted to determine the functions of the job and the requisite KSAs?

2. Once job requirements were established, were selection techniques (or predictors) chosen that adequately assess the degree to which applicants possess these abilities?

3. Are other equally useful selection techniques available that have been found to have less disparate impact?

4. Are good performance measures, also based on careful job analysis, available?

5. Are there data relating scores on the predictors to performance on the job (or some other valued outcome)?

6. Are there data relating scores on the entire selection system to performance on the job?

7. Were these validity studies (used to determine the relationships between scores and performance) conducted using accepted and well-established practices?

8. Is there any evidence that any of these relationships differ as a function of the age, race, or gender of the people involved?

The answer to all of these questions should be yes except for question 3, which should be answered no. If the questions don't elicit these answers, then the potential for incurring legal problems exists. Question 8 has no "right" answer. If the relationships obtained DO vary as a function of any of these characteristics, there will be a need to examine exactly how this affects the decisions that will be made. If the answer is no, the situation will be much simpler. The human resource manager must be able to help the organization change the system and thus avoid legal problems.

selection errors is minimized (and the number of hits maximized) when the relationship between scores on a predictor and performance on the job is at its strongest. That is, the greater the validity of a predictor, the fewer the selection errors we make. Another way of looking at this situation would be to imagine that half the selection decisions were errors. More specifically, imagine that half the people selected turned out to be unsuccessful and half the people rejected would have been successful. This outcome is exactly what we would expect if we selected applicants purely on the basis of chance (the flip of a coin, for example). If the relationship between the predictor and job performance grew stronger, the number of errors would decrease. But saying that the predictor was valid (i.e., we were doing better than chance) doesn't tell us how much better than chance we are doing or what that situation is worth to the organization.

Utility analysis is an attempt to determine the extent to which a selection system provides real benefit to the organization. This method assesses the practical payoff for any selection system. Although the use of any valid predictor should increase the hit rate to better than what would happen if selections were left to chance, other factors must be considered in assessing utility. First, the organization must consider the cost. A firm might be able to increase its hit rate by 10 percent by using a selection system that costs

Utility analysis *is an attempt to determine the extent to which a selection system provides real benefit to the organization.*

$100,000 per applicant to implement. But is this selection system worth it? The simple answer appears to be no, but it's actually more complicated. What if the job in question were an airline pilot? What would it be worth it to you, as a consumer, to be 10 percent more comfortable that the person flying your plane was really capable of doing so? Therefore, an organization needs to consider both the cost of the selection system and the cost of a selection error.

The firm also needs to determine a definition of success and then estimate what percentage of applicants would be successful under different scenarios. In fact, for many low-level jobs the probability of success for a random group of applicants is probably much higher than 50 percent. In such cases, it may be difficult to increase the hit rate significantly for the selection system, and it may be relatively inexpensive to make a selection error. Therefore, many selection systems, even though they are valid, might have little utility. More detailed information about utility analysis and some formulas available for computing utility are available in Appendix 2. You may not be interested in understanding the formula, but it is important that all human resource managers understand that they must be able to justify the expense of the systems they create by showing how the improved selection system contributes to the bottom line. Whether the system is evaluated in terms of decreased accidents and turnover or increased productivity, human resource managers must demonstrate utility.

Chapter Summary

Recruiting is the process of developing a pool of qualified applicants who are interested in working for the organization and from which the organization might reasonably select the best individual or individuals to hire for employment. Organizational goals in recruiting are to optimize, in various ways, the size of the pool of qualified applicants and to offer an honest and candid assessment to perspective applicants of what kinds of jobs and what kinds of opportunities the organization can potentially make available to them.

Internal recruiting is the process of looking inside the organization for existing qualified employees who might be promoted to higher-level positions. The three most common methods used for internal recruiting are job posting and supervisory recommendations. External recruiting involves looking to sources outside the organization for prospective employees. Different methods are likely to be used by an organization engaged in external recruiting. These include the general labor pool, direct applicants, referrals, advertisements, employment agencies, and colleges and universities.

Many organizations today are finding that it is increasingly important to provide perspective employees with what is called a realistic job preview. Realistic job previews might involve providing job applicants with an opportunity to actually observe others performing the work.

The selection process involves three clear, distinct steps: gathering information about the members of the pool of qualified recruits, evaluating the qualifications of each applicant from among the recruiting pool, and making the actual decision about which candidate or candidates will be offered employment with the organization. The basic selection criteria that most organizations use in deciding whom to hire are education and experience, skills and abilities, and personal characteristics. Firms must also decide whether to focus on fit or skills.

Organizations use various techniques for gathering information about job candidates. The most common are employment applications and background checks, employment tests, work simulations, and employment interviews. Each of these techniques has its unique strengths and weaknesses, but each can also play an important role in selection.

After subjecting the pool of qualified applicants to the organization's selection process, it is then necessary to make a final selection decision. Most organizations choose to rely on several selection techniques and, in fact, may use all or most of the selection techniques discussed in this chapter. Managers also strive to avoid various selection errors.

It is important that the organization understand the legal context in which it can recruit and select new employees and that it evaluate its selection and placement activities periodically.

Key Points for Future HR Managers

- Recruitment is the process by which qualified applicants are attracted to the organization.

- Although it is important to have more applicants than openings, it is not helpful to have too many applicants per opening.

- Recruitment from within is preferable because of the motivational value.

- External recruitment is necessary for entry-level jobs and brings new ideas into the organization.

- Internal recruiting techniques include job postings and supervisory recommendations.

- External recruiting techniques include word of mouth, advertisements, public and private employment agencies, college placement offices, and executive search firms.

- Electronic recruiting is having a major impact on both internal and external recruiting because it allows companies to reach a wider range of applicants and it is cost-effective, but it does come at a cost in terms of administrative burdens and the fact that not everyone has access to a computer.

- Realistic job previews involve telling people the truth about the job before they begin. Realistic job previews have been found to increase performance and reduce turnover.

- Selecting qualified employees for open jobs is one of the most important aspects of the human resource manager's job.

- There are two basic types of selection errors—selecting someone who ultimately fails, and failing to select someone who would have been successful. Both are problematic and there are tradeoffs between the two types of errors.

- Potential criteria for selection include education, experience, skills, abilities, personal characteristics, and "fit."

- Techniques available for selection include application blanks, employment tests (including cognitive ability tests, psychomotor tests, personality tests, and integrity tests), work simulations, interviews, personal recommendations, and physical examinations. Several of these are now available widely, via computer and the Internet.

- Assessment centers are used for managers and are settings where each candidate is evaluated on multiple criteria by multiple judges—usually higher-level managers. Although these centers are good at predicting future performance, there are some issues involved and they are expensive.

- Selecting employees is one of the most important functions of the human resource manager. The success of these activities can be evaluated by conducting a formal utility analysis, which can assess whether the costs associated with the selection system can be justified by cost savings and/or productivity gains.

Key Points for Future General Managers

- The goal of recruiting is to generate qualified applicants for jobs.

- Recruiting can be either internal or external, and each has advantages and disadvantages.

- Decisions about the best methods for external (or internal) recruiting should be based on the kind of applicants the firm wants to attract.

- Electronic recruiting is revolutionizing the recruiting field. It is cost-effective and allows the firm to

reach a broad range of applicants, but it can increase administrative costs.

- Realistic job previews involve telling applicants both the positive and negative aspects of the job. Some applicants may be frightened by this information, but these are people who would not have been successful anyway. The use of realistic job previews has been linked to more positive attitudes about the job, higher performance, and lower turnover rates for a wide variety of jobs.

- Applicants decide which jobs to apply for and to accept based on the extent to which they feel they will fit with the company (in addition to considering basic issues such as compensation, benefits, and terms of employment).

- Selection is one of the most important functions carried out by the HR Department.

- No selection system is perfect, and decisions have to be made about which types of errors are the most and the least costly.

- Selection systems should be based on careful job analysis information.

- Decisions must be made about the basis for selection decisions. It is especially important to decide the extent to which people should be selected on the basis of their fit with the organization.

- Many techniques are available for selecting individuals. Each has some advantages and some drawbacks. An ideal system would combine several of these techniques into a single system, but there is no one best way to select people, and when any technique is used for making a selection decision, including interviews, it is treated as a "test" for legal purposes and must be validated.

- Using tests that are not valid (and not reliable) is irrational and can lead to serious legal problems.

- There are methods available, all falling under the general category of utility analysis, which can allow an assessment of whether the costs of a selection system are justified by increased productivity or decreased costs.

Review and Discussion Questions

1. Compare and contrast the advantages and disadvantages of internal versus external recruiting.

2. Identify and describe the basic methods used by organizations for external recruiting.

3. What is a realistic job preview? What function does it serve?

4. How would you feel if you thought you deserved to be promoted, but instead the organization hired someone from outside and made that person your boss? What would you do?

5. Which recruiting methods are most likely to attract your attention?

6. What are the general steps in the selection process?

7. What are the most common selection criteria that organizations use when making selection decisions?

8. Identify and describe several popular selection techniques.

9. Can you identify various kinds of jobs where experience is more important than education? Where education is more important than experience?

10. Which selection techniques would you feel most confident in using? Least confident in using? Why?

CLOSING CASE

Hiring High-Risk Employees Can Pay Off for Business

When most people think of new employees starting to work for an organization, they most likely imagine only the brightest, most highly motivated, and most upstanding and respectable applicants being chosen for employment. But with surprising frequency, these new employees may in fact be former drug addicts, alcohol abusers, welfare recipients, and homeless people. What could prompt a business to hire from these ranks as it expands its workforce? The reasons run the gamut from absolute necessity to social conscience. Regardless of the organization's motive, however, many managers report that with a little extra attention and cau-

tion, new employees chosen from what might be considered high-risk labor pools can actually pay big dividends.

One example is Candleworks, a small candle-making company based in Iowa City, Iowa. The firm's owners, Lynette and Mike Richards, didn't want to hire high-risk employees at first. Instead, they tried to follow the conventional wisdom of hiring only the best and the brightest. The problem, however, was that they simply couldn't find enough "qualified" workers from this pool who were interested in working long hours for relatively low wages. Unfilled jobs and high turnover eventually forced the owners to look elsewhere for employees and, in near desperation, they took a big chance on hiring one applicant who was undergoing treatment for alcohol abuse.

As it turned out, because this employee had few other opportunities, he greatly valued his job and was very appreciative of the trust placed in him by the Richardses. He eventually became a highly committed and valuable employee. Because of this positive experience, the Richardses subsequently began to recruit and hire high-risk employees systematically and routinely, and these individuals are now the foundation of the workforce at Candleworks.

Ken Legler, owner of Houston Wire Works, a Texas-based enterprise, has also experienced a major labor shortage. Legler's solution has been to tap into a works program sponsored by the Texas Department of Corrections. Depending on the situation, convicts may be bused to and from a work site, or work may instead be shipped to and from a prison. Convicts receive training in how to perform the necessary work and are paid (usually at the minimum wage rate) for their work.

But not all employers use high-risk employees purely out of necessity. For example, Microboard Processing, Inc. (MPI), a small New England electronics firm, makes giving troubled people a second chance a basic part of its business philosophy. MPI is owned and managed by Craig Hoekenga. Hoekenga has always had a strong sense of social responsibility and believes that his best way of making a contribution to society is by offering second chances to high-risk employees.

Indeed, almost one-third of MPI's employees today might be classified as high-risk. They include former welfare recipients, people who have never held a steady job, convicted felons, and former drug addicts. Hoekenga insists that at least 10 percent of the firm's new hires each year be from one of these high-risk categories. While the firm also hires plenty of "conventional" employees—those with respectable backgrounds and solid work histories—Hoekenga considers his high-risk workers to be the backbone of the company.

For example, Ruth Tinney recently applied for employment at MPI. At the time of her application, she had not worked for several years and had spent the three previous years on welfare. Hoekenga gave her a two-week trial, and now she has a regular position as an assembly-line worker. He can also point to numerous other success stories throughout his business, and he can describe many former employees who were essentially rehabilitated while working at MPI but who then left for other jobs—for advancement opportunities, relocation to another part of the country, and so forth.

But not all of his new hires succeed, of course. He estimates that about two or three employees out of every ten he hires eventually fail. For example, one former drug addict who had worked at the firm for over a year returned to drug abuse and went back to jail. Hoekenga points out that he has to give newly hired, high-risk employees a while to learn the ropes. Many, for example, have never held a steady job and do not understand or appreciate the need for regular and prompt attendance. Consequently, they may come in late for work and/or not show up regularly.

Therefore, MPI allows them considerable latitude in absenteeism and tardiness during the first few weeks. Each instance of tardiness or absenteeism is followed by a conversation with Hoekenga or a supervisor. In these conversations, Hoekenga and his supervisors stress the need for punctual and regular work schedules and focus on the need for improvement. Their goal is to teach their high-risk employees proper work habits during the first six months of employment. After that time, the firm takes a much harder line and cuts people less and less slack. But the ones who make it feel an especially strong sense of loyalty and appreciation toward Hoekenga and his company and make enormous contributions to the firm's continuing profitability and growth.[52]

Case Questions

1. What do you see as the major advantages and disadvantages of hiring high-risk employees?

2. What differences in employment strategies exist between firms like Candleworks and MPI?

3. The examples cited in this case involve smaller businesses. How might a big corporation like IBM or Ford try to hire high-risk employees?

Building HR Management Skills

Purpose: The purpose of this exercise is to give you insights into effective and ineffective recruiting via advertisements.

Step 1: Obtain a section of a newspaper (no longer than one page) that contains numerous recruiting ads. Working alone, identify the one ad that you think is most effective and the one ad that you think is least effective. Jot down on a piece of paper your reasoning for each choice.

Step 2: Form pairs with your classmates. Exchange ad pages with the student in your pair. Pick two ads from the student's paper, the ones that you think are most and least effective. Again, jot down your rationale.

Step 3: Each of you should next reveal your own choices for most and least effective recruiting ads, along with your rationales for your choices.

Step 4: This step is optional. Your instructor may ask for a few examples of particularly effective and less effective ads to be shared with the entire class.

Ethical Dilemmas in HR Management

Assume that after working for several years you returned to graduate school to take some advanced courses and earn a master's degree as a way of improving both your specific job skills and your overall prospects for career advancement. While your degree program was relatively technical in nature, you did take a course in industrial psychology. One of the topics covered in this course was personality testing and measurement. As a term paper for this course, you thoroughly studied and reviewed the most popular personality tests used by companies as selection techniques.

You recently completed your degree and are now looking for a new position. You are especially interested in working for one particular company, and this firm is also actively considering you. As part of its selection process, the firm has requested that you complete a battery of tests, including some personality measures. Because you (1) understand these tests so well and (2) have a good understanding of the type of person the firm is looking for, you know that you can answer the questions in the personality measure so as to make you a near-perfect candidate for the job. On the other hand, you also know that the personality traits the company is seeking, and on which you can score highly, are not exactly descriptive of your own personality. But you also believe that you are so highly motivated that you will excel if given the right opportunity.

Questions

1. What are the ethical issues in this situation?

2. What are the basic arguments for and against "cheating" on the personality tests?

3. What do you think most job seekers would do? What would you do?

HR Internet Exercise

Several Internet sites are dedicated to employment opportunities for job seekers. Use a search engine to locate the addresses for three different sites of this type. As you visit each site, try to place yourself in the role of a job seeker looking for employment in each of the following three areas:

1. Production manager in a manufacturing plant

2. Sales representative for a consumer products group

3. Restaurant manager

Questions

1. Are there any differences in ease of use and perceived value for job searches among the three sites?

2. Are there any differences in ease of use and perceived value for each of the three kinds of jobs being searched?

3. Identify the basic quality requirements in such sites to maximize their potential value to a job seeker.

CONTINGENT WORKERS, RELIABILITY, AND VALIDITY

Part Two has discussed numerous issues and HR activities that involve decision making. For instance, we described information needed to make human resource decisions, organizational form and structure, recruitment and selection, and diversity. This Taking HR to the Next Level section focuses on two related areas, contingent workers and reliability and validity.

Contingent Workers

In 2006, as the price of gasoline rose to near record levels, the large energy and oil companies found themselves needing to increase their workforces to keep up with the increases in demand. But only a few years earlier, the price of a barrel of crude oil had gotten so low that a restaurant attached to a petroleum club in Texas had to suspend its policy of selling its featured steak at the price of a barrel of crude oil—selling a steak for such a low price would have bankrupted the club. Of course, during the time of low oil prices, the major oil and energy companies were busy reducing their workforces and shutting down operations. Although this example is a bit extreme, many organizations find that they go through similar cycles every few years. That is, they recruit, select, and train new employees when things go well, only to lay off many of them when there is a downturn in business. Are there any alternatives to these "boom or bust" cycles that are costly for everyone involved?

> **Contingent workers** are any type of nonpermanent employee hired by the organization during times of peak demand and who can be easily dismissed when that peak is over.

Some organizations have begun trying to soften the impact of business cycles by employing **contingent workers:** any type of nonpermanent employee hired by the organization during times of peak demand and that can be easily dismissed when that peak is over. These contingent workers have no long-term ties to the organization, nor does the organization make any long-term investments in these employees. The employees work for the organization when demand is high and move on when the demand slackens (although, of course, the organization may see some of these employees as desirable enough to offer them permanent employment).

The use of contingent workers has increased dramatically in recent years. As a result, the issues relating to their use have become more complex. We will discuss some types of contingency workers that might be employed, but we will also "take HR to the next level" by discussing various legal and managerial issues associated with their use, as well as a model suggesting when they might be most effective.

Forms of Contingent Work Relationships Categories of contingent workers include temporary employees (usually hired through an outside agency), independent contractors, on-call workers, and contract and leased employees. Another category is part-time workers. For example, Citigroup makes extensive use of part-time sales agents to pursue new clients.[1] As noted above, about 10 percent of the U.S. workforce currently works in one of these alternative forms of employment relationships, but experts suggest that this percentage is increasing at a consistent pace.

> **Temporary workers** are usually hired through an outside agency; they join the organization to work for a specific period of time, rather than with the expectation of permanent or continued employment.

Temporary workers are usually hired through an outside agency; they join the organization to work for a specific period of time, rather than with the expectation of permanent or continued employment. A major advantage of temporary employment to the organization is that such workers can usually be paid a lower rate, although they are now more likely to be entitled to the same benefits as full-time workers.[2] Considerable flexibility comes from the fact that employees themselves realize their jobs are not permanent and therefore the organization can terminate their relationship as work demands mandate.[3] On the other hand, temporary employees tend not to understand the organization's culture as well as do permanent employees. In addition, they are not as likely to be as productive as are permanent full-time employees of the organization.

Leased workers are part of a pool of employees provided by a leasing firm to the hiring firm for a fee paid to the leasing firm. This pool of employees usually constitutes a group or crew intended to handle all or most of the organization's work needs in a particular area. For example, an organization might lease a crew of custodial and other maintenance workers from an outside firm specializing in such services. These workers appear in the organization every day at a predetermined time and perform all maintenance and custodial work. To the general public, they may even appear to be employees of the firm occupying the building. In reality, however, they work for a leasing company. As should be clear, this really involves the strategy of outsourcing, discussed in Chapter 1.

Part-time workers are those individuals who routinely expect to work less than forty hours a week. This approach affords the organization a great deal of flexibility since these workers are routinely called on to work different schedules from week to week, thereby allowing the organization to cluster its labor force around peak demand times and have a smaller staff on hand during down times. Part-time workers are common in organizations like restaurants. Wait staff, bus persons, kitchen help, and other employees of such an organization might be college students who want to work only fifteen or twenty hours a week to earn spending money.

Independent contractors are basically consultants who work for an organization on a specific project and then leave for another project and another organization. They are usually hired for a specific period of time, however, and so afford a bit less flexibility than do part-time workers, but they can often bring a unique set of skills that would be difficult to replace but that are needed only for a short period of time.

On-call workers are employees of the organization who do not normally work full-time. Instead, they are expected to be "on-call," which means that they must be available on short notice, whenever the organization requires them. This alternative affords perhaps even more flexibility than that provided by part-time workers since the workers must be available for duty at all times, but only work when needed.

Advantages and Disadvantages of Using Contingent Workers Companies that use contingent and temporary workers face several advantages and disadvantages. The primary advantage that most companies seek to achieve with the use of contingent workers is cost savings. For the most part an organization that uses contingent workers does not have to pay for their benefits, such as health insurance, vacation time, and sick days. Usually the agency that provides the contingent workers absorbs these costs. In some arrangements, tax burdens can also be shifted to either the employee him- or herself or to the provider of the contingent worker.

As noted above, another major advantage that companies derive from the use of contingent workers is increased flexibility. Recruiting and hiring permanent workers is a costly proposition. If the organization miscalculates its workforce needs and hires more employees than it can adequately support, it may then face expensive and painful layoffs and downsizing efforts. But using contingent workers helps an organization

Leased workers *are part of a pool of employees provided by a leasing firm to the hiring firm for a fee paid to the leasing firm.*

Part-time workers *are those individuals who routinely expect to work less than forty hours a week.*

Independent contractors *are basically consultants who work for an organization on a specific project for a specific period of time, and then leave for another project and another organization.*

On-call workers *are employees of the organization who do not normally work full-time. Instead, they are expected to be "on-call," which means that they must be available on short notice, whenever the organization requires them.*

address this predicament more effectively. That is, the organization can maintain a permanent and full-time workforce of somewhat less than it really needs to conduct its business and then make up the difference with contingent workers. Then, as its demand for human resources increases or decreases, it can bring in more or fewer contingent workers.

Nonetheless, there are also some disadvantages associated with the use of contingent workers. Perhaps the biggest drawback is that, because the individuals are not employees of the firm, they are likely to have less commitment and attachment to the organization. When an employee is a permanent and full-time member of a firm's staff and has spent years working for the organization, it follows that she or he will develop a reasonably strong loyalty and commitment to the organization. This loyalty and commitment is a function of well-established working relationships, common and shared experiences, and the security of employment. But none of these characteristics are likely to exist in the work relationship an organization has with contingent workers.

Reliance upon contingent workers can also result in a decrease in productivity. While few studies have been conducted to document this belief scientifically, it seems reasonable to believe that the average contingent worker is not as well versed in the organization and how it conducts its business as is a permanent and full-time employee. That is, the individual contingent worker may possess adequate generalized skills but may lack firm-specific skills. Consequently, the contingent worker may not understand enough about specific organizational procedures and operations to be able to function efficiently, at least during the early period of work.

Another disadvantage is that an organization may fail to develop a strong human resource base of its own if it relies too heavily on contingent workers. In today's environment, an organization can staff almost all skilled positions with contingent workers. But if it takes this course of action, it may end up with few or even no employees of its own who possess some of these fundamental skills. In the short run, this situation might not be a particularly big problem. But in the long term, the organization may face at least some problems of decreased effectiveness as a result of a weaker human resource foundation of its own.

Finally, several court decisions have raised some legal issues associated with the use of contingent workers. As noted earlier, an important reason for employing contingent workers is that they are generally not covered under various benefits plans, especially pensions. But what happens when a firm hires temporary workers and then keeps them on for an extended period of time? A recent article reported that over 29 percent of the workers employed by temp agencies remain on their assignments for a year or longer.[4] At that point, the question becomes who is the primary employer: the temp agency who first hired the individual or the firm that contracted for the individual's services with the temp agency but then kept the employee for an extended period of time?

In the last several years lawsuits were filed against Time-Warner, Microsoft, and FedEx dealing with whether "temporary" employees were entitled to the same benefits (such as pensions) as the permanent employees. The court ruled that the question was determined by the nature of the employment relationship. If the firm itself decides who it will employ, provides the same supervision for temporary workers as for permanent workers, and uses its own payroll system to compensate them, the courts are generally finding that the workers qualify for all other benefits afforded regular employees. Only when the temp agency itself makes the assignment decision, provides at least part of the supervision, and handles compensation do the individuals remain temporary workers. In the case of Microsoft, this meant that over 6,000 temporary workers had to be provided with the same pension benefits as the permanent workers.[5] Clearly these decisions make using contingent workers a bit less attractive.

Managing Contingent and Temporary Workers   Given the widespread use of contingent and temporary workers today, it follows logically that managers should understand how to utilize these kinds of employees more effectively. That is, they need to understand how to manage contingent and temporary workers.

One key to the effective management of contingent and temporary workers is careful planning. Even though one of the presumed benefits of using contingent workers is flexibility, it is still important for managers to try to use such workers in a relatively smooth and coordinated fashion. Rather than having to call in contingent workers sporadically and with no prior notice, it is beneficial for the organization to be able to bring in specified numbers of contingent workers for well-defined periods of time, and this approach calls for thoughtful planning. A second important part of managing contingent and temporary workers more effectively is to understand and acknowledge the advantages and disadvantages described in the preceding section. That is, the organization needs to recognize what it can and can't achieve from the use of contingent and temporary workers. Expecting too much from such workers, for example, is a mistake that the manager should avoid.

Third, it is important that managers carefully assess the real cost of using contingent workers. For example, we noted above that many firms adopt this course of action as a way of saving labor costs, and the organization should be able to document precisely its labor costs savings. It can document this information by looking at how much it would be paying people in wages and benefits if they were on permanent staff, comparing this figure with how much they are paying the agency providing the contingent workers, and assessing the difference. But this difference might be misleading. For instance, we also noted above that contingent workers might not be as effective performers as permanent and full-time employees. So comparing employees on a direct cost basis is not necessarily valid. Instead, the organization has to adjust the direct differences in labor costs with the differences in productivity and performance.

Managers also need to articulate and understand fully their own strategies and decide in advance how they intend to manage their temporary workers, specifically focusing on how to integrate these workers into the organization. At a simplistic level, for example, an organization with a large contingent workforce needs to make some decisions about the treatment of contingent workers relative to the treatment of permanent, full-time workers. For example, should contingent workers be invited to the company holiday party? Should contingent workers have the same access to employee auxiliary benefits, such as counseling services or childcare facilities, as do permanent and full-time employees? These questions don't have clear right or wrong answers. The point simply is that managers must understand that they need to develop a strategy for integrating contingent workers according to some sound logic and rationale and then follow that strategy consistently over time.

Managing work relationships is becoming more difficult with such a great reliance on outsourcing. When work is outsourced, the people performing the job are not employees of the company but work for the contractor who provides the service. Yet these workers provide services that customers see as coming from the parent company. So the parent company must manage these people, even though they work for someone else and may be located far away from the parent company. Organizations such as Convergys specialize in providing outsourced services. Their main call center located in Cincinnati, Ohio, handles billing for many firms in the customer care industry, and the company has recently won a $280 million contract to perform many human resource management functions for the State of Florida. The services, of course, will be provided from the headquarters in Ohio.

Human resource architecture
is based on the calculation of two critical terms: the value of human capital (determined by the extent to which an employee helps an organization to accomplish its major strategic objectives); and the uniqueness of human capital (which refers to the ease with which the organization can find another employee with the same skills). These calculations can help an organization decide which jobs need to be performed by permanent employees and which can be performed by other employees.

Human Resource Architecture   There is, fortunately, a proposed model that can aid a manager making strategic decisions about the use of contingent workers. This model, which has been termed **human resource architecture,** is based on the calculation of two critical terms: the value of human capital (i.e., employees) and the uniqueness of human capital.[6] In this view, value is determined by the extent to which an employee helps an organization to accomplish its major strategic objectives. Core assets are those assets that are vital for the organization's strategic position (and are thus more valuable), while peripheral assets are those employees who do not serve those strategic goals directly (and are thus less valuable). Uniqueness refers to the ease with which the organization can find another employee with the same skills—the more difficult it is to replace the skills, the more unique the human capital.

The human resource architecture consists of four quadrants, which are formed by crossing two levels of value (high and low) with two levels of uniqueness (high and low) for human capital (see Figure II.1). In quadrant I, human capital is both valuable and unique. In this quadrant we rely on permanent, full-time employees and work to develop those employees to their full potential. Thus, the organization should hire employees at the entry level (for the most part) and should provide all necessary training and developmental experience. The nature of the psychological contract in this quadrant should focus on the organization and should encourage mutual investment on the part of the employees and the organization.

Quadrant II is where human capital is valuable but not unique. Here the organization should hire employees who have already developed the necessary skills at another organization. Although these employees should also be full-time and permanent, the nature of the psychological contract should be much different. Here, the focus should be on a symbiotic relationship where both parties benefit, but the organization should appreciate that these employees are less likely to be fully committed to the organization, and vice versa.

In quadrant III both value and uniqueness are low. Needed skills are not strategic and many workers possess them, and so the firm would be wise to contract for the services externally. This approach translates into a strong reliance on contract labor, or even temporary and part-time labor, and the psychological contract is transactional. That is, the employees are hired to do a job only and are not expected to have much commitment to (or involvement in) the overall organization. Finally, in quadrant IV human capital is unique but not valuable. Thus, the skills are not critical for achieving strategic objectives, but they are important and not easy to find. In this quadrant the nature of the psychological contract is one where both parties enter a partnership, and part-time and temporary work relationships are likely to be widely used.

To date, little empirical research supports (or refutes) this model, but it does provide a potentially useful framework for organizations deciding where and when nontraditional employment relationships are more likely to be successful.

Reliability and Validity

Reliability and validity are concepts that are important for any psychological type of measurement. That is, these concepts are important for measures of attitudes, beliefs, and values. For purposes of our discussion, though, they are especially important for the selection techniques used by an organization. Regardless of which technique or techniques an organization chooses to use for its selection decisions, it must ensure that those techniques are reliable and valid.

Without such evidence, the organization is exposing itself to the possibility of discrimination. As noted in Chapter 2, if there is evidence of disparate impact, the organization must prove it is not discriminating. This is typically accomplished by demonstrating

FIGURE II.1 Human Resource Architecture

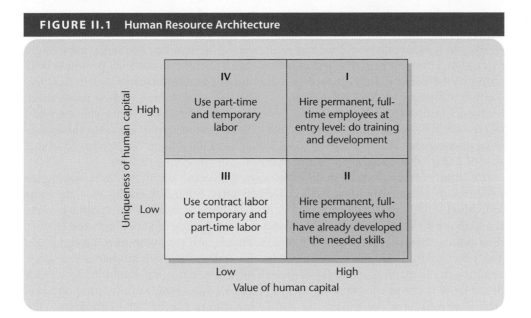

that the selection technique is job related. In practice, this means demonstrating that the selection technique is a valid predictor of performance on the job. Also, as we saw in the discussion of hits and errors in decision making, even without laws concerning discrimination, an organization is wasting its resources if it uses an invalid selection technique. As we discussed and illustrated in Figure 7.6, if the selection techniques results in too many errors, it is not helping the organization and is probably not worth the cost. Techniques of test validation provide more detailed information about the relationship between scores on a selection technique and subsequent performance on the job than we can obtain by just looking at a chart such as Figure 7.6. Therefore, even in countries and cultures where there are no laws concerning discrimination in hiring, test validation provides important information about how useful the selection technique is for helping the organization hire the most successful people. We will begin, however, with a discussion of test reliability, because a test that is not reliable can never be valid. (Refer also to Appendix 2, Data and Research in Human Resource Management.)

Reliability **Reliability** refers to the consistency of a particular selection device. Specifically, it means that the selection device measures whatever it is supposed to measure, without random error. Systematic error may be present, though, so reliability is not the same as accuracy. For example, if your true weight remained constant across three days at precisely 135 pounds, but your bathroom scale indicated you weighed 137 pounds one day, 134 the next day, and 135 pounds the third day, you would have an unreliable scale. It is unreliable not because the scale is usually not accurate, but because the amount and direction of error are random—on the first day the error is +2 pounds, on the second day it is −1 pound, and on the third day the error is zero. If the scale indicated your weight was 2 pounds more than it actually was every single day, your scale would still be inaccurate, but now it would be reliable—it is always off by 2 pounds in the same direction. In fact, you could always learn your true weight by simply subtracting 2 pounds from the weight indicated on your scale.

All measures that organizations use in selection decisions have some degree of error, and all measures are less than perfectly reliable. In the example above, your true

Reliability *refers to the consistency of a particular selection device. Specifically, it means that the selection device measures whatever it is supposed to measure, without random error.*

249

weight is the most important factor in determining what your scale indicates, but there could be cases where the error component was larger than that attributed to your actual weight, and your scale would be useless. In a selection context, this large error might mean that, although person A scores higher on an arithmetic test than person B, who scores higher than person C, these differences are due to random error and, in fact, person C's arithmetic skills are the highest, followed by persons B and A, respectively. Managers responsible for selecting new employees should always learn what part of a given score on a selection technique is due to error and what part is due to the underlying phenomenon they are trying to measure. Reliability, then, can be viewed as that part of a score that is not due to random error.

Reliability can be assessed in different ways. One common method of assessing the reliability of a selection technique is called test-retest reliability. In this case, the same individual or individuals are subjected to the selection technique at two points in time. If a high positive correlation exists between their scores or evaluation between the two time points, then reliability can be inferred. That is, test results seem to be consistent over time and thus are reliable. Any random error component would change over time, resulting in inconsistencies, so the degree of consistency is an indication of how much of the score is due to what is being measured rather than error. Another method of establishing reliability, particularly for employment tests, is called alternate-form reliability. In this case, the organization develops multiple forms of the same instrument and these multiple forms are administered to samples of individuals. To the extent that the alternative forms of the instrument yield the same score, reliability can be inferred again using the same logic as above. In this case, however, reliability is demonstrated across alternate forms and not over time.

Validity   **Validity** refers to the extent to which a measure or indicator is in fact a real reflection of what it is assumed to be. For example, it would make no sense for an organization to use a keyboarding test as a measure of a person's potential ability as a truck driver. The ability to keyboard would have no obvious predictive relationship with an individual's ability to be an effective truck driver, and thus the measure of keyboarding skill lacks validity relative to the job of driving a truck.

The first condition for a measure to be valid is that it be reliable, as described above. If test scores are attributable largely to error, the test cannot be measuring what it is supposed to measure. Beyond this condition, various kinds of validity are relevant to the selection process. One type of validity is **content validity.** Content validity is the extent to which a selection technique such as a test or interview measures the skills, knowledge, and abilities necessary to perform the job. A keyboarding test would, in fact, be a content validity test for the job of secretary. This test replicates conditions for a secretarial job and provides a true reflection of a person's capabilities for performing that job. Content validity is usually assessed using expert judgment.

A second kind of validity is called **construct validity.** Construct validity is the extent to which a relationship exists between scores on the measure and the underlying trait the measure is supposed to tap. For example, if an organization wanted to measure the conscientiousness of applicants but was not happy with existing measures, it might develop its own measure of this personality trait. The question would be whether the measure that was developed really assessed conscientiousness—this issue is fundamental in construct validity.

How would an organization demonstrate that it was really measuring conscientiousness? (Construct validity is never really "proven.") One method would be to administer the measure to employees believed to be conscientious (e.g., they always finish their work) and to employees believed not to be conscientious (e.g., they always leave jobs

Validity *refers to the extent to which a measure or indicator is in fact a real reflection of what it is assumed to be.*

Content validity *is the extent to which a selection technique such as a test or interview measures the skills, knowledge, and abilities necessary to perform the job.*

Construct validity *is the extent to which a relationship exists between scores on the measure and the underlying trait the measure is supposed to tap.*

unfinished). The conscientious group should score much higher than the other group, and, if this were the case, it would suggest construct validity. Another method would be to determine if scores on the measure of conscientiousness were correlated with behaviors (such as staying late at work) that the organization might believe are indicative of conscientious employees. Basically, then, one builds a body of evidence for construct validity by examining relationships such as those described above. The more these relationships are borne out, the more confident managers can be that they are really measuring what they intend to measure.

A third kind of validity that is relevant to selection decisions is **criterion-related validity.** Although construct validity may be the most difficult type of validity to establish, criterion-related validity is most critical to the selection process. Criterion-related validity is the extent to which a particular selection technique can accurately predict one or more elements of performance. Criterion-related validity is most typically demonstrated by establishing a correlation between a test or measured performance in a simulated work environment with measures of actual on-the-job performance. In this approach, the test or performance measure represents a predictor value variable, and the actual performance score itself is the criterion. If this correlation is meaningful (i.e., statistically significant), a relationship exists between test scores and performance, and the test is job related.

Different relationships, or correlations, are illustrated in Appendix 2. As shown in Figure A2.1a we can see that a perfect correlation means perfect prediction. If we were to superimpose the four quadrants from Figure 7.6 upon this figure, we would see that we make *no* errors. That is, everyone who we predict will succeed will be successful and everyone who we predict would fail would fail. Notice that, in Figure A2.1c, we have a zero correlation and we would be wrong as often as we would be right. Figures A2.1d and A2.1e present positive correlations of different strength and, note again, that we would make fewer errors in the case of A2.1c, where the correlation is higher.

Factors Affecting Criterion-Related Validity   Since selection decisions are most closely related to criterion-related validity, it is worth noting some factors that can influence the strength of the relationship between scores on a test and performance on the job—factors other than the idea that the test is simply not related to job performance. First, as noted above, it is important that both the test and other selection device be reliable and that the measure of performance or success be reliable. Unfortunately, as we discussed in Chapter 7, some commonly used selection techniques, such as the interview are often not reliable and, as we will discuss in Chapter 10, many measures of performance are also not very reliable. Even in the case where a selection technique should be able to predict performance perfectly, if the selection technique does not employ a reliable measure or if the measure of performance is not reliable, the correlation we obtain will be much less than perfect (exactly how much less depends upon how unreliable each measure actually is). If both measures are unreliable, the resulting correlation will be quite low.

As a result, human resource management researchers are always looking for better measures of potential predictors of job performance, as well as better measures of job performance itself. There are also some statistical procedures available that can "correct" for unreliability. These procedures can indicate what would have been the correlation between scores on selection techniques and job performance if both measures were perfectly reliable. Since, of course, neither is perfectly reliable, we cannot use these corrected correlations to defend against discrimination charges, since the corrected correlation simply tells us what is possible rather than the existing situation. Such corrected correlation are useful, however, in the sense that they tell us whether or not it is

Criterion-related validity *is the extent to which a particular selection technique can accurately predict one or more elements of performance. Criterion-related validity is most typically demonstrated by establishing a correlation between a test or measured performance in a simulated work environment with measures of actual on-the-job performance.*

worth expanding effort trying to find more reliable measures of these same variables. That is, if we find that a perfectly reliable measure of conscientiousness would be highly correlated with a perfectly reliable measure of performance, there would be strong incentive to develop better measures of conscientiousness and performance.

Correlations between predictor scores and job performance will also be maximized if we have the complete range of both, scores on the predictor (selection technique) and scores on the criterion (job performance). But, oftentimes, organizations do not have the full range of scores for a number of reasons. For example, if someone is doing poorly on the job, especially during their early tenure on the job (which might even be a probationary period), they will likely be fired, or they will quit. Therefore, when the time comes to correlate the scores on the selection device with the measure of performance, we can only calculate this correlation for those people who did well enough to remain on the job. In this case, the scores on the measure of performance is certainly restricted to those people who did well (i.e., we don't have performance measures for those who failed) and, if the selection technique has any ability to predict performance, we probably only have the higher scores on that measure as well. In such a case, we would find that the correlation we obtain is much lower than it should be.

In some cases, organizations attempt to validate selection techniques with their present employees (this is referred to as concurrent validation), giving the test or other selection technique to present employees, and then simply using their most recent performance appraisal as a measure of performance. Clearly this results in restricting the range of performance scores (as well as likely scores on the selection technique), which produces a lower correlation, but organizations sometimes prefer this to the alternative, which is the ideal, if most costly, way to conduct a criterion-related validity study.

When an organization uses a purely predictive validity model, selection decisions are made using whatever selection technique the organization currently relies upon. So, for example, if Acme Company selects people using an interview only, it would continue to make selection decisions on the basis of the interview information only. But, at the same time, if Acme was trying to validate a new selection technique, perhaps using an intelligence test, Acme would administer the intelligence test at the same time as the interview to all applicants. But, Acme would ignore the information from the intelligence test. In fact, if Acme were willing to hire purely at random for a while, this would be even better (for validation, but not for business!). Therefore, Acme would be hiring employees with low test scores, medium test scores, and high test scores as long as they passed the interview. Also, if intelligence were really a predictor of performance on the Acme jobs, this would mean that Acme was also hiring good performers and poor performers.

It is important to step back at this point, to consider what we have just said—the organization would intentionally hire people who would probably fail. Although this seems foolish, Acme would really be in no worse shape than it had been all along, hiring on the basis of the interview. But now, after six months or so (i.e., after the newly hired employees really got a feel for the job), Acme could correlate scores on the intelligence test with performance on the job, knowing that they have maximized the range of scores on both measures. This would increase the chances of finding a strong relationship, which would help Acme in all its subsequent selection decisions.

In any event, validity information helps an organization to know whether it is making good decisions, and, in the United States (and several other countries), this information also provides the basis for a defense against discrimination charges. Organizations that claim that validation of selection techniques is too expensive have simply not accurately calculated the costs and benefits involved.

Managing the Existing Workforce

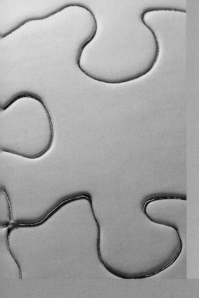

8

Managing the Diverse Workforce

Diversity is a fact of life in organizations today. And while diversity has many benefits, the potential for conflict increases significantly. Different backgrounds, perspectives, customs, and values combine to make it ever more likely that people will disagree and see situations differently.

For example, take the Marriott Marquis Hotel in New York City's Time Square. The hotel employs 1,700 people from seventy countries and who speak forty-seven languages. One major reason for the hotel's diversity is its labor pool—the area is populated by a diverse set of immigrants and these residents often apply for these kinds of jobs. But the hotel managers also strongly believe that the diverse workforce is an asset in part because it fits the multicultural clientele who frequent the hotel.

But managing the diversity at Marriott can be a challenge. For example, consider the case of Jessica Brown, an African-American quality-assurance manager responsible for housekeeping. Brown says that when she rewards other African-Americans, some of her Hispanic employees criticize her for playing favorites. But when she rewards the Hispanic employees, some African-Americans accuse her of ignoring them.

Balancing religious preferences is also complicated. One manager, Victor Aragona, recently sought out a room attendant to fix an overflowing bathtub. The attendant was found prostrate on a towel in the housekeeper's closet bowing to Mecca and saying his daily Islamic prayers. Rather than disturb him, Aragona fixed the bathtub himself.

To help cope with these challenges, Marriott offers frequent training programs in multiculturalism and conflict management. These courses are required for all managers and are open to most nonmanagers as well. Even so, the hotel still finds it necessary to offer periodic and regular refresher courses to help people work together with a minimum of conflict.[1]

> *"[A]ll you can really do is hope [the resentment] goes away eventually. And it usually does."*
>
> (Cynthia Keating, Marriott manager)*

Managers at the Marriott Marquis Hotel face a complex set of challenges and opportunities. On the one hand, the diverse workforce they oversee poses far more complications and complexities than would a more homogenous one. On the other hand, the diverse workforce employed at the hotel also provides competitive advantages and opportunities to cater more effectively to the multinational clientele who frequent the area. Balancing the complications and the benefits of diversity is among the most important workplace issues facing most managers and their organizations today.

This chapter is about workforce diversity in organizations. We begin by exploring the meaning and nature of diversity. We distinguish between diversity management and equal employment opportunity. Next we identify and discuss several common dimensions of diversity. The impact of diversity on the organization is explored. We address how diversity can be managed for the betterment of both individuals and organizations. Finally, we characterize and describe the fully multicultural organization.

The Nature of Workforce Diversity

Workforce diversity has become an important issue in many organizations, both in the United States and abroad. A logical starting point in understanding this phenomenon better is to establish the meaning of the word *diversity* and then to examine why such diversity is increasing today.

The Meaning of Workforce Diversity

Diversity *exists in a group or organization when its members differ from one another along one or more important dimensions.*

Diversity exists in a group or organization when its members differ from one another along one or more important dimensions.[2] If everyone in the group or organization is exactly like everyone else, no diversity exists. But if everyone is different along every imaginable dimension, total diversity exists. In reality, of course, these extremes are more hypothetical than real; most settings are characterized by a level of diversity somewhere between. Thus, diversity is not an absolute phenomenon wherein a group or organization is or is not diverse. Instead, diversity should be conceptualized as a continuum. Therefore, diversity should be thought of in terms of degree or level of diversity along relevant dimensions.[3]

These dimensions of diversity might include gender, age, and ethnic origin, among many others. A group composed of five middle-aged white male U.S. executives has relatively little diversity. If one member leaves and is replaced by a young white female executive, the group becomes a bit more diverse. If another member is replaced by an older African-American executive, diversity increases a bit more. And when a third member is replaced by a Japanese executive, the group becomes even more diverse.

Trends in Workforce Diversity

As we noted earlier, organizations today are becoming increasingly diverse along many different dimensions. Several different factors have accounted for these trends and changes. One factor that has contributed to increased diversity is changing demographics in the labor force. As more women and minorities have entered the labor force, for example, the available pool of talent from which organizations hire employees has changed in both size and composition. If talent within each segment of the la-

Workforce diversity is increasing in virtually all organizations today, regardless of size, industry, or organizational level. New opportunities are being constantly presented to people from all ethic backgrounds, races, or genders, primarily because businesses today recognize that it is in their own best interests to hire and develop the most capable employees possible. PepsiCo, for instance, recently appointed a new CEO—Ms. Indra Nooyi. Before taking over the top spot she proved her capabilities as the firm's CFO and president. When the top job opened, PepsiCo's board knew that Ms. Nooyi was the best person for the job.

bor pool is evenly distributed (for example, if the number of talented men in the workforce as a percentage of all men in the workforce is the same as the number of talented women in the labor force as a percentage of all women in the workforce), it follows logically that, over time, proportionately more women and proportionately fewer men will be hired by an organization compared to the employees who were hired in the past.

A related factor that has contributed to diversity has been the increased awareness by organizations that they can improve the overall quality of their workforce by hiring and promoting the most talented people available, regardless of gender, race, or any other characteristics. By casting a broader net in recruiting and looking beyond traditional sources for new employees, organizations are finding more broadly qualified and better qualified employees from many different segments of society. Thus, these organizations are finding that diversity can be a source of competitive advantage.

Another reason for the increase in diversity has been legislation and legal actions that have forced organizations to hire more broadly. Organizations in the United States were once free to discriminate against women, blacks, and other minorities. Thus, most organizations were dominated by white males. But over the last thirty years or so, various laws have outlawed discrimination against these and other groups. As we detailed in Chapter 2, organizations must hire and promote people today solely on the basis of their qualifications.

A final contributing factor to increased diversity in organizations has been the globalization movement. Organizations that have opened offices and related facilities in other countries have had to learn to deal with different customs, social norms, and mores. Strategic alliances and foreign ownership have also contributed because managers today are more likely to have job assignments in other countries and/or to work with foreign managers within their own countries. As employees and managers move from assignment to assignment across national boundaries, organizations and their subsidiaries within each country thus become more diverse. Closely related to this pattern is a recent increase in immigration into the United States. As illustrated in Figure 8.1, for example,

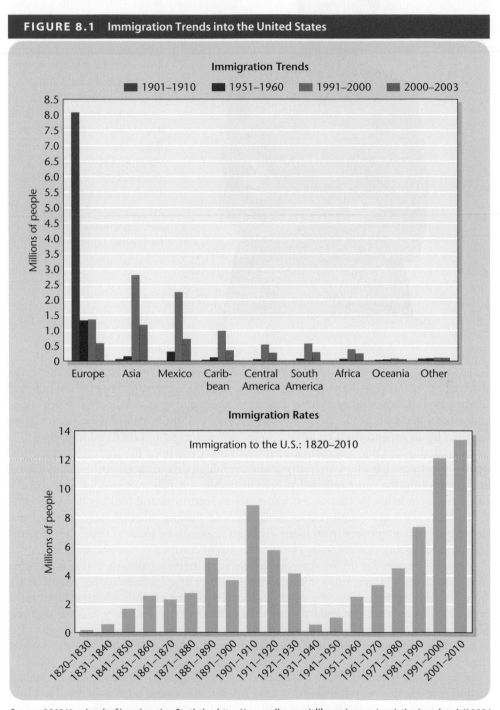

FIGURE 8.1   Immigration Trends into the United States

Source: 2003 Yearbook of Immigration Statistics, http://www.dhs.gov/xlibrary/assets/statistics/yearbook/2003/2003Yearbook.pdf.

immigration declined steadily from 1900 until around 1930 but has been increasing since that time, although the rate of increase has slowed a bit in the last decade.

As a result of recent immigration trends, this has become a very "hot" issue in the United States. According to statistics published by the Department of Immigration (part of the Department of Homeland Security), in 2005 (the last year for which complete data were available) there were over 1 million Mexicans who were in the United States illegally, followed by almost 30,000 people from Central America and just over 3,000 from Asia (out of a total of 1.1 million illegal immigrants total). In May of 2006, President Bush proposed a "Guest Worker" program along with some guidelines for how immigrants living illegally in the United States could gain legal immigrant status. Debate continues over what to do about this problem, but it is clear that managing diversity will become even more important to organizations in the coming years regardless of what legislation the U.S. government eventually passes.

Diversity Management Versus Equal Employment Opportunity

Many managers assume that diversity and equal employment opportunity are the same. In fact, they have completely different meanings. **Equal employment opportunity** means treating people fairly and equitably and taking actions that do not discriminate against people in protected classes on the basis of some illegal criterion. But **diversity management** places a much heavier emphasis on recognizing and appreciating differences among people at work and attempting to provide accommodations for those differences to the extent that is feasible and possible.

Equal employment opportunity *means treating people fairly and equitably and taking actions that do not discriminate against people in protected classes on the basis of some illegal criterion.*

Diversity management *places a much heavier emphasis on recognizing and appreciating differences among people at work and attempting to provide accommodations for those differences to the extent that is feasible and possible.*

Similarities Among People at Work

Regardless of how different people appear to be, almost all employees share some fundamental similarities.[4] For example, most people work to satisfy some set of needs that are almost always based on financial criteria. Most people have a fundamental and basic desire to be treated with respect and dignity by their employer. And third, most people have a capacity for being reasonable and understanding when confronted with reasonable behavior by others and when they recognize all the information relevant to a work setting.

Differences Among People at Work

Many people share some basic set of similar characteristics, but they also display various fundamental differences, a topic that will be discussed more fully in the next major section of the chapter. Common differences include gender, ethnicity, and age. But the list of differences among individuals is much longer and ranges from religious beliefs to dietary preferences to political philosophies.

Identical Treatment Versus Equitable Treatment

In the years immediately following passage of Title VII of the 1964 Civil Rights Act, many human resource managers operated under the assumption that they were required by law to treat everyone equally. But in reality, that assumption is neither the intent of the law nor really even possible. The real essence not only of Title VII but of the more contemporary perspective on workforce diversity is that it is appropriate to acknowledge differences among people as long as people are treated fairly.

Consider religion, for example. A typical company in the United States routinely gives days off to employees for basic Christian holidays such as Christmas. But people who have different religious beliefs may not acknowledge the sanctity of these religious holidays and instead have a different set of days that they associate with strong religious beliefs. Thus, an employer who provides Christian holidays off should also be sensitive to the need to provide important religious holidays off for various employees of different beliefs and faiths. The Whirlpool appliance factory near Nashville, Tennessee, for example, employs about 200 Muslims (about 10 percent of its workforce). The factory found it necessary to adjust its work schedules, cafeteria menus, and dress codes to accommodate workers who pray several times a day; don't eat pork; and wear loose-fitting clothing, head coverings, and sandals.[5]

Men and women are also fundamentally different in various ways that cannot be ignored. For example, on average, men have greater muscle mass than do women and can therefore lift heavier weight. And women have the biological capacity to bear children. Consequently, men and women may need fundamentally different treatment in work organizations. For example, women may need to be given longer periods of time off during the time immediately preceding and after the birth of a child. When a woman chooses to return to work after birth, the organization may need to provide a transitional period during which her work-related demands are lessened at first but then gradually increased over time.

The Americans with Disabilities Act (ADA) presents a serious challenge to managers who try to balance treating everyone the same with treating everyone equitably. The ADA specifically states that an organization cannot discriminate against a person with a disability as long as he or she can perform the essential functions of the job *with* or *without a reasonable accommodation*. Therefore, an employee who requests such an accommodation must be accommodated. At first glance, this situation may not appear problematic because the employee presumably needs this accommodation to perform his or her job. Many of the accommodations requested and granted, such as large-print computer screens, allowances for guide dogs, wheelchair ramps, or amplified phones, don't present a problem.

But what about an accommodation requested by a person with a disability that would be desirable and/or useful to other employees who do not have a disability? An interesting example of this dilemma occurred in early 1998 when the Professional Golf Association (PGA) ruled that Casey Martin, whose serious back problems made walking a golf course dangerous, would be allowed to use a golf cart in tournament play. Although there was disagreement over exactly how much of a difference this accommodation would make, many other golfers claimed that if they too were allowed to ride around the course, they would be less tired and so would play better. In this case, not only did other golfers want the same accommodation that had been granted to Martin, they also felt that it gave him an unfair competitive advantage.

Although Martin's case may be a particularly dramatic example of the problem, we can easily imagine other accommodations requested by a person with a disability would also be valued by other employees or that other employees might perceive the accommodation as an unfair advantage. Even in classroom settings, students often perceive it as unfair when a student with a disability is granted extra time for a test. Coworker resentment over the granting of accommodations can be a problem for all concerned. For the able-bodied employee, these accommodations may be perceived as unjust, leading to dissatisfaction on the job. For the disabled employee, the anticipated resentment may discourage him or her from asking for the accommodation needed to perform the job effectively. The manager's perspective, of course, focuses on the problem of balancing the concerns of the different parties.[6]

Again, the important message is for managers to recognize that differences among people exist. It is important first to acknowledge the differences and then to make reasonable accommodation to deal with these differences. The key issue, however, is to make sure that the acknowledgment and the accommodation are equitable—everyone needs to have an equal opportunity to contribute to and advance within the organization.

Dimensions of Diversity

As indicated earlier, many different dimensions of diversity can be used to characterize an organization. In this section we discuss age, gender, ethnicity, disability, and other dimensions of diversity.

Age Distributions

One key dimension of diversity in any organization is the age distribution of its workers.[7] The average age of the U.S. workforce is gradually increasing and will continue to do so for the next several years. Several factors contribute to this pattern. The baby-boom generation (a term used to describe the unusually large number of people who were born in the twenty-year period following World War II) continues to age. Declining birth rates among the post-baby-boom generations simultaneously account for smaller percentages of new entrants into the labor force. Another factor that contributes to aging of the workforce is improved health and medical care. As a result of these improvements, people can remain productive and active for longer periods of time. Combined with higher legal limits for mandatory retirement, more and more people are working beyond the age at which they might have retired just a few years ago.

How does this trend affect human resource management? Older workers tend to have more experience, may be more stable, and can make greater contributions to productivity. On the other hand, despite the improvements in health and medical care, older workers are nevertheless likely to require higher levels of insurance coverage and medical benefits. As shown in Figure 8.2, accident rates are substantially higher for older workers than for younger workers up to the age of fifty-four. (In most years accident rates continue to increase; however, for the year shown (2005) accident rates actually dropped a bit for workers older than age fifty-four.) Further, the overall number of retirees combined with fewer younger members of the workforce may lead to future labor shortages, even though some workers are staying in the workforce longer.

Gender

As more and more females have entered the workforce, organizations have subsequently experienced changes in the relative proportions of male and female employees. Figure 8.3 highlights trends in gender composition (as well as ethnicity) in the workplace. As the figure shows clearly, the proportion of female employees to male employees has and will continue to increase gradually. For instance, projections show that by 2010 women will comprise 47.9 percent of the workforce, up from 45.2 percent in 1990 and 46.6 percent in 2000.

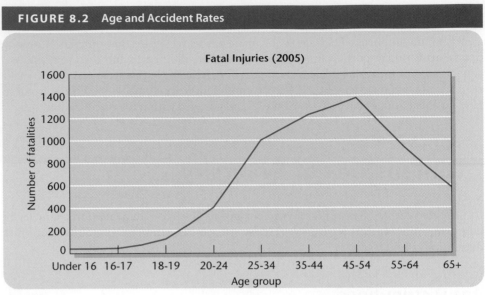

FIGURE 8.2   Age and Accident Rates

Source: Census of Fatal Occupational Injuries, 2005, http://www.bls.gov/iif/oshwc/cfoi/cftb0212.pdf.

The **glass ceiling** *describes a barrier that keeps many females from advancing to top management positions in many organizations.*

These trends aside, a significant gender-related problem that many organizations face today is the so-called glass ceiling, which was introduced in Chapter 5. The **glass ceiling** describes a barrier that keeps many females from advancing to top management positions in many organizations. This ceiling represents a real nonphysical barrier that is difficult to break but is also subtle. While women comprise almost 50 percent of all managers, female CEOs head only 10 of the 500 largest businesses in the United States. Similarly, the average pay of females in organizations is lower than that of males. While the pay gap is gradually shrinking, inequalities are still present.

Why does the glass ceiling exist? One reason is that some male managers are still reluctant to promote female managers. Another is that many talented women choose to leave their jobs in larger organizations and start their own businesses. Still another factor is that some women choose to suspend or slow their career progression to have children.

Ethnicity

Ethnicity *refers to the ethnic composition of a group or organization.*

A third major dimension of cultural diversity in organizations is ethnicity. **Ethnicity** refers to the ethnic composition of a group or organization. Within the United States, most organizations reflect varying degrees of ethnicity and are composed of whites, African-Americans, Hispanics, and Asians. Figure 8.3 also shows trends in the ethnic composition of the U.S. workforce.

The biggest projected changes involve whites and Hispanics. In particular, the percentage of whites in the workforce is expected to drop to 69.2 percent by 2010, down from 73.1 percent in 2000 and 77.7 percent in 1990. At the same time, the percentage of Hispanics is expected to climb to 13.3 percent by 2010, up from 10.9 percent in 2000 and 8.5 percent in 1990. The percentage of blacks is expected to remain relatively stable (10.9 percent in 1990, 11.8 percent in 2000, and 12.7 percent in 2010). Finally, Asians and others are expected to represent 6.1 percent of the U.S. workforce in 2010, up from 4.7 percent in 2000 and 3.7 percent in 1990.

FIGURE 8.3   Changing Composition of the U.S. Workforce

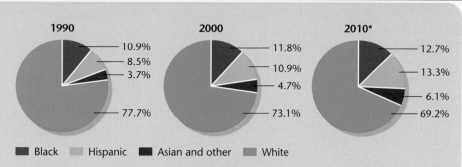

The shifting racial and ethnic makeup of the U.S. work force: number of workers by race and ethnic origin and their share of the total civilian labor force.

Numbers (thousands)	1990	2000	2010*	Percent	1990	2000	2010*
Total	125,840	140,863	157,721	Total	100.0	100.0	100.0
Men	69,011	75,247	82,221	Men	54.8	53.4	52.1
Women	56,829	65,616	75,500	Women	45.2	46.6	47.9
White, non-Hispanic	97,818	102,963	109,118	White, non-Hispanic	77.7	73.1	69.2
Men	53,731	55,359	57,538	Men	42.7	39.3	36.5
Women	44,087	47,604	51,580	Women	35.0	33.8	32.7
Black, non-Hispanic	13,740	16,603	20,041	Black, non-Hispanic	10.9	11.8	12.7
Men	6,802	7,816	8,991	Men	5.4	5.5	5.7
Women	6,938	8,787	11,050	Women	5.5	6.2	7.0
Hispanic origin	10,720	15,368	20,947	Hispanic origin	8.5	10.9	13.3
Men	6,546	8,919	11,723	Men	5.2	6.3	7.4
Women	4,174	6,449	9,224	Women	3.3	4.6	5.8
Asian and other, non-Hispanic	4,653	6,687	9,636	Asian and other, non-Hispanic	3.7	4.7	6.1
Men	2,572	3,570	5,070	Men	2.0	2.5	3.2
Women	2,081	3,116	4,566	Women	1.7	2.2	2.9

*Projection

Source: U.S. Department of Labor, Bureau of Labor Statistics, *Monthly Labor Review,* November 2001, http://www.bls.gov.

As with women, members of the African-American, Hispanic, and Asian groups are generally underrepresented in the executive ranks of most organizations today, as well as in several different occupational groups. And their pay is similarly lower than might be expected. But as is the case for women, the differences are gradually disappearing as organizations fully embrace equal employment opportunity and recognize the higher overall level of talent available to them. Table 8.1 shows trends in different occupations for blacks and Hispanics. For example, the percentage of blacks and Hispanics comprising several different kinds of business roles plus various professional specialties increased substantially from 1983 to 2002.

TABLE 8.1   Employment of Blacks and Hispanics in Selected Occupations, 1983 and 2002*

	Blacks		Hispanics	
	1983	2002	1983	2002
Total workforce, 16 years of age and over	9.3%	10.9%	5.3%	12.2%
Occupation				
Executive, administrative, and managerial	4.7	7.6	2.8	6.3
Officials and administrators in public administration	8.3	13.0	3.8	7.6
Financial managers	3.5	8.4	3.1	6.8
Personnel and labor relations managers	4.9	8.0	2.6	5.1
Purchasing managers	5.1	6.6	1.4	4.7
Managers in marketing, advertising, and public relations	2.7	3.7	1.7	4.9
Managers in medicine and health care	5.0	9.5	2.0	6.2
Accountants and auditors	5.5	9.0	3.3	6.0
Management analysts	5.3	6.2	1.7	2.5
Professional specialty	6.4	8.3	2.5	5.3
Architects	1.6	2.3	1.5	5.2
Engineers	2.7	4.5	2.2	4.0
Mathematical and computer scientists	5.4	7.3	2.6	5.1
Natural scientists	2.6	4.1	2.1	2.9
Physicians	3.2	5.0	4.5	5.8
Dentists	2.4	4.0	1.0	3.3
College and university teachers	4.4	5.4	1.8	5.4
Economists	6.3	6.2	2.7	4.6
Psychologists	8.6	9.5	1.1	3.8
Lawyers	2.6	4.6	0.9	3.1
Authors	2.1	2.3	0.9	3.8
Musicians and composers	7.9	12.9	4.4	5.8
Editors and reporters	2.9	4.7	2.1	3.3

*Data for 1983 and 2002 are not strictly comparable.
Minorities as a percentage of total employed.
Source: Data for 1983: *The Wall Street Journal Almanac 1999,* p. 241. © 1999 Dow Jones and Company, Inc. All rights reserved. Data for 2002: U.S. Department of Labor, Bureau of Labor Statistics, http://www.bls.gov.

Disability

Disability is another significant dimension of diversity. Disabilities can range from hearing impairments to missing fingers or limbs, to blindness, to paralysis. The presence of a disability represents another aspect of diversity in organizations, but among persons who have disabilities, some differences are important as well. That is, unlike

Diversity can be seen along a variety of dimensions. Take Emma Shulman, for example. Ms. Shulman works fifty hours a week recruiting patients for an Alzheimer's treatment center at the New York University Medical Center. Her boss says that it will take two or three people to replace her when she retires. So what makes her so unique? Among other things, her age—she's ninety-two years old. While relatively few people work to this age, more and more people are working beyond traditional retirement ages. And businesses are recognizing that they can greatly benefit from the skills, experiences, and motivation of workers once thought of as "too old."

other dimensions of diversity, reactions to persons with disabilities vary dramatically as a function of several dimensions of the disability. One of these dimensions is termed "origin." That is, if the disability is perceived as being avoidable (for example, someone who has been injured while driving drunk), coworkers are likely to react more negatively to the disability than when the problem was unavoidable (for example, a person who was born blind).

Another dimension is the aesthetic aspect of the disability, with disabilities that are more disfiguring being perceived more negatively. A third and critical dimension refers to the nature of the disability itself. For example, although mental disabilities might be easier to conceal, they are also more frightening to coworkers. Disabilities related to stress or to back injuries are not as physically obvious and so, when individuals with these disabilities request and are granted an accommodation, resentment by coworkers is more likely.[8]

Other Dimensions of Diversity

In addition to age, gender, ethnicity, and disability status, organizations are also confronting other dimensions of diversity. Country of national origin is a dimension of diversity that can be especially important for global organizations. This dimension can be particularly significant when different languages are involved. Single parents, dual-career couples, gays and lesbians, people with special dietary preferences (e.g., vegetarians), and people with different political ideologies and viewpoints also represent significant dimensions of diversity in today's organizations.

The Impact of Diversity on Organizations

No doubt organizations are becoming ever more diverse. But what is the impact of this diversity on organizations? As we will see, diversity provides both opportunities and challenges for organizations. Diversity also plays several important roles in organizations today.

Diversity and Social Change

Diversity can have a significant impact on organizations as a force for social change. This change generally occurs as the composition of an organization's workforce gradually begins to mirror the composition of its surrounding labor market. For example, if a manager in an organization learns to interact effectively with a diverse set of people at work, it follows logically that she or he will be better equipped to deal with a diverse set of people in other settings. And conversely, an individual who is comfortable interacting in diverse settings should have little problem dealing with diversity at work. Thus, diversity in organizations both facilitates and is facilitated by social change in the environment.

Another way that organizations affect social change is through the images they use to promote themselves and their products. An organization that runs print ads showing nothing but white male executives in its workplace conveys a certain image of itself. In contrast, an organization that uses diverse groups as representatives conveys a different image.

Diversity and Competitiveness

Many organizations are also finding that diversity can be a source of competitive advantage in the marketplace. In general, six arguments have been proposed for how diversity contributes to competitiveness.[9] These six arguments are illustrated in Figure 8.4.

The *cost argument* suggests that organizations that learn to cope with diversity will generally have higher levels of productivity and lower levels of turnover and absenteeism. Organizations that do a poor job of managing diversity, on the other hand, will suffer from problems of lower productivity and higher levels of turnover and absenteeism. Because each of these factors has a direct impact on costs, the former organization will remain more competitive than will the latter. Ortho Pharmaceuticals estimates that it has saved $500,000 by lowering turnover among women and ethnic minorities.

The *resource acquisition argument* for diversity suggests that organizations that manage diversity effectively will become known among women and minorities as good places to work. These organizations will thus be in a better position to attract qualified employees from among these groups. Given the increased importance of these groups in the overall labor force, organizations that can attract talented employees from all segments of society are likely to be more competitive.

FIGURE 8.4 Diversity and Competitiveness

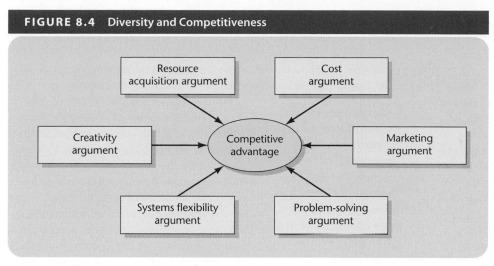

Source: Ricky W. Griffin, *Management,* 9th ed. (Boston: Houghton Mifflin, 2008), p. 154. Copyright © 2008, Houghton Mifflin Company. Reprinted by permission.

The *marketing argument* suggests that organizations with diverse workforces will be able to understand different market segments better than will less diverse organizations. For example, a cosmetics firm like Avon that wants to sell its products to women and blacks can better understand how to create such products and market them effectively if women and black managers are available to provide input into product development, design, packaging, advertising, and so forth.

The *creativity argument* for diversity suggests that organizations with diverse workforces will generally be more creative and innovative than will less diverse organizations. If an organization is dominated by one population segment, its members will generally adhere to norms and ways of thinking that reflect that population segment. They will have little insight or few stimuli for new ideas that might be derived from different perspectives. *HR Around the Globe* explores this idea in more detail. The diverse organization, in contrast, will be characterized by multiple perspectives and ways of thinking and is therefore more likely to generate new ideas and ways of doing things.

Related to the creativity argument is the *problem-solving argument*. Diversity carries with it an increased pool of information. In almost any organization, there is some information that everyone has, and other information that is unique to each individual. In an organization with little diversity, the larger pool of information is common and the smaller pool is unique. But in a more diverse organization, the unique information is larger. Thus, if more information can be brought to bear on a problem, the probability is higher that better solutions will be identified.[10]

Finally, the *systems flexibility argument* for diversity suggests that organizations must become more flexible as a way of managing a diverse workforce. As a direct consequence, the overall organizational system will also become more flexible. Organizational flexibility enables the organization to respond better to changes in its environment. Thus, by effectively managing diversity within its workforce, an organization simultaneously becomes better equipped to address its environment.[11] As we shall see below, however, the truth is a bit more complex than these arguments suggest.

Too Little Diversity?

It's no secret, of course, that many businesses from Japan and South Korea have been highly successful in recent years. But some experts question whether or not the lack of diversity that exists in those firms will still be an advantage in the future. To see how little diversity exists, consider the case of Samsung Electronics, a huge Korean business. The firm's board of directors consists of nineteen members, all male. Fifteen of them have worked for the firm for at least twenty years, and eight even attended the same university. Japan's Honda Motor Co. is quite similar—its board is all Japanese, as is every president of each Honda foreign subsidiary.

Executives at these firms defend their hiring and promotion practices. They argue, for example, that their lack of diversity reduces management conflict, smoothes decision making, and ensures that top management is both loyal to and knowledgeable about the business. It also enhances

"Cohesiveness of corporation is more important to [the] Japanese. They are not well-trained in managing different nationalities. They are more comfortable in [their own] group."

(Kaoru Kobayashi, Japanese professor)*

cohesiveness among key leaders because they tend to see situations the same way and to have similar interests.

But critics point out that the lack of diversity also creates problems. For example, some experts contend that executives from Japan and Korea do not understand people from other cultures and thus treat them cavalierly and with disdain. By not relying more on foreigners, Japanese and Korean firms may also be less knowledgeable about international laws and regulations. And some critics even predict that the lack of executive diversity may dampen creativity and innovation, potentially causing Japanese and Korean firms to be less competitive in the future.

Sources: "Narrow Thinking Limits Competitiveness," *USA Today,* December 28, 2005, p. 1B; "Breaking Up the Good Old Boys," *Wall Street Journal,* February 16, 2006, p. B3; "Men's Club," *Wall Street Journal,* September 26, 1996, pp. A1, A8 (*quote on p. A1); "Tight Little Island," *Forbes,* January 12, 1998, pp. 52–53; "Seoul Is Still Teetering on the Edge," *Business Week,* January 5, 1998, pp. 56–57.

Diversity and Conflict

Diversity in an organization can also become a major source of conflict.[12] This conflict can arise for different reasons. One potential avenue for conflict is when an individual thinks that someone has been hired, promoted, or fired because of her or his diversity status.[13] For example, suppose a male executive loses a promotion to a female executive. If he believes that she was promoted because the organization simply wanted to have more female managers rather than because she was the better candidate for the job, he will likely feel resentful toward both her and the organization itself.

Conflict among whites and blacks within the ranks of the Federal Aviation Administration (FAA) has been a recurring problem. Some blacks have charged that their white supervisors are prejudiced and that blacks are subject to various subtle forms of discrimination. Some whites, however, believe that the government agency has hired some blacks who really aren't qualified for the job of air traffic controller because it cannot attract a significant number of qualified employees.[14]

Another source of conflict stemming from diversity is through misunderstood, misinterpreted, or inappropriate interactions between people of different groups. For example, suppose a male executive tells a sexually explicit joke to a new female executive. He may intentionally be trying to embarrass her, he may be trying clumsily to show her that he treats everyone the same, or he may think he is making her feel like part of the team. Regardless of his intent, however, if she finds the joke offensive, she will justifiably feel anger and hostility. These feelings may be directed only at the offending individual or more generally toward the entire organization if she believes that its culture facilitates such behavior. Of course, sexual harassment itself is both unethical and illegal.

Some evidence suggests that conflict may be especially pronounced between older and younger women in the workplace. Older women may be more likely to have sacrificed family for career and to have overcome higher obstacles to get ahead—they were, in a sense, trailblazers. Younger women, on the other hand, may find that organizational accommodations make it relatively easy for them to balance multiple roles and may also have a less pronounced sense of having to fight to get ahead.[15]

Conflict can also result from other elements of diversity. For example, suppose a U.S. manager publicly praises the work of a Japanese employee for his outstanding work. The manager's action stems from the dominant cultural belief in the United States that such recognition is important and rewarding. But because the Japanese culture places a much higher premium on group loyalty and identity than on individual accomplishment, the employee will likely feel ashamed and embarrassed. Thus, a well-intentioned action may backfire and result in unhappiness.

Conflict can arise as a result of fear, distrust, or individual prejudice. Members of the dominant group in an organization may worry that newcomers from other groups pose a personal threat to their own position in the organization. For example, when U.S. firms have been taken over by Japanese firms, U.S. managers have sometimes been resentful or hostile to Japanese managers assigned to work with them. People may also be unwilling to accept people who are different from themselves. And personal bias and prejudices are still very real among some people today and can lead to potentially harmful conflict.

The Bottom Line on Diversity

Despite the arguments, the data supporting the positive effects of diversity on organizational outcomes is not as clear as one might believe. In fact, a number of studies have found that diversity leads to positive outcomes such as better firm performance and (the absence of) harmful conflict,

Firms that have resisted efforts to diversify their workforce often argue that a diverse workforce can hurt a strong corporate culture. Critics of such firms have argued that maintaining a culture is merely an excuse to discriminate. The clash between diversity and culture has become quite clear at Wal-Mart. Wal-Mart, a company that likes to think of employees as family and vows to treat everyone with respect, is facing a huge discrimination suit on behalf of the firm's female employees. Stephanie Odle, a former assistant manager for Wal-Mart who discovered that she was being paid $10,000 less per year than a male assistant manager, was the catalyst for what will be the largest sex discrimination case (Dukes v. Wal-Mart) in history, covering some 1.5 million current and former Wal-Mart employees. Part of the problem is that the Wal-Mart culture is built upon the Wal-Mart way of doing things. For example, Wal-Mart does not post openings for management training positions because it believes that would be too bureaucratic; store managers are absolutely trusted to promote the most qualified people. Also, there are no companywide statistics on diversity because, again, managers are trusted to do what is right. However, it is alleged that these practices have been partly responsible for the fact that only 14.5 percent of Wal-Mart managers are women while 66 percent of the total workforce is female, and female managers earn an average of $89,000 annually versus almost $106,000 for male managers.

while others have found that diversity results in poorer performance and more conflict, and still others find no relationship between diversity and outcomes such as these.[16] This has led some scholars to propose a nonlinear relationship between diversity and such outcomes as conflict and firm performance.[17]

The arguments all follow lines similar to the following: when diversity is low (i.e., most employees are similar to each other), organizations obtain no benefits from diversity (e.g., creativity), but also suffer no penalties (e.g., greater conflict). As diversity increases, positive gains increase, but the problems increase at a greater rate, so that the most problematic situation is when there is a moderate amount of diversity. However, when a firm becomes truly diverse, to such an extent that there really are no identifiable "minority groups" within the workforce, the positive results of diversity can be truly maximized, while most of the problems disappear. The key here is that, when a firm reaches true diversity, the conflicts and subgroup dynamics disappear as everyone begins to view themselves as members of the same organization rather than members of a subgroup within the organization. Thus, firms experiencing problems because of workforce diversity would be advised to further increase diversity to make the firm truly diverse. It is interesting to note that there is a growing body of research that supports exactly this recommendation.[18]

Managing Diversity in Organizations

Because of the tremendous potential that diversity holds for competitive advantage, as well as the possible consequences of diversity-related conflict, much attention has been focused in recent years on how individuals and organizations can manage diversity better. In the following sections we first discuss individual strategies for dealing with diversity and then summarize organizational approaches to managing diversity.

Individual Strategies for Dealing with Diversity

One key element of managing diversity in an organization consists of actions that individuals themselves can take. Individuals can strive for understanding, empathy, tolerance, and communication.

Understanding   The first element in the strategy is understanding the nature and meaning of diversity. Some managers have taken the basic concepts of equal employment opportunity to an unnecessary extreme. They know that, by law, they cannot discriminate against people on the basis of gender, race, and so forth. Thus, in following this mandate they come to believe that they must treat everyone the same.

But this belief can cause problems when it is translated into workplace behaviors among people after they have been hired. As noted earlier, people are not the same. While people need to be treated fairly and equitably, managers must understand that differences do exist among people. Thus, any effort to treat everyone the same, without regard to their fundamental human differences, only leads to problems. Therefore it is important for managers to understand that cultural factors cause people to behave in different ways and that these differences should be accepted.

Empathy   Related to understanding is empathy. People in an organization should try to understand the perspective of others. For example, suppose a group that has traditionally been composed of white males is joined by a female member. Each male may be a little self-conscious about how to act toward the group's new member and may be interested in making her feel comfortable and welcome. But they may be able to do this even more effectively by empathizing with how she may feel. For example, she may feel disappointed or elated about her new assignment, she may be confident or nervous about her position in the group, and she may be experienced or inexperienced in working with male colleagues. By learning more about these and similar circumstances, the existing group members can facilitate their ability to work together effectively.

Tolerance   A third related individual approach to dealing with diversity is tolerance. Even though managers learn to understand diversity, and even though they may try to empathize with others, the fact remains that they may still not accept or enjoy some aspect or behavior on the part of others. For example, one organization recently reported that it was experiencing considerable conflict among its U.S. and Israeli employees. The Israeli employees always seemed to want to argue about every issue that arose. The U.S. managers preferred a more harmonious way of conducting business and became uncomfortable with the conflict. Finally, after considerable discussion, it was learned that many Israeli employees simply enjoy arguing and see it as part of getting work done. The firm's U.S. employees still do not enjoy the arguing but are more willing to tolerate it as a fundamental cultural difference between themselves and their Israeli colleagues.

Communication   A final individual approach to dealing with diversity is communication. Problems often become magnified over diversity issues because people are afraid or otherwise unwilling to discuss issues that relate to diversity. For example, suppose a younger employee has a habit of making jokes about the age of an elderly colleague. Perhaps the younger colleague means no harm and is just engaging in what she sees as good-natured kidding. But the older employee may find the jokes offensive. If the two do not communicate, the jokes will continue and the resentment will grow. Eventually, what started as a minor problem may erupt into a much bigger one.

For communication to work, it must be two-way. If a person wonders if a certain behavior on her or his part is offensive to someone else, the curious individual should probably just ask. Similarly, if someone is offended by the behavior of another person, he or she should explain to the offending individual how the behavior is perceived and request that it stop. As long as such exchanges are handled in a friendly, low-key, and nonthreatening fashion, they will generally have a positive outcome. Of course, if the same message is presented in an overly combative manner or if a person continues to engage in offensive behavior after having been asked to stop, the problem will escalate. At this point, third parties within the organization may have to intervene. And in fact, most organizations today have one or more systems in place to address questions and problems that arise as a result of diversity. We now turn our attention to the various ways that organizations can indeed manage diversity better.

Organizational Strategies for Dealing with Diversity

Individuals can play an important role in managing diversity, but the organization itself must also play a fundamental role. Through its various policies and practices, people in the organization come to understand which behaviors are appropriate and which are not. Diversity training is an even more direct method for managing diversity. The organization's culture is the ultimate context that diversity must address.

Organizational policies   Managing diversity starts with the policies that an organization adopts because they directly or indirectly affect how people are treated. Obviously, the extent to which an organization embraces the premise of equal employment opportunity determines to a large extent the potential diversity within an organization.

But differences exist between the organization that follows the law to the letter and practices passive discrimination and the organization that actively seeks a diverse and varied workforce.

Another aspect of organizational policies that affects diversity is how the organization addresses and responds to problems that arise from diversity. Consider the example of a manager charged with sexual harassment. If the organization's policies put an excessive burden of proof on the individual being harassed and invoke only minor sanctions against the guilty party, it is sending a clear signal about the importance of such matters. But the organization that has a balanced set of policies for addressing questions like sexual harassment sends its employees a different message about the importance of diversity and individual rights and privileges.

Indeed, perhaps the major policy through which an organization can reflect its stance on diversity is its mission statement. If the organization's mission statement articulates a clear and direct commitment to diversity, everyone who reads that mission statement will grow to understand and accept the importance of diversity, at least to that particular organization.

As a result of some of the issues raised above, people have argued that increased diversity should not be a major goal of most organizations. These individuals are not necessarily arguing that diversity is not worth achieving but simply that so many problems are associated with increased diversity that it should not be a major focus of organizations. Our Point/Counterpoint feature addresses some of these disagreements.

Organizational practices   Organizations can also help manage diversity through various ongoing practices and procedures. Avon's creation of networks for various groups represents one example of an organizational practice that fosters diversity. In general, the idea is that, because diversity is characterized by differences among people, organizations can manage that diversity more effectively by following practices and procedures based on flexibility rather than rigidity.

Benefits packages, for example, can be structured to accommodate individual situations. An employee who is part of a dual-career couple and has no children may require relatively little insurance (perhaps because his spouse's employer provides more complete coverage) and would like to be able to schedule vacations to coincide with those of his spouse. Another employee who is a single parent may need a wide variety of insurance coverage and prefer to schedule his vacation time to coincide with school holidays.

Flexible working hours can help an organization accommodate diversity. Differences in family arrangements, religious holidays, cultural events, and so forth, may each require that employees have some degree of flexibility in their work schedules. For example, a single parent may need to leave the office every day at 4:30 to pick up the children from their daycare center. An organization that truly values diversity will make every reasonable attempt to accommodate such a need.

Organizations can also facilitate diversity by making sure that diversity exists in its key committees and executive teams. Even if diversity exists within the broader organizational context, an organization that does not reflect diversity in groups like committees and teams implies that diversity is not a fully ingrained element of its culture. In contrast, if all major groups and related work assignments reflect diversity, the message is a quite different one.

Diversity training
is specifically designed to enable members of an organization to function better in a diverse workplace.

Diversity training   Many organizations are finding that diversity training is an effective means for managing diversity and minimizing its associated conflict. **Diversity training** is specifically designed to enable members of an organization to function bet-

POINT | COUNTERPOINT

Should Our Society Move from the "Melting Pot" to Pluralism?

 The United States has often been called the "great melting pot" because people from many countries and different cultures can come here and become "Americans." But this means that they lose their own unique cultural identity in exchange for a new identity as Americans. In recent years, some people have argued that this loss of cultural identity is too costly, and that the United States should move to a more pluralistic model to replace the melting pot model.

POINT... The U.S. society should retain the "melting pot" model because...	COUNTERPOINT... The U.S. society should move, instead, toward a model of pluralism because...
It has worked well in the past.	Hostility toward immigrant groups is growing in the United States.
It has allowed immigrants to develop an identity as Americans—something they have in common with all other Americans.	More recent immigrants do not wish to abandon their national identities.
The United States is a stronger, more cohesive society because everyone adopts the same identity.	The United States has lost the richness of the various cultures that can lead to new ideas, new fashions, new foods, new customs, and new approaches to problems.
Other countries with pluralistic structures have also had increased conflict because of this fact (e.g., the Quebecois in Canada).	Other European countries (e.g., Belgium) have had pluralistic traditions without the conflict (at least not recently).
True pluralism will be expensive (signs and classes in multiple languages) and confusing.	True pluralism is worth the expense because it can strengthen the country in so many ways.

So... Perhaps the time has come for the United States to abandon its melting pot mentality. It is possible that, by creating a truly pluralistic society this country might see an injection of culture that has never before been seen here. Yet, with everything that is gained something is lost, and the United States will have to decide if these benefits are worth the loss of a single national identity—assuming that such an identity exists now.

ter in a diverse workplace. This training can take various forms.[19] As discussed in the *HR Legal Brief* feature, diversity training has to be undertaken all too often to remedy specific problems or crises that have erupted. But many organizations find it useful to help people learn more about their similarities and differences for other reasons.

Men and women can be taught to work together more effectively and can gain insights into how their own behaviors affect and are interpreted by others. In one organization, a diversity training program helped male managers gain insights into how various remarks they made to one another could be interpreted by others as being sexist. In the same organization, female managers learned how to point out their discomfort with those remarks without appearing overly hostile.

Similarly, white and black managers may need training to understand each other better. Managers at Mobil noticed that four black colleagues never seemed to eat lunch together. After a diversity training program, they realized that the black managers felt

The Merits of Diversity Training?

Texaco executives made headlines a few years ago when a tape-recorded conversation in which they made racially insulting remarks was made public. About the same time, AT&T came under fire when a company newsletter used images of monkeys to represent people in Africa. And Denny's, the popular restaurant chain, attracted national attention over charges that it discriminated against minority customers and employees.

In each case, company officials made public apologies and offered restitution to those who were most directly offended. Another response from each company was an announcement that key managers throughout the firm must participate in diversity training. Diversity training, as the term suggests, is designed to help individuals better understand people who are different from themselves.

> *"The objective is to help managers and supervisors to understand how unconscious behavior can impact employees, how differences can get in the way of productivity in the workplace and how to leverage diversity as a competitive advantage."*
>
> (Edward N. Gadsden, Jr., Texaco's diversity director)*

Such training is supposed to help people understand the beliefs, values, and life styles of others and to make them more tolerant and accepting of diverse points of view. Many experts believe that a well-planned and well-delivered diversity training program can indeed help people become more tolerant of others. On the other hand, some critics believe that such training addresses only surface-level issues. For example, some of the terms that the Texaco executives used disparagingly had been learned in a diversity program!

Sources: "Does Diversity Training Work?" *USA Today,* March 2, 2006, p. 1B; "Companies Try New Tactics in Diversity Training," *Wall Street Journal,* November 10, 2005, p. B6; "A 3Com Factory Hires a Lot of Immigrants, Gets Mix of Languages," *Wall Street Journal,* March 30, 1998, pp. A1, A12; "Do Diversity Programs Make a Difference?" *Wall Street Journal,* December 4, 1996, p. B1 (*quote on p. B1).

that if they ate together, their white colleagues would be overly curious about what they were talking about. Thus, they avoided close associations with one another because they feared calling attention to themselves.

Some organizations go so far as to provide language training for their employees as a vehicle for managing diversity. Motorola, for example, provides English language training for its foreign employees on assignment in the United States. At Pace Foods in San Antonio, Texas, staff meetings and employee handbooks are translated into Spanish for the benefit of the company's 100 Hispanic employees (out of a total payroll of 350 employees).

Organizational culture   The ultimate test of an organization's commitment to managing diversity is its culture. Unless there is a basic and fundamental belief that diversity is valued, it cannot become a truly integral part of an organization, regardless of what managers say or put in writing. An organization that really wants to promote diversity must shape its culture so that it clearly underscores top management commitment to and support of diversity in all of its forms throughout every part of the organization. With top management support, and reinforced with a clear and consistent set of organizational policies and practices, diversity can become a basic and fundamental part of an organization.

Many organizations today are moving inexorably toward multiculturalism. Myriad legal, social, and business forces are reinforcing this pattern. John Rogers, Jr. is CEO of Ariel Capital Management, the first African American-owned mutual fund company. Mr. Rogers co-hosts an annual seminar to train black directors, and his company sponsors the Ariel Community Academy to help develop entrepreneurial acumen in young people such as these. As more and more talented minorities emerge, multicultural organizations will become increasingly common.

The Multicultural Organization

Many organizations today are grappling with cultural diversity. While organizations are becoming more diverse, there are few truly multicultural organizations. The **multicultural organization** is one that has achieved high levels of diversity, one that can capitalize fully on the advantages of the diversity, and one that has few diversity-related problems.[20] One recent article described the six basic characteristics of such an organization.[21] These six basic characteristics are illustrated in Figure 8.5.

A multicultural organization is one in which diversity and the appreciation of all cultures is simply the way business is done. Some people think of UPS as a somewhat old-fashioned company, and it certainly isn't as splashy as some of its competitors in the shipping industry. But that doesn't mean that UPS is behind the curve in multiculturalism. Jovita Carranza, the company's highest-ranking Hispanic female executive, began working at UPS twenty-seven years ago. She says she never asked for a promotion, but more responsibility came as a result of doing a good job. She now oversees the daily loading and unloading of 1.5 million packages and the 20,000 employees who handle them as they come through UPS Worldport, a four-million-square-foot facility, in Louisville. She notes that there is no diversity officer or diversity committee at UPS. Instead, she notes that diversity and multiculturalism are just part of the way UPS does business.

*The **multicultural organization** is one that has achieved high levels of diversity, one that can capitalize fully on the advantages of the diversity, and one that has few diversity-related problems.*

empathy, tolerance, and communication. Major organizational approaches are through policies, practices, diversity training, and culture.

Few, if any, organizations have become truly multicultural. The key dimensions that characterize organizations as they eventually achieve this state are pluralism, full structural integration, full integration of the informal network, an absence of prejudice and discrimination, no gap in organizational identification based on a cultural identity group, and low levels of intergroup conflict attributable to diversity. Ultimately, the people of any country with a diverse population such as the United States must also decide if a model of pluralism will work on the national level as well.

Key Points for Future HR Managers

■ While equal employment opportunity is the law, effective management of diversity in the workplace is critical for gaining and maintaining competitive advantage.

■ Effective diversity management requires recognition of how people are similar to and how they are different from one another. It also requires respect for the differences that do exist.

■ The workforce is becoming much more diverse. The workforce is aging, more women have entered the workforce, the workforce is becoming more ethnically diverse, and the number of persons with disabilities is rising. Each of these trends presents special challenges to human resource managers.

■ Increased diversity has the potential to allow the firm to acquire more valued employees, to raise levels of productivity, to market its goods and services more effectively to a broader segment of the population, and to increase its levels of creativity. Conflict can also increase as diversity increases.

■ Effective management of diversity and the development of multicultural organizations require a clear and strong commitment from the highest levels in the organization.

Key Points for Future General Managers

■ Managing diversity is critical for the company that wants to remain competitive in the new century. Extremely effective diversity management can lead to a strong competitive advantage as a firm becomes more attractive to a broader set of applicants, has easier access to a broader set of markets, and increases creativity within the firm.

■ Effective diversity management is a full-time job and requires strong and consistent support from top management.

Review and Discussion Questions

1. Define diversity.

2. What are the basic trends in diversity in the United States today? What accounts for these trends?

3. Distinguish between identical treatment and equitable treatment in an organizational setting.

4. What are the four most common bases of diversity that are relevant to managers and their organizations?

5. What trends are apparent regarding age, gender, and ethnicity in the workplace?

6. How does diversity contribute to competitiveness?

7. How does diversity contribute to conflict?

8. Identify and discuss various individual strategies for managing diversity.

9. Identify and discuss various organizational strategies for managing diversity.

10. What is a multicultural organization? Do you think such an organization exists?

CLOSING CASE

The Avon Way

Women have always played an important role at Avon, the largest cosmetics firm in the United States. Starting with the first Avon Lady in 1886, women have long been the foundation of the firm's marketing and sales efforts. And Avon has always employed a lot of women throughout its organization. But control always remained in the hands of the small group of men who ran the company. A series of disastrous decisions and setbacks in the 1980s, however, caused the firm to rethink its philosophies and to promote its best middle managers, many of them women, into the executive ranks. And as a result, Avon has turned itself around. Today the firm is known for both its exemplary financial performance and its acceptance of all people, regardless of their gender, skin color, or age.

Avon's problems started in the 1970s, when its top management team tried to change the firm's strategy. This group of predominantly male managers first ignored their own marketing research about women consumers and shifting career patterns, which had indicated that more women were entering the workforce and seeking professional careers. In particular, they failed to recognize that the personal-care products preferred by women were also changing. Then, in the 1980s, they tried to buck emerging trends and to diversify with a number of ill-conceived acquisitions. Finally, as the firm was on the brink of bankruptcy, a new top management team was brought in. Led by chief executive officer (CEO) Jim Preston, Avon refocused itself on its roots and began to market cosmetics again to a largely female market, albeit a very different market.

But this time the firm adopted new approaches. It decided to recognize and reward managerial talent rather than the gender of the individual manager. As a result, more women were promoted into higher-level positions. In addition, Preston shifted the firm's organization culture to be more accommodating to all its employees—to value differences among people rather than attempting to impose a rigid and controlling model for accomplishing goals. For example, the firm dropped its season-ticket purchases to Knick and Yankee games and replaced them with season tickets for the New York City Ballet and the New York Philharmonic. And the company eliminated its annual hunting retreat, a male bastion of drinking and card playing.

Avon is also moving aggressively into foreign markets. For example, Avon products are now sold in mature markets like western Europe and Japan. In addition, the firm sells its products throughout China, Russia, and eastern Europe. All told, Avon manufactures its products in 18 countries and sells them in 125. Preston credits several key female executives for championing the international push and for making sure that it was done right. And many new managers at the firm have come from international contacts, organizations, and networks that the firm did not previously see as a valuable source of executive talent.

But perhaps the biggest testament to the "new" Avon is its new top management team. In 1999, after Preston's departure, Andrea Jung was named chair and CEO; at the same time Susan Kropf was appointed president and chief operating officer (COO). All told, over half of the firm's top officers are women and more than 40 percent of its global managers are women. Almost half of the firm's board of directors is female. Clearly, Avon is a firm that has changed its own culture and appreciates the power of diversity and multiculturalism.[22]

Case Questions

1. What underlies Avon's commitment to diversity?

2. Why don't more companies follow Avon's lead?

3. Can any of the dimensions of diversity derail Avon's success?

Building HR Management Skills

Purpose: The purpose of this exercise is to help develop increasingly important human resource skills as they relate to multicultural issues and challenges.

Step 1: Read and reflect on the scenario that follows:

Your firm has recently undergone a significant increase in its workforce. Many of the new workers you have hired are immigrants from eastern Europe and

Asia. Several do not speak English very well, but all are hard workers who appear to want to be successful and to fit in with their coworkers.

Recently, however, some problems have come to your attention. Several of your female workers have begun to complain about an increase in sexual harassment. Your supervisors have noticed an increase in tardiness and absenteeism among all your workers. You have decided that some action is needed. You are unsure, however, about how to proceed. Consequently, you have decided to spend a few days thinking about what to do.

Step 2: Respond to the questions that follow:

1. Think of as many causes as you can for each of the two problems you face.

2. Determine how you might address each problem, given the potential array of factors that might have contributed to each.

3. What role might the organization culture be playing in this situation, apart from issues of multiculturalism?

4. What role might multiculturalism be playing in this situation, apart from issues of organization culture?

Ethical Dilemmas in HR Management

 Assume that you are the senior human resource executive in your company. For years your firm had relatively little diversity. The 1,000-member workforce was almost exclusively white and male. But in recent years you have succeeded in increasing diversity substantially. Almost one-third of your employees are now female, while over 40 percent are Hispanic or African-American.

Your firm has recently had some unfortunate financial setbacks. You feel that you have no choice but to lay off about 300 employees for a period of at least six months. If everything goes well, you also expect to be able to rehire them at the end of the six-month period.

You are currently puzzling over what criteria to use in selecting people for layoffs. If you use strict seniority, women and ethnic minorities will bear the brunt of the layoffs because they are almost all among the newest em-

ployees in the firm. If you use strict performance, however, your older and more senior (and predominately white male) workers will bear the brunt because your newer employees have the most current training and job skills. You also wonder what role loyalty should play because many of your older workers could have left for higher-paying jobs a few years ago but chose to stay.

Questions

1. What are the ethical issues in this situation?

2. What are the basic arguments for and against the different criteria in selecting employees to be laid off?

3. What do you think most managers would do? What would you do?

HR Internet Exercise

 One of the most important multicultural challenges facing managers today involves language skills. Assume that you are the human resource manager for a large domestic company. Your firm has recently decided to enter into a joint venture with three foreign companies, one each from France, Germany, and Korea. The terms of this joint venture involve your three partners each sending a team of managers to your corporate headquarters for a period of two years.

You must make sure that your own top management team has the basic language skills in each of the three languages represented among your partners.

With the background information above as context, do the following:

1. Use the Internet to obtain information about language-training programs and methods.

2. Obtain information about one or more programs or methods and decide how you should proceed.

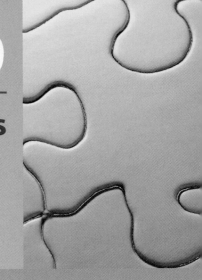

9

Compensation and Benefits

CHAPTER OUTLINE

Developing a Compensation Strategy
Basic Purposes of Compensation
Wages Versus Salaries
Strategic Options for Compensation
Determinants of Compensation
Strategy

Determining What to Pay
Job Evaluation Methods
Pay-for-Knowledge and
Skill-Based Pay

Wage and Salary Administration
Pay Secrecy
Pay Compression

**Basic Considerations in Benefits
Programs**
The Costs of Benefits Programs
Purposes of Benefits Programs

Mandated Benefits
Unemployment Insurance
Social Security
Workers' Compensation

Nonmandated Benefits
Insurance Coverage
Private Pension Plans
Paid Time Off
Other Benefits
Cafeteria-Style Benefits Plans

**Legal Issues in Compensation
and Benefits**

**Evaluating Compensation
and Benefits Programs**

CHAPTER OBJECTIVES

*After studying this chapter you should
be able to:*

■ Describe the basic issues involved
in developing a compensation
strategy.

■ Discuss how organizations develop
a wage and salary structure.

■ Identify and describe the basic
issues involved in wage and salary
administration.

■ Discuss the basic considerations in
understanding benefit programs.

■ Identify and describe types of benefit plans in organizations.

■ Identify and describe basic legal
issues in compensation and benefits.

■ Describe the importance to an
organization of evaluating its compensation and benefit programs.

Nucor is a pioneer in the steelmaking industry, one of the first to make new steel from scrap metal. From a tiny upstart in the 1960s, the company today is the largest producer in the United States, shipping 21 million tons in 2005. The Nucor success story is all about the effective use of human resources.

In the 1960s, then-CEO Ken Iverson transformed the struggling firm with a unique management perspective. His philosophy required that employee earnings be based on productivity and that workers enjoy job security and be treated fairly. These principles created an organization culture that is egalitarian, participative, and decentralized.

Iverson also designed a simple management structure, with few layers and a small staff. General managers supervise department managers, line supervisors, and hourly personnel. There are just four layers and four job titles between a janitor and the current CEO, Daniel DiMicco. Nucor's headquarters staff consists of a mere 65 employees overseeing 12,000 workers, the smallest support staff of any multibillion dollar firm.

Nucor has the best labor relations of any domestic steelmaker. None of the firm's plants are unionized, and employees do not feel they need a union for protection. On its part, Nucor has never engaged in union-busting tactics. Workers' contributions are recognized. In a gesture of appreciation, every single worker's name is printed on the cover of Nucor's annual reports.

Nucor also has an innovative compensation plan. Hourly workers at other mills earn $16 to $21 per hour, yet Nucor's make just $10. However, Nucor gives generous bonuses that are tied to the quality and productivity of the entire shift. Profit sharing adds an extra $18,000 annually. Bonuses and profit sharing in 2005 exceeded $220 million, in some cases, tripling take-home pay.

Compensation for managers is 75 to 90 percent of market average, but performance bonuses can double that amount. However, the hourly workers' bonuses and profit sharing are not offered to managers, creating greater pay equality. Even CEO DiMicco's pay is limited to 23 times the average hourly workers,' compared to the typical CEO who makes 400 times the pay of a low-level worker. Executives have no perks—no company cars, extra holidays, enhanced insurance benefits, or reserved parking spaces.

Employment at Nucor can be lucrative, but high pay isn't guaranteed. If a bad batch of steel is identified before leaving the factory, the workers get no bonus. If the bad steel gets to the customer, they give up three times that amount. Bonuses are also dependent on the cyclical steel market. In 2005, when sales were strong, the average hourly worker made $91,000. In 2003, with steel sales down, the average was $59,000. "In average-to-bad years, we earn less than our peers in other companies," says James Coblin, Nucor's human resources vice president. "That's supposed to teach us that we don't want to be average or bad. We want to be good."

The nonunion workforce is flexible and participative. Workers take the initiative to improve operations in their areas. In fact, worker suggestions are the most important source of new ideas for the firm. Management has pushed decision making down to the lowest possible level. DiMicco refers to his executive vice presidents as "mini CEOs." Workers voluntarily assume responsibility because their pay is tied to overall performance. Trust is so high that divisions regularly compete for high performance, while still maintaining cooperation.

Nucor has grown through more than a dozen acquisitions over the last decade, yet the culture and practices have spread to each newly acquired plant. Leaders are promoted from within, which strengthens the culture. Nucor takes care to persuade new workers of the advantages of its system. At one newly acquired plant, Nucor based pay on the old system but posted what employees would have earned under the new

> *"In average-to-bad years, we earn less than our peers in other companies. That's supposed to teach us that we don't want to be average or bad. We want to be good."*
>
> (James Coblin, Nucor's human resources vice president*)

system. After six months, employees realized the benefits and asked to switch to Nucor's formula.

Workers are passionate about Nucor. One vice president describes himself as "an apostle" for Iverson's methods and says, "Our culture is a living thing. It will not die because we will not let it die, ever." That passion has translated into profitability. Nucor has one of the highest returns to shareholders of almost all Standard & Poor's 500-stock index, at 387 percent over the past five years. Nucor managers routinely credit the workers for Nucor's high performance. General manager Ladd Hall says, "The people in the mills, that's what makes it Nucor."[1]

The amount of value people create for an organization and what the organization gives them as compensation for that value are important determinants of organizational competitiveness. If employers pay too much for the value created by workers, profits (and hence competitiveness) will suffer. But if they pay too little or demand too much from their workers for what they are paying they will suffer in different ways—lower quality workers, higher turnover, employee fatigue and stress, and/or legal sanctions. Clearly, then, managing compensation and benefits are important activities for any organization. And just as clearly, Nucor managers have a keen understanding of the relationship between worker compensation and company performance.

Compensation and benefits refer to the various types of outcomes employees receive for their time at work. **Compensation** is the set of rewards that organizations provide to individuals in return for their willingness to perform various jobs and tasks within the organization. **Benefits** are the various rewards, incentives, and other items of value that an organization provides to its employees beyond wages, salaries, and other forms of financial compensation. The term *total compensation* is sometimes used to refer to the overall value of financial compensation plus the value of additional benefits that the organization provides.

In this chapter we cover the basic concepts of compensation and benefits. We start by examining how compensation strategies are developed, and then turn to the administration of compensation programs, and how organizations evaluate their compensation programs. We then turn our attention to benefits, discussing the basic reasons for benefit plans and describing different types of benefit plans typically found in organizations. We conclude with a discussion of legal issues associated with compensation and benefits and the ways in which organizations can evaluate their compensation and benefit programs.

Compensation *is the set of rewards that organizations provide to individuals in return for their willingness to perform various jobs and tasks within the organization.*

Benefits *generally refer to various rewards, incentives, and other things of value that an organization provides to its employees beyond their wages, salaries, and other forms of direct financial compensation.*

Developing a Compensation Strategy

Compensation should never be a result of random decisions but instead the result of a careful and systematic strategic process.[2] Embedded in the process is an understanding of the basic purposes of compensation, an assessment of strategic options for compensation, knowledge of the determinants of compensation strategy, and the use of pay surveys.

Basic Purposes of Compensation

Compensation has several fundamental purposes and objectives. First, the organization must provide appropriate and equitable rewards to employees. Individuals who work for organizations want to feel valued and want to be rewarded at a level commensurate with their skills, abilities, and contributions to the organization. In this regard, an organization must consider two different kinds of equity. In addition, compensation serves a "signaling" function. Organizations signal to employees what they feel is important for the employee to focus on (and what they feel is less important) by paying for certain kinds of activities or behaviors and not for others. As we discuss in more detail in the next chapter, compensation can serve as an incentive to employees to increase their efforts along desired lines. We turn first to the issues of fairness and equity.

Internal equity in compensation refers to comparisons made by employees to other employees within the same organization. In making these comparisons the employee is concerned that he is equitably paid for his contributions to the organization relative to the way other employees are paid in the firm. For example, suppose a department manager learns that all the other department managers in the firm are paid more than he is. He subsequently looks more closely at the situation and finds that they all have similar experience and responsibilities. As a result, he becomes unhappy with his compensation and likely requests a salary increase. On the other hand, he might discover that he has much less work experience and fewer responsibilities than the other managers and thus concludes that there is no equity problem. Problems with internal equity can result in conflict among employees, feelings of mistrust, low morale, anger, and perhaps even legal action if the basis for inequity is perceived to result from illegal discrimination.

External equity in compensation refers to comparisons made by employees with similar employees at other firms performing similar jobs. For example, an engineer may experience internal equity relative to her engineering colleagues in her work group because she knows they are all paid the same salary. But if she finds out that another major employer in the same community is paying its engineers higher salaries for comparable work, she might be concerned about external equity. Problems with external equity may result in higher turnover (because employees will leave for better opportunities elsewhere), dissatisfied and unhappy workers, and difficulties in attracting new employees.

A critical source of information concerning external equity is the pay survey. **Pay surveys** are surveys of compensation paid to employees by other employers in a particular geographic area, industry, or occupational group. Some wage surveys, especially for executive and managerial jobs, are conducted by professional associations such as the Society for Human Resource Management. The results of these surveys are then made available for all members, which means that employees scan for information about external wages and salaries on their own. Indeed, as discussed more fully in the *HR in the 21st Century* feature titled "Negotiating Salaries on the Web," the Internet is making this practice increasingly common and easy today.

Other organizations also routinely conduct wage surveys. Business publications such as *Business Week, Fortune,* and *Nation's Business* routinely publish compensation levels for various kinds of professional and executive positions. In addition, the Bureau of National Affairs and other government agencies routinely conduct wage surveys within certain occupational groups, certain regions, and so forth. The Bureau of Labor Statistics is also an important source of government-controlled wage and salary survey information. But, in order to obtain the exact data they need, many larger firms design their own pay surveys, while many others rely upon consulting firms to conduct wage and salary surveys on their behalf. This approach allows them to take advantage of the expertise available in such firms and to minimize their own risk and the prospects of making a

Internal equity *in compensation refers to comparisons made by employees to other employees within the same organization.*

External equity *in compensation refers to comparisons made by employees to others employed by different organizations performing similar jobs.*

Pay surveys *are surveys of compensation paid to employees by other employers in a particular geographic area, industry, or occupational group.*

Negotiating Salaries on the Web

Back in the "old days" (probably up to the final years of the twentieth century, in fact) negotiating wages and salaries was typically handled in a meeting between the employee and his or her manager. The same approach was used both for individuals who were being offered their first job with the company and for existing employees who felt they deserved a raise. But in both cases, the manager and the organization usually had the upper hand. This situation stemmed from the fact that both prospective and current employees generally had relatively little knowledge about prevailing wage and salary levels. They usually did not know what others in the firm were being paid, for example, or what similar companies were paying for similar jobs in different parts of the region or country.

But the Internet is rapidly changing all that. Several large websites now provide salary information for interested parties. Among other information, these sites include salary survey data, job listings with specified pay levels, and even customized compensation analyses. Armed with such detailed information, more and more

"The Internet has become the big level playing field for everyone [by exposing businesses that] are way below everyone else as far as pay is concerned."

(Brian Krueger, consultant)*

people today are negotiating better deals for themselves with their employers.

Sometimes the Web can provide even more insights, especially for crafty negotiators. For example, some people have been known to use Internet bulletin boards to track down other individuals who have recently been offered employment with a particular firm, find out how much they were offered, and then use that information as leverage in their own negotiations.

In another unforeseen development, the big-time recruiting firm of Korn/Ferry recently set up its own salary site called Futurestep. But the firm faced internal negotiations when some of its own employees used the site to determine that they themselves were being underpaid! On balance, then, it seems like the Internet will be playing a major role from now on in the kinds of wages and salaries that employees expect and that companies pay.

Source: "How the Internet is Changing the World of HR," *HR Magazine,* February 2006, pp. 34–36; "Using the Web to Get Ahead," *USA Today,* March 4, 2006, p. B3; "Web Transforms Art of Negotiating Raises," *Wall Street Journal,* September 22, 1998, pp. B1, B16 (*quote on p. B16).

significant error or mistake in the conduct of the survey.[3] Figure 9.1 presents a sample section from a pay survey.

Both internal and external equity are clearly important, but there is one additional consideration concerning internal equity. The Equal Pay Act of 1963 stipulates that men and women who perform essentially the same job must be paid the same. Generally speaking, internal equity problems occur when employees on one job feel that they are being undercompensated relative to employees on some other job or jobs within the organization. However, it is illegal to pay a woman less than a man (or vice versa) for performing the same job when no objective basis for such a differential exists. If the organization can prove that such differences are based on differences in performance and/or seniority, the organization can probably avoid litigation, but it takes only the perception by a woman that she is being paid less than a man doing the same job for problems to begin. Also, if some jobs in the organization are performed mostly by men and others mostly by women, differences in pay between the two jobs (real or perceived) must be attributable to differences in job demands or, again, the organization might face legal problems.

It is also important that compensation serve a motivational purpose. By "motivational purpose" we mean that individuals should perceive that their efforts and contributions to the organization are recognized and rewarded. Individuals who work hard

FIGURE 9.1   Example of a Pay Survey

Organization: ABC Trucking
Location: Dallas, TX

Benchmark Jobs	No. of workers (this title)	No. of workers (total)	Average weekly hours	Base Pay			Median total compensation (base pay + benefits)	Industry			
				25th %-tile	50th %-tile	75th %-tile		Mfg.	Trans.	Utilities	Trade
File clerk	10	300	40	$15,000	$20,000	$25,000	$28,000		✓		
Order clerk											
Accounting clerk											

A survey such as this one is sent to other organizations in a given region. In this case, the survey would go to organizations in various industries, but other surveys might be targeted to a specific industry. The jobs that are the focus of the survey should be benchmark jobs, where everyone understands the nature of the job, the content is fairly stable, and the job is likely to be found in a wide variety of organizations. In some surveys, specific benchmark jobs are coded to ensure that everyone reacts to the same job. Also, some surveys ask more specific questions about other areas of compensation. Data from surveys such as this one are then summarized for each job.

and who perform at a high level should be compensated at a level higher than are individuals who do just enough to get by and who perform at only an average or below average rate.[4] If everyone perceives this situation to be true, employees will believe that the reward system is fair and just and that internal equity exists, and they will be more motivated to perform at their highest level. We will discuss some specific models of motivation in Chapter 13, and we will discuss incentive pay plans in Chapter 14.

Organizations must adequately and effectively manage compensation. Compensation to employees is one of the major expenses in most organizations. On the one hand, it is important that employees be appropriately and equitably rewarded. On the other hand, it is important that the organization control its compensation costs. For example, it should be careful not to overpay individuals for the value of their contributions (which could lead to problems with internal equity) or to provide excess or superfluous benefits or rewards.[5] Thus, the ideal compensation system would be one that reflects an appropriate balance of organizational constraints, costs, budgets, income, and cash flow relative to employee needs, expectations, and demands.

The fundamental purpose of compensation, then, is to provide an adequate and appropriate reward system for employees so that they feel valued and worthwhile as organizational members and representatives. Compensation represents more than the number of dollars a person takes home in her or his pay envelope. Instead, it provides a measure of the employee's value to the organization and functions indirectly as an indicator of his or her self-worth.[6]

Wages Versus Salaries

Wages *generally refer to hourly compensation paid to operating employees; the basis for wages is time.*

Fundamental to understanding compensation is the distinction between wages and salaries. **Wages** generally refer to hourly compensation paid to operating employees;

The minimum wage continues to be a controversial subject in the United States. Advocates for increased minimum wages argue that higher wages would allow workers to better support their families, but opponents argue that higher wage costs would make firms less competitive and less likely to hire unskilled workers. In other parts of the world discussions about minimum wages also go on—but the stakes are sometimes substantially different. Wellington Casas is a mine worker at the Muzo emerald mines in Colombia, South America. Colombia is the largest producer of emeralds in the world, and most say that Colombian emeralds are the finest in the world. Yet Casas earns a minimum wage of $130 for twenty days work. He works around-the-clock shifts, breaking only for meals and sleep.

the basis for wages is time. That is, the organization pays individuals for specific blocks of their time. Most organizations calculate wages on an hourly basis. If an individual works eight hours, he or she earns eight hours times the hourly wage rate. But if an individual works only four and a half hours, then she or he makes four and a half times the hourly wage rate. Individuals who are paid on an hourly basis typically receive their income on a weekly or biweekly basis. Most of the jobs that are paid on an hourly wage basis are lower-level and/or operational jobs within the organization.

Rather than expressing compensation on an hourly basis, the organization may instead describe compensation on an annual or monthly basis; when this method is used, compensation is referred to as **salary.** A salary is used to provide compensation not for how much time people spend in the organization but for their overall contributions to the organization's performance. On a given day, for instance, if a manager leaves work a couple of hours early or works a couple of hours late, that time has no bearing on the individual's compensation. She is not docked for leaving early, nor does she get overtime pay for working extra. Salaries are usually quoted on either a monthly or an annual basis (such as $4,000 a month or $48,000 a year). In general, salaries are paid to professional and managerial employees within an organization. Plant managers, product managers, and professional managers in areas such as marketing and finance and accounting, for example, are all likely to be paid on an annual basis.

> **Salary** *is income paid to an individual on the basis of performance, not on the basis of time.*

Strategic Options for Compensation

Most organizations establish a formal compensation strategy that dictates how they will pay individuals. Several decisions are embedded within this strategy. The first decision relates to the basis for pay. Most organizations traditionally based pay on the functions performed on the job. But more recently organizations have begun to rely on skill-based pay and pay-for-knowledge programs. In this way, organizations signal to their employees the relative importance of what someone does on the job versus what they bring to the job.

A second decision in developing a compensation strategy focuses on the bases for differential pay within a specific job. In some organizations, especially those with a strong union presence, differences in actual pay rates are based on seniority. That is, with each year of service in a particular job, wages go up by a specified amount. Therefore, the longer one works on the job, the more that person makes, regardless of the level of performance on the job. Most public school systems use a seniority system to pay teachers—they get a base salary increase for each year of service they accumulate. And as already noted, unions have historically preferred pay based at least in part on seniority.

Sometimes the relationship between seniority and pay is expressed as something called a **maturity curve.** A maturity curve is simply a schedule specifying the amount of annual increase a person receives. This curve is used when the annual increase varies based on the actual number of years of service the person has accumulated. Organizations that use maturity curves might argue that a new person tends to learn more (in part because there is more to learn) than more experienced employees and thus may deserve a larger increase. Meanwhile more senior people may already be earning considerably higher income anyway and also have fewer new tasks to learn. In any event, the assumption under a seniority-based pay system is that employees with more experience can make a more valuable contribution to the organization and should be rewarded for that contribution. These systems also encourage employees to remain with the organization.

In other organizations, differences in pay are based on differences in performance, regardless of time on the job. These systems are generally seen as rewarding employees who are good performers rather than those who simply remain with the organization. For such systems to succeed, however, the organization has to be certain that it has an effective system for measuring performance. Most major companies base at least a portion of individual pay on performance, especially for managerial and professional employees. Performance-based incentives will be discussed in more detail in Chapter 14.

A third decision in developing a compensation strategy deals with the organization's pay rates relative to going rates in the market. As shown in Figure 9.2, the three basic strategic options are to pay above-market compensation rates, market compensation rates, or below-market compensation rates.[7] This decision is important because of the costs it represents to the organization.[8]

A firm that chooses to pay above-market compensation, for example, will incur additional costs as a result. This strategic option essentially indicates that the organization pays its employees a level of compensation that is higher than that paid by other employers competing for the same kind of employees. Of course, it also anticipates achieving various benefits. Some organizations believe that they attract better employees if they pay wages and salaries that are higher than those paid by other organizations. That

*A **maturity curve** is a schedule specifying the amount of annual increase a person will receive.*

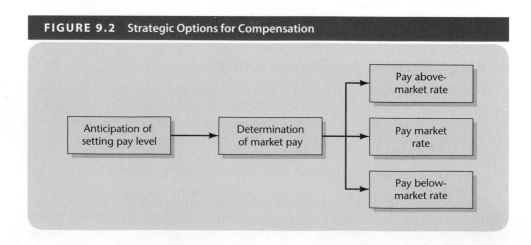

FIGURE 9.2   Strategic Options for Compensation

Anticipation of setting pay level → Determination of market pay → Pay above-market rate / Pay market rate / Pay below-market rate

is, they view compensation as a competitive issue. They recognize that high-quality employees may select from among several different potential employers and that they have a better chance of attracting the best employees if they're willing to pay them an above-market rate. Above-market pay policies are most likely to be used in larger companies, particularly those that have been performing well.

In addition to attracting high-quality employees, an above-market strategy has other benefits. Above-market rates tend to minimize voluntary turnover among employees. By definition, above-market rates mean that an employee who leaves a company paying such wages may have to take a pay cut to find employment elsewhere. Another reason that paying above-market rates might be beneficial is that it can create and foster a culture of elitism and competitive superiority. Cisco Systems, a Silicon Valley computer company, pays higher-than-average salaries specifically as a way of retaining its valued employees in an industry where turnover and mobility are high.

The downside to above-market compensation levels, of course, is cost. The organization simply has higher labor costs because of its decision to pay higher salaries to its employees. Once these higher labor costs become institutionalized, employees may begin to adopt a sense of entitlement, coming to believe that they deserve the higher compensation and thus making it difficult for the organization to be able to adjust its compensation levels down to lower levels. The *HR in the 21st Century* box titled "Minimum Wage . . . or Minimum Wages?" highlights some of the issues associated with minimum-wage compensation when state or local governments impose minimums that are higher than the federal minimum. This situation involves people being paid higher wages and knowing that their wages are better than those earned in many other states.

Another strategic option is to pay below-market rates. The organization that adopts this strategy is essentially deciding to pay workers less than the compensation levels offered by other organizations competing for the same kinds of employees. Thus, it is gambling that the labor cost savings it achieves will offset the low-quality employees it is likely to attract. Organizations most likely to pursue a below-market rate are those in areas with high unemployment. If lots of people are seeking employment and relatively few jobs are available, then many people are probably willing to work for lower wages. Thus, the organization may be able to pay lower than the market rate and still attract reasonable and qualified employees. In other situations, employers may be able to pay below-market rates because of various offsetting factors. For instance, some employers in Hawaii find that the state's beautiful setting and mild weather allows them to pay below-market salaries—some people are willing to work for less money just to be able to live in Hawaii. Again, the benefit to this strategy is lower labor costs for the organization.

On the other hand, the organization will also experience several negative side effects. Morale and job satisfaction might not be as high as the organization would otherwise prefer. Individuals are almost certain to recognize that they are being relatively underpaid, and this situation can result in feelings of job dissatisfaction and potential resentment against the organization. In addition, turnover may also be higher because employees will be continually vigilant about finding better-paying jobs. Compounding the problem even further is the fact that the higher-performing employees are among the most likely to leave, and the lower-performing employees are among the most likely to stay.

Finally, a third strategic option for compensation is to pay market rates for employees. That is, the organization may elect to pay salaries and wages that are comparable to those available in other organizations, no more and no less. Clearly, the organization that adopts this strategy is taking a midrange perspective. The organization assumes that it will get higher-quality human resources than a firm that takes a below-market strategy. At the same time, it is willing to forgo the ability to attract as many high-quality employees as the organization that takes an above-market strategy.

Minimum Wage . . . or Minimum Wages?

Most people are aware that workers in the United States are guaranteed a minimum hourly wage. But not everyone is aware of the fact that some states actually set a higher hourly minimum wage for their in-state workers. All told, twenty-three states and the District of Columbia currently have minimum wages higher than the federal minimum. Several others are also considering setting their own minimums. The current highest hourly minimum is Connecticut's, at $7.65 an hour. Other current examples include Arizona ($6.75), Colorado ($6.85), and Ohio ($6.85). One goal behind most minimum wages set above national levels is to help workers catch up with cost-of-living increases from previous years when wages failed to keep pace with inflation. Another is to compensate for higher-than-average regional living costs.

In another recent development, some cities and counties, especially in high-cost urban areas, have started imposing their own minimum wages, at least for certain kinds of jobs. For example, the city of San Jose, California,

"This isn't a debate about haves and have-nots. It's about what we all want: a good workforce."

(Jan Rigg, spokesperson for a business coalition opposing higher wage minimum)*

mandates that construction workers be paid either $9.50 an hour plus health benefits, or $10.75 an hour without health benefits. And while some cities are committed to the concept of a living wage for their citizens, other cities are more cautious. Some that try it end up abandoning the idea if they see businesses moving to nearby locations or suburbs to avoid the higher wage levels.

Not surprisingly, though, there are conflicting views on this subject. On the one hand, statistics suggest that wages have not kept pace with the cost of living, resulting in an actual reduction in real income. That is, minimum wage hikes have not kept pace with inflation. But critics argue that a higher minimum wage will result in fewer jobs for teenagers and other low-wage earners. Reduced profits (from higher labor costs) may also have a negative effect on the U.S. economy.

Source: "Minimum Wage Laws Multiply in States," *USA Today,* September 13, 2006, p. 1A (*quote on page 1A); "Struggling to Make Ends Meet," *USA Today,* September 5, 2006, p. 3B; "Minimum-Wage Increases Debated Anew," *USA Today,* January 6, 1999, p. 3A.

The advantages and disadvantages of this strategy are also likely to reflect midrange comparisons with the other strategies. That is, the organization will have higher turnover than a firm paying above-market rates but lower turnover than an organization paying below-market rates. An organization that adopts a market-rate strategy is likely to believe it can provide other intangible or more subjective benefits to employees in return for their accepting a wage rate that is perhaps lower than they might be paid elsewhere. For example, job security is one important subjective benefit that some organizations provide.

Employees who perceive that they are being offered an unusually high level of job security may therefore be willing to take a somewhat lower wage rate and accept employment at a market rate. Universities frequently adopt this strategy because they believe that the ambiance of a university environment is such that employees in such organizations do not necessarily expect higher salaries or higher wages. Microsoft also uses this approach. It offsets average wages with lucrative stock options and an exceptionally pleasant physical work environment.

Determinants of Compensation Strategy

Several different factors contribute to the compensation strategy that a firm develops. One general set of factors has to do with the overall strategy of the organization itself. As detailed in Chapter 4, a clear and carefully developed relationship should exist between a firm's corporate and business strategies and its human resource strategy.[9] This connection, in turn, should also tie into the firm's compensation strategy. Thus, a firm in a high-growth mode is constantly striving to attract new employees and may find itself in a position of having to pay above-market rates to do so. On the other hand, a stable firm may be more likely to pay market rates, given the relatively predictable and stable nature of its operations. And finally, an organization in a retrenchment or decline mode may decide to pay below-market rates because it wants to reduce the size of its workforce anyway.[10]

In addition to these general strategic considerations, several other specific factors determine an organization's compensation strategy. One obvious factor is simply the organization's ability to pay. An organization with a healthy cash flow and/or substantial cash reserves is more likely to be able to pay above-market wages and salaries. On the other hand, if the organization suffers from a cash flow crunch, has few cash reserves, and is operating on a tight budget, it may be necessary to adopt a below-market wage strategy. Thus, the organization's ability to pay is an important consideration. During the economic stagnation of recent years, many firms have found themselves in this predicament. In response, several major companies reduced the pay increases they granted to their employees.[11]

In addition, the overall ability of the organization to attract and retain employees is a critical factor. For example, if the organization is located in an attractive area; has several noncompensation amenities; and provides a comfortable, pleasant, and secure work environment, then it might be able to pay somewhat lower wages. But if the organization is located in, for example, a high-crime area or a relatively unattractive city or region, and if it has few noncompensation amenities that it can provide to its employees, it may be necessary to pay higher wages simply as a way of attracting and retaining employees.

Union influences comprise another important determinant of an organization's compensation strategy. If an organization competes in an environment that is heavily unionized, such as the automobile industry, then the strength and bargaining capabilities of the union influence what the organization pays its employees. On the other hand, if the organization does not hire employees represented by unions or if the strength of a particular union is relatively low, then the organization may be able to pay somewhat lower wages and the union influence is minimal or nonexistent.

Determining What to Pay

Once a compensation strategy has been chosen it is necessary to determine exactly what employees on a given job should be paid. The starting point in this effort has traditionally been job evaluation. We will describe this more traditional method first and then introduce a relatively new but increasingly popular approach to determining what to pay.

Job Evaluation Methods

Job evaluation is a method for determining the relative value or worth of a job to the organization so that individuals who perform that job can be compensated adequately and appropriately. That is, job evaluation is mostly concerned with establishing internal pay equity. Several job evaluation techniques and methods have been established.[12] Among the most commonly used are classification, point, and factor comparison systems. We will discuss each of these methods for job evaluation in more detail.

Job evaluation *is a method for determining the relative value or worth of a job to the organization so that individuals who perform that job can be compensated adequately and appropriately.*

The **classification system** *for job evaluation attempts to group sets of jobs together into clusters, often called grades.*

Classification system   An organization that uses a **classification system** attempts to group sets of jobs together into classifications, often called *grades*. After classifying is done, each set of jobs is then ranked at a level of importance to the organization. Importance, in turn, may be defined in terms of relative difficulty, sophistication, or required skills and abilities necessary to perform that job. A third step is to determine how many categories or classifications to use for grouping jobs. The most common number of grades is anywhere from eight to ten, although some organizations use the system with as few as four grades and some with as many as eighteen.

FIGURE 9.3   Job Classification System

Grade GS–1

Grade GS–1 includes those classes of positions the duties of which are to perform, under immediate supervision, with little or no latitude for the exercise of independent judgment:

    A. the simplest routine work in office, business, or fiscal operations; or

    B. elementary work of a subordinate technical character in a professional, scientific, or technical field.

Grade GS–6

Grade GS–6 includes those classes of positions the duties of which are:

    A. to perform, under general supervision, difficult and responsible work in office, business, or fiscal administration, or comparable subordinate technical work in a professional, scientific, or technical field, requiring in either case–
        1. considerable training and supervisory or other experience;
        2. broad working knowledge of a special and complex subject matter, procedure, or practice, or of the principles of the profession, art, or science involved; and
        3. to a considerable extent the exercise of independent judgment; or

    B. to perform other work of equal importance, difficulty, and responsibility, and requiring comparable qualifications.

Grade GS–10

Grade GS–10 includes those classes of positions the duties of which are:

    A. to perform, under general supervision, highly difficult and responsible work along special technical, supervisory, or administrative lines in office, business, or fiscal administration, requiring–
        1. somewhat extended specialized, supervisory, or administrative training and experience which has demonstrated capacity for sound independent work;
        2. thorough and fundamental knowledge of a specialized and complex subject matter, or of the profession, art, or science involved; and
        3. considerable latitude for the exercise of independent judgment; or

    B. to perform other work of equal importance, difficulty, and responsibility, and requiring comparable qualifications.

Source: U.S. Office of Personnel Management

Job classification systems require clear definitions of classes and benchmark jobs for each class. The most widely known example of a job classification system is the General Schedule (GS) system used by the federal government. This system has eighteen grades (or classes). Most federal employees fall into one of fifteen grades, while the top three grades have been combined into a single "supergrade" that covers senior executives.

    The information above outlines the descriptions of three grades from the GS system. An example of a job classified as a GS-1 would be a janitor; an example of a GS-6 job would be a light truck driver; and an example of a GS-10 job would be an auto mechanic. Within each grade are ten pay steps based on seniority, so that the range of salaries for a GS-6 job starts at just under $20,000 a year and goes up to over $25,000 a year.

The U.S. postal system is a good example of an organization that uses the classification system. The U.S. postal system has sixteen job grades, with nine pay steps within each grade. Once the grades have been determined, the job evaluator must write definitions and descriptions of each job class. These definitions and descriptions serve as the standard around which the compensation system is built. That is, once the classes of jobs are defined and described, jobs that are being evaluated can be compared with the definitions and descriptions and placed into the appropriate classification.

A major advantage of the job classification system is that it can be constructed relatively simply and quickly. It is easy to understand and easy to communicate to employees. It also provides specific standards for compensation and can easily accommodate changes in the value of various individual jobs in the organization. On the other hand, the job classification system is more complicated than simple ranking. It is based on the assumption that a constant and inflexible relationship exists between the job factors and their value to the organization. Because of this shortcoming, some organizations find it necessary to group jobs that do not necessarily fit together very well. Figure 9.3 on page 292 presents an example of a job classification system.

Point system   The most commonly used method of job evaluation is the point system.[13] The point system is more sophisticated than either the ranking or the classification system and is also relatively easy to use. The **point system** requires managers to

*The **point system** for job evaluation requires managers to quantify, in objective terms, the value of the various elements of specific jobs.*

The classification system for job evaluation is used in the U.S. federal government and thus applies to jobs in the postal service. Each postal job has a general service (GS) classification, which determines the range of pay for that job. In such a system, everyone understands what aspects of the job are compensated, and while the system is extremely structured, it is easily understood and accepted. George Lacap, a mail sorter (GS–5), is shown here sorting the mail at the San Francisco Processing Center in early December, the busiest time of the year for the postal service.

quantify, in objective terms, the value of the various elements of specific jobs. Using job descriptions as a starting point, managers assign points to the degree of various compensable factors that are required to perform each job. Compensable factors include any aspect of a job for which an organization is willing to provide compensation. For instance, managers might assign points based on the amount of skill required to perform a particular job, the amount of physical effort needed, the nature of the working conditions involved, and the responsibility and authority involved in the performance of the job. Job evaluation simply represents the sum of the points allocated to each of the compensable factors for each job.

Point systems typically evaluate eight to ten compensable factors for each job. It is important that the factors chosen do not overlap one another, that they immediately distinguish between substantive characteristics of the jobs, that they are objective and verifiable in nature, and that they are well understood and accepted by both managers and employees. Not all aspects of a particular job may be of equal importance, so managers can allocate different weights to reflect the relative importance of these aspects to a job. These weights are usually determined by summing the judgments of various independent but informed evaluators. Thus, an administrative job within an organization might result in weightings of required education, 40 percent; experience required, 30 percent; predictability and complexity of the job, 15 percent; responsibility and authority for making decisions, 10 percent; and working conditions and physical requirements for the job, 5 percent.

*The **point manual,*** *used to implement the point system of job evaluation, carefully and specifically defines the degrees of points from first to fifth.*

Because the point system is used to evaluate jobs, most organizations also develop a point manual. The **point manual** carefully and specifically defines the degrees of points from first to fifth. For example, education might be defined as follows: (1) first degree, up to and including a high school diploma, 25 points; (2) second degree, high school diploma and one year of college education, 50 points; (3) third degree, high school diploma and two years of college, 75 points; (4) fourth degree, high school education and three years of college, 100 points; and (5) fifth degree, a college degree, 125 points. These point manuals are then used for all subsequent job evaluation.

*The **factor comparison method*** *for job evaluation assesses jobs, on a factor-by-factor basis, using a factor comparison scale as a benchmark.*

Factor comparison method   A third method of job evaluation is the **factor comparison method.** Like the point system, the factor comparison method allows the job evaluator to assess jobs on a factor-by-factor basis. At the same time, however, it differs from the point system because jobs are evaluated or compared against a standard of key points. That is, instead of using points, a factor comparison scale is used as a benchmark. Although an organization can choose to identify any number of compensable factors, commonly used systems include five job factors for comparing jobs. These factors are responsibilities, skills, physical effort, mental effort, and working conditions.

Managers performing a job evaluation in a factor comparison system are typically advised to follow six specific steps. First, the comparison factors to be used are selected and defined. The five universal factors are used as starting points, but any given organization may need to add factors to this set. Second, benchmark or key jobs in the organization are identified. These jobs are typically representative of and common in the labor market for a particular firm. Usually, ten to twenty benchmark jobs are selected. The third step is to rank the benchmark jobs on each of the compensation factors. The ranking itself is usually based on job descriptions and job specifications determined by a job analysis.

The fourth step is to allocate part of each benchmark's job wage rate to each job factor. This allocation is based on the relative importance of the job factor. Each manager participating in the job evaluation might be asked to make an independent allocation first, without consultation with other managers. Then the managers would meet as a group to develop a consensus about the assignment of monetary values to the various factors. The fifth step in the factor comparison system is to prepare the two sets of ratings based on the ranking and the assigned wages and thus determine the consistency demonstrated by the evaluators. Sixth, a job comparison chart is developed to display the benchmark jobs and the monetary values that each job received for each factor. This chart can then be used to rate other jobs in the organization as compared to the benchmark jobs.

The factor comparison system is a detailed and meticulous method for formally evaluating jobs. Thus it provides a rigorous assessment of the true value of various jobs, which is one of its advantages. It also allows managers to recognize fully how the differences in factor rankings affect the dollars that the organization allocates to compensation for various jobs. On the other hand, the factor comparison method is also extremely complex and difficult to use. Therefore, it is time-consuming and expensive for an organization that chooses to adopt it. A fair amount of subjectivity is involved, and it is possible that people whose jobs are evaluated with this system may feel that inequities have crept into the system either through managerial error or through politically motivated oversight.

Hay and Associates is a well-known compensation consulting firm that often does job evaluations for large organizations. Hay and Associates uses a factor comparison system based on three factors: know-how, problem solving, and accountability.

Pay-for-Knowledge and Skill-Based Pay

The steps, decisions, and processes outlined above still apply to many jobs in most organizations, but recent proposals have suggested a whole different approach to compensation: employees should be rewarded for what they know rather than what they are specifically required to do on the job. The relative advantages and disadvantages of these two philosophies are summarized in the *Point/Counterpoint* feature for this chapter.

Pay-for-knowledge involves compensating employees (usually managerial, service, or professional employees) for learning specific material. For example, this approach might include paying programmers for learning a new programming language or rewarding managers who master a new manufacturing system. These systems can also be designed to pay for learning supervisory skills or for developing more in-depth knowledge about a topic relevant to the organization. Pay-for-knowledge systems reward employees for mastering material that allows them to be more useful to the organization in the future and are based on mastering new technology or mastering information that relates to global issues. These systems tend to be fairly expensive to start because the organization needs to develop methods for testing whether the employee has mastered the information in question. Once the systems are in place, however, the costs are usually not excessive. In addition, these plans have the potential to clash with more traditional incentive systems (see Chapter 14) because employees might choose to perfect and apply knowledge they already have rather than learn new material.[14]

> **Pay-for-knowledge** *involves compensating employees for learning specific information.*

Skill-based pay operates in much the same way as a pay-for-knowledge system, but these plans are more likely to be associated with hourly workers. Instead of rewarding employees who master new material, employees are rewarded for acquiring new skills. Under such a plan, for example, an administrative assistant would be paid for learning how to use spreadsheets. The skills involved can either be for the same job (or in the same job family) or they can be relevant for other jobs in the organization. For example, in manufacturing plants, it is often useful for employees to be cross-trained so that they have the skills to do several different jobs in the plant. This approach affords management a great deal of flexibility in scheduling, and it benefits employees because they can rotate through different jobs (providing some variety) and they acquire skills that may increase their market value if they choose to seek another job.

> **Skill-based pay** *rewards employees for acquiring new skills.*

POINT | COUNTERPOINT

What Should Be the Basis for Compensation?

 The basis for compensation in most organizations is the set of job requirements. That is, employees who are expected to perform more complex, difficult, or dangerous tasks or even numerous tasks are generally paid more than other employees. Thus, the basis for compensation is the set of tasks that are required, and these tasks are usually spelled out in a job description. It has been argued, however, that this set of tasks is not the best basis for compensation. Instead, critics say that we should pay for knowledge, skill, or competency. In other words, we should not pay a person for what he or she does but for what he or she knows. Under these systems an organization specifies the knowledge bases or skills it is willing to pay for; as employees acquire this information and can demonstrate mastery, their compensation increases. We refer to this alternative as knowledge-based pay.

POINT... **We should base compensation on what a person is required to do on his or her job because...**	COUNTERPOINT... **We should base compensation on what a person knows because...**
Assessing what a person does (or should do) is easier than assessing what she or he knows.	Developing a system to certify whether employees have mastered some skill or knowledge base is relatively easy.
Most employees see this approach as a fair basis for compensation, and they can easily see the basis for compensation differences.	The organization pays people for what they can contribute in terms of special knowledge or expertise—employees are paid for what they are worth to the company.
All employees know what is expected of them and how they will be rewarded.	All employees focus on growth and the accumulation of new knowledge or skills as the means to rewards.
Paying people for what they actually do makes sense.	Paying people for what they bring to the job that is useful to the organization makes sense.
What do we do when everyone has mastered all the knowledge bases or skills specified?	Under such a system employees will strive to improve themselves, and the organization will gain flexibility as well as a more knowledgeable workforce.

So... Knowledge-based systems reward people who learn more and acquire more skills that are relevant to the job. In the long run this plan is likely to benefit the company as it tries to grow and react to changes in the environment. However, few data exist either to support or to refute this position. In addition, many bureaucratic systems must be in place to determine requisite skills and to certify mastery of those skills and knowledge bases. It is possible for an employee to master all the specified skills or knowledge bases and, at that point, have the compensation decision become complicated. Nonetheless, if knowledge-based systems can be implemented, they seem to have the potential for aiding long-run competitiveness.

Wage and Salary Administration

Once wages and salaries have been determined, the resulting compensation system must be administered on an ongoing basis. Most organizations call this process **wage and salary administration,** or compensation administration. Much of this administration involves making adjustments to wages and salaries as the result of pay raises or changes in job responsibilities. In addition, in organizations where jobs are arranged in a more hierarchical structure, it is important to implement programs for progression to a higher-level job within a job class. But, in addition, there are certain issues that are related to compensation that must also be addressed as part of this administration process. Two of the most important of these issues involve pay secrecy and pay compression.

Wage and salary administration *is the ongoing process of managing a wage and salary structure.*

Pay Secrecy

Pay secrecy refers to the extent to which the compensation of any individual in an organization is secret or the extent to which it is formally made available to other individuals. Each approach has some merit.[15] On the one hand, advocates of pay secrecy maintain that what an individual is paid is his or her own business and it is not for public knowledge. They also argue that if pay levels are made known to everybody else, then jealousy and/or resentment may result. Indeed, most businesses practice pay secrecy, sometimes to the point of formally forbidding managers from discussing their pay with other people.

On the other hand, some organizations adopt a more open pay system where everyone knows what everyone else makes. The logic behind this strategy is that it promotes equity and motivation. If high performers are known to make more money than low performers, it follows logically that people throughout the organization will be motivated to work harder, under the assumption that they too will be recognized and rewarded for their

Pay secrecy *refers to the extent to which the compensation of any individual in an organization is secret or the extent to which it is formally made available to other individuals.*

THE LIGHTER SIDE OF HR

Pay secrecy is a long-standing practice in many companies today. But some companies seem to be willing to consider open pay systems. At the same time, however, organizations that are interested in open pay systems should be prepared for cries of favoritism, politics, and worse! As shown in this cartoon, for example, workers who are paid less than they think they deserve will likely find reasons to criticize the pay of others, especially upper-level managers whose salaries are likely to be relatively high.

Source: DILBERT by Scott Adams reprinted by permission of United Feature Syndicate, Inc.

contributions. Many publicly funded organizations such as state universities and public schools have open pay systems whereby any interested individual can look at budgets or other information to determine how much any employee is being paid. On the previous page, this issue is given an amusing slant in *The Lighter Side of HR*.

Pay Compression

Pay compression

occurs when individuals with substantially different levels of experience and/or performance abilities are being paid wages or salaries that are relatively equal.

Another problem that some organizations must confront occasionally during wage and salary administration is pay compression. **Pay compression** occurs when individuals with substantially different levels of experience and/or performance abilities are being paid wages or salaries that are relatively equal. Pay compression is most likely to develop when the market rate for starting salaries increases at a rate faster than an organization can raise pay for individuals who are already on the payroll.

For example, suppose that an organization hires a new engineer one year at a starting annual salary of $35,000. The next year the organization wants to hire another engineer in the same field. Overall market conditions demand that such engineers are now worth $37,000 a year, and the organization finds that it has to pay that salary to attract a new engineer. Presumably, the first engineer hired has acquired a year of experience, is performing at a reasonable level in the organization, and ought to be paid more than someone who is just starting. If the organization has the resources to adjust the existing employee's salary up beyond the $37,000 level, then it is likely to avoid any major problems. On the other hand, if internal budget constraints and other considerations limit the organization's ability to adjust the compensation of its existing employees, then pay compression may result.

Indeed, it may even be possible for a newcomer starting in an organization to be paid a higher salary than an individual who has been working for the organization for a year or two. If other employees are aware of this situation, then, again, the possibility for resentment and disappointment is likely to increase. Organizations sometimes have little remedy in the event of pay compression. On the one hand, they have to respond to market shifts if they want to continue to hire at a competitive level. At the same time, their internal resources may limit their ability to maintain pay increases at the same rate that the market rate is increasing. In this case the organization may find it necessary to try to provide other kinds of rewards, such as intangible benefits and recognition, or simply face the consequences of disgruntled employees leaving because they feel they are being underpaid relative to newcomers in the organization.

Basic Considerations in Benefits Programs

As noted above, in addition to wages and salaries, most organizations provide their employees with an array of other indirect compensation, or *benefits*. Although these benefits were once called "fringe benefits" (and a few people still use this expression today), once managers began to fully realize that they were spending more than one-third of wages and salaries in additional expenses on benefits they decided that the word *fringe* might have been understating to employees the true value of these benefits. Hence, most organizations today no longer use the term *fringe benefits* but instead refer to employee benefits, or simply benefits.

The Cost of Benefits Programs

Data from the U.S. Chamber of Commerce provide some insights into the composition of the total compensation paid to a typical employee in the United States. According to these figures, the typical employee costs the company almost $50,000 a year in total compensation. Of this amount, roughly $30,000 is paid for time worked, while the remaining $20,000 is paid for other than time worked and includes vacation time, mandated benefits, pensions, insurance, and so forth.[16]

Hence, it is quite clear that organizations are spending huge amounts of money on benefits. It also appears that many organizations are trying to hold the tide, or even reverse it, by asking employees to bear more of the costs of these benefits. But surely benefits costs will continue to be a large part of labor costs in the United States. It is also interesting to note, however, that despite these statistics, the United States actually ranks rather low in terms of the relative costs of benefits around the world.

These global differences are due almost entirely to the number of mandated benefits, which are based on the different social contracts (guarantees made by the government in return for higher taxes) in place in the respective countries, and they are substantial. For example, the German workweek is 38.3 hours (on average). The German worker works 1,685 hours per year, has forty-two days off, and has mandated benefits costs alone that equal almost 30 percent of wages. For comparison purposes, the average U.S. worker spends forty hours a week at work, spends 1,847 hours a year working, has twenty-three days off a year, and has mandated benefits costs equal to about 10 percent of wages.

Indeed, when Ford first announced its purchase of the Swedish automobile maker Volvo a few years ago, Volvo workers immediately started to express their concerns about the potential loss of their relatively lavish benefits. For example, Volvo's main manufacturing plant in Gothenburg, Sweden, has a sprawling health complex that includes an Olympic-size swimming pool, tanning beds, and tennis courts. The firm spends over $600,000 a year to maintain the center. While Ford's U.S. workers enjoy a strong benefits program, it pales in comparison to the program at Volvo.[17]

In the case of BP-AMOCO, a multinational energy company, the exact benefits offered differ substantially from country to country, and are designed to meet the specific needs (relative to balancing work and family) in the host country. For example, in Egypt, resorts are quite expensive and offering short vacations for families to spend together is helpful. Because Muslims are expected to make the pilgrimage to Mecca at least once during their life (if at all possible), vacation time is a valuable benefit. In Norway, Trinidad, and the United Kingdom, operations tend to be off-shore or in rather remote regions of the country. As a result, employees do not see their families every day and do not generally live at home. Under these circumstances, compressed workweeks are extremely important to employees, as are other benefits such as family days, where families are brought to work sites for visits at company expense.

Purposes of Benefits Programs

In general, benefits programs serve several purposes for the organization. First, many experts believe that organizations willing to spend more money on total compensation are able to attract better-qualified people and/or to convince employees to work harder. The general concept underlying this approach is known as *efficiency wage theory*. This theory suggests that firms can actually save money and become more productive if they pay more because they attract employees who are better or who would be willing to work hard. Little data exist to support or refute this position, but some organizations appear to view wages and benefits as a means of attracting better applicants.

Most experts would also argue that money spent on benefits has an impact on job satisfaction and subsequent turnover. That is, even if employees do not work harder in response to better benefits, they are more likely to remain with a firm that provides better benefits and are more satisfied with that firm. In part, an employee's reactions to specific benefits programs reflect that individual's belief about the value of benefits at the present company as compared with the value of benefits at other companies. As a result, the need to remain competitive with other firms in an industry is a major force driving up the price of benefits. Just as when one airline in a market lowers fares and all others follow suit, once one visible organization in an industry starts offering a given benefit, it is usually not long until its competitors offer similar benefits.

In addition, various social, cultural, and political forces may promote the introduction of new and broader benefits programs. For example, increases in the number of women in the workforce and the rising costs of health care have each affected benefits programs in recent times. Because of the growth in the numbers of female workers, more and more companies offer on-site daycare, dual-parent leave for the birth of a child, and other benefits that make it easier for people to work and have productive careers. Likewise, the health-care environment has prompted growth in benefits programs including health maintenance organizations (HMOs), managed health care, and so forth.

Finally, employee expectations are a driving force in determining what benefits a firm must offer. For example, an organization is not legally required to offer any vacation time. But because this benefit is so desirable and has become common, almost every person who accepts a new job expects that he or she will be given some vacation time. Indeed, most people today would be unlikely to accept a permanent full-time job without this basic benefit. A major implication of these issues, then, is the strategic importance of employee benefits. Their costs are high and their impact is great. Thus, careful planning, monitoring, and communication about benefits are of paramount importance.

Mandated Benefits

Some common benefits are mandated by law. Specifically, a number of laws have been passed that require organizations to offer certain types of benefits to their employees, or to legislate the way benefits plans are administered. In Chapter 2 we discussed several of these, including the Family and Medical Leave Act of 1993, the Pregnancy Discrimination Act of 1978, and the Employee Retirement Income Security Act of 1974. Another significant law, the Social Security Act of 1935, is discussed below. Each of these laws has resulted in mandated benefits or legally restricted the way organizations treated certain benefits. Protection plans are benefits designed to provide protection to employees when their income is threatened or reduced by illness, disability, death, unemployment, or retirement.

Unemployment Insurance

Unemployment insurance was created in the United States as part of the Social Security Act of 1935. The rationale for the act was to protect those people who were experiencing the high levels of unemployment that were pervasive in the United States during the 1930s.

Unemployment insurance is intended to provide a basic subsistence payment to employees who are between jobs. That is, it is intended for people who have stopped working for one organization but who are assumed to be seeking employment with another organization. Employers pay premiums to the unemployment insurance fund. In

Unemployment insurance,
a mandated protection plan, is intended to provide a basic subsistence payment to employees who are between jobs.

An ongoing debate in recent years centers around social security reform. Some people think that the current system is antiquated and needs to be totally overhauled. President George W. Bush, for example, campaigned for a plan under which workers could take a portion of their payroll deduction set aside for social security contributions and instead invest it in other areas such as mutual funds. But others argue that workers want—and need—the security of a guaranteed benefit plan like social security. George Silli, for instance, is a sixty-six-year-old waiter living in Philadelphia. The value of his personal investments in mutual funds dropped by 60 percent in a market downturn in 2000. Mr. Silli is one of many who believe that people are better off with the current social security system.

addition, in the states of Alabama, Alaska, and New Jersey, the employees also pay a contribution to the fund. The premium payment is increased if more than an average or designated number of employees from the organization is drawing from the fund at any given time.

Unemployment insurance and related systems for certain former government workers cover about 120,000,000 employees in the United States. However, some types of positions, such as self-employed workers, farm employees, and employees of nonprofit organizations such as hospitals are excluded from coverage. To be covered by unemployment insurance, an individual must have worked a minimum number of weeks, must now be without a job, and must be willing to accept a suitable position if one is found through the State Unemployment Compensation Commission.

A critical variable in determining when an employee is qualified for receipt of benefits is the circumstances under which he or she became unemployed. In general, if the employee is out of work through no fault of his or her own (as in the case of a layoff), then benefits start almost immediately. But, if the employee quits of his or her own free will or is fired because of poor performance or other legitimate circumstances, then there is usually a longer period of time before the individual becomes qualified for unemployment benefits. Regardless of the starting time, however, compensation is available for only a limited period (typically twenty-six weeks). Extensions beyond this term can also be granted if there is an emergency situation. For example, after Hurricane Katrina, unemployment benefits in most of Louisiana were extended to a full year.

The payment provided is intended to represent about half of what the individual might have been earning had he or she retained the former job, although an upper limit is placed on the benefit paid. As noted above, this program is funded through employer contributions. The tax for this program is 6.2 percent on the first $7,000 earned by each employee. Each state administers this program in its own fashion; however, considerable variation exists in how the laws and provisions are interpreted.

Social Security

Social security *(officially the* **Old Age Survivors and Disability Insurance Program***), another mandated program, was originally designed to provide limited income to retired individuals to supplement their personal savings, private pensions, part-time work, and so forth.*

A second mandated benefit created by the same law is **social security** itself. What most people think of as social security is officially the **Old Age Survivors and Disability Insurance Program.** The initial purpose of this program was to provide some limited income to retired individuals to supplement their own personal savings, private pensions, part-time work, and so forth. Unfortunately, many people have come to view social security as their primary source of retirement income. Problems associated with this assumption are discussed later in this section.

The social security program is funded through employee and employer taxes that are withheld on a payroll basis. At present the percentage of payment is 7.65 percent. Individuals are eligible for partial benefits when they reach the age of sixty-two or full benefits when they reach the age of sixty-five. Effective in 2027, however, individuals will not be able to retire with full benefits until they reach age sixty-seven. If an employee dies before reaching retirement age, a family with children under the age of eighteen receives survival benefits, regardless of the employee's age at the time of her or his death. In addition, an employee who becomes totally disabled before the age of sixty-five is also eligible to receive insurance benefits; Medicare benefits are also provided under this act.

The amount of money any individual is eligible to be paid from the social security system is a function of the average monthly wage that individual earned, weighted toward the latter years of a person's career. In addition, an individual has to have worked a minimum period of time and made a minimum amount of contributions to the system to be eligible to draw full benefits.

In recent years considerable concern has been raised in the United States about the long-term future viability of the social security system. In particular, with longer life expectancies, the increased risk of suffering disability in older age, new work patterns, and new family norms, the demands placed on the social security system have increased significantly. Indeed, the system is paying out more money than it is taking in. Thus, the government must intervene and make some manipulation or adjustment in the system to maintain its viability. In 1998, President Clinton vowed to use any budget surplus to strengthen the social security system and thus ensure its viability for years to come. He failed in his bid to do so, however. Several proposals have been offered for privatizing the system or for allowing employees to invest their own pension funds in the stock market. It is clear that social security will continue to be an issue for the coming years.

Workers' Compensation

Workers' compensation, *another mandated protection program, is insurance that covers individuals who suffer a job-related illness or accident.*

Workers' compensation is also an important legally mandated benefit available to most employees. **Workers' compensation** is insurance that covers individuals who suffer a job-related illness or accident. Employers pay the cost of workers' compensation insurance. The exact premium paid is a function of each employer's past experience with job-related accidents and illnesses. Over 90 million workers in the United States are protected under the Workers' Compensation Insurance Program.

Nonmandated Benefits

Most modern organizations provide other benefits in addition to those mandated by law. Businesses may elect to provide these benefits in order to attract more qualified workers and/or for any of the other reasons noted earlier. In some cases, if an organization does elect to offer a nonmandated benefit, it may be required by law to follow certain guidelines.

Insurance Coverage

Perhaps the most common nonmandated benefit (for full-time employees) is insurance coverage, which has essentially become a "standard" part of any benefit package. In some cases the organization pays all or at least a major portion of the insurance premiums. It is also common, however, for employees to bear a considerable portion of the load themselves. Different kinds of insurance are available. *Health insurance,* of course, is the most common. Because of the dramatic escalation of medical costs over the last several years, this benefit has become increasingly expensive and complicated for many organizations to provide and to maintain. It is estimated that in the United States between 85 and 90 percent of all health-insurance coverage is purchased by employers as group plans covering their employees.[18]

While basic health insurance is the norm, some organizations also provide special programs for prescription drugs, vision-care products, mental-health services, and dental care. For example, today about one-fourth of all employees in the United States at least have the opportunity to purchase dental insurance through their employers. **Health maintenance organizations (HMOs)** are also a growing trend in health-insurance coverage. An HMO is a medical organization that provides medical and health services to employees on a prepaid basis. That is, rather than billing patients or companies for specific services rendered, the initial premium paid to the HMO provides the employee with prepaid coverage of all expenses he or she might incur for health care.

> **Health maintenance organizations (HMOs)** *are medical organizations that provide medical and health services to employees on a prepaid basis.*

A growing trend toward cost containment strategies by organizations has been developed to reduce the huge outflow of funds for medical benefits. These strategies include coordinating benefits across plans and cost sharing. Unfortunately for the employee, cost sharing simply means that he or she has to bear a greater part of the cost of the insurance. In addition, some organizations have become self-funded or self-insured. In most such cases, an organization contracts with an insurance company to provide health benefits, but some companies have been trying to fund their own health-insurance plans. They believe that this arrangement gives them greater control over costs and helps them to avoid state insurance regulations.

Other kinds of insurance coverage include life insurance, long-term disability insurance, and so forth. Life insurance, of course, provides payment to the survivors of an individual who has died or been killed. Disability insurance is designed to supplement workers' compensation insurance and provide continued income in the case of employee disability.

Private Pension Plans

In addition to the pension benefits guaranteed under the Social Security Act, many companies elect to establish **private pension plans** for their employees. These prearranged plans are administered by the organization that provides income to the employee at her or

> **Private pension plans** *are prearranged plans administered by the organization that provide income to the employee at her or his retirement.*

his retirement. Contributions to the retirement plan may come from either the employer or the employee, but in most cases are supported by contributions from both parties. Different retirement plans are available, including individual retirement accounts (IRAs) and employee pension IRAs. In addition, a 401(k) plan allows employees to save money on a tax-deferred basis by entering into salary deferral agreements with their employer.

There are two basic types of pension plans: defined benefit plans and defined contribution plans. Under **defined benefit plans,** the size of the benefit is precisely known and is usually based on a simple formula using input such as years of service. This type of plan is often favored by unions and is closely monitored under ERISA. Although the employee may contribute to these plans, the amount of the contribution has no bearing on the benefits. Under **defined contribution plans,** the size of the benefit depends on how much money is contributed to the plan. This money can be contributed by either the employer alone (noncontributory plans) or the employer and the employee (contributory plans). Most new pension plans are contributory, defined contribution plans.

As we shall see a bit later in the chapter, legal protection dictates how the funds in pension plans are invested. Nonetheless, Enron required its employees to invest the vast majority of their 401(k) funds in Enron stock if Enron were to match their contributions. When Enron declared bankruptcy, the company's stock became almost worthless, which wiped out the retirement savings of many of Enron's employees.

Defined benefit plans *are private pension plans in which the size of the benefit is precisely known and is usually based on a simple formula using input such as years of service.*

Defined contribution plans *are private pension plans in which the size of the benefit depends on how much money is contributed to the plan.*

Paid Time Off

Many organizations also provide their employees with some amount of time off with pay. No U.S. laws mandate this type of benefit, but most employees now expect it. One major type of paid time off is the paid holiday. Most full-time employees receive about ten paid holidays per year. The most common holidays for which workers are paid without having to work include New Year's Day, Memorial Day, Independence Day, Labor Day, Thanksgiving Day, and Christmas. In addition, many other holidays are scheduled to abut a weekend so that people can have a three-day weekend. These additional holidays include President's Day in February, Memorial Day in May, Columbus Day in October, and Veterans Day in November.

Religious holidays (in addition to Christmas) are also often given. Organizations have to be careful with this practice, however, because growing diversity in the workplace is accompanied by an increasingly diverse set of religions and thus religious holidays. An organization has to be sensitive to the fact that it can create problems if it gives time off for some religions but not others. For example, Christianity is the most common religion in the United States. Judaism is second, but Islam is growing rapidly. Each of these three religions has different holidays, both in terms of numbers and dates. An organization that seeks to accommodate members of one or two religions but not all is asking for problems. But accommodating all religions creates other complications. Thus, organizations need to have clear policies and to enforce those policies in a fair and equitable manner.[19]

Paid vacations are also common but are likewise not required by law. Paid vacations are usually a period of one, two, or more weeks when an employee can take time off from work and continue to be paid. Most organizations vary the amount of paid vacation according to an individual's seniority with the organization. For example, it is typical to give an employee one week of paid vacation a year if he or she has three or less years of service with the organization. Following a third anniversary, however, the vacation benefit may increase to two weeks a year. At a later point, perhaps after ten years, it might be increased to three weeks of vacation a year. For the firm's most senior employees, such as those with perhaps twenty or twenty-five years of experience, the benefit may be increased to four weeks of paid vacation a year.[20]

Organizations administer vacation pay in very different ways. Some require employees to take their accumulated vacation time each year. Others are willing to pay employees extra (usually time and a half) for their vacation time if they continue to work instead of taking the time off. Some also allow employees to roll vacation time over into the next year (i.e., to save it for at least some period of time).

Earlier in the chapter, we mentioned that German workers had more extensive benefits than the typical U.S. employee. One area with considerable difference is in the number of days off per year. Although the number of days off is not mandated in the United States or the European Union, many European countries *do* mandate a minimum annual vacation. Table 9.1 illustrates some of the differences from country to country.

Yet another common paid time off plan is sick leave. This benefit is provided when an individual is sick or is otherwise physically unable to perform his or her job duties. Most organizations allow an individual to accumulate sick time on the basis of some schedule, such as one sick day per month worked. Some organizations require that employees submit a doctor's note verifying illness in the event the employee wants to draw sick pay. Other organizations take a more egalitarian approach, however, and require no such documentation, relying instead on employee honesty. One interesting wrinkle in sick-leave policies is that some organizations require the employee to use his or her allocation of sick days or lose them. Under such a system, it would seem illogical for an employee not to take all the sick days allocated during the year.

A final common method of paid time off is personal leave. Sometimes an organization allows an employee to take a small number of days off for personal business. Examples include funerals, religious observances, a marriage, a birthday, or simply a personal holiday. Organizations are usually also required to allow an employee to miss work if he or she is called for jury duty.

Other Benefits

In addition to protection plans and paid time off, some organizations offer various other kinds of benefit programs. For example, Clif Bar is a small company that makes

TABLE 9.1   Minimum Annual Vacation by Law in Different Countries

Country	Minimum Vacation Time
Belgium	4 weeks
Denmark	36 days
France	36 days
Greece	4 weeks
Ireland	3 weeks
Italy	National Collective Bargaining Agreement*
The Netherlands	4 weeks
Portugal	21–30 days

*Unions and the Italian government negotiate minimum annual vacation periods as part of each collective bargaining agreement.
Source: Reprinted from G. Milkovich and J. Newman, *Compensation,* 5th ed. (Chicago, Ill.: Richard D. Irwin, 1996). Copyright © 1996 by The McGraw-Hill Companies. Reprinted with the permission of The McGraw-Hill Companies.

energy bars; its headquarters building in California contains a rock climbing wall that employees can use. In this section we will describe several of the more common of these kinds of benefits.

As noted earlier, many organizations are struggling with ways to reduce health-care costs. In addition to the attempts described earlier, these efforts have also resulted in a different type of benefit known as **wellness programs.** Wellness programs concentrate on keeping employees from becoming sick, rather than simply paying expenses when they do become sick.[21] In some organizations, these programs may be simple and involve little more than organized jogging or walking during lunch breaks. More elaborate programs might include smoking cessation programs, blood pressure and cholesterol screening, and stress-management programs. Some organizations have full-fledged health clubs on site and provide counseling and programs for fitness and weight loss. Although these programs typically take place after work hours (or before), the companies often provide the services for free or at a low cost.

Not only are these plans attractive to employees who appreciate the ease and low costs, but they are usually seen as an excellent investment by the organization. Specifically, many case studies indicate that these programs reduce the number of sick days, reduce medical costs, and improve productivity because the organization gains a more physically fit workforce.[22] An additional group of benefits are often referred to collectively as *life-cycle benefits.* The most common are childcare and eldercare benefits. Thus, these benefits are targeted at different stages in an employee's life.

Childcare   Childcare benefits are becoming extremely popular. In fact, any organization that wants to be considered a family-friendly organization must have some type of childcare benefits, at a minimum. A claim of being family-friendly is increasingly viewed as a competitive advantage.[23] These plans might include scheduling childcare help, referrals to various types of childcare services, or reimbursement accounts for childcare expenses. In many cases, however, they include company-paid daycare. For example, BP-AMOCO International's headquarters in Houston, Texas, has an on-site, freestanding daycare facility. The building had been intended for another use and then had been abandoned. The

> **Wellness programs** *are special benefits programs that concentrate on keeping employees from becoming sick rather than simply paying expenses when they do become sick.*

Some employers seem to be getting increasingly flexible and creative in the kinds of benefits they offer to their employees. Take Electronic Arts for example, a growing maker of electronic games. The firm offers its employees access to this labyrinth outside its corporate headquarters and encourages them to wander through it to relax and recharge their creative energies. Electronic Arts also provides free espresso, sponsors volleyball and basketball games, and even grants seven-week sabbaticals to employees after seven years with the firm.

management at BP-AMOCO purchased the building and contracted with an outside firm to provide daycare services, which are offered at heavily discounted rates for employees. Such a program has a strong impact on employee attitudes and job performance.[24]

Eldercare   Unlike childcare, it is unusual for an organization to have on-site elder-care facilities. Instead, this benefit often takes the form of referrals. It is especially useful for the employee with a disabled parent or one needing constant care. The employee is saved the time and effort of locating these resources, and the resources provided by the organization have presumably been checked first. Long-term health-care insurance is also becoming a more common benefit, and these plans provide for nursing homes or at-home care. The premium is typically paid fully by the employee and, at least for now, these benefits are for the employee or the employee and spouse only.

One of the most controversial issues for benefits programs involves the question of whether to extend benefits to same-sex partners. It has become fairly typical for organizations to extend benefits to spouses of employees, but the move to extend these benefits to life partners or spousal equivalents has been accepted much more slowly.[25] Obviously, objections to such a plan are based on different points of view, but more organizations are coming to believe that it is simply fair to extend benefits to same-sex partners. Chevron's corporate headquarters is located in San Francisco, California, and, in an attempt to be fair and to remain competitive for employees in the local market, the company decided to extend all health and insurance benefits to same-sex partners. Although this move was applauded in San Francisco, employees at headquarters for the firm's production company located in Houston, Texas, were less enthusiastic. The company made it clear, however, that the provision of these benefits is company policy and that they believed that gay and lesbian partners deserved equal treatment on the job, and they invited employees who could not live with this policy to seek employment elsewhere.

In addition, organizations sometimes provide various additional services for their employees. These services may include relocation services and help with mortgage financing, although these benefits are typically available for senior-level employees only. IBM wants to facilitate the ability of its higher-paid senior managers to not have to work beyond a normal retirement age. The company also realizes, in turn, that one constraint many people face when thinking about early retirement is money. Therefore, they offer estate-planning and wealth-accumulation programs for their management employees. An employee might have to pay for these kinds of services him- or herself if they were not provided by the company, so they are rather attractive to employees.

A somewhat different type of service is contained in what are referred to as employee assistance plans (EAPs). These programs are designed to assist employees who have chronic problems with alcohol or drugs or who have serious domestic problems. An increase in the number of programs for mental problems and stress, as well as for bereavement, has also been a recent trend.[26] These programs are typically voluntary and referrals are confidential. Yet the needs of the organization (especially when the personal problem is causing performance problems on the job) must be balanced with the needs of the individual to avoid any stigma attached to having the specific problem.[27]

Finally, employee perquisites are sometimes provided. A *perquisite,* or *perk,* as it is more informally known, is an extra benefit that may or may not have any direct financial value but is considered an important reward by employees. A perk might include a bigger office, a company car, membership in a country club, stock-purchase options, premium insurance coverage, and so forth. Perquisites are usually made available only to members of top management or to certain especially valuable professionals within the organization. Sometimes organizations provide special perquisites that might be available to all employees. For example, some firms might provide the cost of uniforms for a company softball team, a health club on site that all members of the organization can use, a car-pooling service for employees who live some distance from the organization, and similar kinds of perquisites.

Cafeteria-Style Benefits Plans

Most benefits programs are designed for all the employees in an organization. Although the exact benefits may vary as a function of level in the organization, within those levels the plans are generally "one size fits all." **Cafeteria-style benefits plans** allow the employee to choose the benefits that he or she really wants. Thus, under these plans the organization typically establishes a budget indicating how much it is willing to spend per employee on benefits.[28] The employee is then presented with a list of possible benefits and the cost of each. Employees are then free to choose the benefits in any combination they wish. Such an approach should maximize the effectiveness of the benefits program for achieving the organizational goals that we discussed at the beginning of the chapter, and some evidence suggests that cafeteria-style benefits programs can lead to increased satisfaction and reduced turnover.[29]

> **Cafeteria-style benefits plans** *allow the employee to choose those benefits he or she really wants.*

Not surprisingly, perhaps, these plans come with variations. In some cases, the cafeteria menu includes only basic levels of coverage, and the employee must pay (or substitute for other types of coverage) for enhanced coverage. In other cases, the employee is allowed to keep the money not spent on benefits. In yet other plans, the cost to the employee of each benefit is structured so that the employee is rewarded for choosing more cost-effective benefits (e.g., HMO versus more traditional medical plans).

Two serious problems limit the willingness of organizations to adopt cafeteria-style benefits plans, however. The first is the cost of administration. Because every employee has a potentially unique set of benefits, someone has to keep track of what benefits each employee has chosen. It is often typical for the employee to be able to change his or her choices, so the administrative task is further complicated by the fact that the package of benefits can change on an employee-to-employee basis.

The second problem stems from the presumably rational choices an employee makes. For example, if an employee has children who are at the age where children typically need dental braces, the employee will most likely select a dental plan that includes coverage for braces. Because the recipients of this plan are those employees most likely to use it, the provider will charge relatively high prices to both the employee and the organization. And because the employee will probably drop this coverage for a different benefit when his or her children get older, the costs of coverage cannot be amortized across less frequent users. This problem, known as *adverse selection,* can be costly for the organization.

One final consideration in the design of cafeteria-style benefits plans is that employees are *not* always rational in their choices. A younger employee may elect to contribute less to his or her retirement because retirement seems like a distant future event and wait until later in life before increasing the contribution. But given the power of compounding interest, a larger contribution early in life, followed by a smaller contribution later, is actually worth much more at retirement age than a smaller contribution made early in life, followed by a larger contribution made later. Therefore it is extremely important for employees to have full information about the available benefits, and in some cases it may be necessary for the organization to mandate minimum benefits levels in some areas.

Legal Issues in Compensation and Benefits

The major legal issues involved in compensation and benefits were discussed in Chapter 2, but we will review them briefly here. The Fair Labor Standards Act includes provisions for the minimum wage, overtime, and child labor. The first two topics are rather straightforward in most cases, but some issues arise in both areas. One of these issues may be more social than legal, but it certainly has legal implications.

As noted in Chapter 2, not every employee in every organization receives "the" minimum wage. In fact, several minimum wages exist, such as the minimum wage for agricultural jobs, and various states have also established higher minimum wages than the national limit. Even if an employee receives the minimum wage, some argue that it is difficult to live on the minimum wage in the United States in the twenty-first century. If an employee works forty hours a week at $7.25 an hour, he or she earns $290.00 a week, or just over $15,000 a year before taxes, social security, and any insurance or pension deductions. Is this really a living wage in this country? Perhaps not. But raising the minimum wage unilaterally is not so simple. Surely employees are hired because they are willing to work for low wages. In economic terms, their marginal productivity level is equal to their marginal wage rate. In simpler terms, they are worth exactly what the company is paying them. If the firm were forced to pay a higher rate, they simply would not hire these individuals.

It is surely within our power, as a country, to raise the minimum wage. We could raise it to $10.00 an hour and ensure that everyone who has a full-time job can truly support him- or herself. The counterargument that this increase will result in people losing their jobs, however, makes this matter extremely complicated.

The other issue relates to overtime. The laws concerning overtime pay seem straightforward. Employees who work more than forty hours a week must be paid time and a half for all hours in excess of forty, unless they are considered exempt. As explained in Chapter 2, the term *exempt* means that the employee is literally exempt from the overtime provisions, and this term usually applies to managers and professionals. In some organizations, however, employees who are asked to work more than forty hours during a week are not paid overtime but are given time off instead. This time off is referred to as *comp time* and is considered compensation for overtime. Thus, someone who has to work forty-five hours one week might be assigned only thirty-five hours the next week but still receive full pay. Comp time is often not as beneficial to the employee, who would otherwise earn more in total pay, but it is more cost efficient for the organization. And it does give employees something that many of them value—time away from work.

The legal issues related to benefits are a bit more complicated. One important consideration for an organization is to make sure that its benefits plan is qualified. A qualified benefit plan is one where (1) the employer receives an immediate tax deduction for any contributions made, (2) the employee does not incur a tax liability at the time of the employer deduction, and (3) investment returns (such as from stocks and bonds) are accumulated tax-free. Although the requirements for qualification differ for different types of benefits plans, it is critical that the plan be nondiscriminatory: the plan cannot disproportionately favor employees with higher income levels.[30]

Of course, the most important legal issue in this area deals with the Employee Retirement Income Security Act (ERISA) of 1974. We introduced this law in Chapter 2, but it deserves additional attention here. As noted earlier, this law was passed to protect employees who had contributed to their pensions but were unable to collect those benefits later. This situation occurred primarily because of the restrictions that the organizations had placed on employees before they could receive retirement benefits. Specifically, organizations required that employees remain with the company as long as thirty years before they were vested. (**Vesting rights** are guaranteed rights to receive pension benefits.) For example, before 1974 a sixty-year-old employee with twenty-nine years of service would not be entitled to pension benefits if he or she left the company—or even if he or she died—before his or her thirty-year anniversary. Under ERISA, however, vesting rights become operational after six years *at the most,* and employees with less service are still usually eligible to receive some portion of their retirement benefits.

Vesting rights   *are guaranteed rights to receive pension benefits.*

ERISA also provides protection for the funding underlying the pension plan. The Pension Benefit Guaranty Corporation oversees how pension plans are funded and can seize corporate assets to support underfunded plans. In addition, ERISA allows an employee to carry a portion of his or her benefits to another job. This notion of portability is especially important when employees change jobs frequently. ERISA also imposes some minimum requirements for how pension plans are communicated to employees. If an organization does not follow ERISA guidelines, its pension plan will not be qualified as defined above.

Evaluating Compensation and Benefits Programs

Given the enormous cost to an organization of compensation and benefit packages, it is clearly important that managers carefully assess the benefit of these packages for the organization. On the one hand, it is important that the organization provide reasonable compensation and appropriate benefits to its employees. At the same time, it is in the best interests of the stockholders and other constituents of the organization that the firm manage its resources wisely. Thus, it is important to assess this topic periodically to ensure that costs are in line. One method of assessment is through the use of wage surveys, as noted earlier in this chapter. Similar comparisons can also be made for wage structures, benefit packages, and so forth. Any organization can learn the average insurance premium costs, for example, that other organizations are paying. While the organization may not be able to match these premiums, particularly if it has a history of accident claims, illnesses, and so forth, it can nevertheless learn how close its costs are to those of other firms.

Some organizations might find it necessary to audit their overall compensation (i.e., compensation and benefits) programs to determine whether or not they are providing a competitive package. As part of the recruiting process, it is necessary, of course, that the organization is viewed as an attractive place to work if it wants to hire high-quality human resources. Thus, many organizations look to the success (or lack thereof) of their recruiting efforts as providing some indication of how competitive their compensation and benefits packages are.

One final issue must be considered relative to evaluating benefits programs. In many cases, these programs are not as effective as they might be simply because the organization has not communicated effectively with employees about those benefits. Indeed, many organizational surveys suggest that many employees are not fully informed about their benefits. For example, some evidence suggests that awareness about benefits could be increased through communication via several media and that, as awareness increased, so did satisfaction with benefits.[31] The reason for this relationship is underscored by the results of another study, where employees were asked to estimate the value of the employer's contribution to their benefits. When asked about family coverage, the average estimate was only 38 percent of the actual cost of those benefits to the employer.[32] It seems clear that an organization can never expect to appreciate the full advantage of its benefits program when employees underestimate the cost of their benefits by such a large amount.

Chapter Summary

Compensation and benefits programs have several fundamental purposes and objectives. One fundamental purpose is to provide an adequate and appropriate reward system for employees so that they feel valued and worthwhile as organizational members and representatives. Firms can adopt one of three basic compensation strategies to help achieve this goal—pay above-market compensation rates, market compensation rates, or below-market compensation rates. Several different factors contribute to the compensation strategy that a firm develops. The critical source of information that many organizations use in developing compensation strategies is pay surveys.

Once an overall strategy has been chosen, human resource managers must determine what any given job should be paid. The starting point in this effort is job evaluation, a method for determining the relative value or worth of a job to the organization so that individuals who perform that job can be compensated adequately and appropriately. Several job evaluation techniques and methods have been established, although alternative approaches to compensation, such as pay-for-knowledge and skill-based pay are increasingly popular. Continued administration of the wage and salary structure in an organization requires consideration of how to deal with such things as pay secrecy and salary compression.

Benefits take up an ever-larger portion of employers' total compensation costs. Organizations sustain these costs because they believe that competitive benefits packages attract better applicants and help the company retain the employees they have already hired. Although benefits costs are high in the United States, levels of mandated benefits are much higher in Europe and elsewhere. The kinds of benefits that are attractive or appropriate to employees around the world differ considerably. Several laws provide guidelines for how benefits plans should be administered.

Additional laws mandate that all employees must have certain benefits, such as social security, unemployment insurance, and workers' compensation. In addition, many organizations offer optional protection plans such as health and dental insurance coverage and private pension plans.

Paid time off is another important benefit. The most common forms of paid time off are vacation time, holidays, religious days, sick leave, and personal time. This benefit, in particular, varies widely from country to country. Organizations are also becoming more likely to offer benefits in areas such as wellness programs, childcare, eldercare, and employee assistance programs. Finally, some benefits provided by organizations are services and perks that the employee would otherwise have to pay for.

Because needs and preferences differ, some organizations offer cafeteria-style benefits plans in which the employee gets to pick and choose the benefits desired. These programs are expensive to run, but they result in employees getting exactly what they want, which makes the benefits program more cost-effective.

Given the enormous cost to an organization of compensation and benefits packages, it is clearly important that managers carefully assess the advantages of those packages to the organization. One key factor in the administration of benefits programs is communications. Employees often underestimate the cost of the benefits provided for them, and this lack of understanding reduces the effectiveness of any benefits package. Overall, it is clearly important that managers carefully assess the effectiveness of the firm's compensation structure to ensure that organizational and employee interests are optimized.

Key Points for Future HR Managers

- Compensation includes the total set of rewards an organization provides an employee in return for his or her work. Thus, it is more than just a weekly or monthly paycheck.

- Indirect compensation and benefits represent a significant portion of the total compensation paid to employees in the United States. Yet these portions are generally lower here than in many European countries.

- The rise in the cost of benefits is the result of attempts to attract high-quality employees during times of low unemployment, the belief that employees might respond to the provision of more attractive benefits by working harder, and by employee expectations about benefits.

- For compensation programs to be effective, they must account for both external equity (comparisons with employees at the same job at different organizations) and internal equity (the relative pay of employees within the same organization at different jobs), and the organization must decide what it is willing to pay for. For example, it is possible to base pay on seniority, performance, or knowledge, among other things.

- Another critical strategic decision is whether the organization will pay at, above, or below the market wage for a job.

- Pay-for-knowledge programs and skill-based pay systems are newer systems for determining compensation based on what the employee knows rather than on job duties. Under these systems the employee can increase his or her compensation by acquiring new knowledge that is valuable to the organization.

- Pay compression is a problem in many organizations. It occurs when the difference between lower-paying and higher-paying jobs shrinks. It is most likely to occur when market rates are rising quickly, and senior employees are paid only slightly more than new hires.

- A substantial portion of the benefits paid to employees today are mandated by law and cannot be reduced without legislation. Other benefits, such as pensions and medical insurance, are not mandated but are surely expected by employees. The cost of some of these benefits (especially medical insurance) is rising at an alarming rate. Still other optional benefits, such as wellness programs and eldercare, started as a source of competitive advantage but, while costly, they are also becoming part of employee expectations at larger firms.

- Cafeteria-style benefits plans allow for the possibility of using benefits dollars so that they have the greatest positive impact on employee satisfaction. These plans have several disadvantages, however, and so they require careful study before they are implemented.

- It is difficult to assess the effectiveness of indirect compensation plans, but it is critical that the organization communicate clearly to employees what benefits those employees are receiving.

Key Points for Future General Managers

- Critical strategic decisions relate to determining what should be paid to employees and what that rate should be relative to market rates.

- The decision concerning what to pay employees for is probably the most critical, and new pay systems such as pay-for-knowledge and skill-based pay advocate paying employees for what they know rather than what they do.

- All decisions to pay wages and salaries at rates below, above, or at the going market rate should be made with full knowledge of the implications of each decision.

- Indirect compensation and benefits represent a large portion of total compensation costs. Many of the benefits are required by law; others (such as vacations and medical insurance) have become such a strong part of employee expectations that they cannot easily be eliminated.

- Cafeteria-style benefits plans may allow the company to spend its benefits dollars so that the plan has the greatest impact on employee satisfaction, although these plans have some disadvantages.

- Communication is a key part of the indirect compensation strategy, but the link between indirect compensation and any organizational-level outcomes is unclear.

Review and Discussion Questions

1. What is compensation? What are the basic differences between wages and salaries?

2. What are the basic strategic options an organization has for its compensation policies?

3. Identify and summarize the basic methods of job evaluation.

4. Why are job classes needed? How are they developed?

5. How does pay compression develop? Why is it a problem?

6. What are the purposes of employee benefits programs?

7. What benefits are mandated by law?

8. What are the most common benefits not mandated by law?

9. Describe the basic components of the Social Security Act of 1935.

10. What are the key legal issues in managing employee compensation and benefits?

CLOSING CASE

Working by the Hour at General Motors and Wal-Mart

Hourly workers—people who are paid a set dollar amount for each hour or fraction of an hour they work—have long been the backbone of the U.S. economy. But times are changing, and so is the lot of the hourly worker. Like all change, of course, some is for the better, but some is clearly for the worse, at least from the workers' standpoint. And nowhere are these differences more apparent than the contrasting conditions for hourly workers at General Motors (GM) and Wal-Mart.

General Motors, of course, is an old, traditional, industrial company that, up until recently, was the nation's largest employer. For decades, its hourly workers have been protected by strong labor unions like the United Auto Workers (UAW). These unions, in turn, have forged contracts and working conditions that almost seem archaic in today's economy. Consider, for example, the employment conditions of Tim Philbrick, a forty-two-year-old plant worker and union member at the firm's Fairfax plant near Kansas City. He has worked for GM for twenty-three years.

Philbrick makes almost $20 an hour in base pay. With a little overtime, his annual earnings top $60,000. But he is far from the highest-paid factory worker at GM. Skilled-trade workers like electricians and toolmakers make $2 to $2.50 an hour more, and with greater overtime opportunities, they often make $100,000 or more per year. Mr. Philbrick also gets a no-deductible health insurance policy that allows him to see any doctor he wants. He gets four weeks of vacation per year, plus two weeks at Christmas and at least another week in July, when the plant is closed. In addition, he gets two paid twenty-three-minute breaks and a paid thirty-minute lunch break per day. He also has the option of retiring with full benefits after thirty years.

GM estimates that, with benefits, its average worker makes more than $43 an hour. Perhaps not surprisingly,

then, the firm is always looking for opportunities to reduce its workforce through attrition and cutbacks, with the goal of replacing production capacity with lower-cost labor abroad. The UAW, on the other hand, is staunchly opposed to further workforce reductions and cutbacks. And long-standing work rules strictly dictate who gets overtime, who can be laid off and who can't, and myriad other employment conditions for Philbrick and his peers.

But the situation at GM is quite different—in a lot of ways—from conditions at Wal-Mart. Along many different dimensions Wal-Mart is slowly but surely supplanting General Motors as the quintessential U.S. corporation. For example, it is growing rapidly, is becoming more and more ingrained in the U.S. life style, and now employs more people than GM did in its heyday. But the hourly worker at Wal-Mart has a much different experience than do hourly workers at GM.

For example, consider Nancy Handley, a twenty-seven-year-old Wal-Mart employee who oversees the men's department at a big store in St. Louis. Jobs like Handley's are paid between $9 and $11 an hour, or about $20,000 a year. About $100 a month is deducted from her paycheck to help cover the costs of benefits. Her health insurance has a $250 deductible; she then pays 20 percent of her health-care costs as long as she uses a set of approved physicians. Her prescriptions cost between $5 and $10 each. She also has dental coverage; after her $50 deductible, she pays 20 percent of her dental costs. During her typical workday, Handley gets two fifteen-minute breaks and an hour for lunch, but she has to punch out at the time clock and doesn't get paid during these times.

But Handley doesn't feel mistreated by Wal-Mart. Far from it; she says that she is appropriately compensated for what she does. She has received three merit raises in the last seven years, for example, and has considerable job security.

If she decides to try for advancement, Wal-Mart offers considerable potential. For example, several thousand hourly workers a year are promoted to the ranks of management. While the amount of time they must work during their workweek increases, so too does their pay. And Handley is clearly not unique in her views—Wal-Mart employees routinely reject any and all overtures from labor unions and are among the most loyal and committed employees in the United States today.[33]

Case Questions

1. Compare and contrast hourly working conditions at GM and Wal-Mart.

2. Describe the (apparent) wage structures at GM and Wal-Mart.

3. Summarize the basic issues in wage and salary administration that managers at GM and Wal-Mart most likely face.

Building HR Management Skills

Purpose: The purpose of this exercise is to help you assess the issues associated with cafeteria-style benefits programs.

Step 1: Assume that you are the human resource manager of a midsized manufacturing company. Your company currently offers a relatively traditional benefits program. The specifics are as follows:

1. Health insurance: the organization contributes $250 per employee per month, which covers the cost for the employee; the employee pays an additional $50 per month per covered dependent.

2. Dental insurance: the organization contributes $50 per month, which covers the cost for the employee; the employee pays an additional $10 per month per covered dependent.

3. Life insurance: the organization contributes $20 per month for $40,000 in term life insurance; the employee can buy additional units of coverage as a function of annual salary.

4. Vacation: everyone gets two weeks per year.

5. Holidays: everyone gets ten paid holidays per year.

6. Sick time: everyone gets ten sick days per year.

Step 2: Assume that your boss has indicated that the firm wants to adopt a cafeteria-style benefits plan, and that you are to devise such a plan.

Step 3: Outline as many options as you can think of for such a plan. Use the set of benefits listed above as a starting point.

Ethical Dilemmas in HR Management

Assume that you are the human resource manager for a service organization. Your boss recently read that most employees underestimate the value of the benefits provided to them by their employer. He has instructed you to develop a plan for communicating the costs of benefits to your employees. You agree that communicating this information is a good idea; however, he has instructed that you should manipulate the information so that it looks better than the reality.

For example, your firm offers ten sick days per year. The average employee takes only eight days per year and forfeits the unused number of days. Your boss wants you to talk about this benefit as though everyone took their full allotment. Your firm offers two health insurance options: a basic or standard plan and a premium plan. Both the company and the individual pay more if the premium plan is chosen. He wants you to quote only the cost for the more expensive plan, even though more than half of your workers have chosen the standard plan.

When you questioned his ideas, your boss simply said, "These are the potential costs that we could incur for everyone. Just because people don't take all their sick days or they select the basic insurance plan, that's their choice. The company is willing to pay for ten sick days and for the high-end insurance. So we should get credit for being generous."

1. What are the ethical issues in this situation?

2. What are the basic arguments for and against what your boss is instructing you to do?

3. What do you think most managers would do? What would you do?

HR Internet Exercise

Search the Internet for sites devoted to wages and/or salaries. Visit at least six such sites. Two especially good ones are: http://jobsmart.org/tools/salary http://www.careerbuilder.com/JobSeeker/CRC/ Salary Information.htm

Learn as much as possible about each site and then respond to the following questions:

Questions

1. How might you, as a job seeker, use these kinds of websites to ensure that you are paid an equitable wage or salary?

2. How might you, as a human resource manager, use these kinds of websites to ensure that your firm is paying an appropriate wage or salary?

3. What information seems to be common to all the sites you visited?

4. Did you expect to find or would have liked to find certain information that did not appear on the site?

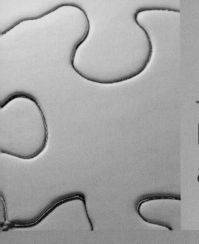

10

Performance Appraisal and Career Management

CHAPTER OUTLINE

CHAPTER OBJECTIVES

After studying this chapter you should be able to:

■ Describe the purposes of performance appraisal in organizations.

■ Summarize the performance appraisal process in organizations.

■ Identify and describe the most common methods that managers use for performance appraisal.

■ Discuss other general issues involving performance appraisal in organizations.

■ Identify and describe the basic legal issues in performance appraisal.

■ Describe the nature of careers in organizations.

■ Discuss human resource management and career management.

■ Identify and discuss basic career development issues and challenges.

For a variety of strategic reasons, financial services giant Merrill Lynch has been overhauling many of its basic business practices. One key area of attention has been on performance management and the firm's reward system. Under the old process, employees were ranked against one another. Rewards were distributed to those with higher performance according to a predetermined formula. This system emphasized competition between employees and forced managers to look for justifications for their ranking choices. It also created tension among employees and between employees and managers.

> *"The conversation really is, how do we work together to improve performance?"*
>
> (Linda Murphy, Director of Global Performance Management, Merrill Lynch)

Today, "the whole emphasis has shifted from one of justifying a rating to one of improving performance," says Linda Murphy, Merrill Lynch's director of global performance management. "We're looking at how we can help the employee improve his or her performance. And because of that, there's much more concentration on the coaching, the feedback, and the conversations that occur between the manager and the employee. . . . The conversation really is, how do we work together to improve performance?" Instead of focusing on the past, the new system looks forward, to improve future performance.

The new process begins with each employee and his or her managers agreeing on a set of performance objectives. The objectives are closely tied to Merrill's business goals. Goals can be adjusted as needed at any time. Feedback is ongoing, with required reviews at midyear and year-end and lots of opportunities for spontaneous suggestions and mentoring. Joint goal setting strengthens the cooperative relationship between manager and worker, while performance measured against standards reduces competition among workers.

To de-emphasize the importance of ratings in this highly competitive industry, the company has moved to a simple three-point scale. Murphy states, "[The new scale] allows the manager to say to the employee, 'The middle category is an acceptable level of performance. Most of us are in that category. Now, let's talk about how, relative to your peers, we can move you up in the rankings.'"

Another important aspect of the new process is the use of 360-degree feedback, where each employee is evaluated by superiors, peers, and clients. Peer reviews are most useful in assessing an employee's performance as a team member, which accounts for about one-third of the overall evaluation at Merrill.

In the brokerage industry, most companies have many limitations on their performance evaluation system, including too much reliance on subjective criteria, reliance on a single criteria, and refusal to publicize the criteria. Merrill, on the other hand, relies on numerous, mostly objective criteria for evaluation, including profit margin, ROE, market share, growth of new businesses, and expense reduction. And its evaluation criteria are published in-house and publicly, through the Internet.

The new system has other benefits, too, including better appeal to a diverse pool of applicants and ease in recruiting and retention. "This is a critical element that will help us be more competitive in the war for talent," says Murphy. Forecasts predict that the brokerage industry will become even more cutthroat over the next few years, increasing pressures for efficiency. If Merrill Lynch can successfully implement an innovative and supportive performance management system, it might be able to outrun this very fast and very resourceful pack.[1]

Virtually all businesses must focus some degree of attention on performance management. Indeed, the effective management of performance may be the difference between success and failure. And many firms, like Merrill Lynch, find it necessary to occasionally adjust how they approach performance management. Performance appraisal systems are designed to provide organizations with the information to manage performance improvement. But, in order to develop employees to their full potential, it is also important that organizations help employees manage their careers. Career management and career development enable employees to grow both personally and professionally. Further, performance appraisals help provide employees with information on how they can best manage their own careers. This chapter is about performance appraisal systems and their implications for how individuals manage their careers. We also cover careers from other perspectives as well.

Performance appraisal
is the specific and formal evaluation of an employee conducted to determine the degree to which the employee is performing his or her job effectively.

Performance management
is the general set of activities carried out by the organization to change (improve) employee performance.

Performance appraisal is the specific and formal evaluation of an employee to determine the degree to which the employee is performing his or her job effectively. Some organizations use the term *performance appraisal* for this process, while others prefer to use different terms such as *performance evaluation, performance review, annual review, employee appraisal,* or *employee evaluation.* The outcome of this evaluation is some type of score or rating on a scale. These evaluations are typically conducted once or twice a year. A related topic, **performance management,** refers to the more general set of activities carried out by the organization to change (improve) employee performance. Although performance management typically relies heavily on performance appraisals, performance management is a broader and more encompassing process and is the ultimate goal of performance appraisal activities. We will touch on some concepts of performance management in this chapter but will discuss these ideas much more fully in Chapters 13 and 14.

Why Organizations Conduct Performance Appraisals

Most people involved in performance appraisals tend to be dissatisfied with them. This tendency is true for both the person being rated and the person doing the rating. We will discuss some of the major reasons for this dissatisfaction in this chapter. But the fact that performance appraisals are so widely used in spite of this dissatisfaction is a strong indicator that managers believe that the performance appraisals are important and that they have a meaningful role to play in organizations. In fact, managers conduct performance appraisals for several different reasons. Organizations also hope to achieve several goals with performance appraisals.[2]

The Importance of Performance Appraisal

As just noted, most managers may be unhappy with various facets of the performance appraisal process, but most would agree that they are nevertheless very important. One reason why appraisals are so important to organizations is that they provide a benchmark for assessing the extent to which recruiting and selection processes are adequate. Recall from earlier chapters that the organization endeavors to recruit and select high-quality employees who are capable of working effectively toward the accomplishment of the organization's goals. Performance appraisal helps managers assess the extent to which they are indeed recruiting and selecting the most appropriate employees. When this information is used in conjunction with performance management techniques, described in more detail in Chapter 14, it can lead to real improvements in the performance of individual employees. Ultimately, organizations try to use this improvement at the level of the individual and translate it into improvements in the performance of the entire organization.

Performance appraisal is also important because it is—or at least should be—fundamentally linked to an organization's compensation system (see Chapter 9). In theory, organizations prefer to provide greater rewards to higher-performing employees and lesser rewards to lower-performing employees. To provide this compensation on a fair and equitable basis, however, it is important that the organization can differentiate between its higher- and its lower-performing employees. Managers want to know that they are giving the appropriate rewards to employees for appropriate reasons. Performance appraisal plays a big role in this process.

Performance appraisal is also important for legal reasons. Organizations must be able to demonstrate that their promotions, transfers, terminations, and reward allocations are based on merit (or the lack thereof), as opposed to some discriminatory factor such as gender or race. Performance appraisal, therefore, is the mechanism by which the organization can provide this documentation. Managers must be able to rely on performance appraisal information to demonstrate that all of their important employment-related decisions have been based on the actual performance of those affected by the decisions. Without proper performance appraisal, an organization is subject to concerns or charges that there is at least the impression that promotions and other rewards may be based on a factor or factors other than actual performance.

Performance appraisal also plays an important role in employee motivation and development (see Chapter 13). Most people want to know how well they are doing so that they can correct their deficiencies, capitalize on their strengths, and improve their overall contributions to their jobs. Again, performance appraisal provides this information to employees. An individual who is told that he or she is doing well on three dimensions of his or her job performance but needs to improve on a fourth dimension recognizes how managers see him or her and knows where to allocate additional developmental work and effort in the future.[3]

Finally, performance appraisal provides valuable and useful information to the organization's human resource planning process. Recall from our discussion in Chapter 5 that assessing the current supply of human resources is an important element in human resource planning. The supply of human resources is most effectively conceptualized, however, from the standpoint of the quality of those human resources. For example, from the standpoint of the actual number of employees needed, an organization may have enough people on its payroll to satisfy its staffing needs. But if many of those individuals are doing a poor job, the organization may need to take a much different approach to its future recruiting and selection activities than if all employees are doing an excellent job. Likewise, knowing the distribution of qualified employees within the organizational system is an important factor for managers to know. And performance appraisal helps provide this information to managers.

Goals of Performance Appraisal

Given the importance of performance appraisal, as documented in the preceding section, the goals of performance appraisal are almost self-evident. For example, a basic goal of any appraisal system is to provide a valid and reliable measure of employee performance along all relevant dimensions. That is, the appraisal results should reflect the true picture of who is performing well and who is not, and they should indicate the areas of specific

Improving employee performance requires more than simply completing a rating form that evaluates the employee's performance. It also requires a formal performance review in which the manager discusses with the employee the employee's strengths and weaknesses, and together they formulate goals for the future. Here, a manager ends a performance review with a smiling employee who now has a better understanding of what she needs to do during the next evaluation period.

strengths and weaknesses for each person being rated. We should note, though, that it is extremely difficult to assess the extent to which an appraisal system accomplishes these goals. Furthermore, it is probably most important that employees have confidence in the reliability and accuracy of the appraisals. In other words, because managers cannot be absolutely sure that appraisals reflect true levels of performance, organizations should not forget the importance of the perceptions of accuracy and fairness. We assume that if appraisals were accurate and meaningful, they would be perceived as such, but the perceptions probably matter the most![4]

In addition, another goal of appraisals is to provide useful and appropriate information for the organization with regard to human resource planning, recruiting and selection, compensation, training, and the legal context. This information can help the organization avoid discrimination against employees on the basis of some irrelevant factor such as gender, age, or ethnicity. Therefore, this goal of performance appraisal specifically and most directly relates to the organization's ability to document any employment-related decisions based on supposed or presumed performance.

The ultimate goal for any organization using performance appraisals, however, is to improve performance on the job. This goal has two parts. First, the organization needs to be able to use performance appraisals for decision making. The relevant decisions might include determining who gets fired, who gets promoted, and how much money employees are paid. The second part of this goal relates to motivation. That is, the appraisal should provide employees with information about their strengths and weaknesses so that they can work to become more effective on the job. These two considerations serve the larger goal of improving performance by affecting motivation. Managers can generally assume that when employees get feedback about areas that need improvement, they will be motivated to make these improvements if they recognize that improving their performance will improve their chances for a promotion, pay increase, or some other important outcome or benefit. At the same time, employees should also gain a clear understanding of where they stand relative to the organization's expectations of them vis-à-vis their performance.

The Performance Appraisal Process

Several tasks are necessary for the performance appraisal process to be successful. Some should be done by the organization, some by the rater(s) (the individual[s] who will be conducting the performance appraisal), and in many organizations by the ratee (the individual whose performance is evaluated). In addition, follow-up and discussion should accompany the process. Although some of this follow-up and discussion may be more accurately considered performance management rather than performance appraisal per se, it is still an integral part of how organizations manage the entire process. Figure 10.1 illustrates the actual performance management system of one major corporation. While some firms might make minor modifications to reflect their philosophies more closely, these general steps are almost always followed. The performance appraisal part of this overall process is highlighted and will be the framework for much of the discussion that follows. In later sections of this chapter, we will address and discuss the remaining parts of the process.

The Role of the Organization

The organization, primarily through the work of its human resource function, develops the general performance appraisal process for its managers and employees to use. One of the first considerations relates to how the information gained from performance appraisals is to be used. For example, will it be used for developmental feedback only? Or will decisions about merit pay and/or other outcomes be based on these ratings as well? It is obviously important that everyone understand exactly what the ratings are to be used for and exactly how they will be used. The organization also generally determines the timing of the performance appraisals. Most organizations conduct formal appraisals only once a year, although some organizations conduct appraisals twice a year or even more frequently for new employees. However frequent the appraisals, the organization and its human resource managers must decide when they will be conducted. The most common alternatives are for appraisals to be done on the anniversary date of each individual employee's hiring or for all appraisals throughout the organization to be conducted during a specified period of time each year.

Conducting appraisals on employment anniversary dates means spreading the appraisals over the entire year. Under this system, supervisors may always have some appraisals to conduct, but they are not necessarily required to complete an excessive number of appraisals at any one time. On the other hand, spreading the appraisals over the year may make it more difficult to make comparisons among employees. Unless managers budget their salary dollars carefully over the entire year, those employees who were reviewed earlier in the year may have a greater opportunity to earn a larger salary increase than those who are reviewed toward the end of the year simply because there may be fewer salary dollars remaining. Conducting all appraisals at the same time (probably near the end of the fiscal year) avoids problems of having to ration salary dollars quite as carefully and makes comparisons among employees easier. But requiring a large

FIGURE 10.1   The Performance Management Process in a Typical Organization

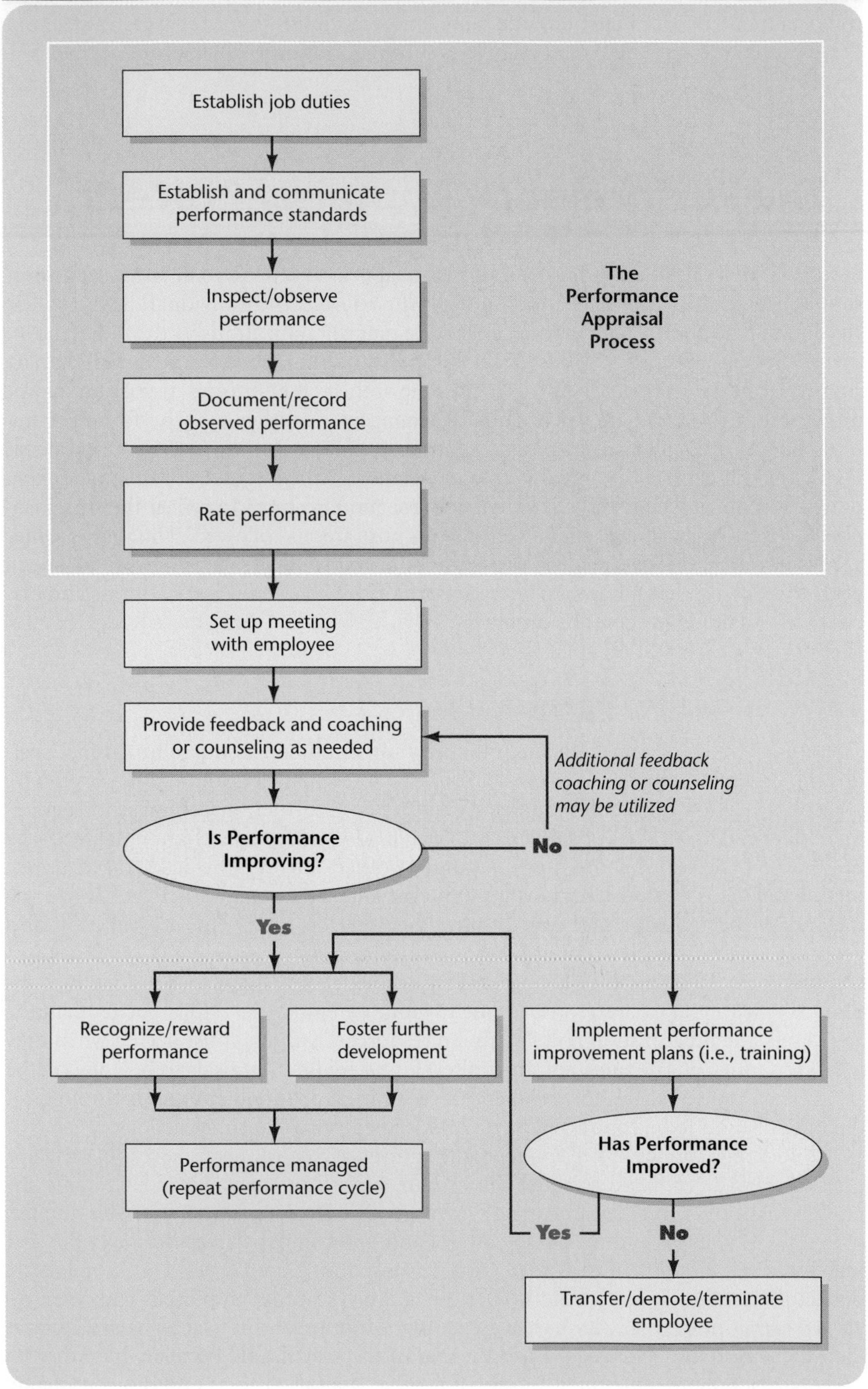

The Performance Appraisal Process

Establish job duties

Establish and communicate performance standards

Inspect/observe performance

Document/record observed performance

Rate performance

Set up meeting with employee

Provide feedback and coaching or counseling as needed

Additional feedback coaching or counseling may be utilized

Is Performance Improving?

No

Yes

Recognize/reward performance

Foster further development

Implement performance improvement plans (i.e., training)

Performance managed (repeat performance cycle)

Has Performance Improved?

Yes   **No**

Transfer/demote/terminate employee

number of appraisals at one time may also make it more likely that a rater will not devote as much time as desired to each appraisal.

The organization is also responsible for ensuring that clear and specific performance standards are available to managers. The organization should also ensure that these standards are communicated carefully to the employees. Although this step involves those individuals performing the ratings as well, the organization must ensure that everyone rates performance using the same set of standards and that employees know what is expected of them. Otherwise, performance appraisal cannot accomplish its goals and the organization may have serious problems by creating a disgruntled workforce and/or exposing itself to legal liabilities.

The Role of the Rater

The rater (traditionally and most typically the supervisor of the employee being appraised) plays the largest role in the appraisal process. As noted above, the organization is responsible for making sure that all raters have clear performance standards, but raters have to help develop and learn those standards. As performance information is acquired about a ratee, the rater also has to compare the information acquired with these standards as a way of evaluating the employee's performance. When making these decisions, the rater must consider the context in which performance occurs so that any extenuating conditions can be taken into consideration. In addition, the rater has to communicate those standards to the ratees so that each individual will know what is expected.

But the rater has a more critical role to play as well. On a day-to-day basis, an employee behaves, or performs, on the job and exhibits many behaviors that might be relevant to performance on that job. The rater's task is to collect information about those behaviors and translate that information into the ratings themselves. Therefore, the rater truly becomes a decision maker who must observe ratee performance and process the information gleaned from the observations. Because most formal appraisals are conducted only once a year, the rater must also somehow store this information in memory, recall what has been stored at the appropriate time, and use the information to provide a set of ratings. This task is potentially difficult and time-consuming.[5] Indeed, as shown in *The Lighter Side of HR,* managers may very well distort their appraisals based on the most recent observations of performance rather than on a long-term perspective.

Once ratings have been completed, it is also usually the rater who must then communicate the results and consequences of the appraisal to the ratee. When the results are somewhat negative, this task may be uncomfortable and is often stressful for managers. This communication process should also include goals for the future and a performance plan for helping the employee improve, thus adding a positive element. This set of activities, of course, is really part of the performance management process. Finally, the rater is ultimately responsible for preparing the employee to perform at desired levels. That is, the supervisor must be sure that the employee knows what is required on the job, has the needed skills, and is motivated to perform at the level desired.

The Role of the Ratee

Although attempts to improve appraisals often focus on the organization or the rater, the ratee also has responsibilities in the appraisal process. First, for performance appraisals to work most effectively, a ratee should have a clear and unbiased view of his or her performance. Problems can occur during the appraisal process if there is disagreement between the rater and the ratee, so it is essential that both parties have all the information they can collect about the ratee's performance. This approach may require

THE LIGHTER SIDE OF HR

A major drawback of annual performance reviews is that some managers tend to be biased by recent behaviors. That is, they remember recent events more clearly and may have fuzzier memories of employee behaviors that are several months old. Consequently, when these managers do performance appraisals of their subordinates, they may rely more heavily on recent behaviors than on older ones. While few managers will be as blatant as the one shown in the cartoon here, they should recognize that milder forms of this behavior can indeed occur, and they should try their best to take a longer and more complete perspective on the appraisal process.

Source: DILBERT reprinted by permission of United Feature Syndicate.

the ratee to acquire information about the performance of coworkers and requires the ratee to gain an understanding about how his or her behavior affects performance. This approach should also allow the ratee to be more receptive to feedback from the rater (especially if it is somewhat negative), which in turn makes it more likely that the ratee will change his or her behavior in response to that feedback.

Who Performs the Performance Appraisal?

Another important aspect of performance appraisal is the determination of who conducts the appraisal and what information will be used. The most common appraisers are shown in Figure 10.2.

FIGURE 10.2   Sources of Information for Performance Appraisal

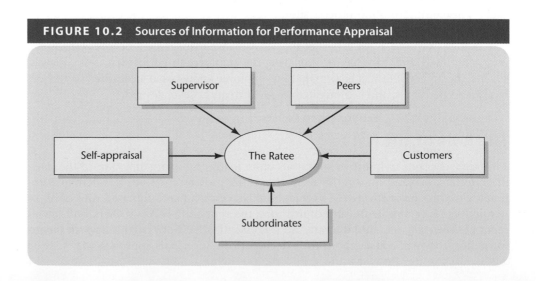

As noted earlier, the individual's supervisor is the most likely rater. Supervisors are perhaps the most frequently used source of information in performance appraisal. The assumption underlying this approach is that supervisors usually have the most knowledge of the job requirements and they have the most opportunities to observe employees performing their jobs. In addition, the supervisor is usually responsible for the performance of his or her subordinates. Thus, the individual supervisor is both responsible for employees' high performance and accountable, perhaps, for their low performance.[6]

At the same time, it should also be recognized that supervisors are not necessarily a perfect source of information. A supervisor may not have as much in-depth job knowledge as might be expected. For example, if the job has changed dramatically over the last few years because of new technology or other factors, the supervisor might not be as familiar with the job as in the past. Likewise, a supervisor may have been promoted from another part of the organization and thus may have never performed the jobs that she or he is supervising. In addition, in some job settings the supervisor may not really have an adequate opportunity to observe the employee performing his or her work. This situation is especially true in outside sales, where sales representatives spend much of their time working alone with customers in the field, out of view of their supervisor.

But these limitations all relate to the supervisor's *ability* to provide a meaningful appraisal. In addition, we must also consider the question of the supervisor's *motivation* to provide such ratings. Motivational issues are involved regardless of who does the appraisal, but it is especially important to realize that supervisors are not always motivated to give the most accurate ratings they can. For example, there is always the possibility that the supervisor is biased (either for or against) the person being rated. Only mixed evidence of systematic bias against members of identifiable groups based on race,[7] age,[8] gender,[9] and disability exists.[10] Nonetheless, a supervisor may be negatively or positively biased toward various workers because of personal liking, attitudes, personal relationships, and so forth. As a result favoritism and/or negative bias may be possible.

Supervisors might also choose to be inaccurate in their ratings because they feel threatened by a particular subordinate and want to prevent him or her from getting ahead, or because the supervisor wants to get rid of a problem subordinate and tries to do so by getting her or him promoted into a different department. In addition, supervisors may be concerned about team member relations and decide to rate all team members the same, regardless of what they deserve, to avoid jealousy or conflict. These and other motivational factors that affect supervisory ratings are discussed in depth by Kevin R. Murphy and Jeanette N. Cleveland,[11] but the main point here is to appreciate that supervisors may choose to be inaccurate in their ratings for a wide range of reasons.

Peers, colleagues, and coworkers represent other potential sources of information for performance appraisal systems. An advantage of using peers in a performance appraisal process is that, by definition, they have expert knowledge of job content and they may also have more of an opportunity than does the supervisor to observe the performance of a given worker on a day-to-day basis. Peers also have a different perspective on the performance of their work: they really understand their own opportunities and limitations regarding performance. Merck and 3M Corporation both use peer evaluations as a major component of their performance appraisal process.

Of course, friendship, group norms, and other personal factors may intervene in this situation. And individuals may see their own performance as being significantly different than others perceive it in the group.[12] Also, in some situations, coworkers might be competing with each other for a promotion (or some other reward), which may affect their motivation to be accurate in their peer evaluations. Because peers or coworkers remain in an ongoing relationship with each other, someone who received poor ratings from his or her coworkers may try to retaliate and rate those coworkers poorly during subsequent evaluations.[13] Nevertheless, peer evaluation is particularly useful in professional organizations such as law firms, architectural firms, academic departments, and so forth. As more and more organizations begin to use work teams for production work, peer evaluations are becoming more widely used in those contexts as well.

A third source of information in the performance appraisal process is subordinates of the individual being appraised. Subordinates are an especially important source of information when the performance of their own manager is being evaluated, and this information is perhaps most useful when the performance appraisal is focused on the manager's leadership potential. That is, if top-level managers in an organization are appraising the performance of a certain middle manager on the basis of his or her leadership potential, then the subordinates of that manager are perhaps the best source of information for evaluating that person's performance. Of course, a major problem with using subordinates as input to the performance appraisal process is that this approach may influence the manager's behavior in the sense that she or he may be more focused on making workers happy and satisfied than in making them perform at a high level.[14] Nonetheless, there has been a great deal of recent interest in so-called upward appraisals and in the ways to make them more effective.[15]

Another source of information in a performance appraisal process is self-evaluation. In many professional and managerial situations, individuals may frequently be asked to evaluate their own performance. The rationale for this approach is that, more than any other person in the organization, an individual is in the best position to understand his or her strengths and weaknesses and the extent to which he or she has been performing at an appropriate level. Of course, the biggest negative aspect of using self-ratings is the tendency on the part of many people to inflate their own performance.

A final source of information in the performance appraisal system is customers. Because of the dramatic increase in the service sector of the U.S. economy in recent years, the use of customers as a source of information in performance appraisal has received much more attention. The inclusion of customers might be accomplished through techniques such as having customers fill out feedback forms or respond to mail surveys whenever they use the services of an organization. Some restaurants, like Red Lobster and Chili's, put brief feedback forms on the table when the customer receives his or her meal check. These forms ask the customer to rate the server, the cook, and so forth, on various characteristics relevant to the meal just consumed. The advantage of this method is that customers are the lifeblood of an organization and it is very helpful to managers to know the extent to which customers feel that employees are doing a good job. On the other hand, this method may be expensive and may be able to tap only certain aspects of an employee's job.

One important detail for any manager to recognize is that each source of performance appraisal information is subject to various weaknesses and shortcomings. As a result, many organizations find it appropriate and effective to rely on different information sources when conducting a performance appraisal. That is, they may gather information from not just supervisors or peers, but both. Indeed, some organizations gather information from all the sources described in this section. This approach, the basis for the chapter-opening vignette, has even gained a new term in the management literature: *360-degree feedback.*

360-degree feedback

is an approach to performance appraisal that involves gathering performance information from people on all sides of the manager—above, beside, below, and so forth.

Organizations that use **360-degree feedback** gather performance information from people on all sides of the manager—above, beside, below, and so forth.[16] By focusing on 360-degree feedback, they obtain information on a person's performance from all perspectives. This approach allows them to match the strengths and weaknesses, the benefits and shortcomings, from each perspective and thus gain a more realistic, overall view of a person's true performance.[17] It is important to recognize, however, that the feedback from the different sources could be inconsistent. Otherwise, there is no value in obtaining evaluations from different sources. But this approach means that the manager has to reconcile different feedback and that the organization probably needs to use these ratings for feedback and development purposes only. If decisions are to be based on these evaluations, the organization would have to decide how to weight the ratings from the different sources.[18] The *Point/Counterpoint* feature for this chapter provides more details about the strengths and weaknesses of this approach to performance appraisal. While it is not a panacea (and in fact few studies have evaluated its effectiveness), variations on 360-degree appraisal systems are likely to continue to be popular for some time.

Regardless of who conducts the appraisals, another important issue to consider when conducting effective appraisals is that organizations typically conduct them once a year. Therefore, the rater who is evaluating a ratee's performance should consider the entire year's performance as part of the evaluation. Thus, the rater must observe and then remember the relevant performance information that occurred over that time.[19] But memories are not perfect. Raters forget what happened, especially if it happened some time ago. Rater memory is therefore a critical factor, limiting the accuracy and effectiveness of performance appraisals. If a rater cannot remember a performance incident, he or she cannot rate it. Note that, although most of the research on rater memory has focused on the supervisor as rater, this issue is important for any rater.

What can be done to address this problem? Several organizations and studies have found a rather simple solution: having raters keep performance diaries (or performance logs) can help.[20] Performance diaries or electronic records of the relevant performance information for a ratee are recorded at the time the behavior occurs. For example, if a supervisor observes an especially effective interaction between a salesperson and a customer, the supervisor notes the salesperson's name, the date, and the time, and then writes a brief description of the interaction. Keeping such diaries for all ratees (and writing down incidents of both good and poor performance when they occur) has at least three important advantages:

1. Raters do not have to rely on their imperfect memories to provide ratings; they can consult their diaries.
2. Raters can provide detailed feedback about the basis for the ratings they give, which should increase the perceptions of procedural fairness.
3. If an employee is discharged for poor performance and the employee subsequently sues the organization, these diaries can serve as the documentation of performance that the organization needs to defend itself in court.

What Gets Rated?

Another important decision to make regarding the design of appraisal systems is what should be rated. The choice of appraisal instruments (discussed below) is related to this issue because some systems are clearly designed to measure some aspects of performance rather than others. But the decision of what to rate should be based more on the needs of the organization than on the choice of rating instrument. Although the decision about what to rate can probably include many factors, three choices are most commonly encountered. All are related to task performance, which will be distinguished from contextual performance later.

It is most common for organizations to rate traits in conducting appraisals. Traits are abstract properties of individuals that generally cannot be observed directly but can be inferred from behavior. For example, many organizations rate employees on their attitude and their initiative. We may or may not agree on what these terms mean, but we can never truly observe something like a person's attitude. Instead, we infer it from his or her behavior. Thus, a rater might believe that an employee who is always smiling has a good attitude, but that may or may not be the reason for the employee's smiling. Rating traits allows an organization to use the same appraisal instrument for all or

POINT | **COUNTERPOINT**

360-Degree Feedback

 A system of evaluation and feedback in which different groups of people evaluate a specific employee is called 360-degree feedback. Typically, an employee might receive ratings and feedback from peers, supervisors, subordinates, and customers or clients. Organizations differ in how they summarize and/or present these data to the employee, and they also differ on whether the ratings are used for feedback only (to be seen only by the employee for his or her personal development) or whether they are used for decision making as well. In either case the logic is that the employee can learn more about how he or she is viewed by a wider range of people, providing a more complete picture.

POINT... **Evaluation systems based on 360-degree feedback are useful because...**	**COUNTERPOINT...** **But such systems cause problems because...**
They provide ratees with information about how they are viewed by other employees.	The ratee then has to determine how to deal with all of this information.
They provide more information for development—working toward improvement or addressing weaknesses—than any other tool.	They are useful for providing a more complete picture, but the amount of information transmitted can be overwhelming.
They recognize that different groups of employees are likely to have different perspectives and thus have different views.	These differences must then be reconciled somehow. Whose view does the ratee rely on primarily if the recommendations conflict? This situation is especially problematic if the appraisals are to be used for decision making.
Ratings and feedback from different groups can be obtained in areas where each group has special insights (e.g., asking customers about the employee's dealings with customers).	Most organizations ask all raters to rate the ratee in all areas.
Ratees tend to view the appraisals as useful and helpful.	Employees probably need help and guidance (e.g., a coach) in figuring out what to do with the potentially conflicting information.
Important organizational decisions can be based on input from multiple sources.	The original proponents of the system recommended that the ratings be used for feedback only, and we have little data on how effective the data are when they are used for decision making. If evaluations conflict, whose recommendations does the organization rely on for making decisions?

So... Appraisal systems based on 360-degree feedback are potentially helpful, especially when they are used for feedback purposes only. When organizations first implement these systems, they are often meant to be used for feedback only. As time goes by and important decisions must be made, however, many organizations begin to use these appraisals for decision making as well. In any case, the different perspectives are likely to result in different evaluations, and so 360-degree systems are most likely to be effective when the employee has a coach to help interpret and sort out the evaluations. We should note, however, that although these systems are becoming extremely popular, their effectiveness is still not known.

most employees, and this approach is based on the assumption that similar traits underlie effective performance for all jobs. It should be noted, however, that an analysis of court cases involving performance appraisals suggests that trait-based appraisals are the most difficult to defend because the courts tend to see them as more subjective than other systems.[21] Also, feedback concerning rating traits is often less instructive and helpful than other types of feedback.

In some cases, organizations base their appraisals on behaviors. These appraisals tend to be based on job analysis, and they tend to be tailored for specific jobs. For example, a ratee may be evaluated on how well he or she follows up on sales leads. These appraisals are still subjective, but they require the rater to evaluate behaviors that he or she can physically observe and therefore they seem more objective. Reliance on behaviors can also lead to an emphasis on processes underlying effective performance. In the example above, one might assume that following up sales leads is part of the process of being an effective salesperson. Providing feedback about behaviors and processes can be instructive and useful because it can help employees to understand how to improve their performance.

The final commonly encountered option is to rate performance based on outcomes. For example, rather than evaluating whether the salesperson has a good attitude or whether the salesperson follows up on leads, an organization could simply tally actual sales. Focusing on outcomes has the advantage of emphasizing the most objective measures of performance available. Also, when these systems are used, they are usually tied to specific goals, which have added benefit (discussed below). Feedback can be relatively straightforward and easy to interpret (i.e., you did or you didn't meet your sales goal), although feedback is even more useful if it includes information on how to improve future performance. Goals can be stated in terms of absolute amounts or in terms of improvement (e.g., increase sales by 10 percent over last year). It is important to set the right goals (goals that help the organization to achieve its objectives), and it is important to monitor the means by which employees meet their goals (i.e., to make sure they act ethically and legally). Appraisal systems built around outcome measures are a reasonable alternative for organizations to consider.

Who Should Be Rated?

A final issue to consider is exactly who should be rated in the appraisal process. Specifically, this issue is connected with the use of work teams. With work teams, the organization must decide whether to evaluate individual performance or team performance, and this issue can become quite complicated.

If individuals are rated and rewarded based on their individual performance, they have less reason to cooperate with other team members to accomplish the team's goals. In some cases, this situation might be desirable. For example, although the Ryder Cup in golf is considered to be a team competition, the team's performance is simply the sum of the scores of individual team members. Therefore, having team members seek to maximize their own performance helps the team as well. In team settings that are structured in a similar manner, the team leader or fellow team members can provide ratings as well.

But in other team settings, it is critical that team members work together toward a common goal. In these cases, it is critical that performance be measured and rewarded only at the team level. One person's performance should not be considered except as part of the whole. Some employees are uncomfortable with this kind of system and believe that they should be recognized for their individual efforts. Also, in such settings, it is possible for one employee to relax and let the other team members carry the workload. This free-rider problem is a real challenge to work teams. Nonetheless, if the team functions as a team rather than as a set of individuals, it is essential that the team's performance is appraised and rewarded.[22]

Methods for Appraising Performance

Different performance appraisal methods and techniques are used in organizations. By their very nature, most appraisals are subjective. That is, we must rely on a rater's judgment of an employee's performance. As a result performance appraisals are also prone to problems of bias (some of which were discussed above) and rating errors (which will be discussed later in this chapter). Raters tend to be uncomfortable passing judgment on employees, and employees generally don't care to be judged in this way. The question then becomes: Why do we rely on these subjective evaluations? Why not rely instead on objective performance information and rate employees on outcome achievement alone?

Several reasons explain why subjective evaluations are far more common than objective performance measures. The biggest reason, however, is relatively simple: for most jobs, and for all managerial jobs, straightforward objective measures of performance do not exist. Even in cases where easy outcome measures might be available, there are often complications. For example, it would seem a relatively simple matter to measure the performance of the manager of a bookstore by calculating total sales or sales per square foot. But a bookstore in an upscale shopping village is more likely to sell a lot of higher-priced hardcover books than is a bookstore in a rural or economically depressed area. If the manager of either store had played a role in choosing the location, this approach might be relevant. But for large chains such as Barnes and Noble or Borders, the corporation chooses the store location. As a result, a major determinant of sales volume is really outside the control of the manager, and so sales figures alone do not provide a good source of information about the manager's performance. A careful evaluation will almost always result in the acknowledgment that many so-called objective measures of performance are based on factors outside the control of the person being evaluated, and so they are not really effective measures of individual performance.

Of course, objective data that do reflect conditions under the control of the individual employee are sometimes available. These data could be sales figures for outside sales employees. In other cases, a rater could measure outcomes such as reductions in complaints. These examples are best suited for outcome-based appraisal methods. In many other cases, however, organizations have no choice but to rely on judgments and ratings. Therefore a great deal of effort has been spent in trying to make these subjective evaluations as meaningful and as useful as possible. Some of the methods that have been proposed are based on relative rankings, while others rely more on absolute ratings.

Ranking Methods Versus Rating Methods

Probably the simplest method of performance appraisal is the **simple ranking method,** which involves having the manager simply rank-order, from top to bottom or from best to worst, each member of a particular work group or department. The individual ranked first is presumed to be the top performer, the individual ranked second is presumed to be the second-best performer, and so on, and the ranking is generally global or based on overall performance. A variation on the ranking method is the **paired comparison method** of performance appraisal, which involves comparing each individual

The **simple ranking method** involves having the manager rank-order, from top to bottom or from best to worst, each member of a particular work group or department.

The **paired comparison method** of performance appraisal involves comparing each individual employee with every other individual employee, one at a time.

employee with every other individual employee, one at a time. This technique is simply an alternative way to generate rankings, however.

Although ranking techniques are simple and easy to implement, there are some serious shortcomings. It is true that organizations who are seeking to make relatively simple decisions such as which person to promote can obtain clear information about the "most promotable" and this is useful. But, even in such cases, if an organization must then turn to the "second most promotable," ranking methods provide no information about the difference between the persons ranked first and second. The absence of such information is even more problematic for the employees who might be told that she or he is the "second best" but is not given any information about how to become the best.

A related technique for performance appraisal is forced distribution, a method that has been in practice for many years.[23] The **forced distribution method** involves grouping employees into predefined frequencies of performance ratings. Those frequencies are

> The **forced distribution method** *involves grouping employees into predefined frequencies of performance ratings.*

HR LEGAL BRIEF

Identifying a Firm's "Worst" Employees

A few years ago Goodyear adopted what was then an increasingly popular approach to performance appraisal that relies heavily on the forced distribution method. But the firm then announced that it would abandon the system that had asked managers to identify the 2,800 employees who make up the worst-performing 10 percent of the company's salaried workforce. What forced the about-face? The tire maker became the target of an age discrimination lawsuit that claimed that it singled out too many older employees as bad workers.

Goodyear became the latest company to put the brakes on so-called ABC employee evaluation systems, which had gained favor with large companies eager to weed out underperforming workers. In March 2002 Ford Motor Company quit handing out C's to its bottom 10 percent and paid $10.6 million to settle an age discrimination suit filed by the same law firm taking on Goodyear.

As is typical of ABC systems, Goodyear gave A's to the top 10 percent of workers, B's to the middle 80 percent, and C's to the bottom 10 percent. Spokesperson Keith Price says that the system was not discriminatory and that the suit filed by Michigan law firm Pitt Dowty McGehee & Mirer had no influence over Goodyear's decision.

As in the Ford case, the Goodyear case gained momentum when the American Association for Retired Persons (AARP), an advocacy group for older Americans (you must be at least fifty years old to be a member) committed itself to provide legal resources to those suing the tire company. The lawsuit named eight plaintiffs aged fifty-

> *"It's pretty blatant that they're trying to get rid of older employees."*
>
> (John Van Hoose, fifty-nine, Goodyear employee who got a C)*

five to fifty-nine, whose annual salaries ranged from $48,700 to $71,700. The lawsuit claimed that hundreds of workers in more than ten states could join if the case was granted class-action status.

Jim Skykora, fifty-five, the youngest and best-paid plaintiff, said in an interview that he designed tires for General Motor's vehicles and has had all eleven of his projects approved in the past four years. He was graded a B– a year ago, then was downgraded to a C and told that he was at risk of being fired.

The plaintiffs' lawyers plan to go ahead with their lawsuit to find out if a disproportionate number of older workers have been fired or denied raises and bonuses during the eighteen months that Goodyear's system was in place. Goodyear's Price says that even if the company was inadvertently discriminating, the human resources department would have seen statistics showing that too many older workers were being singled out. That is not the case, Price says. The court ultimately agreed with Goodyear and dismissed the case. But while some companies are retreating from ABC appraisal systems, General Electric (GE) remains an outspoken advocate and has no plans to abandon it. Spokesperson Gary Sheffer says GE has never been sued over it.

Source: "Goodyear to Stop Labeling 10% of Its Workers as Worst" by Del Jones from *USA Today,* September 12, 2002. Copyright © 2002 *USA Today.* Reprinted with permission. *Quote from John Russell, "Goodyear Backs Down," *Beacon Journal,* September 12, 2002, p. A15; See Cathleen Flahardy, "Companies Should Get Their Policies in Order to Avoid Potential Age Discrimination Lawsuits," InsideCounsel.com., November 18, 2006.

determined by the organization in advance and are imposed on the rater. For example, a decision might be made that 10 percent of the employees in a work group can be grouped as outstanding, 20 percent as very good, 40 percent as average, 20 percent as below average, and the remaining 10 percent as poor. The manager then classifies each employee into one of these five performance classifications based on the percentage allowable. For example, if the manager has twenty employees, then two of those employees can be put in the top and bottom categories, four employees can be put in the second from the top and second from the bottom categories, and the rest will fit into the middle category. The forced distribution method is familiar to many students because professors who grade on a so-called bell or normal curve are using this method.

An advantage of this system is that it results in a normal distribution of performance ratings, which many people see as inherently fair. Also, from the organization's perspective, if employees are to receive merit pay increases, a forced distribution ensures control over how much money is spent on merit pay. On the other hand, the distribution that is being imposed may have no relationship to the true distribution of performance in the work group. For example, many more employees than 10 percent may deserve to be rated as outstanding, and so the forced distribution may result in perceptions of unfairness and may even result in employees losing motivation. It might also be that *all* the employees are performing at acceptable levels, but the forced distribution methods, as well as the other ranking methods, force the rater to make distinctions that might not really be meaningful. The *HR Legal Brief* feature for this chapter (on page 331) discusses another potential pitfall regarding the forced distribution approach (called the ABC employee evaluation system in the feature). As a result, most organizations rely instead on some type of absolute judgments and employ a system of performance ratings rather than rankings.

Specific Rating Methods

A **graphic rating scale** *consists of a statement or question about some aspect of an individual's job performance.*

One of the most popular and widely used performance appraisal methods is the graphic rating scale. A **graphic rating scale** simply consists of a statement or question about some aspect of an individual's job performance. Following that statement or question is a series of answers; the rater must select the one that fits best. For example, one common set of responses to a graphic rating scale is *strongly agree, agree, neither agree nor disagree, disagree,* and *strongly disagree.* These descriptors or possible responses are usually arrayed along a bar, line, or similar visual representation, and this representation is marked with numbers or letters that correspond to each of the descriptors.

Figure 10.3 illustrates a graphic rating scale. One of the appealing features about graphic rating scales is that they are relatively easy to develop. A manager simply needs to brainstorm or otherwise develop a list of statements or questions that are presumably related to indicators of performance relevant to the organization. A wide array of performance dimensions can be tapped with various rating scales on the same form. Each of the descriptors on the rating form is accompanied by a number or a letter for responses. Most graphic rating scales have ranges of 1 to 5 or 1 to 7, although occasionally a scale may use only 1 to 3 or perhaps as many as 1 to 9 alternatives.

To develop a performance measure, the manager simply adds the points for a particular employee's graphic scale items to obtain an overall index of performance (which is why these scales are sometimes referred to as summated ratings). For example, if an appraisal instrument contains five graphic rating scales and each has a possible range of 1 to 5, then the potential performance scores for an individual can range from a minimum of 5 (when the individual receives an evaluation of 1 on each item) to a maximum of 25 (when the individual receives a 5 on each dimension). The specific dimensions measured by graphic rating scales should be based on job analysis, but this approach is not typically taken. Instead, to have a single instrument that can be used

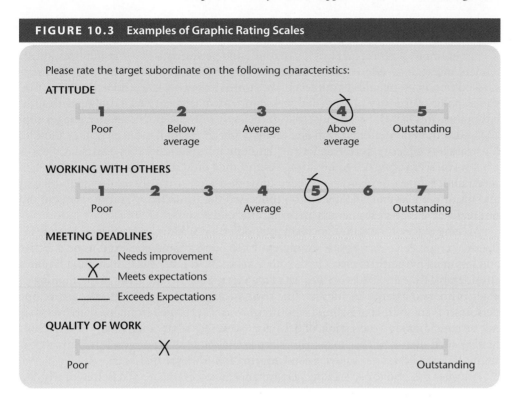

FIGURE 10.3   Examples of Graphic Rating Scales

Please rate the target subordinate on the following characteristics:

ATTITUDE

1 — 2 — 3 — ④ — 5

| Poor | Below average | Average | Above average | Outstanding |

WORKING WITH OTHERS

1 — 2 — 3 — 4 — ⑤ — 6 — 7

| Poor | | | Average | | | Outstanding |

MEETING DEADLINES

_____ Needs improvement

__X__ Meets expectations

_____ Exceeds Expectations

QUALITY OF WORK

Poor ———————X————————————————— Outstanding

with all or most employees in an organization, graphic rating scales typically measure performance relative to traits or behaviors such as initiative or problem-solving capabilities or even attitudes. Also, in some cases, the organization might add an overall performance scale in addition to scales for the specific dimensions.

Although they are popular, graphic rating scales have problems. Managers may tend to go down the list of items and circle all the points at one end or the other of the scale. As we will see later, this pattern results in errors of what is called leniency or severity. On the other hand, some managers tend to circle primarily midpoints on the scale. This approach results in what is called central tendency. In all these cases, the real problem is a range restriction. It has also been suggested that graphic rating scales are particularly prone to the problem where an evaluation in one area or a general impression about the ratee influences ratings on all scales. This problem, which will also be discussed later in the chapter, is usually called halo error. Another shortcoming of the graphic rating scale is the tendency for managers to attribute perhaps too much precision and objectivity to them. That is, because numbers can be added and divided, a person may end up with a score such as 4.25 or 3.65. Thus, people may perceive that the results are more objective and precise than they are in reality.

A somewhat different type of rating instrument involves the use of the **critical incident method.** (Recall from Chapter 5 that this method can also be used as a job analysis technique.) A critical incident is simply an example or instance of especially good or poor performance on the part of the employee.[24] Organizations that rely on this method often require raters to recall such instances on the job and then describe what the employee did (or did not do) that led to success or failure. Thus, this technique provides rich information for feedback to the employee and defines performance in fairly clear behavioral terms. In other cases, managers are asked to keep a log or diary in

*The **critical incident method** relies on instances of especially good or poor performance on the part of the employee.*

which they record examples or critical incidents that they believe reflect good and bad performance on the part of individual employees.[25]

For example, a critical incident illustrating good performance by a gasoline station attendant might be as follows: "On Monday, January 15, you were observed to have fully restocked certain merchandise counters in the store without being instructed to do so. And you also illustrated very pleasant and service-oriented behavior when dealing with three customers. You handled each quickly and efficiently but gave each customer the prompt and courteous attention that each one wanted." On the other hand, a critical incident to illustrate less effective performance for the same job might be: "On Thursday, February 15, you were observed to be sitting behind the counter reading a newspaper when merchandise inventory stocking needed to be done. You were also observed to be curt and blunt with several customers. You processed their purchases quickly, but you did not really give each customer any personal attention."

An advantage of the critical incident method is that it allows managers to provide individual employees with precise examples of behaviors that are believed to be effective and less effective performance. On the other hand, the critical incident method requires considerable time and effort on the part of managers because they must maintain a log or diary of these incidents. In addition, the method may make it difficult to compare one person with another. That is, the sample of behaviors developed from one employee may not be comparable to the sample of behaviors acquired for another. In any event, maintaining such diaries or logs may help raters in making evaluations and providing clear feedback regardless of how they use the information from the diaries.[26]

Another method for appraising performance involves the use of a **Behaviorally Anchored Rating Scale (BARS)**.[27] BARS appraisal systems (also known sometimes as behavioral expectation scales) represent a combination of the graphic rating scale and the critical incident method. They specify performance dimensions based on behavioral anchors associated with different levels of performance. Figure 10.4 presents an example of a BARS. As shown in the figure, the performance dimension has different behavioral examples that specify different levels of performance along the scale.

Developing a BARS is a complicated and often expensive process. Generally these scales are developed by the same managers who eventually use them to evaluate employees. First, the managers must develop a pool of critical incidents that represent various effective and ineffective behaviors on the job. These incidents are then classified into performance dimensions, and the dimensions that the managers believe represent a particular level of performance are used as behavioral examples, or anchors, to guide the raters when the scales are used. At each step, an incident is discarded unless the majority of managers can agree on where it belongs or what level of performance the incident illustrates.[28] The manager who then uses the scale has to evaluate an employee's performance on each dimension and determine where on the dimension the employee's performance fits best. The behavioral anchors serve as guides and benchmarks in helping to make this determination.

A significant advantage of a BARS system is that it dramatically increases reliability by providing specific behavioral examples to reflect effective and less effective behaviors. Because the managers themselves develop the scales, they tend to be more committed to using them effectively, and the process of developing the scales helps raters develop clearer ideas about what constitutes good performance on the job. The process of developing a truly effective BARS is extremely expensive and time-consuming, and so these scales are rarely used in their pure form. Instead, some modified BARS procedures are often adopted in an attempt to reap some of the benefits without incurring the costs.

A related measure of performance is the **Behavioral Observation Scale (BOS)**.[29] Like a BARS, a BOS is developed from critical incidents. Rather than using only a sample of behaviors that reflect effective or ineffective behavior, a BOS uses substantially

*A **Behaviorally Anchored Rating Scale (BARS)** is an appraisal system that represents a combination of the graphic rating scale and the critical incident method.*

*A **Behavioral Observation Scale (BOS)** is developed from critical incidents like a BARS but uses substantially more critical incidents to define specifically all the measures necessary for effective performance.*

FIGURE 10.4 Behaviorally Anchored Rating Scales

PERFORMANCE DIMENSION 1.
Interpersonal skills: Instructor's ability to establish rapport with students in and out of the classroom.

7 —

— Instructor encourages students to ask questions.

⑥ —

— Instructor comes down to the level of the students.
Instructor maintains an informal relationship with the students.

5 —

4 —

— Instructor doesn't draw out students who don't ask questions.

3 —

2 —

— Instructor "puts down" students who ask questions.
Instructor lowers students' self-esteem.

1 —

Here is an example of a BARS for one dimension of teacher performance. This scale was developed by one of the authors with the students in his class.

more of the behaviors to define specifically all the measures necessary for effective performance. A second difference between a BOS and a BARS is that a BOS allows managers to rate the frequency with which the individual employee has exhibited each behavior during the rating period. The manager then averages these ratings to calculate an overall performance rating for the individual. While the BOS approach is an improvement over the limitations of the BARS approach, it takes even more time and can be even more expensive to develop.

Earlier in the chapter, we noted that it might be reasonable to evaluate an employee based on outcomes. In fact, another popular method of appraising performance that does focus on outcomes is a **goal-based** or **management-by-objectives (MBO)** system.[30] Management by objectives is the most popular term used for this approach, although many companies that use it develop their own label to describe the system in their organization. In an MBO system, a subordinate meets with his or her manager and together they set goals for the subordinate for a coming period of time, often one year. These goals are usually quantifiable, objective, and almost always written down. During the year, the manager and the subordinate meet periodically to review the subordinate's performance relative to attaining the goals. At the end of the year, a more formal meeting is scheduled. During that meeting the actual degree of goal attainment is assessed. The degree of goal attainment then becomes the individual's performance appraisal. That is, if an individual has attained all the goals that she or he set for her- or himself, then employee performance is deemed to be very good. On the other hand, if not all goals were accomplished and the individual is directly responsible for that performance deficiency, then her or his performance is judged to be less than adequate or acceptable.

A **goal-based** or **management-by-objectives (MBO)** *system is based largely on the extent to which individuals meet their personal performance objectives.*

Goal-based systems are often seen as the best alternative available for rating performance, but care must be taken when these systems are used. Specifically, the kinds of behaviors specified in the goal-setting process are exactly what the employee will tend to focus on. Therefore it is critical that the organization really wants to encourage these particular behaviors. For example, if a sales representative's goals are stated in terms of dollar volume of sales, he or she might exert a lot of pressure on customers to increase the dollar volume of merchandise they're ordering in a coming period to boost his or her performance measures. At the same time, however, the sales representative may also hurt the firm's relationship with the customer if too much pressure is applied or if the customer ends up ordering more merchandise than is really needed. Thus, an important long-term goal may be sacrificed for the achievement of a short-term goal. The only solution to this type of potential problem is to emphasize the need for care in setting goals.

One relatively new innovation in performance appraisal methods is the use of computer monitoring. It is now possible to monitor electronically how employees are spending their time and how productive they are. These systems are now used widely with customer-service representatives and reservations clerks. In fact, you may have heard a telephone recording (after you pressed the right numbers to get the service you wanted) stating, "This call may be monitored for quality purposes." This recording is an indication that electronic monitoring is taking place. For example, it is possible to track how many calls an employee receives, how long each call takes, and (with minimal input) the outcome of those calls. It is also possible to track when an employee is not at his or her phone station, which has caused some people to raise serious questions about invasion of privacy.[31] Although only a limited number of studies have investigated the effectiveness of this method, it seems as though the approach can be effective without triggering negative reactions on the part of employees—at least under certain circumstances.[32] While we need to know a great deal more about the effects of computer monitoring on individuals, the fact remains that this approach is being used with growing frequency in the workplace, and it is likely to become even more popular in the future.[33]

Which System Is Best?

Despite the time and effort that have gone into developing and improving performance appraisal systems, it is difficult to find much advantage for any one system over the others.[34] We shall discuss issues of rating errors later in the chapter, and much research has focused on the susceptibility of different types of rating instruments to different types of errors. But this research has been inconclusive, and it is somewhat misguided. As noted at the beginning of this chapter, the ultimate reason for conducting performance appraisal is to improve performance. Therefore, it is difficult to suggest which system is best because it is difficult to predict how a set of employees will react to a given system. The human resource manager must take what is known about each type of system and decide how well the system fits into the culture and operations of the organization.

Thus, performance appraisal systems are neither good nor bad; these systems work or they don't for a particular organization. It is probably advisable to have some employees and supervisors involved in the development of any system so that they feel a sense of ownership. But the critical issue is how the organization uses the information collected in the performance appraisal. In fact this issue is at the heart of the performance management process, and we shall discuss it in more detail later. For now, though, it is safe to say that when employees perceive the appraisal system as fair and just, they work harder to make it work and they respond more constructively to the ratings they receive, thus making the system work.

General Issues in Performance Appraisal

We noted earlier that all the participants in the appraisal process tend to be dissatisfied with the process. Several issues that arise when we try to appraise performance contribute to this dissatisfaction, and we will discuss some of these problems below. One issue that has been getting more attention over the past few years, and is different from most of the other issues we will discuss, deals with exactly what should be appraised.

Contextual Performance

Typically, performance appraisal systems assess performance on aspects of one's job. That is, the areas for which the employee receives ratings are those areas the employee has been told are part of his or her job. Recently, a great deal of interest has focused on what has been termed contextual performance, which brings a different dimension to the question of what should be appraised.[35] **Contextual performance** refers to tasks an employee does on the job that are not required as part of the job but that nevertheless benefit the organization in some way (we introduced this topic in the previous chapter). These behaviors might include staying late at work, helping coworkers get their work done, and any of the behaviors that benefit the general good of the organization. These behaviors are often referred to as organizational citizenship behaviors.[36] Because these behaviors are never stated as formal requirements of the job, the employee is never formally told that he or she is expected to do these tasks. They might be told informally, however, that such behaviors are valued by the organization in general and/or the manager in particular. In any event, they do benefit the organization and raters do consider them when conducting employee evaluations.[37]

How important are contextual performance behaviors in determining the overall ratings an employee receives? A recent study indicates that, although they are important, they are not as important as task behaviors (or even as important as counterproductive behaviors), but they do matter.[38] The next question is, How important are these behaviors? Clearly, the organization benefits if someone engages in these behaviors, and therefore they represent part of an employee's overall contribution to the organization. On the other hand, they are not required of anyone. Some, especially union members, argue that it is inherently unfair to evaluate someone on something that is not part of his or her job. Perhaps that assertion is true, but it seems that, consciously or not, raters do take these behaviors into account. We can speculate about whether or not reliance on contextual performance behaviors can serve to discriminate unfairly against certain groups of employees. For example, a single parent may not be able to volunteer for overtime. Should he or she be penalized for this situation? There are no clear answers to how we should treat contextual performance, but it is clear that we need to learn a lot more about the premise for ratings and the importance of behavior at work that is not required.

Deficiencies in Appraisal Methods

In addition, it is important to recognize that all performance measurement techniques and appraisal approaches are subject to one or more weaknesses or deficiencies as well.[39] One deficiency is known as projection. **Projection** occurs when we tend to see in

Contextual performance *refers to tasks an employee does on the job that are not required as part of the job but that still benefit the organization in some way.*

Projection *occurs when we tend to see in others characteristics that we ourselves have and that we think contribute to effectiveness.*

others characteristics that we ourselves have and that we think contribute to effectiveness. That is, we tend to judge people like ourselves to be higher performers than we do people who are less like ourselves. The basis for similarity may be demographic characteristics (for example, race, gender, or age) or other characteristics (for example, the college the individual attended or his or her personal appearance, life style, etc.).

Contrast error *occurs when we compare people against one another instead of against an objective standard.*

Another performance deficiency is contrast error. **Contrast error** occurs when we compare people against one another instead of against an objective standard. For example, suppose a particular employee is a good performer but not an outstanding one. If that individual happens to work in a group of people where everyone else is a relatively weak performer, the "average" individual may appear to be a better performer than he or she really is. Likewise, if the same person works in a group of exceptionally strong performers, the person may be seen as a poorer performer than might otherwise be the case.

A **distributional error** *occurs when the rater tends to use only one part of the rating scale.*

Managers who conduct performance appraisals are also prone to make what is called **distributional errors.** A distributional error occurs when the rater tends to use only one part of the rating scale. Sometimes the distributional error may be *severity,* which occurs when the manager gives low ratings to all employees by holding them to an unreasonably high standard. The opposite error is *leniency,* which occurs when a manager assigns relatively high or lenient ratings to all employees.[40] A *central tendency* distributional error occurs when the manager tends to rate all employees as average, using only the middle part of a rating scale.

A **halo error** *occurs when one positive performance characteristic causes the manager to rate all other aspects of performance positively.*

A final type of error that may occur is what is known as either halos or horns. A **halo error** occurs when one positive performance characteristic causes the manager to rate all other aspects of performance positively. For example, suppose a given employee always comes to work early and is always full of energy and enthusiasm at the beginning of the workday. The manager may so appreciate this behavior that he or she gives the employee

Organizations are increasingly concerned with contextual performance as well as with the more traditional task performance. Whereas task performance refers to the assigned tasks and responsibilities that come with the job, contextual performance refers to things an employee does for the good of the organization that go above and beyond job requirements. Dr. Larry Nathanson, an Emergency Room doctor at Boston's Beth Israel Deaconess Medical Center is an excellent case in point. Although his primary job is to provide emergency care for patients who come to the emergency room, he realized that the usual dry-erase board was an ineffective tool for keeping track of ER patients. He initiated an effort to replace the board with a new system called an "electronic dashboard," which electronically monitors patients and their needs. Hospital officials estimate that this new system saves thirty minutes in processing time for each patient, which is important given that 60,000 patients visit the hospital's emergency room each year.

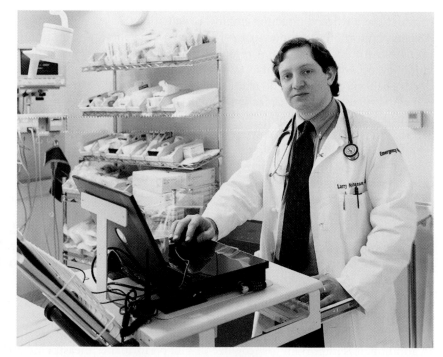

a high performance rating on all other aspects of performance, even when those other aspects may be only average or merely adequate.[41] The opposite of a halo error is a **horns error.** In this instance, the manager tends to downgrade other aspects of an employee's performance because of a single performance dimension. For example, the manager may feel that a given employee does not dress appropriately and views that characteristic negatively. As a result, the manager may also give the individual low performance ratings on other performance dimensions when higher ratings are justified.

> *A **horns error** occurs when the manager downgrades other aspects of an employee's performance because of a single performance dimension.*

But there is one additional point that should be discussed relative to these rating errors. Using the term *error* implies that there is a correct rating and that the observed rating in some cases is incorrect. So, for example, when we discuss leniency error, we observe that the ratings are "too high." That implies that we know how high the ratings really should be—but we don't. We really never have correct answers (sometimes referred to as "true scores") when we look at a set of ratings, so we really don't know whether a rating or set of ratings reflects reality or a rating error. Therefore, what we observe might be leniency or it might simply mean that the employee is really good. This fact makes it difficult to suggest that organizations take extraordinary measures to reduce "errors."

Nonetheless, these rating "errors" such as leniency and halo sometimes make it difficult to differentiate between different employees, or to accurately identify the strengths and weaknesses of a given employee. Furthermore, employees (ratees) might be less likely to perceive a set of lenient ratings as accurately reflecting their performance, and so may not be willing to work to improve their performance. As a result, organizations often do work to reduce rating error. One method for error reduction is to train managers to overcome these weaknesses. For example, sometimes pointing out to managers their tendency to commit distributional errors or contrast errors may be sufficient to enable those managers to do a better job. A related method for improving the accuracy of performance evaluations is the so-called rater accuracy training. This approach (also called frame of reference training) attempts to emphasize for managers the fact that performance is multidimensional in nature and to train those managers with the actual content of various performance dimensions.[42]

As noted earlier in the chapter, even if a rater can be trained to avoid errors and to provide accurate ratings, he or she may simply choose to be inaccurate in the ratings he or she gives. Therefore it is critical that organizations do whatever they can to reward raters for doing a good job in performance appraisal by reinforcing the fact that these appraisals are important. It may also be important to punish raters who do not take the task seriously. It is important to realize that a rater who really wants to be inaccurate or unfair can probably find a way to do so, whatever systems an organization puts in place. That is why it is so important for the organization to do what it can to convince raters that it is in their own best interests to do the best job they can in appraising employee performance.

Follow-up to Appraisals

Once an organization has collected performance appraisal data, it must then decide exactly what to do with the information collected. As noted earlier, appraisal information is often the basis for decisions about salary increases and promotions among others, and so the appraisal information must be provided to those individuals making these decisions. It is also critical that the employee being rated receives feedback (as well as some type of coaching) about how well he or she was evaluated.

We suggested earlier that the primary reason for organizations conducting appraisals is to improve employee performance, and ultimately organizational performance. Therefore it is also important that some consequences be attached to both effective and ineffective performance. Programs designed to develop such attachments are usually considered part of the performance management process, and this will be discussed, along with other performance enhancement techniques, in Chapter 14. Furthermore, Chapter 13 will discuss how various models and theories of motivation help to inform organizations about how to best manage employee performance in order to improve that performance. For now, though, it must suffice to say that there must be some follow-up to the appraisal process. If employees believe that appraisals are simply put away in a file cabinet, it will be difficult to motivate raters to do a good job and it will be even more difficult to motivate ratees to work toward improvement. Those outcomes can only be accomplished when there are consequences for performance, and we will return to this topic in Chapter 14.

Evaluating the Performance Appraisal Process

At the beginning of this chapter, we noted the strategic importance of the performance appraisal system. Clearly the organization must monitor the extent to which it is conducting its performance appraisals effectively, adequately, and appropriately. As with selection, performance appraisal must be free from bias and discrimination.

Beyond these stipulations, however, the performance appraisal system must also help the organization identify its strongest performers so that they can be appropriately rewarded and efforts can be made to retain them. It should also identify low performers so that their performance deficiencies can be remedied through training or other measures. Periodic audits of the performance appraisal system by trained professionals can be an effective method for assessing the effectiveness and appropriateness of the performance appraisal process used by the organization.

Because performance appraisal feeds into the performance management process, and because the ultimate goal of this process is to improve performance on the job, managers should be able to see real improvements in organizational performance if the process is working. This improvement may take the form of fewer errors in production, fewer returns in sales, improved performance appraisals, or lower levels of absenteeism or turnover. In the long run, however, these outcomes are not critical to the organization unless they translate into some improvement in overall firm performance. That is, if performance appraisal and performance management systems are doing what they were designed to do, the organization as a whole should perform better.

Legal Issues in Performance Appraisal

When performance appraisals are used as the basis for human resource decisions (as in the case of merit pay or promotion decisions), they are considered the same as any other test under the law. This designation includes decisions about layoffs based on performance. Therefore, appraisals that show evidence of disparate impact must be validated the same as any selection technique. This principle was first established in *Brito* v. *Zia Company,*[43] and was reinforced as part of the decision in the *Albermarle Paper Company* case discussed earlier in the text (see Chapter 2).

As noted above, performance appraisal decisions are known to suffer from various types of biases and problems. Also noted earlier in the chapter was the fact that ratings based on traits tend to have ambiguous standards, and so they are probably more prone to these biases. It is difficult to validate appraisal decisions using the methods described in Chapter 6 (i.e., content validity, construct validity, and criterion-related validity). Therefore it is critical that the organization can demonstrate that the ratings provided are in areas that are "job related," that raters can observe the behaviors they are rating, and that raters received some training to help them do a better job with rating performance. It is worth noting that, if an appraisal system is used for providing feedback only, it is not subject to these same legal requirements.

The Nature of Careers

Most people have a general idea of the meaning of *career*. For instance, people generally agree that careers have something to do with the work a person does in an organization, but they also recognize that a career is a broader and more general concept than a single job or task in an organization.

The Meaning of Career

We define a **career** as the set of experiences and activities that people engage in related to their job and livelihood over the course of their working life. This definition, then, suggests that a career includes the various specific jobs that a person performs, the kinds of responsibilities and activities that comprise those jobs, movements and transitions between jobs, and an individual's overall assessment of and feelings of satisfaction with these various components of her or his career.

A **career** *is the set of experiences and activities that people engage in related to their job and livelihood over the course of their working life.*

Most people have historically thought of the various components making up a person's career as having some degree of interrelation. This perspective stems from the fact that, in the past at least, people generally wanted to work for a single organization and spent most of their work life within that single organization. Presumably, if they performed effectively and were successful at their work, they advanced up the organizational hierarchy. Even when people changed jobs, they tended to work for other organizations in the same industry. For example, while Lee Iacocca is perhaps best remembered for saving Chrysler several years ago, at earlier times in his career he worked for both General Motors and Ford.

But in recent times, conceptualizations of careers have become considerably more general. Because of organizational downsizing efforts and innovations in strategies such as outsourcing and shared services, considerably more change has occurred in the work patterns of individuals than in the past.[44] For instance, people are likely to leave an organization in one industry and go to work for an organization in a totally different industry, and they may also spend some time between jobs and organizations consulting or working in otherwise independent contractor-type positions.

More and more frequently, people are taking breaks from their work. These breaks include sabbaticals, discretionary periods of unemployment, and similar activities that may make a positive contribution to a person's overall work life but do not involve formal employment by an organization. People who return to school to enhance their education now more than ever before are likely to consider that period of their lives as part of their career.

Carol Thompson spent years working in her practice as a licensed clinical social worker. She saw private patients and worked for the courts in San Francisco, and she found her work very rewarding if rather draining. When she finally decided to retire from her practice after closing it down gradually over several years, she was not ready to totally "retire." She responded to a call for volunteers at the Botanical Gardens at the University of California at Berkeley, and eventually began taking classes in horticulture. She is now a full-time volunteer, working with professional botanists on plant propagation at the Botanical Gardens. She says that this new work has reinvigorated her and is quite rewarding. In this decision to find something to do after retirement, Thompson is not alone. It is estimated that in 2005, 38 percent of men and 33 percent of women aged fifty-five to sixty-four were employed full- or part-time while receiving pensions from previous employers.

Traditional Career Stages

Exploration *is the first traditional career stage and involves identifying interests and opportunities.*

A long-time, generally accepted view of a career included stages that a typical individual progresses through. As shown in Figure 10.5, the first stage is called **exploration.** During this period of a person's life, he tries to identify the kind of work that he is interested in doing. This period of a typical person's career starts in his mid- to late teens and lasts through his mid- to late twenties. It generally encompasses the time when he tries to assess his own interests, values, preferences, and career opportunities and to relate them to what he thinks represents a feasible career option for himself. His course work in school and his first jobs play an important role in the exploration stage of career development.

For example, it is not uncommon for someone who anticipates majoring in a certain field of study to change his major once he begins taking courses in that area. Sometimes people take their first job in a particular field only to discover it's not what they expected it to be and then begin to look for alternative options. Of course, sometimes people are perfectly happy with the outcome of the exploration stage. They find that the coursework of their field is indeed of interest to them and their first job assignment is exciting, challenging, and just what they expected it to be.

*The **establishment** stage of the traditional career model involves creating a meaningful and relevant role in the organization.*

*The **maintenance** stage involves optimizing talents or capabilities.*

The second stage of a typical career is called the **establishment** stage. During this period, the individual begins to create a meaningful and relevant role for herself and the organization. She may, for example, become a valuable member of a work team, achieve success and recognition by her superior, and be acknowledged by the organization as someone whom the company values and wants to retain. While considerable range in terms of age and time exists in this stage, it generally encompasses the period of time when an individual is in her late twenties through her mid- to late thirties.

The **maintenance** stage is the next stage in a typical career. During this period, the individual begins to reach a level in the organization that optimizes his talents or

FIGURE 10.5   The Traditional Model of Career Stages

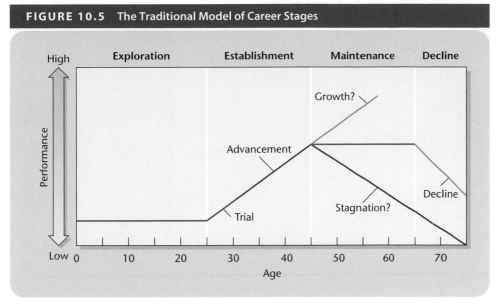

Source: Adapted from *Careers in Organization,* by Douglas T. Hall. Copyright © 1976 by Scott, Foresman, and Co. Reprinted by permission of Douglas T. Hall and Lyman Porter.

capabilities. Not everyone can become a CEO, however, and only a small percentage of the total workforce in any organization attains the rank of top executive. Thus, for many employees, this stage also marks a midcareer plateau. Many successful managers, especially in larger companies, may never progress beyond the rank of middle manager, and so end their careers on this plateau, but nevertheless enjoy careers considered to be highly productive and worthwhile. Individuals in the maintenance stage of their career must often devote extra effort to learning new job skills and remaining current in their professional skills and abilities. They are also frequently called on to fill mentoring roles in which they help newcomers to the organization to get their feet on the ground and to launch their own careers.[45]

Finally, the fourth stage of a typical career is the **disengagement** stage. During this period, the individual gradually begins to pull away from her work in the organization, her priorities change, and work may become less important to her. Consequently, she begins thinking more and more about leaving the organization and finding other sources for fulfilling her personal needs and goals. Some employees may evolve toward part-time work status, some retire from the organization, some simply cut back on their activities and responsibilities.

*The fourth traditional career stage, **disengagement,** involves the individual gradually beginning to pull away from work in the organization. Priorities change and work may become less important.*

New Views of Career Stages

Of course, in the contemporary era of downsizing and layoffs, sometimes people go through these four stages of career development in a relatively short period of time. People may find themselves disengaging from the organization at a relatively young age, and they may also anticipate beginning the entire process again by seeking new opportunities, new challenges, and new interests.[46] Many experts agree that while the traditional model of careers summarized above still has conceptual value, a new perspective such as the one shown in Figure 10.6 is a more accurate representation of career stages now and in the future.

This model also suggests a progression of career stages, but it focuses more on "career age" (i.e., how long a person has been in a particular job) rather than chronological age

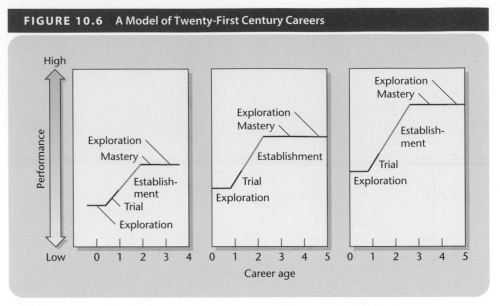

FIGURE 10.6   A Model of Twenty-First Century Careers

Source: Douglas T. Hall, "Protean Careers in the 21st Century," *Academy of Management Executive,* Vol. 10, No. 4, p. 9. Copyright © 1996 by Academy of Management. Reprinted by permission of the Academy of Management via Copyright Clearance Center.

and directly incorporates the premise of multiple career stages. The model describes career stages of exploration, trial, and establishment, followed by another period of exploration. This second level of exploration in turn is likely to take the person away from the current career and into a new one where the process begins again.

At each stage in the person's career he or she faces a different set of issues and decisions.[47] At the beginning of one's career there are issues about making the transition from a student to an employee. This involves questions about one's self-identity, and these questions also influence decisions about exactly what career someone plans to enter. Individuals may choose to enter certain careers because they are considered "hot," or because of general economic trends. They also choose careers because they are more consistent with their own interests, education, and values.

Once a career has been chosen and the person begins to build on that career, a different set of issues emerges. Most of these issues relate to trying to establish the proper balance between work and family life. It is at this point in one's career where these issues become more salient and the individual must deal with the potential tradeoff between working hard to build and advance a career, and establishing lasting relationships with others, including building a strong family life. Also, at this stage, decisions are more frequent regarding whether or not the person should remain with a given firm or move to a different organization. The decision as to how best to advance one's career in terms of moving is, of course, also tied to the growing importance of balancing work and family. By the time a person reaches some sort of midcareer point, there are often questions about the worth of continuing to work on one's career, and new questions about self-identity emerge (sometimes leading to a "midlife crisis").

Issues Facing Older Workers and the Decision to Retire

As workers continue to age there are new issues to deal with, and some of them relate to potential age discrimination. As noted in Chapter 2, persons over forty years of age are protected by the Age Discrimination in Employment Act, but the fact remains that many people assume that abilities and job performance decline with age. In fact, the evidence regarding such declines is rather mixed and generally weak. For example, although there is evidence of declines in abilities such as motor coordination and dexterity, the relationship between age and the levels of these abilities almost completely disappears when we control for education and job type. Furthermore, there is no evidence of any meaningful relationship between age and such abilities as intelligence, verbal ability, or numerical ability.[48] Perhaps more critically, there is almost no relationship between age and job performance—in fact, some studies have found a curvilinear relationship between age and performance where performance is highest when a worker is youngest and when a worker gets older.[49]

In any event, eventually older workers must confront the decision to retire. In truth, however, the decision to retire is not as simple as it once was. Today, there is really a whole continuum of choices available to a person contemplating retirement. The person can actually retire, take a pension, and begin some other nonwork activities (the traditional view of retirement), but this is becoming less common. More commonly, individuals retire and then take on full-time work at another organization, or retire and then take on part-time work, or work as a consultant, either at their former employer or somewhere else. Over time, they may reduce the amount of time they spend at work until they gradually move into full retirement, but retirement has become much more of a process than an event.[50]

Nonetheless, a number of factors are related to the decision to retire (or to begin the retirement process). For example, individuals are more likely to retire when they have the financial resources needed to maintain their preretirement life styles, and they are more likely to retire when their health makes continuing to work excessively burdensome. Individuals are also more likely to retire when their spouses have retired. In addition, several factors are related to adjustment after retirement. Of course, as noted above, many people tend to continue with some type of "bridge work," and these people generally adjust well to retirement. Also individuals who have structured leisure activities and those who do volunteer work tend to adjust better to retirement. But one of the most important factors related to adjustment is one's health. Individuals who avoid serious health problems adjust better, in part, because they can engage in the kinds of activities outlined above.

In conclusion, a person's career can be viewed as extending past the time of full-time work, as it becomes more difficult to tell who is really retired and who is simply doing some type of bridge work in preparation for full retirement. Although issues relating to retirement have always been important, they will become even more so in the future. The aging workforce, combined with longer life spans and longer productive work careers, means that the issues will become much more important for the HR manager in the future.

Human Resource Management and Career Management

Most successful organizations and managers today recognize that careers don't simply happen; they must be planned and managed. Part of the responsibility for this career planning resides with the organization, and the feedback from the appraisal process is a critical factor in this process. But the individual her- or himself must also play a role in this process.[51] This section examines the organizational and individual perspectives on careers shown in Figure 10.7.

Organizational and Individual Perspectives on Careers

Organizations are generally responsible for determining the jobs that people will perform for the organization, the pattern of interrelationships between jobs in an organization, the kinds of people who will be hired for those jobs, the development of those individuals to prepare them for more meaningful jobs, and the decisions regarding the movement of people from one job to another. Clearly, it is in the organization's best interest to take an active role in career management for people in the firm, and for this reason career management is often part of the larger performance management process.[52]

The organization can take steps from the outset to facilitate career management. For example, in Chapter 7 we discussed the idea of selecting individuals not because of their match with the requirements of a specific job but because of their fit with the organization. Despite any other problems associated with this selection strategy, it seems helpful for career management because the organization presumably hires individuals who fit different jobs. In fact, even when organizations select individuals for a specific job, it is still possible to do so with subsequent career moves in mind. That is, if an entry-level position is not particularly demanding, it is possible for an organization to hire people whose skills and abilities match a higher-level job that they might be expected to move into later. This practice can be defended as long as the employee will likely move up to the higher-level job eventually.

If an organization does indeed help its employees plan and manage their careers more effectively, it can expect to achieve several benefits. It will find itself with a larger pool of talented individuals. In addition, this workforce will generally be more satisfied and motivated because they will have recognized the opportunities that the organization has provided for them and the care with which their job assignments are managed. When an organization finds that it must reduce the size of its workforce, it will have a better understanding of which individuals are more likely to contribute to the success and effectiveness of the organization itself.

On the other hand, if the organization does a poor job with managing the careers of people in the organization, it will face several difficulties. The quality of its talent pool might vary in inefficient and erratic ways. That is, it might have an abundance or surplus

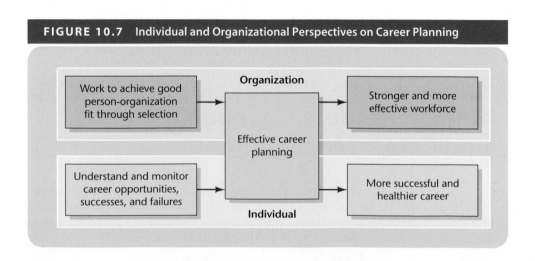

FIGURE 10.7   Individual and Organizational Perspectives on Career Planning

of highly talented and qualified employees in some areas and at some levels of the firm but have a shortage of talented and capable people at other levels or areas of the organization. In addition, the workforce of such an organization might be more dissatisfied and unmotivated because people are not given appropriate promotion opportunities and/or are not placed in appropriate positions. When the organization needs to transfer people or lay people off, it may be unsure about who can handle the new assignments.

Individuals obviously have an important stake in their own careers. They experience most directly the benefits and rewards of successful careers and incur the costs and frustrations of unsuccessful careers. A person's perceived and experienced career success or failure is also likely to have a major impact on his or her self-esteem and similar indications of self-worth.

A person who understands and carefully monitors his or her career is likely to understand the reasons behind his or her successes and failures. That is, this individual will know why she or he has been promoted or not and will have an accurate assessment of future promotion prospects and possibilities. In addition, an individual who accepts responsibility for managing her or his career will also be better prepared to deal with an unanticipated career setback such as job loss or demotion.

But many people are surprisingly uninformed and uninvolved in their own careers. They accept jobs and go to work but pay relatively little attention to their roles in the organization beyond the scope of a specific job. Thus, they may have little understanding about how they landed in a particular position and may have little understanding about what their next position is likely to be and how they might prepare themselves for that position when they are placed in it.

The Importance of Career Planning

Career planning is clearly important to both organizations and employees. Furthermore, effective career planning requires careful coordination between individual employees and the organization itself. Usually human resource managers represent the organization in the career planning process. General Electric and Shell Oil are known to be especially effective in the area of career planning and development for their managers. In general, most career planning systems involve the steps shown in Figure 10.8.

The first step is generally called the **individual assessment phase.** As the term suggests, individual assessment requires that individuals analyze carefully what they perceive to be their own abilities, competencies, skills, and goals. Many organizations provide employees with forms or questionnaires to help them develop this information. These forms may be tests or personality inventories, or they may simply be open-ended questions for the individual to answer.

*The **individual assessment phase** of career planning requires that individuals analyze carefully what they perceive to be their own abilities, competencies, skills, and goals.*

FIGURE 10.8   Steps in Career Planning

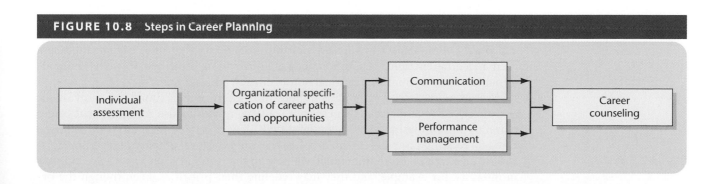

The organization also plays an important role in career planning. From the organization's standpoint, human resource managers should develop specifications about where individuals in each position might be most likely to advance. That is, a determination might be made about where a person in a particular job category is likely to be promoted in one of two or three other job categories. Thus, the organization is specifying potential career paths that an individual might take up the organizational hierarchy.[53] Shell's career-path model, for example, is available to managers on the firm's corporate intranet. The organization must also integrate its performance management system with its career management system. That is, a person should not expect to progress automatically from one job to another along a certain path but instead recognize that this movement will be determined in part by his or her performance effectiveness. That is, occupying a certain job for a few years may potentially lead to a promotion into a particular area, but that potential doesn't make such a progression automatic. If an individual does poor work in the first job, for example, the individual may be demoted, terminated, or transferred laterally into another job without a promotion.

Communication is also an important part of this process. For example, the organization may know the paths that are most likely to be followed from one position to another and may be able to gauge the probability or likelihood that a specific individual will follow this path or a prescribed path for a promotion to another position. But if this information isn't communicated to the individual employee, then it is of little or no value to anyone.

Career counseling *involves interaction between an individual employee or manager in the organization and either a line manager or a human resource manager.*

The final step in effective career planning is **career counseling.** As the term suggests, career counseling involves interaction between an individual employee or manager in the organization and either a line manager or a human resource manager. This counseling session typically involves frank and open dialogue, with the goal of making sure that the individual's assessment and the organization's assessment of the individual's role and prospects in the organization are congruent. We will discuss career counseling programs in more detail later in this chapter.

The Consequences of Career Planning

When an organization does an effective job of career planning, both it and its employees can expect to achieve numerous benefits. As noted earlier, for example, effective career development and management can result in a more effective workforce and employees who are more motivated and satisfied with their organization. But the organization that engages in effective career management should also expect to achieve cost savings. A higher level of person-job fit should be achieved, with the resulting benefits of lower absenteeism, lower turnover, and a more satisfied and productive workforce. The organization's costs of identifying managers for promotion should be lowered because that identification is part of its regular and ongoing career development processes.

Individuals in organizations that handle career planning effectively should also achieve numerous benefits. They should have a better understanding of their place in the organization, and they should avoid the feelings of resentment or betrayal that occur when people expect to succeed and find out in fact that their organization sees them in a different light. In addition, they can make more informed decisions about alternative career options, educational opportunities, and so forth.

Even though career planning is important to both organizations and individuals, and effective career planning benefits both, everyone should also recognize that career planning has limitations and potential pitfalls. For example, no amount of sophisticated forecasting can predict with absolute certainty the level of talent, expertise, motivation, or interest a given individual will have in the future. People experience changes in interests, for example, and they may redefine their priorities. Even though the organization and the individual may expect that the individual will be capable of performing a certain job in the future, it may turn out that both parties are wrong.

The organization's future human resource needs can also change. For example, it may become more successful or less successful than it originally envisioned, or it may decide on new strategies to pursue. Or new managers may come in and want work done differently than in the past. And new opportunities may present themselves to both the individual and the organization. For instance, an organization may have a certain current member of its workforce who has been tapped to assume an important position in a couple of years. But a substantially stronger individual for that same position may unexpectedly emerge. In this case, the organization may have to alter its original strategy, even at the risk of alienating the individual originally tapped for the job.

Similarly, individuals sometimes find new opportunities at unexpected times. Both an individual and the organization, for instance, may expect that individual to take a certain job in the future. But another organization may appear on the scene to lure the individual away, perhaps at a substantially higher salary. In this instance, the individual is likely to be happy with this turn of events because he or she will have a new position and a higher salary. The organization, on the other hand, may face disruption and may have to alter its existing plans. Unanticipated mergers and acquisitions can also result in changes in career opportunities. For example, when Amoco was acquired by British Petroleum (BP) a few years ago, the new organization found itself with a surplus of qualified managers and had to offer early retirement incentives to some of them. Others were presented with unanticipated opportunities for new assignments that were substantially different from what they expected. For example, a senior Amoco manager based in Houston, Texas, had been on a career path that did not include the possibility of an international assignment. But shortly after the integration of the firms, this manager was offered a promotion to a new job in London.

Career Development Issues and Challenges

Regardless of the career stages for individual employees, many organizations who are sincerely interested in more effective career management for their employees deal with and address various issues and challenges. In this section we introduce and describe some of these issues and challenges in more detail.

Career Counseling Programs

As already noted, career counseling programs are important to an organization interested in career development for its employees. Such programs usually address a wide variety of career-related issues and are readily accessible to people in the organization. Some programs are formal while others are considerably informal.

Formal career counseling programs usually take the form of workshops, conferences, and career development centers. In some cases, the organization establishes general-purpose career counseling programs that are available to all employees. They may also create special programs targeted for certain categories of employees. Among the more popular special programs are counseling programs for fast-track managers, women managers, and minority managers. These special programs serve various purposes in addition to addressing the specific needs of certain categories of employees. They also help to integrate those employees into the mainstream of the overall organization, and they create important networking opportunities for these individuals.

Organizations also have informal counseling programs. Much of this counseling takes the form of one-on-one interactions between an employee and the employee's supervisor and typically occurs during the performance appraisal period. For example, when supervisors appraise and evaluate the performance of a subordinate and then provide performance feedback to that individual, part of the conversation also deals with issues such as promotion prospects, skill development, and so forth. Sometimes employees may simply drop by the human resource department for advice on career-related questions and issues. When drop-ins are common, it is important for the human resource department to fulfill its center of expertise role to be able to provide useful and accurate information.

Dual-Career and Work-Family Issues

Back in the 1950s and into the 1960s, most married couples in the United States were characterized by roles that gave the male partner's career precedence over the female partner's career. That is, the family tended to live where the husband needed to live. When the husband was given a job transfer, his decision to take it wasn't usually ques-

When a person reaches the midcareer stage, he or she is often faced with dual career challenges as well as work-family conflicts. Women especially are forced to deal with the conflicts between raising a family and managing a career. Liz Ryan, shown here with her five children, founded World Women in Technology (WorldWIT; www.worldWIT.org) to help them. The organization, which she runs from her home, has 20,000 members and forty discussion groups designed to help women deal with the conflicts between career and family. Ryan manages to juggle both WorldWIT and her own consulting business, which requires her to travel. Ryan says she hates the phrase "work-life balance" because it implies a stable state of equilibrium that no one ever really achieves.

tioned. And if the wife happened to be employed outside the home, it was assumed that she would resign from her job and that the family would move.

But as more and more women entered the workforce, primarily beginning in the mid- to late 1960s, this pattern changed substantially. For many married couples now the wife's career is on an equal footing with the husband's or perhaps may be given precedence over that of the husband. Thus, when organizations offer a transfer to an employee, they must be prepared to deal with the complexities associated with another career. The entire process of career planning must take into consideration the fact that another career must often be managed simultaneously.

Perhaps related to this trend is the growing concern over balancing family needs with the demands of work. As noted above, as dual-career and single-parent employment increases, these concerns pose yet another challenge to career management, especially in the midcareer stages.[54] First, concerns over family-friendly work practices (such as childcare, eldercare, and flexible work schedules) have an influence over the choices that employees make concerning where to work. In fact, many organizations are now advertising their family-friendly practices as a means of competing for employees.[55] Also, it is increasingly clear that concerns at home and with the family affect an employee's behavior at work. Stress over how to arrange for childcare or who will care for an ailing parent can cause the employee problems at work. Relieving these pressures allows the employee to concentrate more on the job and so more fully realize his or her career potential.[56]

Finally, evidence shows that work stressors influence family stress, which in turn is related to long-term health.[57] Thus, as the workforce becomes more diverse, organizations have to recognize that both dual-career issues and concerns over work-family balance will become increasingly important factors for determining career success and must be considered as part of career management. Some of these issues will be taken up in more detail later in this chapter.

Evaluating Career Management Activities

The ultimate goals of career management are to have employees reach their full potential at work, enjoy productive and satisfying work careers, and then make a successful transition to retirement. Full appreciation of career management activities on the part of the employee may not come until after retirement. But as employees are increasingly unlikely to spend their entire careers in a single organization, success in retirement is much more likely to be a function of the individual's own career management efforts (as well as the good fortune to remain healthy through the retirement years). For a large number of employees, especially those in higher-status jobs or those for whom work is an important part of self-image, leaving one's career does not mean the end of work. For these employees, managing the transition to what have been called "bridge" jobs (and eventually to full retirement) is most important for their continued satisfaction.[58]

Therefore, career management activities can be judged only by their success at any one point in time. If an employee is satisfied with his or her career at this point, then career management must be judged successful up to that point. We have focused primarily on actions the organization can take to manage this process, but clearly a great deal also depends on the employee's efforts at managing his or her career. Employees who go into careers for which they are not well suited (either in terms of abilities or temperament) will obviously be more likely to suffer dissatisfaction with their careers.

Although organizational career management efforts are important, the successful management of one's career depends heavily on the employee's efforts to assess his or her own abilities and interests accurately and to formulate a plan for what a successful career should look like.

Chapter Summary

Performance appraisal and career management are two tools used by organizations to begin the process of performance improvement. Performance appraisal is the specific and formal evaluation of an employee conducted to determine the degree to which the employee is performing his or her job effectively. Careers are the set of experiences that one has through his or her work life. The management of that career is critical for employee development.

Performance appraisals are important because they ensure that recruiting and selection processes are adequate, play an important role in training, can help link performance with rewards, demonstrate that important employment-related decisions are based on performance, and can promote employee motivation and development. They also provide valuable and useful information to the organization's human resource planning process. The ultimate goal for any organization using performance appraisals is to improve performance on the job.

The organization, primarily through the work of its human resource function, develops the general performance appraisal process, including issues of timing, for its managers and employees to use. The organization is also responsible for ensuring that clear and specific performance standards are available to managers and employees.

Both the rater and the ratee have specific responsibilities. Raters can include the supervisor, peers, colleagues, coworkers, subordinates of the individual being appraised, the individual him- or herself, and customers and clients. When all of these raters are used, the appraisal is called 360-degree feedback.

Several methods can be used to assess performance, ranging from ranking systems to rating systems employing Behaviorally Anchored Rating Scales (BARS), Behavioral Observation Scales (BOS), and goal-based or management-by-objectives systems. All of these methods are subject to one or more weaknesses or deficiencies, and no system is ideal for all settings. Also, regardless of the approach used, once the appraisal is completed, the next major activity is the provision of feedback to the employee, in the hopes of improving performance and guiding the employee's self-development. Part of that self-development must be focused on career management.

A career is the set of experiences and activities that people engage in related to their job and livelihood over the course of their working life. Traditionally, individuals were seen as progressing through a series of career stages that include exploration, establishment, maintenance, and disengagement. A more recent perspective refocuses career stages on career age and acknowledges the likelihood of multiple careers, and this more recent perspective also recognizes that retirement is a part of the career progression.

Successful careers don't just happen; they must be planned and managed by both the organization and the individual employee. Career planning requires careful coordination between individual employees and the organization itself. Even though career planning is important and beneficial to both organizations and individuals, everyone should also recognize that career planning has limitations and potential pitfalls.

In many ways, the early career stages faced by an individual are the most tumultuous. Regardless of whether they are taking their first jobs or whether they are moving into one job after a long period of employment elsewhere, new entrants into an organization always feel a certain degree of uncertainty and apprehension about their new employer. Thus, an important starting point for human resource managers interested in managing the careers of their employees more effectively is understanding some of the early career problems that such employees often encounter.

After an individual completes the first few years of a job successfully, many of the early career problems may have been addressed. But some problems still loom on the horizon for these individuals once they reach the midcareer stage. The most common midcareer problem faced by most individuals in corporations today is what is generally referred to as the midcareer plateau.

In the latter stages of a person's career, it is perhaps

even more important for the organization to provide career management services. Many of these services try to solve the problems people face in the later stages of their careers. Many of these problems revolve around issues associated with retirement.

Regardless of the career stage of each employee, many organizations that are sincerely interested in more effective career management for their employees deal with and address various issues and challenges. Career counseling programs are important to an organization interested in career development for its employees. Such programs usually address a wide variety of career-related issues and are readily accessible to people in the organization. Dual-career and work-family issues are also an important part of today's career management activities and concerns.

The success of career management activities can only be judged according to their success at any one point in time. If an employee is satisfied with his or her career at one point, then career management must be judged successful up to that point.

Key Points for Future HR Managers

- Performance appraisal serves several purposes in organizations, but the primary purpose for conducting appraisals is to improve employee performance and thus improve organizational effectiveness.

- The rater in the appraisal process has the ultimate responsibility for how well an appraisal system works, and raters can and do distort appraisals.

- Raters can be chosen from several sources, but ideally the person best able to assess performance in an area should be the person to conduct the appraisal.

- Multisource or 360-degree appraisals combine ratings data from multiple sources. Although these appraisals are potentially useful for feedback purposes, they are problematic when used for decision making, and no evidence exists to suggest that these appraisals are more effective than alternative methods. It is clear, however, that 360-degree appraisals are more costly to conduct.

- Performance appraisals can focus on behaviors, traits, or outcomes. Although each can provide useful information, appraisals designed around outcomes, stated in terms of goals, may be more useful than others.

- Teams provide a real challenge for performance appraisals, and in some cases it is best to assess the team. In other cases, it is best to assess individual team members.

- Many alternative methods are available for the actual design of an appraisal system. Years of research have indicated no clear advantage to any of these methods, with the possible exception of goal-based appraisals.

- It is important to consider the role of contextual performance in the appraisal context. Although this approach refers to behaviors that are not formally evaluated, they are also behaviors that are critical for the organization.

- Several appraisal errors, such as halo error, are commonly discussed, but it is no longer clear that these are truly errors, or that organizations should exert a great deal of effort to reduce them.

- Regardless of the appraisal system used, performance management is critical to achieve the most important goal for the process—the improvement of performance, and this process begins with providing feedback to the employee.

- The nature of careers is changing, but it is still important to recognize that effective human resource management requires career planning, not just filling jobs.

- Dual-career and work-family issues will remain the most challenging aspects of career planning in the new century.

Key Points for Future General Managers

- Appraisal systems should always be designed so that they have the greatest likelihood of improving individual and organizational performance.

- Raters must be convinced that it is in their best interests to be fair and accurate in appraisals. No type of system can replace rater motivation to do a good job.

- Although 360-degree appraisals are popular, evidence does not support their effectiveness relative to other, less expensive methods, and it is problematic to use 360-degree appraisals for decision making.

- In team settings, decisions must be made about whether appraisals and feedback should focus on the whole team or on individual members.

- Contextual performance refers to those behaviors that we do not evaluate formally but that must occur for the organization to function effectively. Decisions have to be made about how to treat contextual performance.

- Clear evidence shows that one appraisal system is not more effective than any other type of appraisal system, although there is some reason to believe that goal-based systems may offer some advantages over the alternatives.

- Feedback does not always have the desired effect on performance. Sometimes providing feedback can hurt subsequent performance.

- Although the traditional career may be dead, it is still critical to think through and plan an employee's entire career and help the employee to manage that career.

Review and Discussion Questions

1. Identify and briefly describe the basic steps in performance appraisal.

2. What are the basic goals of performance appraisal?

3. Summarize the roles of the organization, the rater, and the ratee in performance appraisal.

4. Who are the most common raters in the performance appraisal process?

5. Identify and critique the basic methods for performance appraisal.

6. How might feedback interviews and meetings be conducted most effectively?

7. What is a career?

8. Compare and contrast the traditional and emerging career models. Which model are you most comfortable with? Why?

9. If you are soon becoming a new career entrant, what issues are you most concerned about? How might an employer help you deal with these issues?

10. Would you like to have an international assignment as part of your career? What issues and concerns might you have about such a possibility?

CLOSING CASE

Accelerated Performance Reviews May Improve Retention

Most organizations have traditionally conducted performance appraisals for everyone on a routine schedule, either once a year near the anniversary of each employee's hiring date or during one common period when everyone was evaluated. A schedule was especially true for new employees, who were told at the start of their employment when their first review would be. Part of the logic underlying this system was that newcomers were considered to be on probation until their first review. In addition, organizations felt that new employees might need an extended period of time to learn their jobs and to have a reasonable time in which to establish their capabilities.

From the standpoint of the newcomers themselves, they often saw value in the recognition that they had ample time to learn their jobs before they would be evaluated. On the other hand, they also knew that, because increased compensation and/or promotions are usually tied to perfor-

mance appraisals, they had little opportunity to seek a pay raise or to be given greater job responsibilities until that first review had been completed. Thus, the standard review cycle had both pluses and minuses for new employees.

In recent years, though, this cycle has been gradually altered in some firms. And this change has come about in large part because of the tight labor market in certain areas, especially rapidly growing high-tech firms. Because the highly skilled workers these firms need are well aware of their value to prospective employers, some of the more enterprising and self-assured candidates have started requesting—or in some cases demanding—promises of earlier reviews to have an opportunity to ratchet up their salaries more quickly. The practice of early reviews has also started spreading outside the high-tech environment to include areas such as banks, accounting firms, and insurance companies.

These firms are finding that by offering earlier reviews,

they have a better chance of landing the top prospects. A guaranteed review after six months is rapidly become an expectation in the eyes of some of the most promising recruits. For example, one recent survey of executive search firms found that over 27 percent of new management positions currently being filled come with the assurance of an initial six-month review. But one factor that is often overlooked in this trend is that the recruit still has to ask for the earlier performance review. If he or she does not, the company is likely to stick with its normal one-year cycle.

So, can the cycle take place any faster? Absolutely. For example, consider the case of software programmer David Parvin, a recent college graduate courted by Cougar Mountain Software, a Boise, Idaho, company. Parvin learned that Cougar Mountain provided performance reviews of its new hires after thirty days. But Parvin wanted it even faster, so he demanded a two-week review. And sure enough, during his first two weeks on the job, he so impressed his bosses that they gave him a 7.1 percent pay raise. During his first eighteen months on the job, he continued to request frequent reviews, earning a total of six raises and one major promotion.

While this cycle may seem extreme, one reason it has worked is that Cougar Mountain has a history of rapid reviews. Indeed, about 10 percent of its new hires get a raise after thirty days, and almost all get a raise within three months. The firm's managers also believe that this practice helps Cougar Mountain retain its most valuable employees. In an industry with extremely high turnover, Cougar Mountain's turnover among all its employees is only about 10 percent; among its very best employees, it is an incredible 1 percent.

Of course, this approach can also create some problems. In addition to the extra administrative time and expense needed to manage such an appraisal and salary adjustment system, potential morale problems can occur with other employees. To address this concern, some companies require those who will be getting frequent reviews to keep their arrangement a secret in the hope of avoiding problems with other employees. But word is still likely to get out, especially if more than just a few new employees are getting this special attention.

For the future, there seems to be a difference of opinion about whether or not this practice will continue. Some experts predict that as soon as the tight labor market begins to loosen (for example, when firms stop adding new jobs), firms will quickly move to drop the frequent review process. Others believe just the opposite will occur, and that firms may well come to value the flexibility that this system affords and will want to apply it to everyone. That is, as long as they review and reward their highly valued workers on an accelerated schedule, they may be able to slow the process for less valued workers. Thus, a well-established worker with a history of being judged as adequate may be evaluated even less frequently—and get fewer raises—than is the case today.[59]

Case Questions

1. What do you see as the advantages and disadvantages of frequent performance appraisals?

2. Under what circumstances would you envision wanting more frequent reviews? Under what circumstances would you prefer just the opposite?

3. What is your prediction about the future of rapid performance appraisal cycles?

Building HR Management Skills

 Purpose: The purpose of this exercise is to help you develop insights into the process of developing performance appraisal methods and systems. As background, conceptualize how performance appraisal works in a typical course such as the one you are taking now: the instructor is the rater and the students are the ratees. Instructors generally use some combination of exams, tests, papers, cases, and/or class participation as the basis for evaluation and then provide the formal appraisal in the form of a letter grade.

Step 1: Your instructor will ask you to form small groups of four to five members.

Step 2: Working with your group members, develop three alternative methods that an instructor might use to evaluate your performance. Try to match your methods to those discussed in this chapter whenever possible.

Step 3: Evaluate each method you developed in terms of its potential usefulness. Identify the strengths and weaknesses of each method relative to the traditional system.

Step 4: Discuss and develop responses for the following questions:

1. What barriers might exist to the adoption of one of the new methods you developed?

2. What limitations characterize the traditional system? Do any of your methods overcome these limitations?

3. At your school, do students evaluate instructors? If so, how might the current method be improved?

4. Does 360-degree feedback have any relevance in the classroom?

Ethical Dilemmas in HR Management

 Assume that you are a marketing executive in a major corporation. You need to hire a new staff member to fill a position that has just been created. The members of your current staff are not interested in the position, do not have the requisite skills for the position, or already have comparable or better positions. Thus, the person you select will come from outside your work group.

You have asked the human resource department to help identify three possible candidates from inside the organization. You have met with each of these people and thoroughly reviewed their educational backgrounds, experience, performance appraisals, career paths, and other qualifications. You have eliminated one person because of lack of fit, but you now face a complicated decision between the other two. Specifically, you see them as relatively equal in terms of potential. The real problem, however, is one of diversity and equal opportunity.

One candidate is a black female. You are personally committed to equal opportunity for minorities and have a reputation for helping members of protected classes whenever appropriate. You are familiar with this candidate's current boss. You see that the candidate has received performance appraisals consistently in the range of 3.8–4.2 on your firm's 5-point rating scales. But because of your knowledge of her boss, you know that these numbers really mean that her performance has been in the range of 4.2–4.6 (her boss rates everyone on the low side—in your opinion, about 0.4 point below where others would rate them).

The other candidate is a white male. This individual's performance appraisal ratings have been in the range of 4.0–4.4. You also know this person's boss very well, and believe that these scores are pretty accurate as is because his boss always does a fair, objective, and equitable job in her performance appraisals.

Your dilemma is whether to select the white male on the basis of the numbers or to select the black female on the basis of what you think the numbers really mean. While you have the authority to make this decision yourself, you also want to make sure that you can defend it in the event that the individual not selected questions how and why you chose the other individual for the position.

Questions

1. What are the ethical issues in this situation?

2. What are the basic arguments for and against selecting each candidate?

3. What do you think most managers would do? What would you do?

HR Internet Exercise

@ Many different human resource consulting firms offer services in the area of performance appraisal, including advice on how to install systems, how to use 360-degree feedback, forms to use, and so forth. Assume that you have just taken the position of senior human resource executive for a large manufacturing business and believe that its current performance appraisal system is inadequate. Your plan is to scrap the current system and replace it with a new one. Because you are both quite busy with other problems and also have little direct experience with performance appraisal yourself, you are interested in engaging the services of a consulting firm to help.

Using a search engine, search the Web for the following key terms: *performance appraisal, performance assessment, performance management,* and any other version of the term that you think is appropriate. Locate several consulting firms that might offer the services you need.

Review each site thoroughly, and then narrow your list to the three most promising. Finally, list the additional information you want to have before selecting one.

Questions

1. What role does the Internet serve when selecting a consulting firm for a purpose such as the one described above?

2. How realistic do you think the information on the Web is for reviewing and selecting a service provider for the purpose described above?

3. Compare notes with your classmates and see if any of you chose some of the same firms. Compare your evaluations of each.

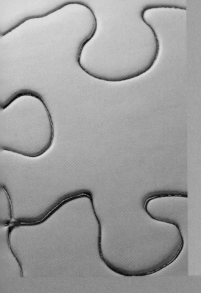

11

Managing Labor Relations

CHAPTER OBJECTIVES

After studying this chapter you should be able to:

■ Describe the role of labor unions in organizations.

■ Identify and summarize trends in unionization.

■ Discuss the unionization process.

■ Describe the collective-bargaining process.

■ Discuss how labor agreements are negotiated.

■ Summarize how labor agreements are administered.

■ Discuss labor unions and social issues.

Sometimes it takes three, not two, to tango. Management and a large labor union (the "two") recently needed federal intervention (the "third") to partially cajole and partially coerce them to reach a labor agreement. The two key parties in the conflict were the International Longshore and Warehouse Union and the Pacific Maritime Association (representing twenty-nine West Coast ports). The problems began when their labor agreement was coming to an end and a new one was being discussed.

According to the port association, as a new labor contract was being negotiated, the union instructed its workers to begin a systematic work slowdown to improve its bargaining position. The union, for its part, argued that it simply told its members to work in strict accordance with all existing safety and health rules because the employers were bargaining in bad faith. In response, the port association imposed a lockout, which prevented all port workers from getting to their job sites.

> *"It's a disaster. Our Christmas merchandise . . . is sitting in boats or over in Asia."*
>
> (Robin Lanier, spokesperson for Target)*

The resulting chaos was near-disastrous for the U.S. economy, which was struggling at the time. Foreign automobile parts sat on ships, forcing several assembly plants to be idle. Toys and other holiday merchandise bound for retailers across the country sat in cargo hulls. And fruits, vegetables, and other perishables began to rot. Finally, after ten days, President Bush invoked federal legislation to force the ports to reopen, and a federal mediator stepped in to help the two sides reach an agreement.

Eventually, as the year drew to a close, the two sides began to compromise with the help of the federal mediator. The resulting agreement increased worker pension benefits and required employers to pay all insurance costs for the workers. But the ports also received union authorization to develop new productivity-enhancing technologies and to cut 400 marine clerk jobs. And early the next year the union members voted overwhelmingly to accept a new five-year contract.[1]

The Pacific Maritime Association and its managers had to contend with one of the most significant challenges facing many businesses today—dealing with organized labor in ways that optimize the needs and priorities of both the business and its employees. When this challenge is handled effectively and constructively, both sides benefit. But when relationships between an organization and its unions turn sour, both sides can suffer great costs. In the chapter-opening vignette, workers lost ten days of income. The ports also lost millions of dollars in revenues, and the shock waves spread across several different industries.

In this chapter, we focus on the management of labor relations. We start by assessing the role of labor unions in organizations. We examine trends in unionization and describe the unionization process itself. Collective bargaining is discussed, followed by a description of the issues involved in negotiating labor agreements, and the chapter closes with a discussion of the administration of labor agreements.

The Role of Labor Unions in Organizations

Labor relations *is the process of dealing with employees who are represented by a union.*

A **labor union** *is a legally constituted group of individuals working together to achieve shared, job-related goals, including higher pay and shorter working hours.*

Collective bargaining *is the process by which managers and union leaders negotiate acceptable terms and conditions of employment for those workers represented by the unions.*

Labor relations can be defined as the process of dealing with employees who are represented by a union. A **labor union,** in turn, is a legally constituted group of individuals working together to achieve shared job-related goals. As we will see later, these goals often include issues such as higher wages, enhanced benefits, and/or better working conditions. **Collective bargaining,** a specific aspect of labor relations discussed more fully later in this chapter, is the process by which managers and union leaders negotiate acceptable terms and conditions of employment for those workers represented by the unions.[2] Although *collective bargaining* is a term that technically and properly is applied only in settings where employees are unionized, similar processes, of course, often exist in nonunionized settings as well. In these cases, however, they are likely to be labeled employee relations rather than labor relations.

Historical Development of Unions

Figure 11.1 shows the major historical events in the emergence and growth of labor unions in the United States. Indeed, the historical formation of labor unions closely parallels the history of the country itself. For example, the earliest unions in the United States emerged during the Revolutionary War. These unions were called craft unions. By "craft unions" we mean that each such union limited itself to representing groups of workers who performed common and specific skilled jobs. For example, one of the first unions—the Journeyman Cordwainers Society of Philadelphia—was formed by shoemakers in Philadelphia in 1794. The union's goal was to enhance the pay and working conditions of all shoemakers.

Many of the earliest unions were localized in nature and often confined their activities to a single setting. But in 1834 the first national unions in the United States began to emerge. Throughout the remainder of the nineteenth century, one major union after another began to appear. Among the most significant were the National Typographical Union in 1852, the United Cigar Makers in 1856, and the National Iron Molders in 1859. The nineteenth century ended with thirty national unions, with a combined membership of around 300,000 individuals.

The **Knights of Labor** *was an important early union that expanded its goals and its membership to include workers in numerous fields rather than a single industry.*

The first major union to have a significant impact in the United States, however, was the **Knights of Labor,** which was founded in 1869. Like most other unions, the Knights

FIGURE 11.1   A Historical Time Line of Unionization in the United States

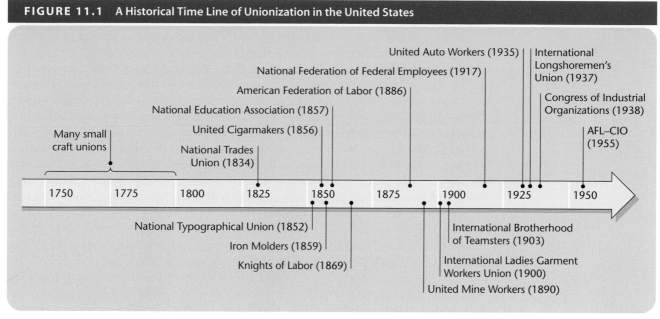

Source: Ricky Griffin and Ronald Ebert, *Business*, 3rd ed., Copyright © 2000. Reprinted by permission of Pearson Education, Upper Saddle River, NJ.

originally represented crafts and sought to improve the lot of its members. But unlike most other national unions that restricted their organizing activities to a single craft or job, the Knights of Labor expanded its goals and its membership to include workers in numerous fields. Their objective was quite simple—the leaders of the Knights of Labor believed that if they could control (or represent) the entire supply of skilled labor in the United States, their ability to negotiate favorable wages would be significantly enhanced. Members joined the Knights directly, as opposed to a later model where members joined a separate union that was affiliated with other more specific unions loosely coordinated under an umbrella organization.

The Noble and Holy Order of the Knights of Labor (the union's full name) admitted anyone to membership, regardless of race or creed (which typically were important considerations for membership in unions at the time), except for those they considered to be "social parasites" (such as bankers). In addition to improving wages, the Knights of Labor sought to replace capitalism with worker cooperatives. The union enjoyed incredible growth for several years, growing from 52,000 members in 1883 to 700,000 members in 1886. But internal strife about goals and disagreement over what should replace the capitalist model all led to the eventual demise of the Knights of Labor. The single event that contributed most to its demise, however, was a mass meeting in Chicago's Haymarket Square on May 4, 1886. The meeting was held to protest some earlier violence stemming from an attempt to establish an eight-hour workday. When the May 4 meeting was over, further violence left 200 wounded and resulted in the hanging of several leaders of the Knights. By the end of the century, the Knights of Labor had all but disappeared from the labor scene.

Even as the Knights of Labor union was dying, however, its replacement was already beginning to gather strength. The **American Federation of Labor (AF of L)** was founded in 1886 by Samuel Gompers. Like the Knights of Labor, the American Federation of Labor was composed of various craft unions. Unlike the Knights of Labor, the AF of L sought not to get involved in legislative and political activities, but instead focused its efforts on improved working conditions and better employment contracts. Also unlike the Knights

The **American Federation of Labor (AF of L)** *was another early union; it focused its efforts on improved working conditions and better employment contracts rather than getting involved in legislative and political activities.*

of Labor, the AF of L served as an umbrella organization, with members joining individual unions affiliated with the AF of L, as opposed to joining the AF of L itself.

While the AF of L focused exclusively on the "business" of unions, several more radical and violent union movements developed after the demise of the Knights of Labor. For example, under the leadership of Eugene V. Debs, the American Railway Union (ARU) battled the railroads (especially the Pullman Company—of Pullman car fame), mostly over wages, and many people were killed during strike violence. Debs also became a leader of the Socialist Party and actually ran for president of the United States on the Socialist ticket in 1920. The Industrial Workers of the World consisted mostly of unskilled workers and advocated extreme violence as a means of settling labor disputes. The mining companies and textile mill owners with which they battled also believed in violence as a means of settling labor disputes, and many people were killed during strikes organized by the "Wobblies," as they were called. The union's opposition to U.S. involvement in World War I led to its being prosecuted for treason and most of the leaders being jailed.

For the more mainstream organized labor movement, many of these fringe groups were too radical, and workers preferred the businesslike approach of the AF of L. As a result, the AF of L grew rapidly throughout the early decades of the twentieth century. Indeed, by the end of World War I, it had a total membership of more than 5 million individuals. Over the next several years, however, membership in the AF of L began to decline, and by the mid-1930s its membership stood at approximately 2.9 million members.

One of the weaknesses of the AF of L was its continued focus on crafts. That is, only skilled craftspersons performing specifically defined jobs were allowed to join. During the 1930s, however, a new kind of unionization began to emerge that focused on industrial unionization. Rather than organizing workers across companies or across industries based on their craft, this new type of union activity focused on organizing employees by industry, regardless of their craft, skills, or occupation.

Another important early union was the **Congress of Industrial Organizations (CIO),** *which focused on organizing employees by industry, regardless of their craft, skills, or occupation.*

In the late 1930s, John L. Lewis of the United Mine Workers led a dissenting faction of the AF of L to form a new labor organization called the **Congress of Industrial Organizations (CIO).** The CIO was the first major representative of the new approach to unionization noted above. The CIO quickly began to organize the automobile, steel, mining, meatpacking, paper, textile, and electrical industries. By the early 1940s, CIO unions had almost 5 million members.

In the years following World War II, union memberships in the AF of L and the CIO, as well as other unions, gradually increased. However, a series of bitter strikes during that same era also led to public resentment and calls for union reform. And Congress did indeed intervene to curtail the power of unions. The AF of L and the CIO then began to contemplate a merger as a way of consolidating their strength. Eventually, in 1955, the AFL-CIO was formed, with a total membership of around 15 million employees. In 2005, however, citing unhappiness with the strategic direction of the AFL-CIO, two of its largest member unions, the Service Employees International Union and the International Brotherhood of Teamsters, withdrew from the parent organization and set out on their own.[3]

Overall, union membership since 1955 has been quite erratic, and we will discuss that fact more fully in the next section. The *Point/Counterpoint* feature for this chapter highlights some of the basic arguments for and against the viability of unions today and sheds some light on the question of whether or not unions still have a role in contemporary society. Next, we will examine the legal context of unions and common union structures.

Legal Context of Unions

Partly because of the tumultuous history of labor unions in the United States, various laws and other regulations have been passed. Some are intended to promote unionization and union activities, while others are intended to limit or curtail union activities,

The legal context of labor unions is an important backdrop for all labor relations. Moreover, this context is strongly rooted in the historical evolution of labor relations. For example, the Taft-Hartley Act (more formally known as the Labor Management Relations Act) was passed in 1947 to curtail and limit certain union practices. These protesters are members of the International Ladies' Garment Workers Union. They are picketing nonunion garment shops in downtown Los Angeles in 1948 as a demonstration of their strength. Some of their signs are clearly directed at the Taft-Hartley Act and Taft himself. But the law remains intact and still plays an important role in labor relations today.

but early legislation simply dealt with the question of whether or not unions were legal. As early as 1806, the local courts in Philadelphia declared the Cordwainers to be, by its very existence, in restraint of trade and thus illegal. This Cordwainer Doctrine, as it became known, dominated the law's view of unions until 1843, when the Massachusetts Supreme Court, in *Commonwealth* v. *Hunt,* ruled that unions were not by their very nature in restraint of trade but that this issue had to be proven in each individual case. This court decision led to increased union activity, but organizations responded by simply firing union organizers. After the Sherman Antitrust Act was passed in 1890, businesses once again sought (successfully) court injunctions against unions for restraint of trade. By the 1920s organizations also sought to identify union leaders as communists to reduce public sympathy toward them and to give the government an excuse to control the unions.

By the end of the 1920s, the country was in the grip of the Great Depression and the government soon intervened in an attempt to end work stoppages and start the economy on the road to recovery. The first significant piece of legislation was the **National Labor Relations Act,** which was passed in 1935. This act is more commonly referred to as the **Wagner Act** and still forms the cornerstone of contemporary labor relations law; it was discussed earlier in Chapter 2. The basic purpose of the Wagner Act was to grant power to labor unions and to put unions on a more equal footing with managers in terms of the rights of employees. It gives workers the legal right to form unions, to bargain collectively with management, and to engage in group activities such as strikes to accomplish their goals. This act also forces employers to bargain with properly elected

*The **National Labor Relations Act,** passed in 1935 and more commonly referred to as the **Wagner Act,** granted power to labor unions and put unions on a more equal footing with managers in terms of the rights of employees.*

Are Labor Unions Still Necessary?

Labor unions were initially formed to try to equalize the power between labor and management. Because management controlled more resources, labor had power only if individual workers united in a concerted effort. This approach allowed workers to enjoy the rights they deserved and to deal with management as equals. Some people claim that unions have become too powerful and too interested in political agendas that are not always in the country's best interests. Others simply argue that labor is now the equal of management, and because effective management requires granting workers power and discretion, unions are simply no longer needed.

POINT... Labor unions are no longer needed in the United States because...	**COUNTERPOINT...** But labor unions still serve an important function and so are needed because...
Employees already have clear rights, and nonunion companies often offer better pay and conditions than do unionized companies.	Employees without unions have only the rights management chooses to grant, rather than the rights the workers might actually deserve. Would nonunion companies offer those levels of pay and benefits without the continued threat of unionization?
Unions raise pay without regarding costs and so hurt U.S. competitiveness.	What is the good of improving competitive position if it comes at the cost of jobs and fair pay for U.S. employees?
Unions are largely corrupt.	Many unions do have a history of corruption, but extensive efforts have been aimed at cleaning up this problem.
Union leaders pursue political agendas that are at odds with the interests of their members.	Individual workers often see only their own interests and don't understand how some policies can hurt other workers; thus, in the long run, they hurt themselves as well.
Unions interfere with more progressive management efforts aimed at improving competitiveness in international markets.	Union-management cooperation has led to situations where competitive advantage has been gained. The auto company Saturn claims that cooperation with the UAW has led to lower production costs and better quality—sources of competitive advantage. The key is to get unions involved in decision making.

So... It is reasonable to suggest that unions still have a function, and the threat of unionization probably continues to play a role in management decisions to implement more enlightened policies. But the role of unions will probably need to change (and already is changing). Unions need to become strategic partners with management to help ensure that U.S. companies survive and prosper—which is in everyone's best interest. But unions must also continue to fight for employee rights and to serve as the voice of employees who believe they have been wronged by management. It will be interesting to see how unions change, or whether they even manage to do so. If they do not adapt, they may well become obsolete.

union leaders and prohibits employers from engaging in certain unfair labor practices, including discriminating against union members in hiring, firing, and promotion.

The Wagner Act also established the **National Labor Relations Board (NLRB)** to administer its provisions. Today the NLRB still administers most labor law in the United States. For example, it defines the units with which managers must collectively bargain and it oversees most elections held by employees that will determine whether or not they will be represented by a union.

The **National Labor Relations Board (NLRB)** *administers most labor law in the United States.*

In the previous section, we noted congressional activity in the years following World War II that curtailed the power of the unions. The most important piece of legislation in this era was the **Labor Management Relations Act,** also known as the **Taft-Hartley Act,** which was passed in 1947. This act was a response to public outcries against a wide variety of strikes in the years following World War II. The basic purpose of the Taft-Hartley Act was to curtail and limit union practices. For example, the Taft-Hartley Act specifically prohibits practices such as requiring extra workers solely as a means to provide more jobs and refusing to bargain with management in good faith. It also outlawed an arrangement called the **closed shop,** which refers to a workplace in which only workers who are already union members may be hired by the employer.

The **Labor Management Relations Act,** *also known as the* **Taft-Hartley Act,** *was passed in 1947 in response to public outcries against a wide variety of strikes in the years following World War II; it curtailed and limited union powers.*

A **closed shop** *refers to a workplace in which only workers who are already union members may be hired by the employer.*

Section 7 of the Taft-Hartley Act also allowed states, if they wished, to restrict union security clauses such as closed-shop agreements. Roughly twenty states took advantage of this opportunity and passed laws that also outlawed **union shop agreements** (where a nonunion member can be hired but must join the union within a specified time to keep his or her job) and various other types of union security agreements. These laws are known as right-to-work laws, and the states that have adopted them (located predominantly in the Southeast) are known as right-to-work states.[4]

A **union shop agreement** *includes various types of union security agreements in addition to a requirement that a nonunion member can be hired, but he or she must join the union within a specified time to keep his or her job.*

The Taft-Hartley Act also established procedures for resolving strikes deemed threatening to the national interest. For example, the president of the United States has the authority under the Taft-Hartley Act to request an injunction to prohibit workers from striking for sixty days. The idea is that, during this so-called cooling-off period, labor and management stand a greater chance of resolving their differences. For example, in February 1997 the union representing the pilots at American Airlines announced that its members had voted to strike. Within minutes of this announcement, President Clinton invoked the Taft-Hartley Act and ordered the union to cancel its strike. His argument was that American Airlines is the nation's largest air carrier and a shutdown would be extremely detrimental to national interests. In addition, the Taft-Hartley Act extended the powers of the NLRB. For example, following passage of the act, the NLRB was also given the power to regulate unfair union practices.

A final significant piece of legislation affecting labor relations is the **Landrum-Griffin Act,** which was passed in 1959, and was also discussed in Chapter 2. Officially called the **Labor Management Reporting and Disclosure Act,** this law focused on eliminating various unethical, illegal, and undemocratic union practices. For instance, the Landrum-Griffin Act requires that national labor unions elect new leaders at least once every five years, and that convicted felons cannot hold national union office (which is why Jimmy Hoffa was removed as president of the Teamsters union). It also requires unions to file annual financial statements with the Department of Labor. And finally, the Landrum-Griffin Act stipulates that unions provide certain information regarding their internal management and finances to all members.

The **Landrum-Griffin Act** *(officially called the* **Labor Management Reporting and Disclosure Act***) was passed in 1959 and focused on eliminating various unethical, illegal, and undemocratic union practices.*

Union Structures

All organizations have their own unique structure, and so do large labor unions. But most unions have some basic structural characteristics in common. Figure 11.2 shows the basic structure of most unions. The cornerstone of most labor unions, regardless of

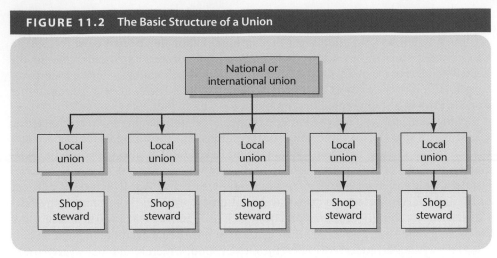

FIGURE 11.2   The Basic Structure of a Union

Source: Ricky Griffin and Ronald Ebert, *Business,* 3rd ed. Copyright © 2000. Reprinted by permission of Pearson Education, Upper Saddle River, NJ.

Locals   *are unions organized at the level of a single company, plant, or small geographic region.*

The **shop steward,**   *an elected position in a local union, is a regular employee who functions as a liaison between union members and supervisors.*

their size, is the local union, more frequently referred to as a local. **Locals** are unions organized at the level of a single company, plant, or small geographic region. Each local has an important elected position called the shop steward. The **shop steward** is a regular employee who also functions as a liaison between union members and supervisors.

Local unions are usually clustered by geographic region and coordinated by a regional officer. These regional officers in turn report to and are part of a national governing board of the labor union. The national affairs of a large union are generally governed by an executive board and a president. These individuals are usually elected by members of the union themselves. This election takes place at an annual national convention that all union members are invited to and are encouraged to attend.

The president is almost always a full-time union employee and may earn as much money as the senior manager of a business. The executive board functions much more like a board of directors and is generally composed of individuals who serve on the board in addition to their normal duties as employees of an organization. Just as a large business has various auxiliary departments (such as a public relations and a legal department), so too do large national unions have auxiliary departments. These auxiliary departments may handle issues such as the legal affairs of the union. They may oversee collective bargaining issues and may provide assistance and services to the local unions as requested and needed.

Trends in Unionization

While understanding the historical, legal, and structural context of labor unions is important, so too is an appreciation of other trends regarding union membership, union-management relations, and bargaining perspectives. These topics are each discussed in the sections that follow. *HR in the 21st Century* also describes some interesting trends in unionization.

Trends in Union Membership

Since the mid-1950s labor unions in the United States have experienced increasing difficulty in attracting new members. While millions of U.S. workers still belong to labor unions, union membership as a percentage of the total workforce has continued to decline at a steady rate. For example, in 1977, over 26 percent of U.S. wage and salary employees belonged to labor unions. But today, that figure is about 12.5 percent of those workers. If government employees are excluded from consideration, then less than 10 percent of all wage and salary employees in private industry currently belong to labor unions. Yet, it is interesting to note that membership figures essentially remained steady from 2004 to 2005. Although it is too early to know if the trend in membership declines is ending (or even reversing), it does suggest that unions are by no means "dead." These union membership trends are shown in Figure 11.3.

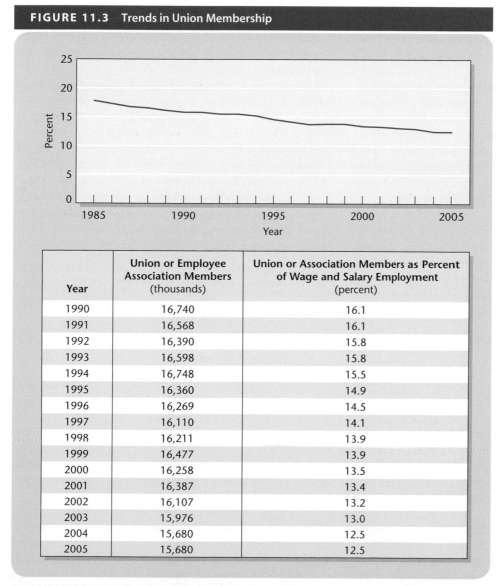

FIGURE 11.3   Trends in Union Membership

Year	Union or Employee Association Members (thousands)	Union or Association Members as Percent of Wage and Salary Employment (percent)
1990	16,740	16.1
1991	16,568	16.1
1992	16,390	15.8
1993	16,598	15.8
1994	16,748	15.5
1995	16,360	14.9
1996	16,269	14.5
1997	16,110	14.1
1998	16,211	13.9
1999	16,477	13.9
2000	16,258	13.5
2001	16,387	13.4
2002	16,107	13.2
2003	15,976	13.0
2004	15,680	12.5
2005	15,680	12.5

Source: U.S. Department of Labor, Bureau of Labor Statistics, 2006.

HR IN THE 21ST CENTURY

Emerging Trends in Unionization

As noted in the text, unionization among U.S. workers has been on the decline for some time and will probably continue in that direction for the foreseeable future. Although unionization in the service sector of the economy has increased, this trend has been more than offset in the rest of the economy. Will unions disappear? Probably not, but they may look different in the next century than they have looked in the past. For example, some experts suggest that a basic transformation in unionism and the relationship between unions and management is already taking place. And nowhere is this more evident than in the U.S. automobile industry.

"... [S]ome experts suggest that a basic transformation in unionism and the relationship between unions and management is already taking place."

One major reason often cited for the lack of global competitiveness by U.S. automakers is high labor costs. Over a period of decades, companies like Ford and General Motors routinely agreed to higher wages and more lucrative benefits in order to avoid costly strikes. But because foreign competitors—especially those in Asia—have maintained lower labor costs, they can make automobiles for $2,000–$4,000 cheaper than can their American competitors.

Ford, in particular, has had to become increasingly inventive to address this problem. On the one hand, the firm has desperately needed to lower its labor costs; but on the other hand, its powerful unions have negotiated such high levels of job security that Ford has found it difficult to either lower wage and benefits costs or to reduce the size of its workforce. But a recent—and dramatic—development may allow the firm to turn the corner.

Working in concert with the UAW and its other unions, Ford devised eight different plans under which it could basically "buy out" workers and end their employment with the company. One option was for workers to accept a one-time cash payment ranging from $35,000 to $140,000 (depending on years of service, age, and how close the employee was to retirement). Another option offered up to $15,000 per year for four years to be applied to college tuition and expenses, plus half of the employee's salary and benefits for that same four-year period. Yet another included tuition and 70 percent of salary for two years.

During the enrollment period that lasted throughout 2006, 38,000 employees—about 46 percent of its unionized workforce—accepted one of the packages. This reduction in force, in turn, has several potential consequences. For one thing, Ford incurred short-term costs of several billion dollars. For another, it will provide substantial flexibility in the future for the firm to increase and reduce its workforce to align with market demand. And for yet another, the long-term influence of its major unions, especially the UAW, will likely evolve into more of a partnership than its traditional antagonistic relationship.

Sources: "Ford Says 38,000 Have Taken Buyouts," *Wall Street Journal,* November 29, 2006, pp. B1, B14; "38,000 Ford Workers Take Buyout Offers," *USA Today,* November 29, 2006, pp. 1B, 2B.

Just as union membership has been declining, so has the percentage of successful union-organizing campaigns. In the years immediately following World War II and continuing through the mid-1960s, for instance, most unions routinely won certification elections. In recent years, however, labor unions are winning certification fewer than 50 percent of the times when workers are called on to vote. From most indications then, the power and significance of labor unions in the United States, while still quite formidable, is significantly lower than it was just a few decades ago. Several factors explain the declining membership in labor unions today.

One common reason is the changing composition of the workforce itself. Traditionally, union members have been predominantly white males in blue-collar jobs. But as most people are aware, today's workforce is increasingly composed of women and ethnic minorities. These groups have a much weaker tradition of union affiliation, so their members are less likely to join unions when they enter the workforce. A corollary to these trends has to do with the fact that much of the workforce has shifted toward

Union-management relations continue to undergo profound change. To many observers Andy Stern is the new face of labor. Stern is the president of the Service Employees International Union (SEIU), the fastest growing union in the country. Stern made national headlines and angered many traditional labor leaders when he led the movement for several large unions, including SEIU, to withdraw from the AFL-CIO and launch a new union federation. His approach hinges on partnerships with business rather than strikes; he also is aggressively expanding the scope of the union to multinational firms and actively using modern technology such as blogs and webcasts to communicate with workers.

geographic areas in the South and toward occupations in the service sector that have also been less heavily unionized.

A second reason for the decline in union membership in the United States is more aggressive anti-unionization strategies undertaken by businesses.[5] The National Labor Relations Act and other forms of legislation specify strict management practices vis-à-vis labor unions; nevertheless, companies are still free to pursue certain strategies intended to eliminate or minimize unionization. For example, both Motorola and Procter & Gamble now offer no-layoff guarantees for their employees and have created a formal grievance system for all workers. These arrangements were once available only through unions. But because these firms offer them without any union contract, employees are likely to see less benefit from joining a union.

Some companies have also tried to create a much more employee-friendly work environment and strived to treat all employees with respect and dignity. One goal of this approach has been to minimize the attractiveness of labor unions for employees. Many Japanese manufacturers that have set up shop in the United States have successfully avoided unionization efforts by the United Auto Workers by providing job security, better wages, and a work environment in which employees are allowed to participate in the management of the facilities.

Trends in Union-Management Relations

The gradual decline in unionization in the United States has been accompanied by some significant trends in union-management relations. In some sectors of the U.S.

economy, perhaps most notably the automobile and steel industries, labor unions still remain strong. In these areas, unions have a large membership and considerable power vis-à-vis the organizations in which their members work. The United Auto Workers, for example, is still one of the strongest unions in the United States today.

But in most sectors of the economy, labor unions are clearly in a weakened position; as a result many have had to take a much more conciliatory stance in their relations with managers and organizations.[6] This situation contrasts sharply with the more adversarial relationship that once dominated labor relations in this country. For instance, unions recognize that they don't have as much power as they once held and that it is in their best interests, as well as the best interests of the workers they represent, to work with management as opposed to working against management. Hence, union-management relations are in many ways better today than they have been in years. Although this improvement is attributable in large part to the weakened power of unions, most experts would agree that union-management relations have still improved.[7]

But this does not mean that unions are dead, or that unions and management do not still struggle with more basic issues as well as newer issues. In August of 2003 Verizon Communications faced a strike by the Communication Workers of America (CWA) and several other unions representing 85,000 employees. The issues were an interesting mix of traditional union concerns and some of the more recent concerns discussed above. For example, telephone operators and customer-service representatives complained that they were forced to work overtime and that the lack of sufficient break time had led to undue stress on the job. This "stress in the workplace" issue is surely typical of the more recent union issues. But there were also problems with pay raises, and the fact that the company was shifting jobs to lower-paying regions of the country.

There was one additional issue at stake that never made it to the bargaining table. The CWA, which represents about 75,000 Verizon employees, has been trying to unionize Verizon Wireless as well. The wireless communications sector has thus far resisted unionization, and since that sector is extremely competitive, Verizon has been fighting hard to keep it that way.

The strike lasted fifteen days. Verizon found that, in the high-tech sector of the economy, it was difficult to replace the striking workers, and that they needed to get their workers back on the job. As a result, the union won on most issues, including a 12 percent wage increase and a 14 percent pension increase over the three-year contract. The company also granted stock options to every union employee for the first time in the company's history. The company won some freedom to move around employees in return for some job security promises, and service reps were guaranteed "close time" when they could shut down their station to relieve stress. But the unspoken issue remains unresolved as the CWA continues to try to unionize the Wireless employees. The strike, and the way it was settled, illustrates that, while basic issues can still lead to labor problems, the world of labor-management relations is indeed changing. It also illustrates that there may be cases where union power is not as low as had been reported. Specifically, in a competitive industry where there is a strong demand for well-trained, well-educated workers, the American union movement may find it has more leverage than has been the case for many years.

..ds in Bargaining Perspectives

..ding on the trends identified in the two previous sections, bargaining perspectives .ve also altered in recent years. For example, in the past most union-management bargaining situations were characterized by union demands for dramatic increases in wages and salaries. A secondary issue was usually increased benefits for union members. But now unions often bargain for different goals, such as job security. Of special interest in this area is the trend toward moving jobs to other countries to take advantage of lower labor costs. Thus unions might want to restrict job movement, whereas companies might want to maximize their flexibility vis-à-vis moving jobs to other countries.[8]

As a result of organization downsizing and several years of relatively low inflation in this country, many unions today opt to fight against wage cuts rather than strive for wage increases. Similarly, organizations might be prone to argue for less health care and other benefits for workers, and a common union strategy today is simply to attempt to preserve what workers currently have. Unions also place greater emphasis on improved job security for their members. An issue that has become especially important in recent years has been to focus on improved pension programs for employees.

The Unionization Process

The laws discussed earlier, as well as various associated regulations, prescribe a specific set of steps that employees must follow if they want to establish a union. These laws and regulations also dictate what management can and cannot do during an effort by employees to form a union.

Why Employees Unionize

Why do employees choose to join labor unions? In the simplest of terms, the answer is really straightforward: they believe that they are somehow better off as a result of joining a union.[9] More precisely, employees are more likely to unionize when they are dissatisfied with some aspect of their job, they believe that a union can help make this aspect of the job better, and they are not philosophically opposed to unions or to collective action.[10]

But the real answer is much more complex. In the early days of labor unions, people chose to join them because their working conditions were so unpleasant in many cases. In the eighteenth and nineteenth centuries, in their quest to earn ever-greater profits, some business owners treated their workers with no respect. They often forced their employees to work long hours, and minimum-wage laws and safety standards did not exist. As a result, many employees worked twelve, fifteen, or eighteen hours a day and sometimes were forced to work seven days a week. The pay was sometimes just pennies a day and employees received no vacation time or other benefits. They worked totally at the whim of their employer; if they complained about working conditions, they were dismissed. Thus, people initially chose to join labor unions because of the strength that lay in the numbers associated with the large-scale labor unions.

In many parts of the United States and in many industries, these early pressures for unionization became an ingrained part of life. Union values and union membership expectations were passed down from generation to generation. This trend typified many industrialized northern cities such as Pittsburgh, Cleveland, and Detroit. In general, parents' attitudes toward unions are still an important determinant for whether or not an employee elects to join a union.[11] As noted earlier, strong unionization pressures still exist in some industries today, such as the automobile industry, the steel industry, and other economic sectors relying on heavy manufacturing.

Steps in Unionization

Several prescribed steps must be followed if employees are to form and join a labor union. These general steps are shown in Figure 11.4 and are described in more detail below.

First, employees must exhibit some interest in joining a union. In some cases, this interest may arise from among current employees who are dissatisfied with some aspects of the employment relationship. In other instances, existing labor unions may send professional union organizers to nonunionized plants or facilities to create interest in unionization.[12]

If interest in forming a union exists, the National Labor Relations Board is asked to define the bargaining unit. The **bargaining unit** refers to the specifically defined group of employees who will be eligible for representation by the union. For example, a bargaining unit might be all nonmanagement employees in an organization or perhaps all clerical workers at a specific site within the organization.

The **bargaining unit** *refers to the specifically defined group of employees who are eligible for representation by the union.*

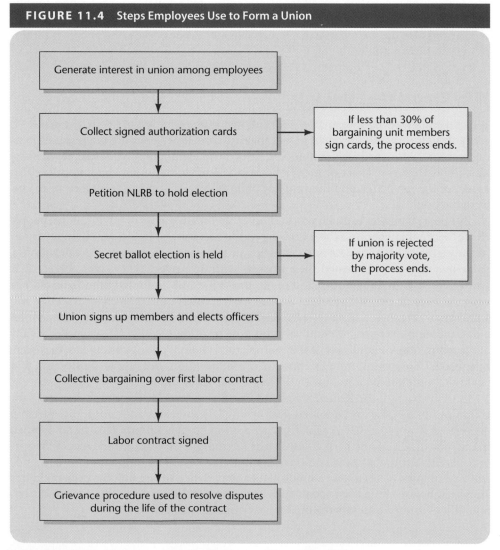

FIGURE 11.4   Steps Employees Use to Form a Union

Generate interest in union among employees

↓

Collect signed authorization cards → If less than 30% of bargaining unit members sign cards, the process ends.

↓

Petition NLRB to hold election

↓

Secret ballot election is held → If union is rejected by majority vote, the process ends.

↓

Union signs up members and elects officers

↓

Collective bargaining over first labor contract

↓

Labor contract signed

↓

Grievance procedure used to resolve disputes during the life of the contract

Source: Ricky Griffin, *Management,* 9th ed. (Boston: Houghton Mifflin, 2008), p. 393. Copyright © 2008 by Houghton Mifflin Company. Reprinted with permission.

Once the bargaining unit has been defined, organizers must then strive to get 30 percent of the eligible workers within the bargaining unit to sign authorization cards requesting a certification election. Signing an authorization card does not necessarily imply that the individual signing the card wants to join a union. Rather, the authorization card simply indicates the individual's belief that a union election should be held. If organizers cannot get 30 percent of the workers to sign authorization cards, then the process ends.

But if the required number of signatures is obtained, the next step in forming a union is for organizers to petition the NLRB to conduct an election. The NLRB sends one or more representatives, depending on the size of the bargaining unit, to the facility and conducts an election. The election is always conducted via secret ballot. If a simple majority of those voting approve union certification, then the union becomes the official bargaining agent of the eligible employees. But if a majority fails to approve certification, the process ends. In this instance, organizers cannot attempt to hold another election for at least one year.[13]

If the union becomes certified, then its organizers create a set of rules and regulations that govern the conduct of the union. They also elect officers, establish a meeting site, and begin to recruit members from the labor force in the bargaining unit to join the union. Thus, the union comes into existence as a representative of the organization's employees who fall within the boundaries of the bargaining unit.

Decertification of Unions

Just because a union becomes certified, however, does not necessarily mean that it will exist in perpetuity. Under certain conditions an existing labor union may be decertified. A company's workers, for example, might become disillusioned with the union and may even come to feel that they are being hurt by the presence of the union in their organization. They may believe that the management of the organization is trying to be cooperative and to bargain in good faith but that the union itself is refusing to cooperate.

For decertification to occur, two conditions must be met. First, no labor contract can currently be in force (that is, the previous agreement must have expired and a new one not yet been approved). Second, the union must have served as the official bargaining agent for the employees for at least one year. If both these conditions are met, employees or their representatives can again solicit signatures on decertification cards. As with the certification process, if 30 percent of the eligible employees in the bargaining unit sign the decertification cards, then the NLRB conducts a decertification election. Again, a majority decision determines the outcome. Thus, if a majority of those voting favor decertification, the union is then removed as the official bargaining agent for the unit. Once a union has been decertified, a new election cannot be requested for certification for at least one year.

The Collective-Bargaining Process

When a union has been legally certified, it becomes the official bargaining agent for the workers it represents. Collective bargaining can be thought of as an ongoing process that includes both the drafting and the administration of a labor agreement.

Preparing for Collective Bargaining

By definition, collective bargaining involves two sides: management representing the employing organization and the labor union representing its employees. The collective-bargaining process is aimed at agreement on a binding labor contract that will define various dimensions of the employment relationship for a specified period of time. Thus it is incumbent on both management and union leaders to be adequately prepared for a bargaining and negotiation period because the outcome of a labor negotiation will have long-term effects on both parties.

Management can take several actions to prepare for collective bargaining. For example, the firm can look closely at its own financial health to work out a realistic picture of what it can and cannot offer in terms of wages and salaries for its employees. Management can also conduct a comparative analysis to see what kinds of labor contracts and agreements exist in similar companies and research what this particular labor union has been requesting—and settling for—in the past.

The union can and should undertake several actions to be effectively prepared for collective bargaining. It too should examine the financial health of the company through sources such as public financial records. Like management, the union can also determine what kinds of labor agreements have been reached in other parts of the country and can determine what kinds of contracts other divisions of the company or other businesses owned by the same corporation have negotiated recently.

Setting Parameters for Collective Bargaining

Mandatory items *including wages, working hours, and benefits, must be included as part of collective bargaining if either party expresses a desire to negotiate one or more of them.*

Permissive items *may be included in collective bargaining if both parties agree.*

Another part of preparing for collective bargaining is prior agreement about the parameters of the bargaining session. In general, two categories of items may be dealt with during labor contract negotiations. One set of items, as defined by law, consists of **mandatory items.** Mandatory items include wages, working hours, and benefits. If either party expresses a desire to negotiate over one or more of these items, the other party has to agree.

Almost any other aspect of the employment relationship is also subject to negotiation, provided both sides agree. These items are called **permissive items.** For example, if the union expresses an interest in having veto power over the promotion of certain managers to higher-level positions and if, for some reason, the company were willing to agree to this demand as a point of negotiation, then it would be permissible to enter this point into the negotiations.

But some items are not permissible for negotiation under any circumstances. For example, in a perfect world management might want to include a clause in the labor contract specifying that the union promises not to strike. However, legal barriers prohibit such clauses from being written into labor contracts, and therefore this item would not be permissible.

Negotiating Labor Agreements

After appropriate preparation by both parties, the negotiation process itself begins. Of course, barriers may also arise during this phase, and bargaining impasses may result in strikes or other actions.

The Negotiation Process

Generally speaking, the negotiation process involves representatives from management and the labor union meeting at agreed-on times and at agreed-on locations, and working together to attempt to reach a mutually acceptable labor agreement. In some instances, the negotiation process itself might be relatively brief and cordial. But in other instances it might be lengthy, spanning weeks or perhaps even months, and it might also be quite acrimonious. For example, the labor agreement reached between the team owners and the union representing baseball players that was settled in late 1996 took several years to negotiate and was interrupted by a strike by the baseball players.

A useful framework for understanding the negotiation process refers to the bargaining zone, which is illustrated in Figure 11.5.[14] During preparations for negotiation, both sides are likely to attempt to define three critical points. For the organization, the bargaining zone and its three intermediate points include the employer's maximum limit, the employer's expectation, and the employer's desired result on items being negotiated. For example, the organization might have a zero increase in wages and benefits as a desired result (also known as management's "target point"). But it also recognizes that this desired result is unlikely and so what it expects is to have to provide a modest increase in wages and benefits totaling perhaps 4 to 5 percent. But if preparations are done thoroughly, managers also know the maximum amount they are willing to pay, which might be as high as 7 or 8 percent (management's "resistance point"). Note that, in this example, management would rather suffer through a strike than pay more than an 8 percent pay increase.

On the other side of the table, the labor union also defines a bargaining zone for itself that includes three points. These three points include the union's minimum acceptable limit on what it will take from management (the union resistance point: the settlement level below which the union will strike), its own expectations about what management is likely to agree to, and the most it can reasonably expect to get from management (the union target point). For instance, the labor union might feel that it has to provide a minimum increase of 2 to 3 percent in wages and benefits to its members. They expect a settlement of around 5 percent but would like to get 9 or 10 percent. In the spirit of bargaining, they may make an opening demand to management as high as 12 percent.

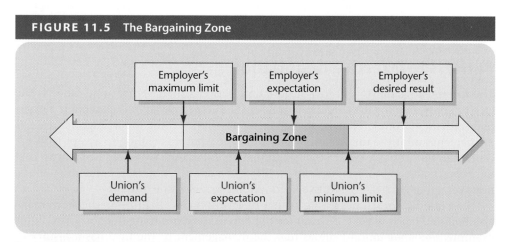

FIGURE 11.5   The Bargaining Zone

Source: Ricky Griffin and Ronald Ebert, *Business,* 3rd ed. Reprinted with permission of Pearson Education, Upper Saddle River, NJ.

Hence, during the opening negotiation session, labor might inform management that it demands a 12 percent wage and benefit increase. And the employer might begin by stating emphatically that no increases should be expected. Assuming, however, that some overlap exists between the organization's and the union's demands and expectations in the bargaining zone (a positive settlement zone), and assuming that both sides are willing to compromise and work hard at reaching an agreement, it is likely that an agreement will in fact be attained. Where exactly within that range the final agreement falls depends on the relative bargaining power of the two parties. This power is a function of many factors, such as negotiating skills, data on other settlements, and the financial resources needed either to call for (for the union) or to survive (for management) a strike.

Much of the actual negotiations revolve around each party trying to discover the other's resistance point without revealing its own. Because this point represents the least favorable settlement the party is willing to accept, the opponent who discovers that point then makes a "final" offer exactly at the resistance point. For example, if the union discovers that management is willing to go as high as 8 percent before breaking off negotiations and facing a strike, the union would then make an offer at 8 percent and indicate that this was its final offer. Management would rather pay 8 percent than have a strike, so they should settle at 8 percent, which is actually the most favorable contract the union could have possibly won. Incidentally, once a party makes a true final offer, they cannot back away from that position without losing face in the negotiations. Parties usually leave themselves some room for further negotiations and use statements such as the following: "I cannot imagine our members accepting anything less than an 8 percent raise, and I'm sure they would walk out on strike if we came back with less."

The resulting agreement is not necessarily the end of the bargaining process. First, the new contract agreement must be ratified by the union membership. If the union membership votes to reject the contract (which typically reflects internal union politics more than anything else), the parties must return to the bargaining table. But even before the union membership votes, a final step in the bargaining process must be followed. As soon as an agreement is reached, both parties begin to make public statements about how tough a negotiator the other party was. Both acknowledge that they really wanted a lot more and that they hope they can live with this agreement, but that the other party was such a good negotiator that this agreement was the best they could come up with. This posturing helps both parties "sell" the agreement to their constituencies and also allows both parties to maintain their image as a strong negotiator no matter how one-sided the final agreement might be. Once ratified, this agreement then forms the basis for a new labor contract.

Barriers to Effective Negotiation

The foremost barrier to effective negotiation between management and labor is the lack of an overlap for the bargaining zones of the respective sides (i.e., there is a negative settlement zone). That is, if management's upper limit for a wage increase is 3.5 percent and if the union's minimum limit for what it is willing to accept is 5 percent, then no overlap exists in the bargaining zones and the two sides will almost certainly be unable to reach an agreement. Beyond such differences in bargaining zones, however, other barriers to effective negotiation can also come into play.

For example, sometimes a long history of acrimonious relationships between management and labor make it difficult for the two sides to negotiate in good faith. If, for example, the labor union believes that the management of the firm has a history of withholding or distorting information and that management approaches negotiations from the standpoint of distrust and manipulation, then the union will be suspicious of

Negotiations between management and labor are an integral part of union-management relations. Dick Shoemaker (left) is the chief negotiator for General Motors, while Ron Gettelfinger is the president of the United Auto Workers (UAW). The two are shown here addressing other representatives of GM, the UAW, and the media during a recent contract negotiation.

any proposal made by management and may in fact be unwilling to accept almost any suggestion made by management. Of course, the same pattern can occur for the other side, with management exhibiting extreme distrust of the labor union.

Negotiations can also be complicated by inept negotiators and poor communication between negotiators. Effective negotiation is a critical skill and one that not everyone possesses. Thus, if managers select as a representative someone who doesn't understand the negotiation process, then difficulties are likely to arise.

As a result of diligent negotiation, however, management and labor should be able to agree on a mutually acceptable labor contract. On the other hand, if management and labor cannot agree on a new contract or one to replace an existing contract after a series of bargaining sessions, then either side or both sides might declare that they have reached an impasse. An **impasse** is simply a situation in which one or both parties believe that reaching an agreement is not imminent.

*An **impasse** is a situation in which one or both parties believe that reaching an agreement is not imminent.*

Resolving Impasses

If labor and management have reached an impasse, several actions can be taken by either side or both sides in an attempt to break the impasse. The basic objective of most of these tactics is to force the other side to alter or redefine its bargaining zone so that an accord can be reached.

The most potent weapon that the union holds is the potential for a strike. A **strike** occurs when employees walk off their jobs and refuse to work. In the United States, most strikes are called economic strikes because they are triggered by impasses over mandatory bargaining items such as salaries and wages. During a strike, workers represented by the union frequently march at the entrance to the employer's facility with signs explaining their reasons for striking. This action is called **picketing** and is intended to elicit sympathy for the union and to intimidate management.

Two less extreme tactics that unions sometimes use are boycotts and slowdowns. A **boycott** occurs when union members agree not to buy the products of a targeted employer. A **slowdown** occurs when workers perform their jobs at a much slower pace

*A **strike** occurs when employees walk off their jobs and refuse to work.*

***Picketing** occurs when workers representing the union march at the entrance to the employer's facility with signs explaining their reasons for striking.*

*A **boycott** occurs when union members agree not to buy the products of a targeted employer.*

*A **slowdown** occurs when workers perform their jobs at a much slower pace than normal.*

than normal. A variation on the slowdown occurs when union members agree, sometimes informally, to call in sick in large numbers on certain days, an action called a sickout. Pilots at American Airlines engaged in a massive sickout in early 1999, causing the airline to cancel thousands of flights before a judge ordered the pilots back to work.

Some kinds of strikes and labor actions are illegal. Foremost among these illegal actions is the so-called wildcat strike. A **wildcat strike** occurs during the course of a labor contract and is usually undertaken in response to a perceived injustice on the part of management. Because strikes are not legal during the course of a binding labor agreement, a wildcat strike is also unauthorized, at least theoretically, by the strikers' union.

Management also has certain tactics that it may employ in its efforts to break an impasse. One possibility is called a lockout. A **lockout** occurs when the employer denies employees access to the workplace. Managers must be careful when they use lockouts, however, because the practice is closely regulated by the government. A firm cannot lock out its employees simply to deprive them of wages or to gain power during the labor negotiations. Suppose, however, that the employer can meet a legitimate business need by locking out its employees. If this business need can be carefully documented, then a lockout might be legal. For example, in 1998 ABC locked out its off-camera employees because they staged an unannounced one-day strike during a critical broadcasting period.[15] Almost half of the 1998–1999 NBA season was lost when team owners locked out their players over contract issues.[16] Management occasionally uses temporary workers or replacements for strikers. These individuals are called *strikebreakers*. Conflict sometimes erupts between strikebreakers attempting to enter an employer's workplace and picketers representing the interests of the union at the employer's gates.

Sometimes the various tactics described above are successful in resolving the impasse. For instance, after workers have gone out on strike, the organization may change its position and indeed modify its bargaining zone to accommodate potentially larger increases in pay. After management experiences a strike, it sometimes realizes that the costs of failing to settle are greater than previously believed, and so managers are willing to give more to avoid a longer strike (i.e., their resistance point has shifted). But in many situations other alternatives for resolving an impasse are also available. Common alternatives include the use of mediation and arbitration.

In **mediation** a neutral third party, called the mediator, listens to and reviews the information presented by both sides. The mediator then makes an informed recommendation and provides advice to both parties about what she or he believes should be done. For example, suppose the impasse centers around wage increases, with the union demanding 8 percent and the company willing to pay only 5 percent. The mediator listens to both sides and reviews all the evidence, and may subsequently conclude that because of the financial profile of the company and because of other labor negotiations in other industries, 5 percent is both fair and all the organization can afford to pay. This advice is then provided to both sides. The union doesn't have to accept this information, however, and can continue its efforts to exact a higher wage increase from the employer.

Another alternative to resolving impasses is arbitration. In **arbitration** both sides agree in advance that they will accept the recommendations made by an independent third-party arbitrator. Like a mediator, the arbitrator listens to both sides of the picture and presents and reviews all the evidence. But in arbitration, the information that results is placed in the form of a proposed settlement agreement that the parties have agreed in advance to accept. Thus, a settlement is imposed on the parties and the impasse is ended. But some believe that arbitrators tend to impose settlements that "split the difference." If both parties believe that the arbitrator has proposed such a settlement, they have an incentive to stick to their original positions and not move toward a settlement because such a move shifts the middle further away from their target point.[17] As such, the threat of arbitration may "chill" the negotiation process and actually make a negotiated settlement less likely.

A **wildcat strike** *occurs during the course of a labor contract and is usually undertaken in response to a perceived injustice on the part of management.*

A **lockout** *occurs when an employer denies employees access to the workplace.*

In **mediation** *a neutral third party, called the mediator, listens to and reviews the information presented by both sides and then makes an informed recommendation and provides advice to both parties about what she or he believes should be done.*

In **arbitration** *both sides agree in advance that they will accept the recommendations made by an independent third-party arbitrator.*

An alternative form of arbitration has therefore been proposed that should induce the parties, it is argued, to negotiate a settlement by potentially imposing strikelike costs on both parties.[18] Under **final-offer arbitration,** the parties bargain until impasse. At that point, the two parties' final offers are submitted to the arbitrator. Under traditional arbitration, the arbitrator is then free to impose a settlement at any point he or she wishes. But under final-offer arbitration, the arbitrator has only two choices for the imposed settlement—the two parties' final offers. That is, the arbitrator must select either one or the other party's final offer *as the imposed settlement.* Thus, the party that does not bargain in good faith may get everything he or she wants in the arbitrator's decision but may just as easily lose everything. Under such a system, the parties are more willing to try to reach a settlement on their own rather than go to the arbitrator. Professional baseball uses final-offer arbitration to resolve contract disputes between individual players and owners.

> *Under **final-offer arbitration,** the parties bargain until impasse and then the two parties' final offers are submitted to the arbitrator.*

Administering Labor Agreements

Another key clause in the labor contracts negotiated between management and labor defines how the labor agreement will be enforced. In some cases, enforcement is clear. If the two sides agree that the company will increase the wages it pays to its employees by 2 percent a year over the next three years according to a prescribed increase schedule, then there is little opportunity for disagreement. Wage increases can be calculated mathematically and union members will see the effects in their paychecks. But other provisions of many labor contracts are much more subjective in nature and thus are more prone to misinterpretation and different perceptions.

For example, suppose a labor contract specifies how overtime assignments are to be allocated in the organization. Such allocation strategies are often relatively complex and suggest that the company may have to take into account various factors, such as seniority, previous overtime allocations, the hours or days in which the overtime work is needed, and so forth. Now suppose that a supervisor in the factory is attempting to follow the labor contract and offers overtime to a certain employee. This employee, however, indicates that before he or she can accept, he or she must check with a spouse or partner to learn more about previous obligations and commitments. The supervisor may feel a time crunch and be unable to wait as long as the employee would like. As a result, the supervisor gives the overtime opportunity to a second employee. The first employee may feel aggrieved by this course of action and elect to protest.

When such differences of opinion occur, the individual labor union member takes the complaint to her or his shop steward, a union officer described earlier in this chapter. The shop steward listens to the complaint and forms an initial impression. The shop steward has the option of advising the employee that the supervisor handled the matter appropriately. But other appeal mechanisms are also available so that the employee, even if refuted by the shop steward, still has channels for appeal.

Of course, if the shop steward agrees with the employee, she or he may also follow prescribed methods for dealing with the situation. The prescribed methods might include starting with the supervisor to listen to his or her side of the story and then continuing along the lines of appeal up the hierarchy of both the labor union and the company. In some cases, mediation and arbitration may be instigated in an effort to resolve the disagreement. For example, some of the potential resolutions to the grievance described above would be to reassign the overtime opportunity to the employee who was asked first. Or the overtime opportunity may stay with the second employee but the first employee would also receive overtime pay.

Labor Unions in the Twenty-First Century

Earlier in this chapter we discussed the historical roots of the U.S. labor movement. We noted that the labor movement in this country focused on bread-and-butter issues such as wages and hours of work, unlike the labor movement in many European countries. Early American unionists were less concerned with social issues and, partially as a result, a labor party in the United States never drew much interest. Unions and union members supported political candidates who favored their goals, and unions have spoken out on any number of political issues. But for the most part the issues in which U.S. labor unions became involved were pretty close to the basic issues facing U.S. labor. This situation is clearly changing, however.

U.S. labor unions have become quite vocal in several areas where they have traditionally been silent. For example, union leaders in this country have spoken out against child labor in Third World countries and the general exportation of jobs to lower-paying countries. Union positions on these issues represent union self-interests to some extent. For example, moving manufacturing jobs to Mexico also means that U.S. unions will lose members. But there is more to this issue than obvious self-interest. These public positions have changed the way many people think about unions. Although union membership has declined over the past several decades, these changes can enhance the power of labor unions and thus affect the relationship between unions and management. A wide array of issues has attracted the involvement of the U.S. labor movement, but we will focus on only a few. Note, however, that these issues are simply meant to be illustrative of the new scope of union interests in this country. As we discuss in the *Taking HR to the Next Level* feature in Part Three, human resource managers themselves are beginning to be concerned about a similar set of issues.

"Replacement" Sources of Labor

We discussed the trends to export jobs overseas in both Chapters 3 and 4. The U.S. labor movement has become quite interested in these trends, and has generally argued for how this results in the loss of jobs in the United States. But overseas labor markets are only one source of "replacement" laborers. Labor unions in the United States have also voiced concern over the use of other such sources.

For example, in 2005 there were roughly one million people serving time in federal, state, or local prisons. Many of these inmates work in paid jobs, although they are paid much less than the minimum wage (we will discuss this in more detail in the *Taking HR to the Next Level* feature at the end of Part Three). The fact that these inmates are paid less makes it possible for the goods they produce to be sold for less, which can cause a serious problem for unskilled jobs in the general population. Furthermore, many critics of the U.S. prison system argue that these prison jobs do not prepare prison inmates for outside jobs once they are released and so do not lessen the rate of subsequent arrest and incarceration. Thus, the U.S. labor movement and its advocates argue that this system needs to be reformed to provide more rights to prison laborers and to ensure that prison labor does not take away civilian population jobs, which in the long run can lead to increased crime.

Unions have become much more involved in social issues over the past few years. One of the issues that unions have spoken out against is the use of prison labor. Here, a group of inmates at the Central California Women's Facility, near Fresno, work on circuit boards for Joint Venture Electronics, which employs fifty-five inmates. The inmates at the facility are excited about working on this job because it actually pays minimum wage. The other job available to inmates in this facility is working in the state-sponsored denture lab for $.33 an hour. Of course, assemblers of circuit boards on the outside would earn several times the minimum wage, so relying on convict labor reduces company costs. But it also reduces the number of jobs available to non-inmates—which could lead to more crime.

Contingent Workers   Another source of "replacement labor" is the pool of contingent workers, discussed earlier in Chapter 6. Perhaps it is not surprising that U.S. unions have taken a stand on the topic of contingent workers. Under U.S. labor laws, contingent workers are considered independent contractors or self-employed laborers, and in 1998 these self-employed workers numbered about 10.3 million—or approximately 8 percent of the workforce.[19] As independent contractors, these workers are not covered by most employment and labor laws. In fact, to be covered by almost any legislation related to employment, a person must have some type of employment relationship with an entity, which is not the case for most contingent workers. This problem will become more serious as more organizations turn to contingent workers as a way of managing the demand for labor.

Clearly, organized labor has a vested interest in opposing the reliance upon these groups of potential "replacement" laborers. Although the representatives of the unions focus on the social implications of these practices, and probably are concerned about these social costs, it is clear that labor unions have more to lose in these cases than do some others. Nonetheless, U.S. labor unions have been able to form coalitions with other community groups who oppose the use of prison labor, or are concerned about exporting jobs overseas, and they have become very vocal in this movement. As a result, labor unions have gained a great deal of credibility as guardians of middle class jobs.

Unions and the Electronic Age

The Internet presents many interesting challenges for U.S. labor unions. The most obvious challenge stems from the fact that computers and new technology often mean that work can be done by fewer employees. We noted earlier that companies have been trying to move more production sites to foreign countries where labor costs are lower and where U.S. unions have no input. Thus, unions would lose members. At the same time, the introduction of technology is also reducing the number of workers and the number of union members. Although unions must oppose some of these technological advances for the sake of their members' jobs if nothing else, they cannot simply reject these advances wholesale. It is clear in many cases that the firms involved will lose business and perhaps even be forced out of business if they cannot keep pace with the technology (and cost control) of their competitors. Such outcomes are not desirable from the unions' perspective either, and so the U.S. labor movement is in a difficult position.

But changes in technology have also posed a much different set of challenges for unions and for the management of firms with unionized employees. For example, many firms who fear unionization efforts have no-solicitation rules at work. These rules simply mean that no employee can solicit other employees on company time for any cause except United Way campaigns. That is, under such rules, employees cannot sell candy for the high school band, raffle tickets for a new car, or even tickets for a church dinner. An important aspect of these rules is that they also outlaw any attempts by union organizers to solicit employees to sign cards appointing the union as sole bargaining agent. Organizations are usually vigilant about no-solicitation rules because they stop union-organizing efforts at work.

But the Internet presents a challenge to these no-solicitation rules. It is much more difficult to monitor solicitation on the Internet, and some of this solicitation may even come from outside the firm. If the company fails to stop these forms of solicitation, can they still legally stop union solicitation at work? Can unions use the Internet to solicit union membership if they do so from outside the company? Recent NLRB rulings and opinions have not clarified the answers to these questions. For example, if the organization allows employees to use the Internet (even if the computers are company owned) to post thank-you notes, it may be forced to allow union solicitation as well. The NLRB will have to deal with these issues in the coming years, but the key seems to be nondiscrimination. That is, companies cannot (apparently) forbid employees from using the Internet for union solicitation if companies allow employees to use the Internet for other non-business-related purposes.[20] In any case, the Internet has complicated the problem of solicitation—by any party—on the job.

It seems, however, that unions have generally seen Internet solicitation as a useful tool in a different setting. In many high-tech firms, it is common to outsource work and for people to work at home. In these situations, employees rarely meet face-to-face. How can a union hope to organize these workers? A recent article has pointed out that unions in the Silicon Valley area have been successful in using the Internet for union-organizing campaigns.[21] They have been active in trying to organize a wide variety of contingent workers in the area, and they successfully organized janitorial workers across firms in the Silicon Valley through Internet solicitation. This approach has enabled union organizers to reach workers they couldn't meet personally, and it plays on the fact that many workers at all levels in this area have easy access to computers. Unions in the Silicon Valley area have also used Internet-based campaigns to mount successful boycotts against some firms.

Finally, unions have found that the Internet has had a significant impact on the way they conduct their own internal business. It is now possible for unions in this country to communicate immediately with union leaders and members from around the world. This development has made unions more democratic in their internal policies. It has also enabled unions to mobilize international resources to deal with issues that all union members face wherever they work, such as the lower wages and looser labor regulations associated with agreements under the World Trade Organization.

It remains to be seen how unions will be able to use and be challenged by computers and the electronic age in the coming years. It is already clear, however, that new electronic technology has been a mixed blessing for the U.S. labor movement. While technology continues to threaten jobs, it also allows unions to reach workers in ways that were never possible before. It is not yet clear that computers will be able to revitalize the union movement in the United States, but they certainly seem capable of breathing new life into that movement.

Chapter Summary

Labor relations is the process of dealing with employees who are represented by a union. A labor union is a legally constituted group of individuals working together to achieve shared job-related goals. Collective bargaining is the process by which managers and union leaders negotiate acceptable terms and conditions of employment for those workers represented by the unions. The historical formation of U.S. labor unions closely parallels the history of the United States itself. Many laws and other regulations have been passed, some of which are intended to promote unionization and union activities; others are intended to limit or curtail union activities. Like any large organization, labor unions also have structures that facilitate their work.

Since the mid-1950s labor unions in the United States have experienced increasing difficulty in attracting new members. Indeed, while millions of U.S. workers still belong to labor unions, union membership as a percentage of the total workforce has continued to decline at a steady rate. Unions recognize that they don't have as much power as they once held and that it is in their best interests, as well as the best interests of the workers they represent, to work with management as opposed to working against management. Bargaining perspectives have also altered in recent years.

Employees must follow a specific set of steps if they want to establish a union. First, employees must express some interest in joining a union. If interest exists in forming a union, the National Labor Relations Board (NLRB) is asked to define the bargaining unit. Once the bargaining unit has been defined, organizers must then strive to get 30 percent of the eligible workers within the bargaining unit to sign authorization cards requesting a certification election. If organizers cannot get 30 percent of the workers to sign authorization cards, then the unionization process ends. But if the required number of signatures is obtained, the next step in forming a union is for organizers to petition the NLRB to conduct an election. If the union becomes certified, then its organizers create a set of rules and regulations that will govern the conduct of the union. Under certain conditions, an existing labor union may be decertified.

Collective bargaining involves management representing the employing organization and the labor union representing its employees. The collective-bargaining process is aimed at agreement on a binding labor contract that will define various dimensions of the employment relationship for a specified period of time. One important part of preparing for collective bargaining is prior agreement on the parameters of the bargaining session.

Generally speaking, the negotiation process involves representatives from management and the labor union meeting at agreed-on times and at agreed-on locations, and working together to attempt to reach a mutually acceptable labor agreement. A useful framework for understanding the negotiation process is the bargaining zone. Of course, numerous barriers to effective negotiation exist, and several methods are available for both management and labor to use in their attempts to overcome an impasse.

A key clause in the labor contracts negotiated between management and labor defines how the labor agreement will be enforced. While some enforcement issues are relatively straightforward, others may rely heavily on a formal grievance procedure.

Key Points for Future HR Managers

- Despite declines in union membership, unionization of employees remains a reality for many large firms in the United States and even more so internationally.

- The relationship between unions and management is strictly regulated by law, and these regulations are much more comprehensive in Europe and other parts of the world.

- Although some evidence suggests that union-management relations are improving in the United States, other evidence suggests that, in some cases, these relations are getting worse.

- Most employees join unions because they are dissatisfied with the way they are treated and they feel that management is not responsive to their concerns. Some employees join unions, though, because of social norms and the fact that unions helped their parents.

- Effective human resource practices can reduce the desire of employees to unionize, but organizations are limited in what they can do to prevent unionization. Also, while unions can be decertified, management cannot advocate decertification.

- Collective bargaining is a reality in unionized firms, and many critical issues must be part of the bargaining process with the union.

- When bargaining fails, slowdowns, strikes, and lockouts are possible alternatives.

- Third-party intervention, in the form of mediation and arbitration, is becoming common in labor-management disputes.

- Although U.S. labor unions continue to be concerned with basic issues of wages and work conditions, the labor movement has become much more involved in social issues in recent years and has become a vocal advocate for social change.

- The Internet may change the way unions do business and the way management must relate to unions.

Key Points for Future General Managers

- Unions have traditionally played an important role in improving working conditions for U.S. workers, and many workers still view unions in this light. Therefore, if a firm has a union, it may be difficult to vote it out; if a firm does not have a union, it may be more difficult than some managers believe to keep a union out.

- Some firms have found unions to be helpful partners as they explore new ways to organize work, while others have found unions to be tenacious opponents to any change. It is important to think seriously about the kind of relationship management wants to have with unions.

- A well-developed legal framework is in place to guide management in dealing with unions, and enforcement of these laws has been fairly consistent over the years.

- Unions have become effective at calling for social reform, and such actions have increased their popularity in the media.

Review and Discussion Questions

1. Discuss the historical evolution of labor unions in the United States.

2. Identify and briefly explain each of the major laws affecting unionization in the United States.

3. What is a shop steward?

4. Is your state a right-to-work state? What are your personal opinions about this issue?

5. Discuss trends in unionization.

6. What steps would you take to increase union membership?

7. Summarize the basic steps employees must follow to create a union.

8. What is the bargaining zone?

9. Identify and describe the three general areas that relate to collective bargaining.

10. Identify and discuss the methods for resolving impasses.

CLOSING CASE

Winning the Battle but Losing the War?

It's Sunday of Memorial Day weekend in Flint, Michigan. A line of big flatbed trucks pulls up to the delivery doors of the General Motors (GM) Flint Metal Center. Drivers and crew members get out and look around nervously. A few minutes later the big doors are open and more than a dozen two-ton metal dies, valued at over $300,000 each, are loaded on the

trucks. When they are all loaded and tied down, the drivers and crew members again look around nervously, then get back into the trucks and drive off.

Was this incident a serious case of industrial espionage? After all, these dies are used to turn sheets of steel into the hoods and fenders of the new GMC Sierra pickup trucks and are extremely valuable. Or perhaps it was the work of the United Auto Workers (UAW). After all, the union had been feuding with GM over the new trucks, with GM trying to cut labor costs by reducing the workforce and the union fighting to save jobs and keep them from moving to Mexico. In truth, the real culprits were neither the competition nor the union. GM itself "stole" the dies from one of its own plants that was being threatened with a strike.

In June 1998 the UAW had threatened to shut down the metal-stamping plant. The threat of a shutdown represented a major concern for GM because this particular plant was being set up to make fenders and bumpers for a new truck model that had the potential to be the best-selling and highest-profit-margin vehicle in GM's 1999 lineup. As a result, GM couldn't risk losing production time because of a strike and was simply taking extreme measures to protect itself.

The dies and other key components for the new trucks were secretly stored in old factories—and even a few bowling alleys—in the area and were then shipped to another stamping plant in Mansfield, Ohio. The Ohio plant had a contract with GM that would not allow a strike at that critical time, and so GM could produce the needed parts if the Flint plant were closed. GM later justified its actions on the grounds that the truck was its most promising new product in a long time and it was crucial that it be available at the start of the new model year. The UAW, on the other hand, felt that it was fighting for jobs for its workers and against trends by GM to move auto jobs outside the United States.

GM did get the trucks out on time, but it also endured one of the costliest strikes in its history. The dispute was so bitter, the loss of jobs so substantial, and the concessions made by GM so sweeping that it is not clear who ultimately "won." As explained more fully below, the heart of the issue involved the loss of jobs by U.S. workers. So, on June 5, 1998, 25,000 workers from the firm's Flint, Michigan, plants went on strike. The strike spread quickly and lasted until July 28. By the time the strike was settled, GM estimated that it lost $2.2 billion in sales and even more in terms of lost market share, making it the costliest labor battle GM had fought in decades.

GM had argued earlier that the project would result in 20,000 new jobs across five plants. But UAW officials countered that the accompanying efficiencies and automation could also result in the long-term reduction of 50,000 jobs, and even more jobs would be moved to Mexico and Asia. The UAW also alleged that GM had not followed through on promises to spend millions on modernizing U.S. plants because, it claimed, the company was planning to shift more production to other countries. Therefore, the UAW was opposing GM at every step of the way. In fact, there had been strikes the previous year that were also called in reaction to this plan.

During one of these earlier strikes at a Pontiac, Michigan, plant, a union official commented that, to settle the strike, the union made several concessions, including agreeing to have repairpersons fix problems with the trucks while they were still on the assembly line instead of at the end of the line. This "concession" sounds more like the enlightened employee involvement systems described in this chapter: it would give the workers more say on when and what type of repairs were needed. But the union claimed that these systems have not worked at GM due to a lack of trust. As the union official put it, stopping the line by pulling the "stop-line cord" to make repairs often got workers in trouble with management.

GM was trying to circumvent these labor problems by shifting production to sites that were less likely to be disrupted by work stoppages. The dies that had been spirited away on the Sunday of Labor Day weekend, were finally returned to the plant on July 26, but by that point, the strike had been going on for some time and had become ugly. In fact, during the course of the strike, GM had attempted to have the strike declared illegal and then, failing in that, threatened to stop medical benefits for striking workers—an unheard-of move!

When the fifty-four-day strike finally ended, it was difficult to see what GM had won. The union did agree to new work rules that would increase productivity at the Flint stamping plant, and it also agreed to settle several other disputes that would ensure labor peace until the national contract expired. But in return, GM had to agree to invest about $180 million in plant modernization and to hold on to several plants that were planned for divestiture. Perhaps more critically, the relationship between the UAW and GM had been damaged. It is not clear if it can be improved, although UAW vice president William Shoemaker urged cooperation in a speech he made before 2,000 GM managers. On the other hand, employees at the Lordstown, Ohio, GM plant have complained that they are being pressured to increase productivity or GM will move most of the jobs from that plant to Mexico.

The real issue, then, is whether the relationship between unions and management is really changing. Cases of increased cooperation and partnering have occurred. But unions see membership dwindling and jobs being shifted to other countries, so they are unlikely to view the situation as one where "everyone wins." In the coming years, GM will have to reduce its workforce and cut labor costs if it is to retain its leadership in the auto industry. Both Ford and Daimler-Chrysler are already way ahead in modernization. If GM can accomplish this modernization with the cooperation of the UAW, it will truly signal the beginning of a new era in union-management relations, but for now it may just be business as usual.[22]

(continued)

Case Questions

1. Which side do you think had a better argument for its position, General Motors or the United Auto Workers?

2. Which side do you think won? Why?

3. What general insights can be gleaned from this case regarding labor-management relations?

Building HR Management Skills

Purpose: The purpose of this exercise is to help you understand the bargaining process and how the bargaining-zone model can help facilitate negotiation and bargaining.

Step 1: Your instructor will divide the class into an even number of small groups. Half the groups will be designated as management and the other half as labor. Assume that you are about to negotiate and bargain over a potential wage increase.

Step 2: Your instructor will provide each group with information corresponding to the three parts of the bargaining-zone model as it applies to your role.

Step 3: Your group should spend a few minutes discussing the best way to handle negotiations so you can meet or exceed your expectations.

Step 4: Your instructor will pair teams of labor negotiators with teams of management negotiators. Within a time limit specified by your instructor, engage in bargaining until you reach an agreement (if possible).

Step 5: Each group should share its negotiated agreement on the wage increase with the rest of the class.

Step 6: Respond to the following questions:

1. Explain differences and/or similarities in negotiated agreements.

2. How useful did you find the bargaining-zone model? Without using this model, would your bargaining have been more or less difficult?

3. Can you see other areas of applicability besides collective bargaining for the bargaining-zone model?

Ethical Dilemmas in HR Management

Assume that you work for a midsized non-union company. The firm is facing its most serious union-organizing campaign in years, and your boss is determined to keep the union out. He has just given you a list of tasks that should thwart the efforts of the organizers. For example, he has suggested the following:

- Whenever you learn about a scheduled union information meeting, you should schedule a worker appreciation event at that same time. He wants you to offer free pizza and barbecue and to give cash prizes. The winners have to be present to receive their prizes.

- He wants you to look at the most recent performance evaluations of the key union organizers and to terminate the one with the lowest overall evaluation.

- He wants you to make an announcement that the firm is seriously considering new benefits such as on-site childcare, flexible work schedules, telecommuting options, and exercise facilities. While you know the firm is indeed looking into these benefits and several others, you also know that ultimately what is provided will be far less lavish than your boss wants you to intimate.

When you questioned the ethics and legality of these practices, he responded by saying, "Look, all's fair in love and war, and this is war." He went on to explain that if the union wins, the company might actually shut down its domestic operations altogether and move all its production capacities to lower-cost foreign plants. He concluded by saying that he was really looking out for the benefit of the employees, even if he had to play hardball to help them. And indeed, while you can see through his hypocrisy, you also recognize that there is some potential truth in his warning—if the union wins, jobs may actually be lost.

Questions

1. What are the ethical issues in this situation?

2. What are the basic arguments for and against taking extreme measures to fight unionization efforts?

3. What do you think most managers would do in this situation? What would you do?

HR Internet Exercise

 Both the AFL-CIO and the NLRB maintain websites to help explain what they do and why. Visit each of their websites at these addresses:
http://www.aflcio.org/
http://www.nlrb.gov/

Questions

1. What specific information can you find on each site that might be of benefit to you as a manager?

2. What specific information can you find on each site that might be of benefit to you as an individual worker interested in forming a union?

3. What improvements might you suggest to make each website more effective for its intended audience?

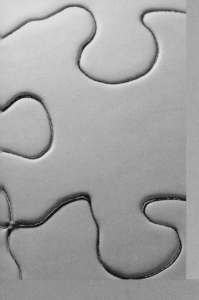

12

Safety, Health, Well-Being, and Security

CHAPTER OBJECTIVES

*After studying this chapter you should
be able to:*

■ Identify and discuss the central
elements associated with employee
safety and health.

■ Describe the basic issues involved in
the physical work environment.

■ Discuss health- and stress-
management programs.

■ Identify and describe the most
important HR-related security issues
in organizations.

FedEx provides air cargo express services, moving everything from an urgent business letter to a human heart for transplant. FedEx employs thousands of aircraft, vehicles, and workers in dozens of countries. At FedEx's Memphis airport hub, the company typically processes 5 million packages—per day—and up to 7.5 million items per day during holidays. Looking around on a recent, typical night, Reginald Owens, Sr., vice president, admits it may look like controlled chaos, but in reality "is a well-conditioned, well-organized machine."

> *"Everything we do, we're*
>
> *managing to a time clock."*
>
> (G. Dunavant, managing director for global operations control, FedEx)

But clearly, jobs at FedEx can be stressful. For example, FedEx package handlers and couriers must sort, load, and deliver a variety of different kinds of packages under tight deadlines. Moreover, they often work outside with heavy machinery on day and night shifts, and are required to use physical coordination, strength, speed, and attention to detail.

Call center employees face different sources of stress. They don't lift or sort packages, and they work in a more controlled environment. But they also answer a high volume of calls and must do so with accuracy, courtesy, and speed. Employee performance is sometimes evaluated by supervisors who listen in on calls.

Even managers at FedEx experience stress. Executive vice president T. Michael Glenn explains that performance is critical: "We've got to work our people pretty hard to guarantee that every child gets her Christmas doll on time." Nightly deadlines contribute to the urgency, and managing director for global operations control John G. Dunavant says, "Everything we do, we're managing to a time clock."

In addition, the business environment is characterized by intense competition with UPS and DHL, a high need for security, and unpredictable weather. Each of these elements further adds to stress. High stress can cause mental and physical problems and reduce motivation. These consequences, in turn, can lead to increased absenteeism and turnover, burnout, and loss of productivity. FedEx competes in a customer-oriented service industry, where these consequences could be devastating.

FedEx uses two strategies to effectively address employee stress. First, it tries to reduce the stress inherent in its jobs to the extent that is possible. For example, the company conducts time-and-motion studies to identify less tiring ways of completing tasks. Employees are then trained in the proper techniques. Employee suggestions are also used to redesign jobs to make them less stressful. Automated tools, such as bar code scanners and computerized package tracking systems, handle some of the repetitive tasks.

FedEx's second strategy helps employees more effectively cope with stress. Job duties can be modified if an employee needs a temporary break. Company benefits include paid sick time and leave, and assistance with stressful life events such as birth, adoption, or death. An employee assistance program also provides counseling and help for legal, financial, mental health, relationship, childcare, and eldercare problems.

While stress seems inevitable at FedEx, the company's strategies do seem to at least partially offset this stress. As one indicator of how well the company helps its employees, for example, FedEx has been named as one of the best companies for workers by *Fortune, ComputerWorld,* the *Wall Street Journal,* and *Business Ethics.*[1]

Most people don't think a great deal about their safety or health when they go to work. They assume that their employer has done whatever is possible to make the workplace as safe and as healthy as it can be. And while many routinely experience stress, many people don't see it as something they can really control. Further, since September 11, 2001, some American workers have experienced more concern about their physical security at work, as well as at home. Also, the truth is that many accidents do occur in the workplace and that many workplaces are actually not very healthy. This chapter is about ways in which organizations and human resource managers can make the workplace environment safe and healthy. As we shall see, there are some legal pressures (recall the Occupational Safety and Health Act of 1970, described in Chapter 2) operating to make workplaces safe, and there are also some very practical issues that lead human resource managers to keep workplaces healthy and secure.

Employee Safety and Health

An organization tries to create and maintain a safe and healthy workplace for many reasons. For one thing, it's simply an ethical and socially responsible position—no one would accept the premise that it's acceptable for employees to get hurt or become sick because of their working conditions. But there are also a number of other very specific reasons as well. First, recall from our discussion in Chapter 9 that mandated workers' compensation provides insurance coverage for employees who are hurt or who become ill on the job. The insurance premium an organization pays for this coverage is determined by several factors, including the value of the claims paid out to employees of the firm. In other words, firms that have fewer accidents and workers' compensation claims actually pay lower premiums. Furthermore, the Occupational Safety and Health Act (OSHA) can impose fines against organizations that have unsafe workplaces. Finally, lost time due to accidents or illness costs organizations a great deal of money; therefore, it is simply good business to maintain a safe and healthy workplace. An important step in this process is to identify and eliminate safety and health hazards on the job.

Safety hazards refer to those conditions in the work environment that have the potential to cause harm to an employee. **Health hazards,** on the other hand, are elements of the work environment that more slowly and systematically, and perhaps cumulatively, result in damage to an employee's health. Thus, a poorly connected string of wiring that might result in electrical shock to an employee poses a safety hazard, whereas continuous and ongoing exposure to chemicals that may increase the risk of cancer represents a health hazard.

These risks do not seem to be equally likely in all types of businesses or occupations. In fact, some types of work are much more likely to experience injuries than others. Table 12.1 lists several of the most dangerous occupations in the United States. For example, in 2004 there were 85 reported fatalities among logging workers. This resulted in a fatality rate of 92.4 per 100,000 workers. Likewise, there were 307 fatalities among U.S. farmers and ranchers, with a resultant fatality rate of 37.5 per 100,000 workers.

Common Workplace Hazards and Threats

First, we address some of the more frequent causes of accidents and then describe some of the more pervasive health hazards. One major category of factors that can cause ac-

Safety hazards   *refer to those conditions in the work environment that have the potential to cause harm to an employee.*

Health hazards   *are characteristics of the work environment that more slowly and systematically, and perhaps cumulatively, result in damage to an employee's health.*

TABLE 12.1   Most Dangerous Occupations in the United States, 2004

| | National Data | | |
Occupation Title	Fatality Rate*	Reported Fatalities	Most Frequent Cause
Logging workers**	92.4	85	Contacts with objects
Aircraft pilots and flight engineers***	92.4	109	Transportation incidents
Fishers and related fishing workers	86.4	38	Transportation incidents
Structural iron and steel workers	47.0	31	Falls
Refuse and recyclable material collectors	43.2	35	Transportation incidents
Farmers and ranchers	37.5	307	Transportation incidents
Roofers	34.9	94	Falls
Electrical power-line installers and repairers	30.0	36	Exposure to harmful substances
Driver/sales workers and truck drivers	27.6	905	Transportation incidents
Taxi drivers and chauffeurs	24.2	67	Assaults and violent acts

*per 100,000 employed
**includes fallers, operators, and scalers
***employment includes commercial pilots, but wage is only for commercial pilots
Source: Workforce Explorer Washington, October 25th 2005. http://www.workforceexplorer.com/article.asp?PAGEID=94&ARTICLEID=5703.

cidents in the workplace is the characteristics of the physical environment. At a general level, of course, accidents can happen anywhere. People can slip on wet flooring or a loose piece of carpeting or can drop something heavy on a foot in almost any setting. But in manufacturing settings, several specific conditions of the work environment might prove to be potentially dangerous. Among the more common are unguarded or improperly guarded machines. In this instance, "guarding" refers to a shield or other piece of equipment to keep body parts from coming in contact with moving machine parts, such as gears or conveyor belts.

Defective equipment and tools can cause accidents. Poor lighting and poor or improper ventilation can also be dangerous. Improper dress poses a hazard. For example, if a person wears loose clothing, she or he runs the risk that the clothing might get caught in the moving part of a machine. Sharp edges around machinery can be a hazard. And finally, poor housekeeping resulting in dirty or wet floors, improperly stacked materials, and congested storage areas can result in accidents. Of course, hazards are not restricted to manufacturing settings; they can occur in almost any work setting. For example, home-office safety must be a concern for businesses that allow telecommuting.[2]

Personal actions of individual employees can also represent a common workplace hazard. Among the more frequently described and identified personal actions that result in accidents include taking unnecessary risks, failing to wear protective equipment such as goggles or gloves, using improper tools and equipment for specific jobs, taking unsafe shortcuts, and simply engaging in foolish horseplay. Any of these actions has the potential to bring harm or injury to people in the workplace quickly and without warning. These kinds of actions caused an excessive number of injuries for years at Georgia-Pacific, as detailed later in this chapter's *Closing Case.*

Dysfunctional behavior
refers to any behavior at work that is counter-productive. These behaviors may include theft and sabotage, for example, as well as sexual and racial harassment.

Other forms of **dysfunctional behavior** may be even more costly for an organization. Theft and sabotage, for example, result in direct financial costs for an organization. Sexual and racial harassment are also costly to an organization, both indirectly (by lowering morale, producing fear, and driving off valuable employees) and directly (through financial liability if the organization responds inappropriately).

Workplace violence and aggression are also growing concerns in many organizations. People who are having problems coping with stress may vent their difficulties by yelling at or harassing their colleagues. They may also engage in other destructive behaviors such as damaging company property or physically assaulting their boss or a coworker. Violence by disgruntled workers or former workers results in dozens of deaths and injuries each year.[24]

But it is also possible that stress has some positive effects on behavior at work. Several studies[25] have suggested that not all stress is the same and that some sources of stress can actually lead to positive outcomes at work.[26] Also, it has been argued that without stress, there is little stimulation and employees can become bored. This perspective leads to the question, Is it possible to have too little stress on the job? The *Point/Counterpoint* feature for this chapter presents some different views on this question.

Wellness Programs in Organizations

Institutional programs
for managing stress are undertaken through established organizational mechanisms.

Two basic organizational strategies for helping employees manage stress are institutional programs and collateral stress programs. **Institutional programs** for managing stress are undertaken through established organizational mechanisms. For example,

POINT | COUNTERPOINT

Not Enough Stress?

 Is stress always a bad thing? Considerable evidence suggests that more stress is not always related to decreased job satisfaction and physical problems. In fact, in some cases, stress can be seen as representing a challenge to the employee and can be quite stimulating. Given this finding, it is not clear whether we should be advocating more or less stress on the job, and some suggest that stress should be increased in some cases.

POINT... We should always seek to reduce the levels of stress on the job because...	**COUNTERPOINT...** Sometimes we can have too little stress and should increase the stress on the job because...
High levels of stress have been related to burnout and physical problems.	Overcoming some stress results in feelings of mastery.
High levels of stress are related to dissatisfaction and turnover.	Dealing effectively with stress is important for the development of managers.
High levels of stress lead to declines in performance on the job.	Jobs with no stress also present no challenge, which leads to boredom.

So... We can have too much stress on the job, but we should also consider the possibility of too little stress and stimulation. The key is to identify the levels of stress that lead to challenge and stimulation but do not reach the levels of producing burnout and dissatisfaction.

properly designed jobs and work schedules, as discussed earlier, can help ease stress. Shiftwork, in particular, can cause major problems for employees because they have to adjust their sleep and relaxation patterns constantly. Thus, the design of work and work schedules should be a focus of organizational efforts to reduce stress.

The organization's culture can also be used to help manage stress. Some organizational cultures, for example, have a strong norm against taking time off or going on vacation. In the long run, such norms can cause major stress. Thus, the organization should strive to foster a culture that reinforces a healthy mix of work and nonwork activities. Supervision can play an important institutional role in managing stress. A supervisor is a potential major source of overload. If made aware of their potential for assigning stressful amounts of work, supervisors can do a better job of keeping workloads reasonable.

In addition to their institutional efforts aimed at reducing stress, many organizations are turning to collateral stress programs. A **collateral stress program** is an organizational program created specifically to help employees deal with stress. Organizations have adopted stress-management programs, health-promotion programs, and other kinds of programs for this purpose. More and more companies are developing their own programs or adopting existing programs of this type. For example, Lockheed Martin offers screening programs for its employees to detect signs of hypertension, and Hospital Corporation of America offers its employees four cents a mile for cycling, sixteen cents a mile for walking or jogging, and sixty-four cents a mile for swimming.

Collateral stress programs *are organizational programs created specifically to help employees deal with stress.*

Many firms today also have employee fitness programs. These kinds of programs attack stress indirectly by encouraging employees to exercise, which in turn is presumed to reduce stress. On the negative side, this kind of effort costs considerably more than stress-management programs because the firm must invest in exercise facilities. Still, more and more companies are exploring this option. Both Tenneco and L. L. Bean, for example, have state-of-the-art fitness centers available for their employees' use.

Organizations try to help employees cope with stress through other kinds of programs. For example, existing career development programs like that at General Electric are used for this purpose. Other companies use programs promoting everything from humor to massage as antidotes for stress. Of course, little or no research supports some of the claims made by advocates of these programs. Thus, managers must take steps to ensure that any organizational effort to help employees cope with stress is at least reasonably effective.

Given the widespread adoption of wellness and stress-reduction programs, it is important to understand how effective these programs are. Much of the "evidence" supporting their effectiveness is anecdotal, with employees reporting how much better they feel when they are allowed to participate in wellness programs. But, such data, although encouraging, cannot substitute for more rigorous evaluations of these programs. Unfortunately, a recent report from the Society for Human Resource Management (SHRM), suggests that many of the programs being established may not be as effective as they could be.[27]

The problem appears to be that many companies, especially smaller firms with more limited resources, do not have comprehensive wellness programs. Instead, they focus on one or two health risks (such as high blood pressure), are not continued over the long run, and tend to focus on salaried employees who are already generally healthier than other employees. The report also suggests that top leadership in the organization must support these programs, and must develop a culture where employees feel valued, in order for these programs to be effective. Finally, the report cites several examples of successful programs (for example, at 3M and at General Mills), where the corporation has partnered with a health-care organization (such as the Mayo Clinic) to ensure that employees have access to good assessment tools as well as programs that can help them deal with their specific health problems, and that there is adequate follow-up. Although it may not be easy for every organization to implement all of these features, it would seem that these are the keys to more effective wellness programs.

AIDS in the Workplace

Acquired immune deficiency syndrome (AIDS) has become a major problem in the world today. AIDS is relevant to employers for several reasons. An employee with AIDS must cope with a life-threatening medical issue, but it is also important to that individual's coworkers. Unfortunately, there is no clear-cut solution for dealing with this issue. Individuals who publicly disclose their condition increase the potential for retaliation from coworkers—many people fear the disease and may shun those who have it. And the organization faces various privacy-related issues.

An organization that wants to deal with this issue must start by developing and implementing a comprehensive AIDS policy. As a premise for developing a policy, however, all employers must keep in mind certain points. First, it is illegal to ask an applicant if she or he has AIDS. Some states allow organizations to require applicants to take an AIDS test, whereas other states do not. Regardless of the outcome, an employee can be denied employment on the basis of AIDS only if it is determined that the applicant cannot perform the job. As long as the individual who is already hired is capable of performing the job, he or she cannot be terminated or placed on leave. All medical information regarding the individual and her or his condition must be kept absolutely confidential.

In general, organizations can adopt three strategies in trying to deal with AIDS from a management perspective. One strategy is to categorize AIDS under a comprehensive life-threatening illness policy. In this instance, AIDS is treated like terminal cancer or any other life-threatening illness. The organization can then apply the same sorts of insurance coverage provisions, early-retirement and leave provisions, and so forth.

Another strategy is to form an AIDS-specific policy. This action is completely legal for an organization to contemplate as long as neither the intent nor the implementation of the policy results in discrimination against people on the basis of an AIDS condition. In general, most companies that form an AIDS-specific policy do so in an affirmative way. That is, the essence of the policy is to affirm the organization's stance that employees with AIDS are still entitled to work, receive benefits, and be treated comparably to all other employees.

The third approach that some companies take is to have no policy at all, an approach taken by far too many companies. The organization either doesn't want to confront the necessity for having an AIDS policy, is afraid to confront the need for such a policy, or doesn't know how to approach such a policy. In any of these events, managerial ignorance can potentially result in serious problems for both the employer and the employees.

Security Issues

The need to live in a safe and secure environments is one of the basic needs driving human behavior (as will be discussed in Chapter 13). But security can be threatened (or guaranteed) in many different ways at work. For example, individuals working in organizations with low accident rates are more likely to feel secure about their safety on the job. But even individuals working on relatively dangerous jobs can feel more secure if the organization (or someone else) is concerned about their safety. Thus, employees

The terrorist attacks on September 11, 2001 and subsequent events have led to dramatic changes in business security. For instance, many organizations have been looking at better ways to protect their employees in the event of future terrorist attacks. Stanford University professor Lawrence Wein is helping to figure out more effective strategies by developing mathematical models that will help security experts better predict potential terrorist targets as well as the best responses should a business be hit by a terrorist attack.

working at nuclear power facilities may feel quite secure because the organization, as well as the federal government, constantly monitors their environment for any threats.

On the other hand, announcements about impending layoffs, or actual layoffs, are likely to increase feelings of insecurity concerning employment.[28] Once layoffs have been announced, many employees will remain feeling insecure for quite some time as they wonder when the next series of cutbacks will be announced. Finally, organizations typically offer insurance plans and pensions in an effort to make employees feel more secure about an uncertain future.

But a different type of security issue has become much more salient to employees in the United States since September 11, 2001. The threat of bombings or kidnappings is not new to the world, but Americans have traditionally felt as though these were concerns only when they were traveling abroad but not when they were at their jobs. During the 1970s there were many kidnappings of executives visiting Latin America, and even some countries in Europe. Organizations began training drivers in evasion tactics, and firms such as GTE bought executives inexpensive plastic briefcases to take when they travel outside the United States, based on the belief that terrorists would target individuals wearing expensive clothes or carrying expensive briefcases. In countries such as Israel, an everyday commute on the bus is far from relaxing, as terrorists have repeatedly bombed these buses. In London, riders on the Underground (subway) were often searched in an attempt to stop IRA bombings. But such threats were quite foreign to U.S. workers.

Of course, there had been an earlier terrorist attack in the United States. On the morning of April 19, 1995, a bomb located in a van parked outside, exploded at the Murrah Federal Building in downtown Oklahoma City. That explosion killed 168 people in what was termed the worst terrorist attack on U.S. soil. But that incident did not threaten the basic security of the U.S. population. The bombing could be blamed on one or two irrational men who were certainly not declaring war on the United States.

The attack on the World Trade Center, however, changed all that. As we discussed in Chapter 2, one reaction to this attack has been a rash of legislation that falls under the heading of Homeland Security. The issues about security versus privacy were also discussed earlier and will be debated for years to come. But these new concerns over security have also had an impact on the human resource management functions in many organizations. For example, most U.S. firms have always been willing to hire non-U.S. citizens for certain types of jobs, and to help those new employees attain the proper status with immigration officials. But in the post-9/11 environment, many companies have been less willing to hire foreigners, especially those from the Middle East. In fact, many American universities have also become less willing to recruit students from certain parts of the world, and the U.S. government has made it more difficult for any potential students and employees to obtain visas. The issue with foreign students has become especially serious, since several of the attackers at the World Trade Center were in this country on student visas. To the extent that these concerns and practices eliminate from consideration potentially qualified employees and students, they hurt the ability of businesses to recruit the best-qualified people available.

Concerns over security have also made many Americans less willing to travel abroad—especially to areas that are potentially dangerous. While these concerns have been present for quite some time, the new feelings of vulnerability have resulted in U.S. business leaders being even less willing to travel to certain parts of the world on business. This, in turn, has necessitated an increased reliance upon teleconferencing and other substitutes for face-to-face meetings. But the reluctance to travel abroad also makes it more difficult to manage overseas operations and makes it more difficult to give managers expatriate assignments.

In addition, most U.S. firms are now engaging in high-level emergency preparedness planning. The World Trade Center attacks wiped out the entire financial records of some firms. Other companies lost employee records and other critical data. Although most large firms have always had backup systems in place, heightened security concerns have led organizations to develop multiple backup systems, as well as information technology systems that are not tied to a single location.

But perhaps the greatest impact of September 11 has been on the general sense of well-being of many Americans. Americans are now subject to constant reminders of threat levels (color-coded for ease of interpretation), and there are repeated warnings of potential threats and the message that Americans must be more vigilant. But since there are really no specific instructions given as to what should be the target of that vigilance, such warnings really serve primarily to increase the stress levels of everyone involved.

In August of 2005 Hurricane Katrina struck the Gulf Coast of the United States, breached the levees in New Orleans, and resulted in a large portion of New Orleans being under water for weeks. Recent surveys of stress in the city of New Orleans suggest that self-reported stress, as well as the incidence of psychosomatic symptoms have increased dramatically, and security has become a major concern for many New Orleanians. In general, then, people all over the world are feeling less secure than they did twenty years ago, but perhaps the greatest change has come in the United States where most people believed that they were immune from the security threats they now deal with every day.

Chapter Summary

There are many reasons why modern organizations are more concerned about employee safety and health issues than ever before. Lost work time and increased insurance costs are among the most important but, for whatever reasons, organizations are very interested in ways to keep employees safe, healthy, and secure.

As such, organizations are interested in ways of managing the work environment to make it safer. Basic issues involve actions that the organization can and should take to control or eliminate safety hazards and health hazards. Safety hazards refer to those conditions in the work environment that have the potential to cause harm to an employee. Health hazards are those characteristics of the work environment that more slowly and systematically, and perhaps cumulatively, result in damage to an employee's health. OSHA authorized the U.S. government to create and enforce various standards regarding occupational safety and health.

In addition, the actual physical environment in which an employee works is also extremely important. Many aspects of the physical environment may affect an employee's attitudes and behavior on the job and can affect employee health and well-being. Work hours reflect one such aspect. Illumination, temperature, and office and work-space design are also important.

Stress is a person's adaptive response to a stimulus that places excessive psychological or physical demands on him or her. The stimuli that cause stress are called stressors. Organizational stressors are various factors in the workplace that can cause stress. Four general sets of organizational stressors are task demands, physical demands, role demands, and interpersonal demands. If the stress is positive, the result may be more energy, enthusiasm, and motivation. Three other sets of consequences that can result from stress are individual consequences, organizational consequences, and burnout. But it is important to note that not everyone experiences stress in the same way, and there are also individual differences in the effects that stress has on employees. Two basic organizational strategies for helping employees manage stress are institutional programs and collateral stress programs. In addition, organizations develop programs to reduce the threat of various diseases at work, including AIDS.

Finally, security concerns have emerged as a real issue for employees. The United States has probably seen the greatest change in stress due to security concerns, because such concerns were not salient to Americans in the past. But, especially since the September 11 attacks, U.S. firms have become much more security conscious, as have most Americans.

Key Points for Future HR Managers

- Occupational safety and health is important because of legal requirements and also because of its impact on productivity and employee attitudes.

- Managing the physical work environment is another critical aspect of the human resource function.

- Decisions about shiftwork, illumination, temperature, and workplace design can have a significant impact on employee productivity, employee health, employee safety, and employee attitudes toward their jobs.

- Stress at work plays a major role in employee health, attitudes, and productivity, and much of this stress comes from the way work is designed.

- There are important individual differences in terms of how one experiences stress and what are the effects of stress.

- AIDS in the workplace will continue to be an important health issue.

- Security issues are becoming extremely important, especially for U.S. firms and their employees.

Key Points for Future General Managers

- Employee safety is not only a matter of the law, it is good business because it reduces costs and increases productivity.

- The physical work environment is critical for productivity, health, safety, and employee attitudes.

- Stress on the job could be the result of job demands, physical demands, role demands, and interpersonal demands.

- Stress can have many negative effects, although there are individual differences in how people experience stress.

- Security concerns at work have become much more important, especially in the United States.

Review and Discussion Questions

1. What are the differences between safety hazards and health hazards?

2. Review the list of injury-prone jobs and dangerous occupations in Table 12.2. Identify five other jobs that you think might also belong on each list.

3. Research the OSHA guidelines and regulations that relate most directly to your current or anticipated job.

4. Would you prefer a job that required you to work relatively long hours but provided relatively more days off from work each week, or a job that required relatively fewer hours per day but also provided relatively fewer days off? Why?

5. Describe the kind of physical environment in which you would most like to work.

6. What are the primary causes and consequences of stress in organizations?

7. What are the primary stressors that affect you now? How do you respond to stress?

8. Identify people you know who respond differently to stress? What seems to be the basis for their differences?

9. Would the presence of an on-site wellness center influence your decision to work for a particular organization?

10. In general, increased security seems to come at the expense of personal freedom. In your opinion, is this a reasonable trade-off?

CLOSING CASE

Safety Comes to Georgia-Pacific

Georgia-Pacific Corporation is the world's largest distributor of building products (such as wood panels, lumber, and gypsum products) and among the five-largest manufacturers of packaging materials, correspondence paper (such as office printing products and stationery), wood pulp, and tissue paper. The firm is based in Atlanta, Georgia, and has more than 100 distribution centers scattered across North America. It controls more than 6 million acres of timberland in the United States and Canada. Its annual revenues generally run about $20 billion.

Forest-products businesses have never been known for their safe, pleasant, and comfortable work environments. Paper mills, sawmills, and plywood factories, for example, are generally characterized by constant, deafening noise; huge, razor-toothed blades, shredders, and grinders; long chutes loaded with rumbling tons of lumber; and giant vats full of boiling water and caustic chemicals. The products they make are awkward in size, heavy, and often full of painful splinters, and the machinery used to make them requires frequent maintenance and close contact with sharp edges and dangerous moving parts.

Throughout much of its history, Georgia-Pacific had an unenviable accident record, even for what experts see as a highly dangerous and hazardous industry. For example, between 1986 and 1990 the firm averaged nine serious injuries per year per 100 employees, and twenty-six workers lost their lives on the job. Two factors contributing to these statistics were unrelenting pressure to keep productivity high and a macho organization culture that promoted risk-taking and bravado.

For example, top management continually reinforced the importance of keeping production lines moving, no matter what. As a result, workers would often attempt to perform routine maintenance or repair broken equipment parts without shutting down the line. And if they didn't have a pair of safety gloves handy, they would carry around heavy—and sharp—saw blades with their bare hands rather than "waste" an extra few minutes to take appropriate safety precautions. Indeed, one observer noted that you weren't considered a real Georgia-Pacific "mill guy" unless you were missing a finger or two!

But this situation started to change a few years ago when a new top management team came in. The new managers were appalled by the firm's poor safety record and vowed to make it a source of pride rather than a source of embarrassment. The starting point was creating a task force charged with learning more about operating practices that contributed to accidents and then figure out how to change those practices. The next step was altering the firm's basic culture so that it reinforced safe rather than risky practices and behaviors. And finally, Georgia-Pacific implemented an array of new rules and regulations that explicitly promoted safe work and punished those responsible for unnecessarily hazardous or dangerous actions.

So far, the results have been impressive. Accident rates have dropped consistently for each of the past fifteen years, and few workers lose their lives anymore. At one of the firm's most hazardous plants, injuries run about only 0.7 per 100 workers annually. OSHA indicates that this ratio is about one-third the injury rate at the average bank! And the company has realized that being more cautious and following safer work procedures has boosted its productivity rather than lowering it. Stopping a production line to correct a problem usually takes only a few minutes, whereas stopping it because of an accident or injury might shut down production for hours—or even days.

Injury rates now play a major role in the performance evaluation and compensation for all supervisors and managers at Georgia-Pacific. Safety equipment is an absolute requirement. One top manager, for example, happily tells the story of how he was recently chewed out by an hourly worker while visiting a sawmill because he carelessly stepped too close to a dangerous piece of equipment. All employees in the mills have to wear earplugs, hardhats, goggles, gloves, and steel-toed shoes at all times. Failure to follow these regulations can result in immediate dismissal. And indeed, Georgia-Pacific is so proud of its achievements in safety that it's working to extend the same principles used to make these changes to other areas of its business, including quality and customer service.[29]

Case Questions

1. Why do you think Georgia-Pacific has been so successful in reducing its accident and injury rates?

2. What other industries and businesses might benefit from the same kind of approach?

3. Research Georgia-Pacific's most recent safety statistics and see if the firm is still doing as well.

Building HR Management Skills

Purpose: The purpose of this exercise is to help you appreciate the various workplace hazards that organizations must confront.

Step 1: Select three jobs that you would predict to be relatively dangerous. Select three other jobs that you would expect to be relatively safe.

Step 2: Next, carefully consider each of the six jobs you selected and identify two of the biggest safety and/or health hazards that might affect each one.

Step 3: Finally, briefly describe how you might go about reducing or eliminating the safety and/or health hazards identified in step 2.

Questions

1. Are there any jobs that face no workplace hazards or threats?

2. Are there any dangerous jobs that simply cannot be made less hazardous?

3. See if you can find any data online about the real hazards or threats facing the jobs you identified.

Ethical Dilemmas in HR Management

You are the owner/manager of a small software enterprise. You employ a total of 150 people, all of whom have stock options in the business. Working in consultation with several of your designers, you are closing in on a major breakthrough with a software product that can dramatically reduce manufacturing costs for firms in several different industries. You are also aware, however, that several larger competitors are working hard to develop the same basic technology. If your firm is to achieve the breakthrough first, a major push is needed. You are sitting in your office weighing the following basic facts:

1. All of your employees are on the verge of exhaustion; each one has been putting in sixty to eighty hours per week for the last four months, and no one ever takes a day off. You know that a couple of employees are drinking more than normal, and at least three are reportedly having marital difficulties.

2. You estimate that another six to eight weeks of intense work and long hours will likely allow your firm to get the new product up and running first.

3. If your firm is the first to get the new software finished, everyone in the firm will reap a huge financial reward. The most senior employees (and you, of course) will likely become millionaires; even the newest employees should see their stock options increase in value to near $100,000 more than their current value.

4. It will take an all-or-nothing effort if you are to succeed. That is, you cannot cut back on work schedules or give people time off, or else you will fall behind your competitors. Every single worker will need to work hard until the project is finished, or else you might as well give up now.

You see yourself as having two options. On the one hand, you can cut back on the workload and reduce the stress and pressure on your employees. While your firm would almost certainly lose the race for the software breakthrough, the company is nevertheless quite profitable and your employees earn an above-market income. Other opportunities for major breakthroughs may occur in the future. On the other hand, you can keep the work pace as it is; after all, it's only for a few more weeks and then everyone will share in what will likely be a major reward.

Questions

1. What are the ethical issues in this situation?

2. What are the basic arguments for and against continuing an all-out push to achieve the breakthrough?

3. What do you think most owners/managers would do? What would you do?

HR Internet Exercise

The Occupational Safety and Health Administration (OSHA), part of the U.S. Department of Labor, maintains an extensive website. Start by visiting the site at http://www.osha.gov/.

Now, assume that you have just been placed in charge of workplace safety for a midsized manufacturing firm plagued by a high rate of injuries and accidents. Based on your review of the OSHA website, respond to the following questions:

Questions

1. How helpful do you think the OSHA website might be to you in lowering your plant's accident and injury rate?

2. What parts of the site do you think are most and least helpful?

3. Do you think a manager in your position can rely solely on the OSHA website to deal with problems, or will other information be required?

KNOWLEDGE, SOCIAL ISSUES, AND HUMAN RESOURCE MANAGEMENT

In Part Three we have learned about compensation and benefits, performance appraisal and development, labor relations, and health, well-being safety, and security. The common theme across these topics is that they all relate in one way or another to the role of human resource management in managing the workforce. In this *Taking HR to the Next Level*, we examine two additional topics that also relate to this theme. First we discuss the ways in which firms can manage the knowledge function; next we describe HR and social issues.

Managing the Knowledge Function

Traditionally, most organizations thought of their product as some tangible type of "goods." That is, steel companies produced steel, and auto companies produced autos. Over time, however, the economies in many countries, including the United States, shifted from a focus on manufacturing to a focus on services, and so the orientation shifted to the production of "goods and services." But, in today's economy, many organizations are now really trading in knowledge. Investment firms are selling their special knowledge about how to manage a portfolio and plan for retirement or some other goal; consulting firms are selling expertise in dealing with the many management problems that face organizations, and many other types of businesses are actually dealing primarily in knowledge rather than any goods or services.

With these shifts also came the recognition that knowledge was also a commodity within an organization that needed to be managed and leveraged. Furthermore, as the nature of work and business changed, many organizations found that that they were employing a larger number of "knowledge workers" who required some special handling. In this section, we focus on the notion of organizational learning, which is an important part of the internal knowledge management function, as well as some issues associated with the management of knowledge workers.

Organizational Learning **Organizational learning** refers to the process by which an organization "learns" from past mistakes and adapts to its environment. Over time, rules and procedures change based on experience, but this change is still based on individual learning. That is, individuals learn how to adapt and change, and then interact with one another so that the new information gained can be shared and distributed throughout the organization. As a result, a shared vision and interpretation of the information is developed throughout the organization, and the change permeates the entire organization. At this point, the organization can be said to have "learned" how to be more effective.

A few points are important to remember. First, the process begins with individual learning and change. If there is no individual learning, there can be no organizational learning. Second, whereas the individual learning process is a cognitive one, organizational learning depends more upon social processes and sharing of information. Thus, individual learning is a necessary but not sufficient condition for organizational learning to occur.[1]

The process of organizational learning, then, involves the acquisition of new knowledge by the organization. Again, it is not enough that individuals acquire this knowledge.

Organizational learning
refers to the process by which an organization "learns" from past mistakes and adapts to its environment.

They must then communicate with other organizational members to ensure that this knowledge is available throughout the organization. And the organization must use this information to adapt. There is a strong belief that organizations that can manage this change—that is, organizations that can acquire information and adapt—can gain significant competitive advantage versus their competitors.[2]

For example, large conglomerates such as General Electric or Viacom typically grow by acquiring other firms. Each time these firms make an acquisition, they must figure out how to best integrate the new employees into the firm, and how to marry the culture of the acquired firm with the culture of the parent firm. Presumably, these large conglomerates made mistakes over the years in both the targets for their acquisitions, and how they managed the acquisition after it was completed. But they also probably learned from their experience and got better at it over time. This is a case of organizational learning, and learning how to better target and manage acquisitions would clearly give the conglomerate an advantage over its competitors.

Furthermore, a firm can gain important new knowledge as a result of a merger or acquisition. Thus, for example, a large firm may be contemplating entering a new market in China, but the firm lacks the expertise (or knowledge) on how to enter that difficult market successfully. The large firm (Company A) could acquire the needed information by sending key employees to some source where they can learn the needed skills, or it can acquire those skills directly by acquiring individuals who already possess the needed skills. That is, the large firm can look for another firm (Company B) that has already mastered the China market. Then Company A can either try to hire the experts away from Company B, or if the expert knowledge is widely held throughout Company B, it can access the expertise throughout the firm via a merger, a joint venture, or a complete acquisition of Company B.

Finally, we should note the concept of organizational memory and the role it plays in organizational learning. **Organizational memory** refers to the collective, institutional record of past events. In order for an organization to "learn" from past events, it must be possible to "recall" those events in some way. Some of these things are written down or stored electronically, so that there is a physical record of the events surrounding a recent merger, or some change in legislation, or any other event from which someone might learn a lesson. These physical records then serve as the organizational memory. But there are also many cases where this information is not formally recorded. Instead, one or more people who were there when the event happened become the organizational memory. These individuals are the repository for information that can help the organization to learn from experience and to avoid repeating mistakes.

Thus, an organization can gain access to new information through a variety of ways. Once this information is shared and distributed throughout the organization so that all employees now share a view of what this information means and how it can be used to change, organizational learning is said to have occurred. When this information and its interpretation also become part of the organizational memory, change and adaptation can continue for some time. This type of learning and the adaptation that it involves will clearly be critical to firms as they try to compete effectively in the twenty-first century.

Managing Knowledge Workers Traditionally, employees added value to organizations because of what they did or because of their experience. As we enter the information age in the workplace, however, many employees add value simply because of what they know.[3] This new reality creates new problems and challenges for managing work relationships.

The Nature of Knowledge Work Employees who add value simply because of what they know are usually referred to as **knowledge workers,** and how well these employ-

Organizational memory
refers to the collective, institutional record of past events. In order for an organization to "learn" from past events, it must be possible to "recall" those events in some way. They may be written or stored electronically, or these events may be stored only in the memories of the individuals involved.

Knowledge workers *are employees who add value simply because of what they know.*

414

ees are managed is seen as a major factor in determining which firms will be successful in the future.[4] Knowledge workers include computer scientists, engineers, and physical scientists, and they provide special challenges for the human resource manager. They tend to work in high-technology firms and are usually experts in some abstract knowledge base. They often believe they have the right to work autonomously and they identify more strongly with their profession than they do with any organization—even to the extent of defining performance in terms recognized by other members of their profession.[5]

As the importance of information-driven jobs grows, the need for knowledge workers will also grow. But these employees require extensive and specialized training, and not everyone is willing to make the human capital investments necessary to move into these jobs. In fact, even after knowledge workers are on the job, retraining and training updates are critical so that their skills do not become obsolete. It has been suggested, for example, that the "half-life" for a technical education in engineering is about three years. Failure to update the required skills by the end of that time not only results in the organization losing competitive advantage but also increases the likelihood that the knowledge worker will go to another firm that is more committed to updating these skills.[6]

Compensation and career development policies for knowledge workers must also be specially tailored. For example, in many high-tech organizations, engineers and scientists have the option of entering a technical career path that parallels a management career path. This option allows the knowledge worker to continue to carry out specialized work without taking on management responsibilities; at the same time the organization offers the knowledge worker compensation that is equivalent to the compensation available to management. Also, in many high-tech organizations, salary adjustments within various classifications for management workers are most frequently based on maturity curves rather than on performance. That is, because performance is difficult to quantify for these employees, and because a great deal of research and development (R&D) activity may not have an immediate payoff, salary is based on the employee's years of work experience. The assumption is that, in a technical area, more experience makes the employee more valuable to the organization.[7]

But in other high-tech firms, the emphasis is on pay for performance, with profit sharing based on projects or products developed by the knowledge workers. In addition, the tendency in most firms employing these workers is to reduce the number of levels of the organization to allow the knowledge workers to react more quickly to the external environment and to reduce the need for bureaucratic approval.[8]

Special Issues with Knowledge Worker Management   It is clear that the demand for knowledge workers has been growing dramatically in recent years. As a result, organizations that hire these workers need to introduce regular market adjustments (upward) to employee pay if they want to retain them. This approach is especially critical in an area where demand is growing because entry-level wages for these employees are skyrocketing. Once an employee accepts a job with a firm, he or she is more subject to the internal labor market, which is not likely to grow as quickly as the external market for the knowledge workers. As a result, the longer an employee remains with a firm, the further behind the market rate his or her pay falls—unless it is regularly adjusted.

Of course, the growing demand for these workers also results in organizations going to rather extreme measures to attract them in the first place.[9] High starting salaries and sign-on bonuses are common. British Petroleum Exploration was recently paying starting petroleum engineers with undersea platform drilling knowledge (not experience, just knowledge) salaries in the six-figure range, with sign-on bonuses of over $50,000 and immediate profit sharing. Even with these incentives, human resource managers from the organization complained that in the Gulf Coast region, they could not retain these specialists because the young engineers would leave to accept a sign-on bonus with a competitor after just a few months.

But these phenomena occur in times when unemployment is relatively low, and the demand for certain types of knowledge workers is relatively recent. As time goes on and college students learn about the salaries paid to these specialists, more of them will gravitate to programs in areas such as undersea drilling. More universities will respond with larger and larger programs in these and other areas to accommodate the new demand. As a result, enough of these specialists will be available in a few years to meet the demand, and the frenzy over hiring and retaining these employees will subside.

This information takes time to filter down to new students, and some students are already on the academic track in these areas. Therefore, the future will likely see a surplus of ocean-drilling engineers, for example. This situation will drive salaries down, which in the long run will discourage new students from making the human capital investments needed to perform these jobs. Then another shortage of these knowledge workers will trigger a new round of efforts to attract and retain those employees who are available. While these patterns greatly complicate the lives of human resource professionals, organizations will have to do better long-term planning so they can manage the supply and demand of knowledge workers rather than react to the labor market conditions. The knowledge base about the issues related to managing knowledge workers is growing, and organizations can build competitive advantage by better utilizing the knowledge resources they have.[10] These skills will be critical to human resource managers in the new century.

An Expanded View of Knowledge Work Our discussion thus far has concentrated on employees who have knowledge-related jobs, known as knowledge workers. But organizations are increasingly coming to view "knowledge" more broadly: as the ultimate source of competitive advantage. That is, according to a popular view of strategic management known as the resource-based view of the firm, firms gain competitive advantage by developing resources that are rare, valuable, and difficult to copy or substitute.[11] Traditionally, these resources were considered to be technology or specialized suppliers, for example, but more recent thinking suggests that intangible resources based on knowledge and the capabilities of workers is a more sustainable source of competitive advantage. Thus, any employee who can bring some unique insights to the job is potentially seen as a source of competitive advantage. As a result, most employees are viewed as knowledge workers and should be rewarded and valued because of the knowledge they possess.

Elsewhere (*Taking HR to the Next Level,* Part One) we discussed how expatriate workers were critical for knowledge transfer to and from the headquarters and the overseas operation. This discussion reflected the expended view of knowledge work and the importance of competing on the basis of knowledge. Likewise, we discussed the role of human resource management in mergers and acquisitions (also in *Taking HR to the Next Level,* Part One) but focused on human resource management during the process. An expanded view of knowledge work also acknowledges that critical employees and the knowledge they possess may actually be the reason for an attempted acquisition or merger. That is, if a certain company is known for its marketing techniques or its innovations in technology, another firm may attempt to acquire that knowledge through a merger or an acquisition. It is important to note that, in such cases, it is exactly these employees with that specialized knowledge who will probably have the most options open to them and so are more likely to leave when they face the uncertainty of a merger or acquisition. Therefore, in cases where a merger or acquisition is being planned to acquire certain employees, it is even more critical that the acquiring firm manages the process in such a way as to reduce uncertainty and turnover.

In any case, it seems as though more and more organizations are beginning to view themselves as competing on the basis of knowledge. As this view expands, the importance of knowledge workers, as well as the importance of all workers who possess specialized knowledge will grow. This will lead to increased competition for these employees and will place a great premium on the ability to attract and retain such employees in the future.

HR and Social Issues

In this section of the book, we discussed the importance of safety and health issues, the role of unions in the human resource management process, as well as issues related to compensation, performance appraisals, and career management. These are all topics that have traditionally been part of what we consider to be the core of human resource management. But in recent years, many human resource managers have also begun thinking about how human resource management practices impact social issues. Indeed, one recent study found that human resource executives in the United States (as well as in Australia, China, and India) are more likely to be in charge of implementing and monitoring issues associated with social issues and social responsibility than any other functional executive.[12]

There is an increasing awareness that the needs of the organization can be met even while addressing the needs of the employees or of society as a whole,[13] and there is also an increasing concern with social issues in general. In fact, this is one area where management and organized labor can often come together, and furthermore, labor unions in the United States have been especially successful at using these issues to change their image into one of a group of people concerned about conditions around the world. We discuss some areas where there is evidence of this new concern and what it means as we take HR to the next level.

Prison Labor   Most of us do not spend a lot of time thinking about what prison inmates do with their time, but in most cases they work at jobs inside the prisons. Traditionally, these jobs included manufacturing automobile license plates, repairing roads, or doing the laundry for other state institutions, but that situation has been changing. As we noted in Chapter 11, this is a source of concern for the U.S. labor movement, but it is increasingly a source of concern for human resource managers as well.

First, the number of prisoners involved has been changing. In 1990 there were approximately 66,000 federal prisoners and 708,000 state and local prisoners. By 2006, those numbers had risen to 155,000 federal inmates and 1.95 million state and local inmates. Many of these inmates work at paid jobs, but they earn somewhat less than workers on the outside. In fact, in 1991, prison wages ranged from $0.23 to $1.15 per hour on a federal pay scale, although more than half these workers earned $0.40 per hour or less.[14] Second, the laws regulating where and how the goods produced by inmate labor can be sold have been changing, thus making it easier to sell products produced by inmates on the open market.

The fact that goods produced at such a low cost can compete openly with goods produced by workers who are paid a minimum wage is potentially a serious threat to the jobs of low-paid, unskilled workers in the general population.[15] In fact, some argue that prison labor contributes little to the gross domestic product (GDP) but has a substantial effect on the employment opportunities and wages of high school dropouts in this country.[16] These same critics also argue that these jobs do not prepare prison inmates for outside jobs once they are released and so do not lessen the rate of subsequent arrest and incarceration.

What should we do? Clearly, several different issues are involved. One relates to the problem of allowing products produced by prisoners (who are paid less) to compete with products that are produced by employees who earn a legal wage. Although companies may need incentives to hire prison workers, allowing these goods to compete more freely in the open market may actually be a problem. Other organizations can see this as a way to gain some advantage, and eventually, we can see a very heavy reliance upon prison labor. Also, we must think about what we would like to have inmates do while they are in prison. For some, who will never be released, this may not be a problem. But, for others, perhaps it is important that the work they do while in prison will help them to get and hold jobs on the outside. Furthermore, the employees should probably be paid what their work is really worth.

A Living Wage   In Chapter 2 and later in Chapter 9, we discuss the minimum wage noting that there is some controversy over whether the minimum wage should be raised. But how does a person earning the national minimum wage of $7.25 live? That person will earn $290 per week or just over $15,000 per year. It is difficult to imagine how someone would live on that, never mind support a family. Instead, there are those within our country who suggest that we should work, instead, toward paying employees a "living wage"—that is enough to allow a family to live above the poverty level. It is interesting to note that this is exactly what several states have done. For example, the minimum wage in California is $8.50 an hour, while the rate in Alaska is $7.15 and, effective January 2007, the minimum wage in Connecticut will be $7.65 an hour, and it will be $7.25 an hour in Hawaii. These are attempts to ensure that working people can live at some reasonable level, but they may not be enough.

In New Orleans, after Hurricane Katrina, there was a shortage of workers for jobs in fast-food restaurants. As a result, Burger King was offering $10 an hour to start and a $5,000 signing bonus if the employee worked for one year. But Katrina destroyed much of the lower-middle-class housing that had been available in New Orleans, and the housing that remained was expensive even at these higher wages. Therefore, even these wages could not attract a sufficient number of employees for some time.

The challenge, then, is how we should determine what someone is paid. The traditional human resource management approach would be either to conduct some type of job evaluation (we discuss some of these in Chapter 9), or do a survey to determine the "going rate" in a given market. The living wage movement would suggest that this is not adequate and that organizations owe their employees the ability to live a reasonable life. Of course, opponents argue that if a state (or a firm) pays above market rate, they will need to either charge more for their goods (making them less competitive) or accept lower profits. Therefore, no rational business person would move to these states. Instead, by this argument, states such as Kansas and Ohio (with state minimum wages below the national level) or states such as Mississippi and Louisiana (with no state minimum wage laws) should be the most prosperous, but they aren't. Florida continues to grow in terms of both population and business, and Nevada (which has a state law at the level of the national law) is usually ranked as the best state for business in the United States.

But should human resource managers be social activists? Should they argue for a living wage as opposed to a more competitive wage? As with all the issues discussed in this section, the answers to these questions depend on the person and his or her values. For some of our readers, it will be difficult not to speak out.

Immigration   During the spring of 2006, there were literally hundreds of demonstrations involving hundreds of thousands of people dealing with U.S. immigration policy.

The Congress had been debating how to deal with the large number of illegal immigrants in the United States and many people were angry. Interestingly, this was also an important issue for human resource managers, since much of their work touches on issues that are important for immigrants—both legal and illegal.

The concerns during 2006 were with illegal immigrants. These are people who entered the country illegally but who were living (and often working) in this country. These workers are typically willing to accept lower wages, and they are really in no position to complain about their working conditions. Therefore, they are the perfect target for anyone who wishes to exploit them. Why would someone do that? There are several reasons.

First, as noted, these workers are willing to work for lower wages. This allows organizations and employers to hold down labor costs. These workers are also usually quite willing to work hard, and so they may be especially productive. In some cases, these workers are also willing to perform jobs that other workers are unwilling to do. In addition, even if they are paid exploitative wages, they are probably earning more than they could earn in their home countries. So what is the problem?

As with several of the issues we have been discussing, one problem is that U.S. citizens (or legal immigrants) who need to work to support a family will either not find jobs or will be forced to work for lower wages because the organization can always go to the illegal immigrant if necessary. Also, these illegal immigrants cannot really support their families on the wages they earn. But the immigration problem is actually even more complex. During the 1960s and 1970s, countries in Europe, especially Germany, found that there was actually a shortage of workers who were willing to perform unskilled jobs. The Germans invited thousands of Turks and Greeks to enter Germany as "guest workers." They could remain in Germany legally, and they were paid a fair wage. Over time, this program led to a number of social problems, however, and after the German reunification, the Germans focused more on integrating the citizens of the former East Germany into their economy. In 2006 President Bush recommended a similar solution for this country, although he allowed for a mechanism whereby the guest workers could eventually become citizens as well.

How do organizations find employees to perform undesirable and unskilled jobs? Could older, retired workers perform some of them? What do we owe employees, even if they are guests? Do we owe them full benefits? Job security? Education? Is the solution simply to make sure that everyone is paid a living wage so that there would be no advantage to a firm hiring illegal immigrants? Finally, how do all of these issues impact those who entered the United States legally and are pursuing normal channels to become citizens?

Security Issues   Since September 11, 2001, the United States has become much more conscious of security issues. We discussed some implications of these concerns in Chapter 2, but, as noted in Chapter 12, there are also some very direct HR implications for this heightened concern over security.

Most human resource managers would argue that an organization needs to hire the best people in order to be competitive. But what if the "best" person for a job happens to be a young single male from a Middle Eastern country not particularly friendly to U.S. policies? The simple response is that such a person would probably have difficulty getting the necessary permission to enter this country and get a job. This represents a potentially serious constraint on a firm's ability to hire the best employees.

On the other hand, the U.S. government has formed a new agency, the Transportation Security Administration, to deal with security at airports. These employees are supposed to screen baggage and look out for suspicious situations in an attempt to prevent another

September 11 episode. This decision has created an interesting selection problem, however, for government HR experts. What kind of person do we want performing these tasks? What should their qualifications be? How do we deal with the fact that these employees are required to be vigilant for a situation that will occur (hopefully) very infrequently, which can lead to boredom and low vigilance. How do we recruit, select, and train employees to carry out these functions for salaries that are unlikely to attract the most qualified applicants? The future of how we deal with homeland security will depend largely on how well we are able to deal with these very specific human resource management issues.

Enhancing Performance

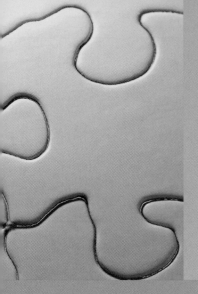

13

Motivation at Work

CHAPTER OBJECTIVES

After studying this chapter you should be able to:

- Describe the basic model of performance.

- Discuss motivation and human needs.

- Identify the basic process models of motivation and describe an integrative model of motivation.

- Describe two other important theories of motivation.

- Discuss additional issues in motivation.

The U.S. government and citizens give generously, donating billions of dollars to troubled regions desperate for aid and assistance. Yet one of the biggest contributions from Americans isn't money, it's time. Each year 64.5 million Americans volunteer, collectively investing 3.4 billion hours. Volunteers derive satisfaction from their efforts. In addition, corporations that support volunteers are very effective in recruiting and retaining workers, making profitable business connections, and promoting excellent corporate public relations.

Corporate-sponsored volunteers work within the United States and abroad. For example, at drug manufacturer Pfizer, workers volunteered to provide services to low-income communities from the Philippines to the Bronx. Cisco Systems, a networking provider, sent an executive to Southeast Asia for a year. He set up wireless networks to coordinate aid workers throughout the region. Microsoft employee Frank Schott visited a refugee camp in Kosovo and came away convinced that his company needed to help. Schott says, "It's very hard to go on a mission to a refugee camp and go out of there without thinking, 'Gosh, we've got to do something.'" Microsoft built a software system to register refugees, making it easier for families to reunite, and then sent 400 employees to Kosovo to implement it.

Robert Nardelli, former CEO of Home Depot, participated personally in building schools and playgrounds and sponsored a program in which Home Depot employees volunteered 250,000 hours in 2004. He noted that IBM, Target, UPS, and Avon, among other firms, have strong corporate volunteering programs. "Each corporation should play to its strength. The specific tactics should be tied to the specific skills of the corporation," said Nardelli. "For us . . . it's about building things."

Beth Miller runs a consulting firm that formerly provided information consulting services. When the company couldn't recruit enough skilled programmers in a tight job market, it began a corporate-sponsored volunteering program. The program was so successful that it became a full-time concern for Miller, whose company now helps corporations form philanthropy partnerships with nonprofits. Miller found that the volunteering program made recruiting easier, reduced turnover, and enabled employees to develop in skills and leadership, leading her to believe that volunteering increases worker satisfaction. "Satisfied employees are worth their weight in gold," according to Miller. "[A volunteering] program would be especially appealing to Generation Y—those socially conscious workers now in their twenties who grew up doing community service."

Volunteering can motivate workers by increasing their sense of self-esteem, fulfilling their need for achievement, and satisfying other higher-level needs. Workers whose companies support volunteering feel pride in their employer, too. And corporations clearly benefit, as do communities in need. When asked about whether companies that support corporate volunteering are promoting a cause or their own self-interest, Nardelli says, "They're inseparably linked. Not only does a corporation have to provide financial value, it also has to build itself on values."[1]

> *"Satisfied employees are worth their weight in gold."*
>
> (Beth Miller, chairwoman, MA&A Group)

Motivation *determines how a person will exert his or her effort. It represents the forces operating on the person to exert effort, as well as the direction in which that effort will be exerted.*

Why do some people choose to volunteer their time for important causes and others do not? Even more germane, if two people are equally capable of performing the same task, why might one consistently outperform the other? We might say that one tries harder, or exerts more effort, but what we really mean is that one person is more motivated than the other to perform well. **Motivation** determines how a person will exert his or her effort. More specifically, it represents the forces operating on the person to exert effort, as well as the direction in which that effort will be exerted. One person might work hard at academics while another person might work hard at sports. Both are motivated, but the direction of their motivation is quite different and it will produce much different outcomes.

Motivation at work is a critical determinant of what will occur on the job. An effective manager must not only motivate employees to exert *some* effort, but he or she must also make sure that the effort is exerted in a way that produces organizationally valued outcomes. The human resource manager must design systems that make it more likely that employees will exert effort in these desirable ways. The key, then, is to understand how we can motivate people to engage in behaviors we desire. As we shall discuss, a number of models or theories of motivation have been proposed as a way of accomplishing this. We will review some of these theories and discuss some strengths and weaknesses of each. But there is no one model of motivation guaranteed to work in all situations for all people. Instead, several models of motivation provide us with some insights into how to motivate people, and taken together, we can formulate a set of clear suggestions about how human resource managers could develop systems that improve work motivation, which will lead to improved performance and will help develop competitive advantage for the firm.

Through four generations of the Smucker family and 105 years of making great jams, jellies, and other goodies, J. M. Smucker knows a few things about how to motivate and retain good employees. For instance, the Orville, Ohio, company grants unlimited paid time off to employees who want to volunteer. Here Brenda Dempsey, Smucker's corporate communications director, instructs an economics class at Orville High School. This sort of community-building program has a broad range of direct and indirect benefits.

A Basic Model of Performance

For most of us, the possibility of playing basketball like Michael Jordan or playing piano like Elton John has very little to do with motivation. We simply lack the necessary talent to perform at those levels (and few do). Hence, it should be clear that any level of performance on any task is not solely a function of motivation—it is a joint function of ability, motivation, and context. The human resource manager must play a critical role in determining two of these critical elements, the ability and the motivation sides of performance. (The third element, context, refers to such things as equipment and materials. While Elton John can certainly play piano and might be motivated to do so at any given time, if his piano is poorly tuned or has broken strings he will still not be able to play well. Context, however, is usually not the purview of human resources.)

Specifically, the human resource management decisions we discussed in Part Two of this book dealt with the determinants of ability on the job. If the human resource manager collected the right information about the job requirements, recruited qualified people and then selected the best among these recruits, and trained them on exactly what they were required to do, it is quite likely that all the employees in the firm will be capable of performing their jobs at a reasonably high level of proficiency. The difference between employees who performed at a mediocre level and those who performed at a higher level, then, would be a function of motivation alone.

Of course, no human resource manager does a perfect job of recruiting or selecting of training, and so not everyone may be capable of performing at the level the organization desires. For some of these employees, though, they may still be able to reach desired performance levels by exerting an extraordinary level of effort. That is, high levels of motivation can compensate for lower levels of ability—at least up to a point. In a similar fashion, if an employee was extremely talented (or able), she or he might be able to perform at a desired level while exerting very little effort. So, either ability or motivation can compensate for the other up to a point. But in order to maximize performance we need to have a workforce that is fully capable of doing their jobs and a system that motivates them to exert their highest levels of effort. For the remainder of this chapter, we will assume that the human resource manager has staffed the organization with capable people and that the only issue is how to motivate them to do their best work.

Motivation and Needs

Everyone has needs that they attempt to satisfy. For most of us, on a day-to-day basis, these needs are pretty simple and are relatively easy to satisfy—we stop at a drinking fountain when we are thirsty or get a candy bar or piece of fruit when we are hungry. But what about more serious needs that might truly be capable of determining behavior? For example, what if you found yourself abandoned on a desert island (like Tom Hanks in the movie *Castaway*)? Probably the first thing you would do, once you figured out that you couldn't get off the island, would be to search for food and water. Hunger and thirst, at this level, are critical and basic needs that must be satisfied in order to survive. Once you located food and water you would probably begin working on some shelter and only then might you begin searching to see if there was anyone else on the island (or you might begin talking to a soccer ball as Tom Hanks did). Through all of this, you would probably not worry much about how you looked or how others might

Need-based theories

are theories of motivation that focus on what motivates a person, rather than on how that motivation occurs.

Hierarchy of Needs

Probably the best known of the need-based theories, this model, proposed by Abraham Maslow, specifies five levels of needs that are capable of motivating behavior—physiological, security, social, esteem, and self-actualization.

Prepotent   *needs, according to Maslow's theory, are those specific needs (of the five levels in the model) that are capable of motivating behavior at any given point in time.*

view your behavior if they could see you. That is, all your behavior would be aimed at satisfying some basic needs in life, and only after these were satisfied would you begin thinking about other, less critical needs. This view includes several **need-based theories** of motivation.

Some readers will recognize that the discussion above is similar to Maslow's **Hierarchy of Needs.** Abraham Maslow proposed this well-known theory of motivation over sixty years ago,[2] and it has been quite popular ever since. The basic hierarchy model is presented in Figure 13.1, and illustrates the five categories of needs arranged from the most basic needs at the bottom to the more complex needs at the top. The lowest level of needs is labeled "Physiological Needs," and includes such things as the need for food or water. The next level of needs is labeled "Security Needs," and includes anything involving safe and secure environment. This is followed by "Social Needs," which include the need to have meaningful interactions and relationships with others. Next comes "Esteem Needs," which include the need to have a positive view of yourself, and finally comes "Self-Actualization Needs," or the need to reach your personal potential.

According to the model, only one level of need is capable of motivating behavior at any given time. This level of need is said to be **prepotent.** Thus, if we are truly starving (rather than just in need of a snack), we will not worry about shelter or other people until we get something to eat. Only after we find food, and satisfy our physiological needs, will we worry about security. Therefore, the other important aspect of the theory is that humans are said to move neatly up the hierarchy, one need at a time. There is some disagreement as to whether the theory suggests that anyone can be completely self-actualized, although at one point in time Maslow did propose a list of people he suggested were self-actualized, including the pope and Eleanor Roosevelt. The following *HR in the 21st Century* provides another possible illustration. It certainly reinforces the idea that a variety of needs motivate different people.

Maslow's theory is useful because it focuses on needs and suggests that not everyone would be motivated by the same set of needs at any one time. Thus, from an organizational point of view, if we tried to motivate employees by meeting their esteem needs

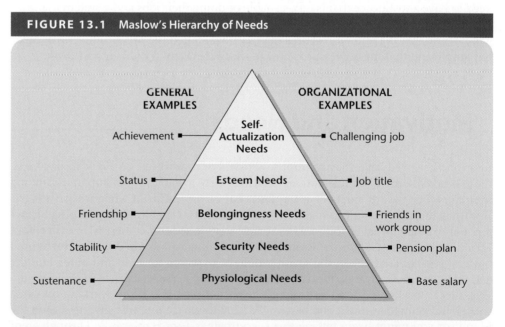

FIGURE 13.1   Maslow's Hierarchy of Needs

Source: Adapted from Abraham H. Maslow, "A Theory of Human Motivation," *Psychological Review,* 1943, vol. 50, pp. 374–396.

HR IN THE 21ST CENTURY

The Noble Choice

Why would a person give up the opportunity to work in a nice environment and earn a great income for a job that pays little and is set in places that are likely to be dangerous? Ask the volunteers who choose to join Doctors Without Borders. When an Indian Ocean tsunami struck Asia in 2005, volunteers from Doctors Without Borders were the first responders. When civil wars broke out in Sudan and Congo, Doctors Without Borders went. They also went to an earthquake site in Pakistan, an election in Haiti that ended in bloodshed, and flooded regions in Guatemala where hundreds were homeless.

> *"It's amazing. I think working with starving people is the best thing I've done."*
>
> (Lisabeth List, Doctors Without Borders volunteer nurse)*

Doctors Without Borders was started in France in 1971. Its members responded to crises in seventy countries in 2005. Volunteers are physicians and other healthcare professionals, in addition to experts in communications, information technology, water and sanitation engineering, and distribution. The organization recruits volunteers through word of mouth and public relations. Applicants must have specialized and professional qualifications as well as personal characteristics such as adaptability, teamwork, commitment, and ability to function under stress. Volunteers are expected to work continuously, in primitive and stressful conditions, often with people who may be afflicted with dangerous contagious diseases. Volunteers may also have to work in hostile areas and under armed guards, and employees are sometimes the target of violence—five workers were killed in a 2004 ambush in Afghanistan. Doctors Without Borders members tell of working seven days a week, for ten to sixteen hours daily, and being threatened with automatic weapons in Rwanda and Somalia.

Why are highly qualified people, who could be earning top salaries in more conventional and comfortable jobs, volunteering to work under brutal conditions for so little compensation? And why do 70 percent of the members return for more duty after their first year's experience? Although experienced volunteers qualify for a small salary and benefits, the pay is low, even compared to that of other nonprofits and NGOs.

What most Doctors Without Borders volunteers cherish most is the chance to make a difference in someone's life. "There is nothing like seeing a child deathly skinny and watching that child become healthy," states Lisabeth List, a volunteer nurse. "It's amazing. I think working with starving people is the best thing I've done." Other members mention the career opportunities and valuable experience they gained as MSF volunteers, including everything from patient care to training to advising local governments.

Surgeon Wei Cheng and his wife Karin Moorhouse recently wrote *No One Can Stop the Rain,* a book about their Doctors Without Borders volunteer experience in Angola. By writing this book, they fulfill their commitment to *temoinage,* or bearing witness. They discuss their motives: "The flickering light of humanity we witness almost daily in this world of conflict and tragedy is not about to be extinguished, but rather can be given new energy through the efforts of ordinary people. . . . [T]he rewards are tremendous. The [Angolans'] ability to endure in terrible circumstances touched us to the core. Our experience was both inspiring and humbling."

Sources: "As Disaster Follows Disaster, Relief Groups Feel the Strain" *New York Times,* October 13, 2005, p. 1A (*source of quote); "Afghan Aid Killings: Suspect, No Arrests," *New York Times,* April 10, 2005, p. 3B; Doctors Without Borders website: www.doctorswithoutborders.org on December 5, 2006; Karin Moorhouse and Wei Cheng, *No One Can Stop the Rain* (San Francisco: Insomniac Press, 2005).

(perhaps by assigning grand titles or giving people more prestigious office locations such as the corner office), this would only be effective for employees for whom these needs were important. This plan would not work for employees who were focused on more basic needs that might be satisfied by a pay increase (rather than a larger office).

There has been considerable research done on Maslow's theory[3] and the results of that research suggest that people are motivated by more than one level of need at any point in time, and that people do not always march neatly up the hierarchy, but sometimes move down the hierarchy as well. In fact, some years later, Clayton Alderfer proposed a variation

ERG theory   *is a need-based theory of motivation proposed by Alderfer that involves three, rather than five levels of needs, and also allows for someone to regress from a higher-level need to a lower-level need.*

on Maslow's theory, which he called **ERG theory.** Alderfer's theory substituted three levels of needs for Maslow's five (and he labeled them Existence Needs, Relatedness Needs, and Growth Needs). These three levels simply collapse Maslow's five categories into three, but the more important aspect of Alderfer's theory is that he suggested that people might move either up or down the hierarchy and he allowed for multiple levels of needs being prepotent. So, once we satisfy our Existence Needs, and move up to Relatedness Needs, if those Relatedness Needs are not being satisfied (i.e., they are being frustrated), we will regress backward and Existence Needs will again be prepotent. Thus, this theory would suggest that individuals who cannot find meaningful relationships might spend their time accumulating money instead.

But, whichever model we accept, the important thing to remember is that not everyone will be motivated by the same things at any one time, and that need satisfaction is an important source of motivation. Before leaving these models, though, it is worth commenting on the role of money in need-based models of motivation. Money has the potential for satisfying all of the needs proposed by Maslow (and Alderfer). If we are not on a desert island, we probably satisfy hunger and thirst by buying food and water at the supermarket, which requires money. Security needs are satisfied by a home (which we must pay for), and by things such as insurance and a pension (which also require money).

Social needs are satisfied by having friends. But money also plays a role; having money, for instance allows us to have the leisure time to meet friends as well as to spend time in settings where we might interact with other people. Money also brings us status, which helps to satisfy esteem needs. Furthermore, even if most people are not self-actualized by simply earning more,, they may be self-actualized by being able to contribute a new wing to a museum, or by paying for an artist to appear at the local opera—activities which require money.

Dual factor theory   *is a need-based Theory proposed by Herzberg, which identifies motivators and hygiene factors as two sets of conditions at work that can satisfy needs. The research on this theory provides little empirical support for the model, however.*

We should also note that there are other need-based theories of motivation as well. Among these, the best known is probably Herzberg's **dual factor theory,**[4] which identifies motivators and hygiene factors as two sets of conditions at work that can satisfy needs. The research on this theory provides little empirical support for the model, however,[5] and so we will not discuss it in any detail. We will note, however, that the "motivator" side of this theory provides the basis for much of the work that has been done in the area of job enrichment, which we will discuss in some detail in Chapter 14.

Need-based theories only explain part of the story of motivation, however. Needs can help us understand what will motivate someone, but they do not tell us much about how the person becomes motivated or how the person decides where to exert his or her effort. To understand more about that, we need to turn to the various process-based models of motivation.

Process Theories of Motivation

Process theories   *are motivation theories that focus on how a person becomes motivated and what they are motivated to do, rather than on what motivates them.*

Process theories of motivation are concerned with *how* a person becomes motivated to perform in a certain way. These theories also tell only part of the story and we really need to integrate some aspects of need-based theories with some aspects of process theories to understand human motivation better. We will attempt such integration at the end of this chapter.

Reinforcement Theory

Reinforcement theory is probably the most basic process theory, but its simplicity, as well as its effectiveness and applicability to work settings make this an important theory to discuss. Stated quite simply, **reinforcement theory,** usually associated with B. F. Skinner,[6] proposes that all behavior is a function if its consequences. Figure 13.2 presents the model of behavior that underlies reinforcement theory. The model has three components only—stimulus, response, and outcomes. The *stimulus* refers to something in the environment that cues the person about a behavior. A soft drink machine is a stimulus reminding us that we might be thirsty and might want to buy a drink. The *response* is the behavior that the person exhibits when she or he encounters the stimulus. In the case of the soft drink machine, the person might take out a dollar and put it in the machine. The *outcomes* refer to the consequences that follow the response. So, once we put a dollar in the machine, several things might happen: the machine might reject the dollar and send it back out; the machine might take the dollar and deposit a soft drink; or the machine might take then dollar and keep it without depositing the drink.

Reinforcement theory suggests that the response a person makes to the stimulus is a function of what he or she expects will happen. This means that reinforcement theory is really about learning behaviors through some type of experience. So, if the last time you deposited a dollar in a soft drink machine you received the drink you wanted (a positive outcome), the next time you encounter a soft drink machine and feel thirsty you are likely to deposit a dollar again (i.e., repeat the behavior). If your dollar was rejected the last time you tried (really, no outcome), you might try again, although if your money is rejected over and over, eventually you might stop even trying to buy a soft drink from a machine. If the machine "ate" your dollar last time (a negative outcome), you will be less likely to repeat the behavior this time and so you probably won't deposit another dollar.

Note that the key here is that we learn what consequences to expect over time, and these expectations guide our behavior. If we apply this to a work context, we can think about a supervisor asking an employee to stay late to work on a special project. Assuming the employee agrees, it is possible that the supervisor will be grateful, praise the employee, and perhaps even give the employee some time off. This would represent a positive outcome for the employee and, the next time the supervisor asked for someone to stay late, this employee would be very likely to volunteer.

On the other hand, the supervisor might say and do nothing following the employee's late-night assignment. If this were the case, the employee might or might not be willing to stay late again but, eventually, if the supervisor continued to ignore the employee's staying late, he or she would no longer be willing to remain and work. Finally, the supervisor could respond by suggesting that, since the employee obviously has nothing else to do, she or he should stay late tomorrow night as well. This would represent a negative outcome for the employee and he or she would not be likely to stay late ever again. Now let us assume that the organization would like all its employees to be willing to stay late, so that agreeing to work late is a desirable behavior. These scenarios can then be reduced to a simple set of rules, illustrated on the next page in Figure 13.3.

Reinforcement theory *is a process theory, usually associated with B. F. Skinner, proposing that all behavior is a function if its consequences.*

FIGURE 13.2 Stimulus-Response-Outcome Model of Behavior

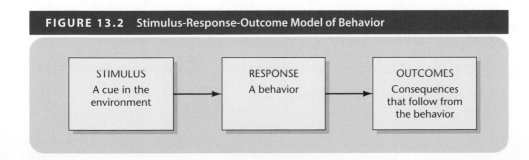

FIGURE 13.3   Reinforcement and Behavior

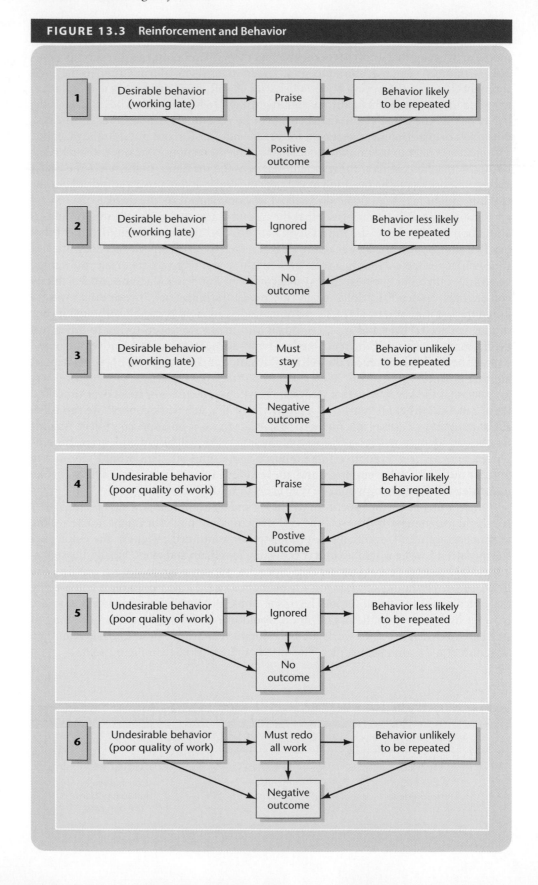

The first scenario in Figure 13.3 is known as **positive reinforcement** and represents a very positive situation from the organization's perspective. The rewards are likely to lead to the employee volunteering more frequently, which is what the organization desires. The second scenario pictured is known as **extinction** and, in this case, extinction is not what the organization wants since it will eventually result in the employee not volunteering to stay late. The third scenario is known as **punishment,** which, in this case, is disastrous for the organization since it almost guarantees that the employee (as well as any other employee who sees what is going on) will never volunteer to stay late again.

Notice that Figure 13.3 also presents three scenarios where the behavior involved is undesirable (poor quality work). Scenarios 4, 5, and 6 are also referred to as positive reinforcement, extinction, and punishment respectfully, but now the consequences for the organization are quite different. Here, the positive reinforcement scenario (4) is disastrous since it will almost ensure that poor quality work continues. The extinction scenario (5) is reasonably good for the organization (although there are some issues that we will discuss a bit later), and the punishment scenario (6) is actually the best for the organization.

The relationships illustrated in these scenarios actually hold up quite well in empirical testing[7] so there are clear lessons to be learned from reinforcement theory. First, it is critical that the supervisor know what behaviors are desired and not desired on the part of the employee. Then, the supervisor must make sure that there are consequences for all behaviors and that desired behaviors are followed by positive consequences and undesired behaviors are followed by negative consequences (or perhaps, no consequences). The stronger the links between the behavior and the consequences perceived by the employee, the more likely will the supervisor get the behavior that he or she desires. When a supervisor works to simultaneously eliminate undesired behavior (through punishment or extinction) and to reward desired behavior, this is known as **behavior modification.** However, there are some critics who question the ethics of behavior modification. Our *Point/Counterpoint* feature highlights some of these basic arguments.

You may wonder why anyone would possibly reward undesired behavior, and yet it happens all the time—although presumably unintentionally. In the preceding examples, a supervisor would probably not actually praise an employee for poor quality, but the

Positive reinforcement   *is a term from reinforcement theory and refers to the situation where a behavior is followed by positive consequences and so is likely to be repeated.*

Extinction   *is also a term from reinforcement theory and refers to the situation where a behavior is followed by no consequences and eventually disappears.*

Punishment   *is yet another term from reinforcement theory and refers to a situation where a behavior is followed by negative consequences and so is not repeated.*

Behavior modification   *is the combination of positive reinforcement with either punishment or extinction so that an undesired behavior disappears and is replaced with a desired behavior.*

Steve Bennett is CEO of Intuit, a software manufacturer that sells financial programs such as TurboTax and Quicken. Bennett, shown here, is a true believer in incentive pay and employee recognition programs. In fact, the company spends about 1.5 percent of its total compensation budget on employee recognition programs. In a company of over 6,000 employees, this represents a major investment. For example, employee Alan Hampton designed and built a data center for the company. He received a thank you e-mail that linked him to a website where he learned that the appreciation included an all expenses paid weekend trip with his wife to Monterey Bay, California.

POINT | COUNTERPOINT

Reinforcement Versus Free Will

 Advocates of the usefulness of reinforcement theory would argue that it is possible to elicit almost any response from a person, or to eliminate any response a person might elicit, by the judicious use of contingent rewards and punishment. But, if one takes that argument to its logical conclusion, this would suggest that there is essentially no such thing as free will and that ideal societies would be ones where leaders managed behavior so that citizens acted responsibly. What if we could do this at work? Would it be desirable? What costs would we incur if we could accomplish this?

POINT... **Organizations should actively attempt to modify employees' behavior at work because...**	**COUNTERPOINT...** **Organizations should foster employee free will and so not try to modify behavior at work because...**
It would enable employees to be more productive.	Employees will resist attempts to modify their behavior and so be less productive.
This could eliminate conflict at work and all its negative consequences.	Some conflict at work is useful.
It would be possible to establish policies and rules that benefit most people most of the time.	Employees are adults and should be allowed to make their own choices about what benefits them the most.
If left to their own devices, employees will behave in a way that is best for their own self interests rather than for the interests of the firm or their coworkers.	Individuals behaving to maximize their own best interests is economically rational, and organizations should work to align their interests with those of its employees.
Such systems of social engineering have been described as "utopian" by some authors (such as B.F. Skinner in *Walden II*).	Other authors have described such systems of control as much more problematic (such as George Orwell in *1984*).

So... Even though organizations cannot completely control employees' behavior, the real issue is whether they should even try. The answer seems to be that some degree of control is desirable, but that organizations must allow employees to make their own decisions in the end. People react well to being treated as adults and having their own wishes respected—and one can imagine that a world ruled by the goals of productivity and efficiency could be quite grim.

supervisor could reward that behavior in other ways. Perhaps the supervisor would respond to poor-quality work by losing faith in the employee's ability to perform good-quality work and ask someone else (presumably more trustworthy) to redo the work. Alternatively, the supervisor may simply assign his job to someone else in the future, and if the job is one that is not really desirable, this would be a reward to the employee who performs poorly.

We also need to say a bit more about the relative merits of extinction versus punishment as a means of eliminating undesirable behavior. Punishment is quite effective because, when done properly, it establishes a strong link between a behavior and a negative outcome. We learn not to touch exposed wires because we get a shock when we do; we learn to avoid hot surfaces because we get burned when we touch them.

But we do not always need to punish someone in order to get a behavior to disappear. For example, some children act out in school because their classmates laugh and so reward them. If we can remove the laughter (the reward), the behavior will eventually be extinguished (i.e., it will disappear). So extinction is a more benign means to remove undesired behavior, although it takes a bit longer to work. Also, extinction will not work with certain types of behavior. Smoking is a good example of the problem. If we want a loved one to stop smoking (because we believe it to be unhealthy), ignoring the behavior will not result in the person's quitting smoking. Why not? Because smoking is itself rewarding. That is, the person is not smoking because she or he expects to get rewarded by others (surely not in today's environment), but because nicotine is addictive and smoking satisfies the craving for nicotine. If we ignore the smoking, the person is actually being rewarded because he or she is getting the drug they crave. We can only stop someone from smoking by punishing them for it, or by finding a substitute source of nicotine that is less harmful (e.g., a nicotine patch).

It is also important to note that punishment (and positive reinforcement) work best when there is a strong link between behavior and consequences. That is, *every* time the undesired behavior is exhibited it is punished. But that is quite difficult to manage and it requires a great deal of monitoring. Furthermore, if someone realizes that undesired behavior is only punished when it is "caught," then the person is motivated to not get caught, rather than to cease the behavior. This is how we explain the fact that motorists often speed until they see a police officer. As a result, it is easier, and more pleasant if we can change behavior by focusing on positive reinforcement rather than on punishment. Employees are drawn to supervisors who reward them, but hide from supervisors who punish them—and it is difficult to supervise employees who are hiding!

Finally, although rewards and punishment are most effective when they are administered following every behavior (also referred to as *continuous reinforcement*), they can still work if they are administered some time but not others. **Partial reinforcement** means rewarding a behavior only some times, but not others (it can be applied to punishment as well, but the reward case is simpler). Specifically, the rewards are administered on some schedule that dictates when the reward is administered and when it is not. These schedules can vary on two dimensions, so that there are four different schedules of reinforcement that can be used, as illustrated in Table 13.1. First, there are interval schedules versus ratio schedules. **Interval schedules** reinforce behavior as a function of the passage of time. A schedule where someone was rewarded every ten minutes as long as they were exhibiting desired behavior would be an interval schedule. **Ratio schedules** reinforce behavior as a function of how many times it occurs. For example, rewarding someone every fifth time a desired behavior occurs would be an example of a ratio schedule. But in addition, the ratio or the interval can either be fixed or variable. That is, the number of times the behavior must be displayed or the amount of time that must pass before a reward is given can be constant over time, or it can change. Therefore, we can have **fixed interval schedules** such as when employees are paid once every two weeks as long as they continue to do their jobs; or we can have a **variable interval schedule** such as when employees are promoted as a function of time with the firm, but the amount of time between promotions can vary substantially. We can also have a **fixed ratio schedule** such as the case where an employee is paid on a piece rate where he or she is paid one dollar for every ten units produced; or we can have a **variable ratio schedule** such as bonus system based on performance, where the number of units that must be produced to obtain a bonus can vary over time.

From the perspective of the human resource manager, or even the general manager, there are a few things about these partial reinforcement schedules that are worth noting. First, if we are trying to shape an employee's behavior through reinforcement, it will take longer for the employee to "learn" the correct behavior under any partial reinforcement schedule as compared to a continuous reinforcement schedule, and it will take even longer

Partial reinforcement *means rewarding a behavior only some times, but not others (it can be applied to punishment as well, but the reward case is simpler).*

Interval schedules *are partial reinforcement schedules where behavior is reinforced as a function of the passage of time. A schedule where someone was rewarded every ten minutes as long as they were exhibiting desired behavior would be an interval schedule.*

Ratio schedules *are partial reinforcement schedules where behavior is reinforced as a function of how many times the behavior occurs. For example, rewarding someone every fifth time a desired behavior occurs would be an example of a ratio schedule.*

Fixed interval schedules *are interval schedules where the amount of time that must pass before a reward is given is constant over time.*

Variable interval schedules *are interval schedules where the amount of time that must pass before a reward is given can change from one reward period to another.*

Fixed ratio schedules *are ratio schedules where the number of times a behavior must occur before it is rewarded remains constant over time.*

Variable ratio schedules *are ratio schedules where the number of times a behavior must occur before it is rewarded changes over time.*

for the employee to learn a behavior under any variable schedule. On the other hand, we might also be concerned about a learned behavior disappearing because we fail to reinforce it for a while. Here we are interested in how resistant to extinction any learned behavior might be, and any partial reinforcement schedule is more resistant to extinction than a continuous reinforcement schedule, and furthermore, any variable schedule (i.e., variable ratio or variable interval) is more resistant to extinction than any fixed schedule. Finally, ratio schedules, since they reward individual responses, result in higher levels of behavior (such as higher productivity) than do interval schedules, and variable ratio schedules produce more consistent levels of behavior (e.g., output) than do fixed ratio schedules, since employees will slow down right after receiving a reinforcement and speed up again as they anticipate the next reinforcement.[8] All of this is summarized in Table 13.1.

Expectancy Theory

Expectancy theory, sometimes referred to as **VIE theory,**[9] is a fairly complex theory from a cognitive perspective, because it casts the employee in the role of decision maker. It developed from early work in psychology,[10] as well as basic economic theory, which assumes that people work to maximize their personal (positive) outcomes. Expectancy theory is concerned with three components and the links among them. The components are termed *effort, performance,* and *outcomes* and are used in the usual ways. The links among these three, however, are more central to the theory.

The first link is between effort and performance and is sometimes referred at as the "expectancy" term. Specifically, the **effort-to-performance expectancy** is the person's perception of the probability that an increase in effort will result in an increase in performance. This can range from 0 to 1.0. Expectancy is zero when the employee believes that increasing effort will definitely not increase performance, and this could be the result of a task that is too easy ("I can perform at the highest level with no effort") or a task that is too difficult ("No matter how hard I try I cannot do any better"). Clearly, ability plays a role in determining this expectancy term, since a lack of ability (due to poor selection or poor training) will always result in a low level of expectancy.

The second link is between performance and outcomes and is sometimes referred to as the "instrumentality" term. Specifically, the **performance-to-outcomes expectancy (instrumentality)** is the person's perception of the probability that improved performance will lead to certain outcomes. Operationally, this is viewed as a correlation coefficient indicating that as performance improves, the chances of gaining outcomes can either go up (a positive correlation), remain unchanged (a zero correlation), or go down (a negative correlation). As such, the values can range from +1.0, through 0, to −1.0. We will explain how this works as soon as we discuss the final link in the model.

Expectancy theory *(or* **VIE theory***) is a fairly complex process theory of motivation that casts the employee in the role of decision maker. Basically, an employee decides whether or not to exert effort depending on the outcomes he or she anticipates receiving for those efforts, based on calculations made concerning expectancies, instrumentalities, valences, and the links among these three components.*

Effort-to-performance expectancy *(or* **expectancy***) is the person's perception of the probability that an increase in effort will result in an increase in performance. This can range from 0 to 1.0.*

Performance-to-outcomes expectancy *(or* **instrumentality***) is the person's perception of the probability that improved performance will lead to certain outcomes. Operationally, this is viewed as a correlation coefficient indicating that as performance improves, the chances of gaining outcomes can either go up (a positive correlation), remain unchanged (a zero correlation), or go down (a negative correlation).*

TABLE 13.1   Effects of Different Partial Reinforcement Schedules

Schedule	Time to Learn	Resistance to Extinction	Productivity[a]
Continuous	Shortest	Least resistant	Average
Fixed interval	Longer	Resistant	Lowest
Variable interval	Longest	Most resistant	Next lowest
Fixed ratio	Longer	Resistant	Next highest
Variable ratio	Longest	Most resistant	Highest

[a]Productivity refers to the number of desired responses or behavior exhibited.

The final piece of the model is not really a link between two other components, but an extra component. **Valence** refers to the attractiveness or unattractiveness an outcome has for a person. Thus, as noted above, there might be many outcomes associated with work and some of these might be quite attractive, while others may be rather unattractive. For example, good performance might be associated with receiving a raise, which would be attractive to most people. But poor performance might be associated with being fired, which would presumably be unattractive. Another way of stating this would be to suggest that improving performance *increases* the chances of receiving a raise (thus a positive correlation or instrumentality), but *decreases* the chances of being fired (thus a negative correlation or instrumentality), and have no impact on the chances of winning the lottery (thus a zero correlation or instrumentality). Valences can thus be positive, negative, or neutral, and it is possible to specify that some outcomes are more positive (or negative) than others.

Note that all the terms in expectancy theory are based on a person's perceptions. That is, we are less interested in whether, in fact, a person's efforts will result in increased performance, but more interested in whether the person believes that to be the case. Of course, if individuals' perceptions are incorrect, they will learn this over time and adjust their perceptions, but it is essential to remember that we are dealing with perceived links here, not the actual relationships between the components in the model.

Figure 13.4 illustrates the way the model works and indicates that the model is used to estimate the "force" operating on the employee to increase her or his effort. Note that in the example, the expectancy is set at 1.0, suggesting that there is a certainty that increased effort will lead to improved performance. There are also three outcomes in the example, two positive (pay raise and winning the lottery) and one negative (getting fired), and that winning the lottery is more attractive than getting a pay raise. The key here, though, is the instrumentality term. Although winning the lottery is attractive, improved performance is not associated with increased chances of winning the lottery, and so this drops from consideration (zero times three is zero), suggesting that winning the lottery does not play a role in an employee's decision to increase effort at work. Notice too that getting fired is a negative outcome, but that increased performance decreases the chances of getting fired, producing a negative instrumentality. When we multiply two negatives we get a positive, suggesting here that increasing performance makes it less likely that an employee will be fired, which is really a benefit of improved performance.

In the example, the force is calculated to be positive, which suggests that the employee should increase effort on the job. We could imagine a situation where the force would be negative (suggesting there would be no chance of improving effort since it would result in bad things only) or a situation where the force would be less positive, and so it would

Valence   *refers to the attractiveness or unattractiveness an outcome has for a person.*

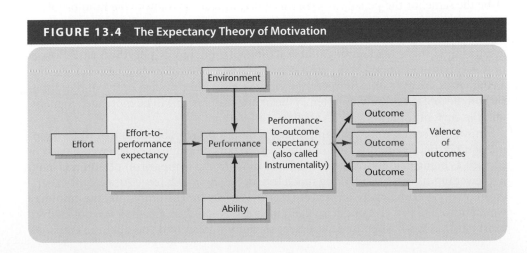

FIGURE 13.4   The Expectancy Theory of Motivation

be less likely, but still somewhat likely, that the employee would increase effort. Note too that if any term in this model goes to zero, the resulting force goes to zero. This also makes sense since there would be no reason for an employee to increase effort if (a) performance was unlikely to improve as a result of that effort, or (b) there were no outcomes associated with any improved performance, or (c) increased performance would result in some good outcomes but these would be canceled out by negative outcomes.

Research on expectancy theory supports the general logic of the theory, but not many of the specific mechanisms, and suggests that the theory is much more rational and calculating than are most employees.[11] A number of variations on expectancy theory also have been proposed,[12] the most comprehensive of which was put forth by Naylor, Pritchard, and Ilgen[13] and which we will discuss later in the context of performance enhancement interventions. In any case, expectancy theory has important lessons for the human resource manager. First, this theory underscores the importance of selecting the right employees for the job and then training them so that they can perform their jobs effectively. The theory also suggests that it is important for the organization to have as many desirable outcomes associated with improved performance as possible, and finally, the theory suggests that organizations can best influence performance by establishing clear links between increased performance and rewards. This will be the basis for our discussion of incentive pay plans in Chapter 14.

Equity Theory

Equity theory *is concerned with a person's perceived inputs to a (work) setting and the outcomes they receive from that setting. The theory suggests that everyone calculates the ratio of inputs to outcomes, almost the way one would consider a return on any investment.*

J. Stacey Adams developed another somewhat narrow but very useful process theory called equity theory.[14] **Equity theory** is most concerned with a person's perceived inputs to a (work) setting and the outcomes they receive from that setting. The theory suggests that everyone calculates the ratio of inputs to outcomes, almost the way one would consider a return on any investment. But, once individuals calculate this ratio for themselves, they then must determine if their ratio (or rate of return) is "fair." They try to determine this by comparing their ratio to the perceived ratio of some other comparison person. Note that the target for this comparison could be anyone an employee chooses to use—it could be a coworker, a supervisor, a friend, or even an ideal that does not really exist. The employee then compares his or her input/outcome ratio to the ratio of this other person to determine whether the employee's ratio is fair. Employees will be most likely to be motivated when they believe they are being treated fairly, which in the case of this theory is defined as *equitably*.

Figure 13.5 illustrates the comparison process and also illustrates the potential results of the comparison process. Note neither the actual inputs nor the actual outcomes need to be the same for the person to perceive equity; instead it is simply the ratio or rate of return on investment. So an employee may perceive that a coworker is earning more money, but still perceive equity if the employee believes that the coworker is making greater inputs to the work setting. These additional inputs could take the form of longer hours worked, greater effort on the job, or additional education or experience. As long as the ratios are the same, however, the employee should perceive equity and exert effort on the job; specifically, as noted in the figure, the person will be motivated to maintain the current situation.

In some cases, however, the employee's ratio is less favorable than that of the comparison person. Again, this could be the case even if the employee perceived herself or himself as being paid more, if the employee thought the comparison person was making fewer inputs (such as working much less, or having much less education or experience). As long as the ratio, or rate of return, was less for the employee, the employee would be said to perceive underpayment inequity. Not only is an employee not likely to exert effort at work when underpayment inequity is perceived (because the employee

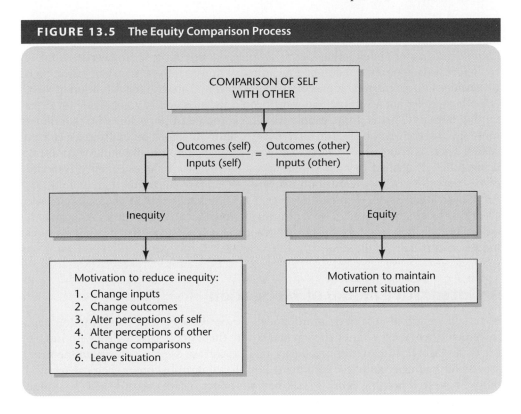

FIGURE 13.5   The Equity Comparison Process

COMPARISON OF SELF
WITH OTHER

$$\frac{\text{Outcomes (self)}}{\text{Inputs (self)}} = \frac{\text{Outcomes (other)}}{\text{Inputs (other)}}$$

Inequity

Equity

Motivation to reduce inequity:
1. Change inputs
2. Change outcomes
3. Alter perceptions of self
4. Alter perceptions of other
5. Change comparisons
6. Leave situation

Motivation to maintain
current situation

feels that any effort will not be "fairly" rewarded), but the employee will also work to restore equity. That is, the employee will try to either reduce his or her inputs (e.g., exert *less* effort), increase his or her outcomes (e.g., ask for a raise), or try to influence the comparison person to either reduce outcomes or increase inputs (unlikely to be successful). Thus, perceived underpayment inequity can present a real problem for a manager trying to enhance performance. Also, we must note again that this is all based on perceived inequity, so that, in reality, the employee in question might be treated quite fairly, but the fact that the employee doesn't perceive that to be the case will present problems.

Another potential situation is the case where the employee's input/outcome ratio is more favorable than that of the comparison person. The situation is known as overpayment inequity. There is some debate over whether anyone really perceives overpayment inequity, since it would be easy to justify the overpayment as actually being deserved ("I guess I do work a lot harder"), and research support for overpayment inequity is mixed at best.[15] But, according to the theory, an employee facing overpayment inequity should also seek to restore equity, which would be easiest to do by increasing her or his inputs in the situation.

Equity theory can be quite useful to the human resource manager because it makes it clear that any rewards associated with effort or performance will be evaluated, in part, for their fairness as well as their innate attractiveness. That is, giving someone a raise for a job well done may not be very motivating if another employee received a larger raise for a similar job. Whether or not overpayment inequity really exists, the human resource manager needs to be aware of this potential problem with underpayment inequity. Also, if the employee perceiving underpayment inequity were a woman (or a member of any protected class), and the comparison person were a white male *and* the employee perceived underpayment inequity, she would also be likely to sue under the Equal Pay Act (see

Chapter 2)—even though she is being paid fairly relative to the male employee. You may recall that equity theory is also the basis for much of the discussion of justice and fairness in Chapter 2, suggesting that this is indeed a useful theory to keep in mind.

Before leaving our discussion of equity theory, however, there is an important point to consider. Our discussion here, as in Chapter 2, revolved around the definition of "fair." In both cases, we are assuming that most people consider equity a good rule for determining fairness. That is, most people would assume that the person who contributes more should receive more. But this is really an assumption based on our western cultural values. There is evidence to suggest that other cultures are more likely to judge fairness using a rule of equality,[16] which would suggest that everyone shares equally in any outcomes regardless of their contributions. Still others have suggested that, in some settings, individuals prefer a rule of need; that is, individuals should share in outcomes according to what they need.[17] We are not suggesting that any one rule is better than the others, but it is important for the human resource manager to realize that not everyone judges what is "fair" in the same way.

An Integrative Model of Motivation

Although we will discuss a few more models of motivation, need-based models, reinforcement theory, expectancy theory, and equity theory collectively deal with most of the issues facing a human resource manager. In each case, we have presented the major aspects of the theory and have commented on the empirical support each has received, but we have said nothing about which theory is better. That is because each has something to offer, and each has weaknesses as well. But we can integrate the useful information provided by each theory to develop a single, integrative model that will make it easier to discuss what the human resource manager should understand about motivation.

First, we should note that few of these theories actually conflict with each other. That is, they tend to deal with different aspects of the motivational process, and it is rare that two theories would make different predictions about a situation that could not be easily resolved.[18]

Next we should note that the five categories of needs from Maslow can be easily mapped onto the three categories used in ERG theory, so the only issue is how many categories of needs we wish to consider. Finally, although expectancy theory is much more complex than reinforcement theory, both theories would lead us to make the same basic recommendations—that we strengthen the links between performance and gaining valued outcomes. With these comments in mind, Figure 13.6 presents a possible integration of the various motivational theories we have discussed thus far.

The basic notion here is that an employee will exert effort on the job *only if* that effort will lead to improved performance, if that performance will lead to rewards (which depends upon whether or not the improved performance will help the organization meet its goals) and if those rewards are considered to be fair *and* satisfy important needs of the employee.

Other Important Theories

Two other theories or models of motivation are important to discuss, although they do not fit neatly into the integrative framework we just presented.

FIGURE 13.6   An Integrative Model of Motivation

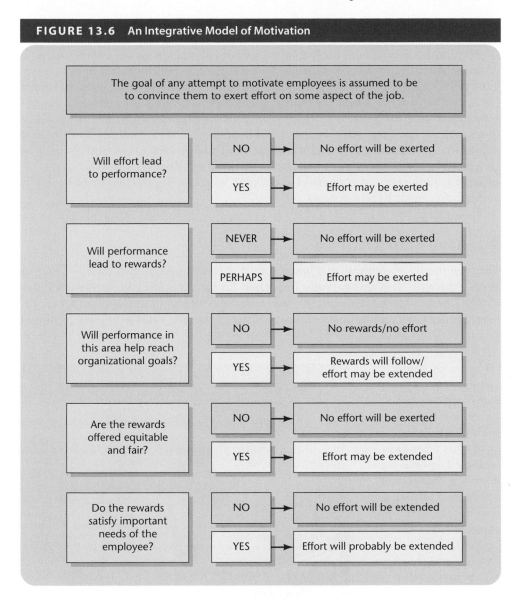

The goal of any attempt to motivate employees is assumed to be to convince them to exert effort on some aspect of the job.

Will effort lead to performance?
- NO → No effort will be exerted
- YES → Effort may be exerted

Will performance lead to rewards?
- NEVER → No effort will be exerted
- PERHAPS → Effort may be exerted

Will performance in this area help reach organizational goals?
- NO → No rewards/no effort
- YES → Rewards will follow/ effort may be extended

Are the rewards offered equitable and fair?
- NO → No effort will be exerted
- YES → Effort may be extended

Do the rewards satisfy important needs of the employee?
- NO → No effort will be extended
- YES → Effort will probably be extended

Goal Theory

One of these is **goal theory,** first proposed by Ed Locke.[19] Goal theory is fairly simple because it is based on the premise that people with goals work harder than people without goals. Beyond that, the theory suggests that not all goals are created equal, and that goals which are difficult and yet specific and concrete will motivate employees best. So, for example, a goal to "work harder" is not very specific or concrete and so would not be very likely to motivate effort. Goals such a "reducing waste by 10 percent" or "increasing sales by 15 percent," on the other hand, are quite specific and should lead to increased effort. This is because employees will know exactly how to exert effort and exactly what direction that effort should take, and they will also be able to monitor their own progress toward meeting those goals. Also, difficult goals are preferable to easy goals, because an employee does not need to exert much effort to meet an easy

Goal theory *is a fairly simple model of motivation, first proposed by Locke, and based on the premise that people with goals work harder than people without goals. Beyond that, the theory suggests that not all goals are created equal, and that goals which are difficult and yet specific and concrete will motivate employees best.*

goal. Impossible goals, on the other hand, are not good, since eventually the employee will realize that he or she cannot ever attain the goal and will stop trying.

The empirical evidence is rather supportive of goal theory across a wide variety of settings.[20] Goal theory has been used as the basis for some performance appraisal systems (see Chapter 10), and is very useful as part of a performance management system (which we will discuss in Chapter 14). In order for goals to be effective, though, the employee must accept the goal as his or her own. This has led some to suggest that goal setting should be done jointly by managers and their subordinates,[21] although others have argued that joint goal setting is helpful but not essential, as long as the employee can be convinced to accept the goal and internalize it.[22] We will discuss some other issues associated with the type of goals set in Chapter 14 when we discuss the use of theory in performance management systems.

Agency Theory

Agency theory   *addresses potential conflicts of interests among different groups of stakeholders in an organization. The name of the theory, and some of its basic principles, is derived from the fact that, in most modern organizations, the individuals who own a firm don't actually run it on a day-to-day basis. Problems arise when the interests of the owners (the principals) are in conflict with the interests of the managers (agents).*

The final model of motivation is based almost entirely in economics and is known as **agency theory.**[23] This theory is also important for the incentive pay plans we will discuss in Chapter 14, but it is especially useful in the design of incentive plans for executives. Agency theory addresses potential conflicts of interests among different groups of

Carin Knickel, general manager of Conoco's Rocky Mountain region, knows the petroleum business from one end to the other. When she inherited a slow-moving unit, she got things going by creating a "climate of inspiration." The key was getting each of her key people to present detailed goals each month in front of their peers, who were instructed to act as coaches. It worked. Now she's steering everyone toward what she terms "break-through goals."

stakeholders in an organization. The name of the theory, and some of its basic principles, is derived from the fact that, in most modern organizations, the individuals who own a firm don't actually run it on a day-to-day basis. Thus, we can think about the owners (including the stockholders) as being the principals for a firm and the management as being their agents. The theory is concerned with the conflicts that arise from this division, and the fact that what is in the best interests of the principals is not always in the best interests of the managers. Yet, when an owner hires a manager, the owner really does assume that the manager will act as his or her agent and work for the best interest of the owner.

In fact, principals and agents differ on a number of important issues. Agents are less likely than principals to take risks when they make decisions, because their livelihood tends to depend upon the business being successful; agents are also more likely than principals to focus on a short time horizon because it is usually easier to affect firm performance in the short run, and the agents may not be working for the firm in the long run. Yet it is not easy for the principals to monitor all the decisions made by the agents, and the agents often have more information about the day-to-day business than do the principals.

Empirical research on agency theory is less concerned with supporting the theory, but research has demonstrated that agents do often behave in ways that are inconsistent with the goals of the owners, consistent with the theory.[24] As noted, executive compensation and executive incentive plans are the areas where agency theory is most often applied, but the human resource manager can learn more from agency theory than just how to structure executive compensation plans. The basic logic underlying agency theory can be applied to a wide variety of settings where different groups of individuals may have conflicting interests. Managers versus union representatives, supervisors versus hourly employees, and research and development scientists versus accountants are all instances where we might find groups within an organization who have conflicting goals. Agency theory can provide guidance on how to change some parameters of any such situation so that we can align the interest of the groups involved. This is often done with incentives or even with appraisal systems; however the problem is approached, agency theory provides human resource managers with a useful framework for trying to deal with conflicts of interest so that everyone works toward the common organizational goals.

Additional Issues in Motivation

Thus far, we have discussed the major theories of motivation that have been applied to the work setting. A few additional issues related to motivation, however, deserve our attention, even though they are not associated strongly with any of the theories discussed.

Intrinsic Motivation

Most models and theories of motivation are concerned primarily with extrinsic motivation, which requires an external agent to administer a reward that is separate from the actual task or job being performed. This is in contrast to **intrinsic motivation.** As others have stated it, "Intrinsic motivation is the motivation to do work because it is interesting, engaging, or possibly challenging."[25] The factors usually associated with high levels of intrinsic motivation at work include a sense of self-determination at work (i.e., I am doing the work because I want to rather than because someone else is rewarding me), feelings that one's skills are being utilized, and generally positive feelings about the work.[26]

Intrinsic motivation *is the motivation to do work because it is interesting, engaging, or possibly challenging, rather than because someone is rewarding us to do the work.*

Many businesses today are interested in promoting creativity and innovation. High-tech giant Texas Instruments is on the leading edge of creating a culture that promotes creativity and idea generation among its employees. This team of Texas Instruments engineers recently developed a new technology for dramatically cutting the power consumption of portable electronic devices like computers and cell phones.

Thus, performing work that is interesting and challenging can be its own reward, and this is the basis for much of the work on job enrichment that will be discussed in the next chapter. We can easily think of examples of individuals expending a great deal of time and effort at tasks for which they receive no reward other than the satisfaction of doing something interesting. Typically, we think of these as hobbies or leisure activities, but there are also jobs that people would probably be willing to perform for free, if they simply had the opportunity to perform the job.

But what if we added extrinsic rewards, such as contingent pay, to jobs that were already challenging and interesting? At first glance, this would seem to represent a great opportunity to improve productivity. It would seem reasonable that, if the extrinsic rewards are administered properly (consistent with the theories discussed earlier), this would improve extrinsic motivation, which would then work with the intrinsic motivation that came from the challenging job, and the organization would have a highly motivated employee. There is evidence to suggest that this would not be the case, however. In fact, the results from a series of studies[27] suggest that the introduction of extrinsic rewards actually serves to destroy intrinsic motivation. Although there is still room to question this outcome,[28] it is quite clear that intrinsic and extrinsic motivation do not simply interact or add together to form a higher level of motivation.

It is also clear that some types of motivation do not require any intervention on the part of a manager. There are certain types of tasks and jobs for which performing the job is its own reward. This type of motivation does not fit neatly into any of the theories we have discussed, but it will play an important part in the next chapter as we discuss other ways to enhance performance.

Creativity

At first glance, it might seem that the topic of creativity is misplaced here. After all, only a few very gifted people are truly creative, and there are very few jobs where one can really be creative on the job. Yet creativity has been suggested as one of the outcomes of intrinsic motivation. Furthermore, and more critically, scholars have begun using a broader definition of creativity at work that encompasses many more employees than we would initially expect.

The most commonly used definition of **creative behavior** at work involves doing things that are innovative and that provide some value for the organization.[29] Zhou and George talk about creativity as the process of generating new and useful ideas concerning new products, services, manufacturing methods, and administrative processes.[31] Given this broad definition, almost any employee at almost any job could be creative at work.

In line with this broader view, a great deal of attention has been focused on how to motivate employees to be more creative at work. As noted above, one factor that has been linked to creativity at work is intrinsic motivation. That is, if we can design jobs to be more challenging and interesting, it is more likely that employees will engage in creative behaviors at work. Interestingly, Amabile has argued that extrinsic motivating factors that serve primarily as information for the employee can also lead to creative behavior at work, as long as they do not threaten the employee's feelings of competency.[32]

Thus, the human resource manager can do things to enhance the creativity of any employee. As noted earlier, we will discuss the topic of job enrichment in some detail in the next chapter, but there are some other factors that have been found to be related to creativity at work that can also be affected by human resource management policies. For example, informative and constructive feedback has been found to be related with high levels of creativity at work,[33] while another study found that structuring jobs in ways that are consistent with the creativity requirements of those jobs (e.g., allowing more autonomy for jobs requiring more creativity) led to increased satisfaction on the job.[34] Also, in an interesting development, Zhou and George reported that, under the right circumstances, job dissatisfaction was related to creativity at work.[35] Specifically, they found that dissatisfied employees, who were also committed to remain with the organization, were more likely to engage in creative behavior at work when they received useful feedback from coworkers and when perceived organizational support for creativity was high.

Therefore, clearly a human resource manager can do things to encourage creative behavior from employees—from all employees. But, before leaving the topic, we need to make one additional point. The definition of creative behavior, introduced above, suggests that ideas or behaviors should be both innovative and useful to the organization. It would seem reasonable, however, that employees might generate a number of ideas that are innovative but are not really useful to the organization. It is critical that the organization react to such ideas in a positive way. That is, an employee puts him- or herself in a certain amount of risk when he or she proposes an innovative approach to a problem. If the management reacts badly, and belittles the employee for an idea that is not very useful, the employee is not likely to come forward with new ideas in the future, and overall creativity is likely to be suppressed. Therefore, it is critical that the organization maintain a climate of openness and make an employee feel comfortable to suggest a "useless" idea. Only when employees feel safe in this way will they be willing to propose the kinds of creative solutions that the organization needs.[36]

Creative behavior *involves doing things, at work, that are innovative and that provide some value for the organization.*[30]

Chapter Summary

Motivation refers to the efforts employees exert at work. Individuals' performance is a function of both their ability to perform a task and their motivation to exert effort on that task. Thus it is critical that human resource managers understand how they might motivate employees to exert effort toward reaching an organization's strategic goals.

There are a number of models or theories of motivation that can provide some help. Need-based theories are more concerned with *what* motivates people, and

Maslow's Hierarchy of Needs is the best known of these theories. The most important lesson human resource managers can learn from these need theories is that, at any one time, different employees may be motivated by different things as they try to satisfy different needs.

Process theories of motivation are more concerned with *how* people become motivated. Reinforcement theory, expectancy theory, and equity theory are three process theories that can be useful to human resource managers. The insights from these three theories plus the insights from need-based theories can be combined to form a more integrative view of motivation at work. In this view, employees will be motivated to exert effort on their jobs when they believe their effort can lead to improved performance, and that improved performance will be rewarded with outcomes that are fair and that can satisfy basic needs.

Goal theory and agency theory are two other theories of motivation that can be useful to the human resource manager. Finally, it is important to realize that all motivation at work does not follow from the introduction of some type of reward. Intrinsic motivation is an important source of motivation at work, and this motivation is derived from having people work on jobs that are challenging and interesting.

Intrinsic motivation is also related to creative behavior at work, which can be exhibited by almost any employee. Creativity also depends upon informative feedback and a climate where it is safe for people to make mistakes.

The most important application of all these theories comes with attempts to enhance performance. The next and final chapter is devoted to discussing various techniques for performance enhancement, and we will discuss and critique each of them from the framework of the various theories of motivation discussed in this chapter.

Key Points for Future HR Managers

- Motivating employees to increase their efforts at work is not a simple process.

- Rewards and incentives should always be designed with the realization that different employees have different needs.

- Making rewards (and punishment) contingent upon behavior is critical for any type of motivation.

- Employees value rewards that are fair.

- Employees will work harder when they have specific goals that are difficult (but not impossible) to reach.

- It is important to align the goals of the organization with the goals of the employees.

- Intrinsic motivation is also important for motivation at work.

- It is possible to motivate creativity at work.

Key Points for Future General Managers

- Employee motivation is essential for organizational success.

- Reward systems must be designed to motivate the behaviors that the organization really desires.

- Managing employee behavior is easiest when there is a strong link between desired behaviors and outcomes that are important to the employee.

- It *is* possible to motivate employees by increasing intrinsic motivation.

- It *is* possible to increase creativity at work.

Review and Discussion Questions

1. What are the three basic determinants of performance on a task?

2. Identify and summarize the five basic need categories included in Maslow's hierarchy of needs.

3. Compare and contrast Maslow's need hierarchy and Alderfer's ERG theory.

4. What is the primary distinction between need-based theories and process theories of motivation?

5. Identify and describe the three basic forms of reinforcement that most directly influence behavior in organizations.

6. What are the four primary schedules of reinforcement?

7. Identify and summarize the basic elements of expectancy theory and discuss how they relate to one another.

8. How does equity theory relate to organizational rewards?

9. Describe how goal theory relates to employee motivation.

10. What is intrinsic motivation? How is it different from extrinsic motivation?

Motivational Silos

Experienced managers refer to "the silo effect," in which various departments within an organization or across organizations act as if each were a stand-alone unit, ignoring important shared resources and interactions. One "silo effect" area that is a constant concern for many corporations is the tense, even hostile relationship that often exists between workers in the sales and marketing departments.

To an outsider, sales and marketing may appear to be compatible and harmonious complements—both, after all, are a bridge between the organization and its customers. Yet in many, if not most, organizations, salespeople claim that marketers are too abstract, too academic, too focused on creativity and not focused enough on outcomes. But most of all, they claim that marketing staff don't understand sales, because they never have to interact directly with a customer. On the other side, marketers claim that salespeople are too egotistical, too focused on making the sale at any cost, and don't understand the organization's strategy.

According to Christopher Kenton, president of the marketing firm Cymbic, neither the marketers nor the salespeople understand the relationship that should exist between them. Kenton explains the ideal relationship as similar to that between professional sports coaches and their players. "Every year [coaches] get fired while flashy players get fame and million-dollar contracts. Marketers are coaches and salespeople are players. Whatever role you choose, you need to understand that it's meaningless without your partner. If you fail to recognize you're joined at the hip, your team will lose."

How then can organizations inspire marketers and salespeople so that employees in each department are motivated, satisfied, and productive? CollabNet, a unique software company, provides a great answer. Marketing and sales departments cooperate. This requires marketing to start viewing the sales department, not the buyer, as their customer. "[Sales] is our customer. They're the ones who will be in front of the client," says CollabNet's marketing vice president Bernie Mills. "And treating sales as a customer means understanding their requirements." Rather than resenting the other department, each unit is encouraged to see the different yet equitable treatment they both receive.

Managers in both units realize that the probability of success and rewards is greater when both take on tasks that will benefit the other department. Marketing staff, for example, go on sales calls with salespeople. They meet customers, they watch negotiations, they begin to understand how to build a relationship with a customer. When CollabNet's marketing department created a sales kit for a new product launch, salespeople were involved in every aspect of the process. Mills says, "We showed up at the launch with a sales kit already [approved] by sales." These techniques ensure that the resources marketing provides are helpful and needed by the salespeople.

Sales is also doing more to support marketing. As part of a sales call, salespeople now ask questions about competing products and customer expenditures to gain useful market research for the marketing department. With constant customer contact, salespeople hear bits of market intelligence that might be useful to marketing staff, and now the relationship between the two units ensures that the intelligence is passed on.

The sales and marketing personnel seem very satisfied with the new way of conducting business. "I love our marketing department," says CollabNet salesperson Bart Tilly. "They're great." Tilly lists more participation and collaboration in sales calls, meetings, and strategy formulation as some of the ways that marketing provides support to sales. Marketing vice president Mills describes himself as "thrilled" by the developments and gives the credit for the initial collaborative efforts to his counterpart in sales.

According to Mills, both departments have a lot to gain through collaboration and shared goal setting. "Sales is selling one-to-one. Marketing is selling one-to-many. For sales, that means selling deal-to-deal, quarter-to-quarter, while marketing needs to focus on the longer-term picture," Mills asserts.

"We need to understand and respect that difference." Mills still sees marketing as responsible for the big picture, but adds, "Marketing needs to lead with a listening ear. Marketing doesn't need to have all the good ideas, they just need to recognize them." Sounds like CollabNet has already recognized the best idea of all—collaboration.[37]

Case Questions

1. Describe the jobs of salesperson and marketer at a typical firm in terms of the employee needs that are being met. Then describe the jobs of salesperson and marketer at CollabNet in terms of met needs. What are the differences?

2. Use equity theory to compare inputs and outcomes for a salesperson and a marketer at CollabNet. In your opinion, does equity exist? Why or why not?

3. Based on what you read in the case, does worker satisfaction seem to lead to higher performance at CollabNet? Or does higher performance lead to satisfaction? Explain.

Building HR Management Skills

Purpose: The purpose of this exercise is to provide you with insights into how to apply equity and justice in the workplace.

Step 1: Assume you are the manager of a group of professional employees in the electronics industry. One of your employees, David Brown, has asked to meet with you. You think you know what David wants to discuss, and you are unsure about how to proceed. You hired David about ten years ago. During his time in your group, he has been a solid, but not an outstanding, employee. His performance, for example, has been satisfactory in every respect, but seldom exceptional. As a result, he has consistently received average performance evaluations, pay increases, and so forth. Indeed, he actually makes a somewhat lower salary today than do a few people in the group with less tenure but with stronger performance records.

The company has just announced an opening for a team leader position in your group, and you know that David wants the job. He feels that he has earned the opportunity to have the job on the basis of his consistent efforts. Unfortunately, you see things a bit differently. You really want to appoint another individual, Becky Thomas, to the job. Becky has worked for the firm for only six years, but she is your top performer. You want to reward her performance and think that she will do an excellent job. On the other hand, you do not want to lose David because he is a solid member of the group.

Step 2: Using the previous information, answer the following questions:

1. Using equity theory as a framework, how do you think David and Becky are likely to see the situation?

2. Outline a conversation with David in which you will convey your decision to him. What will you say?

3. What advice might you offer Becky in her new job? About interacting with David?

4. What other rewards might you offer David to keep him motivated?

Ethical Dilemmas in HR Management

As noted in the chapter, some companies try to control—and even alter—workers' behavior through systematic rewards and punishments for specific behaviors. In other words, they first try to define the specific behaviors they want their employees to exhibit (such as working hard, being courteous to customers, stressing quality) and the specific behaviors they want them to eliminate (wasting time, being rude to customers, ignoring quality). Then they try to shape employee behavior by linking reinforcement to desired behaviors and punishment to undesired behaviors.

Assume that you are the new human resources manager in a medium-sized organization. Your boss has just ordered you to implement a behavior-modification program by creating an intricate network of rewards and punishments to be linked to specific desired and undesired behaviors. You, however, are uncomfortable with this approach. You regard behavior-modification policies to be too much like experiments on laboratory rats. Instead, you would prefer to use rewards in a way that is consistent with expectancy theory—that is, by letting employees know in advance how they can most effectively reach the rewards they most want. You have tried to change your boss's mind but to no avail. She says to proceed with behavior modification with no further discussion.

Questions

1. What are the ethical issues in this case?

2. What do you think most managers would do in this situation?

3. What would you do?

HR Internet Exercise

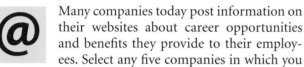

Many companies today post information on their websites about career opportunities and benefits they provide to their employees. Select any five companies in which you have a personal interest. Visit their websites and learn as much as you can about their career opportunities and their benefits. If any of them do not provide this information, continue exploring until you find information on five different companies.

Questions

1. Critique the promotion opportunities as described in terms of their motivational impact on you personally.

2. Critique the benefits packages as described in terms of their motivational impact on you personally.

3. If you were advising the firm on how to improve the motivational impact of their websites, what would you tell them?

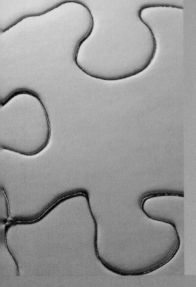

14

Performance Enhancement Techniques

CHAPTER OBJECTIVES

After studying this chapter you should be able to:

- Describe the relationships among performance measured at different levels within an organization.

- Discuss basic concepts of training and development and understand the difference between the two.

- Describe and critique various methods of delivering training material.

- Discuss how job redesign can help motivate improved performance.

- Describe the role of incentive pay.

- Identify different programs for individual-based and team-based incentive plans.

- Discuss the best ways to deliver performance feedback and the issues involved with feedback.

- Describe the basic operation of the ProMES system.

- Discuss how organizations evaluate performance enhancement programs.

Myriad articles, books, and television shows suggest that many Americans are unhappy at work. Increased competition, longer hours, an uncertain economy, technology that allows workers to work continuously—all of these have been blamed for the trend. Employees of video game maker Electronic Arts, for example, claim they routinely work between sixty-five and eighty-five hours a week, without overtime pay, which has led to some unhappy workers and at least one lawsuit. The consequences for businesses, in terms of increased turnover, lost efficiency, low morale and so on, is high, and the consequences for workers are even worse. Although statistics are inconclusive, observers report that white-collar injuries, illnesses, and even suicides related to work have risen recently. One study in 2000 found that 23 percent of male stockbrokers were clinically depressed, three times the national average for U.S. men.

Yet there are also many people who are motivated by and fully engaged with their work. One study describes 40 percent of American workers as excited about their jobs, eager to begin work on Monday mornings, and loving what they do. In many cases, happy workers have jobs that are easy to love. Sandor Zombori was working as an engineer but always longed to cook. He walked away from his job, invested his savings in a restaurant, and twenty years later is the owner and chef at an award-winning restaurant. "All the time, I am soaking it up, like a sponge, trying to learn as much as I can," Zombori explains. Artists, game

> *"As the parent of a toddler, it's exciting to have the coolest job at preschool."*
>
> (Robert Sunday, associate marketing manager, General Mills)

inventors, knitters, and architects have a passion to express themselves and to learn, which often leads to career happiness.

For others, more traditional careers hold rewards. Robert Sunday, associate marketing manager of Cheerios brand at General Mills, says about his job, "I truly love it! As the parent of a toddler, it's exciting to have the coolest job at preschool." For college professors, nurses, bank loan officers, and executive assistants, job happiness comes from satisfying intellectual curiosity, helping others, giving back to the community, and feeling needed. Sometimes the job can be defined to increase satisfaction. Richard Karlgaard is the publisher of *Forbes* magazine. He enjoys acting as an editor at large and writing about technology, while leaving most of the financial reporting to others.

But still, there are individuals who don't find their jobs rewarding and who can't change the job itself. In these cases, looking elsewhere may be the best option. Mary Lou Quinlan was the CEO of a New York advertising agency, the pinnacle of her profession, but chose to quit and start a small consulting business. The pay is less but she is happier. "Finally, I'm doing something I can picture doing for a long, long time," Quinlan says. Harvard University lecturer Laura Nash agrees that individuals can be happier in their personal and professional lives if they separate notions of success and money. If you can't be a star ballerina, Nash recommends, "you can start a ballet company or design a new ballet shoe, or even supply shoes to the dancers."[1]

As our opening vignette suggests, people can respond to their work in many different ways. These responses, in turn, contribute to how motivated they are to perform, how prepared they are to perform, and, ultimately, to organizational effectiveness. In our last chapter we described numerous theoretical models and frameworks for understanding employee motivation. In this chapter we examine the next step—the techniques that managers can use to capitalize on employee ability and motivation to enhance performance. In many ways this chapter is the culmination of much of what we have discussed throughout the book. Effective human resource management deals with ways to recruit, attract, retain, and reward employees. But the ultimate goal of all these activities must be to enhance organizational performance.

Note that we are suggesting an ultimate goal of organizational performance rather than simply individual or even group performance. Yet many of the techniques available for performance enhancement focus on the individual or group, and more or less assume that if individual performance improves, so will firm performance, but this is not necessarily the case. Therefore, we will begin by discussing some issues associated with the relationship between individual-level and firm-level performance, and this will serve as a background for our discussion of specific performance enhancement techniques, including different kinds of work arrangements, incentive and performance-based pay, and performance management and rewards. We conclude with a discussion of how managers can best evaluate their performance enhancement programs.

Organizations that can fully engage their employees and utilize various practices to enhance their motivation are often among the most successful firms in their industry. Take this Apple executive, Jonathan Ive, for example. Ive has played a major role in designing the newest iPod, as well as the firm's iPhone. He credits his success and the success of his team to their passionate feelings about their work.

Enhancing Performance at Different Levels

Performance in any organization exists at multiple levels. The most basic level of performance is at the level of the individual employee, and this is the level that most people find easiest to conceptualize. In fact, in Chapter 10, we discussed primarily measures and models of individual-level performance. That is, most appraisal techniques are concerned with determining how many products a person assembles or how many they sell *as individual contributors*. We can usually aggregate this up to the group or department level by simply combining sales or productivity data for individuals, but when we move up to the organizational level, things become more complicated. Of course, we can still talk about how many products are produced by the firm, or what a company's total sales are for a quarter, but this is often not very meaningful data.

For example, sales representatives might sell a lot of a product, but they may need to lower their prices so much that the firm is not profitable. Also, not all product lines are equally profitable so that one person can sell less and actually generate more profit for a firm than another person who sells more. But it makes little sense to talk about profitability at the level of the individual because profits depend largely on costs that can often be computed only at the firm level. As a result, a performance management or enhancement intervention designed to improve sales might not actually improve firm performance. There is no simple answer to the question of how to translate individual-level performance to organizational-level performance, but the key seems to be adopting a systems approach. That is, the firm can focus on individual-level performance but must do so in a systematic way that recognizes the interrelationships among individuals and the need to coordinate across individuals.[2]

It is critical that these performance enhancement interventions ultimately improve **firm-level performance.** This is the level that determines the long-term survival of the firm, generates profits for potential profit sharing, and determines the company's stock price. As you read through the rest of this chapter, it is important to keep this in mind: regardless of the level of performance targeted by a specific intervention, these interventions are effective only as long as they also improve organizational performance. With this as background, we can now review a number of techniques that have been shown to improve performance at some level within the organization.

Firm-level performance *is an indication of the likelihood of long-term survival of the firm. Performance at this level generates profits for potential profit sharing, and determines the company's stock price.*

Training and Development

Training and development activities within an organization are a very basic type of performance enhancement intervention. Training and development represent a fundamental investment in the employees who work for an organization, with the overall goal of improving their ability to make contributions to the firm's effectiveness. Employee **training** can be defined as a planned attempt by an organization to facilitate employee learning of job-related knowledge, skills, and behaviors. **Development,** on the other hand, usually refers to teaching managers and professionals the skills needed for both present and future jobs. Thus, each has a slightly different orientation.[3]

Training usually involves teaching operational or technical employees how to do their jobs more effectively and/or more efficiently. Teaching telephone operators to help customers more efficiently, showing machinists the proper way to handle certain kinds of tools, and demonstrating for short-order cooks how to prepare food orders

Training *can be defined as a planned attempt by an organization to facilitate employee learning of job-related knowledge, skills, and behaviors.*

Development *usually refers to teaching managers and professionals the skills needed for both present and future jobs.*

systematically are all part of training, and all these activities are aimed at helping the organization function more effectively.

For example, suppose that a small manufacturing company has a workforce of machinists and other operating employees who are currently capable of working at 85 percent of plant capacity. That is, the space, equipment, and technology in the plant may be potentially capable of producing, say, 100,000 units of output per day; the existing workforce, however, can turn out only 85,000 units per day. Because of anticipated growth in product demand, managers want to be prepared to meet this demand when it occurs by boosting the plant's level of potential performance. That is, they want their workforce to be able to produce more without having to hire new employees or invest in new equipment or technology. As a first step, the organization might want to work toward achieving 95 percent of capacity—or 95,000 units per day—using existing employees and facilities. Thus, these existing employees will need to be trained in more efficient work methods, with the ultimate goal of making them more productive. Such an approach should work as long as the workers have the ability they need to perform at this higher level of productivity.

Whereas training focuses on specific job-related skills, development is aimed at helping managers improve more general skills such as time management, motivating

Does training employees pay off? The answer is certainly "yes." In fact, the cost of NOT *training employees can be very high. Tom Farmer arrived at a hotel where he had a "guaranteed" reservation. It was two o'clock in the morning and the hotel was fully booked, leaving Farmer without a room. He insisted that the hotel clerk find him another room, but the clerk refused. When he returned home, Farmer sent an e-mail message to the hotel manager and to some of his friends. He named the hotel and stated simply "Yours is a very bad hotel." Within days the e-mail was being forwarded around the world, and the hotel chain's executives were extremely concerned. They contacted Farmer and asked what they could do. His response was simple: "Train your hotel's workers."*

employees, and solving problems. IBM helps develop its new first-line managers with an extensive nine-month training program called Basic Blue, which covers such topics as people management, HR policies, and leadership development. Program participants complete six months of online e-learning before traveling to this Learning Center next door to headquarters in Armonk, New York, for the continuation of the program. Almost 20,000 IBM managers worldwide have attended the program since its inception in 1999. Similarly, Halliburton provides six weeks of development annually for its top executives under a program it calls the Presidential Leadership Seminar.

Rather than focusing on specific job-related skills, development is more generally aimed at helping managers better understand and solve problems, make decisions, and capitalize on opportunities.[4] For example, managers need to understand how to manage their time effectively. Thus, some management development programs have a component dealing with time management. Other management development programs may help managers better understand how to motivate employees (for example, to get the employees discussed above to exert extra effort). Thus, managers do not necessarily return from development programs with a specific new operational method for doing their job more effectively. Instead, they may return with new skills that may be of relevance to them in a general sense at some point in the future. They may have a better understanding of how to work more effectively, how to motivate their employees better, and how to make better decisions, and they may possess a more complete understanding of how the overall organization functions and their role within it. Development is often considered a human resource function in most organizations, but because of its strategic nature and importance, one or more senior executives are usually given specific responsibility to ensure that management development is approached systematically and comprehensively.

There are several basic steps in the design of any training or development intervention, and these are illustrated in Figure 14.1. The process should begin with a needs analysis. That is, human resource managers responsible for training and development must determine the organization's true needs vis-à-vis training. This analysis generally focuses on two issues: the organization's job-related needs and the capabilities of the current workforce. The organization's needs are determined by the nature of the work that the organization needs to have performed. That is, what knowledge, skills, and abilities must the organization's workforce have to perform the organization's work most effectively?

As part of this analysis, the manager must carefully assess the company's strategy, the resources it has available for training, and its general philosophy regarding employee training and development. By "philosophy," we mean the extent to which the organization views training as a true investment in human resources or simply as a necessity to alter or change a specific outcome or criterion measure. Workforce analysis involves a careful assessment of the capabilities, strengths, and weaknesses characterizing the organization's

FIGURE 14.1 Assessing Training and Development Needs

Needs analysis
- Organization's job-related needs
- Capabilities of existing workforce

→ Setting training and development goals →

Determining approach
- In-house programs
- Outsourced programs

current workforce. That is, it is important to understand the extent to which the organization's workforce is skilled or unskilled, motivated or unmotivated, committed to the organization or not, and so forth. Furthermore, it is important for the organization to decide that it wishes to train employees for the present or to be more proactive and train the employees for what is expected to come in the future.

Once these needs are assessed, whether through direct observation, or some type of survey or interview process, the organization must then determine its goals for training and development. Unless a manager knows what to expect from the training it is difficult (if not impossible) to determine how effective any training or development activity has been. For example, consider the case of an insurance claims office. Assume that claims adjusters are processing insurance claims at an average rate of six business days per claim. Responses and feedback from customers suggest that some customers are becoming unhappy because they would like to have their claims processed more quickly. Using this information and other relevant data, the human resource manager—working in conjunction with operating managers—might decide that an appropriate and reasonable goal would be to cut the average processing time from six days down to four days. Thus, a "four-day processing average" becomes the goal of this particular training endeavor.

The next step in the process is to decide between in-house versus outsourced training. Many larger organizations, such as Texas Instruments and Exxon Mobil, have large training staffs, and so the organization itself assumes the responsibility for training and developing its employees, and thus assures that the content of its training and development efforts are precisely and specifically tailored to fit the organization's needs. Alternatively, outsourcing training activities enables a firm to draw upon expertise not available inside, in order to maximize training effectiveness. But outsourced programs tend to be more general and even generic, and thus have less applicability and direct relevance to the organization's needs.

Finally, once the organization has decided on whether to conduct training and development in-house or through outsourcing, it must decide upon the specific techniques to be used. For some situations, organizations might prefer to rely upon various work-based programs. *Work-based programs* tie the training and development activities directly to performance of the tasks. The most common method of work-based training is *on-the-job training*. This approach to training can help an organization to achieve a return on the labor cost of the employee almost immediately, assuming that the individual is capable of performing at a minimal level of competency. Also, direct training costs may be lower because the organization may not need to hire dedicated trainers or send employees to training programs.[5] Two other types of work-based training are apprenticeship programs and vestibule training. *Apprenticeships* involve a combination of on-the-job training and classroom instruction, and *vestibule training* involves a work-simulation situation in which the job is performed under a condition that closely simulates the real work environment.

Instructional-based programs are also quite common, especially the *lecture or discussion approach*. In these situations, a trainer presents the material to those attending the program in a lecture format; although lectures continue to play a role in most training programs, there is evidence that their use has been declining, and they are being replaced with training outside the classroom, primarily using electronic technologies.[6]

Another instructional-based program for training and development is *computer-assisted instruction*. In this situation, a trainee sits at a personal computer and operates software that has been developed specifically to impart certain material to the individual. The major advantage of this method is that it allows self-paced learning, and immediate feedback can be given to the trainee.[7]

Another method that involves basic instruction as a training device is *programmed instruction*. In recent years, these activities have become computerized, but remain self-paced and with self-assessment. Also, in recent years, all of these approaches have been affected by changes in training technology. Video teleconferencing allows a trainer in a centralized location to deliver material live via satellite hookup to remote sites in different locations; the training can thus be delivered effectively but without the travel costs necessary in transporting people to a common training site. Interactive videos involve presenting information on a monitor from a central serving mechanism, DVD, CD-ROM, or website. The trainee interacts with the system via a mouse or keyboard. Feedback can be provided when inadequate responses or improper answers are given, and the trainee can skip material that has already been learned.

Job Redesign

A much different approach to enhancing organizational performance is through the redesign of jobs. Specifically, this technique involves changing—redesigning—jobs so that the work itself will motivate employees to exert greater effort. This motivation is stimulated by making the job more interesting and/or challenging. We will discuss five motivational approaches to the redesign of work: job rotation, job enlargement, job enrichment, the job characteristics approach, and work teams. As we shall see, the use of work teams is a bit different in its intent. Although a driving consideration is still to help motivate employees to work harder, this approach is also concerned with designing more effective ways of doing a job, and it has a great deal of applicability in today's organizations.

Job rotation involves systematically moving employees from one job to another. A worker in a warehouse might unload trucks on Monday, carry incoming inventory to storage on Tuesday, verify invoices on Wednesday, pull outgoing inventory from storage on Thursday, and load trucks on Friday. Thus, the jobs do not change; instead, workers move from job to job. For this very reason, however, job rotation has not been very successful in enhancing employee motivation or satisfaction. Jobs that are amenable to rotation tend to be relatively standard and routine. Workers who are rotated to a "new" job may be more satisfied at first, but the novelty soon wanes. Although many companies (among them American Cyanamid, Bethlehem Steel, Ford, Prudential Insurance, TRW, and Western Electric) have tried job rotation, it is most often used today as a training device to improve worker skills and flexibility.

Based on the assumption that doing the same basic task over and over is the primary cause of worker dissatisfaction, **job enlargement** was developed to increase the total number of tasks that workers perform. As a result, all workers perform a wide variety of tasks, presumably reducing the level of job dissatisfaction. Many organizations have used job enlargement, including IBM, Detroit Edison, AT&T, the U.S. Civil Service, and Maytag. At Maytag, for example, the assembly line for producing washing-machine water pumps was systematically changed so that work originally performed by six workers, who passed the work sequentially from one person to another, was performed by four workers, each of whom assembled a complete pump. Although job enlargement does have some positive consequences, they are often offset by several disadvantages: (1) training costs usually rise; (2) unions have argued that pay should increase because the worker is doing more tasks; and (3) in many cases, the work remains boring and routine even after job enlargement.

A more comprehensive approach, **job enrichment,** assumes that increasing the range and variety of tasks alone is not sufficient to improve employee motivation.[8] Thus, job enrichment attempts to increase both the number of tasks a worker does and the control the worker has over the job. To accomplish this objective, managers remove some controls from the job; delegate more authority to employees; and structure the work in complete, natural units. These changes increase the subordinates' sense of responsibility. Another

Job rotation *involves systematically moving employees from one job to another.*

Job enlargement *was developed to increase the total number of tasks workers perform based on the assumption that doing the same basic task over and over is the primary cause of worker dissatisfaction.*

Job enrichment *attempts to increase both the number of tasks a worker does and the control the worker has over the job.*

part of job enrichment is to assign new and challenging tasks continually, thereby increasing the employees' opportunity for growth and advancement.

AT&T was one of the first companies to try job enrichment. In one experiment, eight typists in a service unit prepared customer-service orders. Faced with low output and high turnover, management determined that the typists felt little responsibility to clients and received little feedback. The unit was changed to create a typing team. Typists were matched with designated service representatives, the task was changed from ten specific steps to three more general steps, and job titles were upgraded. As a result the number of orders delivered on time increased from 27 percent to 90 percent, the need for messenger service was eliminated, accuracy improved, and turnover became practically nil.[9] Other organizations that have tried job enrichment include Texas Instruments, IBM, and General Foods. Problems have been found with this approach, however. For example, analysis of work systems before enrichment is needed but seldom performed, and managers rarely deal with employee preferences when enriching jobs.

The **job characteristics approach** is an alternative to job specialization in that it does take into account the work system and employee preferences.[10] It is also one of the most widely used and widely studied approaches to job design. As illustrated in Figure 14.2, the job characteristics approach suggests that jobs should be examined and improved along five core dimensions:

The **job characteristics approach** *is an alternative to job specialization that takes into account the work system and employee preferences; it suggests that jobs should be diagnosed and improved along five core dimensions.*

1. *Skill variety:* the number of tasks a person does in a job
2. *Task identity:* the extent to which the worker does a complete or identifiable portion of the total job
3. *Task significance:* the perceived importance of the task
4. *Autonomy:* the degree of control the worker has over how the work is performed
5. *Feedback:* the extent to which the worker knows how well the job is being performed

The higher a job rates on these five dimensions, the more employees will experience various psychological states. Experiencing these states, in turn, presumably leads to high motivation, high-quality performance, high satisfaction, and low absenteeism and turnover. Finally, a variable called *growth-need strength* is presumed to affect how the model works for different people. People with a strong desire to grow, develop, and expand their capabilities (indicative of high growth-need strength) are expected to respond strongly to the presence or absence of the basic job characteristics; individuals with low growth-need strength are expected not to respond as strongly or consistently.

Several studies have been conducted to test the usefulness of the job characteristics approach. The Southwestern Division of Prudential Insurance, for example, used this approach in its claims division. Results included moderate declines in turnover and a small but measurable improvement in work quality. Other research findings have not supported this approach as strongly. Thus, although the job characteristics approach is one of the most promising alternatives to job specialization, it is probably not the final answer.

Work teams represent a much different way of approaching job design. Under this arrangement, a group is given responsibility for designing the work system to be used in performing an interrelated set of jobs. These groups are sometimes referred to as self-directed work teams or autonomous work teams, and they are permanent parts of the organizational architecture. In these teams, the group itself decides how jobs will be allocated. For example, the work team assigns specific tasks to members, monitors and controls its own performance, and exercises autonomy over work scheduling.

A **work team** *is an arrangement in which a group is given responsibility for designing the work system to be used in performing an interrelated set of jobs.*

The original impetus for the reliance on work teams comes from a famous series of studies conducted in England by the Tavistock Institute and dealing with the coal-mining industry.[11] The researchers determined that it was important for miners to have social interaction, and so they suggested that the miners work in teams. The researchers also identified and suggested several changes in the actual coal-mining jobs themselves. As it turned out, the job changes were also conducive to team settings in that they in-

FIGURE 14.2   The Job Characteristics Model of Job Design

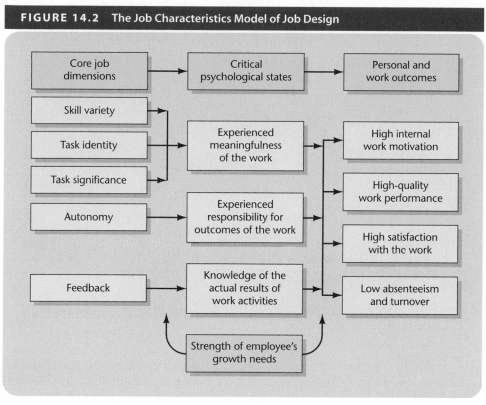

Source: J. R. Hackman and G. R. Oldham, "Motivation Through the Design of Work: Test of a Theory," from *Organizational Behavior and Human Performance,* Vol. 16, 1976, pp. 250–279. Reprinted with permission from Elsevier.

creased the need for coordination. After the jobs were changed and the workers formed into teams, performance in the mines improved considerably, and the miners reported more satisfaction and increased motivation. Hence, in some settings, teams make a great deal of sense. But work teams are not without problems, and they certainly are not the answer in all cases.

For example, if work is designed to be done by teams, then all rewards must be based on team performance; that is, we cannot reward individuals in true team work settings. This may decrease the motivation of some employees, especially those who might exert exceptional effort, only to see less effort exerted by fellow team members. Finally, in situations where we cannot identify the work product of any single individual, there is greater likelihood of "shirking," or simply not exerting effort with the assumption that someone else will get the work done. These problems may not argue against team work, but they do underscore the importance of making sure that the situation really calls for team work.

Alternative Work Arrangements

Another approach to performance enhancement comes with allowing employees more flexibility in their working arrangements. The assumption here is that if employees can work in ways that better suit their lifestyles, they will be less distracted and more likely

Teams are increasingly common in the workplace as organizations realize that certain tasks are best handled by a group of individuals working together toward a common goal. Of course, this model of accomplishing tasks has been around for a long time in other settings. For example, the yacht racing crew pictured here is a team. Although each person has a specific task to carry out, the boat will only perform well if everyone does his or her job and coordinates with every other crew member. This particular example also illustrates the advantages and potential disadvantages of working in teams. It is difficult to imagine sailing such a large boat with only one person, or with a group of people who do not work well together. Yet in the flurry of activity it is difficult to monitor behavior to ensure that each person does his or her best as part of the team. Thus it is important that each team member understand and be committed to the goals of the team in order for the team to be successful.

Flexible work hour plans
are plans where employees usually must still work a full forty hours per week and, typically, they must work five days a week, but where they have control, however, over the starting and ending times for work on each day.

to be productive. But these interventions are also designed to affect organizational-level performance by simply reducing costs and increasing efficiency. Thus, traditionally, employees came to a specific workplace and were expected to be physically present at work five days a week, eight hours a day, unless the nature of the job was such that the employee was required to spend time on the road. In modern organizations, however, it is becoming increasingly common for people to work on a schedule other than five days/forty hours and/or to work at a place other than the office or place of business.

Alternate Work Schedules

The two most common alternatives to the traditional workweek are programs known as flexible work hours and compressed workweeks. Employees working under **flexible work hour plans** usually must still work a full forty hours per week and, typically, they must work five days a week. The employees have control, however, over the starting and ending times for work on each day. In almost every case, there is a core time each day when every employee must be at work. During these hours the organization can schedule meetings or any other activities that require coordination among employees. The remaining hours (flextime) can be made up in any way that the employee prefers. For example, if a company's core time is 10:00 A.M. until 2:00 P.M., everyone is expected to be at work during those hours. But starting times might be anywhere between 7:00 A.M. and 10:00 A.M., and quitting times might be anywhere between 2:00 P.M. and 7:00 P.M. Under such a plan, the core time represents twenty hours a week, and the employee is free to work the remaining twenty hours in any fashion within the stated constraints.

Figure 14.3 illustrates how an organization might function with one type of flexible work schedule. This organization has defined 6:00 A.M.–9:00 A.M., 11:00 A.M.–1:00 P.M., and 3:00 P.M.–7:00 P.M. as flexible time, and 9:00 A.M.–11:00 A.M. and 1:00 P.M.–3:00 P.M. as core time. A worker choosing option 1 (i.e., the early riser) comes to work at 6:00 A.M., takes an hour for lunch, and is finished for the day at 3:00 P.M. Option 2, perhaps more attractive for those not considered to be morning people, involves starting work at 9:00 A.M., taking two hours for lunch, and working until 7:00 P.M. Option 3 is closest to a standard

FIGURE 14.3   Flexible Work Schedules

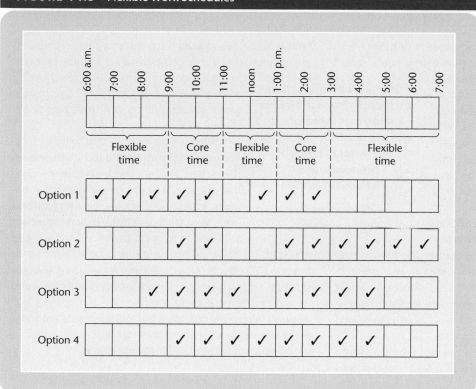

workday, starting at 8:00 A.M., taking an hour at lunch, and leaving at 5:00 P.M. Finally, option 4 involves starting at 9:00 A.M., taking no lunch, and finishing at 5:00 P.M. Note that in every case, however, each employee works during the core time periods.

These plans are believed to reduce stress because the employee does not have to travel during peak commuting times and can have more control over the commute.[12] They are also believed to increase job satisfaction because the employee is given more control over the work environment and a stronger feeling that he or she is trusted by the organization.[13] They are not as feasible in organizations that place a strong emphasis on teams; otherwise, no serious problems associated with their use are reported. The following *HR in the 21st Century* feature provides additional perspectives on flexible work schedules.

Compressed workweeks are arrangements in which the employee works the required number of hours (typically forty) but does so in less than five days. For example, a four-day, ten-hour-a-day work schedule is fairly common, and schedules that involve four days with twelve hours a day, followed by four days off, are also fairly common. The employee gains the flexibility of three days off a week, presumably making it less likely that he or she will lose work time to deal with personal business. These schedules are also well suited for employees who work at sites that are difficult to get to, such as offshore drilling rigs. These schedules are not for everyone, however, and longer workdays are related to increased accidents in some settings.[14] Nonetheless, compressed workweeks are extremely popular with some employees.

Both of these alternative schedule plans are growing in popularity, and few problems seem to be associated with them (except as noted). These alternative schedules present some unique challenges to the human resource manager, however. As noted above, flexible

Compressed workweeks
are arrangements in which the employee works the required number of hours (typically forty) but does so in less than five days. For example, a four-day, ten-hour-a-day work schedule is fairly common.

HR IN THE 21ST CENTURY

Creating Humane Work Schedules

Sixty-hour workweeks used to be the norm in the United States; now eighty hours is not uncommon. But working longer hours doesn't always increase productivity. One recent study showed that U.S. workers were less productive per hour worked than those from countries with shorter workweeks, including France and Germany. Experts hypothesize that overworked employees become tired, stressed, and less motivated. Lowell Bryan, a McKinsey & Company partner, claims, "We've created jobs that are literally impossible. The human cost is profound, and the opportunity cost is also great in terms of organizational effectiveness." Problems made worse by overwork are costly and can include injuries, mistakes, rework, workplace violence, stress-related diseases, absenteeism, and high turnover.

Some companies are actively seeking ways to offer a more reasonable work-life balance. Fox News, for example, split the job of one senior executive between two individuals, who both work full-time and share responsibilities equally. The editorship of the *Los Angeles Times* was once held by one person, but now three workers do the job. Part-time work is another increasingly popular option.

> *"We've created jobs that are literally impossible. The human cost is profound, and the opportunity cost is also great in terms of organizational effectiveness."*
>
> (Lowell Bryan, McKinsey & Company partner)*

JetBlue allows key managers to work part-time schedules in exchange for reduced compensation. In many cases it's not hard to implement these new working arrangements. Law associates can handle fewer cases; auditors can work with fewer clients.

It's accepted wisdom that willing workers are plentiful, no matter how demanding the schedule, but most companies note that there is a shortage of qualified managers. Increasingly, people want time off and are willing to give up money and career advancement to get it. Both men and women now talk freely in many companies about wanting to "have it all," referring to a career and a rewarding life outside of work. As these conversations become more widespread and more intense, perhaps U.S. companies will respond. Alternate, flexible work arrangements are more acceptable to workers, and they can also create a more motivated, productive, and loyal workforce.

Sources: "Nice Work If You Can Get It," *Business Week,* January 9, 2006, pp. 56–57; Jody Miller and Matt Miller, "Get a Life!" *Fortune,* November 28, 2005, pp. 109–124 (* quote); Danielle Sacks, "Scenes from the Culture Clash," *Fast Company,* January 2006, pp. 28–31.

schedules are often not feasible in organizations that rely heavily on teams. In fact, whenever one employee's work depends on input from another employee, these schedules may be a problem. Even when they are not a problem, flexible schedules reduce the amount of time that employees interact with their coworkers, which makes it more difficult to develop a strong culture or even a strong esprit de corps.

Although employees are at work the same number of hours as before and have the opportunity to interact with coworkers, compressed workweeks present similar challenges because the stress of longer hours may make social interaction less likely, and the greater number of days off may also affect some social aspects of the job. The human resource manager must try to find ways to replace socializing activities with other experiences so that employees, especially new employees, can learn more about their coworkers and can become more fully socialized into the organization.

Alternate Work Sites

In addition to employees working on alternate schedules, employees performing their work at a location other than the place of business, most likely at home, is a growing trend. Home work and telecommuting are two popular variations on this theme. Table 14.1

shows the number and distribution of people currently working under an alternative work arrangement. *Home work programs* include arrangements that are often referred to as cottage industries. In the earliest days of the industrial revolution, before many factories were built, employees would take parts back home to their cottages and manufacture them, then return them to a central point where they could be assembled. Similar types of cottage industries still exist for the manufacturing of small and not very complex items.

It is more common, however, to operate in what can be called an electronic cottage. Employees take office work home with them and complete it on home computers. They

TABLE 14.1   Employed Workers with Alternative Work Arrangements by Occupation and Industry (Percentage Distribution for 2005)

Characteristic	Workers with Alternative Arrangements			
	Independent Contractors	On-Call Workers	Temporary Agency Workers	Workers Provided by Contract Firms
Total,16 years of age and over (in thousands)	10,342	2,454	1,217	813
Management, professional & related occupations	39.9	35.6	20.3	39.6
Service Occupations	13.7	22.1	15.6	26.2
Sales and Office occupations	20.5	12.6	26.9	7.2
Natural Resources, Construction & Maintenance Occupations	19.7	16.9	7.1	21.8
Production, Transportation & Material Moving Occupations	6.1	12.7	30.1	5.2
Industry Total, 16 years of age and over (in thousands)	10,342	2,454	1,217	813
Agriculture & related industries	2.6	0.6	-	0.2
Mining	0.1	1.0	0.5	0.2
Construction	22.0	12.2	3.4	16.5
Manufacturing	3.2	4.8	28.4	14.1
Transportation and utilities	3.9	8.4	3.1	4.0
Wholesale trade	2.1	2.1	5.4	3.4
Retail trade	8.9	5.6	2.1	3.1
Information	2.0	1.8	1.8	4.0
Financial Activities	10.4	3.4	4.1	6.8
Profession & Business Services	2.0	1.8	1.8	4.0
Education & Health Services	8.7	33.8	11.1	15.7
Leisure & Hospitality	4.5	10.4	1.8	4.5
Other Services	9.9	3.8	2.9	0.3
Public Administration	0.3	4.4	2.8	16.6

Source: U.S. Department of Labor, Bureau of Labor Statistics

can then return to the office to collect more work. They are connected to that office via a modem, fax machine, and e-mail. These arrangements can even result in a virtual office and are becoming especially popular with people who want (or need) to work but do not wish to work full-time or who have other responsibilities such as child- or eldercare.[15]

Telecommuting is simply the logical extension of the electronic cottage. Under this arrangement, employees may do almost all of their work at home and may even receive assignments electronically. This arrangement provides employees with the ultimate in flexibility because they can choose the hours they work and even the location. A growing body of evidence suggests that this arrangement increases job satisfaction and even productivity, and it also allows organizations to use the services of individuals who may not be able to work at a given site.[16] For example, an employee can live many hours from his or her office if he or she performed most of the work via telecommuting. Finally, larger organizations can save considerable amounts of money if they do not need large (or any) real office space. Cisco Systems, a pioneer in telecommuting, estimates that, by allowing employees to work at home, it has boosted productivity by 25 percent, lowered its own overhead by $1 million, and retained key knowledge workers who might have left for other jobs without the flexibility provided by the firm's telecommuting options.[17]

Alternative work sites present a more serious challenge to the human resource manager. In the past, the AFL-CIO has complained that home work arrangements allow management to impose unfair working conditions on employees, and it also makes it more difficult for unions to organize workers. So unions continue to oppose these arrangements. As with alternative work schedules, communication among employees is difficult under these arrangements, and it is extremely difficult for a new employee to become socialized. But in fact little socialization may be possible if many of the employees are working under nontraditional work arrangements and many are working at home.

In addition, some individuals may simply lack the self-discipline to get the work done in a completely unconstrained environment, although the available evidence suggests that this outcome is not much of a problem. What does seem to be a problem is that these alternative work sites are likely to increase employees' sense of alienation at work.[18] They have no social connections and no support from coworkers, and so loyalty or commitment to the organization is unlikely to develop. Companies are trying, however, to overcome these problems. For example, Merrill Lynch allows potential telecommuters a two-week dry run to see how they like it. Aetna assigns each of its telecommuters an office buddy to help those working at home to stay in touch with what's going on at the office. And America West even arranges monthly potluck dinners to maintain social interaction among employees who work at home.[19]

Incentives and Performance-Based Rewards

Merit pay is pay awarded to employees on the basis of the relative value of their contributions to the organization.

Merit-pay plans are compensation plans that formally base at least some meaningful portion of compensation on merit.

Yet another approach to enhancing performance is by explicitly tying rewards, especially pay, to performance. That is, organizations try to reinforce certain types of behaviors and outcomes (recall our discussion in Chapter 13) by tying compensation directly to measures of performance or productivity. There are many plans to allow this to be done.

The most basic form of incentive compensation is merit pay. **Merit pay** generally refers to pay awarded to employees on the basis of the relative value of their contributions to the organization. Employees who make greater contributions are given higher pay than those who make lesser contributions. **Merit-pay plans,** then, are formal compensation plans that base at least some meaningful portion of compensation on merit.

The most general form of the merit-pay plan is to provide annual salary increases to individuals in the organization based on their relative merit. Merit, in turn, is usually determined or defined based on the individual's performance and overall contributions to the organization. Recall that in Chapter 10 we discussed various methods for evaluating employee performance. We noted, as well, that performance appraisal had the most meaning to employees if it was subsequently connected with a reward such as a salary increase. However, it is important for the organization to have valid and reliable measures for merit. Merit generally refers to performance, but for the plan to have motivation and performance effects, people throughout the organization must have a clear understanding of what the firm means by the term merit. Otherwise, the plan will not only not be effective in improving performance, it may cause problems with employees' perceptions of justice.

Another basic approach is based on systems of *skill-* and *knowledge-based pay.* Recall from Chapter 9 that, under these systems, instead of rewarding employees for increased performance they are rewarded for the acquisition of more skills or knowledge. But these skills or this knowledge is related to what the organization believes it will need in the future. Thus, in effect, the organization is rewarding the employee for increasing his or her capacity to perform well in the future, while more traditional merit-pay systems reward employees for achieving some level of performance, but this performance is defined by what the organization needs (or wants) right now. Although problems are associated with these systems and their administration, they offer an alternative to more traditional merit-pay systems and provide a more strategic long-term focus for the organization.[20] In addition, they allow the organization to move employees toward focusing on more than just basic productivity.[21]

Incentive compensation systems are among the oldest forms of performance-based rewards. For example, as noted earlier, some companies used individual piece-rate incentive plans over 100 years ago.[22] Under a piece-rate incentive plan, the organization pays an employee a certain amount of money for every unit she or he produces. For example, an employee might be paid $1.00 for every dozen units of product that she or he completed successfully. But such simplistic systems fail to account for factors such as minimum-wage levels, and they rely heavily on the assumptions that performance is under an individual's complete control and that the individual employee does a single task continuously throughout his or her work time. Thus, most organizations that try to use incentive compensation systems today use more sophisticated methods, and we will now discuss some of these.

Individual Incentive Pay Plans

Generally speaking, **individual incentive plans** reward individual performance on a real-time basis. That is, rather than increasing a person's **base salary** at the end of the year, an individual instead receives some level of salary increase or financial reward in conjunction with demonstrated outstanding performance in close proximity to when that performance occurred. Individual incentive systems are most likely to be used in cases where performance can be objectively assessed, in terms of number of units of output or similar measures, rather than on a subjective assessment of performance by a superior.

Some variations on a piece-rate system are still fairly popular. Although many of these systems still resemble the early plans in most ways, a well-known piece-rate system at Lincoln Electric illustrates how an organization can adapt the traditional model to achieve better results. For years Lincoln's employees were paid individual incentive payments based on their performance. However, the amount of money shared (or the incentive pool) was based on the company's profitability. A well-organized system allowed employees to make suggestions for increasing productivity. Motivation was provided in

Individual incentive plans *reward individual performance on a real-time basis.*

The **base salary** *of an employee is a guaranteed amount of money that the individual will be paid.*

the form of a reward equaling one-third of the profits (another third went to the stock-holders and the last third was retained for improvements and seed money). Thus, the pool for incentive payments was determined by profitability, and an employee's share of this pool was a function of his or her base pay and rated performance based on the piece-rate system.

Lincoln Electric was most famous, however, because of the stories (which were apparently typical) of production workers receiving a year-end bonus payment that equaled their yearly base pay.[23] In recent years, Lincoln has partially abandoned its famous system for business reasons, but it still serves as a benchmark for other companies seeking innovative piece-rate pay systems.

*A **sales commission** is an incentive paid to salespeople.*

Perhaps the most common form of individual incentive is the **sales commission** that is paid to salespeople. For example, sales representatives for consumer products firms and retail sales agents may be compensated under this type of commission system. In general, the person might receive a percentage of the total volume of attained sales as her or his commission for a period of time. Some sales jobs are based entirely on commission, while others use a combination of base minimum salary with additional commission as an incentive. Notice that these plans put a considerable amount of the salespersons' earnings at risk. Although organizations often have drawing accounts to allow the salesperson to live during lean periods (the person then "owes" this money to the organization), if he or she does not perform well, he or she will not be paid much. The portion of salary based on commission is simply not guaranteed and is paid only if the employee's sales reach some target level.

Finally, organizations occasionally may use other forms of incentives to motivate employees. For example, a nonmonetary incentive such as additional time off or a special perk might be a useful incentive. A company might establish a sales contest in which the sales group that attains the highest level of sales increase over a specified period of time

THE LIGHTER SIDE OF HR

Organizations often use incentives to attract and retain workers. As shown in this cartoon, however, managers need to remember that because people have different needs, the same incentives do not always work for everyone. For example, some people may want a bigger office, while others might want greater flexibility over working hours and conditions. And someone may even occasionally be motivated by something such as control of the office thermostat!

cathy®   **by Cathy Guisewite**

Source: Cathy © 1998 Cathy Guisewite. Reprinted with permission of Universal Press Syndicate. All rights reserved.

receives an extra week of paid vacation, perhaps even at an arranged place such as a tropical resort or a ski lodge.[24] *The Lighter Side of HR* illustrates one humorous example of how such incentives might be used to attract new employees.

As with merit systems, incentive compensation systems have some shortcomings and weaknesses. One major shortcoming is that they are practical only when performance can be measured easily and objectively. Most managerial work does not fit this pattern and, in fact, is often characterized by ambiguous performance indicators that are difficult to assess. Thus, it may be much more difficult to provide valid and appropriate incentives for these individuals. Individual incentives are also likely to focus attention on only a narrow range of behaviors, perhaps at the expense of other behaviors. Consider, for example, a sales representative in a department store. This sales representative may be able to maximize his or her pay by greeting every customer aggressively, trying continually to sell them items that they may or may not need, and overlooking deficiencies or shortcomings in the product offered for sale. In such cases, sales representatives sometimes make grandiose claims that have no basis in reality and may stretch the truth to the point of creating totally inaccurate expectations. Thus, the individual sales representative may maximize her or his income in the short term, but at the cost of poor morale among other less aggressive salespeople and increasingly dissatisfied customers.

Team and Group Incentive Plans

In addition to incentive plans designed to improve individual performance, there are plans that focus on group or team performance. These programs are particularly important for managers to understand today because they focus attention on higher levels of performance, and because of the widespread trends toward team- and group-based methods of work and organizations.[25] The Point/Counterpoint feature for this chapter underscores some of the basic issues between individual and team-based incentive systems.

A fairly common type of group incentive system is an approach called **gainsharing.** Gainsharing programs are designed to share the cost savings from productivity improvements with employees. The underlying assumption of gainsharing is that employees and the employer have the same goals and thus should share in incremental economic gains,[26] consistent with our discussion of agency theory in Chapter 13.

In general, organizations that use gainsharing start by measuring team- or group-level productivity. It is important that this measure is valid and reliable and that it truly reflects current levels of performance by the team or group. The team or work group itself is charged with attempting to lower costs and otherwise improve productivity through any measures that its members develop and that its manager approves. Resulting cost savings or productivity gains that the team or group is able to achieve are then quantified and translated into dollar values. A predetermined formula is used to allocate these dollar savings between the employer and the employees themselves. A typical formula for distributing gainsharing savings is to provide 25 percent of the dollar savings to the employees and 75 percent to the company.

One specific type of gainsharing plan is an approach called the **Scanlon plan.** This approach was developed by Joseph Scanlon in 1927. The Scanlon plan has the same basic strategy as gainsharing plans because teams or groups of employees are encouraged to suggest strategies for reducing cost. However, the distribution of these gains is usually tilted much more heavily toward employees, with employees usually receiving between two-thirds and three-fourths of the total cost savings that the plan achieves. The cost savings resulting from the plan are not given just to the team or group that suggested and developed the ideas, but are instead distributed to the entire organization.

Gainsharing *is a team- and group-based incentive system designed to share the cost savings from productivity improvements with employees.*

Scanlon plans *are gainsharing plans (where teams or groups of employees are encouraged to suggest strategies for reducing costs in which the distribution of gains is tilted much more heavily toward employees and across the entire organization.*

Team Versus Individual Incentives

 Incentives are meant to shape employee behavior in some desired direction. For example, if organizations want employees to produce more units, they would pay them for each additional unit (over some minimum) that they produce. Under such a system, employees learn to maximize their rewards by behaving in a way desired by the organization. But as organizations increase the extent to which work is done by teams, the incentive situation becomes more complex. Should organizations reward the behavior of individual team members as if they were independent employees, or should they focus on team behaviors instead? In the latter situation, organizations would reward behaviors exhibited by the team as a whole, rather than behaviors exhibited by any individual team member.

POINT... Organizations should base incentives on individual behavior because...	COUNTERPOINT... Organizations should base incentives on team behavior because...
Individual effort is the easiest to monitor, and individual behaviors are the easiest to specify.	They are ultimately interested in changing the behavior of the team when work is done by teams.
Any team performance must be a function of the effort and performance of individual team members.	Team effectiveness requires more than just the efforts of individuals to perform their own jobs. It also requires people to be concerned with team spirit and communication.
If individuals are not rewarded for their effort, they will be less motivated to exert effort.	If team members are rewarded for individual performance, each member will seek to maximize his or her own performance, even to the detriment of team effectiveness.
If individuals are not responsible for achieving performance goals, there is a good chance that no one will feel responsible.	Individuals will not exert effort to maintain effective team functioning unless they are rewarded, and this effort can be rewarded only at the team level.
There will always be free riders who will not exert effort if the job is being done by others, and anything but individual-based incentives will unjustly reward these free riders.	The free-rider problem can be addressed by the rest of the team, which can exert group pressure on nonperforming members.

So... As organizations move more toward team work, they must establish incentives so that team-level goals and objectives are accomplished. Efforts to do so by implementing individual-based incentives will almost certainly fail because individual goals may be independent of or even in conflict with team goals. Nonetheless, if organizations ignore rewards for individual efforts, team performance levels are likely to drop. The key, then, is to combine the two. One possibility is to implement team-level incentives and then to allow the team, as a group, to provide incentives to individual team members for their individual efforts.

In addition to gainsharing and Scanlon plans, other systems are also used by some organizations. Some companies, for example, have begun to use true incentives at the team or group level. As with individual incentives, team or group incentives tie rewards directly to performance. And like individual incentives, team or group incentives are paid as they are earned rather than being added to employees' base salaries. The incentives are distributed at the team or group level, however, rather than at the individual level. In some cases, the distribution may be based on the existing salary of each employee, with incentive bonuses being given on a proportionate basis. In other settings, each team or group member receives the same incentive pay.

Some companies also use nonmonetary rewards at the team or group level. These rewards come most commonly in the form of prizes and awards. For example, a company might designate the particular team in a plant or subunit of the company that achieves the highest level of productivity increase, the highest level of reported customer satisfaction, or a similar index of performance. The reward itself might take the form of additional time off (as described earlier in this chapter) or a tangible award such as a trophy or a plaque. In any event, however, the reward is given to the entire team and serves as recognition of exemplary performance by the entire team.

Other kinds of team- or group-level incentives go beyond the contributions of a specific work group. These incentives are generally organizationwide. One long-standing method for this approach is profit sharing. In **profit sharing,** some portion of the company's profits is paid at the end of the year into a profit-sharing pool that is distributed to all employees. This amount is either distributed at the end of the year or put into an escrow account and payment is deferred until the employee retires.

> **Profit sharing** *is an incentive system in which, at the end of the year, some portion of the company's profits is paid into a profit-sharing pool, which is then distributed to all employees.*

The basic rationale behind profit-sharing systems is that everyone in the organization can expect to benefit when the company does well. During bad economic times, however, when the company is perhaps achieving low or no profits, then no profit sharing is paid out. This situation sometimes results in negative reactions from employees who come to feel that the profit sharing is really part of their annual compensation.

Various types of *stock-based incentives* are also a way to tie incentives to the performance of the firm, although these are more typically used with executive employees rather than hourly employees. For example, in many companies, executives may be given a certain number of *stock options,* which enable them to purchase shares of the company's stock at a fixed price. Thus, under a **stock-option plan** an executive may be given 1,000 options to purchase the firm's stock at $5.00 per share (the current trading price) for up to one year. If the stock price rises to $6.00 a share (presumably because of something the executive did), the employee can exercise his or her option: buy the shares at $5.00, sell them at $6.00, and make a $1,000.00 profit.

> A **stock-option plan** *is an incentive plan established to give senior managers the option to buy the company stock in the future at a predetermined fixed price.*

Alternatively, some firms offer **stock purchase plans,** which are typically offered to all the employees of a firm rather than just the executives. Many start-up firms, especially in high-tech sectors, also offer restricted stock plans, which are really used as a retention tool rather than as a performance incentive. Under these plans, employees are entitled to the stock only if they remain with the company for a specified period of time. If they leave before that time, they have no rights to the shares of stock.

> **Stock purchase plans** *are typically offered to all the employees of a firm rather than just the executives, and serve more as a retention tool. Under these plans, employees are entitled to the stock only if they remain with the company for a specified period of time. If they leave before that time, they have no rights to the shares of stock.*

Employee stock ownership plans (ESOPs) represent another group-level reward system that some companies use. Under the ESOP, employees are gradually given a major stake in the ownership of a corporation. The typical form of this plan involves the company taking out a loan, which is then used to buy a portion of the company's own stock in the open market. Over time, company profits are then used to pay off this loan. Employees, in turn, receive a claim on ownership of some portion of the stock held by the company based on their seniority and perhaps their performance. Eventually, each individual becomes an owner of the company.

> **Employee stock ownership plans (ESOPs)** *are group-level reward systems in which employees are gradually given a major stake in the ownership of a corporation.*

While group reward systems can be effective in some situations, they are also subject to difficulties. For example, not every member of a group may contribute equally to the group's performance. But if the group incentive system distributes rewards equally to group members, then people may feel that some factors beyond individual performance dictate the distribution of rewards. Also, for incentive plans based on firm profitability, employees may not see how their efforts lead to increased profits (often referred to as a *line-of-sight problem*). In fact, many factors that are beyond the employees' control can affect profitability. Thus, the links among effort, performance and outcomes, as specified by expectancy theory, are often quite weak, thus resulting in little motivation. In addition, a limitation noted earlier in our discussion on profit sharing is that employees may come to view the group-level incentive as a normal part of their compensation and consequently be unhappy or dissatisfied if that reward is withheld one year.

Stock-based programs have special problems, since the employees incentives are tied to the price of the stock. An employee, especially an executive, may therefore make decisions or take actions that might result in a short-term increase in the stock price, while causing long-term problems for firm performance. Also, stock programs are effective only so long as the price of the stock is rising—or at least not falling. In the example given earlier, if the employee has the option to buy the stock at $5.00 per share, and price of the stock goes down to $4.00 a share, there is no incentive value and no reason for the employee to exercise the option. In such cases, the stock options are said to be "below water."

Finally, a recent scandal illustrates how organizations can manipulate stock options.[27] A high-tech company, Brocade Systems, Inc., granted employees stock options when they joined the company in 1999. This was a start-up company, and the initial offering price was $2.37, which was also the option price for employees at that time. The stock quickly rose (to over $133 a share), making those options quite valuable. But then the high-tech bubble burst in 2002, and the share price plummeted. Employees who joined the firm later were also offered options, but at the selling price in effect when they were hired. As the stock price continued to drop, these later options became eventually worthless (i.e., under water). The management at Brocade then asked employees to change their employment date to make it later than it actually was—at a time when the stock's price was low—so that the employees would qualify for option prices that were low enough for the options to still have some value. The article reporting the scandal noted that similar (but less egregious) practices were carried out by many high-tech firms, but a follow-up piece indicated that the former CEO and several others who were involved were being charged with both civil and criminal securities fraud.[28]

Performance Management and Feedback

There are also a series of programs and interventions that are referred to as *performance management techniques,* which are somewhat more specific than the programs we have been discussing thus far. We will discuss two of these that were introduced in the previous chapter—behavior modification and goal setting—and we will also discuss some issues associated with feedback, which is a key component of many of these performance management interventions.

Performance Management Techniques

Recall our discussion of reinforcement theory in Chapter 13. The basic notion underlying this theory is that all behavior is a function of its consequences—whether actual or anticipated—and so we can shape behavior by arranging for the "right" set of consequences. We also noted that positive reinforcement was designed to reward desirable behaviors that we wanted to see repeated, while punishment and extinction were techniques to discourage behaviors that were less desirable. *Behavior modification,* as discussed in the preceding chapter, is the systematic and simultaneous application of positive reinforcement and either punishment or extinction (or both). The basic notion is that it is not enough to eliminate undesirable behaviors unless we can also provide the person with a new set of desirable behaviors.

For example, perhaps an organization is concerned that employees are spending too much time standing around a coffee vending machine. Productivity is suffering because employees are talking and socializing rather than working. The company could begin by taking out the coffee machine (removing an incentive for congregating), and might even install a loud piece of equipment in the space to make it uncomfortable for employees to remain there for long. But, at the same time, the firm could provide free coffee, delivered to workstations on a cart, but only to people actually working. The idea here would be to discourage congregating and socializing *and* to encourage people remaining at their workstations.

One key to any successful behavior modification plan is to make sure that the employee can see strong links between his or her behavior and the consequences that can follow. The other, more critical component, however, is to make absolutely sure that desirable behaviors are never punished and that undesirable behaviors are never rewarded. Too often, supervisors reward the wrong behaviors and punish the behaviors they should be rewarding. One of the authors of this text recently had to put together a faculty committee for a task that no one really wanted to carry out. When he suggested a certain faculty member, he was told that it was unwise to assign that faculty member to any committees because the person didn't usually show up for meetings. Instead, it was suggested, he should assign a different faculty member who always showed up for meetings. This apparently had been a long-standing practice and yet no one could understand why it was so difficult to get the first faculty member to perform any service activities. The author, of course, assigned the first faculty member to the committee and actually released the second faculty member from one or two committee assignments.

We also discussed *goal theory* in the previous chapter and indicated that this theory was very useful for managing performance as well as simply motivating it. Recall that goal theory suggests that employees will exert the greatest effort when they have specific, difficult goals to work toward. Thus, from a performance management perspective, managers should provide employees with difficult, specific goals, and then reward them when those goals are achieved. The earlier discussion also included consideration of some issues in choosing the "right" goal, but, for the present discussion, it is extremely important that all parties can agree on what is the "right" goal.

Quite often, when employees (and managers) are asked to think about goals, they tend to focus on things that can be readily counted. That is not necessarily bad, since such goals are often concrete and specific, but they can simply be wrong. We can think about a police officer who is told by her supervisor that she should set goals for her job and so she decides to set a goal of ten arrests per week. This goal is concrete, specific, and presumably difficult, but what purpose would be served if the officer spent her time trying to arrest as many people as she could? Would that reduce crime or increase public perceptions of safety? Probably not, unless she was arresting truly dangerous criminals. But it would be easier to arrest people for petty crimes, or even to arrest people who could never be convicted. Thus, the officer could meet her goal every week and still perform her job poorly in a more objective sense. Note that we wouldn't want the goal to be a reduction of crimes either, or the officer would have no incentive to accurately report (or even respond to) all the crimes committed.

In the case of police officers, perhaps goals should be stated in terms of public perceptions, but there are many other examples of goal setting that reflect this problem. Think about a customer service representative whose goal might be to respond to fifty customers a day (and therefore has no incentive to really deal with any of their problems), or a repair person whose goal is to respond to fifty calls a day, or even a teacher whose goal is to have the highest percentage of students passing a course (and therefore has no incentive to fail anyone regardless of how little they have learned). The key here is that any goal chosen as part of a performance management system must be aligned with the higher-level, strategic goals of the organization. Ideally, one can think about these goals as "cascading down" so that at each level in the organization the performance goals that are set will influence the goals at the next lower level. In terms of goal accomplishment, we can think about the goals cascading upward so that goals met at one level help the next level to meet its goals and so on up to the strategic level.

Performance feedback plays an important role in both behavior modification and goal setting, and it is also seen as a useful tool in its own right for performance management. But many managers do a poor job in this area, in part because they don't understand how to provide feedback properly and in part because they don't enjoy it. Almost by definition, performance appraisal in many organizations tends to focus on negatives, and, as a result, managers may have a tendency to avoid giving feedback because they know an employee who hears negative feedback may be angry, hurt, discouraged, or argumentative. But clearly, if employees are not told about their shortcomings, they have no reason to try to improve and have no guidance concerning how to improve. Therefore, it is critical that a rater provide feedback, and so it is important to understand how he or she might do it better.

One method of improving performance feedback is to provide feedback on a regular basis via feedback interviews. Instead of providing feedback annually, in tandem with the annual performance appraisal interview, it might be more appropriate for managers to provide feedback on an ongoing basis. Feedback might be provided on a daily or weekly basis, depending on the nature of the job, and should focus on various

The performance review is the place for a manager to provide feedback for the employee, but it is also the place for the employee to promote his or her accomplishments during the evaluation period. As Dana Hall, a managing director of hedge fund Lighthouse Partners, discovered, women such as herself often have difficulty communicating clearly their own accomplishments and overall value to a company. Since realizing this difficulty was holding her back in her career, she worked to improve it. Now she helps other women executives manage their careers better by teaching them how to be more effective self-promoters.

characteristics of performance, including both effective and ineffective performance.[29] In fact, if managers remember that the goal of performance management is changing employee behavior, they should also recognize the fact that they clearly are more likely to effect change with more frequent feedback, and this approach is consistent with both behavior modification and goal setting.

Another useful method for improving performance feedback is to have the individual appraise his or her own performance in advance of an appraisal interview. This method involves having employees think about their own performance over the rating period and helps sensitize them to areas where they have done both a good and an ineffective job. This method also lends efficiency to the process because the manager and the subordinate may be able to focus most of their time and effort in a performance appraisal interview on those areas of performance assessment where they disagree. That is, if the manager and the subordinate both agree that certain elements of the subordinate's performance are very good and that certain other elements need improvement, it may be possible to spend little time discussing those elements and to focus more energy on the performance areas that are in disagreement.

It is also important during a performance feedback interview to encourage participation and two-way communication. Some managers are prone to lecture a subordinate on the outcome of the performance appraisal interview. The basic nature of the meeting, then, involves the manager telling the subordinate how he or she has been evaluated and then concluding the interview. As a result, the subordinate may feel threatened and that she or he had no voice in the process. Participation and two-way dialogue, however, allows the individual to express her or his own feelings and opinions about job performance and to provide other kinds of feedback as appropriate.[30]

It is also important for the manager to try to balance positive and negative feedback. As already noted, many managers tend to focus on the negative. In reality, however, employees are likely to have many positive characteristics related to performance as well. Thus, while the manager must clearly address the negative performance characteristics noted in the appraisal, these negative attributes should be balanced against praise and recognition of the positive aspects of the employee's performance.

Also, throughout the interview and the performance management process, it is essential that the manager take a developmental and problem-solving orientation to the process. That is, it is important not to focus on the individual as a person by saying things like, "You are a bad employee." Instead, the focus should be on providing developmental feedback targeted at behavior, not on the individual him- or herself. A simple distinction between saying things like, "You are a poor performer" versus "Your performance is not acceptable" can help keep the focus on behavior and not on the individual.

The performance appraisal interview should conclude with a future-oriented discussion of what will happen next. This discussion often includes topics such as setting goals for correcting performance deficiencies and discussing the possibility of pay raises, promotion prospects, and similar kinds of awards. Of course, if performance is judged to be deficient, the feedback interview may focus on topics such as the establishment of a probationary period (after which employment may be terminated), the development of a training strategy for improving performance, and so forth. Regardless of the level of present performance, this interview setting should provide a time when the rater and the employee discuss future performance goals for the employee. If the organization uses a goal-based appraisal system, this discussion may be automatic. Even if a different type of appraisal model is used, it is helpful for the employee to have clear and specific goals for improving future performance. These goals, along with continued and regular feedback, should constitute the critical part of any performance management program.

Even with these recommendations, however, feedback is not always as effective as we would like to believe. Many of today's recommendations and practices are based on the assumption that, if done properly, they will provide employees with feedback about their job performance. Several years ago, however, a study reviewed the research on the effectiveness of feedback interventions, beginning with early studies from the nineteenth century.[31] This study found that, although feedback was effective in almost two-thirds of the cases, feedback was not effective in the rest. In fact, in a large number of cases, providing feedback to employees actually lowered subsequent performance. This result was independent of the nature of the feedback (i.e., whether the feedback was positive or negative), which suggests that any feedback can, under certain conditions, have a negative effect on subsequent performance.

The study found that feedback was more likely to have a negative effect when the employee was new to a job, the job was extremely complex, ways to improve performance were not discussed, or goals for the future were not considered. The study also reported that feedback must focus the employee's attention on the task at hand. When feedback is provided so that the employee can take it personally, the feedback is much more likely to interfere with rather than enhance subsequent performance. Thus, the recommendations above will help ensure that feedback has the desired effect.

ProMES

Some of the techniques and interventions we have described are best suited for enhancing individual performance (which hopefully will result in ultimate improvements in firm performance), while others could be used with groups as well. Furthermore, we have been discussing these techniques relative to how they can improve some type of performance, but it is also possible to establish systems that can reduce turnover or absenteeism. These outcomes might well be related to firm performance as well, but it is critical that such a link be established. In fact, if any performance enhancement technique is doing what it was designed to do, the organization as a whole should perform better. One such technique allows for the consideration of a wide range of outcomes and is concerned directly with team or organizational performance.

Productivity Measurement and Evaluation System (ProMES) *is a program developed to improve group- or firm-level productivity. This approach incorporates ideas from goal setting, with incentives for improvement, and is based on a model of motivation similar to expectancy theory.*

The **Productivity Measurement and Evaluation System (ProMES)** incorporates ideas from goal setting to feedback, and it includes incentives for improvement.[32] More important, it includes a method for tying performance at the individual and group level to organizational productivity. Specifically, team members work with outside experts to literally map the relationship between a given outcome and productivity. For example, let's assume that a group is focusing on reducing turnover. In most cases reducing turnover will lower costs and boost productivity (as discussed in Chapter 6). But also in most cases the incremental value of reducing turnover will be greatest when turnover is high; similarly, when turnover is low further reductions will likely have a smaller impact. This pattern of diminishing returns is shown in the sample ProMES curve illustrated in Figure 14.4.

The curve shows that in this hypothetical example the group has a current annual turnover rate of 20 percent and that there is a known baseline level of units currently being produced (it doesn't matter what this baseline is, only that it is known). The team has also calculated that if turnover can be reduced from 20 percent to 15 percent the number of units produced will increase by 20 percent. An additional reduction in turnover from 15 percent to 10 percent will achieve another 10 percent increase in units produced (a 30 percent increase in total). But yet another 5 percent turnover reduction from 10 percent to 5 percent increases the number of units produced by only an additional 3 percent (33 percent total). Further reductions in turnover from 5 percent to 3 percent and 1 percent yields a unit increase of only 1 percent each.

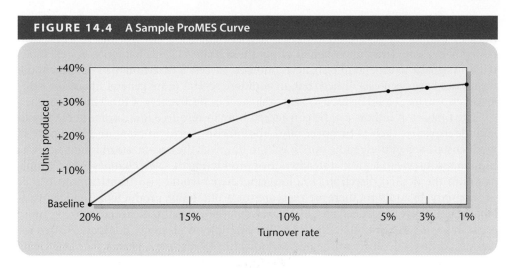

FIGURE 14.4   A Sample ProMES Curve

Now, understand that reducing turnover is likely to have costs associated with it, such as paying higher wages, paying bonuses for longevity, and so forth. The initial costs of reducing turnover from 20 percent to 15 percent will almost certainly be outweighed by the increased unit production of 20 percent. The additional costs for reducing turnover from 15 percent to 10 percent for an additional 10 percent increase in production may or may not be a cost-effective decision. But almost certainly the cost for reducing turnover from, say, 5 percent to 1 percent for only a 2 percent increase in unit production will end up costing more money than is gained. Of course, the point along the diminishing returns curve where costs begin to outweigh benefits must be calculated for each individual work setting.

The other important part of the ProMES process involves the various "connections" among the components. The procedure is based on a model of motivation[33] that is similar to the expectancy model discussed in the previous chapter. Thus, these connections are concerned with the relationship between effort and performance and between performance and attaining outcomes, as well as the link between obtaining outcomes and satisfying needs. The model and the technique are also based on the assumption that individuals and groups have a pool of resources (and effort) that they can assign to different activities, and the technique is designed to help them understand which activities they should focus upon to increase firm productivity. The system has been widely adopted (especially in Europe)[34] and has been quite successful, and it is one of the few performance enhancement techniques that focuses on performance above the level of the individual.

Evaluating Performance Enhancement Programs

Any discussion of how a firm evaluates the effectiveness of these performance enhancement techniques must really become a discussion of how one measures firm performance. When we think about individual performance we can think about units produced, or total sales, or some index of waste, but measuring organizational-level performance is much more difficult. First, any true measure of organizational success must tie back to the organization's strategic goals. Thus, the simplest way to assess firm performance is to determine whether or not those strategic goals were met. For example, if a firm's goal is to expand into six new countries, success is determined by whether those businesses have been established. But, in addition, several more general indices of firm-level performance could be used to help evaluate the effectiveness of these interventions.

The first set of indices can be considered human resource indicators. These would include measures such as turnover rates, absenteeism, accident rates, and even general labor costs. Each of these indicators speaks to how well the organization is managing its human resources, and, given a steady rate of production or sales, changes in these indicators in the desired direction (i.e., lowering them) would also translate into higher profitability. In addition, there are measures of profitability, productivity, and controllable costs. These measures are, in fact, related, with specific measures making more sense in some businesses than in others. For example, food service companies often focus on controllable costs as the major indicator of success, whereas manufacturing firms often focus on some measure of productivity that includes output as well as the cost of production.

Finally, organizations also use a set of financial and accounting indicators. One of these is the stock price, which presumably reflects the market's view of a firm's success, although there are surely other factors that could affect stock price as well. Market share is another similar indicator of success, with the assumption that market share translates into market power and so has some ability to influence prices or costs. Indices such as "return on investment" or "return on assets" are more explicit financial indicators that speak to the rate of return on either corporate investment.

There is no clear rationale for why one of these indices should be favored over the others, and each provides useful information for a firm trying to measure its success. Therefore, when an organization is interested in gauging the effectiveness of a performance enhancement technique, it makes sense to examine multiple indicators. One could even think of these as forming a type of hierarchy: if the intervention is working, individual performance should increase, one or more corporate human resource measures should improve, and these should translate into higher rates of return and higher stock prices. An important caveat, however, is to note that many of these indicators can be affected by a wide variety of factors, so that changes in any one index may not be a good measure of how effective the intervention has really been.

Chapter Summary

Performance in any organization exists at multiple levels. The most basic level of performance is at the level of the individual employee, and this is the level that most people find easiest to conceptualize. However, performance enhancement techniques are ultimately aimed at improving firm-level performance.

Training and development activities within an organization are a very basic type of performance enhancement intervention. Employee training is a planned attempt by an organization to facilitate employee learning of job-related knowledge, skills, and behaviors. Development refers to teaching managers and professionals the skills needed for both present and future jobs.

A much different approach to enhancing organizational performance is through the redesign of jobs. Specifically, this technique involves changing—redesigning—jobs so that the work itself will motivate employees to exert greater effort. This motivation is stimulated by making the job more interesting and/or challenging. There are five motivational approaches to the redesign of work:

job rotation, job enlargement, job enrichment, the job characteristics approach, and work teams.

Another approach to performance enhancement comes with allowing employees more flexibility in their working arrangements. The two most common alternatives to the traditional workweek are programs known as flexible work hours and compressed workweeks. Employees working under flexible work hour plans usually must still work a full forty hours per week and, typically, they must work five days a week. Compressed workweeks are arrangements in which the employee works the required number of hours (typically forty) but does so in less than five days. Allowing employees to perform their work at a location other than the place of business, most likely at home, is a growing trend.

Yet another approach to enhancing performance is by explicitly tying rewards, especially pay, to perform-

ance. There are many plans to allow this to be done. These include merit pay, skill- and knowledge-based pay, individual incentive plans, and group or team incentive plans. The latter include gainsharing and the Scanlon plan. Organizationwide methods include profit sharing, stock-option plans, stock purchase plans, and employee stock ownership plans (ESOPs).

There are also a series of programs and interventions that are referred to as performance management techniques. These include behavior modification and goal setting. Performance feedback plays an important role in both behavior modification and goal setting and is also seen as useful tool, in its own right, for performance management. The Productivity Measurement and Evaluation System (ProMES) incorporates ideas from goal setting to feedback, and it includes incentives for improvement.

Key Points for Future HR Managers

- Performance can occur at different levels within the organization, and it is important to identify the level at which performance improvements are desired.

- It is important to identify the best training and development technique for enhancing performance in any situation.

- Jobs can be redesigned to make them more motivating, but this must be more than simply adding tasks.

- Establishing alternative work schedules can enhance performance on some jobs.

- Allowing employees to work from a site other than an office or factory can enhance performance.

- Incentives can enhance performance, but they must be tied to the right behaviors and must target performance at the right level.

- There are various techniques for performance management but even techniques such as providing feedback don't always produce the desired effects.

- Interventions such as ProMES can enhance performance as well.

- All performance enhancement interventions must be evaluated to determine if they improve performance at the desired level within the organization.

Key Points for Future General Managers

- Improving individual-level performance does not automatically result in improved corporate-level performance.

- Different performance enhancement techniques such as training and development can be effective for some jobs but not others.

- Redesigning jobs along certain lines can improve motivation without increasing pay.

- There are pros and cons associated with both individual- and group-level incentives.

- Feedback is not always effective.

- Some organizational-level interventions have been shown to be effective in improving performance.

- Any performance enhancement technique must be evaluated as to its effectiveness.

Review and Discussion Questions

1. Distinguish between training and development.

2. What are the basic steps in employee training?

3. Identify and summarize the five basic approaches to job redesign.

4. Among the various alternative work scheduling options, which would you prefer to follow?

5. How strong is your interest in having an alternate work site, such as working from home? Why?

6. Identify the most common forms of individual incentive pay plans.

7. Identify the most common forms of team and group incentive plans.

8. Many managers do a poor job of providing performance feedback to their employees. Why do you think this is true?

9. Summarize ProMES.

10. Describe as precisely as you can the kind of performance enhancement system that would be most likely to motivate you.

CLOSING CASE

Enhancing Performance at HP

Imagine an organization that must attract and retain a skilled workforce to stay at the forefront of technological innovation. Imagine further that highly qualified workers are scarce, expensive, and switch employers readily. What can this organization do to motivate its employees?

Hewlett Packard (HP), a provider of computer products and services, knows. "Being known as a great place to work makes it easier to attract top talent," reads HP's website. "For us, being a great place to work is good business." The challenge is great. HP employs more than 140,000 workers worldwide in every function. Alternative work arrangements are one effective way to motivate such a diverse group of employees.

HP provides a "flexible, supportive environment to manage work and personal life demands, including flexible time, telecommuting, and job-sharing," according to its website. Vice president of diversity and work/life Sid Reed acknowledges that motivation can result from alternative work arrangements. "We very definitely see that employees feel empowered when they are able to work in a schedule and a location that suits their needs. They have some flexibility to really integrate in a positive way their personal life and their work life," Reed asserts.

One motivated employee is Kristy Ward, a marketing manager. With more than two decades at HP, she has experienced several types of alternative work arrangements and is currently job sharing. "Much of what I've been able to do seems uncommon in the rest of the industry," Ward relates. "I talk to my friends that work at other companies. They don't have the same alternatives. . . . That has really added to my loyalty to the company."

Ward explains that HP determines each individual's optimal work environment based on the employee's and the company's needs: "Some have the two-minute commute,

downstairs in the house. Others still drive to be able to be in a work environment with other employees. There's a lot of personal preference." HP engineer Cheryl Marks says, "One of the reasons I stay with HP is because they allow me to telework. I get burned out if I can't be as productive as I want to be." Nikki Cheatham telecommutes and estimates it takes her roughly half as much time to absorb complex information at home than in her office cubicle. For just $3,500, HP set up a telework arrangement for a systems engineer with a physical handicap to work at home. The company helped this valuable worker keep his job and saved the cost of finding a replacement.

Among the significant benefits to employees are shorter or nonexistent commuting times, the ability to control their level of interaction with others, and support for family or personal needs. Yet the benefits to the organization are just as great or greater. In addition to support for recruiting and retention, alternative work arrangements can help to increase diversity by encouraging employees with various needs. Reed says, "It's a part of the overall inclusion and diversity strategy. . . . We support employees so that they can contribute to their full potential." Other advantages are the lowered costs for office and parking space, the ability to hire the best talent regardless of location, the ease in forming virtual teams, and the capacity to better manage emergencies such as storms or power failures.

Yet surely the greatest benefit to the organization is the increased motivation experienced by workers when they feel supported by their employer. *ComputerWorld* magazine recently surveyed 17,000 high-tech professionals and found that access to leading technology, training, and flexible workplaces were the top three issues of concern. HP employees show that flexibility is becoming more popular at the firm—telecommuting has grown from 10 percent in 1999 to virtually 100 percent today. Many are also trying other alternatives such as job sharing and part-time work.

Tom Johnson, an HP human resources manager, says, "We have enough hard data and anecdotal evidence to suggest telework can increase productivity, [but] most important is fit." Another human resource manager, Darryl Roberts, characterizes telework as an "employee-driven business decision," a win-win agreement between HP and employees. Ward would certainly agree, as she states with evident satisfaction, "The nice thing about HP is you can do what suits your work style."[35]

Case Questions

1. What types of employees are likely to be motivated by alternative work arrangements? Why?

2. Consider HP's use of flextime, job sharing, and telecommuting. What are some of the potential drawbacks or limitations of these approaches? What can HP do to prepare for, reduce, or eliminate these negative outcomes?

3. In your "job" as a student, do you think you would be more or less effective if you had the opportunity to telecommute (or do more telecommuting, if you already use distance learning)? Explain your answer.

Building HR Management Skills

Purpose: This exercise will help you develop a better understanding of the underlying issues in job redesign.

Step 1: Begin by thinking of three different jobs, one that appears to have virtually no enrichment, one that seems to have moderate enrichment, and one that appears to have a great deal of enrichment. These jobs might be ones that you have personally held or ones that you have observed and about which you can make some educated or informed judgments.

Step 2: Evaluate each job along the five dimensions described in the job characteristics theory.

Step 3: Next, see if you can identify ways to improve each of the five dimensions for each job. That is, see if you can determine how to enrich the jobs by using the job characteristics theory as a framework.

Step 4: Finally, meet with a classmate and share results. See if you can improve your job enrichment strategy based on the critique offered by your classmate.

Step 5: Using the background information about the three jobs you examined as context, answer the following questions.

1. What job qualities make some jobs easier to enrich than others?

2. Can all jobs be enriched?

3. Even if a particular job can be enriched, does that always mean that it should be enriched?

4. Under what circumstances might an individual prefer to have a routine and unenriched job?

Ethical Dilemmas in HR Management

Assume you are a manager for a manufacturing company. For years your low-wage workers have complained because their jobs are boring. At the same time, you also know that the highly specialized nature of each job maximizes efficiency and allows you to pay relatively low wages (because it's easy to replace anyone who leaves).

You recently interviewed for a job with another company. Even though you decided not to take the position,

you did have a chance to tour and study that firm's production facilities. You learned that your firm could actually change the jobs in your factory in ways that would make them more stimulating and enjoyable for your workers. But you also know that you would lose a relatively small degree of efficiency. In addition, because the jobs would be a bit more challenging, you might have to pay higher wages.

You have two choices. One is to keep the jobs in your

plant as they are currently designed (maximizing efficiency and minimizing wage costs) but keep a bored and disinterested workforce. The other is to redesign the jobs in the plant (losing some efficiency and perhaps increasing labor costs), but your workers would find their jobs more enjoyable and challenging.

Questions

1. What are the ethical issues in this situation?

2. What are the basic arguments for each course of action?

3. What do you think most managers would do? What would you do?

HR Internet Exercise

 There are many different methods and approaches for creating alternative work arrangements. Identify five companies that are of particular interest to you. These might be firms that you would be interested in working for, or firms with a large facility in your town.

Begin this exercise by visiting the home pages of each firm. Learn as much as you can about each firm's alternative work arrangements programs. In addition to their home pages, conduct some searches using such key words as "[firm name], flexible work, telecommuting," and so forth.

Questions

1. How easy or difficult is it to learn about a firm's work arrangements online?

2. Based on what you could learn, which firm seems to have the best program? The poorest?

3. Did you learn of any other alternative arrangements beyond those discussed in this chapter?

PSYCHOLOGICAL CONTRACTS AND WORK; HUMAN RESOURCE MANAGEMENT AND EXECUTIVES

This section focuses on two important issues that also relate to performance in organizations. We first discuss psychological contracts and work, and then we examine human resource management and executives.

Psychological Contracts and Work

No one argues that the fundamental relationship between employers and employees has not changed dramatically over the last several years. Likewise, the expectations that both sides have concerning the relationship are now different. In many firms, employees no longer trust their employer to treat them fairly and equitably. And employers often believe their employees act too much in their own self-interests. As a result, the very nature of the employment relationship continues to evolve in various ways.

Many Americans grew up with clear expectations concerning the relationship they would have with the organization where they worked. Traditional models of this relationship suggested that an employee could expect to have a job as long as he or she worked hard and followed the rules. Employees understood that they were expected to exhibit loyalty and commitment to the organization. These contributions from the employee, along with inducements from the organization, formed the basis of the relationship between the employee and the organization. But, as mentioned, today the nature of this relationship has been changing and continues to change.

When we consider the relationship between the organization and the employee, we can talk about the basic legal employment contract, the psychological contract between employee and employer, or the social contract that involves both these parties plus the government. But in each case, the nature of these contracts is not what many people today grew up to expect. As a result, a much wider variety of relationships between organization and employee are possible in today's workplace, and the nature of these varied relationships poses a new set of challenges for the human resource manager. We take up some of these issues in this discussion.

Employee Rights in the Workplace   To appreciate the new reality concerning the relationship between employer and employee, it is useful to briefly discuss some notions of employee rights, since this is often the starting point for the employee. In the United States, the foundation for our general ideas about individual rights lies in our Constitution, and this is generally true in any country. But, in addition, in different countries there are statements about employee rights at work, and these are often different from the statement of individual rights in a constitution.

For example, the foundation of workplace rights in the United States is the **employment-at-will doctrine,** which was discussed earlier in the book (Chapter 6). The concept of employment-at-will suggests that people work at the sole discretion of their employer and thus can be terminated at any time for any reason. This viewpoint, however, represents one extreme perspective on employee rights in the workplace. Essentially, the employment-at-will doctrine suggests that individuals have relatively few rights.

In fact, however, many of the laws and regulations governing human resource management that have been described earlier, most notably in Chapter 2, have been created to help define, maintain, and preserve various employee rights. For example, discrimination

The **employment-at-will doctrine** *is a nineteenth century common law rule that allows an employer to terminate an employee, at any time, for any reason (good or bad) or for no reason at all. This rule still guides most terminations in the United States, although there are exceptions to this doctrine.*

law essentially gives people the right to work without being evaluated on the basis of non-job-relevant factors such as gender or race. Similarly, minimum-wage legislation gives people the right to expect a certain base level of compensation for their work. And labor law gives employees the right to organize and join a labor union under certain prescribed circumstances. As we discussed in Chapter 3, there are other sets of employment laws in other countries that define the relationship between employer and employee in even more detail.

But, in general, an employee's rights in any organizational setting are determined in part by the law and in part by the nature of the contract between the employee and the employer. In unionized settings, these contracts are quite formal and clear about the nature of the relationships. Formal, well-articulated contracts are common in other settings (e.g., professional sports). But in most employment settings, the rules governing the relationship are not so clear, nor are they as well specified. Nonetheless, we can discuss the notion of a psychological contract that governs all relationships at work.

The Nature of Psychological Contracts

A **psychological contract,** which is illustrated in Figure IV.1, can be defined as the set of expectations held by an employee concerning what he or she will contribute to the organization (referred to as contributions) and what the organization, in return, will provide to the employee (referred to as inducements). Thus, psychological contracts define the most basic relationship that employees expect to have with an organization. Note the use of the term "expect." This is important because psychological contracts shape the expectations of both parties concerning what they will get and give in the employment relationship.

These contracts are typically not written, so they are not formal contracts in any legal sense and are not enforceable in court. Nonetheless, an organization that believes an employee has violated his or her commitment and reduced contributions below an acceptable level often disciplines or terminates that employee. On the other hand, an employee who feels the organization has violated its commitment to provide inducements either reduces contributions to the company or leaves. Note that the employee's contributions include intangibles such as loyalty, and so a reduction in contributions might

A **psychological contract** *is the set of expectations held by an employee concerning what he or she will contribute to the organization, and what the organization will provide to the employee in return.*

FIGURE IV.1   The Psychological Contract

Contributions from the individual	Inducements from the organization
• Effort • Ability • Loyalty • Skills • Time • Competencies	• Pay • Job security • Benefits • Career opportunities • Status • Advancement opportunities

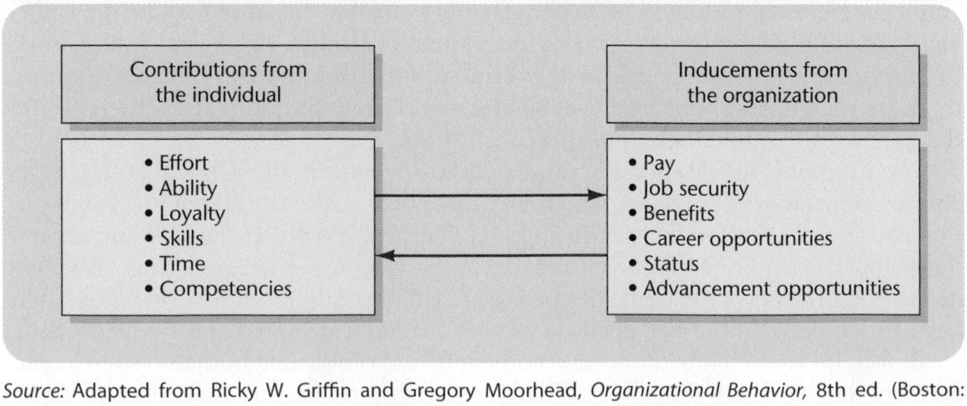

Source: Adapted from Ricky W. Griffin and Gregory Moorhead, *Organizational Behavior,* 8th ed. (Boston: Houghton Mifflin, 2007, p. 59. Copyright © Houghton Mifflin Company. Reprinted with permission.

not be simply a reduction in effort or output but a basic change in attitude toward the organization.

Not all psychological contracts are the same, of course. Some experts have characterized these contracts as falling on a continuum from *transactional* to *relational*.[1] Contracts that are more transactional in nature typically involve a shorter time horizon, contain specific obligations, and stress financial inducements or inducements that can be converted into money (e.g., salary, benefits). Contracts that are more relational in nature involve longer and indeterminate time horizons and nonspecific and wide-ranging obligations, and stress nonfinancial (e.g., socioemotional) inducements as well as financial inducements. These latter contracts are much more fluid and so are more likely to change over time.

Traditionally, one of the inducements offered by an organization was employment security. The basic understanding was that, if an employee continued to contribute to the organization, he or she could expect to remain employed. Although some have argued (probably correctly) that this kind of employment security was never really an inducement offered by U.S. corporations, the fact that many employees perceived it to be the case is enough for it to become part of their view of the contract.[2]

But, as noted in earlier chapters, this inducement has not been available to employees over the last few years because downsizing and layoffs have become common. In many cases, organizations have tried to substitute training and development opportunities for job security. In other words, the organization was admitting that hard work no longer guaranteed a job, but if the organization was considering laying off a worker who was productive, they would at least provide that employee with some skills and competencies that would make him or her more employable elsewhere. Thus, even if the nature of the contract had not changed, the terms of the psychological contract often had.

But for many employees this shift represented a violation of the contract. As a result, employees felt they could reduce their contributions and their obligations to the organization.[3] As long as unemployment was rising, the employee could not afford to reduce effort on the job or to reduce output for fear of being fired. Instead, the employee reduced contributions in the areas of loyalty and commitment. To some extent this change made the terms of the contract less specific (and more transactional in nature), but again, the real change was in the terms of the psychological contract.

At the end of the 1990s, however, unemployment in the United States was at an all-time low. Employees no longer needed to fear losing their jobs because other jobs were available. Therefore, it was possible to reduce effort and output on the job, but this possibility was not the worst of it for organizations. As unemployment shrunk, organizations found they again had to compete for employees. The reduced rate of population growth also began to play a role in reducing the supply of workers in the economy. (We will discuss special problems with certain types of employees below.) Instead of work-force reductions, organizations began to think about ways of retaining employees, and retention bonuses and sign-on bonuses became more popular. But the beginning of the twenty-first century has brought a return to cutbacks and rising unemployment. As a result, employees are much more concerned with the rights they have.

As we noted above, the terms of the psychological contract have already changed. As a result, employees feel less loyalty and attachment to an organization and so are quite willing to be lured away by competing offers. The changing terms of the psychological contract may now become a bigger problem for the organization than it was for the employees who had felt violated when they lost their jobs, regardless of the levels of their contributions. These changes in the psychological contract will clearly be one of the major challenges facing organizations in the new millennium. This challenge will be even more difficult to meet as organizations come to realize that they can no longer offer lifetime employment as an inducement after employees have experienced how empty the inducement was a few years earlier.

Contract Violation The greatest concerns over psychological contracts come when the contract is violated—by either party. Needless to say, there is often disagreement about whether the contract was really violated, but all parties agree that these contracts often are violated by one party or the other. These perceived violations can lead to employers giving lower performance ratings to employees and to employees feeling less satisfied and committed to the employer.[4] Thus, it is important for both parties to view the psychological contract in similar terms and to perceive the same set of inducements and obligations.

Unfortunately, there is often a misalignment in the ways in which the two parties view the psychological contract. Research findings suggest that, although employers and employees often agree on the general terms of the contract and the nature of the work relationship, employers often focus on intangibles in terms of their obligations, while employees often focus on tangible outcomes such as fair pay in terms of their expectations. Furthermore, the research evidence suggests that each party believes it has done a better job in carrying out its end of the deal than does the other party. Thus, each party is more likely to believe that the other party is falling short in terms of its obligations to the agreement.[5]

Given the important consequences of contract violation, it is critical that we learn more about the way parties enter into and perceive psychological contracts. Unfortunately, given the fact that these contracts are often unwritten and exist primarily in the minds of the parties, it is unlikely that we will ever be able to eliminate the incidents of perceived violation of contracts. This is especially troubling when we realize the extent to which employment relationships depend upon these contracts. Beginning with the basic employment agreement, and moving through issues of reward systems, safety and health on the job, and overseas assignments, much of the exchange between employees and employers is in the form of an unwritten psychological contract.

*A **social contract** is a set of expectations concerning contributions and inducements between the employee, the employer, and the government.*

The Nature of Social Contracts A **social contract** simply refers to expanding the relationship between employer and employee to include a third party—the government. This view recognizes that public policies such as minimum-wage levels, taxes, union-management relations, and health-care provisions are an important part of the relationship between employer and employee. For example, we discussed in Chapter 9 how many of the benefits given by organizations are mandated by law. These mandated benefits are an important part of a total benefits package. (And, in fact, we noted that mandated benefits in the United States are relatively low compared to benefits in most European countries.) Therefore, an employee should expect that, in exchange for his or her efforts and loyalty, the organization would provide, at a minimum, those benefits mandated by law.

But the terms of the social contract are changing. Some of the nontraditional work relationships discussed below have resulted in more employees not having even basic benefits usually mandated by law. Years of organizational downsizing have led to many workers not having any type of health insurance. (Even employees who have started their own businesses are less likely to be covered by health-insurance plans.) As a result, the government may need to do more to ensure a minimum safety net for all employees. President Clinton's attempt to provide minimum mandated health-care benefits early in his second term was a concrete manifestation of this growing concern. The Dunlop Commission report, released in 1995, noted that workplace productivity and a hardworking labor force are important assets for any nation and that the government should move to protect these assets, suggesting increased government involvement.[6]

Increased government involvement in providing benefits and guaranteeing worker rights will surely have implications for human resource managers. At the very least it will require increased paperwork and record keeping, but it will also likely involve newer restrictions on how employees can be treated at work. In fact, some have argued that the "new" social contract should have organizations no longer competing on the basis of costs but instead pursuing a high-productivity, high-wage strategy that allows a voice for all employees.[7] Such a strategy would surely change the nature of the human resource function in organizations.

Human Resource Management and Executives

Quite simply stated, many human resource management practices and techniques do not work well with top executives. Of course, it is extremely important to identify the "right" person for a top-level job and then to retain that person, but the methods for achieving those goals are often quite unique to the executive. For example, candidates for executive positions are identified almost exclusively through "headhunters" or executive search firms (see Chapter 7). Once candidates are identified, the selection process almost always involves a very in-depth individual assessment rather than the use of normal interviews or any type of test. Appraisal for executives is typically done on the basis of mutually agreed upon goals that usually relate to firm performance indicators such as profitability or stock price. But the area of human resource management that is most important for executives deals with their compensation. Therefore, we will concentrate primarily upon the issue of executive compensation, discussing techniques and methods, as well as some of the issues that arise in this area.

Standard Forms of Executive Compensation Most senior executives receive their compensation in two forms. One is a base salary. As with the base salary of any staff member or professional member of an organization, the base salary of an executive is a guaranteed amount of money that the individual will be paid. For example, in 2005, the Walt Disney Company paid its chairperson and chief executive officer (CEO), Robert Iger, $1,500,000 in base salary.[8]

Above and beyond this base salary, however, most executives receive one or more forms of incentive pay. The traditional method of incentive pay for executives is in the form of bonuses. Bonuses, in turn, are usually determined by the performance of the organization. Thus, at the end of the year, some portion of a corporation's profits may be diverted into a bonus pool. Senior executives then receive a bonus expressed as a percentage of this bonus pool. The CEO and president are obviously likely to receive a larger percentage bonus than a vice president. The exact distribution of the bonus pool is usually specified ahead of time in the individual's employment contract. Some organizations intentionally leave the distribution unspecified so that the board of directors has the flexibility to give larger rewards to those individuals deemed most deserving. Robert Iger of Disney received a bonus of $8,239,941 in 2005.

Special Forms of Executive Compensation Many executives receive other kinds of compensation beyond base salary and bonuses. One form of executive compensation that has received a lot of attention in recent years has been the stock option and all its variations. We discuss some of the issues associated with stock options in Chapter 14, but there is a great deal more detail that is relevant. A stock-option plan is established to give senior managers the option to buy the company stock in the future at a predetermined, fixed price. The basic idea underlying stock-option plans is that if the executives contribute to higher levels of organizational performance, then the company stock should increase. Then the executive can purchase the stock at the predetermined price that, theoretically, should be lower than its future market price. The difference then becomes profit for the individual. Disney's Robert Iger received various stock options potentially worth as much as $11,956,854.

Stock options continue to grow in popularity as a means of compensating top managers. Stock options are seen as a means of aligning the interests of the manager with those of the stockholders, and if they don't cost the organization much (other than some possible dilution of stock values), they will probably be even more popular in the future. In fact, a recent study by KPMG Peat Marwick indicates that for senior management whose salary exceeds $250,000, stock options represent the largest share of the salary mix (relative to salary and other incentives). When we consider all of top management (managers with an annual salary over $750,000), stock options comprise a full 60 percent of their total compensation. The KPMG Peat Marwick report also indicates that, even among exempt employees at the $35,000-a-year level, stock options represent 13 percent of total compensation.

Agency theory arguments are often cited as the rationale for stock-option plans. The owners of the firm (typically the stockholders) want to increase firm profitability, but the CEO does not necessarily have any incentive to work toward maximizing profits. By basing a considerable portion of the CEO's compensation on stock, however, the interests of the CEO are presumably aligned more closely with the interests of the owners, and everyone works toward the same goal. For instance, in 2005 Indra Nooyi, CEO of PepsiCo, received a base salary of $837,067—relatively low by CEO standards. However, she also received options valued at slightly over $30 million.[9]

Some critics have noted that CEO and firm interests are not really aligned, however, until the CEO or executive actually exercises the stock option. Up to that point, the executive might actually even have an incentive to lower stock prices in the short run, in the hope of being offered more options at the lower price of the stock.[10] Recent events have also raised additional serious questions about the use of stock options as incentives for executives. For example, a big part of the Enron scandal involved executives withholding critical financial information from the markets, cashing in their stock options (while Enron stock was trading at $80 a share), and then watching as the financial information was made public and the stock fell to less than $1 a share.

Of course, these actions were found to be illegal, but they raise questions in the public's mind about the role of stock options and about the way organizations treat stock options from an accounting perspective. Most organizations have *not* treated stock options as liabilities, even though that's exactly what they are when they are exercised. By not carrying stock options as liabilities, the managers can overstate the value of the company, which, of course, can help raise the stock price. Finally, when stock markets generally fell during the middle of 2002, many executives found that their options were worthless because the price of the stock fell below the option price. When stock options go "under water" in this way, they have no value to anyone.

In recent years, in part due to the problems just noted, alternative forms of stock-based rewards are being explored. General Electric, for instance, recently decided to ban stock options as part of the compensation package for its chairman and CEO (currently Jeffrey Immelt). Essentially, Mr. Immelt now has a substantial portion of his compensation expressed as "performance share units" and tied to a number of specific financial performance indicators. These performance indictors include both short-term and long-term components. If he and the company meet the targets, the performance share units are converted into regular stock. But if the targets are not met, then Mr. Immelt's compensation remains simply his base salary plus the possibility of a straight financial bonus. Microsoft has adopted a similar approach.[11]

Aside from stock-option plans, other kinds of executive compensation are used by some companies. Among the more popular are such perquisites as memberships in private clubs, access to company recreational facilities, and similar kinds of benefits. Some organizations occasionally make low- or no-interest loans available to senior executives. These loans are often given to new executives whom the company is hiring from other companies and serve as an incentive for the individual to leave his or her current job to join a new organization.

Criticisms of Executive Compensation   Executive compensation has recently come under fire for various reasons. One major reason is that the levels of executive compensation attained by some managers simply seem too high for the average shareholder to understand. It is not uncommon for a senior executive of a major corporation to earn a total income from his or her job in a given year well in excess of $1 million. Sometimes the income of chief executive officers can be substantially more. Coca-Cola's Douglas Daft earned a total of $55 million in 2001 from all sources combined. Thus, just as the typical person has difficulty comprehending the astronomical salaries paid to some movie stars and sports stars, so too would the average person be aghast at the astronomical salaries paid to some senior executives. Table IV.1 summarizes the compensation packages for the twenty highest-paid CEOs in the United States in 2001.

Executive compensation in the United States also seems far out of line with that paid to senior executives in other countries. For example, compensation for foreign CEOs has only recently crept into the seven-figure range, their annual bonuses are much smaller, and they seldom participate in lavish stock-option plans like those enjoyed by their U.S. counterparts. Looking at the total package clouds the compensation comparisons a bit. For example, Figure IV.2 shows the complete package of executive perquisites for seven countries. While U.S. executives clearly top the list, their counterparts tend to receive more vacation and sick time, plus a car or car allowance.

Compounding the problem created by perceptions of executive compensation is the fact that little or no relationship seems to exist between the performance of the organization and the compensation paid to its senior executives.[12] Certainly if an organization performs at an especially high level and its stock price is increasing consistently, then most observers would agree that the senior executives responsible for this growth should be entitled to attractive rewards.[13] However, it is more difficult to understand situations when executives are paid huge salaries and other forms of rewards when their companies are performing at only a marginal level, yet this fact is fairly common today. For example, Oracle's CEO Lawrence Ellison recently pocketed over $700 million from the sale of previously granted stock options, but during the same year the value of Oracle stock dropped by 57 percent.

Given the recent interest in stock options, it is perhaps not surprising that the government pays close attention to stock options; but, in fact, the federal government started passing legislation regulating the use of stock options as part of compensation in the 1920s and has continued doing so ever since. The government first regulated stock options as compensation in 1923. In that year, the U.S. Treasury ruled that when an employee exercised a stock option, it would be taxed as income. Specifically, the employee would be taxed on an amount equal to the value of the stock at the time the option was exercised, less the cost of the option. In 1939 the Internal Revenue Service (IRS) modified this view somewhat, stating that stock options would be treated as income only if the company *intended* the option to be compensation at the time it was issued. Stock options intended as gifts, on the other hand, would be treated as gifts (i.e., they would not be taxed). By 1945, however, the IRS dropped this distinction and taxed options as income regardless of the intent of the parties involved.

TABLE IV.1 The Twenty Highest Paid CEOs—2005

Rank	Company	Executive	Salary ($mil)	Bonus ($mil)	Other ($mil)	Stock Gain ($mil)	Total Comp ($mil)
1	Capital One Financial	Richard D Fairbank	0	0	0.15	249.27	249.42
2	Terry S Semel	Yahoo	0.60	0	0	229.95	230.55
3	Cendant	Henry R Silverman	3.30	12.32	6.70	117.64	139.64
4	KB Home	Bruce Karatz	1.09	5.0	11.07	118.37	135.53
5	Lehman Bros Holding	Richard S Fuld Jr	0.75	13.75	33.21	74.96	122.67
6	Occidental Petroleum	Ray R Irani	1.30	3.64	38.23	37.56	80.73
7	Oracle	Lawrence J Ellison	0.98	6.50	0.96	66.89	75.33
8	Symantec	John W Thompson	0.80	1.68	0.29	69.07	71.84
9	Caremark Rx	Edwin M Crawford	1.60	3.20	1.03	63.84	69.66
10	Countrywide Financial	Angelo R Mozilo	2.47	17.27	0.62	48.59	68.95
11	Cisco Systems	John T Chambers	0.35	1.30	0.01	61.33	62.99
12	Ryland Group	R Chad Dreier	1.00	16.50	15.72	23.25	56.47
13	Coach	Lew Frankfort	0.83	1.24	5.74	48.18	55.99
14	Hovnanian Enterprises	Ara K Hovnanian	1.02	10.93	7.54	28.35	47.83
15	Sunoco	John G Drosdick	1.10	2.64	16.43	26.02	49.15
16	Toll Brothers	Robert I Toll	1.30	27.32	0.42	12.27	41.31
17	Target	Robert J Ulrich	1.57	5.0	1.31	31.74	39.63
18	Dell	Kevin B Rollins	0.87	2.09	0.01	36.35	39.31
19	Marathon Oil	Clarence P Cazalot Jr	1.08	2.80	9.91	23.70	37.48
20	Yum Brands	David C Novak	1.17	3.06	0.99	32.21	37.42

Source: Forbes (http://www.forbes.com/lists/2006/12/TotComp_1.html)

In 1934 the Securities Exchange Act required "insiders" to reveal information about their stockholdings and also restricted profits that were based on privileged information. The Revenue Act of 1950 first recognized the nature of "restricted" options, which could be sold only after a certain period of time had elapsed. In deciding that profits from the sale of these restricted stocks would not be taxed as regular (current) income but as long-term capital gains (taxed according to a schedule across multiple years), Congress moved in favor of stock options as a form of managerial compensation. Nonetheless, over the next two decades Congress began to reverse its position, and by 1969 all stock options would be treated the same for tax purposes, and all profits would be taxed as income.

But as the government tightened legislation regulating stock options, the stock market itself stagnated. By 1970 long-term incentives (such as stock options) accounted for only about 15 percent of executive compensation. The market remained sluggish through 1980, and stock options lost their popularity. But when the stock market began to regain its vitality in 1981, stock options were once again an important part of

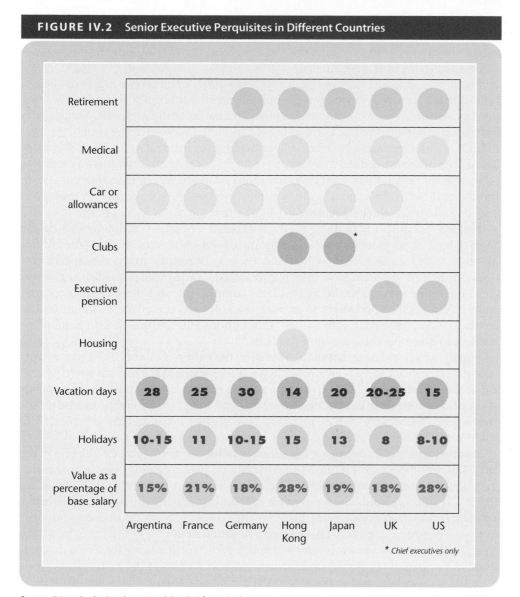

FIGURE IV.2 Senior Executive Perquisites in Different Countries

	Argentina	France	Germany	Hong Kong	Japan	UK	US
Retirement			●	●	●	●	●
Medical	●	●	●	●		●	●
Car or allowances	●	●	●	●	●	●	
Clubs				●	●*		
Executive pension		●				●	●
Housing				●			
Vacation days	28	25	30	14	20	20-25	15
Holidays	10-15	11	10-15	15	13	8	8-10
Value as a percentage of base salary	15%	21%	18%	28%	19%	18%	28%

* Chief executives only

Source: "How Perks Stack Up Worldwide" from *Forbes,* May 19, 1997, p. 162. Reprinted by permission of *Forbes* Magazine © Forbes, Inc., 1997.

compensation. Both the Economic Recovery Act of 1981 and the Tax Reform Act of 1986 included major provisions regulating stock options.

Stock options became even more popular in the 1990s, and legislation through the 1990s lowered many tax rates. Nonetheless, in 1994, while the average compensation for a worker in the United States increased by 2.0 percent, the average income for a *Fortune* 100 firm increased by 16 percent. As a result, Congress became very interested in executive compensation and thus in stock options. Consequently, from 1994 until 1996, a series of laws reduced some of the benefits of stock options for both the manager and the organization. That trend ended in 1996, however, as Republicans took control of both houses of Congress. Legislation since that time has made it easier for companies to give stock options to their employees (since these transactions were no longer subject to as many regulations) and reduced the maximum tax rate on long-term capital gains to 20 percent.

But all this appeared to be at risk during 2000–2002, when several highly publicized bankruptcies occurred. Enron, for example, declared bankruptcy while its CEO Ken Lay enjoyed the gains from the stock options he had recently exercised. Similar tales from other companies led to a strong belief for many that something should be done about how stock options were treated. Specifically, the Financial Accounting Standards Board (FASB) recommended that firms be required to carry stock options on corporate balance sheets as liabilities. That is, corporations would be forced to share information about exactly what those stock options were worth (which is itself open to some controversy) and to list these items as real liabilities that affect the firm's bottom line.

Political pressure in the Republican-dominated Congress apparently caused the FASB to back down from its position. This move is highly unusual because the FASB is supposed to be removed from politics. Nonetheless, the result is that no changes in how stock options are reported have been implemented. Some business leaders (especially those interested in stockholder rights) have complained, and these complaints may make executives more reluctant to exercise stock options under some circumstances. For the present, however, it is likely that stock options will continue to be a popular ingredient in executive compensation packages.[14]

Finally, we should note that the gap between the earnings of the CEO and the earnings of a typical employee is enormous. First, the very size of the gap has been increasing in the United States. In 1980 the typical CEO earned forty-two times the earnings of an ordinary worker, but by 1990 this ratio had increased to eighty-five times the earnings of an ordinary worker. In Japan, on the other hand, in 1990 a typical CEO made less than twenty times the earnings of an ordinary worker.[15]

Another concern is the impact this differential has for the typical employee. On the one hand, he or she may not believe that the CEO is making eighty-five times the contribution made by the typical employee, or at least that no one could be working eighty-five times as hard. This perception may lead to resentment and other problems on the job, and evidence suggests that such large dispersions result in decreased satisfaction, willingness to collaborate, and overall productivity.[16] On the other hand, the typical employee may view this huge salary as a prize worth aiming for. From this perspective, pay structures are seen as tournaments, and the bigger the prize, the more intense the competition, and so the greater the effort and productivity. Some evidence in fact supports this position, indicating that managers cannot really be sure of the effects of these income gaps.[17]

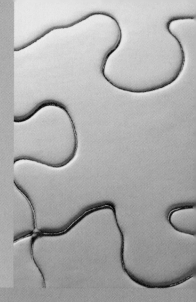

Appendix **1**

Human Resource Information Systems

The human resource manager's job requires a large number of decisions. These decisions, in turn, require access to a large amount of information. In simple cases, we can imagine an HR manager reading and analyzing the files for the ten applicants for a recent job opening and deciding who should receive an offer. Perhaps the position for which these applicants are applying is a new one within the organization, and so at some point the HR manager must determine the appropriate compensation for this position relative to other jobs within the firm. Furthermore, this new position may be the result of a new strategic initiative that requires information about the kinds of skills and abilities available inside the organization.

Clearly, these decisions require that various kinds of information be available for the HR manager. As we will see, there is also a fair amount of information that might be useful to new employees once they join the organization and to other individuals who may have to make very different kinds of decisions but might still need to know something about the current human resources in the organization. The need for this kind of information, in an easily accessible and ready-to-use form, is at the heart of human resource information systems.

What Are Human Resource Information Systems (HRISs)?

A human resource information system is a special form of a more general kind of information system. Thus we begin by briefly examining the nature of information technology in general, and then we focus more specifically on human resource information systems and their role in organizations.

The Nature of Information Technology

Information technology refers to the resources used by an organization to manage information that it needs to carry out its mission. Information technology is generally of two types—manual or computer based. All information technology, and the systems that it defines, has five basic parts. One part is the *input medium,* the device that is used to add data and information into the system. For example, an optical scanner at Kroger enters point-of-sale information. Likewise, someone can also enter data through a keyboard. And when people apply for jobs in an organization, their resumes and/or job applications might be scanned into the firm's information system.

The data that are entered into the system typically flow first to a processor. The *processor* is the part of the system that is capable of organizing, manipulating, sorting, or performing calculations or other transformations with the data. Most systems also have one or more *storage devices*—a place where data can be stored for later use. External disks, "thumb drives," hard drives, and CD-ROMs are common forms of storage devices. As data are transformed into usable information, the resulting information must be communicated to the appropriate person by means of an *output medium.* Common ways to display output are video displays, printers, other computers, and fax machines.

Finally, the entire information technology system is operated by a *control system*—most often software of one form or another. Simple systems in smaller organizations can use off-the-shelf software. Microsoft and Mac have general operating systems that control more specialized types of software. For example, Microsoft Word remains a popular system for word processing, while Microsoft Excel is a very popular program for handling spreadsheets. Of course, elaborate systems of the type used by large businesses require a special customized operating system. Some firms create their own information system for human resources, whereas others buy existing software commercial products.[1] And when organizations start to link computers together into a network, the operating system must be even more complex.

Human Resource Information Systems

A human resource information system, as noted above, is a special form of information system oriented directly at an organization's HR management needs. That is, a human resource information system (or HRIS) is the entire set of people, procedures, forms, and data used to acquire, store, analyze, retrieve, distribute, and use information about an organization's human resources. The system is, therefore, much more than just computer hardware and software (although these components are critical to an effective HRIS). Finally, the major goal of the system is to provide needed information that is timely and accurate and to provide it in a way that it is useful to persons making HR-related decisions. Although many organizations develop their own systems, there are also packages, such as *PeopleSoft,* that are commercially available and that can handle most HRIS needs.

In essence, the information contained in an HRIS is information that has always been available in books, reports, records, or forms. The key difference, though, is that the information is now computerized. There is no longer any need for paper forms or reports, for instance, and decision makers should be able to locate and access easily and exactly the information they need. For example, if there is a need to know exactly how many people are working in an area (the "head count"), when they began working with the company (perhaps to determine potential wage costs), or even the average number of dependents employees have (perhaps to project benefit costs), the person charged with obtaining the information should be able to access a computer database and retrieve the desired information.

Thus the specific nature of any HRIS will depend upon the needs of the organization. Organizations will differ, for example, in terms of what information they actually need to retrieve, and therefore need to store, as part of the HRIS. Some organizations may focus on race and gender characteristics of the workforce, while others might be concerned about accidents and work days lost. Furthermore, organizations will differ in terms of how they need the information to be presented. Some may need information at the aggregate level, about the organization as a whole (numbers of employees, average wages, average hours, and so on), while others might need more information about individuals (a person's work history, skills profile, and so on). The remainder of this appendix discusses some specific uses of HRISs in organizations, as well as some specific ideas about the kinds of information that might be needed. Finally, we will discuss some of the moral, ethical, and legal issues that are involved with setting up and using an HRIS.

Potential Uses of HRISs

Of course, the potential types of output from an HRIS depend on the nature of the input. But the decision concerning what information to input depends on how the system will be used. Ultimately, the HRIS should help the organization in its strategic planning process, but there are a number of other more focused applications.

HR Functions

At a very basic level, the HRIS can be used by the organization and its members to help them more effectively manage the employment relationship. For example, from the standpoint of the organization, the HRIS can be used in HR planning. Job openings can be posted as part of its recruiting efforts. Applications can be scanned (as already noted) and stored. Performance appraisal information can also be stored, as can the employee's history of training and development activities. Career path, compensation, and benefit information can also be an integral part of the HRIS. Individual employees should be able to scan the HRIS for new job possibilities within the organization and be better informed about training opportunities and benefit options.

Record Keeping and Report Generation

Perhaps the most common application of an HRIS, however, involves the generation of reports, especially reports that must be prepared on a regular basis. A good example of this would be the EEO-1 report on current employees that many organizations are required to file with the government. Data must be presented for all jobs using the following categories: officials and managers, professionals, technicians, sales workers, office and clerical, (skilled) craft workers, (semiskilled) operatives, (unskilled) laborers, and service workers. For each job category the organization is required to report how many incumbents can be classified as white (not of Hispanic origin), black (not of Hispanic origin), Hispanic, Asian or Pacific Islander, and Native American or Native Alaskan. Furthermore, the organization must report numbers within these groups for male and female employees separately.

Also, many organizations are required to regularly submit "eight factor" reports, which indicate both the availability and utilization of employees within the same categories (for both jobs and employees) as in the EEO-1 report. These reports depend on the same types of information as the EEO-1 reports, and an HRIS is extremely useful in supplying that information. Other reports requiring HRIS input involve the evaluation of training programs. Computation of cost-benefit ratios for these programs requires information about which training programs an employee has gone through, and some evaluation of past and current levels of job performance, turnover, or absenteeism. In fact, virtually any evaluation that deals with absenteeism and turnover data, or with any type of productivity data, requires input from an HRIS.

But perhaps the area where the most report generation activity requiring an HRIS takes place is the compensation and benefits area. For example, to "price" jobs, an organization needs data on how the jobs score on various compensable factors, as well as data on what other organizations are paying. The results of the wage surveys for comparison data and the results of the job evaluation are likely to be kept in an HRIS and thus made available to compensation analysts. Also, once jobs are priced, an HRIS can provide the data needed to compare current compensation rates with those generated through the pricing process and to indicate which jobs should have their compensation adjusted. HRIS data are also used to determine withholdings and generate rates of take-home pay for employees. In such cases the system must be flexible enough to deal with changes in the tax codes or in the number of dependents.

Similarly, recall that in Chapter 9 we discussed the idea of a cafeteria benefits program. These systems provide an allowance for benefits that employees can "spend" on any mix of benefits they want. It is virtually impossible to implement such a system and keep track of choices and changes in choices and allocations without an HRIS, and data from these systems are needed to provide reports to employees. Even without a cafeteria system,

HRIS data are needed to generate annual reports informing employees of their present benefits and the value of those benefits. Here again, flexibility is vital, as choices and options are likely to change.

One final example of an area where an HRIS is critical is in the area of planning. Specifically, as an organization plans for its human resource needs for the following year (as discussed in Chapter 5), it needs information about planned changes in operations and the implications of those changes for human resources. But the organization also needs to know about its available human resources and what types of skills and experiences the present workforce possesses. Inventories of skills and experience provide a challenge not only because of the amount of information required but also because of the way the information is encoded and used.

In most of the other examples we have discussed, the kind of data required for the system is pretty clear. That is, if managers need to know the number of women in a certain job, encoding this information is straightforward. However, to prepare an inventory of skills and experiences, managers need to first decide which skills and experiences are relevant for the decisions to be made. Then they must decide exactly what information about those skills and experiences to include. For example, a manager might simply want to note whether an employee has had a certain job assignment or not. Or the manager might want to know how long the assignment lasted and how successful the employee was on the job. In the area of skills, an organization might simply rely upon self-reports that an employee can speak French, for example. But more complex systems might include information about scores on a French test or might indicate the level of speaking ability. Thus HRISs used for planning require the organization to make many more decisions than do systems used for other types of decisions.

These examples provide some idea of the range of information that might be included in an HRIS and what kinds of decisions this information might be used for. Nonetheless, the actual range of possibilities is almost endless, as organizations determine what kinds of information they need to have access to in order to make the decisions that need to be made. But regardless of the kinds of information included, a number of other issues must be considered as an organization designs and implements an HRIS.

Issues and Concerns in the Use of HRISs

Regardless of the exact information an organization retains in its HRIS and regardless of how that information is used, the fact that the organization collects and stores a large amount of information about its employees, and that this information can be easily retrieved, raises a number of other issues and concerns. Some of these are related to legal questions concerning privacy and the invasion of privacy, whereas others are related to the ethics of storing and retrieving personal information about employees.

Legal Issues

Most of the legal issues concerning HRISs are related to privacy. The Fourth Amendment to the U.S. Constitution guarantees protection from unreasonable search and seizure. The ability of an organization (or its representatives) to search an employee's files without his or her permission might well violate that protection. In addition, the

Fifth Amendment provides protection against self-incrimination, and if an organization searches through an employee's personnel files and finds incriminating information, this action could be viewed as a violation of that protection.

As noted in Chapter 2, most of the legislation in the privacy area has been enacted by states, but the Privacy Act of 1974 requires federal agencies to open their personnel files for employee inspection. Furthermore, the law enables the employee to correct any incorrect or misleading information in those files, *and* allows the employee to prevent the use of the information in those files for anything other than its original intent. Several lawmakers have suggested that this protection be extended to employees in private industry, but such legislation has not yet been formally proposed. It seems clear, however, that in the future organizations might have more difficulty in deciding what kinds of information to keep about employees and how to use that information, which will have a substantial impact on the design of HRISs.

The Privacy Protection Study Commission was established in 1977 to determine which safeguards needed to be put in place to protect employee rights in this area. The commission has suggested a number of steps to help organizations protect employee rights as they set up HRISs. These include:

1. Organizations should collect and store only job-relevant information in their information systems.
2. Organizations should limit or completely avoid storing subjective information about employees (such as appraisal information) in their information systems.
3. Organizations should provide employees with information about exactly how their records will be used.
4. Organizations should allow employees to access their records and files and to correct any incorrect information.
5. Organizations should strictly limit internal access to employee information.
6. Organizations should strictly limit and always document the release of information to anyone outside the organization without employee approval.[2]

Clearly, these suggestions would significantly limit the organization's ability to rely on information systems for decision making, and the potential conflicts between an employee's rights to privacy and an organization's need to have information will continue to be an important issue.

Ethical Issues

Some legal restrictions already in place potentially limit the information an organization can store about employees and how that information is used. And these restrictions are likely to increase over time. But in addition to legal restrictions, a number of ethical considerations should guide the design and use of an HRIS.

For example, organizations are restricted in the information they can collect about an employee's health at the time of hiring. However, once a person is an employee, an organization might routinely collect and store information about insurance claims that possibly contain information about health issues. Likewise, organizations should not ask applicants (or even current employees) about any disabilities they might have. On the other hand, employees who have disabilities may be able to request certain accommodations in order to carry out their jobs. Furthermore, the organization would be likely to store information about these accommodations, especially if they dealt with hours or conditions of employment. But retaining such information in an employee's file could jeopardize opportunities in the future if some decision maker discovers the employee's "hidden" disability (for example, a learning disability).

Even if there were no tangible results of this information becoming known, coworkers might begin treating the employee differently. Therefore, the question arises of whether or not the organization should keep this kind of information. Clearly, there might be good reasons to keep such information, and doing so is probably legal, but the information could cause embarrassment or discomfort to the employee if it were known. Again, the solution to such dilemmas probably lies with tighter restrictions on who can access an employee's file. But of course, as these restrictions grow, the chances increase that someone who might need to have access to some information will be denied access because he or she would then also have access to more sensitive information.

Conclusions

As organizations become more complex and as the amount of information they need increases, the need for automated information systems increases dramatically. The organization must determine what kinds of information it will need by deciding what kinds of decisions it will make based on the HRIS information and who will actually make the decisions. Because these needs are likely to change over time, it is also necessary to build in a certain amount of flexibility.

But the ultimate flexibility would involve having a maximum amount of information available for every employee and then making this information accessible by every employee. Such a system would almost certainly violate an employee's rights to privacy and might well cause the employee embarrassment. Weighing the present and future organizational needs for information against the employee's rights and well-being will remain a major challenge for designers of HRISs.

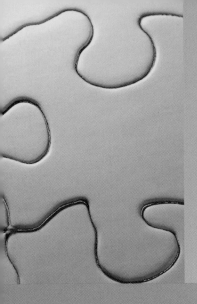

Data and Research in Human Resource Management

Many aspects of the HR manager's job require decisions to be made. Throughout this text we have tried to provide information about the nature of these decisions, as well as insights into potential solutions. But even after a decision is made, the job is not complete—it is still necessary to evaluate the decision. That is, the HR manager (or perhaps someone else in the organization) needs to determine whether the implemented decision or program worked as intended. To be able to evaluate the decision effectively, the HR manager needs some appreciation and understanding of research, data, and data analysis. Note that in this day of computerization, HR managers do not usually need to actually perform specific statistical tests, but they must be able to decide which data to collect and determine which tests to run; then they must be able to interpret the results.

This appendix provides an overview of some of these issues. Although the principles discussed here apply to a wide variety of settings, we place them in the context of HR decisions and HR programs. In addition, we discuss in some detail two HR issues of a fairly technical nature that are also mentioned in the body of the text—validity generalization and utility analysis. First, though, we discuss a general issue that underlies all research in the social sciences, including HR research: causality.

Determining Causal Relationships

When an HR manager implements a new pay plan as a means of reducing turnover and then observes that turnover has, in fact, been reduced, the manager would probably like to believe that the new pay plan *caused* the reduction in turnover. This desire to believe the new pay plan was responsible for the change in turnover is especially true if the new pay plan was implemented in one division, perhaps as a pilot project, and the organization must now decide whether to implement the plan throughout the organization. At first glance the issue may seem to be quite simple. Turnover was high (say, 15 percent), a new pay plan was implemented, and turnover subsequently went down (perhaps to 8 percent). What else could have caused the drop in turnover?

This is exactly the right question to be asking, but the answer is not obvious. Any number of factors other than the new pay system could conceivably influence turnover in the organization. For example, when unemployment rates are high, turnover generally drops in all organizations as employees see few alternatives to their present jobs. When unemployment rates are lower, alternatives are available, and so an unhappy employee might feel more secure in acting on the basis of his or her dissatisfaction. Therefore, if the local unemployment rate increased around the time the new pay plan was implemented, reduced employment alternatives, rather than the new pay plan, may have caused the turnover rate to change. In fact, in this case, if the organization had done nothing, the turnover rate would still have gone down as a result of the rise in unemployment.

Another possibility is that disgruntled employees have been leaving the organization at a fairly constant rate. However, at some point all the disgruntled employees have already quit, and all that are left are the satisfied employees who are not likely to quit. Perhaps this point occurred at about the same time the new pay plan was implemented. Here again, the turnover rate would have dropped even if the organization did nothing.

In yet one more scenario, perhaps the employees believed that the management didn't really care much about them, and so their leaving was in response to a perceived neglect. When the organization introduced a new pay system, the management signaled to the employees that it did care about them. But the important thing was the fact that the management did *something* for the employees, rather than the specific nature of the new pay plan. Here, turnover would not have gone down if the organization did nothing, but a much less expensive intervention that communicated concern on the part of the management might have been equally effective.

To establish that a causal relationship exists, we must be able to effectively rule out all other rival plausible explanations for the changes we have observed. If any or all of the explanations discussed above (or some other explanation) are possible, we cannot say with certainty that the new pay plan caused the reduction in turnover. In fact, under such a set of circumstances we cannot say exactly what caused the reduction in turnover.

Many times, when we want to examine the impact of some program on an outcome of interest, we simply examine the relationship between a variable corresponding to the program and a variable corresponding to the outcome of interest. For example, if an organization is interested in training employees as a means of increasing satisfaction (since the employees would have more skills and be able to do a wider variety of jobs), an HR manager might decide to correlate the amount of training employees have with their levels of satisfaction. This task would involve determining whether employees with more training were also more satisfied with their jobs. Assuming that the HR manager would find such a relationship, she or he might conclude that training causes higher levels of satisfaction and so recommend companywide training programs. (We discuss correlations in more detail a bit later.)

But again, there would be problems with such a statement. Because the HR manager did not provide the training (and so had no control over who was trained or how much training a person received), many other factors could explain the relationship observed. Perhaps being more satisfied on the job leads an employee to make more investments for the sake of the company, including seeking training. Thus increased satisfaction caused increased training, rather than vice versa. Alternatively, perhaps more highly motivated employees were more likely to seek training and more likely to be happy on the job. In this case, training would not have caused satisfaction, and satisfaction would not have caused employees to seek training. Instead, a third variable (the level of employee motivation) caused both, the seeking of training and the increase in satisfaction.

Therefore, we state again that we can make causal statements (changes in *a* caused changes in *b*) only when we have ruled out all plausible alternative explanations. Furthermore, we can never make causal statements when our conclusions are based on a correlation between two variables. Instead, if we wish to make causal statements, we need to be able to control for these alternative explanations. How do we do that? The simple answer is that we need to conduct an experiment in which two groups are equivalent on everything that might possibly be relevant, especially on levels of overall satisfaction. Then we introduce a treatment (for example, a new pay plan) to one group (at random), but not the other. After a suitable period of time, we measure the levels of satisfaction in the two groups. If the level of satisfaction (following the intervention) is higher in the group that received the new pay plan, we can be relatively sure that the new pay plan caused satisfaction to increase.

We have just described a true experiment that allowed us to make a causal statement. It is often difficult to conduct true experiments in organizational settings, but some variations are easier to carry out. The discussion of these different designs is beyond the scope of the present discussion. Nevertheless, without some type of experiment, we cannot make statements of the type that "*a* causes *b*."

Common HR Research Issues

Whether or not some type of experiment will be conducted, a number of issues must be considered whenever an organization does HR research. We will discuss sampling, measurement, and statistical issues in the context of various types of HR research issues. Again, these subjects are complex, and we can provide only an introduction to them here. The interested reader is encouraged to look for additional material.[1]

Samples and Sampling

In Chapter 7 we introduced the idea of validation as it relates to selection—demonstrating that persons who scored higher on some test (or other selection device) also performed better on the job. To demonstrate such a relationship (and so validate the test), we typically collect information on test scores and subsequent (or current) performance and then calculate a correlation to determine the extent of any relationship. Presumably, an organization could give this test to every employee and obtain performance information for every employee, but this would be extremely time-consuming. The organization would be more likely to collect these data from some subset of employees, which we call a "sample." The organization would then determine the extent of the relationship in the sample data and infer that the same relationship holds true for the rest of the population.

Before discussing any details about samples, we must point out that even if the organization decided to test and collect performance data from every employee, sampling would still be involved. That is, managers are not really interested in the relationship between test scores and job performance for current employees—the organization already knows how well they are performing. Instead, managers want to use any information about test scores and performance with future applicants. If a relationship exists between the two, managers would use the test scores of applicants to predict their later performance on the job and hire only those expected to perform well. Therefore, managers would be using the relationship between scores and performance in current employees and assume that the same relationship would hold for new applicants.

For this logic to work, the sample must be representative of the population of interest. If we use current employees to compute a relationship that we hope will apply to later applicants, our current employees must be representative of future applicants. If, for example, our present employees are mostly white males and we expect many future applicants to be nonwhite and/or females, we can be pretty certain that our sample is not a good one for predicting performance of later applicants.

Effective sampling procedures allow television networks to predict the outcome of elections early in the evening. When network executives tell us that 75 million families watched the last Super Bowl, they base this statement on the viewing patterns of a small sample of "typical" families—referred to as "Nielsen families" because of the name of the firm that compiles the ratings.

One of the most famous blunders based on poor sampling occurred during the presidential election of 1948. Harry Truman was running against a Republican named Thomas Dewey. Pollsters conducted an opinion poll to try to predict the outcome of the election. They sought a "representative" sample of all Americans they could poll and decided to draw the sample from local phone directories. The polls indicated that Dewey would be the easy winner, and everyone was surprised when Truman won handily. The problem was with the sample used in the polls. In 1948 many Americans did not own a phone because they could not afford one. Therefore, the phone directory only provided information about phone owners—not the general population. People with more money were more likely to own phones, and traditionally people with more money are more likely to vote Republican. The sample was therefore biased in that it overrepresented Republicans. Had the sample been more representative, the outcome would have been different. Modern pollsters have become much more sophisticated about drawing samples, and in fact, the phone directory might provide a much more representative sample of Americans today than it did in 1948.

Measurement Issues

If we were interested in measuring someone's height, we could do so with a yardstick and be pretty sure that we got it right. We can measure time and distance with amazing precision as well. But when we try to measure someone's level of ability, or personality or intelligence, we begin to have difficulties. In addition to measuring the level of someone's conscientiousness (for example), we are also measuring a lot of other things we don't really want to measure. This is the problem of unreliability we discussed in Chapter 7. Eventually, we could be measuring so many of these unwanted things that we are not measuring conscientiousness at all. We also discussed the validity problem in Chapter 7.

If we are interested in seeing whether a test for conscientiousness is related to performance on the job, we have to be sure that we can measure both conscientiousness and performance in a meaningful way. If our test is somehow biased, or requires a high level of reading ability, for example, we will have problems, since the test is supposed to measure conscientiousness, not reading ability. As a result, we might conclude that conscientiousness does predict job performance when we have really only found that reading ability predicts job performance. Likewise, if we do not have a good measure of job performance (see Chapter 10), we may conclude that our test predicts performance on the job when it really only predicts a person's gender, since men consistently are rated higher on our (flawed) performance measure even when they do not perform better than women. Using the test in this case would then result in selecting only men, which, in this case, would almost certainly be illegal.

Statistical Issues

Despite our discussion of causality, the single most common statistical test used in HR is the correlation coefficient. A correlation coefficient indicates the degree of linear relationship between two sets of scores. When scores on, say, a test and job performance are correlated, we know that changes in test scores are associated with changes in job performance. If the correlation is positive, we further know that higher test scores are associated with higher levels of performance. The stronger the relationship, the higher the correlation, and the closer changes in one are associated with changes in the other. Notice that we are not saying that the test scores cause the changes in performance. Instead, we simply note that those who score higher also tend to perform better. In fact, correlations are used in settings where we do not have experimental designs and so we cannot assess causality.

Correlations can also be negative. The sign (positive or negative) indicates nothing about the strength of the relationship, only the nature of the relationship. When a correlation is negative it means that higher scores on one variable are associated with lower scores on the other. For example, we know that employees who are more satisfied on their jobs should be absent less frequently. Therefore, if we took a sample of employees, measured their job satisfaction, and noted how many days they missed work in the past year, we should find that those with higher satisfaction scores were absent fewer days—a negative correlation.

FIGURE A2.1   Diagrams Illustrating the Scatter Plots for Five Correlation Coefficients

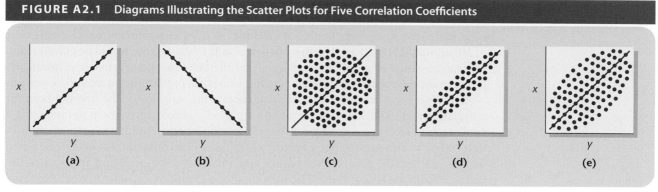

These diagrams illustrate correlations of 1.00 (a), –1.00 (b), zero (c), .80 (d), and .10 (e).

The strength of the correlation coefficient indicates the strength of the relationship between the two sets of scores. Correlations can range from –1.00 through 0 to +1.00. Since the sign of the correlation only tells us the direction of the relationship, we can see that a correlation of 0 indicates no relationship between the variables, whereas a correlation of 1 indicates the strongest relationship possible. In fact, a correlation of 1.00 is also referred to as a perfect correlation. It means that for every unit of change in one variable, there is exactly one unit of change in the other. Because the relationship is perfect, we can also perfectly predict the scores on one variable from the scores on the other variable. To help illustrate this principle and to help make the concept of correlations clearer, we have presented some correlation coefficients in Figure A2.1.

The first three diagrams illustrate correlations that are either perfect or 0. Specifically, these are the scatter plots that would correspond to each correlation. A scatter plot is obtained by simply graphing each person's scores on the two variables *x* and *y* (where *x* might be scores on a test and *y* might be job performance). For example, we have indicated the point corresponding to a person who scored 80 on *x* and 90 on *y*. Every other point in the scatterplot was determined in exactly the same way. You may wonder why if the correlation between the two variables is perfect, the person whose scores we have illustrated does not have exactly the same score on both variables. In order to explain that, we need one more piece of information that is presented in the figure.

Notice that in each case we draw a line, called the regression line, through the scatter plot. This represents the best straight-line fit to the information in the graph. The linear equations represented by those lines are always of the form $y = bx + c$ where *y* is the score on variable *y*; *x* is the score on variable *x*; *c* is a constant; and *b* is the regression coefficient, or the *slope* of the line. The constant term simply allows the scores on the two variables to differ by some constant and is also referred to as the *y intercept*, since it marks the point at which the line crosses the vertical axis. The slope of the line is a ratio of the number of units of change in one variable to the number of units of change in the other. In all the examples provided here, the slope is equal to 1.0. This slope is simply the easiest to illustrate and indicates that in the best-fitting line one unit of change in *x* is associated with one unit of change in *y*. The *y* intercept, or constant, in each case is 10, indicating that the two variables change on different scales, but that these scales differ by exactly 10 units. Thus for each case except for the negative correlation, the equation for the best-fitting regression line would be equal to

$$y = 1.0(x) + 10$$

In the first example, where there is a perfect and positive correlation, the best-fitting line fits the data perfectly—all the points on the scatter plot line up exactly on the regression line. Our equation would lead us to predict that for any value of x, if we simply add 10, we will get a corresponding value for y. In the first case, our predictions are exactly right each time, since every point is on the line. So if we knew someone had a score on x of 30, we would predict a score on y of 40, and in the first case we would be exactly right. The nature of the equation and prediction are the same for the negative correlation, except that the equation would have a negative slope, but prediction would still be perfect.

The regression line for the third correlation is the same as for the first but here the correlation is 0. Thus knowing a score on x provides absolutely no help in predicting a score on y. In fact, we can see that someone scoring 50 on x could score anywhere from 0 to 100 on y. This same range of predicted values will be obtained for every value of x. Notice here that the points in the scatter plot form more of a circle and, in any case, deviate far from the straight line. The only predictions we can make in all cases are those based on the simple linear regression equation, and the further the points deviate from the straight line, the less accurate our predictions until we reach this case, where the correlation is 0, and our predictions are no better than we could obtain if we just chose random numbers.

The remaining two graphs illustrate correlations greater than 0, but less than 1.00. In both cases the points in the scatter plot deviate from our best-line regression line, but the degree of deviation is quite different. In the fourth illustration, the correlation is computed to be = .80. Although prediction is not perfect here, notice the points do not deviate much from the regression line. As in the other cases, if a person had a score of 50 on x, we would predict that he or she should score 60 on y. Because prediction cannot be perfect here, we are not always right. But notice that a person scoring 50 on x will score somewhere between 55 and 65 on y. We predicted a score of 60, and we were off, but not by much. Thus, knowing someone's score on x does not perfectly predict the score on y, but it narrows things down considerably.

The final illustration involves a correlation of + .10. Here the points of the scatter plot deviate quite a bit from the regression line, and so we would expect predictions to be less accurate. The person scoring 50 on x would still be predicted to score 60 on y, but in fact, persons scoring 50 on x score anywhere from 10 to 90 on y. This is still better than the accuracy of prediction when the correlation is 0, but not by much, and we can predict very little about scores on y from scores on x.

Another statistical test that is encountered in HR is known as a t-test. This test, which compares two groups in terms of their mean scores, may well be used in experimental designs as a means of determining causality. For example, if we were interested in whether a group that had received a training program produced more "units" than one that wasn't trained (but was otherwise comparable to aid in determining causality), we would use a t-test to compare the mean levels of output in the two groups. If the trained group produced more units and the difference were greater than we would expect by chance alone (determined by comparing our obtained t-value with some critical value from a table), we would conclude that the training did cause an increase in output.

If, instead, there were three groups, we would need to employ a related but slightly different statistical test. So if we wanted to compare the output of a group receiving traditional training, a group receiving computer-aided training, and a group receiving no training, we could compare the mean levels of output for the three groups simultaneously, using a statistical test called analysis of variance (ANOVA). This technique would be preferable to conducting a series of t-tests among all the possible pairs of groups for a number of reasons that are beyond the scope of this discussion. Suffice it to say, however, that in this case ANOVA would be the best test to use. If we determined that the means differed at a level beyond what we would expect by chance, we would still need to conduct some follow-up (post hoc) tests to determine exactly which means differed from which other means.

These, then, are the statistical tests basic to HR operations. Using the right test, along with proper sampling techniques and sound measurement, allows HR managers to answer the questions needed to carry out their job effectively. Many of these questions deal with the evaluation of programs or interventions. That is, if an organization introduces a new appraisal or compensation program, the firm wants to be sure that the new program is accomplishing what was intended. An HR manager often deals with questions of this type, and the tools and techniques discussed here make it more likely that the manager can provide the organization with the answers it needs.

Other Technical Issues in HR Research

In addition to using statistics and research techniques to answer specific questions, there are also at least two areas in which an HR manager needs some specialized technical expertise related to the treatment of data. We focus on the issues of validity generalization and utility analysis. In both cases the HR manager needs to understand something about data and analysis in order to provide the best services possible to the organization.

Validity Generalization

When we discussed test validation in Chapter 7, we discussed it in terms of separate validation efforts for each test on each job. In fact, organizations and courts have traditionally viewed the validation process this way. Each test must be validated for each job. Yet, at some level we recognize that this approach may be unnecessary. For example, let us say that State Farm Insurance Company develops a test to select insurance agents and goes through the process of validating the test. Let us say further that State Farm relies on a test of clerical abilities that is generally available to any interested organization. Now if Allstate decides to use the same abilities test to select its insurance agents, does it need to conduct a separate validity study? It would seem reasonable to assume that if scores on the test were related to performance at State Farm, they should be related to performance at Allstate as well.

In fact, Allstate would be able to "borrow" State Farm's validity data, and even rely on it in court if necessary, as long as Allstate could demonstrate through job analysis that the job requirements and the settings in the two firms were the same. In fact, in the simplest and least controversial form of validity generalization, one firm uses the validity study results of another firm, but both firms are interested in using the same test to select persons for the same job.

An extension of this type of validity generalization involves the use of the Position Analysis Questionnaire (or PAQ), which was designed to describe a wide variety of jobs using a common set of job dimensions (see Chapter 5). The developers of the PAQ extended some earlier work on synthetic validity[2] and argued that it was possible to show relationships between tests and job dimensions, just as one usually demonstrated relationships between tests and the entire job. If one could establish such relationships (that is, performance on a test was related to performance on some aspect of a job) and if a general set of job dimensions could be used that was believed to underlie all jobs, it would be possible to "construct" validity data for any job. That is, it would be possible to determine which job dimensions were important for a given job and then put together a selection battery by combining those tests that were related to performance on each dimension.

In fact, such a system has been developed for use with the PAQ and was introduced in Chapter 5. This system (which is referred to as job component validity) allows an organization to conduct a job analysis of a job, using the PAQ, and then rely on the already established relationships to construct a recommended test battery for use in selecting persons for the job in question. Although limited, the available information suggests that these recommendations, in fact, prove to be valid for the job in question when this is tested empirically.[3] Thus this approach would allow an organization to piece together validity information for a variety of jobs and tests and would require job analysis, rather than a formal validation study, to support the use of a test or tests in a selection setting. Whether the courts will accept this broader application is not clear.

The most far-reaching proposal for validity generalization, however, has been proposed by Frank Schmidt and John Hunter.[4] These authors and their associates have compiled an enormous amount of data clearly indicating that many of the differences we observe in the validity of a given test, across different jobs, can be attributed to problems of unreliability and measurement, rather than to true differences in the predictability of performance. In fact, these arguments even suggest that certain types of cognitive ability tests (such as intelligence tests), and certain other types of tests, are related to performance on *virtually all* jobs. Furthermore, these tests predict performance better than alternatives do, and so there is no need to conduct any validity studies. An organization can simply use these tests for selection and know it is selecting the best people.[5]

These arguments, although supported by a great deal of data, have not been completely accepted by the courts and are quite controversial. The controversy has been generated not only because these arguments obviate the need for separate validity studies but also because they propose tests such as intelligence tests, which tend to have adverse impact, as the best predictors of performance across a wide variety of jobs.

Utility Analysis

Test validation is concerned with demonstrating that persons who score higher on some test also perform better on some job. Once this relationship has been established, an organization can use the test to select applicants by hiring only those who score above a certain cutoff on the test. This approach will result in the organization hiring more people who are ultimately successful and fewer persons who would ultimately fail on the job. Therefore, the organization can be said to be improving its selection system and selecting better people. But how much better is the selection system, and how much better are the people selected? Utility analysis attempts to answer these critical questions.

For example, we do not need very sophisticated models to conclude that if 95 percent of the persons hired without the use of a test are successful, then even if the test is valid, if it improves the success rate to 96 percent, but costs the firm hundreds of thousands of dollars to administer, it probably is not worth the additional cost. Over the years a number of approaches to assessing utility have been proposed. An early approach used a series of charts (the Taylor Russell tables) that indicate the improvement in the selection of successful applicants by using a test with specified validity, given the percentage of successful employees selected without using the test and the selection ratio (explained below).[6] But this approach failed to consider the costs associated with selection. Therefore, more complete utility models have been proposed that do consider the costs associated with selection, training, or whatever intervention is being evaluated.

An early utility model that considered costs was proposed by Hubert Brogden[7] and is presented below. The original model had a problem calculating one critical component, but subsequent versions, as well as other models that further refined the basic relationships,[8] could be used to express exactly how much (in dollars) a new selection system or training program was worth to an organization. Conceptually, the model is as follows (mathematically, the model must be expressed differently):

$$\text{Savings per person selected} = z_y SD_y - \text{Cost of selecting the person}$$

The cost of selecting a person is the product of the cost of testing each applicant (which includes both actual testing costs and recruiting costs) and the selection ratio, or the ratio of applicants per job opening. If there were ten applicants for each job opening, the selection ratio would be 1/10 or .10. The greater the selection ratio, the more applicants per job, which allows the organization to be more selective, but also increases the cost of testing. So, if the cost to test each applicant is $10, and the selection ratio is .10, the cost to select an individual is $100 (plus recruiting costs). If the selection ratio goes to 1/100, the cost to select an individual becomes $1,000 (plus recruiting costs).

The remaining terms in the expression require some explanation as well. The term z_y refers to the mean criterion score (in standard score units) of those selected. Basically, this value indicates how successful those selected with the test in question might be. The SD_y term refers to the variance in performance on the job, expressed in dollar terms. If this term is high, the performance, or output, of a high-performing individual is worth a lot more to the organization than the performance of a low-performing individual. In such a case the value to the company of selecting high-performing individuals would go up. But in other cases the difference between the value of a high- and low-performing employee might not be so great. The value of the SD_y term would be reduced, and the utility of the test would be less. That is, in such a case, high-performing employees would be worth less to the organization relative to low-performing employees as compared to a case where the utility of the test was high. More complete illustrations of the use of utility analyses can be found elsewhere,[9] but these analyses are an important weapon for HR managers who wish to demonstrate that their efforts yield financial returns to the organization.

Endnotes

Chapter 1

1. Anne Fisher, "Building a Better Reputation," *Fortune,* March 6, 2006, pp. 65–78; Matthew Boyle, "The Right Stuff," *Fortune,* March 4, 2002, pp. 85–86; Matthew Boyle, "The Shiniest Reputations in Tarnished Times," *Fortune,* March 4, 2002, pp. 70–72; Wendy Zellner, "Southwest: After Kelleher, More Blue Skies," *BusinessWeek,* April 2, 2001, p. 45; "America's Top 500 Companies," *Forbes,* April 14, 2003, pp. 144–172; "At 35, Southwest's Strategy Gets More Complicated," *USA Today,* July 11, 2006, pp. 1B, 2B.

2. Robert M. Grant, "Toward a Knowledge-Based View of the Firm," *Strategic Management Journal,* 1996, Vol. 17, pp. 109–122.

3. Jeffrey Pfeffer, "Producing Sustainable Competitive Advantage Through the Effective Management of People," *The Academy of Management Executive,* February 1995, pp. 55–69; Peter Cappelli and Anne Crocker-Hefter, "Distinctive Human Resources Are Firms' Core Competencies," *Organizational Dynamics,* Winter 1996, pp. 7–22.

4. See Charles R. Greer, *Strategy and Human Resources* (Englewood Cliffs, N.J.: Prentice-Hall, 1995), for an overview of the strategic importance of human resources.

5. Robert R. Blake, "Memories of HRD," *Training & Development,* March 1995, pp. 22–28.

6. Randall S. Schuler, "Repositioning the Human Resource Function: Transformation or Demise?" *The Academy of Management Executive,* August 1990, pp. 49–60.

7. Pamela Babcock, "America's Newest Export: White-Collar Jobs," *HRMagazine,* April 2005, pp. 50–57.

8. For an excellent review of some of the problems involved in selecting employees in the context of high-security settings, see Paul R. Sackett, Neal Schmitt, Jill E. Ellingson, and Melissa Kabin, "High-Stakes Testing in Employment, Credentialing, and Higher Education," *The American Psychologist,* April 2001, pp. 302–418.

9. "Life Goes On," *HRMagazine,* September 2002, pp. 42–49.

10. Daniel Wren, *The Evolution of Management Thought,* 5th ed. (New York: Wiley, 2005).

11. Thomas A. Mahoney, "Evolution of Concept and Practice in Personnel Administration/Human Resource Management (PA/HRM)," *Journal of Management,* 1986, Vol. 12, No. 2, pp. 223–241.

12. Frederick W. Taylor, *Principles of Scientific Management* (New York: Harper, 1911).

13. Oliver E. Allen, "This Great Mental Revolution," *Audacity,* Summer 1996, pp. 52–61.

14. J. M. Fenster, "How General Motors Beat Ford," *Audacity,* Fall 1992, pp. 50–62.

15. Wren, *The Evolution of Management Thought.*

16. Elton Mayo, *The Human Problems of an Industrial Civilization* (New York: Macmillan, 1933).

17. Abraham Maslow, "A Theory of Human Motivation," *Psychological Review,* July 1943, pp. 370–396.

18. Douglas McGregor, *The Human Side of Enterprise* (New York: McGraw-Hill, 1960).

19. James H. Dulebohn, Gerald R. Ferris, and James T. Stodd, "The History and Evolution of Human Resource Management," in Gerald R. Ferris, Sherman D. Rosen, and Harold T. Barnum (eds.), *Handbook of Human Resource Management* (Cambridge, Mass.: Blackwell, 1995), pp. 18–41.

20. Dave Ulrich, "A New Mandate for Human Resources," *Harvard Business Review,* January–February 1998, pp. 124–133.

21. Brian Becker and Barry Gerhart, "The Impact of Human Resource Management on Organizational Performance: Progress and Prospects," *Academy of Management Journal,* August 1996, pp. 779–801; Russell A. Eisenstat, "What Corporate Human Resources Brings to the Picnic: Four Models for Functional Management," *Organizational Dynamics,* Autumn 1996, pp. 7–22.

22. John W. Kendrick, *Understanding Productivity: An Introduction to the Dynamics of Productivity Change* (Baltimore, Md.: Johns Hopkins University Press, 1977).

23. Ross Johnson and William O. Winchell, *Management and Quality* (Milwaukee, Wis.: American Society for Quality Control, 1989).

24. Rudy M. Yandrick, "Help Employees Reach for the Stars," *HRMagazine,* January 1997, pp. 96–100.

25. Michelle Martinez, "Prepared for the Future," *HRMagazine,* April 1997, pp. 80–87.

26. For an interesting contrast between large and small firms and human resource management activities, see Allison E. Barber, Michael J. Wesson, Quinetta M. Roberson, and M. Susan Taylor, "A Tale of Two Job Markets: Comparing the Hiring Practices of Large and Small Organizations," *Personnel Psychology,* 1999, Vol. 52, pp. 841–861.

27. For an excellent review, see John W. Boudreau, "Utility Analysis for Decisions in Human Resource Management," in Marvin D. Dunnette and Leatta M. Hough (eds.), *Handbook of Industrial and Organizational Psychology,* Vol. 2, 2nd ed. (Palo Alto, Calif.: Consulting Psychologists Press, 1991), pp. 621–745.

28. See, for example, Mark A. Huselid, "The Impact of Human Resource Management Practices on Turnover, Productivity, and Corporate Financial Reporting," *Academy of Management Journal,* 1996, Vol. 39, pp. 779–801.

29. Lotte Bailyn, "Patterned Chaos in Human Resource Management," *Sloan Management Review,* Winter 1993, pp. 77–89.

30. Martha Finney, "Degrees That Make a Difference," *HRMagazine,* November 1996, pp. 74–82; Bruce Kaufman, "What Companies Want from HR Graduates," *HRMagazine,* September 1994, pp. 84–90.

31. Steve Bates, "Facing the Future," *HRMagazine,* July 2002, pp. 26–32.

32. Brian D. Steffy and Steven D. Maurer, "Conceptualizing and Measuring the Economic Effectiveness of Human Resource Activities," *Academy of Management Review,* 1988, Vol. 13, No. 2, pp. 271–286.

33. For example, see John E. Delery and D. Harold Doty, "Modes of Theorizing in Strategic Human Resource Management: Tests of Universalistic, Contingency, and Configurational Performance Predictions," *Academy of Management,* August 1996, pp. 802–835.

34. Sources: *Hoover's Handbook of Private Companies 2006* (Austin, Tex.: Hoover's Business Press, 2006), pp. 154–155; Brian O'Reilly, "The Rent-A-Car Jocks Who Made Enterprise #1," *Fortune,* October 28, 1996, pp. 125–128; "Enterprise Takes Idea of Dressed for Success to a New Extreme," *Wall Street Journal,* November 20, 2002, p. B1.

Chapter 2

1. "Workers File Suit Over Long Hours," Associated Press news story published in the *Bryan-College Station Eagle,* August 3, 2002, pp. B1, B7.

2. David Israel, "Learn to Manage the Legal Process," *HRMagazine,* July 1993, pp. 83–87.

3. "HR and the Government," *HRMagazine,* May 1994, pp. 43–48. See also J. Ledvinka, *Federal Regulation of Personnel and Human Resource Management* (Boston, Mass.: Kent, 1982).

4. Jon M. Werner and Mark C. Bolino, "Explaining U.S. Court of Appeals Decisions Involving Performance Appraisal: Accuracy, Fairness, and Validation," *Personnel Psychology,* Spring 1997, pp. 1–24.

5. See Philip E. Varca and Patricia Pattison, "Evidentiary Standards in Employment Discrimination: A View Toward the Future," *Personnel Psychology,* Summer 1993, pp. 239–250.

6. *Diaz* v. *Pan American World Airways, Inc.,* 442 F. 2d 385 (5th Cir. 1971).

7. James E. Jones, William P. Murphy, and Robert Belton, *Discrimination in Employment,* 5th ed., American Casebook Series (St. Paul, Minn.: West Publishing Co., 1987, p. 381).

8. *Griggs* v. *Duke Power Company,* 401 U.S. 424 (1971).

9. Technically, neither guilt nor innocence is determined in civil cases. Instead, the defendant is judged to either be liable for discrimination or not liable for discrimination. We will use the terms *guilty* and *innocent* occasionally, however, because readers are more comfortable with these terms.

10. *Wards Cove Packing Co., Inc.* v. *Antonio,* U.S. Sup. Ct. 1387 (June 5, 1989).

11. *McDonnell-Douglas Corporation* v. *Green,* 411 U.S. 792 (1973).

12. "Culture of Racial Bias at Shoney's Underlines Chairman's Departure," *Wall Street Journal,* December 21, 1992, p. A1.

13. "When Quotas Replace Merit, Everybody Suffers," *Forbes,* February 15, 1993, pp. 80–102.

14. *Bakke* v. *The Regents of the University of California at Davis,* 438 U.S. 265 (1978).

15. *United Steelworkers of America, AFL-CIO* v. *Weber,* Sup. Ct. (1979); 443 U.S. 193; 99 S. Ct. 2721; 61 L. Ed. 2d 480.

16. *Wygant* v. *Jackson Board of Education,* Sup. Ct. (1986); 106 S. Ct. 1842; 90 L. Ed. 2d 260.

17. *Local 93 of the International Association of Firefighters, AFL-CIO, C.L.C.* v. *City of Cleveland,* Sup. Ct. (1986); 106 S. Ct. 3063, 92 L. Ed. 2d 405.

18. *U.S.* v. *Paradise,* Sup. Ct.; 478 US 1019; 106 S. Ct. 3331, 92 L. Ed. 2d737 (1986).

19. *Einsley Branch, NAACP* v. *Seibels,* 60 F. 3d 717 (11th Cir. 1994).

20. *Hopwood* v. *State of Texas,* 78 F. 3d 932 (5th Cir. 1996).

21. Jonathan A. Segal, "Sexual Harassment: Where Are We Now?" *HRMagazine,* October 1996, pp. 68–73; Gerald D. Block, "Avoiding Liability for Sexual Harassment," *HRMagazine,* April 1995, pp. 91–94.

22. *Meritor Savings Bank, FSB* v. *Vinson et al.,* Sup. Ct.; 477 U.S. 57 (1986).

23. *Harris* v. *Forklift Systems* 510 U.S. 17 (1993).

24. Jonathan A. Segal, "Proceed Carefully, Objectively to Investigate Sexual Harassment Claims," *HRMagazine,* October 1993, pp. 91–95.

25. *Scott* v. *Sears Roebuck,* 798 F. 2d 210 (7th cir. 1986).

26. *Oncale* v. *Sundowner Offshore Servs.,* 96 Sup. Ct. 568, 523 U.S. 75; S. Ct. 998; 140 L. Ed. 2d 201 (1998).

27. "Justices' Ruling Further Defines Sexual Harassment," *Wall Street Journal,* March 5, 1998, p. B1.

28. "How to Shrink the Pay Gap," *BusinessWeek,* June 24, 2002, p. 151.

29. *Johnson* v. *Mayor and City Council of Baltimore,* Sup. Ct. 105; S. Ct. 2727; 86 l. Ed. 2d 286 (1985).

30. "Recent Suits Make Pregnancy Issues Workplace Priorities," *Wall Street Journal,* January 14, 1998, p. B1.

31. The most noteworthy of these are the *Wards Cove* (1989) case discussed earlier, *Patterson* v. *McLean Credit Union* [109 S. Ct. 2363 (1989)] and *Pricewaterhouse* v. *Hopkins* [109 S. Ct. 1775 (1989)].

32. Most of these issues were decided in *EEOC* v. *Arabian American Oil Co.,* 89 Sup. Ct. 1838, 1845; 498 U.S. 808; 111 S. Ct. 40; 112 L. Ed. 2d 17 (1990).

33. Francine S. Hall and Elizabeth L. Hall, "The ADA: Going Beyond the Law," *The Academy of Management Executive,* February 1994, pp. 17–26.

34. Albert S. King, "Doing the Right Thing for Employees with Disabilities," *Training & Development,* September 1993, pp. 44–46.

35. "Disabilities Act Abused?" *USA Today,* September 25, 1998, pp. 1B, 2B.

36. Michael Barrier, "A Line in the Sand," *HRMagazine,* July 2002, pp. 35–43.

37. "Court Narrows Disability Act," *USA Today,* June 23, 1999, p. 1A.

38. For a review and a discussion of the determinants of this problem, see Adrienne Colella, "Coworker Distributive Fairness Judgments of the Workplace Accommodation of Employees with Disabilities," *Academy of Management Review,* 2001, Vol. 26, No. 1, pp. 100–116.

39. David Stamps, "Just How Scary Is the ADA?" *Training,* 1995, Vol. 32, pp. 93–101.

40. Michelle Neely Martinez, "FMLA—Headache or Opportunity?" *HRMagazine,* February 1994, pp. 42–45.

41. Jonathan A. Segal, "'Traps to Avoid in FMLA Compliance," *HRMagazine,* February 1994, pp. 97–100. See also Timothy Bland, "The Supreme Court Reins in the FMLA (Slightly)," *HRMagazine,* July 2002, pp. 44–48.

42. John Montoya, "New Priorities for the '90s," *HRMagazine,* April 1997, pp. 118–122.

43. David Israel, "Check EEOC Position Statements for Accuracy," *HRMagazine,* September 1993, pp. 106–109.

44. William R. Tracey, "Auditing ADA Compliance," *HRMagazine,* October 1994, pp. 88–93.

45. David C. Ankeny and David Israel, "Completing an On-Site OFCCP Audit," *HRMagazine,* March 1993, pp. 89–94.

46. "Maryland First to OK 'Wal-Mart Bill,'" *USA Today*, January 13, 2006, p. 1B; "SEC to Propose Overhaul of Rules On Executive Pay," *Wall Street Journal*, January 10, 2006, p. A1.

47. *Electromation* v. *NLRB*, US Court of Appeals for the 35 F. 3d 1148 (7th Cir. 1994).

48. *E.I. Du Pont de Nemours and Company* v. *NLRB*, 12 F. 3d 209 (5th Cir. 1993).

49. "Fewer Employers Are Currently Conducting Psych and Drug Tests," *HR Focus*, October 2000, p. 78.

50. Stephanie Overman, "Splitting Hairs," *HRMagazine*, August 1999, pp. 42–48.

51. "Laws, Juries Shift Protection to Terminated Employees," *USA Today*, April 2, 1998, pp. 1B, 2B.

52. "What to Do with Bad News," *HRMagazine*, July 2002, pp. 58–63.

53. Sources: "The *Seinfeld* Firing," *Wall Street Journal*, May 11, 1998, p. A20; "Ex-Miller Executive Wins Award in 'Seinfeld' Case," *Wall Street Journal*, July 16, 1997, p. B13.

Chapter 3

1. *Hoover's Handbook of World Business 2006* (Austin, Tex.: Hoover's Business Press, 2006); "In Mexico, a GM Worker Springs into the Middle Class," *Wall Street Journal*, July 29, 1998, pp. B1, B4; Ricky W. Griffin and Michael W. Pustay, *International Business—A Managerial Perspective*, 5th ed. (Upper Saddle River, N.J.: Prentice-Hall, 2007); Thomas L. Friedman, *The World Is Flat* (New York: Farrar, Straus, and Giroux, 2005).

2. Martha I. Finney, "Global Success Rides on Keeping Top Talent," *HRMagazine*, April 1996, pp. 68–74.

3. Gregory D. Chowanec and Charles N. Newstrom, "The Strategic Management of International Human Resources," *Business Quarterly*, Autumn 1991, pp. 65–70.

4. Griffin and Pustay, *International Business*.

5. Richard M. Steers, "The Cultural Imperative in HRM Research," in Albert Nedd (guest ed.), Gerald R. Ferris, and Kendrith M. Rowland (eds.), *Research in Personnel and Human Resources Management* (Supplement 1: International Human Resources Management) (Greenwich, Conn.: JAI Press, 1989), pp. 23–32.

6. Geert Hofstede, *Culture's Consequences: International Differences in Work-Related Values* (Beverly Hills, Calif.: Sage Publishers, 1980).

7. Nakiye Boyacigiller, "The Role of Expatriates in the Management of Interdependence, Complexity, and Risk in Multinational Corporations," *Journal of International Business Studies*, Vol. 21, No. 3, pp. 357–382.

8. See Richard Posthuma, Mark Roehling, and Michael Campion, "Applying U.S. Employment Discrimination Law to International Employers: Advice for Scientists and Practitioners," *Personnel Psychology*, Fall 2006, pp. 705–739.

9. Sakhawat Hossain and Herbert J. Davis, "Some Thoughts on International Personnel Management as an Emerging Field," in Albert Nedd (guest ed.), Gerald R. Ferris, and Kendrith M. Rowland (eds.), *Research in Personnel and Human Resources Management* (Supplement 1: International Human Resources Management) (Greenwich, Conn.: JAI Press, 1989, pp. 121–136).

10. Griffin and Pustay, *International Business*.

11. Ibid.

12. "The High Cost of Expatriation," *Management Review*, July 1990, pp. 40–41.

13. Cynthia Fetterolf, "Hiring Local Managers and Employees Overseas," *The International Executive*, May–June 1990, pp. 22–26.

14. "Bringing Back the Beetle," *Forbes*, April 7, 1997, pp. 42–44.

15. "What We Earn . . ." *Time*, November 2, 2006, p. 86.

16. Carla Johnson, "Save Thousands per Expatriate," *HRMagazine*, July 2002, pp. 73–77.

17. Winfred Arthur, Jr., and Winston Bennett, Jr., "The International Assignee: The Relative Importance of Factors Perceived to Contribute to Success," *Personnel Psychology*, Fall 1995, pp. 99–113.

18. J. Steward Black, Hal B. Gregersen, and Mark E. Mendenhall, *Global Assignments* (San Francisco, Calif.: Jossey-Bass, 1992).

19. See, for example, Ian Torbion, "Operative and Strategic Use of Expatriates in New Organizations and Market Structures," *International Studies of Management and Organization*, 1994, Vol. 24, pp. 5–17.

20. "Global Managers Need Boundless Sensitivity, Rugged Constitutions," *Wall Street Journal*, October 13, 1998, p. B1.

21. "Firms in Europe Try to Find Executives Who Can Cross Borders in a Single Bound," *Wall Street Journal*, January 25, 1991, p. B1.

22. "Younger Managers Learn Global Skills," *Wall Street Journal*, March 31, 1992, p. B1.

23. "As Costs of Overseas Assignments Climb, Firms Select Expatriates More Carefully," *Wall Street Journal*, January 9, 1992, pp. B1, B6.

24. J. Stewart Black and Hal B. Gregersen, "The Right Way to Manage Expats," *Harvard Business Review*, March–April 1999, pp. 52–62; see also Carla Johnson, "Save Thousands per Expatriate," *HRMagazine*, July 2002, pp. 73–77.

25. For example, see Paula Caligiuiri, MaryAnne Hyland, Aparna Joshi, and Allon Bross, "Testing a Theoretical Model for Examining the Relationship Between Family Adjustment and Expatriate Work Adjustment," *Journal of Applied Psychology*, 1998, Vol. 83, pp. 598–614.

26. Margaret Shaffer and David Harrison, "Expatriates' Psychological Withdrawal from International Assignments: Work, Nonwork, and Family Influences," *Personnel Psychology*, 1998, Vol. 51, pp. 87–96.

27. See review by Denis Ones and Chockalingam Viswesvaran, "Personality Determinants in the Prediction of Expatriate Job Success," in D. Saunders and Z. Aycan (eds.), *New Approaches to Employee Management*, 1994, Vol. 4, pp. 63–92; and the study by Paula Caligiuri, "The Big Five Personality Characteristics as Predictors of Expatriate's Desire to Terminate the Assignment and Supervisor-Rated Performance," *Personnel Psychology*, 2000, Vol. 53, pp. 67–88.

28. See G. W. Florkowski and D. S. Fogel, "Expatriate Adjustment and Commitment: The Role of Host-Unit Treatment," *International Journal of Human Resource Management*, 1999, Vol. 10, pp. 783–807.

29. For a more complete discussion of this potential problem, see Soo Min Toh and Angelo DeNisi, "Host Country National Reactions to Expatriate Pay Policies: A Proposed Model and Some Implications," *Academy of Management Review*, 2003, Vol. 28, pp. 606–621.

30. "Companies Use Cross-Cultural Training to Help Their Employees Adjust Abroad," *Wall Street Journal*, August 9, 1992, pp. B1, B6.

31. Paul Vanderbroeck, "Long-Term Human Resource Development in Multinational Organizations," *Sloan Management*

Review, Fall 1992, pp. 95–99; See also Carl Fey, Antonina Pavlovskaya, and Ningyu Tang, "A Comparison of Human Resource Management in Russia, China, and Finland," *Organizational Dynamics,* Vol. 33, No. 1, 2004, pp. 79–97.

32. Kathryn Tyler, "Targeted Language Training Is Best Bargain," *HRMagazine,* January 1998, pp. 61–68.

33. Frank Jossi, "Successful Handoff," *HRMagazine,* October 2002, pp. 48–52.

34. K. Cushner and Richard Brislin, *International Interactions: A Practical Guide* (Thousand Oaks, Calif.: Sage Publishing, 2000).

35. Simca Ronen, "Training the International Assignee," in I.L. Goldstein and Associates, *Training and Development in Organizations* (New York: Jossey-Bass, 1989), p. 418.

36. Richard M. Hodgetts and Fred Luthans, "U.S. Multinationals' Compensation Strategies," *Compensation & Benefits Review,* January–February 1993, pp. 57–62.

37. Michael J. Bishko, "Compensating Your Overseas Executives, Part 1: Strategies for the 1990s," *Compensation & Benefits Review,* May–June 1990, pp. 33–43.

38. "For Executives Around the Globe, Pay Packages Aren't Worlds Apart," *Wall Street Journal,* October 12, 1992, pp. B1, B5.

39. Stephanie Overman, "In Sync," *HRMagazine,* March 2000, pp. 86–92.

40. See Carla Johnson, "Save Thousands per Expatriate," *HRMagazine,* July 2002, pp. 73–77.

41. Robert O'Connor, "Plug the Expat Knowledge Drain," *HRMagazine,* October 2002, pp. 101–107.

42. Andrea Poe, "Welcome Back," *HRMagazine,* March 2000, pp. 94–105.

43. National Foreign Trade Council report, cited in Carla Johnson, "Save Thousands per Expatriate," *HRMagazine,* July 2002, pp. 73–77.

44. Sources: "Gentlemen, Start Your Engines," *Fortune,* June 8, 1998, pp. 138–146; James Aley and Matt Siegel, "The Fallout from Merger Mania," *Fortune,* March 2, 1998, pp. 26–56; "Labor Holds a Key to Fate of Daimler-Chrysler Merger," *Wall Street Journal,* May 7, 1998, pp. B1, B18; "Oil Companies Pump Out $50 Billion Merger Deal," *USA Today,* August 12, 1998, pp. 1B, 2B.

Chapter 4

1. "The Starbucks Strategy," *Washington Post,* September 1, 2002, pp. E1, E6; "Brewing a British Coup," *USA Today,* September 16, 1998, pp. 1D, 2D; Jennifer Reese, "Starbucks—Inside the Coffee Cult," *Fortune,* December 9, 1996, pp. 190–200 (*quote on p. 196); *Hoover's Handbook of American Business 2006* (Austin: Hoover's Business Press, 2006), pp. 806–807.

2. Charles R. Greer, *Strategy and Human Resources* (Englewood Cliffs, N.J.: Prentice-Hall, 1995).

3. The points in the debate are best explained in Brian Becker and Barry Gerhart, "The Impact of Human Resource Management on Organizational Performance: Progress and Prospects," *Academy of Management Journal,* August 1996, pp. 779–801. The different sides are represented in Mark A. Huselid, "The Impact of Human Resource Management Practices on Turnover, Productivity, and Corporate Financial Reporting," *Academy of Management Journal,* 1995, Vol. 38, pp. 635–672; John Delery and D. Harold Doty, "Modes of Theorizing in Strategic Human Resource Management: Tests of Universalistic, Contingency, and Configurational Perfor-

mance Predictions," *Academy of Management Journal,* 1995, Vol. 38, pp. 802–835; and Patrick Wright, Dennis Smart, and Gary McMahan, "Matches Between Human Resources and Strategy Among NCAA Basketball Teams," *Academy of Management Journal,* Vol. 38, No. 5, pp. 1052–1074.

4. To read more about this model, see Jay Barney, "Firm Resources and Sustained Competitive Advantage," *Journal of Management,* 1991, Vol. 17, pp. 99–120; and Jay Barney, "Is the Resource-based 'View' a Useful Perspective for Strategic Management Research? Yes," *Academy of Management Review,* 2001, Vol. 26, pp. 41–56.

5. See Charles W. L. Hill and Gareth R. Jones, *Strategic Management: An Analytical Approach,* 7th ed. (Boston, Mass.: Houghton Mifflin, 2007).

6. Janine Nahapiet and Sumantra Ghoshal, "Social Capital, Intellectual Capital, and the Organizational Advantage," *Academy of Management Review,* 1998, Vol. 23, pp. 242–266.

7. Catherine M. Daily and Charles Schwenk, "Chief Operating Officers, Top Management Teams, and Boards of Directors: Congruent or Countervailing Forces?" *Journal of Management,* 1996, Vol. 22, No. 2, pp. 185–208.

8. S. A. Kirkpatrick and Edwin A. Locke, "Direct and Indirect Effects of Three Core Charismatic Leadership Components on Performance and Attitudes," *Journal of Applied Psychology,* 1996, Vol. 81, pp. 36–51; see also Harry G. Barkema and Luis R. Gomez-Mejia, "Managerial Compensation and Firm Performance: A General Research Framework," *Academy of Management Journal,* 1998, Vol. 41, pp. 135–145.

9. See, for example, Donald C. Hambrick and Sidney Finkelstein, "Managerial Discretion: A Bridge Between Polar Views on Organizations," in L. L. Cummings and B. Staw (eds.) *Research in Organizational Behavior,* Vol. 9 (Greenwich, Conn.: JAI Press, 1987, pp. 369–406); or Sidney Finkelstein and Donald Hambrick, "Top Management Team Tenure and Organizational Outcomes: The Moderating Role of Managerial Discretion," *Administration Science Quarterly,* Vol. 35, 1990, pp. 484–503.

10. Hill and Jones, *Strategic Management: An Analytical Approach.*

11. Brian Becker and Barry Gerhart, "The Impact of Human Resource Management on Organizational Performance: Progress and Prospects," *Academy of Management Journal,* August 1996, Volume 39, No. 4, pp. 779–801.

12. Donald Laurie, Yves Doz, and Claude Sheer, "Creating New Growth Platforms," *Harvard Business Review,* May 2006, pp. 80–92.

13. David M. Schweiger and James P. Walsh, "Mergers and Acquisitions: An Interdisciplinary View," in Kenneth Rowland and Gerald Ferris (eds.), *Research in Personnel and Human Resource Management,* Vol. 8 (Greenwich, Conn.: JAI Press, 1990), pp. 41–107.

14. David M. Schweiger and Angelo DeNisi, "Communications with Employees Following a Merger: A Longitudinal Field Study," *Academy of Management Journal,* 1991, Vol. 34, pp. 110–135.

15. Hill and Jones, *Strategic Management: An Analytical Approach.*

16. Jay Barney and Ricky W. Griffin, *The Management of Organizations* (Boston, Mass.: Houghton Mifflin, 1992).

17. Russell A. Eisenstat, "What Corporate Human Resources Brings to the Picnic: Four Models for Functional Management," *Organizational Dynamics,* Autumn 1996, pp. 7–21.

18. John O. Whitney, "Strategic Renewal for Business Units," *Harvard Business Review,* July–August 1996, pp. 84–98.

19. Raymond E. Miles and Charles C. Snow, *Organizational Strategy, Structure, and Process* (New York: McGraw-Hill, 1978).

20. Michael Porter, *Competitive Strategy* (New York: Free Press, 1980).

21. Robert L. Cardy and Gregory H. Dobbins, "Human Resource Management in a Total Quality Organizational Environment: Shifting from a Traditional to a TQHRM Approach," *Journal of Quality Management,* 1996, Vol. 1, No. 1, pp. 5–20.

22. Henry Mintzberg, "Patterns in Strategy Formulation," *Management Science,* October 1978, pp. 934–948.

23. David Fiedler, "Know When to Hold 'Em," *HRMagazine,* August 2002, pp. 89–94.

24. Edilberto F. Montemayor, "Congruence Between Pay Policy and Competitive Strategy in High-Performing Firms," *Journal of Management,* 1996, Vol. 22, No. 6, pp. 889–912.

25. David Lepak and Scott Snell, "The Human Resource Architecture: Toward a Theory of Human Capital Allocation and Development," *Academy of Management Journal,* Vol. 24, No. 1, pp. 31–48; David Lepak and Scott Snell, "Examining the Human Resource Architecture: The Relationships Among Human Capital, Employment, and Human Resource Configuration," *Journal of Management,* 2002, Vol. 28, No. 4, pp. 517–544; David Lepak and Scott Snell, "Managing the Human Resource Architecture for Knowledge-Based Competition," in Susan Jackson, Michael Hitt, and Angelo DeNisi (eds.), *Managing Knowledge for Sustained Competitive Advantage: Designing Strategies for Effective Human Resource Management* (San Francisco, Calif.: Jossey-Bass, 2003), pp. 127–154.

26. Peter Bamberger and Avi Fiegenbaum, "The Role of Strategic Reference Points in Explaining the Nature and Consequences of Human Resource Strategy," *Academy of Management Review,* October 1996, pp. 926–958.

27. Richard L. Daft, *Organization Theory and Design* (St. Paul, Minn.: West, 2007).

28. John Purcell and Bruce Ahlstrand, *Human Resource Management in the Multi-Divisional Company* (Oxford: Oxford University Press, 1994).

29. Terrence E. Deal and Allan A. Kennedy, *Corporate Cultures: The Rights and Rituals of Corporate Life* (Reading, Mass.: Addison-Wesley, 1982).

30. Jay Barney, "Organizational Culture: Can It Be a Source of Sustained Competitive Advantage?" *Academy of Management Review,* July 1986, pp. 656–665.

31. See, for example, David Jemison and Sim Sitkin, "Corporate Acquisitions: A Process Perspective," *Academy of Management Review,* 1986, Vol. 11, No. 1, pp. 145–163; or Nancy Napier, "Mergers and Acquisitions, Human Resource Issues and Outcomes: A Review and Suggested Typology," *Journal of Management Studies,* 1989, Vol. 26, No. 3, pp. 271–289.

32. See discussion of this strategy in Bruce Nissen, "The 'Social Movement' Dynamics of Living Wage Campaigns," in Paula Voos (ed.), *Proceedings of the 53rd Annual Meeting of the Industrial Relations Research Association,* Industrial Relations Research Association, Washington D.C., January 2001, pp. 232–240.

33. Lawrence Hrebiniak, "Obstacles to Effective Strategy Implementation," *Organizational Dynamics,* Fall 2006, pp. 12-31.

34. Gary Johns, "The Essential Impact of Context on Organizational Behavior," *Academy of Management Review,* 2006, Vol. 31, No. 2, pp. 386–408.

35. Denise Rousseau, "Changing the Deal While Keeping the People," *The Academy of Management Executive,* February 1996, pp. 50–61.

36. Elizabeth Wolfe Morrison and Sandra L. Robinson, "When Employees Feel Betrayed: A Model of How Psychological Contract Violation Develops," *Academy of Management Review,* January 1997, pp. 226–256; Sandra Robinson, Matthew Kraatz, and Denise Rousseau, "Changing Obligations and the Psychological Contract," *Academy of Management Journal,* 1994, Vol. 37, No. 1, pp. 137–152.

37. Murray Barrick and Michael Mount, "The Big Five Personality Dimensions and Job Performance: A Meta-Analysis," *Personnel Psychology,* 1991, Vol. 44, No. 1, pp. 1–26.

38. Leslie DeChurch and Michelle Marks, "Leadership In Multiteam Systems," *Journal of Applied Psychology,* 2006, Vol. 91, No. 2, pp. 311–329.

39. Several critical measurement issues are raised in Barry Gerhart, Patrick Wright, Gary McMahan, and Scott Snell, "Measurement Error in Research on Human Resources and Firm Performance: How Much Error Is There and How Does It Influence Size Estimates?" *Personnel Psychology,* 2000, Vol. 53, No. 4, pp. 803–834.

40. See, for example, Mark A. Huselid, "The Impact of Human Resource Management Practices on Turnover, Productivity, and Corporate Financial Reporting," *Academy of Management Journal,* 1995, Vol. 38, pp. 635–672; or Rajiv Banker, Joy Field, Roger Schroeder, and Kingshuk Sinha, "Impact of Work Teams on Manufacturing Performance: A Longitudinal Study," *Academy of Management Journal,* 1996, Vol. 39, No. 4, pp. 867–890.

41. Sources: Brian Grow, "Renovating Home Depot," *BusinessWeek,* March 6, 2006, pp. 50–58; Jennifer Reingold, "Bob Nardelli Is Watching," *Fast Company,* December 2005, pp. 58–60; George Stalk, Rob Lachenauer, and John Butman, *Hardball: Are You Playing to Play or Playing to Win?* (Cambridge, Mass.: Harvard Business School Press, 2004).

Taking HR to the Next Level 1

1. See Ricky Griffin and Michael Pustay, *International Business,* 5th Edition (Upper Saddle River, NJ: Prentice-Hall, 2008).

2. See for example, Jean Hailey, "The Expatriate Myth: Cross-Cultural Perceptions of Expatriate Managers," *The International Executive,* 1996, Vol. 38, pp. 255–271; or Mark Vatiokis, M. Clifford, and J. McBeth, "The Lure of Asia," *Far Eastern Economic Review,* 1994, Vol. 157, pp. 32–34.

3. Christopher Barlett and Sumatra Ghoshal, "Building Competitive Advantage Through People," *MIT Sloan Management Review,* 2002, Vol. 43, pp. 34–41.

4. Michael Hitt, R. Duane Ireland, and Robert Hoskisson, *Strategic Management: Competitiveness and Globalization,* 3rd ed. (Cincinnati: South-Western College Publishers, 2005).

5. Angelo DeNisi, Soo Min Toh, and Brian Connelly, "Maximizing the Expatriate–Host Country National Relationship for Successful International Assignments," in M. J. Morley, N. Heraty, and D. Collings (eds.), *International HRM and International Assignments* (Hampshire, United Kingdom: Palgrave Macmillan Publishers, 2006), pp. 147–171.

6. N. Malhotra, "The Nature of Knowledge and the Entry Mode Decision," *Organization Studies,* 2003, Vol. 24, pp. 937–959.

7. See discussion in Dennis Briscoe and Randall Schuler, *International Human Resource Management,* 2nd ed. (London, UK: Routledge, 2004).

8. See review by Gunter Stahl, Mark Mendenhall, Amy Pablo, and Mansour Javidan, "Sociocultural Integration in Mergers and Acquisitions," in Gunter Stahl and Mark Mendenhall (eds.), Mergers *and Acquisitions: Managing the Culture and*

Human Resources (Stanford, Calif.: Stanford University Press, 2005), pp. 3–16.

9. See discussion of various reasons for success and failure of mergers and acquisitions in A. T. Kearney, *White Paper on Post Merger Integration,* KPMG Report, 1998.

10. For further discussion of these processes see H. Tajfel and J. C. Turner, "An Integrative Theory of Intergroup Conflict," in W. Austin and S. Worchel (eds.), *The Social Psychology of Intergroup Psychology* (Monterey, Calif.: Brooks-Cole, 1979), pp. 33–47.

11. David Schweiger and Angelo DeNisi, "The Effects of Communication with Employees Following a Merger: A Longitudinal Field Experiment," *Academy of Management Journal,* 1991, Vol. 34, pp. 110–135.

12. For more detail a further discussion of these processes in the context of a merger or acquisition, see Angelo DeNisi and Shung Jae Shin, "Psychological Communication Interventions in Mergers and Acquisitions," in Gunter Stahl and Mark Mendenhall (eds.), *Mergers and Acquisitions: Managing the Culture and Human Resources* (Stanford, Calif.: Stanford University Press, 2005), pp. 228–249.

Chapter 5

1. Adapted from "While Hiring at Most Firms Chills, Wal-Mart's Heats Up," from *USA Today,* August 26, 2002, p. 3B. Copyright © 2002 *USA Today.* Reprinted with permission. See also *Hoover's Handbook of American Business 2006* (Austin: Hoover's Business Press, 2006), pp. 910-912.

2. Lee Dyer, "Human Resource Planning," in K. Rowland and G. Ferris (eds.), *Personnel Management* (Boston, Mass.: Allyn & Bacon, 1982), pp. 52–77.

3. R. G. Murdick and F. Schuster, "Computerized Information Support for the Human Resource Function," *Human Resource Planning,* 1983, Vol. 6, No. 1, pp. 25–35.

4. Taylor H. Cox and Stacy Blake, "Managing Cultural Diversity: Implications for Organizational Competitiveness," *The Academy of Management Executive,* August 1991, pp. 45–56.

5. "The Geography of Work," *Time,* June 22, 1998, pp. 98–102.

6. Carla Johnson, "Developing a Strong Bench," *HRMagazine,* January 1998, pp. 92–97.

7. "P&G Will Make Jager CEO Ahead of Schedule," *Wall Street Journal,* September 10, 1998, pp. B1, B8. *Hoover's Handbook of American Business 2006* (Austin: Hoover's Business Press, 2006), pp. 706-708.

8. "Firms Plan to Keep Hiring, Spending," *USA Today,* January 26, 1995, p. B1.

9. "Firms Find Ways to Grow Without Expanding Staffs," *Wall Street Journal,* March 18, 1993, pp. B1, B2.

10. Donald Laurie, Yves Doz, and Claude Sheer, "Creating New Growth Platforms," *Harvard Business Review,* May 2006, pp. 80-92.

11. "When UPS Demanded Workers, Louisville Did the Delivering," *Wall Street Journal,* April 24, 1998, pp. A1, A10; *Hoover's Handbook of American Business 2006* (Austin: Hoover's Business Press, 2006), pp. 873-874.

12. "Layoffs on Wall Street Will Bruise Big Apple," *USA Today,* October 15, 1998, p. 1B; "Its Share Shrinking, Levi Strauss Lays Off 6,395," *Wall Street Journal,* November 4, 1997, pp. B1, B8.

13. See especially, Roger Griffeth, Peter Hom, and Stefan Gaertner, "A Meta-Analysis of Antecedents and Correlates of Employee Turnover: Update, Moderator Tests, and Research Implications for the Next Millennium", *Journal of Manage-*

ment, 2000, Vol. 26, pp. 463-488; and Charlie Trevor, "Interactions Among Actual Ease of Movement Determinants and Job Satisfaction in the Prediction of Voluntary Turnover", *Academy of Management Journal,* 2001, Vol. 44, pp. 621-638.

14. For a more detailed discussion of this phenomenon, applied to human resource management, see Edward Lazear, *Personnel Economics for Managers* (New York: Wiley, 1998).

15. E. J. McCormick, *Job Analysis: Methods and Applications* (New York: American Management Association, 1979).

16. Greer, *Strategy and Human Resources.*

17. A. S. DeNisi, "The Implications of Job Clustering for Training Programmes," *Journal of Occupational Psychology,* Vol. 49, pp. 105–113.

18. K. Pearlman, "Job Families: A Review and Discussion of Their Implications for Personnel Selection," *Psychological Bulletin,* Vol. 87, pp. 1–27.

19. McCormick, *Job Analysis: Methods and Applications.*

20. U.S. Department of Labor, Employment, and Training Administration, *The Revised Handbook for Analyzing Jobs* (Washington, D.C.: U.S. Government Printing Office, 1991).

21. Frank Landy and Joseph Vasey, "Job Analysis: The Composition of SME Samples," *Personnel Psychology,* Vol. 44, No. 1, 1991, pp. 27–50.

22. Ibid.

23. U.S. Department of Labor, Employment, and Training Administration, *The Revised Handbook for Analyzing Jobs.*

24. E. A. Fleishman, *Manual for the Ability Requirements Scale* (MARS, revised) (Palo Alto, Calif.: Consulting Psychologists Press, 1991).

25. For example, see J. E. Morsh, *Job Types Identified with an Inventory Constructed by Electronics Engineers* (Lackland Air Force Base, San Antonio, Tex. U.S. Air Force Personnel Research Laboratory, 1966).

26. S. A. Fine and W. W. Wiley, *An Introduction to Functional Job Analysis* (Kalamazoo, Mich.: W. E. Upjohn Institute for Employment Research, 1971).

27. E. J. McCormick, P. R. Jeanneret, and R. C. Mecham, "A Study of Job Characteristics and Job Dimensions as Based on the Position Analysis Questionnaire (PAQ), *Journal of Applied Psychology,* 1972, Vol. 56, pp. 347–368.

28. McCormick, *Job Analysis: Methods and Applications.*

29. See, for example, E. J. McCormick, P. R. Jeanneret, and R. C. Mecham, " A Study of Job Characteristics and Job Dimensions as Based on the Position Analysis Questionnaire (PAQ)," *Journal of Applied Psychology,* 1972, Vol. 56, pp. 347–368; or E. J. McCormick, A. S. DeNisi, and J. B. Shaw, "The Use of the Position Analysis Questionnaire (PAQ) for Establishing the Job Component Validity of Tests," *Journal of Applied Psychology,* 1978, Vol. 64, pp. 51–56.

30. A. S. DeNisi, E. T. Cornelius, and A. G. Blencoe, "A Further Investigation of Common Knowledge Effects on Job Analysis Ratings: On the Applicability of the PAQ for All Jobs," *Journal of Applied Psychology,* 1987, Vol. 72, pp. 262–268.

31. Walter Tornow and Patrick Pinto, "The Development of a Managerial Job Taxonomy: A System for Describing, Classifying, and Evaluating Executive Positions," *Journal of Applied Psychology,* 1976, Vol. 61, pp. 410–418.

32. J. C. Flanagan, "The Critical Incident Technique," *Psychological Bulletin,* Vol. 51, pp. 327–358.

33. Norman Peterson, Michael Mumford, Walter Borman, P. Richard Jeanneret, Edwin Fleishman, Kerry Levin, Michael Campion, Melinda Mayfield, Frederick Morgeson, Kenneth Pearlman, Marilyn Gowing, Anita Lancaster, Marilyn Silver,

and Donna Dye, "Understanding Work Using the Occupational Information Network (O*NET): Implications for Practice and Research," *Personnel Psychology,* 2001, Vol. 54, pp. 451–492.

34. Milan Moravec and Robert Tucker, "Job Descriptions for the 21st Century," *Personnel Journal,* June 1992, pp. 37–40.

35. Karen Cook and Patricia Bernthal, *Job/Role Competency Practices Survey Report* (Bridgeville, Pa.: Development Dimensions Incorporated, 1998).

36. For an excellent review of the various issues associated with competency modeling, the reader is referred to Jeffrey Shippman, Ronald Ash, Mariangela Battista, Linda Carr, Lorraine Eyde, Beryl Hesketh, Jerry Kehoe, Kenneth Pearlman, Erich Prien, and Juan Sanchez, "The Practice of Competency Modeling," *Personnel Psychology,* 2000, Vol. 53, pp. 703–740.

37. *Albermarle Paper Co. v. Moody,* Sup. Ct. of the U.S., 1975, 422 U.S. 405, 95 S. Ct. 2362, L. Ed. 2d. 280.

38. For a complete discussion of these sources of inaccuracy, see Frederick Morgeson and Michael Campion, "Social and Cognitive Sources of Potential Inaccuracy in Job Analysis," *Journal of Applied Psychology,* 1998, Vol. 82, pp. 627–655.

39. Richard Arvey, "Sex Bias in Job Evaluation Procedures," *Personnel Psychology,* 1986, Vol. 39, pp. 315–335.

40. *Electromation Inc.* v. *National Labor Relations Board,* 1992.

41. Sources: "These Six Growth Jobs Are Dull, Dead-End, Sometimes Dangerous," *Wall Street Journal,* December 1, 1994, pp. A1, A8; *Hoover's Handbook of American Business 2006* (Austin, Tex.: Hoover's Business Press, 2006). See also the continuing television series *Dirty Jobs.*

Chapter 6

1. Lisa Takeguchi Cullen, "Where Did Everyone Go?" *Time,* November 18, 2002, pp. 64–66 (*quote on p. 65); "Lower Paid Workers Face Job Cuts," CNN Money website, cnn-money.com; "Pink Slip Blizzard," CBS News website; *Hoover's Handbook of American Business 2006* (Austin: Hoover's Business Press, 2006).

2. "Living Overtime: A Factory Workaholic," *Wall Street Journal,* October 13, 1998, p. B1.

3. Gilbert Nicholson, "Get Your Benefit Ducks in a Row," *Workforce,* September 2000, pp. 78–84.

4. Lee Phillion and John Brugger, "Encore! Retirees Give Top Performance as Temporaries," *HRMagazine,* October 1994, pp. 74–78.

5. See especially David Lepak and Scott Snell, "The Human Resource Architecture: Toward a Theory of Human Capital Allocation and Development," *Academy of Management Review,* 1999, Vol. 24, pp. 31–48.

6. See Sylvia Roch and Linda Shanock, "Organizational Justice in an Exchange Framework: Clarifying Organizational Justice Distinctions," *Journal of Management,* April 2006, pp. 299–322.

7. J. Stacy Adams, "Inequity in Social Exchange," in L. Berkowitz (ed.), *Advances in Experimental Social Psychology,* Vol. 2 (New York: Academic Press, 1965), pp. 267–299.

8. Gerald Leventhal, "The Distribution of Rewards and Resources in Groups and Organizations," in L. Berkowitz and W. Walster (eds.), *Advances in Experimental Social Psychology,* Vol. 9 (New York: Academic Press, 1976), pp. 91–131.

9. Joel Brockner and Batia Wiesenfeld, "An Integrative Framework for Explaining Reactions to Decisions: Integrative Effects of Outcomes and Procedures," *Psychological Bulletin,* 1996, Vol. 120, pp. 189–298.

10. Robert Bies and Joseph Moag, "Interactional Justice: Communication Criteria of Fairness," in R. Lewicki, B. Sheppard, and M. Bazerman (eds.), *Research on Negotiations in Organizations,* Vol. 1 (Greenwich, Conn.: JAI Press, 1986), pp. 43–55.

11. Jerald Greenberg, "The Social Side of Fairness: Interpersonal and Informational Classes of Organizational Justice," in R. Cropanzano (ed.), *Justice in the Workplace: Approaching Fairness in Human Resource Management* (Hillsdale, N.J.: Erlbaum, 1993), pp. 79–103.

12. Wayne Cascio, Clifford Young, and James Morris, "Financial Consequences of Employment Change Decisions in Major U.S. Corporations," *Academy of Management Journal,* 1997, Vol. 40, pp. 1175–1189.

13. For example, see Dan Worrell, Wallace Davidson, and Varinder Sharma, "Layoff Announcements and Stockholder Wealth," *Academy of Management Journal,* 1991, Vol. 34, pp. 662–678.

14. Joel Brockner, "The Effects of Work Layoffs on Survivors: Research, Theory and Practice," in B. Staw and L. Cummings (eds.), *Research in Organizational Behavior,* Vol. 10. (Greenwich, Conn.: JAI Press, 1988), pp. 213–215.

15. American Management Association, *Corporate Job Creation, Job Elimination, and Downsizing: Summary of Key Findings* (New York: American Management Association, 1997).

16. Fay Hansen, "Employee Assistance Programs (EAPs) Grow and Expand Their Reach," *Compensation and Benefits Review,* March–April 2000, p. 13.

17. See, for example, Meg Bryant, "Testing EAPs for Coordination," *Business and Health,* August 1991, pp. 20–24; or Barbara Pflaum, "Seeking Sane Solutions: Managing Mental Health and Chemical Dependency Costs," *Employee Benefits Journal,* 1992, Vol. 16, pp. 31–35.

18. James Smith, "EAPs Evolve to Health Plan Gatekeepers," *Employee Benefit Plan Review,* 1992, Vol. 46, pp. 18–19.

19. M. R. Buckley and W. Weitzel, "Employment at Will," *Personnel Administrator,* 1988, Vol. 33, pp. 78–80.

20. *Toussaint* v. *Blue Cross and Blue Shield of Michigan,* 408 Michigan, 529, 292 N.W. 2d 880 (1980).

21. *Fortune* v. *National Cash Register,* 364 Massachusetts 91, 36 N.E. 2d 1251 (1977).

22. This approach was pioneered by Union Carbide; see A. B. Chimezie, Osigweh Yg, and William Hutchinson, "To Punish or Not to Punish: Managing Human Resources Through Positive Discipline," *Employee Relations,* March 1990, pp. 27–32. For a more complete picture, see Dick Grove, *Discipline Without Punishment* (New York: American Management Association, 1996).

23. See, for example, Michael Abelson and Barry Baysinger, "Optimal and Dysfunctional Turnover: Toward an Organizational Level Model," *Academy of Management Review,* 1984, Vol. 9, pp. 331–341.

24. On the positive side, job satisfaction has been defined as the positive feeling that "results from the perception that one's job fulfills . . . one's important job values." See Edwin Locke, "The Nature and Causes of Job Dissatisfaction," in M. Dunnette (ed.), *Handbook of Industrial and Organizational Psychology* (Chicago, Ill.: Rand McNally, 1976), pp. 901–969.

25. For an excellent review of this literature, see Charles Hulin, Mary Roznowski, and Dan Hachiya, "Alternative Opportunities and Withdrawal Decisions," *Psychological Bulletin,* 1985, Vol. 97, pp. 233–250.

26. The original model was presented in William Mobley, "Intermediate Linkages in the Relationship Between Job Satisfaction and Employee Turnover," *Journal of Applied Psychology,* 1977, Vol. 62, pp. 237–240. A refined model was later presented in Peter Hom and Roger Griffeth, "A Structural Equations Modeling Test of a Turnover Theory: Cross Sectional and Longitudinal Analysis," *Journal of Applied Psychology,* 1991, Vol. 76, pp. 350–366.

27. John Sheridan and Michael Abelson, "Cusp-Catastrophe Model of Employee Turnover," *Academy of Management Journal,* 1983, Vol. 26, pp. 418–436.

28. Thomas Lee and Terrence Mitchell, "An Alternative Approach: The Unfolding Model of Voluntary Employee Turnover," *Academy of Management Review,* 1994, Vol. 19, pp. 51–89.

29. Terrence Mitchell, Brooks Holtom, Thomas Lee, Christopher Sablynski, and Miriam Erez, "Why People Stay: Using Job Embeddedness to Predict Voluntary Turnover," *Academy of Management Journal,* 2001, Vol. 44, pp. 1102–1121.

30. Richard Arvey, Thomas Bouchard, Neal Segal, and Len Abraham, "Job Satisfaction: Genetic and Environmental Components," *Journal of Applied Psychology,* 1989, Vol. 74, pp. 187–193.

31. See, for example, Barry Staw, Nancy Bell, and J. Clausen, "The Dispositional Approach to Job Attitudes: A Lifetime Attitudinal Test," *Administrative Science Quarterly,* 1986, Vol. 31, pp. 56–78; and Timothy Judge, "Does Affective Disposition Moderate the Relationship Between Job Satisfaction and Affective Turnover?" *Journal of Applied Psychology,* 1993, Vol. 78, pp. 395–401.

32. Barry Gerhart, "How Important Are Dispositional Factors as Determinants of Job Satisfaction? Implications for Job Design and Other Personnel Programs," *Journal of Applied Psychology,* 1987, Vol. 72, pp. 493–502.

33. See Locke, "The Nature and Causes of Job Dissatisfaction," for a review of the literature on these determinants of job satisfaction.

34. Bruce Meglino, Elizabeth Ravlin, and Cheryl Adkins, "A Work Values Approach to Corporate Culture: A Field Test of the Value Congruence Process and Its Relationship to Individual Outcomes," *Journal of Applied Psychology,* 1989, Vol. 74, pp. 424–433.

35. For an excellent review of the relationship between leader behavior and employees' reactions, such as satisfaction, see Victor Vroom, "Leadership," in M. Dunnette (ed.), *Handbook of Industrial and Organizational Psychology* (Chicago, Ill.: Rand McNally, 1986), pp. 560–663.

36. Rick Hackett and Robert Guion, "A Re-evaluation of the Job Satisfaction-Absenteeism Relation," *Organizational Behavior and Human Decision Processes,* 1985, Vol. 35, pp. 340–381.

37. Richard Mowday, Richard Steers, and Lyman Porter, "The Measurement of Organizational Commitment," *Journal of Vocational Behavior,* 1979, Vol. 14, pp. 224–247.

38. See, for example, Chester Schriesheim, "Job Satisfaction, Attitudes Towards Unions, and Voting in a Union Representation Election," *Journal of Applied Psychology,* 1978, Vol. 63, pp. 548–553; for a somewhat more complex model that still focuses on job dissatisfaction, see Stuart Youngblood, Angelo DeNisi, Julie Molleston, and William Mobley, "The Impact of Worker Attachment, Instrumentality Beliefs, Perceived Labor Union Image, and Subjective Norms on Voting Intentions and Union Membership," *Academy of Management Journal,* 1994, Vol. 15, pp. 576–590.

39. The original research is summarized in Dennis Organ, *Organizational Citizenship Behavior: The Good Soldier Syndrome* (Lexington, Mass.: Heath, 1988).

40. See Walter Borman, "Job Behavior, Performance and Effectiveness," in M. Dunnette and L. Hough (eds.), *Handbook of Industrial and Organizational Psychology,* Vol. 1, 2nd ed. (Palo Alto, Calif.: Consulting Psychologists Press, 1991), pp. 271–326.

41. See the discussion in Susan Jackson, Donald Schwab, and Randall Schuler, "Toward an Understanding of the Burnout Phenomenon," *Journal of Applied Psychology,* 1986, Vol. 71, pp. 630–640. For an update and a more complex model, see Evangelia Demerouti, Arnold Bakker, Friedhelm Nachreiner, and Wilmar Schaufei, "The Job Demands-Resources Model of Burnout," *Journal of Applied Psychology,* 2001, Vol. 86, pp. 499–512.

42. See Locke, "The Nature and Causes of Job Dissatisfaction," for a review.

43. Patricia Smith, Lorne Kendall, and Charles Hulin, *The Measurement of Satisfaction in work and Retirement* (Chicago, Ill.: Rand McNally, 1969).

44. Theodore Kunin, "The Construction of a New Type of Attitude Measure," *Personnel Psychology,* 1955, Vol. 8, pp. 65–78.

45. Sources: Andrea Poe, "Keeping Hotel Workers," *HRMagazine,* February 2003, pp. 91–93; "America's Top 500 Companies," *Forbes,* April 14, 2003, pp. 144–172.

Chapter 7

1. "Screener Shortage Causes Long Wait at Airport," *Palm Beach Post,* April 18, 2006, p. A1; "9.11.02," *BusinessWeek,* September 16, 2002, pp. 34–38; "Airport Screening Hits Barrier: No Staff," Associated Press wire story as published in the *Bryan-College Station Eagle,* July 29, 2002, p. A3 (*quote on p. A3); "Feds Take Over Airport Screening," *USA Today,* November 18, 2002, pp. 1A, 2A.

2. James A. Breaugh. *Recruitment: Science and Practice* (Boston, Mass.: PWS-Kent, 1992).

3. Robert Bretz, Jr., and Timothy Judge, "The Role of Human Resource Systems in Job Applicant Decision Processes," *Journal of Management,* 1994, Vol. 20, No. 3, pp. 531–551.

4. Allison Barber, Christina Daly, Cristina Giannatonio, and Jean Phillips, "Job Search Activities: An Examination of Changes Over Time," *Personnel Psychology,* 1994, Vol. 47, pp. 739–750.

5. Timothy Judge and Robert Bretz, "Effects of Work Values on Job Choice Decisions," *Journal of Applied Psychology,* Vol. 77, No. 3, pp. 261–271.

6. "Right Here in Dubuque," *Forbes,* March 29, 1993, pp. 86–88.

7. Andy Bargerstock and Hank Engel, "Six Ways to Boost Employee Referral Programs," *HRMagazine,* December 1994, pp. 72–77.

8. "Software Firm Tests College Job Hopefuls," *USA Today,* April 8, 1993, pp. B1, B2.

9. Beth McConnell, "Companies Lure Job Seekers in New Ways," *HR News,* April 2002, pp. 1–5.

10. Peter Cappelli, "Making the Most of Online Recruiting," *Harvard Business Review,* March 2001, pp. 139–146.

11. Bill Leonard, "Online and Overwhelmed," *HRMagazine,* August 2000, pp. 37–42.

12. Candee Wilde, "Recruiters Discover Diverse Value in Websites," *Informationweek,* February 7, 2000, pp. 144.

13. Kuhn and Mikal Skuiterud, "Job Search Methods: Internet Versus Traditional," *Monthly Labor Review,* October 2000, pp. 3–11.

14. Cappelli, "Making the Most of Online Recruiting."

15. J. P. Wanous and A. Colella, "Organizational Entry Research: Current Status and Future Directions," in K. Rowland and G. Ferris (eds.), *Research in Personnel and Human Resource Management* (Greenwich, Conn.: JAI Press, 1989).

16. "It's Not Easy Making Pixie Dust," *BusinessWeek,* September 18, 1995, p. 134.

17. B. M. Meglino and A. S. DeNisi, "Realistic Job Previews: Some Thoughts on Their More Effective Use in Managing the Flow of Human Resources," *Human Resource Planning,* 1987, Vol. 10, pp. 157–167.

18. Jean Phillips, "Effects of Realistic Job Previews on Multiple Organizational Outcomes: A Meta-Analysis," *Academy of Management Journal,* 1998, Vol. 41, pp. 673–690.

19. R. A. Dean and J. P. Wanous, "Effects of Realistic Job Previews on Hiring Bank Tellers," *Journal of Applied Psychology,* 1984, Vol. 69, pp. 61–68.

20. B. M. Meglino, A. S. DeNisi, S. A. Youngblood, and K. J. Williams, "Effects of Realistic Job Previews: A Comparison Using Enhancement and Reduction Previews," *Journal of Applied Psychology,* 1988, Vol. 73, pp. 259–266.

21. B. M. Meglino, A. S. DeNisi, and E. C. Ravlin, "The Effects of Previous Job Exposure and Subsequent Job Status on the Functioning of Realistic Job Previews," *Personnel Psychology,* 1993, Vol. 46, pp. 803–822.

22. See Neal Schmitt and Ivan Robertson, "Personnel Selection," *Annual Review of Psychology,* 1990, Vol. 41, pp. 289–319.

23. Michael Stevens and Michael Campion, "The Knowledge, Skill, and Ability Requirements for Teamwork: Implications for Human Resource Management," *Journal of Management,* 1994, Vol. 20, No. 2, pp. 503–530.

24. M. R. Barrick and M. K. Mount, "The Big Five Personality Dimensions and Job Performance: A Meta-Analysis," *Personnel Psychology,* 1991, Vol. 44, pp. 1–26.

25. It is not always clear that recruiters and interviewers can effectively distinguish between the two types of fit. See, for example, Amy Kristof-Brown, "Perceived Applicant Fit: Distinguishing Between Recruiters' Perceptions of Person-Job and Person-Organization Fit," *Personnel Psychology,* 2000, Vol. 53, pp. 643–672.

26. Orlando Behling, "Employee Selection: Will Intelligence and Conscientiousness Do the Job?" *Academy of Management Executive,* February 1998, pp. 77–86.

27. J. E. Hunter and R. F. Hunter, "Validity and Utility of Alternative Predictors of Job Performance," *Psychological Bulletin,* Spring 1984, pp. 72–98.

28. C. J. Russell, J. Mattdson, S. E. Devlin, and D. Atwater, "Predictive Validity of Biodata Items Generated from Retrospective Life Experience Essays," *Journal of Applied Psychology,* 1990, Vol. 75, pp. 569–580.

29. See "Can You Tell Applesauce from Pickles?" *Forbes,* October 9, 1995, pp. 106–108 for several examples.

30. J. E. Hunter, "Cognitive Ability, Cognitive Aptitudes, Job Knowledge, and Job Performance," *Journal of Vocational Behavior,* 1986, Vol. 29, pp. 340–362.

31. A. R. Jensen, *Bias in Mental Testing* (New York: Free Press, 1980).

32. M. K. Mount and M. R. Barrick, *Manual for the Personal Characteristics Inventory* (Iowa City, Iowa: 1995).

33. Daniel P. O'Meara, "Personality Tests Raise Questions of Legality and Effectiveness," *HRMagazine,* January 1994, pp. 97–104.

34. See L. M. Hough, "The Big Five Personality Variables—Construct Confusion: Description Versus Prediction," *Human Performance,* 1992, Vol. 5, pp. 139–155; for an opposing view, see J. E. Hunter and R. F. Hunter, "Validity and Utility of Alternative Predictors of Job Performance," *Psychological Bulletin,* 1984, Vol. 96, pp. 72–98.

35. "Employers Score New Hires," *USA Today,* July 9, 1997, pp. 1B, 2B.

36. P. R. Sackett, "Integrity Testing for Personnel Selection," *Current Directions in Psychological Science,* 1994, Vol. 3, pp. 73–76.

37. R. C. Hollinger and J. P. Clark, *Theft by Employees* (Lexington, Mass.: Lexington Books, 1983).

38. U.S. Congress, Office of Technology Assessment, *The Use of Integrity Tests for Pre-Employment Screening* (Washington, D.C.: U.S. Government Printing Office, 1990); S. W. Gilliland, "Fairness from the Applicant's Perspective: Reactions to Employee Selection Procedures," *International Journal of Selection and Assessment,* 1995, Vol. 3, pp. 11–19.

39. Michael McDaniel, Deborah Whetzel, Frank Schmidt, and Steven Maurer, "The Validity of Employment Interviews: A Comprehensive Review and Meta-Analysis," *Journal of Applied Psychology,* 1994, Vol. 79, No. 4, pp. 599–616.

40. "Think Fast!" *Forbes,* March 24, 1997, pp. 146–151.

41. Elaine Pulakos and Neal Schmitt, "Experience-Based and Situational Interview Questions: Studies of Validity," *Personnel Psychology,* 1995, Vol. 48, pp. 289–308.

42. M. A. McDaniel, D. L. Whetzel, F. L. Schmidt, and S. D. Maurer, "The Validity of Employment Interviews: A Comprehensive Review and Meta-Analysis," *Journal of Applied Psychology,* 1994, Vol. 79, pp. 599–616.

43. *Watson v. Fort Worth Bank and Trust,* 108 Sup. Ct. 2791 (1988).

44. See Thomas Dougherty, Daniel Turban, and John Callender, "Confirming First Impressions in the Employment Interview: A Field Study of Interviewer Behavior," *Journal of Applied Psychology,* 1994, Vol. 79, No. 5, pp. 659–665.

45. Paul Falcone, "Getting Employers to Open Up on a Reference Check," *HRMagazine,* July 1995, pp. 58–63.

46. "Think Fast!" *Forbes,* March 24, 1997, pp. 146–151.

47. Annette C. Spychalski, Miguel A. Quinones, Barbara B. Gaugler, and Katja Pohley, "A Survey of Assessment Center Practices in Organizations in the United States," *Personnel Psychology,* Spring 1997, pp. 71–82.

48. Justin Martin, "So, You Want to Work for the Best . . . ," *Fortune,* January 12, 1998, pp. 77–85.

49. See especially *Washington* v. *Davis,* Sup. Ct.; 426 U.S. 229; S. Ct. 2040, L. Ed. 2d 597 (1976).

50. See, for example, *Albermarle Paper Company* v. *Moody,* Sup. Ct.; 422 U.S. 405; 95 S. Ct. 2362, 45 L. Ed. 2d 280 (1975); *Connecticut* v. *Teal,* Sup. Ct.; 457 U.S. 440; 102 S. Ct. 2525; L. Ed. 2d 190 (1982); and *Watson* v. *Fort Worth Bank and Trust,* Sup. Ct.; 487 U.S. 977; 108 S. Ct. 2777; L. Ed. 2d 827 (1988).

51. C. R. Williams, C. E. Labig, and T. Stone, "Recruitment Sources and Posthire Outcomes for Job Applications and New Hires," *Journal of Applied Psychology,* 1993, Vol. 78, pp. 163–172.

52. Sources: "Extreme HR: Pushing the Limits of Risk," *Boston Globe,* July 5, 2005, p. B1; "Worker Shortage Forces Small Businesses into Creative Hiring," *USA Today,* October 30, 1998, pp. 1B, 2B; "Making Risky Hires into Valued Workers," *Wall Street Journal,* June 19, 1997, pp. B1, B2.

Taking HR to the Next Level 2

1. "Citibank Hitches Itself to Primerica's Team to Peddle Accounts," *Wall Street Journal,* April 19, 1999, pp. A1, A6.

2. Gilbert Nicholson, "Get Your Benefit Ducks in a Row," *Workforce,* September 2000, pp. 78–84.

3. Lee Phillion and John Brugger, "Encore! Retirees Give Top Performance as Temporaries," *HRMagazine,* October 1994, pp. 74–78.

4. "When Is a Temp Not a Temp?" *BusinessWeek,* December 7, 1998, pp. 90–92.

5. George Flynn, "Temp Staffing Carries Legal Risk," *Workforce,* September 1999, pp. 56–62.

6. The term was introduced by the authors who originally presented the model. See David P. Lepak and Scott A. Snell, "The Human Resource Architecture: Toward a Theory of Human Capital Allocation and Development," *Academy of Management Review,* 1999, Vol. 24, pp. 31–48.

Chapter 8

1. "The 40 Best Companies for Diversity," *Black Enterprise,* June 12, 2006, pp. 18-22; "How One Hotel Manages Staff Diversity," *Wall Street Journal,* November 20, 1996, pp. B1, B11 (*quote on p. B11); *Hoover's Handbook of American Business 2006* (Austin, Tex.: Hoover's Business Press, 2006), pp. 904–905; "In a Factory Schedule, Where Does Religion Fit In?" *Wall Street Journal,* March 4, 1999, pp. B1, B12; Roy Johnson, "The 50 Best Companies for Blacks & Hispanics," *Fortune,* August 3, 1998, pp. 94–106.

2. David A. Thomas and Robin J. Ely, "Making Differences Matter: A New Paradigm for Managing Diversity," *Harvard Business Review,* September–October 1996, pp. 79–90.

3. Dora C. Lau and J. Keith Murnighan, "Demographic Diversity and Faultlines: The Compositional Dynamics of Organizational Groups," *Academy of Management Review,* 1998, Vol. 23, No. 2, pp. 325–340.

4. Frances J. Milliken and Luis L. Martins, "Searching for Common Threads: Understanding the Multiple Effects of Diversity in Organizational Groups," *Academy of Management Review,* 1996, Vol. 21, No. 2, pp. 402–433.

5. "In a Factory Schedule, Where Does Religion Fit In?" *Wall Street Journal,* March 4, 1999, pp. B1, B12.

6. Adrienne Colella, "The Work Group Perspective: Co-Worker Responses to Group Member Accommodations," in D. Harrison (chair), "Implementing What Matters Most: Multiple Stakeholders in Accommodating People with Disabilities at Work. All-Academy Symposium," presented at annual meeting of the Academy of Management, San Diego, Calif., August 1998.

7. Barbara L. Hassell and Pamela L. Perrewe, "An Examination of Beliefs About Older Workers: Do Stereotypes Still Exist?" *Journal of Organizational Behavior,* 1995, Vol. 16, pp. 457–468.

8. For a more complete discussion of these dimensions, see Diane L. Stone and Adrienne Colella, " A Model of Factors Affecting the Treatment of Disabled Individuals in Organizations," *Academy of Management Review,* 1996, Vol. 21, pp. 352–401.

9. Based on Taylor H. Cox and Stacy Blake, "Managing Cultural Diversity: Implications for Organizational Competitiveness," *The Academy of Management Executive,* August 1991, pp. 45–56; see also Gail Robinson and Kathleen Dechant, "Building a Business Case for Diversity," *The Academy of Management Executive,* August 1997, pp. 21–30.

10. C. Marlene Fiol, "Consensus, Diversity, and Learning in Organizations," *Organization Science,* August 1994, pp. 403–415.

11. Douglas Hall and Victoria Parker, "The Role of Workplace Flexibility in Managing Diversity," *Organizational Dynamics,* Summer 1993, pp. 5–14.

12. Janice R. W. Joplin and Catherine S. Daus, "Challenges of Leading a Diverse Workforce," *The Academy of Management Executive,* August 1997, pp. 32–44.

13. "As Population Ages, Older Workers Clash with Younger Bosses," *Wall Street Journal,* June 13, 1994, pp. A1, A8.

14. "Pursuit of Diversity Stirs Racial Tension at an FAA Center," *Wall Street Journal,* December 3, 1998, pp. A1, A8.

15. "Generational Warfare," *Forbes,* March 22, 1999, pp. 62–66.

16. For a review of these results, see Francis Milliken and Louis Martins, "Searching for Common Threads: Understanding the Multiple Effects of Diversity in Organizational Groups," *Academy of Management Review,* 1996, Vol. 21, pp. 402–433; or Belle Rose Ragins and Jorge Gonzalez, "Understanding Diversity in Organizations: Getting a Grip on a Slippery Construct," in J. Greenberg (ed.), *Organizational Behavior: The State of the Science* (Mahwah, N.J.: Erlbaum, 2003).

17. See for example, Christopher Earley and Elaine Mosakowski, "Creating Hybrid Team Cultures: An Empirical Test of Transnational Team Functioning," *Academy of Management Journal,* 2000, Vol. 43, pp. 26–49.

18. Earley and Mosakowski, op. cit.; Orlando Richard, Tim Barnett, Sean Dwyer, and Ken Chadwick, "Cultural Diversity in Management, Firm Performance, and the Moderating Role of Entrepreneurial Orientation Dimensions," *Academy of Management Journal,* 2004, Vol. 47, pp. 255–266.

19. Karen Hildebrand, "Use Leadership Training to Increase Diversity," *HRMagazine,* August 1996, pp. 53–57.

20. Patricia L. Nemetz and Sandra L. Christensen, "The Challenge of Cultural Diversity: Harnessing a Diversity of Views to Understand Multiculturalism," *Academy of Management Review,* 1996, Vol. 21, No. 2, pp. 434–462.

21. This discussion derives heavily from Taylor H. Cox, "The Multicultural Organization," *The Academy of Management Executive,* May 1991, pp. 34–47.

22. Sources: "Alpha Females," *Fortune,* November 14, 2005, pp. 125-170; "If Women Ran the World, It Would Look a Lot Like Avon," *Fortune,* July 21, 1997, pp. 74–79; *Hoover's Handbook of American Business 2006* (Austin, Tex.: Hoover's Business Press, 2006), pp. 202–203.

Chapter 9

1. "About Us," Nucor website, www.nucor.com, on November 9, 2006; "The Art of Motivation," *BusinessWeek,* May 1, 2006, pp. 57–62 (*quote on p. 60); Gretchen Morgenson, "Companies Not Behaving Badly," *New York Times,* October 9, 2005, p. B3; "Reinventing the Mill," *New York Times,* October 22, 2005, p. B5.

2. Kathryn Tyler, "Compensation Strategies Can Foster Lateral Moves and Growing in Place," *HRMagazine,* April 1998, pp. 64–69.

3. Emily Pavlovic, "Choosing the Best Salary Surveys," *HRMagazine,* April 1994, pp. 44–48.

4. J. Stacey Adams, "Inequity in Social Exchange," in L. Berkowitz (ed.), *Advances in Experimental Social Psychology* (New York: Academic Press, 1965), pp. 267–299.

5. Jeffrey Pfeffer, "Six Dangerous Myths About Pay," *Harvard Business Review,* May–June 1998, pp. 109–119.

6. See "Is Minimum Wage Minimum Life?" Associated Press news story, January 23, 1995, as published in the *Bryan-College Station Eagle,* p. B1.

7. Brian S. Klaas and John A. McClendon, "To Lead, Lag, or March: Estimating the Financial Impact of Pay Level Policies," *Personnel Psychology,* 1996, Vol. 49, No. 1, pp. 88–98.

8. Edward E. Lawler III, "The New Pay: A Strategic Approach," *Compensation & Benefits Review,* July–August 1995, pp. 145–154.

9. Sandra O'Neal, "Aligning Pay with Business Strategy," *HRMagazine,* August 1993, pp. 76–80.

10. Charles Greer, *Strategy and Human Resources* (Englewood Cliffs, N.J.: Prentice-Hall, 1995).

11. "Many Companies Lower Pay Raises," *USA Today,* April 4, 2002, p. 1B.

12. Judith Collins and Paul Muchinsky, "An Assessment of the Construct Validity of Three Job Evaluation Methods: A Field Experiment," *Academy of Management Journal,* 1993, Vol. 36, No. 4, pp. 895–904.

13. Ibid.

14. G. D. Jenkins and N. Gupta, "The Payoffs of Paying for Knowledge," *National Productivity Review,* 1985, Vol. 4, pp. 121–130.

15. Adrienne Colella, Ramona Paetzold, Asghar Zardkoohi, and Michael Wesson, "Exposing pay secrecy," *Academy of Management Review,* 2007, Vol. 32, pp. 35–56.

16. Bureau of National Affairs, U.S. Chamber of Commerce data, September 1, 2006.

17. "Detroit Meets a 'Worker Paradise,'" *Wall Street Journal,* March 3, 1999, pp. B1, B4.

18. Richard Wolfe and Donald Parker, "Employee Health Management: Challenges and Opportunities," *The Academy of Management Executive,* 1994, Vol. 8, No. 2, pp. 22–31.

19. For a recent discussion of these issues, see Maureen Minehan, "Islam's Growth Affects Workplace Policies," *HRMagazine,* November 1998, p. 216.

20. Mina Westman and Dov Eden, "Effects of Respite from Work on Burnout: Vacation Relief and Fade-Out," *Journal of Applied Psychology,* August 1997, pp. 516–527.

21. "Employer Benefit Surveys Target Unhealthy Habits," *USA Today,* May 28, 1998, p. 1B.

22. S. Caudron, "The Wellness Pay Off," *Personnel Journal,* July 1990, pp. 55–60.

23. Shirley Hand and Robert Zawacki, "Family-Friendly Benefits: More Than a Frill," *HRMagazine,* October 1994, pp. 74–79.

24. E. E. Kossek and V. Nichol, "The Effects of On-Site Child Care on Employee Attitudes and Performance," *Personnel Psychology,* 1992, Vol. 45, pp. 485–509.

25. "Gay Employees Win Benefits for Partners at More Corporations," *Wall Street Journal,* March 18, 1994, p. A1.

26. Rudy Yandrick, "The EAP Struggle: Counselors or Referrers?" *HRMagazine,* August 1998, pp. 90–91.

27. W. J. Sonnenstuhl and H. M. Trice, *Strategies for Employee Assistance Programs: The Crucial Balance* (Ithaca, N.Y.: Cornell University ILR Press, 1990).

28. Melissa Barringer and George Milkovich, "A Theoretical Exploration of the Adoption and Design of Flexible Benefit Plans: A Case of Human Resource Innovation," *Academy of Management Review,* April 1998, pp. 305–324.

29. A. E. Barber, R. B. Dunham, and R. A. Formisano, "The Impact of Flexible Benefits on Employee Satisfaction: A Field Study," *Personnel Psychology,* 1992, Vol. 45, pp. 55–57.

30. For a more in-depth discussion of the requirements and advantages of qualification, see Michael Sarli, "Nondiscrimination Rules for Qualified Plans: The General Test," *Compensation and Benefits Review,* September 1991, pp. 56–67.

31. H. W. Hennessey, P. L. Perrewe, and W. A. Hochwarter, "Impact of Benefit Awareness on Employee and Organizational Outcomes: A Longitudinal Field Experiment," *Benefits Quarterly,* 1992, Vol. 8, No. 2, pp. 90–96.

32. M. Wilson, G. B. Northcraft, and M. A. Neale, "The Perceived Value of Fringe Benefits," *Personnel Psychology,* 1985, Vol. 38, pp. 309–320.

33. Sources: *Hoover's Handbook of American Business 2006* (Austin, Tex.: Hoover's Business Press, 2006); "'I'm Proud of What I've Made Myself Into—What I've Created,'" *Wall Street Journal,* August 28, 1997, pp. B1, B5; "'That's Why I Like My Job . . . I Have an Impact on Quality,'" *Wall Street Journal,* August 28, 1997, pp. B1, B8.

Chapter 10

1. "Merrill Invests in Human Capital," *Wall Street Journal,* February 14, 2006, p. B4; Dayton Fandray, "Managing Performance the Merrill Lynch Way," *Workforce Management,* May 2001, pp. 36–40 (quotation); Paul Hodgson, "The Wall Street Example—Bringing Excessive Executive Compensation into Line," *Ivey Business Journal,* May/June 2004, pp. 16–18; Jeffrey Rothfeder, "The Road Less Traveled—Merrill Lynch and Co.," *CIO Insight,* March 1, 2004, p. 35; Emily Thornton, "The New Merrill Lynch, " *BusinessWeek,* May 5, 2003, pp. 78–80.

2. See Chapter 8 in Charles R. Greer, *Strategy and Human Resources* (Englewood Cliffs, N.J.: Prentice-Hall, 1995), for a review of the strategic importance of performance management in organizations.

3. W. Timothy Weaver, "Linking Performance Reviews to Productivity and Quality," *HRMagazine,* November 1996, pp. 93–98.

4. A. S. DeNisi, *Cognitive Approach to Performance Appraisal: A Program of Research* (London: Routledge, 1996).

5. For several excellent reviews of these "cognitive" decision-making processes on the part of the rater, see A. S. DeNisi, T. P. Cafferty, and B. Meglino, "A Cognitive Model of the Performance Appraisal Process," *Organizational Behavior and Human Decision Processes,* 1984, Vol. 33, pp. 360–396; and D. R. Ilgen and J. M. Feldman, "Performance Appraisal: A Process Focus," in B. Staw and L. Cummings (eds.), *Research in Organizational Behavior,* Vol. 5 (Greenwich, Conn.: JAI Press, 1983).

6. Arup Varma, Angelo S. DeNisi, and Lawrence H. Peters, "Interpersonal Affect and Performance Appraisal: A Field Study," *Personnel Psychology,* Summer 1996, pp. 341–360.

7. K. Kraiger and K. Ford, "A Meta-Analysis of Ratee Race Effects in Performance Rating," *Journal of Applied Psychology,* 1985, Vol. 70, pp. 56–65.

8. See, for example, J. N. Cleveland, R. M. Festa, and L. Montgomery, "Applicant Pool Composition and Job Perceptions: Impact on Decisions Regarding an Older Applicant," *Journal of Vocational Behavior,* 1988, Vol. 32, pp. 112–125.

9. For example, see the review by V. F. Nieva and B. Gutek, "Sex Effects in Evaluations," *Academy of Management Review,* 1980, Vol. 5, pp. 267–276.

10. A. Colella, A. S. DeNisi, and A. Varma, "A Model of the Impact of Disability on Performance Evaluations," *Human Resource Management Review,* 1997, Vol. 7, pp. 27–53.

11. Kevin R. Murphy and Jeanette N. Cleveland, *Understanding Performance Appraisal: Social, Organizational, and Goal-Based Perspectives* (Thousand Oaks, Calif.: Sage Publications, 1995).

12. Forest J. Jourden and Chip Heath, "The Evaluation Gap in Performance Perceptions: Illusory Perceptions of Groups and

Individuals," *Journal of Applied Psychology,* 1996, Vol. 81, No. 4, pp. 369–379.

13. Angelo S. DeNisi, W. Alan Randolph, and Allyn G. Blencoe, "Potential Problems with Peer Ratings," *Academy of Management Journal,* 1983, Vol. 26, pp. 457–467.

14. Leanne Atwater, Paul Roush, and Allison Fischtal, "The Influence of Upward Feedback on Self- and Follower Ratings of Leadership," *Personnel Psychology,* Spring 1995, pp. 35–59.

15. See, for example, Alan Walker and James Smither, "A Five-Year Study of Upward Feedback: What Managers Do with Their Results Matters," *Personnel Psychology,* 1999, Vol. 52, pp. 393–423.

16. For a good review of the work in this area, see David Waldman and Leanne Atwater, *The Power of 360-Degree Feedback: How to Leverage Performance Evaluations for Top Productivity* (Houston, Tex.: Gulf Publishing, 2000).

17. James M. Conway, "Analysis and Design of Multitrait-Multirater Performance Appraisal Studies," *Journal of Management,* Vol. 22, No. 1, pp. 139–162.

18. For an in-depth discussion of these problems, see Susan Haworth, "The Dark Side of Multi-Rater Assessments," *HRMagazine,* May 1998, pp. 106–112; or Angelo DeNisi and Avraham Kluger, "Feedback Effectiveness: Can 360-Degree Appraisals Be Improved?" *Academy of Management Executive,* Vol. 14, pp. 129–139.

19. See discussions of these processes in Walter Borman, "Exploring the Upper Limits of Reliability and Validity in Job Performance Ratings," *Journal of Applied Psychology,* 1978, Vol. 63, pp. 135–144; and Angelo DeNisi, Thomas Cafferty, and Bruce Meglino, "A Cognitive Model of the Performance Appraisal Process," *Organizational Behavior and Human Decision Processes,* 1984, Vol. 33, pp. 360–396.

20. See, for example, H. John Bernardin and C. S. Walter, "Effects of Rater and Training and Diary Keeping on Psychometric Errors in Ratings," *Journal of Applied Psychology,* 1977, Vol. 62, pp. 64–69; or Angelo DeNisi, Tina Robbins, and Thomas Cafferty, "The Organization of Information Used for Performance Appraisals: The Role of Diary Keeping," *Journal of Applied Psychology,* 1989, Vol. 74, pp. 124–129.

21. For an excellent review of some relevant court cases, see Jon Werner and Mark Bolino, "Explaining U.S. Courts of Appeals Decisions Involving Performance Appraisal: Accuracy, Fairness, and Validation," *Personnel Psychology,* 1997, Vol. 50, pp. 1–24.

22. For a more complete discussion of the proper focus for appraisals in different settings, see Angelo DeNisi, "Performance Appraisal and Control Systems: A Multilevel Approach," in K. Klein and S. Kozlowski (eds.), *Multilevel Theory, Research, and Methods in Organizations,* SIOP Frontiers Series (San Francisco, Calif.: Jossey-Bass, 2000), pp. 121–156.

23. E. D. Sisson, "Forced Choice: The New Army Rating," *Personnel Psychology,* 1948, Vol. 1, pp. 365–381.

24. J. C. Flanagan, "The Critical Incident Technique," *Psychological Bulletin,* 1954, Vol. 51, pp. 327–358.

25. J. C. Flanagan and R. K. Burns, "The Employee Performance Record: A New Appraisal and Development Tool," *Harvard Business Review,* September–October 1955, pp. 95–102.

26. H. J. Bernardin and C. S. Walter, "The Effects of Rater Training and Diary Keeping on Psychometric Errors in Ratings," *Journal of Applied Psychology,* 1977, Vol. 62, pp. 64–69; A. S. DeNisi, T. Robbins, and T. P. Cafferty, "The Organization of Information Used for Performance Appraisals: The Role of Diary Keeping," *Journal of Applied Psychology,* 1989, Vol. 74, pp. 124–129.

27. P. C. Smith and L. M. Kendall, "Retranslation of Expectations: An Approach to the Construction of Unambiguous Anchors for Rating Scales," *Journal of Applied Psychology,* 1963, Vol. 47, pp. 149–155.

28. H. J. Barnardin, M. B. LaShells, P. C. Smith, and K. M. Alvares, "Behavioral Expectation Scales: Effects of Development Procedures and Formats," *Journal of Applied Psychology,* 1976, Vol. 61, pp. 75–79.

29. G. P. Latham, C. H. Fay, and L. M. Saari, "The Development of Behavioral Observation Scales for Appraising the Performance of Foremen," *Personnel Psychology,* 1979, Vol. 33, pp. 815–821.

30. For an excellent review of the variations on these methods, see Chapter 4 in H. J. Bernardin and R. W. Beatty, *Performance Appraisal: Assessing Human Behavior at Work* (Boston, Mass.: PWS-Kent, 1984).

31. See, for example, Joseph Mishra and Susan Crampton, "Employee Monitoring: Privacy in the Workplace?" *SAM Advanced Management Journal,* 1998, Vol. 53, p. 4.

32. See Elizabeth Douthitt and John R. Aiello, "The Role of Participation and Control in the Effects of Computer Monitoring on Fairness Perceptions, Task Satisfaction, and Performance," *Journal of Applied Psychology,* 2001, Vol. 86, pp. 867–874.

33. American Management Association, *Workplace Monitoring and Surveillance: A 1999 AMA Survey* (New York: American Management Association, 2000).

34. See, for example, reviews by Frank Landy and James Farr, "Performance Rating," *Psychological Bulletin,* 1980, Vol. 87, pp. 72–102; or Angelo DeNisi, *A Cognitive Approach to Performance Appraisal* (London: Routledge, 1996), pp. 1–20.

35. W. C. Borman, "Job Behavior, Performance, and Effectiveness," in M. D. Dunnette and L. Hough (eds.), *Handbook of Industrial and Organizational Psychology,* Vol. 2, 2nd ed. (Palo Alto, Calif.: Consulting Psychologists Press, 1991); W. C. Borman and S. J. Motowidlo, "Expanding the Criterion Domain to Include Elements of Contextual Performance," in N. Schmitt and W. Borman (eds.), *Personnel Selection in Organizations* (San Francisco, Calif.: Jossey-Bass, 1993).

36. D. W. Organ and K. Ryan, "A Meta-Analytic Review of Attitudinal and Dispositional Predictors of Organizational Citizenship Behavior," *Personnel Psychology,* 1995, Vol. 48, pp. 775–802.

37. J. M. Werner, "Dimensions That Make a Difference: Examining the Impact of In-Role and Extrarole Behaviors on Supervisory Ratings," *Journal of Applied Psychology,* 1994, Vol. 79, pp. 98–107.

38. Maria Rotundo and Paul Sackett, "The Relative Importance of Task, Citizenship, and Counterproductive Performance to Global Ratings of Job Performance: A Policy-Capturing Study," *Journal of Applied Psychology,* 2002, Vol. 87, pp. 66–80.

39. Neal P. Mero and Stephan J. Motowidlo, "Effects of Rater Accountability on the Accuracy and the Favorability of Performance Ratings," *Journal of Applied Psychology,* 1995, Vol. 80, No. 4, pp. 517–524.

40. Jeffrey S. Kane, H. John Bernardin, Peter Villanova, and Joseph Peyrefitte, "Stability of Rater Leniency: Three Studies," *Academy of Management Journal,* 1995, Vol. 38, No. 4, pp. 1036–1051.

41. Walter C. Borman, Leonard A. White, and David W. Dorsey, "Effects of Ratee Task Performance and Interpersonal Factors on Supervisor and Peer Performance Ratings," *Journal of Applied Psychology,* 1995, Vol. 80, No. 1, pp. 168–177.

42. Juan I. Sanchez and Phillip De La Torre, "A Second Look at the Relationship Between Rating and Behavioral Accuracy in Performance Appraisal," *Journal of Applied Psychology,* 1996, Vol. 81, No. 1, pp. 3–10.

43. *Brito* v. *Zia Company,* 478 F. 2d 1200 (10th Cir. 1973).

44. Manuel London, "Redeployment and Continuous Learning in the 21st Century: Hard Lessons and Positive Examples from the Downsizing Era," *The Academy of Management Executive,* November 1996, pp. 67–79.

45. Adrianne H. Geiger-DuMond and Susan K. Boyle, "Mentoring: A Practitioner's Guide," *Training & Development,* March 1995, pp. 51–55.

46. Douglas T. Hall, "Protean Careers of the 21st Century," *The Academy of Management Executive,* November 1996, pp. 8–16.

47. For a discussion of a wide variety of issues at every stage in one's career, see Daniel Feldman (ed.), *Work Careers: A Developmental Perspective* (San Francisco: Jossey-Bass, 2002).

48. Bruce Avolio and David Waldman, "Variations in Cognitive, Perceptual, and Psychomotor Abilities Across the Working Life Span: Examining the Effects of Race, Sex, Experience, Education, and Occupational Type," *Psychology and Aging,* 1994, Vol. 9, pp. 430–442.

49. See for example, reviews by Glen McEvoy and Wayne Cascio, "Cumulative Evidence of the Relationship Between Employee Age and Job Performance," *Journal of Applied Psychology,* 1989, Vol. 74, No. 1, pp. 11–17; and Susan Rhoades, "Age-related Differences in Work Attitudes and Behavior: A Review and Conceptual Analysis," *Psychological Bulletin,* Vol. 93, pp. 328–367.

50. Terry Beehr, "The Process of Retirement: A Review and Recommendations," *Personnel Psychology,* 1986, Vol. 39, No. 1, pp. 31–55.

51. Gregory K. Stephens, "Crossing Internal Career Boundaries: The State of Research on Subjective Career Transitions," *Journal of Management,* 1994, Vol. 20, No. 2, pp. 479–501.

52. Suzyn Ornstein and Lynn A. Isabella, "Making Sense of Careers: A Review 1989–1992," *Journal of Management,* 1993, Vol. 19, No. 2, pp. 243–267.

53. Kenneth R. Brousseau, Michael J. Driver, Kristina Eneroth, and Rikard Larsson, "Career Pandemonium: Realigning Organizations and Individuals," *The Academy of Management Executive,* November 1996, pp. 52–66.

54. M. Ferber, B. O'Farrell, and L. Allen, *Work and Family: Policies for a Changing Workforce* (Washington, D.C.: National Academy Press, 1994).

55. H. Morgan and K. Tucker, *Companies That Care: The Most Family-Friendly Companies in America, What They Offer, and How They Got That Way* (New York: Simon & Schuster, 1991).

56. S. Zedeck and K. L. Mosier, "Work in Family and Employing Organizations," *American Psychologist,* 1990, Vol. 45, pp. 240–251.

57. V. J. Doby and R. D. Caplan, "Organizational Stress as Threat to Reputation: Effects on Anxiety at Work and at Home," *Academy of Management Journal,* 1995, Vol. 38, pp. 1105–1123.

58. P. B. Doeringer, "Economic Security, Labor Market Flexibility, and Bridges to Retirement," in P. B. Doeringer (ed.), *Bridges to Retirement* (Ithaca, N.Y.: Cornell University ILR Press, 1990), pp. 3–22.

59. Sources: "Early Performance Reviews: Taking the Bad With the Good," *Wall Street Journal,* March 3, 2006, p. B6;"Getting a Jump Start With an Early Review," *USA Today,* November 13, 2005, p. 1B; "New Hires Win Fast Raises in Accelerated Job Reviews," *Wall Street Journal,* October 6, 1998, pp. B1, B16; "Your Year-End Review Doesn't Have to Be Quite That Horrible," *Wall Street Journal,* December 23, 1997, p. B1.

Chapter 11

1. "29 Ports All Stopped Up," *USA Today,* October 1, 2002, p. 3B (*quote on p. 3B); "West Coast Ports Still Closed as Talks Break Down," *USA Today,* October 2, 2002, p. 1B; "West Coast Port Labor Contract Ratified," *The Journal of Commerce,* January 24, 2003, p. 1.

2. David Lipsky and Clifford Donn, *Collective Bargaining in American Industry* (Lexington, Mass.: Lexington Books, 1981).

3. "Two Rebel Unions Split From AFL-CIO," *USA Today,* July 26, 2005, pp. 1B, 2B.

4. Alabama, Arkansas, Florida, Georgia, Iowa, Kansas, Kentucky, Louisiana, Mississippi, Nebraska, Nevada, North Carolina, North Dakota, South Carolina, South Dakota, Tennessee, Texas, Utah, Virginia, and Wyoming are right-to-work states, although a state can change its status on this issue at any time.

5. "Companies Counter Unions," *USA Today,* September 1997, pp. 1B, 2B.

6. Edward E. Lawler III and Susan A. Mohrman, "Unions and the New Management," *The Academy of Management Executive,* 1987, Vol. 1, No. 3, pp. 65–75.

7. "Reinventing the Union," *Wall Street Journal,* July 27, 2006, p. B1, B2.

8. "Why Mexico Scares the UAW," *BusinessWeek,* August 3, 1998, pp. 37–38.

9. Clive Fullagar, Paul Clark, Daniel Gallagher, and Michael E. Gordon, "A Model of the Antecedents of the Early Union Commitment: The Role of Socialization Experiences and Steward Characteristics," *Journal of Organizational Behavior,* 1994, Vol. 15, pp. 517–533.

10. Stuart Youngblood, Angelo DeNisi, Julie Molleston, and William Mobley, "The Impact of Worker Attachment, Instrumentality Beliefs, Perceived Labor Union Image, and Subjective Norms on Voting Intentions and Union Membership," *Academy of Management Journal,* 1984, Vol. 27, pp. 576–590.

11. J. Barling, E. K. Kelloway, and E. H. Bremermann, "Pre-employment Predictors of Union Attitudes: The Role of Family Socialization and Work Beliefs," *Journal of Applied Psychology,* 1991, Vol. 75, pp. 725–731.

12. "Some Unions Step Up Organizing Campaigns and Get New Members," *Wall Street Journal,* September 1, 1995, pp. A1, A2.

13. See Jeanette A. Davy and Frank Shipper, "Voter Behavior in Union Certification Elections: A Longitudinal Study," *Academy of Management Journal,* 1993, Vol. 36, No. 1, pp. 187–199, for a discussion of some of the determinants of individual voting behavior in union elections.

14. Adapted from R. E. Walton and R. B. McKersie, *A Behavioral Theory of Labor Negotiations* (New York: McGraw-Hill, 1965). Note that we have used the terminology used by those authors, which is adapted from game theory. The reader might encounter different terms in other treatments of bargaining, but the concepts are the same as those described here.

15. "ABC Locks Out Striking Employees," *USA Today,* November 3, 1998, p. B1.

16. Phil Taylor, "To the Victor Belong the Spoils," *Sports Illustrated,* January 18, 1999, pp. 48–52.

17. H. S. Farber and H. C. Katz, "Interest Arbitration, Outcomes, and the Incentive to Bargain," *Industrial and Labor Relations Review,* 1979, Vol. 33, pp. 55–63.

18. P. Feuille, "Final Offer Arbitration and the Chilling Effect," *Industrial Relations,* 1975, Vol. 14, pp. 302–310.

19. See Kevin Banks, "Contingent and Informal Workers in North America: Workplace Human Rights," *Proceedings of the 53rd Annual Meeting of the Industrial Relations Research Association,* New Orleans, 2001, pp. 90–98.

20. For a complete discussion of the issues and the rulings in this area, see Camille Olson and Michael Rybick, "Spotlight on Union Organizing: 'No Solicitation No Distribution' and Related Rules in the Age of E-mail and the Internet," *Legal Report* (published by Society of Human Resource Managers), May–June 2002, pp. 5–7.

21. Nathan Newman, "Union and Community Mobilization in the Information Age," *Perspectives on Work,* 2002, Vol. 6, No. 2, pp. 9–11.

22. Sources: "What's Really Behind GM's Strike? A Battle Over a Hot New Truck," *Wall Street Journal,* July 28, 1998, pp. A1, A5; "What Price Peace?" *BusinessWeek,* August 10, 1998, pp. 24–25; "GM Might Stop Benefits for Workers," *USA Today,* June 26, 1998, p. B1; "Rivals Make Strides After Nasty Strike," *USA Today,* December 16, 1998, pp. B1, B2.

Chapter 12

1. "FedEx Philosophy," "Team Member Benefits," FedEx website, www.fedex.com on October 5, 2006; "HR's Push for Productivity," *Employee InfoLink,* August 23, 2002, pp. 19–26; Claudia H. Deutsch, "Planes, Trucks and 7.5 Million Packages: FedEx's Big Night," *The New York Times,* December 21, 2003, p. BU 1 (quotation); Shu Shin Luh, "Asian Employers Give Workers Training, Respect and Merit Pay," *The Asian Wall Street Journal,* March 14, 2005, p. 25.

2. "Working at Home Raises Job Site Safety Issues," *USA Today,* January 29, 1998, p. 1A.

3. "Labor Secretary's Bid to Push Plant Safety Runs into Skepticism," *Wall Street Journal,* August 19, 1994, pp. A1, A5.

4. R. S. Haynes, R. C. Pine, and H. G. Fitch, "Reducing Accident Rates with Organizational Behavior Modification," *Academy of Management Journal,* 1988, Vol. 25, pp. 407–416.

5. "In an Amoco Lab, Researchers Hunt for Colleagues' Killer," *USA Today,* April 13, 1999, p. 8D.

6. Myron D. Fottler, "Employee Acceptance of a Four Day Work Week," *Academy of Management Journal,* 1977, Vol. 20, pp. 656–668.

7. S. Ronen and S. B. Primpts, "The Compressed Work Week as Organizational Change: Behavioral and Attitudinal Outcomes," *Academy of Management Review,* 1981, Vol. 6, pp. 61–74.

8. A. Purach, "Biological Rhythm Effects of Night Work and Shift Changes on the Health of Workers," *Acta Medica Scandinavia,* 1973, Vol. 152, pp. 302–307.

9. S. Zedeck, S. E. Jackson, and E. S. Marca, "Shift Work Schedules and Their Relationship to Health, Adaptation, Satisfaction, and Turnover Intentions," *Academy of Management Journal,* 1983, Vol. 26, pp. 297–310.

10. G. B. Meese, M. I. Lewis, D. P. Wyon, and R. Kok, "A Laboratory Study of the Effects of Thermal Stress on the Performance of Factory Workers," *Ergonomics,* 1982, Vol. 27, pp. 19–43.

11. E. VanDeVliert and N. W. Van Yperen, "Why Cross National Differences in Role Overload? Don't Overlook Ambient Temperature," *Academy of Management Journal,* 1996, Vol. 39, pp. 986–1004.

12. D. G. Hayward, "Psychological Factors in the Use of Light and Lighting in Buildings," in J. Lang, C. Burnette, W. Moleski, and D. Vachon (eds.), *Designing for Human Behavior: Architecture and the Behavioral Sciences* (Stroudsburg, Penn.: Dowden, Hutchinson, & Ross, 1974), pp. 120–129.

13. R. I. Newman, D. L. Hunt, and F. Rhodes, "Effects of Music on Employee Attitude and Productivity in a Skateboard Factory," *Journal of Applied Psychology,* 1956, Vol. 50, pp. 493–496.

14. G. R. Oldham, A. Cummings, L. J. Mischel, J. M. Scmidtke, and J. Zhou, "Listen While You Work? Quasi-Experimental Relations Between Personal Stereo Headset Use and Employee Work Responses," *Journal of Applied Psychology,* 1995, Vol. 80, pp. 547–564.

15. G. R. Oldham, "Effects of Changes in Workspace Partitions and Spatial Density on Employee Reactions: A Quasi-Experiment," *Journal of Applied Psychology,* 1988, Vol. 73, pp. 253–258.

16. Karen Danna and Ricky W. Griffin, "Health and Well-Being in the Workplace," *Journal of Management,* 1999, Vol. 19, pp. 125–146.

17. "Workplace Demands Taking up More Weekends," *USA Today,* April 24, 1998, p. 1B.

18. Myron Friedman and Robert Rosenman, *Type A Personality and Your Heart* (New York: Knopf, 1974).

19. James C. Quick and Jonathan D. Quick, *Organizational Stress and Preventive Management* (New York: McGraw-Hill, 1984).

20. David Turnipseed, "An Exploratory Study of the Hardy Personality at Work in the Health Care Industry," *Psychological Reports,* 1999, Vol. 85, pp. 199–1218.

21. Daniel Ganster and John Schaubroeck, "Work Stress and Employee Health," *Journal of Management,* 1991, Vol. 17, pp. 235–271.

22. Debra Nelson and James Quick, "Professional Women: Are Distress and Disease Inevitable?" *Academy of Management Review,* 1985, Vol. 10, pp. 206–213.

23. Richard S. DeFrank and John M. Ivancevich, "Stress on the Job: An Executive Update," *The Academy of Management Executive,* 1998, Vol. 12, No. 3, pp. 55–67.

24. See Anne O'Leary-Kelly, Ricky W. Griffin, and David J. Glew, "Organization-Motivated Aggression: A Research Framework," *The Academy of Management Review,* January 1996, pp. 225–253.

25. See, for example, Wendy Boswell, Julie Olson-Buchanan, and Marcie Cavanaugh, "Investigation of the Relationship Between Work-Related Stress and Work Outcomes: The Role of Felt Challenge, Psychological Strain, and Job Control," paper presented at the Academy of Management meetings, Toronto, Ontario, 2000; and Marcie Cavanaugh, Wendy Boswell, Mark Roehling, and John Boudreau, "An Empirical Examination of Self-Reported Work Stress Among U.S. Managers," *Journal of Applied Psychology,* 2000, Vol. 85, pp. 65–74.

26. See, for example, Cynthia McCauley, Marian Ruderman, Patricia Ohlott, and Jane Morrow, "Assessing the Developmental Components of Managerial Jobs," *Journal of Applied Psychology,* 1994, Vol. 79, pp. 544–560.

27. Kathy Gerchiek, "Report Cites Barriers to Wellness Programs' Effectiveness," *HR News,* June 27, 2006.

28. Joel Brockner, Stephen Grover, Thomas Reed, and Rocki De-Witt, "Layoffs, Job Insecurity and Survivors' Work Effort: Evidence of an Inverted-U Relationship," *Academy of Management Journal,* 1996, Vol. 35, pp. 413–435.

29. Sources: Anne Fisher, "Danger Zone," *Fortune,* September 8, 1997, pp. 165–167; *Hoover's Handbook of American Business 2006* (Austin, Tex.: Hoover's Business Press, 2006), pp. 402–403.

Taking HR to the Next Level 3

1. The relationship between individual and organizational learning is discussed in much more detail in Lois Tetrick and Nancy Da Silva, "Assessing the Culture and Climate for Organizational Learning," in Susan Jackson, Michael Hitt, and Angelo DeNisi (eds.), *Managing Knowledge for Sustained Competitive Advantage* (San Francisco, Calif.: Jossey-Bass, 2003), pp. 333–360.

2. See, for example, Michael Hitt, Barbara Keats, and Sam DeMarie, "Navigating in the New Competitive Landscape: Building Strategic Flexibility and Competitive Advantage in the 21st Century," *Academy of Management Executive,* 1998, Vol. 12, pp. 22–42; and Angelo DeNisi, Michael Hitt and Susan Jackson, "The Knowledge-Based Approach to Sustainable Competitive Advantage," in Susan Jackson, Michael Hitt and Angelo DeNisi (eds.), *Managing Knowledge for Sustained Competitive Advantage* (San Francisco, Calif.: Jossey-Bass, 2003), pp. 3–36.

3. Max Boisot, *Knowledge Assets* (Oxford, England: Oxford University Press, 1998).

4. M. L. Tushman and C. A. O'Reilly, *Winning Through Innovation* (Cambridge, Mass.: Harvard Business School Press, 1996).

5. M. A. Von Glinow, *The New Professionals* (Cambridge, Mass.: Ballinger, 1988).

6. T. W. Lee and S. D. Maurer, "The Retention of Knowledge Workers with the Unfolding Model of Voluntary Turnover," *Human Resource Management Review,* 1997, Vol. 7, pp. 247–276.

7. J. C. Kail, "Compensating Scientists and Engineers," in D. B. Balkin and L. R. Gomez-Mejia (eds.), *New Perspectives on Compensation* (Englewood Cliffs, N.J.: Prentice-Hall, 1987), pp. 278–281.

8. G. T. Milkovich, "Compensation Systems in High-Technology Companies," in A. Klingartner and C. Anderson (eds.), *High Technology Management* (Lexington, Mass.: Lexington Books, 1987).

9. Thomas Stewart, "In Search of Elusive Tech Workers," *Fortune,* February 16, 1998, pp. 171–172.

10. See, for example, the various discussions in the edited volume by Susan Jackson, Michael Hitt, and Angelo DeNisi, *Managing Knowledge for Sustained Competitive Advantage: Designing Strategies for Effective Human Resource Management* (San Francisco, Calif.: Jossey-Bass, SIOP Frontiers Series, 2002).

11. Jay Barney, "Firm Resources and Sustained Competitive Advantage," *Journal of Management,* 1991, Vol. 17, pp. 99–129.

12. Beth McConnell, "HR Implements Corporate Social Responsibility Globally," *HR News,* November 28, 2006.

13. Angelo DeNisi and Carrie Belsito, "Strategic Aesthetics: Wisdom and HRM" in Eric H. Kessler and James R. Bailey (eds.), *Handbook of Organizational and Managerial Wisdom* (Thousand Oaks, Calif.: Sage Publications, 2007), pp. 261–273.

14. Lynn Gibson, "Implications of the FLSA for Inmates, Correctional Institutions, Private Industry and Labor," statement before the U.S. Senate Hearings of the Committee on Labor and Human Resources, October 18, 1993.

15. For a more in-depth discussion of these issues, see Ray Marshall, "Industrial Relations and Inmate Labor," *Proceedings of the 53rd Annual Meeting of the Industrial Relations Research Association,* New Orleans, 2001, pp. 339–348.

16. Jeffrey Kling and Alan Krueger, "Costs, Benefits, and Distributional Consequences of Inmate Labor," *Proceedings of the 53rd Annual Meeting of the Industrial Relations Research Association,* New Orleans, 2001, pp. 349–358.

Chapter 13

1. "Caring for Community," Pfizer website, www.pfizer.com on October 8, 2006;; "Volunteers by Annual Hours," Bureau of Labor Statistics website, September 2004, www.bls.gov; "A Corporate Peace Corps Catches On," *BusinessWeek,* January 31, 2005, pp. 56–58; William J. Holstein, "The Snowball Effect of Volunteer Work," *The New York Times,* November 21, 2004, p. BU12 (quotation); "Tsunami Relief Aid at $6.28 Billion—U.N." *Washington Post,* February 25, 2005, p. 1.

2. Abraham H. Maslow, "A Theory of Human Motivation," *Psychological Review,* 1943, vol. 50, pp. 370–396; Abraham H. Maslow, *Motivation and Personality* (New York: Harper & Row, 1954).

3. Mahmond A. Wahba and Lawrence G. Bridwell, "Maslow Reconsidered: A Review of Research on the Need Hierarchy Theory," *Organizational Behavior and Human Performance,* April 1976, pp. 212–240.

4. Frederick Herzberg, Bernard Mausner, and Barbara Synderman, *The Motivation to Work* (New York: John Wiley and Sons, 1959); Frederick Herzberg, "One More Time: How Do You Motivate Employees?" *Harvard Business Review,* January–February 1968, pp. 53–62.

5. Marvin Dunnette, John Campbell, and Milton Hakel, "Factors Contributing to Job Satisfaction and Job Dissatisfaction in Six Occupational Groups," *Organizational Behavior and Human Performance,* May 1967, pp. 143–174; Charles L. Hulin and Patricia Smith, "An Empirical Investigation of Two Implications of the Two-Factor Theory of Job Satisfaction," *Journal of Applied Psychology,* October 1967, pp. 396–402.

6. B. F. Skinner, *Science and Human Behavior* (New York: Macmillian, 1953), and *Beyond Freedom and Dignity* (New York: Knopf, 1972).

7. Alexander D. Stajkovic, "A Meta-Analysis of the Effects of Organizational Behavior Modification on Task Performance, 1975–95," *Academy of Management Journal,* 1997, vol. 40, no. 5, pp. 1122–1149.

8. Fred Luthans and Robert Kreitner, *Organizational Behavior Modification and Beyond* (Glenview, Ill.: Scott, Foresman, 1985).

9. Victor Vroom, *Work and Motivation* (New York: John Wiley and Sons, 1964).

10. Craig Pinder, *Work Motivation in Organizational Behavior* (Upper Saddle River, N.J.: Prentice Hall, 1998).

11. See Terence R. Mitchell, "Expectancy Models of Job Satisfaction, Occupational Preference, and Effort: A Theoretical, Methodological, and Empirical Appraisal," *Psychological Bulletin,* 1974, vol. 81, pp. 1096–1112; and John P. Campbell and Robert D. Pritchard, "Motivation Theory in Industrial and Organizational Psychology," in Marvin D. Dunnette (ed.), *Handbook of Industrial and Organizational Psychology* (Chicago: Rand McNally, 1976), pp. 63–130, for reviews.

12. cf., Lyman W. Porter and Edward E. Lawler, *Managerial Attitudes and Performance* (Homewood, Ill.: Dorsey Press, 1968).

13. James C. Naylor, Robert D. Pritchard, and Daniel R. Ilgen. 1980. *A Theory of Behavior in Organizations.* New York: Academic Press.

14. J. Stacy Adams, "Inequity in Social Exchange," in L. Berkowitz (ed.), *Advances in Experimental Social Psychology,* vol. 2 (New York: Academic Press, 1965), pp. 267–299.

15. Craig Pinder, *Work Motivation in Organizational Behavior* (Upper Saddle River, N.J.: Prentice Hall, 1998).

16. See Nancy Adler, *International Dimensions of Organizational Behavior,* 3rd ed. (Boston: PWS-Kent), 1997.

17. Priti Pradham Shah, "Who Are Employees' Social Referents? Using a Network Perspective to Determine Referent Others," *Academy of Management Journal,* 1998, vol. 41, no. 3, pp. 249–268.

18. Although there are some instances where reinforcement theory and expectancy theory would seem to be in conflict, mostly dealing with cases of partial reinforcement schedules. A discussion and/or attempted resolution of these differences are far beyond the scope of the present discussion.

19. See Edwin A. Locke, "Toward a Theory of Task Performance and Incentives," *Organizational Behavior and Human Performance,* 1968, vol. 3, pp. 157–189.

20. Gary P. Latham and Gary Yukl, "A Review of Research on the Application of Goal Setting in Organizations," *Academy of Management Journal,* 1975, vol. 18, pp. 824–845.

21. Gary P. Latham and J. J. Baldes, "The Practical Significance of Locke's Theory of Goal Setting," *Journal of Applied Psychology,* 1975, vol. 60, pp. 187–191.

22. Gary P. Latham, "The Importance of Understanding and Changing Employee Outcome Expectancies for Gaining Commitment to an Organizational Goal," *Personnel Psychology,* 2001, vol. 54, pp. 707–720.

23. See Michael Jensen and William Meckling. 1976. Theory of the firm: Managerial behavior, agency costs, and ownership structure. *Journal of Financial Economics,* Vol. 11: 305–360; Eugene Fama. 1980. Agency problems and the theory of the firm. *Journal of Political Economy,* Vol. 88: 288–307; and Eugene Fama and Michael Jensen. 1983. Separation of ownership and control. *Journal of Law and Economics,* Vol. 26: 301–325.

24. See, for example, Richard Johnson, Robert Hoskisson, and Michael Hitt. 1993. Board of director involvement in restructuring: The effects of board versus managerial controls and characteristics. *Strategic Management Journal,* Vol. 14: 33–50; Rita Kosnik. 1990. Effects of board demography and directors' incentives on corporate greenmail decisions. *Academy of Management Journal,* Vol. 33: 129–150; or Edward Zajac and James Westphal. 1994. The costs and benefits of managerial incentives and monitoring in large U.S. corporations: When is more not better? *Strategic Management Journal,* Vol. 15: 121–142.

25. Teresa Amabile, "Stimulate Creativity by Fueling Passion," in E.A. Locke (ed.) *Handbook of Principles of Organizational Behavior* (Oxford, U.K.: Blackwell Publishing, 2000), p. 331.

26. For more information, see Edward Deci and Robert Ryan, *Intrinsic Motivation and Self-Determination in Human Behavior* (New York: Plenum, 1985).

27. For a review of this work, see Teresa Amabile, "Stimulate Creativity by Fueling Passion," in E.A. Locke (Ed.), *Handbook of Principles of Organizational Behavior* (Oxford, U.K.: Blackwell Publishing, 2000), pp. 331–341.

28. For example, see review by James Cameron and William Pierce, "Reinforcement, Reward, and Intrinsic Motivation: A Meta-Analysis," *Review of Educational Research,* 1994, Vol. 64, pp. 363–423.

29. Greg Oldham and Anne Cummings, "Employee Creativity: Personal and Contextual Factors at Work," *Academy of Management Journal,* 1996, Vol. 39, pp. 607–634.

30. Ibid.

31. Jing Zhou and Jennifer George, "When Job Dissatisfaction Leads to Creativity: Encouraging the Expression of Voice," *Academy of Management Journal,* 2001, Vol. 44, pp. 682–696.

32. Teresa Amabile, "Motivational Synergy: Toward New Conceptualizations of Intrinsic and Extrinsic Motivation in the Workplace," *Human Resource Management Review,* 1993, Vol. 3, pp. 185–201.

33. Teresa Amabile and S. Gryskiewicz, "Creativity in the R&D Laboratory," *Technical Report No. 30* (Greensboro, N.C.: Center for Creative Leadership, 1987).

34. Christina Shalley, Lucy Gilson, and Terry Blum, "Matching Creativity Requirements and the Work Environment: Effects on Satisfaction and the Intent to Leave," *Academy of Management Journal,* 2000, Vol. 43, pp. 215–233.

35. Jing Zhou and Jennifer George, 2001, op. cit.

36. For more information see Todd Dewett, *Differentiating Outcomes in Employee Creativity: Understanding the Role of Risk in Creative Performance,* 2002, College Station, Tex., Ph.D Dissertation submitted to the faculty of the Department of Management, Texas A&M University.

37. "Services," CollabNet website, www.collab.net on October 1, 2006; "Reps and Marketers: Across the Great Divide," *BusinessWeek,* May 26, 2004, p. 28; (quotation); "When Sales Meets Marketing: Part I, II, and III," *BusinessWeek,* February 19, 2005, www.businessweek.com on October 7, 2006; "The Collaborator," *Forbes,* March 14, 2005, p. 55.

Chapter 14

1. Daniel Akst, "White-Collar Stress? Stop the Whining," *New York Times,* September 19, 2004, p. BU6; Lisa Belkin, "Take This Job and Hug It," *New York Times,* February 13, 2005, p. W1 (quotation); Claudia H. Deutsch, "Grab the Brass Ring, or Just Enjoy the Ride?" *New York Times,* June 27, 2004, p. BU7; Claudia H. Deutsch, "She Didn't Stop the World, but She Slowed It Down," *New York Times,* February 13, 2005, p. BU6; Claudia H. Deutsch, "Yes, You Can Follow Your Bliss to Anytown, U.S.A." *New York Times,* October 31, 2004, p. BU7; Keith Dunnavant, "Cooking Up a New Life," *BusinessWeek Small Biz,* Fall 2004, pp. 53–55; Randall Stross, "When Long Hours at a Video Game Stop Being Fun," *New York Times,* November 21, 2004, p. BU3; Landon Thomas Jr., "Depression, A Frequent Visitor to Wall St.," *New York Times,* September 12, 2004, pp. BU1, 9.

2. See, for example, Paul Goodman, F. Javier Lerch, and T. Mukhopadhyay, "Individual and Organizational Productivity: Linkages and Processes," in D. H. Harris (ed.), *Organizational Linkages: Understanding the Productivity Paradox* (Washington, D.C.: National Academy Press, 1994), pp. 55–80; Steve Kozlowski, Stan Gully, E. Nason, and E. Smith, "Developing Adaptive Teams: A Theory of Compilation and Performance Across Levels and Time," in Dan Ilgen & Elane Pulakos (eds.), *The Changing Nature of Work and Performance: Implications for Staffing, Personnel Actions and Development* (San Francisco: Jossey-Bass, 1999), pp. 240–292.

3. See Chapter 1 in Charles R. Greer, *Strategy and Human Resources* (Englewood Cliffs, N.J.: Prentice-Hall, 1995), for an overview of the importance of training and development.

4. Paul Chaddock, "Building Value with Training," *Training & Development,* July 1995, pp. 22–25.

5. Jack Stack, "The Training Myth," *Inc.,* August 1998, pp. 41–42.

6. "Training Takes Front Seat at Offices," *USA Today,* January 19, 1999, p. 6B.

7. Jane Webster and Joseph J. Martocchio, "The Differential Effects of Software Training Previews on Training Outcomes," *Journal of Management,* 1995, Vol. 21, No. 4, pp. 757–787.

8. Frederick Herzberg, *Work and the Nature of Man* (Cleveland, Ohio: World Press, 1966).

9. Robert Ford, "Job Enrichment Lessons from AT&T," *Harvard Business Review,* January–February 1973, pp. 96–106.

10. J. Richard Hackman and Greg R. Oldham, *Work Re-design* (Reading, Mass.: Addison-Wesley, 1980).

11. Eric Trist and Kenneth Bamforth, "Some Social and Psychological Consequences of the Longwall Method of Coal-Getting," *Human Relations,* 1965, Vol. 4, pp. 3–38.

12. A. N. Kluger, "Commute Variability and Strain," *Journal of Organizational Behavior,* 1998, Vol. 19, pp. 147–166.

13. D. Denton, "Using Flextime to Create a Competitive Workforce," *Industrial Management,* January–February 1993, pp. 29–31.

14. J. Pearce and R. Dunham, "The 12-Hour Work Day: A Forty-Eight-Hour, Eight-Day Week," *Academy of Management Journal,* 1992, Vol. 35, pp. 1086–1098.

15. S. Greengard, "Making the Virtual Office a Reality," *Personnel Journal,* September 1994, pp. 66–79.

16. S. Cauderon, "Working at Home Pays Off," *Personnel Journal,* November 1992, pp. 40–49.

17. "Making Stay-at-Homes Feel Welcome," *BusinessWeek,* October 12, 1998, pp. 155–156.

18. S. D. Atchison, "The Care and Feeding of 'Lone Eagles,'" *BusinessWeek,* November 15, 1993, p. 58.

19. "Saying Adios to the Office," *BusinessWeek,* October 12, 1998, pp. 152–153.

20. G. D. Jenkins, G. E. Ledford, N. Gupta, and D. H. Doty, *Skill-Based Pay* (Scottsdale, Ariz.: American Compensation Association, 1992).

21. John L. Morris, "Lessons Learned in Skill-Based Pay," *HRMagazine,* June 1996, pp. 136–142.

22. Daniel Wren, *The Evolution of Management Theory,* 4th ed. (New York: Wiley, 1994).

23. C. Wiley, "Incentive Plan Pushes Production," *Personnel Journal,* August 1993, p. 91.

24. "When Money Isn't Enough," *Forbes,* November 18, 1996, pp. 164–169.

25. Jacquelyn DeMattco, Lillian Eby, and Eric Sundstrom, "Team-Based Rewards: Current Empirical Evidence and Directions for Future Research," in L. L. Cummings and Barry Staw (eds.), *Research in Organizational Behavior,* Vol. 20 (Greenwich, Conn.: JAI Press, 1998), pp. 141–183.

26. Theresa M. Welbourne and Luis R. Gomez-Mejia, "Gainsharing: A Critical Review and a Future Research Agenda," *Journal of Management,* 1995, Vol. 21, No. 3, pp. 559–609.

27. Steve Secklow, "How One Tech Company Played with Timing of Stock Options," *The Wall Street Journal,* July 20, 2006, p. A1, A10.

28. Charles Forelle, James Bandler, and Steve Stecklow, "Brocade Ex-CEO, 2 Others Charged in Options Probe," *The Wall Street Journal,* July 21, 2006, A1, A8.

29. Kate Ludeman, "To Fill the Feedback Void," *Training & Development,* August 1995, pp. 38–43.

30. Allan H. Church, "First-Rate Multirater Feedback," *Training & Development,* August 1995, pp. 42+.

31. Avraham Kluger and Angelo DeNisi, "Feedback Interventions: An Historical Review, and Meta-Analysis and a Proposed New Model," *Psychological Bulletin,* 1996, Vol. 119, pp. 254–284.

32. For a full description of the model and its effectiveness, see Robert Pritchard, Steven Jones, Phillip Roth, Karla Stuebing, and Steven Ekeberg, "Effects of Group Feedback, Goal-Setting, and Incentives on Organizational Productivity," *Journal of Applied Psychology* (Monograph), 1988, Vol. 73, pp. 337–358; and Robert Pritchard, Steven Jones, Phillip Roth, Karla Steubing, and Steven Ekeberg, "The Evaluation of an Integrated Approach to Measuring Organizational Productivity," *Personnel Psychology,* 1989, Vol. 42, pp. 69–115.

33. James C. Naylor, Robert D. Pritchard, and Daniel R. Ilgen, *A Theory of Behavior in Organizations* (New York: Academic Press, 1980).

34. For a description of various ProMES projects, see Robert D. Pritchard, H. Holling, F. Lemming, and Barbara Clark (eds.), *Improving Organizational Performance with the Productivity Measurement and Enhancement System: An International Collaboration* (Huntington, N.Y.: Nova Science, 2002).

35. "About Us," "Awards and Recognitions," "Jobs at HP," "Work/Life Navigation," Hewlett Packard Company website, www.hp.com on March 5, 2005; "Alternative Work Arrangements at Hewlett Packard," video case (quotation); "Case Study: Hewlett Packard Company," Commuter Challenge website, 1999, www.commuter.challenge.org on October 5, 2006, Mary Brandel, "Overview: 100 Best Places to Work in IT," *ComputerWorld,* June 14, 2004, www.computerworld.com on October 6, 2006.

Taking HR to the Next Level 4

1. D. M. Rousseau and J. McLean Parks, "The Contracts of Individuals and Organizations," in L. L. Cummings and B. M. Staw (eds.), *Research in Organizational Behavior,* Vol. 15 (Greenwich, Conn.: JAI Press, 1993), pp. 1–43.

2. D. T. Hall and J. E. Moss, "The New Protean Career Contract: Helping Organizations and Employees Adapt," *Organizational Dynamics,* Winter 1998, pp. 22–37.

3. S. L. Robinson, M. S. Kraatz, and D. M. Rousseau, "Changing Obligations and the Psychological Contract: A Longitudinal Study," *Academy of Management Journal,* 1994, Vol. 37, pp. 137–152.

4. See for example, Guillermo Dabos and Denise Rousseau, "Mutuality and Reciprocity in the Psychological Contracts of Employee and Employers," *Journal of Applied Psychology,* 2004, Vol. 89, pp. 52–72; Elizabeth Morrison and Sandra Robinson, "When Employees Feel Betrayed: A Model of How Psychological Contract Violation Develops," *Academy of Management Review,* 1997, Vol. 22, pp. 236–356; Denise Rousseau, *Psychological Contracts in Organizations: Understanding Written and Unwritten Agreements* (Thousand Oaks, Calif.: Sage, 1995).

5. For example, Dabos and Rousseau, op. cit; Jackie Coyle-Shapiro and Irene Kessler, "Exploring Reciprocity Through the Lens of Psychological Contracts: Employee and Employer Perspectives," *European Journal of Work and Organizational Psychology,* 2002, Vol. 11, pp. 69–86.

6. Commission on the Future of Worker-Management Relations, *Final Report* (Washington, D.C.: Department of Labor-Department of Commerce, 1995; also known as the Dunlop Report).

7. R. Marshall, "A New Social Contract," in J. Auerbach and J. Welsh (eds.), *Aging and Competition: Rebuilding the U.S. Workforce* (Washington, D.C.: The National Planning Association, 1994), pp. 207–224.

8. "The Highest-Paid Executives," *Forbes,* July 19, 2006, pp. 274–280.

9. Ibid.

10. T. A. Steward, "The Trouble with Stock Options," *Fortune,* January 1, 1990, pp. 93–95.

11. "Sign of Times: GE Chief Immelt to Get Stock—Not Options," *Wall Street Journal,* September 18, 2003, pp. B1, B4.

12. Harry Barkema and Luis Gomez-Mejia, "Managerial Compensation and Firm Performance: A General Research Framework," *Academy of Management Journal,* 1998, Vol. 41, No. 2, pp. 135–145.

13. Rajiv D. Banker, Seok-Young Lee, Gordon Potter, and Dhinu Srinivasan, "Contextual Analysis of Performance Impacts of Outcome-Based Incentive Compensation," *Academy of Management Journal,* 1996, Vol. 39, No. 4, pp. 920–948.

14. "Corporate Coffers Gush with Currency of an Opulent Age," *Wall Street Journal,* August 10, 1998, pp. B1, B8; "CEO Pay Outpaces Companies' Performance," *USA Today,* March 30, 1998, p. 1B; Wayne Grossman and Robert Hoskisson, "CEO Pay at the Crossroads of Wall Street and Main: Toward the Strategic Design of Executive Compensation," *Academy of Management Executive,* 1998, Vol. 12, No. 1, pp. 43–57.

15. M. Blair, "CEO Pay: Why Such a Contentious Issue?" *The Brookings Review,* Winter 1994, pp. 23–27.

16. J. Pfeffer and N. Langton, "The Effects of Wage Dispersion on Satisfaction, Productivity and Working Collaboratively: Evidence from College and University Faculty," *Administrative Science Quarterly,* 1993, Vol. 38, pp. 382–407.

17. R. G. Ehrenberg and M. L. Bognanno, "The Incentive Effects of Tournaments Revisited: Evidence from the European PGA Tour," *Industrial and Labor Relations Review,* 1990, Vol. 43, pp. 74–88.

Appendix 1

1. Bill Roberts, "Software Selection Made Easier," *HRMagazine,* June 1998, pp. 44–49.

2. Privacy Protection Study Commission, *Personal Privacy in an Information Society* (Washington, D.C.: Government Printing Office, 1977).

Appendix 2

1. For excellent overviews see Floyd J. Fowler Jr., *Survey Research Methods* (Beverly Hills, Calif.: Sage Publications, 1984); and Randall B. Dunham and Frank J. Smith, *Organizational Surveys* (Glenview, Ill.: Scott, Foresman, 1979).

2. M. J. Balma, "The Concept of Synthetic Validity," *Personnel Psychology,* 1959, Vol. 12, pp. 395–396; C. H. Lawshe, and M. D. Steinberg, "Studies in Synthetic Validity I: An Exploratory Investigation of Clerical Jobs," *Personnel Psychology,* 1955, Vol. 8, pp. 291–301.

3. Ernest J. McCormick, Angelo S. DeNisi, and James B. Shaw, "The Use of the Position Analysis Questionnaire (PAQ) for Establishing the Job Component Validity of Tests," *Journal of Applied Psychology,* 1979, Vol. 64, pp. 51–56; John R. Hollenbeck and Ellen M. Whitener, "Criterion-Related Validity for Small Sample Context: An Integrated Approach to Synthetic Validity," *Journal of Applied Psychology,* 1988, Vol. 73, pp. 536–544.

4. Frank L. Schmidt and John E. Hunter, "Development of a General Solution to the Problem of Validity Generalization," *Journal of Applied Psychology,* 1977, Vol. 62, pp. 529–540.

5. Frank L. Schmidt, Deniz S. Ones, and John E. Hunter, "Personnel Selection," *Annual Review of Psychology,* 1992, Vol. 43, pp. 627–670.

6. H. C. Taylor and J. T. Russell, "The Relationship of Validity Coefficients to the Practical Effectiveness of Tests in Selection. *Journal of Applied Psychology,* 1939, Vol. 23, pp. 565–578.

7. Hubert E. Brogden, "When Testing Pays Off," *Personnel Psychology,* 1949, Vol. 2, pp. 171–185.

8. For example, see proposals by Wayne F. Cascio and Robert A. Ramos, "Development and Application of a New Method for Assessing Job Performance in Behavioral/Economic Terms," *Journal of Applied Psychology,* 1986, Vol. 71, pp. 20–28; or John W. Boudreau, "Utility Analysis for Decision Making in Human Resource Management," in Marvin D. Dunnette and Leaetta M. Hough (eds.), *Handbook of Industrial and Organizational Psychology,* Vol. 2 (Palo Alto, Calif.: Consulting Psychologists Press, 1991), pp. 621–745.

9. Wayne F. Cascio, *Costing Human Resources: The Financial Impact of Behavior in Organizations,* 2nd ed. (Boston, Mass: PWS-Kent, 1987).

Glossary

360° feedback   an approach to performance appraisal that involves gathering performance information from people on "all sides" of the manager—above, beside, below, and so forth (10)

ADA   *see* Americans with Disabilities Act

Adaptation model   a popular approach to business strategy; describes different ways businesses can seek to adapt to their environment (4)

ADEA   *see* Age Discrimination in Employment Act

AF of L   *see* American Federation of Labor

Affirmative action   a set of steps, taken by an organization, to actively seek qualified applicants from groups under-represented in the workforce (2)

Age Discrimination and Employment Act (or **ADEA**)   law that prohibits discrimination against employees over the age of 40 (2)

Agency theory   theory concerned with the diverse interests and goals that are held by the organization's stakeholders, including its employees and managers, and the methods through which the organization's reward system can be used to align those diverse interests and goals (13)

Agency theory   theory that there are potential conflicts of interests between the owners (the principals) of an organization and its managers (agents)(13)

American Federation of Labor (or **AF of L**)   an early union; it sought not to get involved in legislative and political activities, but instead focused its efforts on improved working conditions and better employment contracts (11)

Americans with Disabilities Act of 1990 (or **ADA**)   prohibits discrimination based on disability and all aspects of the employment relationship such as job application procedures, hiring, firing, promotion, compensation, and training, as well as other employment activities such as advertising, recruiting, tenure, layoffs, leave, and fringe benefits (2)

Arbitration   conflict resolution process in which both sides agree in advance that they will accept the recommendations made by an independent third party arbitrator (11)

Bargaining unit   refers to the specifically defined group of employees who will be eligible for representation by the union (11)

BARS   *see* Behaviorally Anchored Rating Scale

Base salary   a guaranteed amount of money that the individual will be paid (14)

Behavior modification   the combination of positive reinforcement with either punishment or extinction so that an undesired behavior disappears and is replaced with a desired behavior (13)

Behavioral Observation Scales (or **BOS**)   performance appraisal method developed from critical incidents like BARS but uses substantially more critical incidents to specifically define all of the measures that are necessary for effective performance (10)

Behaviorally Anchored Rating Scales (or **BARS**)   performance appraisal method representing a combination of the graphic rating scale and the critical incident method (10)

Benefits   various rewards, incentives, and other things of value that an organization provides to its employees beyond their wages, salaries, and other forms of direct financial compensation (9)

BFOQ   *see* bona fide occupational qualification

Big five personality traits   traits likely to be more important for job performance than are more traditional personality traits: *neuroticism, extraversion, openness to experience, agreeableness,* and *conscientiousness* (7)

Biodata applications   applications focusing on the same type of information as found in a regular application, but also go into more complex and detailed assessments about that background (7)

Bona fide occupational qualification (**BFOQ**)   legal requirement for performing a particular job such that race, sex, or other personal characteristic legitimately affects a person's ability to perform the job (2)

BOS   *see* Behavioral Observation Scale

Boycott   when union members agree not to buy the products of a targeted employer (11)

Burnout   a general feeling of exhaustion that develops when an individual simultaneously experiences too much pressure and too few sources of satisfaction (12)

Business necessity   a practice that is important for the safe and efficient operation of the business (2)

Business strategy   deals with how the firm will compete in each market where it conducts business (4)

Cafeteria-style benefit plan   plan that allows the employee to choose those benefits he or she really wants (9)

Career   the set of work-related experiences and activities that people engage in related to their job and livelihood over the course of their working life (10)

Career counseling   involves interaction between an individual employee or manager in the organization and either a line manager or a human resource manager (10)

Circadian rhythm   natural cycles that indicate when a body needs to eat or sleep (12)

CIO   *see* Congress of Industrial Organization

Civil Rights Act of 1991   makes it easier for individuals who feel they have been discriminated against to take legal action against organizations and it also provides for the payment of compensatory and punitive damages in cases of discrimination under Title VII (2)

Classification system a job evaluation method attempting to group sets of jobs together into clusters, often called grades (9)

Closed shop a workplace in which only workers who were already union members may be hired by the employer (11)

Cognitive ability test measure of mental skills (7)

Collateral stress programs organizational programs specifically created to help employees deal with stress (12)

Collective bargaining the process by which managers and union leaders negotiate acceptable terms and conditions of employment for those workers represented by the unions (11)

Compensation the set of rewards that organizations provide to individuals in return for their willingness to perform various jobs and tasks within the organization (9)

Compressed workweeks arrangements where the employee works the required number of hours (typically forty), but does so in less than five days (14)

Congress of Industrial Organizations (or **CIO**) an early union which focused on organizing employees by industry, regardless of their craft or skills or occupation. (11)

Contextual performance refers to tasks an employee does on the job that are not required as part of the job but which still benefit the organization in some way (10)

Contrast error occurs when we compare people against one another instead of against an objective standard (7,10)

Corporate strategy strategy that determines what businesses the corporation will operate (4)

Cost leadership strategy strategy that focuses on minimizing costs as much as possible (4)

Creative behavior actions that are innovative and that provide some value for the organization (13)

Critical incident approach job analysis method focusing on those critical behaviors that distinguish between effective and ineffective performers (5)

Critical incident method performance appraisal method relying on instances of especially good or poor performance on the part of the employee (10)

Culture A country's culture is the set of values, symbols, beliefs, and languages that guide human behavior within that country (3, 4)

Defined benefit plan private pension plan in which the size of the benefit is precisely known; is usually based on a simple formula using such input as years of service (9)

Defined contribution plan private pension plan in which the size of the benefit depends upon how much money is contributed to the plan (9)

Development refers to teaching managers and professionals the skills needed for both present and future jobs (14)

Differentiation strategy attempting to develop an image or reputation for products or services that set them apart from competitors (4)

Direct investment occurs when a firm headquartered in one country builds or purchases operating facilities or subsidiaries in a foreign country (3)

Discipline the system of rules and procedures for how and when punishment is administered and how severe the punishment should be (6)

Disengagement fourth stage of the traditional career model; occurs when the individuals gradually begins to pull away from work in the organization, priorities change, and work may become less important (10)

Disparate impact discrimination occurs when an apparently neutral employment practice disproportionately excludes a protected group from employment opportunities (2)

Disparate treatment discrimination exists when individuals in similar situations are treated differently and when the differential treatment is based on the individual's race, color, religion, sex, national origin, age, or disability status (2)

Distributional error occurs when the rater tends to use only one part of the rating scale (10)

Diversification strategy strategy used by companies that are adding new products, product lines, or businesses to their existing core products, product lines, or businesses (4)

Diversity exists in a group or organization when its members differ from one another along one or more important dimensions (8)

Diversity management management that places a much heavier emphasis on recognizing and appreciating differences among people at work and attempting to provide accommodations for those differences to the extent that is feasible and possible (8)

Drug-Free Workplace Act of 1988 law establishing a drug-free workplace and including the requirement, in some cases, for regular drug testing (2)

Dual factor theory need-based theory proposed by Herzberg, which identifies motivators and hygiene factors as two sets of conditions at work that can satisfy needs(13)

Dysfunctional behavior behavior at work that is counter-productive (12)

Education formal classroom training an individual has received in public or private schools and college, university, and/or technical school (7)

Effort-to-performance expectancy (or expectancy) a person's perception of the probability that an increase in effort will result in an increase in performance (13)

Employee leasing an alternative to recruiting in which the organization pays a fee to a leasing company that provides a pool of employees to the leasing firm (6)

Employee Retirement Income Security Act of 1974 (or **ERISA**) law passed to guarantee a basic minimum benefit that employees could expect to be paid upon retirement (2)

Employee stock ownership plan (or **ESOP**) a group level reward system in which employees are gradually given a major stake in ownership of a corporation (14)

Employment application application asking individuals for a variety of bits of information pertaining to their personal and work background (7)

Employment test a device for measuring characteristics of an individual, such as personality, intelligence, or aptitude (7)

Employment-at-will historical premise that suggests that people work at the sole discretion of their employer and thus can be terminated at any time for any reason (6)

Equal employment opportunity means treating people fairly and equitably and taking actions that do not discriminate against people in protected classes on the basis of some illegal criterion (7)

Equal Pay Act of 1963 law requiring that organizations provide men and women who are doing equal work the same pay (2)

Equity theory theory that a person calculates the ratio of inputs to a (work) setting to outcomes they receive from that setting, almost the way one would consider a return on any investment (13)

ERG theory   need-based theory of motivation proposed by Alderfer that involves three, rather than two levels of needs, and also allows for someone to regress from a higher-level need to a lower-level need (13)

ERISA   *see* Employee Retirement Income Security Act

ESOP   *see* employee stock ownership plan

Establishment   second stage of the traditional career model; involves creating a meaningful and relevant role in the organization (12)

Ethics   an individual's beliefs about what is right and wrong and what is good and bad (2)

Ethnicity   refers to the ethnic composition of a group or organization (8)

Ethnocentric staffing model   primarily use parent country nationals to staff higher-level foreign positions (3)

Executive Order 11478   requires the federal government to base all of its own employment policies on merit and fitness and specifies that race, color, sex, religion, and national origin should not be considered (2)

Executive succession   involves systematically planning for future promotions into top management positions (5)

Expatriates   employees who are sent by a firm to work in another country; may be either parent-country nationals or third-country-nationals (3)

Expectancy theory (or **VIE theory**)   a fairly complex process theory of motivation in which the employee decides whether or not to exert effort depending on the outcomes he or she anticipates receiving for those efforts, based on calculations made concerning valences, instrumentalities, expectancies, and the links among these three components (13)

Experience   the amount of time the individual may have spent working, either in a general capacity or in a particular field of study (7)

Exploration   first traditional career stage; involves identifying interests and opportunities (10)

Exporting   the process of making a product in the firm's domestic marketplace and then selling it in another country (3)

External equity   in compensation, refers to comparisons made by employees to others employed by different organizations performing similar jobs (9)

External recruiting   the process of looking to sources outside the organization for prospective employees (7)

Extinction   a term from reinforcement theory referring to the likelihood that a behavior that is followed by no consequences will eventually disappear (13)

Factor comparison method   method of job evaluation assessing jobs on a factor-by-factor basis, using a factor comparison scale as a benchmark (9)

Fair Labor Standards Act   law passed in 1938 that established a minimum hourly wage for jobs (2)

False negatives   applicants who are predicted to fail and are not hired, but who would have been successful if they had been hired (7)

False positives   applicants who are predicted to be successful and are hired but who ultimately fail (7)

Family and Medical Leave Act of 1993   requires employers having more than fifty employees to provide up to twelve weeks unpaid leave for employees after the birth or adoption of a child, to care for a seriously ill child, spouse, or parent, or in the case of an employee's own serious illness (2)

Final offer arbitration   conflict resolution process in which the parties bargain until impasse and then the two parties' final offers are submitted to the arbitrator (11)

Firm-level performance   an indication of the likelihood of long-term survival of the firm, generating profits for potential profit sharing, and determining the company's stock price (14)

First impression error   error that occurs when an interviewer makes a decision too early in the interview process, even when subsequent information indicates the first impression may have been wrong (7)

Fixed interval schedules   interval schedules in which the amount of time that must pass before a reward is given is constant over time (13)

Fixed ratio schedules   ratio schedules in which the number of times a behavior must occur before it is rewarded remains constant over time (13)

Fleishman job analysis system   a job analysis procedure that defines abilities as enduring attributes of individuals that account for differences in performance; it relies on the taxonomy of abilities that presumably represents all the dimensions relevant to work (5)

Flexible work hours plans   plans whereby employees work forty hours per week, and work five days a week, but with the potential for flexible starting and ending times (14)

Focus strategy   strategy undertaken when an organization tries to target a specific segment of the marketplace for its products or services (4)

Forced distribution method   performance appraisal method involving grouping employees into predefined frequencies of performance ratings (10)

Foreign service premium   *see* hardship premium

Four-fifths rule   suggests that disparate impact exists if a selection criterion (such as a test score) results in a selection rate for a protected class that is less than four-fifths (80 percent) of that for the majority group (2)

Functional strategy   deals with how the firm will manage each of its major functions, such as marketing, finance, and human resources (4)

Gainsharing   a team- and group-based incentive system designed to share the cost savings from productivity improvements with employees (14)

Geocentric staffing model   model that puts parent country nationals, host country nationals, and third country nationals all in the same category, with the firm attempting to always hire the best person available for a position (3)

Geographical comparisons   comparisons of the characteristics of the potential pool of qualified applicants for a job (focusing on characteristics such as race, ethnicity, and gender) with those same characteristics of the present employees in the job (2)

Glass ceiling   refers to a barrier that keeps many females from advancing to top management positions in many organizations (8)

Goal based system (or **management by objectives system**)   performance appraisal method based largely on the extent to which individuals meet their personal performance objectives (10)

Goal theory   a fairly simple model of motivation, first proposed by Locke, based on the premise that people with goals work harder than people without goals (13)

Graphic rating scale   performance appraisal method consisting of a statement or question about some aspect of an individual's job performance; the rater provides an evaluation on a numerical scale corresponding to his/her response or answer to the statement or question (10)

Growth strategy   strategy focusing on growing and expanding the business (4)

Halo error   occurs when one positive performance characteristic causes the manager to rate all other aspects of performance positively (10)

Hardiness   ability of an individual to experience less stress when dealing with stressful events, making them more effective in dealing with the stress they do experience (12)

Hardship premium (also called a **foreign service premium**)   an additional financial incentive offered to individuals to entice them to accept a "less than attractive" international assignment (3)

Hawthorne studies   series of research studies that led to the human relations era (1)

Headhunter   an individual working for an executive search firm that seeks out qualified individuals for higher-level positions (7)

Health hazards   those characteristics of the work environment that more slowly and systematically, and perhaps cumulatively, result in damage to an employee's health (12)

Health maintenance organizations (or **HMO**s)   medical organizations that provide medical and health services to employees on a prepaid basis (9)

Hierarchy of Needs   the best known of the need-based theories, Maslow's model specifies five levels of needs that motivate behavior, with the lowest level needing to be met before the next level becomes prominent—physiological, security, social, esteem, and self-actualization (13)

HMO   *see* health maintenance organization

Horns error   occurs when the manager downgrades other aspects of an employee's performance because of one single performance dimension (10)

Hostile work environment   sexual harassment resulting from a climate or culture that is punitive toward people of a different gender (2)

HRIS   *see* human resource information system

Human capital investments   investments persons make in themselves to increase their value in the workplace (5)

Human relations era   supplanted scientific management as the dominant approach to management during the 1930s (1)

Human resource information system   an integrated and increasingly automated system for maintaining a database regarding the employees in an organization (5)

Human resource management   the comprehensive set of managerial activities and tasks concerned with developing and maintaining a qualified workforce—human resources—in ways that contribute to organizational effectiveness (1)

Human resource management system   an integrated and interrelated approach to managing human resources that fully recognizes the interdependence among the various tasks and functions that must be performed (1)

Human resource planning   the process of forecasting the supply and demand for human resources within an organization and developing action plans for aligning the two (5)

Human resources   the people an organization employs to carry out various jobs, tasks, and functions in exchange for wages, salaries, and other rewards (1)

Illegal discrimination   results from behaviors or actions by an organization or managers within an organization that cause members of a protected class to be unfairly differentiated from others (2)

Impasse   a situation in which one or both parties believe that reaching an agreement is not imminent (11)

In-basket exercise   special form of work simulation for prospective managers; consists of collections of hypothetical memos, letters, and notes that require responses (7)

Individual assessment phase   part of career planning requiring that individuals carefully analyze what they perceive to be their own abilities, competencies, skills, and goals (10)

Individual incentive plans   plans that reward individual performance on a real-time basis (14)

Institutional stress management programs   programs for managing stress that are undertaken through established organizational mechanisms (12)

Integrity tests   tests that attempt to assess an applicant's moral character and honesty (7)

Interactional justice   the quality of the interpersonal treatment people receive when a decision is implemented (6)

Internal equity   in compensation, refers to comparisons made by employees to other employees within the same organization (9)

Internal recruiting   the process of looking inside the organization for existing qualified employees who might be promoted to higher level positions (7)

Interval schedules   partial reinforcement schedules in which behavior is reinforced as a function of the passage of time (13)

Intrinsic motivation   the motivation to do work because it is interesting, engaging, or possibly challenging, rather than because there is a reward for doing it (13)

Job analysis   the process of gathering and organizing detailed information about various jobs within the organization so that managers can better understand the processes through which they are most effectively performed (5)

Job analysts   individuals who actually perform job analysis in an organization (5)

Job characteristics approach   an alternative to job specialization that takes into account the work system and employee preferences; it suggests that jobs should be diagnosed and improved along five core dimensions (14)

Job description   a listing of the tasks, duties, and responsibilities that a particular job entails; specifies the major job elements, provides examples of job tasks, and provides some indication of the relative importance in the effective conduct of the job (5)

Job dissatisfaction   the feeling of being unhappy with one's job (6)

Job embeddedness   refers to the fact that some people stay on their jobs, due to other factors, even when they decide they are unhappy and should leave (6)

Job enlargement   developed to increase the total number of tasks workers perform on the assumption that doing the same basic task over and over is the primary cause of worker dissatisfaction (14)

Job enrichment   practice that attempts to increase both the number of tasks a worker does and the control the worker has over the job (14)

Job evaluation   a method for determining the relative value or worth of a job to the organization so that individuals who perform that job can be adequately and appropriately compensated (9)

Job posting   a mechanism for internal recruiting in which vacancies in the organization are publicized through various media such as company newsletters, bulletin boards, internal memos and the firm's Intranet (7)

Job rotation   involves systematically moving employees from one job to another (14)

Job specification   requirement that focuses on the individual who will perform the job and indicates the knowledge, abilities, skills, and other characteristics that an individual must have to be able to perform the job (5)

Joint venture   two or more firms cooperate in the ownership and/or management of an operation on an equity basis (3)

Knights of Labor   an important early union that expanded its goals and its membership to include workers in numerous fields rather than a single one (11)

Knowledge workers   employees whose jobs are primarily concerned with the acquisition and application of knowledge, and they contribute to an organization through what they know and how they can apply what they know (1)

Knowledge, skills, and abilities (or **KSA**)   the fundamental requirements necessary to be able to perform a job (5)

KSA   *see* knowledge, skills, and abilities

Labor Management Relations Act (or **Taft-Hartley Act**) passed in 1947 in response to public outcries against a wide variety of strikes in the years following World War II; curtailed and limited union powers; regulates union actions and their internal affairs in a way that puts them on equal footing with management and organizations (2, 11)

Labor relations   the process of dealing with employees who are represented by a union (11)

Labor union   a legally constituted group of individuals working together to achieve shared job-related goals, including such things as higher pay, and shorter working hours (11)

Landrum-Griffin Act (officially called the **Labor Management Reporting and Disclosure Act**)   law passed in 1959 that focused on eliminating various unethical, illegal, and undemocratic union practices (2, 11)

Licensing   involves one company granting its permission to another company in a foreign country to manufacture and/or market its products in its local market (3)

Line managers   managers directly responsible for creating goods and services (1)

Locals   unions that are organized at the level of a single company, plant, or small geographic region (11)

Lockout   when the employer denies employees access to the workplace (11)

Maintenance   third stage of the traditional career model; involving optimizing talents or capabilities (10)

Management by objectives system   *see* goal based system

Management Position Description Questionnaire (MPDQ)   a standardized job analysis instrument that measures the thirteen essential components of all managerial jobs (5)

Mandatory items   topics that must be included as part of collective bargaining if either party expresses a desire to negotiate

over one or more of them; common examples are wages, working hours, and benefits (11)

Market wage rate   the prevailing wage rate for a given job in a given labor market (5)

Maturity curve   a schedule specifying the amount of annual increase a person will receive (9)

McDonnell-Douglas test   test that is the basis for establishing a prima facie case of disparate impact discrimination (2)

Mediation   conflict resolution process in which a neutral third party, called the mediator, listens to and reviews the information presented by both sides and then makes an informed recommendation and provides advice to both parties as to what she or he believes should be done (11)

Merit pay   pay awarded to employees on the basis of the relative value of their contributions to the organization (14)

Merit pay plans   compensation plans that formally base at least some meaningful portion of compensation on merit (14)

Mission   a statement of how an organization intends to fulfill its purpose (4)

Motivation   the set of forces that causes people to behave in certain ways (4, 13)

Multicultural organization   one that has achieved high levels of diversity, one which is able to fully capitalize on the advantages of the diversity, and one which has few diversity-related problems (8)

National Labor Relations Act (or **Wagner Act**)   passed in 1935; this law granted power to labor unions and put unions on a more equal footing with managers in terms of the rights of employees (2, 11)

National Labor Relations Board (or **NLRB**)   administers most labor law in the United States (11)

Need-based theories   theories of motivation that focus on *what* motivates a person, rather than on how that motivation occurs (13)

NLRB   *see* National Labor Relations Board

Nonrelevancy   a type of error that occurs when an interviewer bases an assessment of an individual's abilities to perform the job on incomplete or inaccurate assessments of the nature of that job (7)

Occupational Information Network (**O*NET**)   a database that provides both basic and advanced job analysis information and, as such), can be viewed as an alternative to conducting job analysis (5)

Occupational Safety and Health Act of 1970 (or **OSHA**) grants the federal government the power to establish and enforce occupational safety and health standards for all places of employment directly affecting interstate commerce (2, 12)

Old Age Survivors and Disability Insurance Program   *see* Social Security

Organization design   refers to the framework of jobs, positions, clusters of positions, and reporting relationships among positions that are used to construct an organization (4)

Organizational citizenship behaviors (**OCBs**)   employee behaviors that are beneficial to the organization but are not formally required as part of an employee's job (6)

Organizational commitment   the degree to which an employee identifies with an organization and is willing to exert effort on behalf of the organization (6)

OSHA   *see* Occupational Safety and Health Act

Outsourcing the process of hiring outside firms to handle basic human resource management functions, presumably more efficiently than the organization (1)

Overtime an alternative to recruiting in which current employees are asked to work extra hours (6)

Paired comparison method performance appraisal method involving comparing each individual employee with every other individual employee, one at a time (10)

PAQ *see* Position Analysis Questionnaire

Partial reinforcement rewarding a behavior only sometimes, not consistently (13)

Part-time workers those individuals who routinely expect to work less than forty hours a week (6)

Patriot Act law passed shortly after the terrorist attacks on September 11, 2001 to expand the rights of the government or law enforcement agencies to collect information about and/or pursue potential terrorists (2)

Pattern or practice discrimination similar to disparate treatment but occurs on a class-wide basis (2)

Pay compression a circumstance in which individuals with substantially different levels of experience and/or performance abilities are being paid wages or salaries that are relatively close together (9)

Pay secrecy refers to the extent to which any given individual's compensation in an organization is secret or if that information is formally made available to other individuals (9)

Pay surveys surveys of compensation paid to employees by other employers in a particular geographic area, an industry, or an occupational group (9)

Pay-for-knowledge involves compensating employees for learning specific material (9)

Performance appraisal the specific and formal evaluation of an employee in order to determine the degree to which the employee is performing his or her job effectively (10)

Performance management the general set of activities carried out by the organization to change (improve) employee performance (10)

Performance-to-outcomes expectancy (or **instrumentality**) a person's perception of the probability that improved performance will lead to certain outcomes (13)

Permissive items items which may be included in collective bargaining if both parties agree (11)

Personality the relatively stable set of psychological attributes or traits that distinguish one person from another (4)

Personality tests measure traits, or tendencies to act, which are relatively unchanging in a person (7)

Personnel departments original name for specialized organizational units for hiring and administering human resources; became popular during the 1930s and 1940s (1)

Personnel management original name for human resource management; grew from the recognition that human resources needed to be managed (1)

Personnel manager manager who worked in the personnel department (1)

Picketing when workers representing a striking union march at the entrance to the employer's facility with signs explaining their reasons for striking (11)

Point manual used to implement the point system of job evaluation; carefully and specifically defines the degrees of points from first to fifth (9)

Point system a job evaluation method requiring managers to quantify in objective terms the value of the various elements of specific jobs (9)

Polycentric staffing model calls for heavy use of host country nationals throughout the organization (3)

Position Analysis Questionnaire (or **PAQ**) a standardized job analysis instrument consisting of 194 items reflecting work behavior, working conditions, or job characteristics that are assumed to be generalizable across a wide variety of jobs (5)

Positive reinforcement a term from reinforcement theory referring to the likelihood that a behavior that is followed by positive consequences will be repeated (13)

Pregnancy Discrimination Act of 1979 protects pregnant women from discrimination in the workplace (2)

Prepotent needs according to Maslow's theory, specific needs (of the five levels in the model) that are capable of motivating behavior at any given point in time (13)

Privacy Act of 1974 legislation allowing employees to review their personnel file periodically to ensure that the information contained therein is accurate (2)

Private pension plan prearranged plan administered by the organization that provides income to the employee upon her or his retirement (9)

Procedural justice perception that the process used to determine an outcome was fair (6)

Process theories motivation theories that focus on how a person becomes motivated and what they are motivated to do, rather than on what motivates them (13)

Productivity an economic measure of efficiency that summarizes and reflects the value of the outputs created by an individual, organization, industry, or economic system relative to the value of the inputs used to create them (1)

Productivity Measurement and Evaluation System (ProMES) a program incorporating ideas from goal setting, with incentives for improvement, and based on a model of motivation similar to expectancy theory that is developed to improve group- or firm-level productivity (14)

Profit sharing an incentive system in which, at the end of the year, some portion of the company's profits is paid into a profit sharing pool which is then distributed to all employees (14)

Progressive disciplinary plans organizational disciplinary programs in which the severity of the punishment increases over time or across the problem (6)

Projection judgment that occurs when we tend to see in others the characteristics that we ourselves have which we think contribute to effectiveness (10)

Projective technique technique that involves showing an individual an ambiguous stimulus, such as an inkblot or a "fuzzy" picture and then asking what he or she "sees" (7)

Protected class group consisting of all individuals who share one or more common characteristic as indicated by that law (2)

Psychological contract the set of expectations held by an employee concerning what he or she will contribute to the organization (referred to as *contributions*) and what the organization, in return, will provide to the employee (referred to as *inducements*) (1, 4)

Psychomotor ability tests measure physical abilities such as strength, eye-hand coordination, and manual dexterity (7)

Punishment negative consequences following unacceptable behavior (6)

Punishment in reinforcement theory, the idea that a behavior that is followed by negative consequences is not likely to be repeated (13)

Purpose an organization's basic reason for existence (4)

Quality   the total set of features and characteristics of a product or service that bears on its ability to satisfy stated or implied needs (1)

Quid pro quo harassment   sexual harassment when the harasser offers to exchange something of value for sexual favors (2)

Rate of unemployment   calculated by the Bureau of Labor Statistics as the percentage of individuals looking for and available for work who are not presently employed (5)

Ratio schedules   partial reinforcement schedules in which behavior is reinforced as a function of how many times the behavior occurs (13)

Realistic job preview   insuring that job seekers understand the actual nature of the jobs available to them (6, 7)

Recruiting   the process of developing a pool of qualified people who are interested in working for the organization and from which the organization might reasonably select the best individual or individuals to hire for employment (7)

Reinforcement theory   a process theory, usually associated with B. F. Skinner, proposing that all behavior is a function if its consequences (13)

Related diversification   strategy used when a corporation attempts to create synergy among the various businesses that it owns (4)

Retrenchment (turnaround) strategy   strategy employed when an organization finds that its current operations are not effective, and major changes are usually needed to rectify the problem (4)

Rightsizing   process of monitoring and adjusting the composition of the organization's workforce to its optimal size (6)

Safety engineers   experts who carefully study the workplace, try to identify and isolate particularly dangerous situations, and recommend solutions for dealing with those situations (12)

Safety hazards   conditions in the work environment that have the potential to cause harm to an employee (12)

Salary   income that is paid to an individual not on the basis of time, but on the basis of performance (9)

Sales commission   an incentive paid to people engaged in sales work (14)

Scanlon plan   a type of gainsharing plan in which the distribution of gains is tilted much more heavily toward employees and across the entire organization (14)

Scientific Management   one of the earliest approaches to management; was concerned with how to structure individual jobs so as to maximize efficiency and productivity (1)

Selection   process concerned with identifying the best candidate or candidates for jobs from among the pool of qualified applicants developed during the recruiting process (7)

Self-report inventory   a paper and pencil measure where an applicant responds to a series of statements that might or might not apply to the person (7)

Semistructured employment interview   type of interview in which all applicants are asked essentially the same questions, although the interviewer is also given the prerogative to ask additional follow-up questions to probe specific answers that the interviewee provides (7)

Shop steward   elected position in a local union; is a regular employee who functions as a liaison between union members and supervisors (11)

Similarity error   error that occurs when the interviewer is more favorably disposed toward the candidate than the candidate's credentials warrant because the interviewee is similar to the interviewer in one or more important ways (7)

Simple ranking method   performance appraisal method involving having the manager simply rank in order from top to bottom or best to worst each member of a particular work group or department (10)

Situational interview   a type of interview, growing in popularity, where the interviewer asks the applicant questions about a specific situation to see how the applicant would react (7)

Skill-based pay   rewards employees for acquiring new skills (9)

Slowdown   job action taken instead of striking, in which workers perform their jobs at a much slower pace than normal (11)

SMEs   *see* subject matter experts

Social Security (officially the **Old Age Survivors and Disability Insurance Program**)   a mandated program originally designed to provide limited income to retired individuals to supplement their own personal savings, private pensions, part time work, and so forth (9)

Stability strategy   strategy that calls for maintaining the status quo (4)

Staff managers   responsible for an indirect or support function which would have costs but whose bottom-line contributions were less direct (1)

Stock option plan   an incentive plan established to give managers the option to buy the company stock in the future at a predetermined fixed price; was once reserved for senior managers only, but is increasingly offered to other managers as well (14)

Stock purchase plans   plans whereby stocks are offered for purchase to all the employees of a firm rather than just the executives, and serve more as a retention tool (14)

Stress   a person's adaptive response to a stimulus that places excessive psychological or physical demands on him or her (4, 12)

Strike   job action in which employees walk off their jobs and refuse to work (11)

Structured employment interview   type of interview in which the same standard questions are asked of all interviewees (7)

Subject matter experts (or **SMEs**)   individuals presumed to be highly knowledgeable about jobs and who provide data for job analysis; they may be existing job incumbents, supervisors, or other knowledgeable employees (5)

Supervisory recommendations   nominations or recommendations for an open position solicited from supervisors in the organization as a mechanism for internal recruiting (11)

Taft-Hartley Act   *see* Labor Management Relations Act

Task analysis inventory   a family of job analysis methods, each with unique characteristics; each focuses on analyzing all the tasks performed in the focal job (5)

Test validity   determination that test scores accurately relate to performance on a job (7)

Theory X and **Theory Y**   important framework reflecting different ways managers can see employees; developed by Douglas McGregor during the human relations movement (1)

Title VII of the Civil Rights Act   portion of the law that states that it is illegal for an employer to fail or refuse to hire or to discharge any individual or to in any other way discriminate against any individual with respect to any aspect of the employment relationship on the basis of that individual's race, color, religious beliefs, sex, or national origin (2)

Top management team   the group of senior executives responsible for the overall strategic operation of the firm (4)

Training a planned attempt by an organization to facilitate employee learning of job-related knowledge, skills, and behaviors (14)

Turnover voluntary or involuntary exit from employment (12)

Type A Personality personality type characterized by being highly competitive and highly focused on work with few interests outside of work (12)

Type B Personality personality type characterized as being less aggressive, more patient, and more easygoing (12)

Unemployment insurance a mandated protection plan intended to provide a basic subsistence payment to employees who are between jobs (9)

Union shop agreement a requirement that a non-union member can be hired, but must join the union within a specified time in order to keep his or her job (11)

Unrelated diversification strategy used when a firm attempts to operate several unique businesses in different, unrelated markets (4)

Unstructured employment interview interview in which the interviewer may have a general idea about what she or he wants to learn about the job applicant but has few or no advance questions that are formally constructed and ready to be asked (7)

Utility analysis the attempt to measure, in more objective terms, the impact and effectiveness of human resource management practices in terms of such metrics as a firm's financial performance. (1)

Utility analysis attempt to determine the extent to which a selection system provides real benefit to the organization (7)

Utilization analysis a comparison of the racial, sex, and ethnic composition of the employer's workforce compared to that of the available labor supply (2)

Valence the attractiveness or unattractiveness an outcome has for a person (13)

Variable interval schedules interval schedules in which the amount of time that must pass before a reward is given can change from one reward period to another (13)

Variable ratio schedules ratio schedules in which the number of times a behavior must occur before it is rewarded changes over time (13)

Verbal warnings the first step in most progressive disciplinary programs—cautions conveyed orally to the employee (6)

Vietnam Era Veterans' Readjustment Act of 1974 law requiring that federal contractors and subcontractors take affirmative action toward employing Vietnam era veterans (2)

Vocational Rehabilitation Act of 1973 law requiring that executive agencies and subcontractors and contractors of the federal government receiving more than $2,500 a year from the government engage in affirmative action for disabled individuals (2)

Wage and salary administration the ongoing process of managing a wage and salary structure (9)

Wages generally refers to hourly compensation paid to operating employees; the basis for wages is time (9)

Wagner Act *see* National Labor Relations Act

Weighted application blank relies on the determination of numerical indices to indicate the relative importance of various personal factors for predicting a person's ability to perform a job effectively (7)

Wellness programs special benefits programs that concentrate on keeping employees from becoming sick, rather than simply paying expenses when they become sick (9)

Wildcat strike strike that occurs during the course of a labor contract (and which is therefore generally illegal) and is usually undertaken in response to a perceived injustice on the part of management (11)

Word-of-mouth recruiting when the organization simply informs present employees that positions are available, and encourages them to refer friends, family or neighbors for those jobs (7)

work simulation involves asking the prospective employee to actually perform tasks or job-related activities that simulate or represent the actual work for which the person is being considered (7)

Work teams an arrangement in which a group is given responsibility for designing the work system to be used in performing an interrelated set of jobs (14)

Worker Adjustment and Retraining Notification (WARN) Act of 1988 law stipulating that an organization employing at least 100 employees must provide notice at least sixty days in advance of plans to close a facility or lay off fifty or more employees (2)

Workers' compensation a mandated protection program, it is insurance that covers individuals who suffer a job related illness or accident (9)

Written warnings the second step in most progressive disciplinary programs—they are more formal warnings given to the employee in writing that become part of the employee's permanent record (6)

Photo and Cartoon Credits

Organization and Product Index

Subject Index